Antique Trader™
Book Collector's
Price Guide

D0101207

Richard Russell

Published by
Antique Trader Books, A Division of

 **krause publications**
An F&W Publications Company

700 East State Street • Iola, WI 54990-0001
715-445-2214 • 888-457-2873
www.krause.com

Please call or write for our free catalog of publications. Our toll-free
number to place an order or obtain a free catalog is 800-258-0929 or
please use our regular business telephone, 715-445-2214.

Library of Congress Catalog Number: 2003105288
ISBN: 0-87349-607-8

Printed in the United States of America

Edited by: Dennis Thornton
Designed by: Brian Brogaard

Not all books pictured on the cover are first editions.
Books in the cover photo are courtesy of Leon Saxeville Library, Pine River, WI.

Dedication:
To Jack Biblo and Sam Colton

Photo Acknowledgments:
Book Castle's-Movie World: Burbank, CA
Bookfellows: Glendale, CA
Book Stop: Albuquerque, NM
Chelsea Book Shop: San Francisco, CA
Iliad Book Shop: North Hollywood, CA
Kayo Books: San Francisco, CA
Kelmscott Book Shop: Baltimore, MD
Lighthouse Books: Monterey, CA
Nicholas Potter Book Seller: Santa Fe, NM
Old Capitol Books: Monterey, CA
Phoenix Books: San Luis Obispo, CA
Mesa Bookshop: Mesa, AZ
Yesterday's Books: Moss Landing, CA

TABLE OF CONTENTS

Section 1

Section 2

Introduction

I love to read. And I hate to work. So in order to get through life with as little trouble as possible, I became a book seller. Now, when people see me reading, they think I'm working. It's a confidence game that I have been able to pursue with some success since 1973. Unfortunately, an unforgiving society doesn't let me stop there. I have had to learn to identify first editions, grade books, and, most importantly, sell them. Over something like 30 years, I think I've got it down. So, I suppose that the next step was inevitable. I had to teach as many people as possible to do these things. Because the more people who knew them, the more people there would be to buy my books. This, of course, would free up more time that I could use to read. Which, in turn, would make everyone think that I was the hardest-working man on the planet.

Books are, perhaps, the king of collectibles. Back in ancient Egypt, before there were any antiques, because we hadn't had enough time for that yet, there were collections of papyrus scrolls in most literate households. For hundreds of years, architects have been designing mansions to include a library. Whenever people became civilized, one of the very first things they did was to come up with some form of book. And collections? Pharaohs had collections, Romans had them, and so has every civilization since someone, somewhere drew a duck to symbolize ... a duck.

Book collecting hasn't been a fad in, oh, about 4,000 years. It's been in fashion and a pretty solid market at least that long. Because of this, and because mankind has produced more books than any other single product, it's easy to collect books and, sometimes, rather profitable. I once collected "fish stories"

from my fellow book sellers. We've all got a couple. The fishes get a bit bigger as time goes on, but at the core, there is a lot of truth. Figuring out the market at the time, I reckoned that, if the stories were only half true, a million dollars in books cost a little more than three thousand dollars. Two of my own come from different sides of the country, about a decade apart. I found this book: King, Stephen. *Salem's Lot*. Garden City, NY: Doubleday & Company, Inc., 1975, in its extremely rare first issue Dust Jacket, in a Goodwill store in Brooklyn, New York, for fifty cents. At the time, its value was about eleven hundred dollars. Today, it goes for more than two thousand. About a decade later, in a garage in Boulder Creek, California, I ran across this: Lovecraft, H.P. *The Outsider and Others*. Sauk City, WI: Arkham House Publishers, 1939. Inflation had escalated prices by then; it cost me three dollars. Its value is twenty-five hundred.

These are not everyday occurrences, but if I didn't buy a book or two every week for less than five dollars whose value exceeded a hundred, I would have become an expert in the bankruptcy process a long time ago. An ordinary occurrence? This book: Von Loher, Franz. *Cyprus, Historical and Descriptive*. London: W.H.Allen, 1878, cost me three dollars last Wednesday. Its value is four hundred and fifty dollars.

I collect books because I love to read. The fact that, with a little knowledge, I can also profit from that makes book collecting about the best hobby I can think of. In my case, it has become a profession. One might even say that, if I were not such a lazy soul, it might even have made me rich. Because, you see, if I dedicated myself to finding and selling books, instead of reading them...well, you get the idea. Sloth is, after all, one of the seven deadly sins.

What I have done here is to collect the tools you need to build a book collection. How to tell if a book is a First Edition and why that is important. Definitions for eldritch terms like verso, recto, and folio. How books are graded. Price guides that are realistic reflections of the market, not pie in the sky auction prices. The reason is simple. The collector is the center of the universe I inhabit. How much I make, what I live on, whether or not I can afford to keep my son in the fancy college he picked out, all these things are determined by book collectors and just how badly they want to add a book to their collection. The more collectors know, the more adept they become, the more likely it is that they will buy my books and those of my fellow booksellers.

Throughout the book, you will see acknowledgments of the pictures, little bits of knowledge that my fellow booksellers have trusted me with. They will tell you how to sell a book to your local antiquarian bookseller, what a book looks like, what you need to know to be a knowledgeable collector. At the end of the book there is a listing of these book sellers. There is probably one near you. And that might, just possibly, be the best thing I can do for you. Consider this book your personal introduction to your friendly, neighborhood book nut.

How the Prices Are Derived

One of the first things I noticed about the used book market was that auction prices rarely reflected what books were bought or sold for on the retail level. An auction price is only indicative of a small group of collectors, dealers, and their agents. Some books are bought very cheaply as none of the bidders are really interested in them. Others get caught up in the frenzy of the auction and go for a good deal more than they can be purchased for in a well-stocked store. It was a rather expensive lesson in that books detailing auction records and prices tend to be rather expensive.

As early as 1976, I began to keep track of the prices in the used book market by noting bookstore prices and subscribing to lists and catalogues of used books. The advent of the Internet increased the number of catalogues and books I could price out. Adding the Internet to my ongoing surveys of bookstores and mail order catalogues allowed me to develop a system for pricing books.

The system is relatively simple. It is based on whole books, as issued. In other words, if the book was issued with a dust jacket or an errata slip, only those books containing them were considered. I then took all of the books that were labeled Mint, As New, Very Fine, Fine or Near Fine, dropped the highest price and lowest price, then averaged the rest. Next, I performed the same operation on books labeled Very Good, and Good. The result should be an accurate reflection of the average retail price of any given book.

In using these prices, you should keep in mind that they are averages. In other words, they mark the midpoint of a series of prices. So when you grade the book (See: Grading) you can reach a pretty accurate and fair price. A new book (unread) will naturally be a bit higher than the price given. On the flip side, a book that the cover does not naturally close on with a few minor problems will be lower, edging toward the Very Good-Good average.

What is a First Edition?

A general definition for a first edition is the first time that a written work appears in a separate cover. This is an elastic definition and can create some disagreement. To take an example:

Paso Por Aqui by Eugene Manlove Rhodes is one of the most famous and sought after Western novels. Its first appearance was in the *Saturday Evening Post* in February 1927. It was published as the second novel in Once in the Saddle by Houghton Mifflin shortly thereafter. It was republished by Houghton Mifflin in 1949 in *The Best Novels and Short Stories of Eugene Manlove Rhodes*. The first edition of Paso Por Aqui, by the definition above, is by the University of Oklahoma, in 1973. However, if you can find *Once in the Saddle* in the first printing, you have a book worth, depending on condition, from $500 to $1,000. The University of Oklahoma "first" is worth from $25 to $50.

So, when you say "first edition" you are basically talking about the first appearance of a piece of writing in book form. Ideally, you want the first printing, the first state (definition of state is in the glossary), complete as it was issued (with errata slips, dust jacket, etc.) This is important to the collector in the same way an original painting is important to an art collector. It represents the first appearance in the real world of the piece of writing.

While it can be said each publisher has a unique way of marking first editions, there are some basic methods:

1. The date on the title page matches the copyright date, and no additional printings are listed on the verso (copyright page).
2. The verso does not list additional printings.
3. "First Edition," "First Printing," "First Impression," "First Issue," or a variation of these is printed on the title page or verso.
4. "First Published (date)" or "Published (date)" is on the verso.
5. A colophon (publisher's logo) is printed on the title page, verso or at the end of the book.
6. A printer's code, basically a line of numbers or letters printed on the verso, shows a "1" or an A at one end or the other, with certain variations.

There are also unique methods that are exclusive to a single publisher or only two or three publishers.

American Publishers Using Method 1

Abelard-Schuman, Ltd.
Alliance Book Corporation
American Publishing Company
Arcadia House
Arco Publishing Co. Inc
Ben Abramson
Argus Books
Atlantic Monthly Press (before 1925)
Beacon Press
Albert and Charles Boni*
Boni & Gaer, Inc.
R.R. Bowker
Brentano's (before 1927)
Brewer & Warren
Brewer, Warren and Putnam
Cameron Associates
G.W. Carlton
The Century Co.*
Edward J. Clode*

Creative Press*
Thomas Y. Crowell*
Crown Publishers
Stephen Daye Press
Dietz Press*
Dodd Mead & Co.*
Duffield & Co.*
Duffield & Greene*
Duke University
Equinox Cooperative Press
Falmouth Publishing House, Inc.
Four Seas Company
William Godwin
Greenberg, Publisher, Inc.
The Hampshire Bookshop, Inc.
Frances P. Harper
Harvard University Press*
Hastings House Publishers, Inc.
Rae D. Henkle Co. Inc.
Hill and Wang
Hillman-Curl, Inc.
Holiday House, Inc.
Henry Holt & Co. Inc.*
Holt, Rinehart & Winston, Inc.*
Horizon Press
Howell Soskin Publishers
Bruce Humphries, Inc.
The Huntington Library*
Indiana University Press *(before 1974)*
Iowa State University Press
Johns Hopkins University Press
Marshall Jones Company*
H.C. Kinsey & Company Inc.
Alfred A. Knopf*
Lantern Press, Inc.
Horace Liveright, Inc.*
Liveright Publishing Corp.*
Loring & Mussey, Inc.*
Lothrop Publishing Company*
Lothrop, Lee & Shepard Co. Inc.*
Louisiana State University Press
John W. Luce & Company*
The Macauley Company
mcdowell obolensky*
McGraw Hill Book Company*
David McKay Co. Inc.

McNally & Loftin, Publishers
Julian Messner
Minnesota Historical Society (after 1940)
Ohio State University Press
Ohio University Press*
Oxford University Press*
Pantheon Books, Inc.*
Payson & Clarke, Ltd.*
Pelligrini and Cudahy
Penn Publishing Company*
William Penn Publishing Company
Western Reserve University
Princeton University Press
G.P.Putnam's Sons*
Rand McNally & Company*
Reilly & Britton Co.*
Reilly & Lee Co. Inc.*
Reynal and Hitchcock Inc.*
Roy Publishers Inc.
Rutgars University Press
Sagamore Press
Sage Books
St.Martin's Press
Henry Schumann Inc.
Charles Scribner's Sons *(before 1929)**
Sears Publishing Company Inc.
Sheridan House Inc.*
Simon & Schuster*
Harrison Smith Inc.*
Harrison Smith & Robert Haas Inc.*
Richard R. Smith*
Southern Illinois University Press
Stackpole Books*
Stanford University Press
State Historical Society of Wisconsin
Stein & Day Publishers
George W. Stewart Publisher Inc.
Frederick Stokes & Co.*
Superior Publishing Company
The Swallow Press*
Alan Swallow, Publisher*
Syracuse University Press
Ticknor and Company*
Ticknor and Fields*
Trident Press*
Twayne Publishers Inc.

University of Alabama Press
University of Arizona Press
University of California Press*
University of Chicago Press*
University of Colorado Press
University of Illinois Press
University of Kentucky Press
University of Miami Press
University of Michigan Press
University of Minnesota Press
University of Nebraska Press
University of North Carolina Press*
University of Pennsylvania Press*
University of Pittsburgh Press
University of Tennessee Press
University of Texas Press
University of Washington Press
Vanguard Press
Ives Washburn Inc.*
G. Howard Watt
Weybright and Talley Inc.
Whittlesey House*
W.A.Wilde Company
Willet, Clarke and Company
H.W.Wilson Company
John C.Winston Co.
A.A.Wyn, Inc.
Yale University Press*
Ziff-Davis Publishing Company

American Publishers Using Method 2

Henry Altemus
American Publishing Company*
Arkham House
The Atlantic Monthly Press *(after 1925)**
Richard G. Badger
Baker & Taylor
A.S. Barnes & Co. Inc,
Barre Publishing Company Inc.
Albert & Charles Boni*
Boni & Gaer Inc.*
Boni & Liveright*

Brewer & Warren *
Brewer, Warren and Putnam*
The Candlelight Press
G.W. Carleton*
Caxton Printers
The Century Co.*
C.M. Clarke Publishing Co.
Edward J. Clode Inc.*
Copeland and Day
Cosmopolitan Book Corporation
Covici-Friede*
Pascal Covici*
Coward-McCann Inc.*
Coward, McCann and Geohegan*
Creative Age Press Inc.*
Dartmouth Publications
The Dial Press*
G.W. Dillingham Company*
Dodd Mead*
B.W. Dodge & Company
Doubleday, Page & Company
Duffield & Co.*
Duffield & Green*
Dunster House Bookshop
Philip C. Duschnes
E.P. Dutton & Co. Inc.*
Eaton & Mains
Fields, Osgood & Co.
The Fine Editions Press
Lawrence J. Gomme
Frances P. Harper
Harvard University Press*
B.W. Huebach
The Huntington Library*
Michell Kennerly
King's Crown Press
Alfred A, Knopf*
John Lane Company
Lee and Shepard*
Little Brown and Company*
Longmans Green & Co.*
Lothrop Publishing Company*
John W. Luce & Company*
The McClure Company*
McClure, Philips & Co.*
Macmillan Inc.*

Macy-Masius*
Frank Maurice
Merlin Press, Inc.
Minton Balch & Co,
Modern Age Books
William Morrow & Co. Inc.
Mycroft & Moran
Walter Neale
Neale Publishing Company
F. Tennyson Neeley
Northwestern University Press
Noyes, Platt & Company
Ohio University Press*
James R. Osgood and Company
Payson & Clarke Ltd.*
The Penn Publishing Company*
G.P. Putnam's Sons*
Reilly & Britton Co.
Fleming H. Revell Company
Roberts Brothers
William Edward Rudge
R.H. Russell
Charles Scribner's Sons *(before 1929)**
Thomas Seltzer
Sheed & Ward Inc.
Sheridan House Inc.*
Sherman French & Company
Silver Burdett Company
Small Maynard and Company
Harrison Smith Inc.*
Harrison Smith & Robert Haas Inc.*
Richard R. Smith*
Something Else Press*
Southwest Press
Stanton and Lee
Frederick Stokes & Co.*
Herbert S. Stone & Co.
Stone and Kimball
The Sunwise Turn
Ticknor and Company*
Ticknor & Fields
Trident Press*
University of California Press*
University of North Carolina Press*
University of Pennsylvania Press
University Press of Virginia

The Viking Press*
Ives Washburn Inc.*
Franklin Watts Inc.*
Way and Williams
Charles L. Webster and Company
H.W. Wilson Company*

American Publishers Using Method 3

Atheneum Publishers
The Atlantic Monthly Press *(after 1925)*
M.Barrows & Company
Bobbs-Merrill Company*
Boni & Liveright*
George Braziller Inc.
Brentano's (after 1927)
Broadside Press
The Century Company*
Citadel Press*
Covici-Friede*
Pascal Covici*
Covici-McGee
Coward-McCann Inc.*
Coward,McCann & Geohegan*
Thomas Y. Crowell*
Delacorte Press*
The Dietz Press
Dodge Publishing Company
George H. Doran & Co.*
Dorrance & Co.*
Doubleday & Co.
Doubleday Doran & Company
Doubleday Page & Company*
Duell, Sloan and Pearce*
Duffield & Co.*
Duffield & Green*
E.P.Dutton & Co. Inc.*
Farrar & Rinehart Inc.*
Farrar Straus*
Farrar Straus & Cudahy*
Farrar Straus and Giroux*
Follet Publishing Company
Gambit
Bernard Geis Associates

Gnome Press
Grove Press
Harcourt Brace etc.*
Hermes Publications*
Hermitage House
Hill & Wang
Henry Holt & Company Inc.*
Holt Rinehart & Winston Inc.*
Claude Kimball Inc.
Claude Kimbal & Willoughby Sharp
Alfred A. Knopf Inc.*
J.B.Lippencott Company*
Little Brown and Company*
Horace Liveright Inc.*
Longmans Green & Co.*
Loring & Massey*
Robert M. McBride & Company
McGraw Hill Book Company*
Macmillan Inc.*
Macrae-Smith Company
Oxford University Press*
L.C. Page & Co.*
Pergamon Press Inc.
Clarkson N. Potter Inc.
Random House Inc.
The Reilly & Lee Co. Inc.*
Reynal and Hitchcock Inc.*
Simon & Schuster*
William Sloane Associates Inc.
Harrison Smith Inc.*
Harrison Smith & Robert Haas Inc.*
Stackpole Books*
Taplinger Publishing Co. Inc.
The Third Press
Trail's End Publishing Inc.
University of Oklahoma Press
University of South Carolina Press
Franklin Watts Inc.*
Wesleyan University Press
World Publishing Company
Zero Press

American Publishers Using Method 4

Richard W. Baron Publishing Company Inc.
Jonathon Cape & Harrison Smith
The Century Company*
Henry T. Coates & Co.
Lewis Copeland Company
Cornell University Press
The John Day Company Inc.*
G.W. Dillingham Company*
Frederick Fell Publishers
Funk & Wagnells Inc.*
Harcourt Brace etc.*
Henry Holt & Company Inc.*
Holt Rinehart & Winston Inc.*
Houghton Mifflin Company*
Lee and Shepard
J.B. Lippencott Company
Lothrop, Lee & Shepard Company Inc.*
Robert M. McBride & Company*
The McClure Company*
McClure Phillips & Co.*
A.C. McClurg & Co.
Macy-Masius*
Moffat Yard and Company
New American Library
L.C. Page & Co.*
Rand McNally & Company*
R.H. Russell
The Swallow Press*
Alan Swallow Publisher*
The Viking Press*
Yale University Press*

American Publishers Using Method 5

The Cardavon Press
The Derrydale Press
George H. Doran & Co.*
Farrar & Rinehart Inc.*
Farrar Straus*
Farrar Straus & Cudahy*
Farrar Straus and Giroux*

American Publishers Using Unique or Semi-unique Methods

D.Appleton & Co. Appleton-Century Crofts*: The print run is at the end of the text, (1) being a First Edition.

Arcadia House: No date on Title page "1" on the verso.

Carrick & Evans Inc.: First Editions have an "A" on the verso.

Thomas Y. Crowell Company Inc.*: The First Edition has a "1" at the foot of the verso.

Harcourt Brace etc.*: No date on Title page "1" on the verso. Also "First Edition" over a line of letters beginning with B.

Harper etc.: Uses all methods except 5. From 1912 to 1971 used a number code for Month and Year, month starting with A-January through M-December J followed by the year alphabetically beginning with M-1912, and returning to A in 1926, and 1951. Code corresponding to copyright date is a First.

Random House: "First Edition" stated over a number line beginning at 2.

Charles Scribner's Sons*: Between 1929 and 1973 an "A" on the verso designated a First. A colophon accompanying the A was fitfully used at the foot of the verso.

Frederick Warne & Co. Inc.: A number 1 at the foot of the verso is a First.

Franklin Watts Inc.*: A number 1 at the foot of the verso is a First.

Printer's Codes

A printer's code may be a simple line of numbers or letters on the verso, or may be more complicated giving such facts as the year or month of publication.

Examples of a first printing:
1 2 3 4 5 6 7 8 9 10

10 9 8 7 6 5 4 3 2 1

A B C D

a b c d e f g

Subsequent printings remove the runs completed, for example:

3 4 5 6 7 8 9 10 is a third printing.

Later printings may carry a single number or a series, the lowest being the current print run for example:

Both 25 26 27   and   25   indicate the twenty-fifth printing.

A more complicated code might read:

1 2 3 4 5 6   91 92 93 94 95

That would be a first printing in the year 1991. You would then check the copyright date to verify a first edition (i.e.: the copyright date would have to be 1991).

The print code indicates a print run. In and of itself it does not always guarantee a first edition, only a first printing that may be a second or special edition of the work.

Cautions

There are many factors in looking for first editions. Publishers are a bit lax in designating them and often use the same plates without variation or with minor variations when they reprint. For more expensive and collectible books, as well as the books of known and collectible authors, the variations are known and noted in bibliographies. The standard in American books is the Bibliography of American Literature (abbreviated BAL). There are, however, a few obvious factors.

Book Club Editions

There are certain "give-aways" to book club editions. First, check the dust jacket, if one is present. Is it priced? If not, be suspicious. Book of the Month Club stamps the back cover on the lower right with some geometric symbol, either printed on the cloth or indented (debossed). Some BOMC editions carry a code (JK5H, for example) near the bottom of the last few pages. Does it feel light? Book clubs use thinner paper. Does it have a headband (small pieces of cloth inside the top, bottom or along the spine)? If not, be suspicious.

Reprint Publishers

Some publishers specialize in reprinting. So, while a book may look like a first edition given any standard of marking, it is a reprint. Grosset and Dunlap, J. Walter Black, A.L. Burt are all reprint publishers and rarely produced original works.

Bookman's Glossary

Advance Reading Copy: Abbreviated ARC. A copy distributed to reviewers, and/or the book trade previous to publication (See also: Uncorrected Proof).

Association copy: A book given to an acquaintance or prominent person by the author, signed or unsigned.

Back matter: Pages following text.

Bands: *1)* Cords on which a book is sewn; *2)* ridges across the spine of a leather-bound book.

Belles lettres: Literature written for purposes of art, usually poetry essays and the like.

Beveled boards: Books bound on boards with slanting (beveled) edges.

Bibliography: *1)* The technique of describing books academically; *2)* the science of books; *3)* a book containing and cataloguing other books by author, subject, publisher, etc.

Blind stamp: Embossed impression on a book cover without ink or gilt.

Boards: Hardbound book covers

Bookplate: Ownership label in a book.

Book sizes:

Atlas folio	16" X 25"
Elephant folio	14" X 23"
Folio	12" X 15"
4to (quarto)	9" X 12"
8vo (octavo)	6" X 9"
12mo (duodecimo)	5" X 71/2"
16mo (Sextodecimo)	41/4" X 63/4"
18mo (Vicesimo:quarto)	4" X 61/4"
24 mo (Tricesimo)	31/2" X 6"

Bosses: Metal ornamentations on a book cover.

Broadside: Printed on one side only.

Buckram: Heavy cloth used in book binding.

Cancels: Any part of the book that has been replaced for the original printing, usually to replace defective leaves.

Chapbook: Small format, cheaply made book.

Codex: Manuscript book, or book printed from a hand-written manuscript.

Colophon: A device used by printers and publishers to identify themselves, like a crest. Used by some publishers to designate a first edition.

Copyright: Literally the right to copy or publish.

Copyright page: Reverse of the title page, also called the "verso."

Curiosa: Books of unusual subject matter, generally used for occult books and sometimes as a euphemism for erotica.

Dedication: Honorary inscription by an author printed with a literary work.

Deposit copy: Copy of the book deposited in the national library to secure copyright.

Detent: Blind stamp used on rear board to designate a book club edition.

Endpapers: Papers preceding and following the front matter, text and back matter of a book.

Erotica: Books dealing with sexual matters.

Ex:library/ex libris: A book formerly in a library/books formerly owned, usually followed by the owner's or former owner's name.

Facsimile: Exact copy or reproduction.

First edition: First appearance of a work, for the most part, independently, between its own covers.

First printing: Product of the initial print run of a work is either a "First Edition," or "First Thus."

First issue: Synonymous with "First Edition."

First impression: Synonymous with "First Edition."

Flexible binding: *1)* a binding of limp material, usually leather; *2)* a binding technique that allows a new book to lie flat while open.

Foreword: Same as introduction.

Format: Basically the number of times the printed original is folded: Folio: once. Quarto: twice. Octavo: thrice. Duodecimo: four times. Sextodecimo: Five times. Vicesimo:quarto: six times. Tricesimo: seven times.

Foxing: Age darkening of paper, also called "age toning."

Free end paper: Blank page(s) between endpaper and front and back matter.

Front matter: Pages preceding text.

Half binding: Usually used with leather as "half:leather" or cloth as "half cloth." Spine and corners are in leather or cloth.

Head band: *1)* small band of cloth inside the back of the spine of a book; *2)* decorative illustration or photo at the head of a page or chapter.

Imprimatur: A license to publish where censorship exists.

Imprint: 1) Publisher's name; 2) printer's name.

In print: Book is available new.

Incunabula: Books produced before 1501.

Interleaved: Blank pages added to book for notes, etc.

Introduction: Preliminary text, also called foreword.

Jacket: Printed or unprinted paper wrapped around a book; also called dust jacket or dust wrapper.

Leaves: Single pages of a bound book.

Library binding: Endpapers as well as first and last signatures reinforced and smythe sewn.

Limited edition: A single edition for which only a limited number of copies are printed before the printing plates are destroyed.

Marginalia: Notes printed in the margin.

n.d: No date: indicates the book has no date of publication or copyright.

n.p.: No place: indicates a book has no printed place of publication.

Nihil obstat: Indicates a book has the sanction of the Roman Catholic Church.

o.p.: Out of print: book is no longer available new.

Pirate(d) edition: Book issued without the consent of the copyright holder, usually in another country.

Points: Additions, deletions or errors that result in identifying points.

Plates: Illustration printed on special paper and bound with the book.

Posthumous: Published after the author's death.

Private press: Publisher, usually small and specialized.

Pseudonym: Pen name or false name used by an author.

Quarter binding: Spine covered in cloth or leather.

Recto: Right hand page usually used to refer to the title page.

Rebind: A book rebound from the original.

Reback: Quarter bind over original binding.

Remainder: Publisher's overstock sold cheaply.

Remainder mark: Any marking used to identify a remaindered book.

Reprint: All printings after the first.

Review copy: Gratis copy of a book sent out for review.

Rubricated: Printed in red and black.

Signature: A folded printed sheet ready for sewing and binding; 2) a letter or number placed on the first page of a signature as a binding guide.

Slip case: A box manufactured to hold a particular book.

State: A change that occurs during a print run, such as the correction of a typo, or a change in the binding or dust jacket.

Tip in: A leaf added on a single page, or glued to a blank page.

Title page: page which gives the title author publisher etc. referred to as the "recto"

Unauthorized edition: Same as pirate edition.

Uncorrected proof: Book issued before the final edit usually used as an advance reading copy or review copy.

Uncut: Leaves that have not been machine cut.

Unopened: Folded edges that have not been cut.

Vanity press: A publisher subsidized by the author.

Variant: Points or states without a known priority.

Verso: Left hand page identified with the copyright page.

Woodcut: Engraving printed from a carved block of wood.

Wormed: Insect damaged.

Wrapper: Separate jacket, or the covers of a paperbound book.

Grading

The first thing to determine in grading a book is the tightness of the binding. This shows the overall wear of the book and, presumably, how often it has been read. To do this, place the book on its spine, open it so that the covers stand at a 45-degree angle, and let go.

* If the book closes completely, the initial grade is fine
* If the book closes and the cover doesn't, the initial grade is near fine.
* If the book opens and the pages fan, the initial grade is very good.
* If the book lies flat open to a page, the book is, at best, good.

Some booksellers deviate here. A fine book may be downgraded to near fine or even very good due to other flaws such as foxing, dog-eared pages, notes in the text, and other factors. My own preference, and that followed by a good many used booksellers, is to begin with the objective standard above and note the other problems separately.

Below these grades are:

* Fair: a good book that is severely worn.
* Poor: a book that is falling apart but readable.

Either of these two grades might also be called a reading copy.

A binding copy is a book that cannot be read, as it is falling apart but is whole and can be rebound into an acceptable book.

I have seen many different conventions for grading books. Most are filled with ambiguous terms such as "crisp." For many years I have recommended the objective system above. It is either because I like to be able to test something, or because I am just too dense to understand what "crisp" means when applied to a book and not an apple.

Pseudonyms

Who is Currer Bell? If you know that, and someone else doesn't, it might just allow you pick up a real bargain. Let's suppose you run across an old set of three volumes titled *The Professor* by Currer Bell and the bookseller wants $300 for them, mainly because they're pretty old (about 145 years old). Should you buy them? I would certainly suggest that you buy, because Currer Bell is the pseudonym used by Charlotte Bronte and a nice set of *The Professor* (London: Smith, Elder & Co., 1857) is worth from $3,200 in Good condition to $6,000 in Fine condition.

There's no real use for a pseudonym that I can determine, but then I'm not privy to the workings of either authors' minds or the publishing process. Suffice it to say that some authors use names other than their own for some eldritch purpose and leave it at that. For the collector, what this means is that you need knowledge of these names and whom they attach themselves to. If you collect, for example, George Sand, it would be nice to know that her real name is Amadine-Aurpre-Lucile Dupin and that she also wrote under the name Jules Sand. (Okay, strike the first statement. If my name were Amadine-Aurpre-Lucile, maybe I'd prefer being called George).

The list below is arranged alphabetically in the left column, with pseudonyms in italics. The right column gives either the pseudonym or real name, again, with pseudonyms italicized.

A	**Matthew Arnold**
A, Dr.	**Isaac Asimov**
Aallyn, Alysse	**Melissa Clarke**
Aaron, Sidney	**Paddy Chayefsky**
Abbott,	**(Charles) Fulton Oursler**
Abdullah, Achmed.	**Alexander Romanoff**
Abramowitz, Joseph	*Joey Adams*
Acre, Stephen	**Frank Gruber**
Acton, R.	**Emily Bronte**
Adams, Andy.	**Walter B. Gibson**
Adams, Joey	**Abramowitz, Joseph**
Adams, Samuel Hopkins	*Warner Fabian*
Adams, William Taylor	*Warren T. Ashton*
	Oliver Optic
Aadoff, Virginia Esther Hamilton	*Virginia Hamilton*
A.E	**George William Russell**
Aghill, Gordon	**Randall Garrett & Robert Silverberg**
Aiken, Conrad	*Samuel Jeake*
Ainslie, Arthur.	**Arthur Welesley Pain**
Ainsworth, Harriet	**Elizabeth Cadell**
Akers, Alan Burt	**Kenneth Bulmer**
Akers, Floyd	**L. Frank Baum**
Alastor	**Edward Alexander Crowley**
Alastor le Demon du Solitude	**Edward Alexander Crowley**

Albano, Peter .... *Andrea Robbins*
Albert, Marvin H. .... *Al Conroy*
Ian McAllister
Nick Quarry
Anthony (Tony) Rome
Alcott, Louisa .... *A.M. Barnard*
Alden, Isabella MacDonald .... *Pansy*
Aldington, Hilda Doolittle .... **Hilda Doolittle**
Aldiss, Brian W................................ *C.C. Shackleton*
Aleichem, Sholem .... **Sholem Yakov Rabinowitz**
Alekseyev, Constantin Sergeyevich .... *Constantin Stanislavsky*
Alexander, Bruce .... *Bruce Cook*
Alexander, ... **Edward Emshmiller**
Alger, Horatio .... *Arthur Lee Putnam*
Julian Starr
Allan, John B. .... **Donald Westlake**
Allen, Charles Grant Blairfindie .... *Grant Allen*
Cecil Power
Olive Pratt Rayne
Joseph Warborough
Martin Leach Warborough
Allen, Grant .... **Charles Grant Blairfindie Allen**
Allen, Hervey .... **William Hervey Allen Jr.**
Allen, Steve .... *William Allen Stevens*
William Christopher Stevens
Allen, William Hervey, Jr................. *Hervey Allen*
Hardly Alum
Allen, Woody .... **Allen Stewart Konigsberg**
Allingham, Margery Louise .... *Margery Allingham Carter*
Maxwell March
Margery Allingham Youngman-Carter
Allison, Clay............................. **Henry John Keevil**
Allison, Clyde .... **William Knowles**
Almquist, John............................. *Victor W. Appleton II*
Alum, Hardly............................. **William Hervey Allen Jr.**
Alzee, Grendon .... **Arthur Leo Zagat**
Ambler, Eric .... *Eliot Reed*
Amery, Francis .... **Brian Stableford**
Ames, Clyde.............................. **William Knowles**
Amis, Kingsley .... *Robert Markham*
William Tanner
Amory, Guy............................... **Ray Bradbury**
Andersen, Hans Christian .... *Christian Walter Killiam*
Anderson, David.......................... **Raymond F. Jones**
Anderson, Maxwell......................... *John Nairne Michaelson*

Anderson, Poul. . . . . *A.A. Craig*
Michael Karageorge
Winston P. Sanders
Anderson, Roberta. . . . . *Fern Michaels*
Andrews, Cicily Isabel Fairfield . . . . *Rebecca West*
Andrews, Cleo . . . . *V.C. Andrews*
Andrews, Elton V. . . . . **Fred Pohl**
Andrews, Felicia . . . . **Charles L. Grant**
Andrews, V.C. . . . . **Cleo Virginia Andrews and Andrew Neiderman**
Andrezel, Pierre . . . . **Karen Christence Blixen-Finecke**
Andrus, L.R. . . . . *Lee Andre*
Angelique, Pierre . . . . **Georges Bataille**
Ankh-af-na-Khonsu . . . . **Edward Alexander Crowley**
Anmar, Frank
William F. Nolan
Ansle, Dorothy Phoebe . . . . *Laura Conway*
Hebe Elsna
Vicky Lancaster
Lyndon Snow
Anstey, F. . . . . **Thomas Anstey Guthrie**
Anthony, Evelyn . . . . **Evelyn Ward-Thomas**
Anthony, John . . . . **John Ciardi** and **John S. Littel**
Ant(h)ony, Peter . . . . **Anthony (Joshua) Shaffer** and **Peter Levin Shaffer**
Anthony, Piers . . . . **Piers Anthony Dillingham Jacob**
Antoine, Eduoard Charles . . . . *Emile Zola*
Antonius, Brother . . . . **William Everson**
Apollinaire, Guillaume . . . . **Wilhelm de Kostrowitski**
Appel, H.M. . . . . **Wayne Rogers**
Appleton, Laurence . . . . **H(oward) P(hillips) Lovecraft**
Appleton, Victor . . . . **Howard R. Garis**
Edward L. Stratemeyer
Appleton, Victor W., II . . . . **Harriet S. Adams**
John Almquist
Neil Barrett
Vincent Buranelli
Sharman DiVono
William Dougherty
Debra Doyle
Steven Grant
James Duncan Lawrence
F. Gwynplaine MacIntrye
James D. Macdonald
Bill McCay
Bridget McKenna
Richard McKenna

Austin, Mary H. . . . . *Gordon Stairs*
Authoress, The . . . . **Edward Alexander Crowley**
Axton, David. . . . . **Dean R. Koontz**
B . . . . **A. C. Benson**
B., C. . . . . **Charlotte Brontë**
B., H. . . . . **Joseph Pierre Hilaire Belloc**
B., J.K. . . . . **John Kendrick Bangs**
Bachman, Richard . . . . **Stephen King**
Baker, Ray Stannard . . . . *David Grayson*
Ballard, K.G. . . . . **Holly Roth**
Bancroft, Laura . . . . **L. Frank Baum**
Bandoff, Hope . . . . **Thomas Anstey Guthrie**
Bangs, John Kendrick . . . .*J.K.B.*
T. Carlyle Smith
Anne Warrington Witherup
Banks, Edward . . . . **Ray Bradbury**
Baphomet, X', ... **Edward Alexander Crowley**
Baraka, Imamu Amiri. . . . . **Leroi Jones**
Barclay, Bil. . . . . **Michael Moorcock**
Barclay, Gabriel. . . . . **C(yril) M. Kornbluth**
Barclay, William Ewert. . . . . **Michael Moorcock**
Barham, Richard . . . . *Thomas Ingoldsby*
Barnard, A.M. . . . . **Louisa May Alcott**
Barnes, ... *Lydia Steptoe*
Barr, Robert . . . . *Luke Sharp*
Barrett, Neil, Jr. . . . . *Victor W. Appleton II*
Barretton, Grandal. . . . . **Randall Garrett**
Barrington, E . . . . **L(ily) Adams Beck**
Barrington, Michael. . . . . **Michael Moorcock**
Barry, Jonathan. . . . . **Whitley Strieber**
Barry, ... **Barry N(orman) Malzberg**
Barshuck, Grego. . . . . **Hugo Gernsback**
Barstow, Mrs. Montague . . . . *Baroness Orczy*
Emma Magdalena Rosalia Maria Josefa Barbara Orczy
Barton, Eustace Robert . . . . *Robert Eustace*
Eustace Rawlins
Bataille, Georges . . . . *Pierre Angelique*
Baum, L(yman) . . . . *Floyd Akers*
Laura Bancroft
John Estes Cook
John Estes Cooke
Hugh Fitzgerald
Suzanne Metcalf
Schuyler Stanton
Schuyler Staunton

Binder, Eando . . . . **Earl Andrew Binder** and **Otto O(scar) Binder**
Binder, Earl Andrew . . . . *Eando Binder*
Jack Binder
John Coleridge
Gordon A. Giles
Dean D. O'Brien
Binder, Jack . . . . **Earl Andrew Binder** and **Otto O(scar) Binder**
Binder, Otto O(scar) (1911-1975) . . . . *Eando Binder*
Jack Binder
John Coleridge
Will Garth
Gordon A. Giles
Dean D. O'Brien Bird, C(ordwainer . . . . **Harlan Ellison**
Bird, Cordwainer . . . . **Philip José Farmer**
Birdwell, Cleo . . . . **Don DeLillo**
Bishop, Alison . . . . *Alison Lurie*
Bishop, George Archibald . . . . **Edward Alexander Crowley**
Black, Ishi . . . . **Walter B(rown) Gibson**
Blair, Eric Arthur . . . . *George Orwell*
Blake, Andrew . . . . **Randall Garrett** and **Larry M(ark) Harris**
Blake, Nicholas . . . . **C(ecil) D(ay) Lewis**
Blake, Patrick . . . . **Clive Egleton**
Bland, E(dith Nesbit) . . . . *Fabian Bland*
E. Nesbit
Bland, Fabian . . . . **E(dith Nesbit) Bland**
Blight, Rose . . . . **Germaine Greer**
Blish, James (Benjamin . . . . *William Atheling Jr.*
Donald Laverty
Marcus Lyons
John MacDougal
Arthur Merlyn
Bliss, Reginald . . . . **H(erbert) G(eorge) Wells**
Blixen-Finecke, Karen Christence . . . . *Pierre Andrezel*
Isak Dinesen
Osceola
Bloch, Robert (Albert) . . . . *Tarleton Fiske*
Will Folke
Nathan
E.K. Jarvis
Wilson Kane
Jim Kjelgaard
Sherry Malone
John Sheldon
Collier Young
Block, ... *Chip Harrison*

Morgan Ives
Brian Morley
Dee O'Brien
John Jay Wells

Bradshaw, William . . . . *Christopher Isherwood*
Bramah, Ernest . . . . **Ernest Bramah Smith**
Branch, Stephen . . . . **Stefan Zweig**
Brand, Max . . . . **Frederick Schiller Faust**
Bridgeport, Robert . . . . **Robert Crichton**
Bridges, Robert . . . . *Droch*
Brinburning, Algernon Robert Charles . . . . **Edward Alexander Crowley**
Brontë, Anne . . . . *Acton Bell*
Lady Geralda
Olivia Vernon
Alexandria Zenobia
Brontë, Charlotte . . . . *C.B.*
Currer Bell
Marquis of Douro
Genius
Lord Charles Wellesley
Brontë, Emily (Jane) . . . . *R. Acton*
Ellis Bell
Brown, Douglas . . . . **Walter B(rown) Gibson**
Brown, Morna Doris (MacTaggart) . . . . *E.X. Ferrars*
Elizabeth Ferrars
Brulls, Christian . . . . **Georges Simenon**
Brune, Madame Bock . . . . **Edward Alexander Crowley**
Brunner, John (Kilian Houston) . . . . *Kilian Houston Brunner*
Kilian Houston
Gill Hunt
Wolfgang Kurtz
John Loxmith
Trevor Staines
Keith Woodcott
Brunner, Kilian Houston . . . . **John (Kilian Houston) Brunner**
Buchanan, Jack . . . . **Joe R. Lansdale**
Buck, Pearl S(ydenstricker) . . . . *John Sedges*
Pearl Sydenstricker Buck Walsh
Budrys, Algirdas Jonas . . . . *Algis Budrys*
David C. Hodgkins
Ivan Janvier
Paul Janvier
Robert Marner
Frank Mason
Jeffries Oldmann

Alger Rome
William Scarff
John A. Sentry
Albert Stroud
Harold Van Dall

Budrys, Algis . . . . **Algirdas Jonas Budrys**

Bupp, Walter . . . . **John Berryman**
Randall Garrett

Buranelli, Vincent. . . . . *Victor W. Appleton II*

Burke, Ralph. . . . . **Randall Garrett** and **Robert Silverberg**

Burke, Robert . . . . **Robert Silverberg**

Burns, Tex . . . . **Louis Dearborn LaMoore**

Burroughs, Edgar Rice. . . . . *Norman Bean*
Craig Shaw Gardner
John Tyler McCulloch
John Tyler McCullough

Burroughs, William S. . . . . *Willy (William) Lee*

C., A.E. . . . . **Edward Alexander Crowley**

C., E.A. . . . . **Edward Alexander Crowley**

C., G.K. . . . . **G(ilbert) K(eith) Chesterton**

C., H. . . . . **Edward Alexander Crowley**

C., J. . . . . **Edward Alexander Crowley**

Cabell, Branch . . . . **James Branch Cabell**

Cabell, James Branch . . . . *Branch Cabell*
Henry Lee Jefferson
Berwell Washington

Cain . . . . **Edward Alexander Crowley**

Caligula . . . . **Edward Alexander Crowley**

Campbell, (John) Ramsey . . . . *Carl Dreadstone*
Jay Ramsay
Errol Undercliffe

Campbell, John W., Jr. . . . . **John Wood Campbell**

Campbell, John Wood . . . . *John W. Campbell Jr.*
Arthur McCann
Don A. Stuart
Karl Van Campen

Campen, Karl Van **John Wood Campbell, Jr.**

Candlestick . . . . **Edward Alexander Crowley**

Canning, Victor . . . . *Alan Gould*

Cannon, Curt . . . . **Salvatore A. Lombino**

Cantab . . . . **Edward Alexander Crowley**

Capp, Al . . . . **Alfred G(erard) Caplin**

Card, Orson Scott . . . . *Dinah Kirkham*
Noam D. Pellume
Bryon Walley

Carey, The Reverend P.D. . . . . **Edward Alexander Crowley**
Carr, D. . . . . **Edward Alexander Crowley**
Carr, H.D. . . . . **Edward Alexander Crowley**
Carr, John Dickson . . . . *Carter Dickenson*
Carr Dickson
Carter Dickson
Roger Fairbairn
Torquemada
Carrington, Hereward . . . . *Nancy Fodor*
Hubert Lavington
Carter, Margery Allingham . . . . **Margery Louise Allingham**
Cartmill, Cleve . . . . *Michael Corbin*
George Sanders
Cary, Arthur Joyce Lunel . . . . *Joyce Cary*
Cary, Joyce . . . . **Arthur Joyce Lunel Cary**
Casey, John . . . . **Sean O'Casey**
Casseres, Benjamin De . . . . **Clark Ashton Smith**
Casside, John . . . . **Sean O'Casey**
Cave, Hugh B. . . . . *Justin Case*
Geoffrey Vace
Cerebellum . . . . **Edward Alexander Crowley**
C.G.R . . . . **Christine G. Rossetti**
Chaney, John . . . . *Jack London*
Chapin, Paul . . . . **Philip José Farmer**
Chapman, Lee . . . . **Marion Zimmer Bradley**
Chapman, ... **Robert Silverberg**
Charles, J.K. . . . . **Georges Simenon**
Charles, Steven . . . . **Charles L(ewis) Grant**
Charteris, Leslie . . . . **Leslie C(harles) B(owyer) Yin**
Charteris, Mary Evelyn . . . . *Lady Cynthia Asquith*
Chatrian, Alexandre . . . . *Erckmann-Chatrian*
Chaucer, Daniel . . . . **Ford Madox Hueffer**
Chayefsky, Paddy . . . . *Sidney Aaron*
Chesbro, George C. . . . . *David Cross*
Chesney, Weatherby . . . . **C(harles) J(ohn) Cutcliffe (Wright) Hyne**
Chester, Miss Di. . . . . **Dorothy L(eigh) Sayers**
Chesterton, G(ilbert) K(eith) . . . . *Arion*
G.K.C.
Chris, Leonard . . . . **Dean (Ray) Koontz**
Christie, Agatha (Mary Clarissa Miller Mallowan. *Agatha Christie Mallowan*
Mary Westmacott
Christilian, J.D. . . . . *Michael Barone*
Al Conroy
Ian MacAlister
Nick Quarry

Anthony (Tony) Rome

Churton, Henry	**Albion W(inegar) Tourgée**
Ciardi, John	*John Anthony*
Clark, Curt	**D(onald) E(dwin) Westlake**
Clarke, Arthur C(harles)	*E.G. O'Brien*
	Charles Willis
Clemens, Samuel Langhorne	*Mark Twain*
Clement, Hal	**Harry Clement Stubbs**
Cleri, Mario	**Mario Puzo**
Clerk, N.W.	**C(live) S(taples) Lewis**
C.M. of the Vigilantes.	**Edward Alexander Crowley**
Cody, John	**Ed(ward) Earl Repp**
Coe, Tucker	**D(onald) E(dwin) Westlake**
Coeli, Sir Meduim	**Edward Alexander Crowley**
Coffey, Brian	**Dean (Ray) Koontz**
Coffin, Peter	**Jonathan (Wyatt) Latimer**
Cole, Burt	**Thomas Dixon**
Coleman, Emmett	**Ishmael Reed**
Coles, Cyril H(enry)	*Manning Coles*
	Francis Gaite
Coles, Manning	**Cyril H(enry) Coles** and **Adelaide F(rancis) O(ke) Manning**
Colette.	**Sidonie-Gabrielle Colette**
Colette, Sidonie-Gabrielle	*Colette*
	Mme Maurice Goudeket
	Mme Henri de Jouvenal
Collins, Hun	**Salvatore A. Lombino**
Collinson, Peter	**Samuel Dashiell Hammett**
Colvin, James	**Michael (John) Moorcock**
Connor, Ralph	**Charles William Gordon**
Conrad, Joseph	**Jósef Teodor Konrad Korzeniowski**
Constant, Alphonse L.	*Eliphas Levi*
Conway, Graham	**Donald A(llen) Wollheim**
Cook, John Estes	**L(yman) Frank Baum**
Cooke, Arthur	**C(yril) M. Kornbluth** and **Robert (Augustine) W(ard) Lowndes**
Cooke, John Estes	**L(yman) Frank Baum**
Cooke, Margaret	**John Creasey**
Cooke, M.E.	**John Creasey**
Cooper, Henry St. John	**John Creasey**
Cooper, James Fenimore	*Jane Morgan*
Copper, Basil	*Lee Falk*
Corbin, Michael	**Cleve Cartmill**
Corelli, Marie.	**Mary MacKay**
Cornwell, David John Moore	*John LeCarré*
Cor Scorpionis	**Edward Alexander Crowley**
Corvais, Anthony	**Ray(mond Douglas) Bradbury**

Corvo, Baron (Frederick) .... **Frederick William Rolfe**
Corwin, Cecil .... **C(yril) M. Kornbluth**
Costa, Henry De .... **Frederik Pohl**
Costler, A. .... **Arthur Koestler**
Counselman, Mary Elizabeth .... *Charles DuBois*
Sanders McCrorey
John Starr
Courtney, Robert .... **Harlan (Jay) Ellison** and **C(harles) Daly King**
Coward, (Sir) Noel (Pierce) .... *Hernia Whittlebot*
Cox, A(nthony) B(erkeley) .... *Anthony Berkeley*
Frances Iles
A. Monmouth Platts
Craig, James .... **Roy. J. Snell**
Craig, Webster .... **Eric F(rank) Russell**
Crane, Stephen .... *Johnston Smith*
Crayon, Geoffrey .... **Washington Irving**
Creasey, John .... *Gordon Ashe*
M.E. Cooke
Margaret Cooke
Henry St. John Cooper
Credo
Norman Deane
Elise Fecamps
Robert Caine Frazer
Patrick Gill
Michael Halliday
Charles Hogarth
Brian Hope
Colin Hughes
Kyle Hunt
Abel Mann
Peter Manton
J.J. Marric
James Marsden
Richard Martin
Rodney Matheson
Anthony Morton
Ken Ranger
William K. Reilly
Tex Riley
Henry St. John
Jimmy Wilde
Jeremy York
Credo .... **John Creasey**
Crichton, Robert .... *Robert Bridgeport*

Crisp, Quentin . . . . **Dennis Pratt**
Cro-Cro . . . . **Edward Alexander Crowley**
Cross, Mary Ann Evans . . . . *George Eliot*
Mary Ann (Marian) Evans
Cross, Stewart. . . . . **Harry Sinclair Drago**
Crow, Levi . . . . **Manly Wade Wellman**
Crowley, Aleister . . . . **Edward Alexander Crowley**
Crowley, (Edward) Aleister . . . . **Edward Alexander Crowley**
Crowley, Edward Alexander . . . . *St. E. of M. and S.A.*
Abhavananda, Alastor (in Greek)
Alastor le Demon du Solitude
The Priest of the Princes Ankh-af-na-Khonsu
Ariel
Gerard Aumont
The Authoress
X', O.T.O. Ireland
Iona and all... Baphomet
The 666, 9'=2'A.'.A.'. Beast
Francis Bendick
George Archibald Bishop
Lord Boleskine
Algernon Robert Charles Brinburning
Madame Bock Brune
A.E.C., E.A.C., H.C., J.C., C.M. of the Vigilantes
Cain
Caligula
A Gentleman of the University of Cambridge
Candlestick
Cantab
The Reverend P.D. Carey
D. Carr
H.D. Carr
Cerebellum
Sir Meduim Coeli
Cor Scorpionis
Cro-Cro
(Edward) Aleister Crowley
Aleister Crowley
Robinson C. Crowley
Saint Edward Aleister
33', 90', X'... Crowley
Cyril Custance
DCLXVI
Marshal de Cambronne
Comte de Fenix

Barbay de Roche(c)h(o)uart
O Dhammaloyou
Adam Dias
Diogenes
Fra H.I. Edinburgh
V.
M.D. English
Felix
Percy Flage
Alice L. Foote
G.H.
O.M. Frater
A Gentile
Georgos
Laura Graham
James Grahame
Mrs. Bloomer Greymare
O.H.
Oliver Haddo
Hamlet
S.C. Hiller
A.C. Hobbs
S. Holmes
Jonathon
Natu Minimus Hutchinson
I.I., K.S.I.
Lemuel S. Innocent
Professor
Imperator Jacobus
K.H.A.K.
Edward Kelly
Dost Achiba Khan
Khaled Khan
Hodgson Y. Knott
Hsüan Ko, Ko Yuen
Sir Maurice E. Kulm
A.L.
Jeanne La Goulue
Nick Lamb
The Brothers Lazarus
LCLXVI
E. Le Roulx
Leo
Doris (Baby) Leslie
A London Physician

Major Lutiy
The Late Major Lutiy
O.M.
Macgregor of Boleskine and Abertarff
John, Junior Masefield
J.McC.
A Mental Traveller
Miles
S.J. Mills
Mohammed, Morpheus
A Mourner Clad In Green
Martial Nay
A New York Specialist
Percy W
P.R.A.S., P.H.B.S... Newlands
Hilda Norfolk
E.G.O.
Panurge
Enid, aged twelve Parsons
Percurabo
Perdurabo
Frater Perdurabo
Prater Perdurabo
Probationer
Prometheus
Prob Pudor
A. Quiller Jr.
Ethel Ramsay
John Roberts
The Author of Rosa Mundi
S.O.S.
H. Sapiens
William, pp. Ouija Board Shakespear
Mahatma Guru Sri Paramahansa Shivaji
Super Sinistram
Six Six Six (666)
The Prophet of the New Aeon Six Six Six (666)
John St. John
Count Vladimir Svaroff
H.K.T.
Alexander Tabasco
Eric Tait
M.S. Tarr
Logos Aionos (in Greek)
Thelema

	Ellery Queen
	Barnaby Ross
d'Antibes, Germain	**Georges Simenon**
Danzell, George	**Nelson S(lade) Bond**
Darragh, J. Thomas	**Edward Everett Hale**
Davidson, Avram	*Ellery Queen*
Davidson, Lawrence H.	**D(avid) H(erbert) Lawrence**
Davies, Walter C.	**C(yril) M. Kornbluth**
Davis, Audrey	**Lauran Paine**
Davis, Frances Louise	*Frances & Richard Lockeridge*
Davis, Gordon	**E(verette) Howard Hunt Jr.**
Davis, Harold A.	*Kenneth Robeson*
DCLXVI	**Edward Alexander Crowley**
Deane, Norman	**John Creasey**
de Cambronne, Marshal	**Edward Alexander Crowley**
de Camp, L(yon) Sprague	*Lymon R. Lyon*
	J. Wellington Wells
De Costa, ...	**Frederik (George) Pohl (Jr.)**
de Fenix, Comte	**Edward Alexander Crowley**
DeFoe, Daniel	**Daniel Foe**
de Hartog, ...	*F.R. Eckman*
Dekker, Eduard Douwes	*Multatuli*
de Kostrowitski, Wilhelm	*Guillaume Apollinaire*
de la Mare, Walter John	*Walter Ramal*
de la Ramée, (Marie) Louise	*Ouida*
de la Torre, Lillian	**Lillian (de la Torre Bueno) McCue**
DeLillo, Don	*Cleo Birdwell*
del Rey, Lester	**P(aul) W. Fairman,**
Demijohn, Thom	**Thomas M(ichael) Disch** and **John T(homas) Sladek**
Deming, Kirk	**Harry Sinclair Drago**
de Natale, Francine	**Barry N(orman) Malzberg**
Denmark, Harrison	**Roger (Joseph) Zelazny**
Denny, Norman	*Bruce Norman*
Dent, Lester	*Maxwell Grant*
	Kenneth Roberts
	Kenneth Robeson
	Tim Ryan
Dentinger, Stephen	**Edward D(entinger) Hoch**
Derleth, August William	*Will Garth*
	Stephen Grendon
	Eldon Heath
	Kenyon Holmes
	J. Sheridan Le Fanu
	Tally Mason
	Michael West

de Roche(c)h(o)uart, Barbay	**Edward Alexander Crowley**
Dersonne, Jacques	**Georges Simenon**
De Voto, Bernard Augustine	*John August*
	Cady Hewes
	Cady Lewes
Dexter, John	**Marion Zimmer Bradley** and **John Coleman**
Dexter, Martin	**Frederick Schiller Faust**
Dhammaloyou, O.	**Edward Alexander Crowley**
Dias, Adam	**Edward Alexander Crowley**
Di Bassetto, Corns	**George Bernard Shaw**
Dick, Philip K(indred)	*Richard Phillips*
Dickens, Charles	*Boz*
	Timothy Sparks
Dickenson, Carter	**John Dickson Carr**
Dickson, Carr	**John Dickson Carr**
Dickson, Carter	**John Dickson Carr**
Dietrich, Robert	**E(verette) Howard Hunt Jr.**
Dinesen, Isak	**Karen Christence Blixen-Finecke**
Diogenes	**Edward Alexander Crowley**
Diomede, John K.	**George Alec Effinger**
Disch, Thomas M(ichael)	*Thom Demijohn*
	Leonie Hargrave
	Cassandra Knye
d'Isly, Georges	**Georges Simenon**
Dissenter, A	**Jonathan Swift**
DiVono, Sharman	*Victor W. Appleton II*
Dixon, Thomas	*Burt Cole*
Doctor, The Good	**Isaac Asimov**
Dodgson, C(harles) L(utwidge)	*Lewis Carroll*
Doenim, Susan	**George Alec Effinger**
Dogyear, Drew	**Edward (St. John) Gorey**
Donovan, Dick	**James Edward Muddock**
Doolittle, Hilda	*Hilda Doolittle Aldington*
	H.D.
	John Helforth
Dorsage, Jean	**Georges Simenon**
Dorsan, Luc	**Georges Simenon**
Dossage, Jean	**Georges Simenon**
Dougherty, William	*Victor W. Appleton II*
Douglas, Leonard	**Ray(mond Douglas) Bradbury**
Douro, Marquis of	**Charlotte Brontë**
Dowdy, Mrs. Regera	**Edward (St. John) Gorey**
Doyle, Debra	*Victor W. Appleton II*
Doyle, John	**Harlan (Jay) Ellison** and **Robert (Ranke) Graves**
Dr. A	**Isaac Asimov**

Dr. Acula . . . . **Forrest J. Ackerman**
Drago, Harry Sinclair . . . . *Stewart Cross*
Kirk Deming
Will Ermine
Bliss Lomax
J. Wesley Putnam
Grant Sinclair
Drapier, M.B . . . . **Jonathan Swift**
Dreadstone, Carl . . . . **(John) Ramsey Campbell** and **Walter Harris**
Dresser, Davis . . . . *Asa Baker*
Matthew Blood
Kathryn Culver
Don Davis
Hal Debrett
Brett Halliday
Anthony Scott
Anderson Wayne
Droch . . . . **Robert Bridges**
Dr. Seuss . . . . **Theodor Seuss Geisel**
Drummond, Walter . . . . **Robert Silverberg**
DuBois, Charles . . . . **Mary Elizabeth Counselman**
Dufault, Joseph Ernest Nephtali . . . . *Will James*
Dumas, Claudine . . . . **Barry N(orman) Malzberg**
Duncan, David John . . . . *Ken Hood*
Dunne, John L. . . . . **H(oward) P(hillips) Lovecraft**
Dunsany, Lord . . . . **Edward John Moreton Drax Plunkett**
Dunstan, Andrew . . . . **A(rthur) Bertram Chandler**
du Perry, Jean . . . . **Georges Simenon**
Dupin, Amandine-Aurore-Lucile . . . . *George Sand*
Jules Sand
Durham, David . . . . **Roy (C.) Vickers**
Durrell, Lawrence (George) . . . . *Charles Norden*
Dwyer, Deanna . . . . **Dean (Ray) Koontz**
Dwyer, K.R. . . . . **Dean (Ray) Koontz**
E., A. . . . . **George William Russell**
Early, Jack . . . . **Sandra Scoppettone**
E.B.W. . . . . **E.B. White**
Eckman, F.R. . . . . **Jan de Hartog**
Eckman, J. Forrester . . . . **Forrest J(ames) Ackerman**
Eddy, Mary Baker . . . . *Mary Baker Glover*
Edgy, Wardore . . . . **Edward (St. John) Gorey**
Edinburgh, Fra H.I. . . . . **Edward Alexander Crowley**
Edmonds, Paul . . . . **Henry Kuttner**
Edwards, Norman . . . . **Terry (Gene) Carr** and **Theodore Edward White**
Edwin, James . . . . **James E(dwin) Gunn**

Effinger, George Alec . . . . *John K. Diomede*
Susan Doenim
Egan, Lesley . . . . **(Barbara) Elizabeth Linington**
Egleton, Clive. . . . . *Patrick Blake*
John Tarrant
Egremont, Michae . . . . **Michael Harrison**
Eisner, Sam . . . . **C(yril) M. Kornbluth**
Eisner, Simon . . . . **C(yril) M. Kornbluth**
Elbertus, Fra . . . . **Elbert Hubbard**
Eldred, Brian . . . . **Ray(mond Douglas) Bradbury**
Elia . . . . **Charles Lamb**
Eliot, George . . . . **Mary Ann Evans Cross**
Elizabeth . . . . **Countess Mary Annette Von Arnim Beauchamp Russell**
Elliott, Bruce . . . . *Maxwell Grant*
Elliot(t), Don. . . . . **Robert Silverberg**
Elliott, William . . . . **Ray(mond Douglas) Bradbury**
Ellis, Landon . . . . **Harlan (Jay) Ellison**
Ellison, Harlan (Jay) . . . . *Lee Archer*
Cheech Beldone
Phil Beldone
C(ordwainer) Bird
Jay Charby
Robert Courtney
Price Curtis
John Doyle
Wallace Edmondson
Landon Ellis
Sley Harson
Ellis Hart
E.K. Jarvis
Ivar Jorgenson
Al Maddern
John Magnus
Paul Merchant
Clyde Mitchell
Nalrah (Nabrah?) Nosille
Bert Parker
Ellis Robertson
Pat Roeder
Jay Solo
Derry Tiger
Harlan White
Elron. . . . . **L(a Fayette) Ron(ald) Hubbard Sr.**
Emsh. . . . . **Edward A. Emshwiller**
Emshwiller, Edward A. . . . . *Ed Alexander*

Emsler
Emsh
Willer

Emsler .... **Edward A. Emshwiller**
Englehardt, Frederick. .... **L(a Fayette) Ron(ald) Hubbard Sr.**
English, V., M.D. .... **Edward Alexander Crowley**
Epernay, Mark .... **John Kenneth Galbraith**
Ericson, Walter .... **Howard (Melvin) Fast**
Erman, Jacques de Forrest .... **Forrest J(ames) Ackerman**
Ermann, Jack .... **Forrest J(ames) Ackerman**
Ermine, Will .... **Harry Sinclair Drago**
Ernst, Paul (Frederick) .... *George Alden Edson*
Kenneth Robeson
Paul Frederick Stern
Esterbrook, Tom .... **L(a Fayette) Ron(ald) Hubbard Sr.**
Esteven (Estevan?), John .... **Samuel Shellabarger**
Eustace, Robert. .... **Eustace Robert Barton**
Evans, E. Everett .... *Harry J. Gardner*
H.E. Verett
Evans, Evan .... **Frederick Schiller Faust** and **Alan Stoker**
Evans, Mary Ann (Marian) .... **Mary Ann Evans Cross**
Everson, William .... *Brother Antonius*
Ewing, Frederick R. .... **Jean Shepherd** and **Edward Hamilton Waldo**
Fabian, Warner .... **Samuel Hopkins Adams**
Fair, A.A. .... **Erle Stanley Gardner**
Fairbairn, Roger. .... **John Dickson Carr**
Fairman, P(aul) W. .... *Adam Chase*
Lester del Rey
Clee Garson
E.K. Jarvis
Ivar Jorgensen
Robert (Eggert) Lee
Paul Lohrman
F.W. Paul
Mallory Storm
Gerald Vance
Falconer, Kenneth .... **C(yril) M. Kornbluth**
Falk, Lee .... **Basil Copper**
Farigoule, Louis .... *Jules Romains*
Farley, Ralph (Milne) .... **Roger S(herman) Hoar**
Farmer, Philip José .... *Cordwainer Bird*
Paul Chapin
Maxwell Grant
Dane Helstrom
Rod Keen

Harry 'Bunny' Manders
William Norfolk
Kenneth Robeson
Jonathan Swift Somers III
Leo Queequeg Tincrowder
Kilgore Trout
John H. Watson MD

Farr, John . . . . **Jack Webb**
Farrell, James T(homas). . . . . *Jonathan Titulesco Fogarty*
Farrell, John Wade. . . . . **John D(ann) MacDonald**
Farren, Richard M. . . . . **(Sir) John Betjeman**
Fast, Howard (Melvin). . . . . *E.V. Cunningham*
Walter Ericson
Simon Kent
Faulcon, Robert. . . . . **Robert (Paul) Holdstock**
Faulkner, William (Cuthbert) . . . . *Ernest V. Trueblood*
Faust, Alexander . . . . **Harry Altshuler**
Faust, Frederick Schiller . . . . *Frank Austin*
George Owen Baxter
Lee Bolt
Max Brand
Walter C. Butler
George Challis
Peter Dawson
Martin Dexter
Evin Evan
Evan Evans
John Frederick
Frederick Frost
Dennis Lawton
David Manning
Peter Henry Morland
Hugh Owen
John Schoolcraft
Nicholas Silver
Henry Uriel
Peter Ward
Fawkes, Farrah . . . . **Andrew J(efferson V.) Offutt**
Fawkes, Guy . . . . **Robert Benchley**
Feinstein, Isidor . . . . *I.F. Stone*
Felix . . . . **Edward Alexander Crowley**
Fenimore, W. . . . . **A(braham Grace) Merritt**
Fenn, Lionel. . . . . **Charles L(ewis) Grant**
Fernandes . . . . **Joyce Carol Oates**
Ferney, Manuel . . . . **Manly Wade Wellman**

Ferrat, Jacques Jean . . . . **Sam(uel Kimball) Merwin Jr.**

Fetzer, Herman . . . . *Jake Falstaff*

Fickling, Forrest E. . . . . *G.G. Fickling*

Fickling, G.G. . . . . **Forrest E. Fickling** and **Gloria Fickling**

Fickling, Gloria . . . . *G.G. Fickling*

Field, Gans T. . . . . **Manly Wade Wellman**

Finney, Jack . . . . **Walter Braden Finney**

Finney, Walter Braden . . . . *Jack Finney*

Fips, Mohammed U(lysses) S(ocrates) . . . . **Hugo Gernsback**

Firth, Violet M(ary) . . . . *Dion Fortune*

Fish, Robert L(loyd) . . . . *A.C. Lamprey*

Robert L. Pike

Lawrence Roberts

Fiske, Tarleton . . . . **Robert (Albert) Bloch**

Fitzgerald, Hugh . . . . **L(yman) Frank Baum**

Flage, Percy . . . . **Edward Alexander Crowley**

Flapdoodle, Phineas . . . . **Henry Miller**

Fleck, Betty . . . . **Lauran Paine**

Fleming, Dorothy Leigh Sayers . . . . **Dorothy L(eigh) Sayers**

Fletcher, George U. . . . . **(Murray) Fletcher Pratt**

Fodor, Nancy . . . . **Hereward Carrington**

Foe, Daniel . . . . *Daniel DeFoe*

Fogarty, Jonathan Titulesco . . . . **James T(homas) Farrell**

Folke, Will. . . . . **Robert (Albert) Bloch**

Follett, Ken(neth Martin) . . . . *Martin Martinsen*

Simon Myles

Zachary Stone

Foote, Alice L. . . . . **Edward Alexander Crowley**

Ford, Ford Madox . . . . **Ford Madox Hueffer**

Forrest, Julian. . . . . **Edward Wagenknecht**

Fortune, Dione . . . . **Violet M(ary) Firth**

Fosse, Harold C . . . . **H(orace) L(eonard) Gold**

Foster, Alan Dean . . . . *George Lucas*

Fountain, Arnold. . . . . **(Charles) Fulton Oursler**

France, Anatole . . . . **Jacques-Anatole-François Thibault**

Franklin, Madeleine L'Engle Camp . . . . *Madeleine L'Engle*

Fraser, Jane . . . . **Rosamunde Pilcher**

Frazer, Andrew . . . . **Milton Lesser**

Frazer, Robert Caine . . . . **John Creasey**

Frazier, Arthur. . . . . **(Henry) Kenneth Bulmer** and **Laurence James**

Frederick, John. . . . **Milward Rodon Kennedy Burge** and **Frederick Schiller**

Faust

Freeling, Nic(h)olas . . . . *F.R.E. Nicholas*

Freeman, Mary E(leanor) Wilkins . . . . *Mary Wilkins*

Mary E(leanor) Wilkins-Freeman

Freeman, R(ichard) Austin . . . . *Clifford Ashdown*
French, Paul . . . . **Isaac Asimov**
Friedan, Betty . . . . **Betty Naomi Goldstein**
Frikell, Samri . . . . **(Charles) Fulton Oursler**
Frost, Frederick . . . . **Frederick Schiller Faust**
Fuentes, Carlos . . . . **Carlos Manuel Fuentes Macías**
Furey, Michael . . . . **Arthur (Henry) Sarsfield Ward**
 Gaite, Francis. . **Cyril H(enry) Coles** and **Adelaide F(rancis) O(ke) Manning**
Galbraith, John Kenneth . . . . *Mark Epernay*
Ganpat . . . . **Martin Louis Alan Gompertz**
Gardner, Craig Shaw . . . . **Edgar Rice Burroughs**
Gardner, Erle Stanley . . . . *A.A. Fair*
Charles M. Green
Grant Holiday
Carleton Kendrake
Charles J. Kenn(e)y
Robert Park
Robert Parr
Les Tillray
Gardner, Harry J. . . . . **E. Everett Evans**
Gardner, Miriam . . . . **Marion Zimmer Bradley**
Gardner, Noel . . . . **Henry Kuttner**
Garis, Howard R. . . . . *Victor Appleton*
Garrett, Gordon . . . . **(Gordon) Randall (Phillip David) Garrett**
Garrett, (Gordon) Randall (Phillip David) . . . . *Gordon Aghill*
Grandal Barretton
Alexander Blade
Alfred Blake
Andrew Blake
Walter Bupp
Ralph Burke
Gordon Garrett
David Gordon
Richard Greer
Larry Mark Harris
Laurence M. Janifer
Ivar Jorgenson
Darrel T. Langart
Blake MacKenzie
Seaton Mckettrig
Clyde (T.) Mitchell
Mark Phillips
Robert Randall
Leonard G. Spencer
S.M. Tenneshaw

Gerald Vance
Barbara Wilson

Garrison, Frederick . . . . **Upton Sinclair**

Garron, Robert A. . . . . **Howard E(lmer) Wandrei**

Garve, Andrew . . . . **Paul Winterton**

Gash, Jonathan . . . . **John Grant MD.**

Gashbuck, Greno . . . . **Hugo Gernsback**

Gaunt, Graham . . . . **John Grant MD.**

Gaylord, Timeus . . . . **Clark Ashton Smith**

Geiger, Hansruedi . . . . *H.R. Geiger*

Geiger, H.R. . . . . **Hansruedi Geiger**

Geisel, Ted . . . . **Theodor Seuss Geisel**

Geisel, Theodor Seuss . . . . *Ted Geisel*
Theo Le Sieg
Dr. Seuss

Genius . . . . **Charlotte Brontë**

Gentile, A . . . . **Edward Alexander Crowley**

Georgos . . . . **Edward Alexander Crowley**

Gérôme . . . . **Jacques-Anatole-François Thibault**

Geralda, Lady . . . . **Anne Brontë**

Gernsback, Hugo . . . . *Grego Barshuck*
Mohammed U(lysses) S(ocrates) Fips
Greno Gashbuck
Gus N. Habergock
Baron Munchausen

Giles, Geoffrey . . . . **Forrest J(ames) Ackerman** and **Walter Gillings**

Giles, Gordon A. . . . . **Earl Andrew Binder** and **Otto O(scar) Binder**

Gill, Patrick . . . . **John Creasey**

Giovanni, Nikki . . . . **Yolande C. Giovanni**

Giovanni, Yolande C. . . . . *Nikki Giovanni*

Gissing, George . . . . **J. Storer Glouston**

Glidden, Frederick (Dilley) . . . . *Luke Short*

Glouston, J. Storer . . . . *George Gissing*

Glover, Mary Baker . . . . **Mary Baker Eddy**

Gold, H(orace) L(eonard) . . . . *Clyde Crane Campbell*
Dudley Dell
Harold C. Fosse
Julian Graey
Leigh Keith

Goldman, William . . . . *Harry Longbaugh*
S. Morgenstern

Goldsmith, Oliver . . . . *James Willington*

Goldstein, Betty Naomi . . . . *Betty Friedan*

Gompertz, Martin Louis Alan . . . . *Ganpat*

Good Doctor, The . . . . **Isaac Asimov**

Gordon, Charles William .... *Ralph Connor*
Gordon, David .... **(Gordon) Randall (Phillip David) Garrett**
Gordon, Verne......................... **Donald A(llen) Wollheim**
Gorki [Gorky], Maxim................... **Aleksei Maksimovich Pyeshkov**
Gorman, Beth .... **Lauran Paine**
Goryan, Sirak .... **William Saroyan**
Goudeket, Mme .... **Sidonie-Gabrielle Colette**
Goulart, Ron(ald Joseph) .... *Josephine Kains*
Jill Kearny
Julian Kearny
Howard Lee
Kenneth Robeson
Frank S. Shawn
Joseph Silva
Con Steffanson]
Gould, Alan.................................... **Victor Canning**
Grady, Tex... **Jack Webb**
Graey, Julian .... **H(orace) L(eonard) Gold**
Graham, Laura .... **Edward Alexander Crowley**
Graham, Tom.............................. **(Harry) Sinclair Lewis**
Grahame, James .... **Edward Alexander Crowley**
Grandower, Elissa .... **Hillary (Baldwin) Waugh**
Grant, Charles L(ewis) .... *Felicia Andrews*
Steven Charles
Lionel Fenn
Simon Lake
Deborah Lewis
Geoffrey L. Marsh
Grant, Joan.................................... **Joan Marshall Kelsey**
Grant, John, MD................................. *Jonathan Gash*
Graham Gaunt
Jonathan Grant
Grant, Maxwell .... **Lester Dent**
Bruce Elliott
Philip José Farmer
Walter B(rown) Gibson
Dennis Lynds
Theodore Tinsley
Grant, Steven .... *Victor W. Appleton II*
Graves, Robert (Ranke) .... *John Doyle*
Barbara Rich
Frank Richards
Graves, Valerie.......................... **Marion Zimmer Bradley**
Gray, Anthony .... **Ernest K(ellogg) Gann**
Grayson, David .... **Ray Stannard Baker**

Greaves, Richard . . . . **George Barr McCutcheon**

Greaves, Robert . . . . **George Barr McCutcheon**

Green, Charles M. . . . . **Erle Stanley Gardner**

Greer, Germaine. . . . . *Rose Blight*

Greer, Richard. . . . . **(Gordon) Randall (Phillip David) Garrett** and **Robert Silverberg**

Gregory, Stephan . . . . **Don(ald Eugene) Pendleton**

Grendon, Stephen . . . . **August William Derleth**

Grenville, Pelham. . . . . **P(elham) G(renville) Wodehouse**

Grey, Carol . . . . **Robert (Augustine) W(ard) Lowndes**

Greymare, Mrs. Bloomer . . . . **Edward Alexander Crowley**

Grile, Dod . . . . **Ambrose (Gwinnett) Bierce**

Grinnell, David . . . . **Donald A(llen) Wollheim**

Grode, Redway . . . . **Edward (St. John) Gorey**

Groener, Carl. . . . . **Robert (Augustine) W(ard) Lowndes**

Guernsey, H.W. . . . . **Howard E(lmer) Wandrei**

Gunn, James E(dwin) . . . . *James Edwin*
Edwin James

Gut, Gom. . . . . **Georges Simenon**

Guthrie, Thomas Anstey. . . . . *F. Anstey*
Hope Bandoff
William Monarch Jones

Gwendolyn, Jacob Tonson. . . . . **Arnold Bennett**

H., E.W.. . . . . **E(rnest) W(illiam) Hornung**

H., H. . . . . **Helen (Maria Fiske) Hunt Jackson**

H., O. . . . . **Edward Alexander Crowley**

Habergock, Gus N. . . . . **Hugo Gernsback**

Haddo, Oliver . . . . **Edward Alexander Crowley**

Haldeman, Joe W(illiam) . . . . *Robert Graham*

Hale, Edward Everett . . . . *J. Thomas Darragh*
Frederic Ingham
New England minister

Hall, James . . . . **Henry Kuttner**

Halliday, Brett . . . . **Davis Dresser**
William John Pronzini

Halliday, Michael . . . . **John Creasey**

Hamilton, Clive. . . . . **C(live) S(taples) Lewis**

Hamlet . . . . **Edward Alexander Crowley**

Hammett, Samuel Dashiell. . . . . *Peter Collinson*

Hammond, Keith . . . . **Henry Kuttner** and **C(atherine) L(ucille) Moore**

Hammond, Ralph . . . . **(Ralph) Hammond Innes**

Hannon, Ezra . . . . **Salvatore A. Lombino**

Harford, Henry . . . . **W(illiam) H(enry) Hudson**

Hargrave, Leonie . . . . **Thomas M(ichael) Disch**

Harker, Jonathan . . . . **Joe R. Lansdale**

Harris, Frank	**John Thomas Harris**
Harris, J.B.	**John Wyndham Parkes Lucas Beynon Harris**
Harris, Joel Chandler	*Uncle Remus*
Harris, Johnson	**John Wyndham Parkes Lucas Beynon Harris**
Harris, John Thomas	*Frank Harris*
Harris, John Wyndham Parkes Lucas Beynon	*John Beynon*
	J.B. Harris
	Johnson Harris
	Max Hennessy
	Lucas Parker
	Lucas Parkes
	Wyndham Parkes
	John Windham
	John Wyndam
	John Wyndham
Harrison, Bruce	**Edgar Pangborn**
Harrison, Chip	**Lawrence Block**
Harson, Sley	**Harlan (Jay) Ellison**
Hart, Ellis	**Harlan (Jay) Ellison**
Hastings, Hudson	**Henry Kuttner** and **C(atherine) L(ucille) Moore**
Hawkins, Sir Anthony Hope	*Anthony Hope*
Haygood, G. Arnold	**Frank G(ill) Slaughter**
H.D.	**Hilda Doolittle**
Heard, Gerald	**H(enry) F(itzgerald) Heard**
Heard, H(enry) F(itzgerald)	*Gerald Heard*
Hearn, Lafcadio	*Yakumo Koizumi*
Heath, Eldon	**August William Derleth**
Heinlein, Robert Anson	*Anson MacDonald*
	Lyle Monroe
	John Riverside
	Caleb Saunders
	Elma Wentz
	Simon York
Heldmann, Richard B(ernard)	*Richard Marsh*
Helstrom, Dane	**Philip José Farmer**
Hemingway, Ernest	*Morgan Llywelyn*
Hennessy, ...	**John Wyndham Parkes Lucas Beynon Harris**
Edgar Henry	**Albion W(inegar) Tourgée**
Henry, O.	**William Sydney Porter**
Heritage, Martin	**Sydney Horler**
Herman, ...	**Ambrose (Gwinnett) Bierce**
Herriott, James	**J.A. Wight**
Herron, Edna	*Ben Aronin*
Hershfield, Harry	**Walter B(rown) Gibson**
Herzog, Emile Salomon Wilhelm	*André Maurois*

Higgins, Jack . . . . **Henry Patterson**
Hiller, S.C. . . . . **Edward Alexander Crowley**
Hill-Lutz, Grace Livingston . . . . *Grace Livingston*
Marcia Macdonald
Hilton, James . . . . *Glen Trevor*
Hindin, Nathan. . . . . **Robert (Albert) Bloch**
Hirschfield, Magnus . . . . **Arthur Koestler**
Hobbs, A.C. . . . . **Edward Alexander Crowley**
Hodemart, Peter. . . . . **Pierre Audemars**
Hogarth . . . . **Rockwell Kent**
Hogarth, Charles . . . . **(Ivor) Ian Bowen** and **John Creasey**
Holding, James . . . . *Ellery Queen Jr.*
Holiday, Grant . . . . **Erle Stanley Gardner**
Hollerbochen . . . . **Ray(mond Douglas) Bradbury**
Holley, Marietta . . . . *Josiah Allen's Wife*
Holmes, Gordon . . . . **M(atthew) P(hipps) Shiel**
Louis Tracy
Holmes, Kenyon. . . . . **August William Derleth**
Holmes, S. . . . . **Edward Alexander Crowley**
Holt, Harmony . . . . **William Rotsler**
Holt, Samue . . . . **D(onald) E(dwin) Westlake**
Hope, Anthony. . . . . **Sir Anthony Hope Hawkins**
Hope, Brian . . . . **John Creasey**
Hopley, George. **Cornell George Hopley-Woolrich**
Hopley-Woolrich, Cornell George . . . . *George Hopley*
William Irish
Cornell Woolrich
Horn, Gertrude Franklin . . . . **Gertrude Franklin (Horn) Atherton**
Horn, Peter. . . . . **C(yril) M. Kornbluth, Henry Kuttner** and **D(avid) Vern**
Hoskin, Cyril Henry . . . . *T. Lopsang Rampa*
House, Brian. . . . . **Robert Ludlum**
Howard, Robert E(rvin) . . . . *Patrick Ervin*
Patrick Howard
Patrick Irvin
Sam Walser
Robert Ward
Howard, Warren F. . . . . **Frederik (George) Pohl (Jr.)**
Hubbard, Ca. . . . . **Elbert Hubbard**
Hubbard, Elbert . . . . *Fra Elbertus*
Cal Hubbard
Hubbard, L(a Fayette) Ron(ald), Sr. . . . . *Elron*
Frederick Englehardt
Tom Esterbrook
Rene Lafayette
Capt. B.A. Northrop

	Kurt von Rachen
Hudson, Jeffrey	**(John) Michael Crichton**
Hueffer, Ford Hermann	**Ford Madox Hueffer**
Hueffer, Ford Madox	*Daniel Chaucer*
	Ford Madox Ford
	Fenil Haig
	Ford Hermann Hueffer
Hughes, Colin	**John Creasey**
Hughes, Sylvia	**Sylvia Plath**
Hunt, Kyle	**John Creasey**
Hunter, Evan	**Salvatore A. Lombino**
Hutchinson, Jonathon, Natu Minimus	**Edward Alexander Crowley**
I., I	**Edward Alexander Crowley**
I., K.S.	**Edward Alexander Crowley**
Iddrissyeh, Achmed Abdullah	**Alexander Nicholayevitch Romanoff**
Iles, Frances	**A(nthony) B(erkeley) Cox**
Incogniteau, Jean-Louis	**Jack Kerouac**
Ingham, Frederic	**Edward Everett Hale**
Ingoldsby, Thomas	**Richard Barham**
Innes, Michael	**J(ohn) I(nnes) M(ackintosh) Stewart**
Innes, (Ralph) Hammond	*Ralph Hammond*
Innocent, Lemuel S.	**Edward Alexander Crowley**
Irish, William	**Cornell George Hopley-Woolrich**
Irvin, Patrick	**Robert E(rvin) Howard**
Irving, Washington	*Geoffrey Crayon*
	Diedrich Knickerbocker
	Launcelot Langstaff
	Jonathan Oldstyle
Isherwood, Christopher	**William Bradshaw**
Ives, Morgan	**Marion Zimmer Bradley**
Jackson, Helen (Maria Fiske) Hunt	*H.H.*
	Saxe Holm
Jacob, Piers Anthony Dillingham	*Piers Anthony*
	Pier Xanthony
Jacobus, Professor, Imperator	**Edward Alexander Crowley**
Jakes, John (William)	*Darius John Granger*
	Alan Payne
	Jay Scotland
	Jay Scotland
	Allen Wilder
James, Edwin	**James E(dwin) Gunn**
James, P(hyllis) D(orothy)	*Phyllis White*
James, Will	**Joseph Ernest Nephtali Dufault**
Janifer, Laurence M.	**(Gordon) Randall (Phillip David) Garrett**
Janson, Hank	**Harry Hobson** and **Michael (John) Moorcock**

Jeake, Samuel. . . . . **Conrad (Potter) Aiken**
Jefferson, Henry Lee . . . . **James Branch Cabell**
Jennings, Gary . . . . *Gabriel Quyth*
Jessel, John . . . . **Stanley G(rauman) Weinbaum**
J.K.B. . . . . **John Kendrick Bangs**
John, David St . . . . **E(verette) Howard Hunt, Jr.**
John, Henry St. . . . . **John Creasey**
Johnson, Benj(amin) F. **James Whitcomb Riley**
Johnson, Mel. . . . . **Barry N(orman) Malzberg**
Jones, James Athearn . . . . *Matthew Murgatroyd*
Jones, Leroy . . . . *Imamu Amiri Baraka*
Jones, Raymond F . . . . *David Anderson*
Jones, William Monarch . . . . **Thomas Anstey Guthrie**
Josephs, Henry . . . . **Robert (Augustine) W(ard) Lowndes**
Josiah Allen's Wife . . . . **Marietta Holley**
Jouvenal, Mme Henri de. . . . . **Sidonie-Gabrielle Colette**
J.T. . . . . **Eric Temple Bell**
Judd, Cyril (M) . . . . . . **Josephine Juliet Grossman** and **C(yril) M. Kornbluth**
K., K.H.A.. . . . . **Edward Alexander Crowley**
Kaiine, Tanith Lee . . . . *Tanith Lee*
Kain, Saul . . . . **Siegfried Sassoon**
Kains, Josephine . . . . **Ron(ald Joseph) Goulart**
Kaler, James Otis . . . . *James Otis*
Kane, Wilson . . . . **Robert (Albert) Bloch**
Karageorge, Michael . . . . **Poul (William) Anderson**
Kastel, Warren . . . . **C(hester) S. Geier** and **Robert Silverberg**
Kavanagh, Paul . . . . **Lawrence Block**
Kearny, Jill . . . . **Ron(ald Joseph) Goulart**
Kearny, Julian . . . . **Ron(ald Joseph) Goulart**
Keefe, Jack . . . . **Ring Lardner Jr.**
Keen, Rod . . . . **Philip José Farmer**
Keiber, Fritz . . . . **Fritz (Reuter) Leiber Jr.**
Keith, Leigh . . . . **H(orace) L(eonard) Gold**
Kelly, Edward . . . . **Edward Alexander Crowley**
Kelsey, Joan Marshall . . . . *Joan Grant*
Kendrake, Carleton . . . . **Erle Stanley Gardner**
Kennerley, Thomas . . . . *Tom Wolfe*
Kenn(e)y, Charles J.. **Erle Stanley Gardner**
Kent, Kelvin . . . **A(rthur) K(elvin) Barnes, C(yril) M. Kornbluth** and **Henry Kuttner**
Kent, Mallory . . . . **Robert (Augustine) W(ard) Lowndes**
Kent, Rockwell . . . . *Hogarth Jr.*
Kent, Simon . . . . **Max Catto** and **Howard (Melvin) Fast**
Kenton, Maxwell . . . . **Terry Southern** and **Mason Hoffenberg**
Kenyon, Robert O. . . . . **Henry Kuttner**

Kerouac, Jack (Jean-Louis Lebrid) .... *Jean-Louis Incognitea*
Kerr, Ben..................................... **William (Thomas) Ard**
Khan, Dost Achiba .... **Edward Alexander Crowley**
Khan, Khaled .... **Edward Alexander Crowley**
Kim .... **Georges Simenon**
Kineji, Maborushi......................... **Walter B(rown) Gibson**
King, Stephen (Edwin) .... *Richard Bachman*
                  John Swithen
Kingsley, Charles ....*Parson Lot*
Kjelgaard, James Arthur .... *Jim Kjelgaard*
Kjelgaard, Jim .... **Robert (Albert) Bloch** and **James Arthur Kjelgaard**
Klass, Philip (J.) .... *Kenneth Putnam*
                  William Tenn
Klausner, Amos ....*Amos Oz*
Knickerbocker, Diedrich..................... **Washington Irving**
Knight, David .... **Richard S(cott) Prather**
Knott, Hodgson Y........................ **Edward Alexander Crowley**
Knowles, William................................... *Clyde Allison*
                  Clyde Ames
Knox, Calvin M. .... **Robert Silverberg**
Knye, Cassandra....... **Thomas M(ichael) Disch** and **John T(homas) Sladek**
Ko, Hsüan .... **Edward Alexander Crowley**
Koestler, Arthur................................. *A. Costler*
              Magnus Hirschfield
                   Vigil
Koizumi, Yakumo.................................. **Lafcadio Hearn**
Konigsberg, Allen Stewart .... *Woody Allen*
Koontz, Dean (Ray)............................... *David Axton*
                 Leonard Chris
                  Brian Coffey
                Deanna Dwyer
                 K.R. Dwyer
                  John Hill
                Leigh Nichols
                Anthony North
                Richard Paige
                 Owen West
                 Aaron Wolfe
Kornbluth, C(yril) M............................. *Gabriel Barclay*
                Edward J. Bellin
                 Arthur Cooke
                 Cecil Corwin
                Walter C. Davies
                 Sam Eisner
                 Simon Eisner

Kenneth Falconer
Will Garth
S.D. Gottesman
Peter Horn
Cyril (M.) Judd
Kelvin Kent
Paul Dennis Lavond
Scott Mariner
Lawrence O'Donnell
Jordan Park
Martin Pearson
Ivar Towers
Dirk Wylie

Korzeniowski, Jósef Teodor Konrad . . . . *Joseph Conrad*
Kosinski, Jerzy (Nikodem) . . . . *Joseph Novak*
Ko Yuen . . . . **Edward Alexander Crowley**
Kulm, Sir Maurice E. . . . . **Edward Alexander Crowley**
Kurtz, Wolfgang . . . . **John (Kilian Houston) Brunner**
Kuttner, Henry . . . . *Edward J. Bellin*
Paul Edmonds
Noel Gardner
Will Garth
James Hall
Keith Hammond
Hudson Hastings
Peter Horn
Kelvin Kent
Robert O. Kenyon
C.H. Liddell
Hugh Maepenn
K.H. Maepenn
Scott Morgan
Lawrence O'Donnell
Lewis Padgett
Woodrow Wilson Smith
Charles Stoddard

L., A. . . . . **Edward Alexander Crowley**
Lafayette, Rene . . . . **L(a Fayette) Ron(ald) Hubbard Sr.**
La Goulue, Jeanne. . . . . **Edward Alexander Crowley**
Lake, ... **Charles L(ewis) Grant**
Lamb, Charles . . . . *Elia*
Lamb, Nick . . . . **Edward Alexander Crowley**
LaMoore, Louis Dearborn . . . . *Tex Burns*
Louis L'Amour
Jim Mayo

L'Amour, Louis	**Louis Dearborn LaMoore**
Lamprey, A.C.	**Robert L(loyd) Fish**
Lang, Andrew	*A Huge Longway*
Langart, Darrel T.	**(Gordon) Randall (Phillip David) Garrett**
Lange, John	**(John) Michael Crichton**
Langstaff, Launcelot.	**Washington Irving**
	James Kirk Paulding
Lansdale, Joe R.	*M. Dean Bayer*
	Jack Buchanan
	Richard Dale
	Jonathan Harker
	Mark Simmons
	Ray Slater
Lantern, The	**Don(ald Robert Perry) Marquis**
Lardner, Ring, Jr.	*Jack Keefe*
	Philip Rush
	Old Wilmer
Lasly, Walt.	**Frederik (George) Pohl (Jr.)**
Latham, Philip	**Robert S(hirley) Richardson**
Lathrop, Francis	**Fritz (Reuter) Leiber Jr.**
Latimer, Jonathan (Wyatt)	*Peter Coffin*
la Torre, Lillian de	**Lillian McCue**
Laumer, (John)	*Anthony Lebaron*
Laurieres, Chrisophe des	**Clark Ashton Smith**
Laverty, Donald.	**James (Benjamin) Blish** and **Damon (Francis) Knight**
Lavington, Hubert.	**Hereward Carrington**
Lawless, Anthony	**Philip MacDonald**
Lawrence, D(avid) H(erbert)	*Lawrence H. Davidson*
Lawrence, James Duncan	*Victor W. Appleton II*
Lawton, Dennis	**Frederick Schiller Faust**
Lazarus, The Brothers	**Edward Alexander Crowley**
LCLXVI	**Edward Alexander Crowley**
Learsi, Rufus	**Shalom Asch** and **Israel Goldberg**
Lebaron, Anthony.	**(John) Keith Laumer**
LeCarré, John	**David John Moore Cornwell**
Lee, Andrew.	**Louis Auchincloss**
Lee, Gypsy Rose	**Georgiana Ann Randolph**
Lee, Tanith	**Tanith Lee Kaiine**
Lee, Willy (William)	**William S. Burroughs**
Leiber, Fritz (Reuter), Jr.	*Fritz Keiber*
	Francis Lathrop
Leinster, Murray	**Will(iam) F(itzgerald) Jenkins**
L'Engle, Madeleine	**Madeleine L'Engle Camp Franklin**
Leo	**Edward Alexander Crowley**
	Sean O'Casey

Lepovsky, Manfred Bennington . . . . *Manford B. Lee*
Ellery Queen
Barnaby Ross]
Le Roulx, E. . . . . **Edward Alexander Crowley**
Le Sieg, Theo . . . . **Theodor Seuss Geisel**
Leslie, Doris (Baby) . . . . **Edward Alexander Crowley**
Lesser, Milton . . . . *Adam Chase*
Andrew Frazer
Darius John Granger
Stephen Marlowe
Jason Ridgway
S.M. Tenneshaw
C.H. Thames
Lessing, Doris (May). . . . . *Jane Somers*
Lester, Irwin . . . . **(Murray) Fletcher Pratt**
Levi, Eliphas . . . . **Alphonse L. Constant**
Lewes, Cady . . . . **Bernard Augustine De Voto**
Lewis, C(ecil) D(ay) . . . . *Nicholas Blake*
Lewis, C(live) S(taples) . . . . *N.W. Clerk*
Clive Hamilton
Jack Lewis
N.W.
Lewis, D.B. Wyndham . . . . *Timothy Shy*
Lewis, Deborah. . . . . **Charles L(ewis) Grant**
Lewis, (Harry) Sinclair . . . . *Tom Graham*
Lewis, Jack. . . . . **C(live) S(taples) Lewis**
Ley, Willy . . . . *Robert Willey*
Lin, Frank . . . . **Gertrude Franklin (Horn) Atherton**
Linington, (Barbara) Elizabeth. . . . . *Anne Blaisdell*
Lesley Egan
Egan O'Neill
Dell Shannon
Littlewit, Humphrey . . . . **H(oward) P(hillips) Lovecraft**
Lockeridge, Frances & Richard. . . . **Frances Louise Davis** and **Richard Orson**
Lofts, Nora . . . . *Juliet Astley*
Peter Curtis
Logue, Christopher . . . . *Count Palmiro Vicarion*
Lomax, Bliss . . . . **Harry Sinclair Drago**
Lombino, Salvatore A. . . . . *John Abbott*
Curt Cannon
Hunt Collins
Ezra Hannon
Evan Hunter
Richard Marsten
Ed McBain

London, Jack. . . . . **John Griffith Chaney**

Long, Frank Belknap, Jr.. . . . . *Lyda Belknap Long*
Leslie Northern

Long, Lyda Belknap . . . . **Frank Belknap Long Jr.**

Longbaugh, Harry. . . . . **William Goldman**

Longway, A Huge . . . . **Andrew Lang**

Loring, Peter. . . . . **Samuel Shellabarger**

Lorraine, Alden. . . . . **Forrest J(ames) Ackerman**

Lot, Parson . . . . **Charles Kingsley**

Loti, Pierre . . . . **L.M. Julien Viaud**

Lovecraft, H(oward) P(hillips). . . . . *Laurence Appleton*
John L. Dunne
Humphrey Littlewit
Archibald Maynwaring
H(enry) Paget-Lowe
Richard Raleigh
Ames Dorrance Rowley
Theobaldus Senectissimus
Edward Softly
Lewis Theobold Jr.
Albert Frederick Willie
Zoilus

Lovesy, Peter . . . . *Peter Lear*

Lowell, James Russell . . . . *Hosea Biglow*

Lowndes, Robert (Augustine) W(ard) . . . . *Arthur Cooke*
S.D. Gottesman
Carl Greener
Carol Grey
Carl Groener
Henry Josephs
Mallory Kent
Paul Dennis Lavond
John MacDougal
Wilfred Owen Morley
Richard Morrison
Michael Sherman
Peter Michael Sherman
Lawrence Woods
Robert Wright

Loxmith, John. . . . . **John (Kilian Houston) Brunner**

Lucas, Victoria . . . . **Sylvia Plath**

Ludlum, Robert . . . . *Brian House*
Jonathon Ryder
Michael Shepherd

Lufts, Norah. . . . . **Lofts, Nora**

Lurie, Alison . . . . **Alison Bishop**
Lutiy, Major . . . . **Edward Alexander Crowley**
Lutiy, The Late Major . . . . **Edward Alexander Crowley**
Lyon, Lymon R.. . . . . **L(yon) Sprague de Camp**
Lyons, Marcus . . . . **James (Benjamin) Blish**
Lyre, Pynchbeck . . . . **Siegfried Sassoon**
M., O. . . . . **Edward Alexander Crowley**
McBain, Ed . . . . **Salvatore A. Lombino**
McCann, Arthur . . . . **John Wood Campbell**
McCay, Bill . . . . *Victor W. Appleton II*
MacCreigh, James . . . . **Frederik (George) Pohl (Jr.)**
McCrorey, Sanders . . . . **Mary Elizabeth Counselman**
McCue, Lillian (de la Torre Bueno) . . . . *Lillian de la Torre*
McCulloch, John Tyler . . . . **Edgar Rice Burroughs**
McCullough, John Tyler . . . . **Edgar Rice Burroughs**
McCutcheon, George Barr . . . . *Richard Greaves*
Robert Greaves
Macdonald, Anson . . . . **Robert Anson Heinlein**
Macdonald, James D. . . . . *Victor W. Appleton II*
Macdonald, John. . . . . **Kenneth Millar**
MacDonald, John D(ann) . . . . *John Wade Farrell*
Scott O'Hara
Peter Reed
MacDonald, John Ross . . . . **Kenneth Millar**
MacDonald, Marcia . . . . **Grace Livingston Hill**
MacDonald, ... *Anthony Lawless*
Filip Macdonald
Martin Porlock
W.J. Stuart
Macdonald, Ross . . . . **Kenneth Millar**
MacDougal, John. . **James (Benjamin) Blish** and **Robert (Augustine) W(ard)**
Lowndes
McGivern, William P(eter) . . . . *Bill Peters*
Macgregor of Boleskine and Abertarff . . . . **Edward Alexander Crowley**
Machen, Arthur . . . . *Leolinus Siluriensis*
Macías, Carlos Manuel Fuentes . . . . *Carlos Fuentes*
McInerny, Ralph (Matthew) . . . . *Edward Mackin*
Monica Quill
MacIntrye, F. Gwynplaine . . . . *Victor W. Appleton II*
MacKay, Mary . . . . *Marie Corelli*
McKenna, Bridget . . . . *Victor W. Appleton II*
McKenna, Richard . . . . *Victor W. Appleton II*
MacKenzie, Blake . . . . **(Gordon) Randall (Phillip David) Garrett**
McKenzie, Ray . . . . **Robert Silverberg**
Mckettrig, Seaton . . . . **(Gordon) Randall (Phillip David) Garrett**

Mackin, Edward	**Ralph (Matthew) McInerny**
MacLeod, Austin.	**William MacLeod Raine**
McNeile, H(erman) C(yril)	*Sapper*
McQuay, Mike	*Victor W. Appleton II*
Maddern, Al	**Harlan (Jay) Ellison**
Maepenn, Hugh	**Henry Kuttner**
Maepenn, K.H..	**Henry Kuttner**
Magnus, John	**Harlan (Jay) Ellison**
Malcom, Dan	**Robert Silverberg**
Mallory, Drew	**Brian (Francis Wynne) Garfield**
Mallowan, Agatha Christie	**Agatha (Mary Clarissa Miller) Christie**
Malone, Sherry.	**Robert (Albert) Bloch**
Malzberg, Barry N(orman)	*Mike Barry*
	Francine de Natale
	Claudine Dumas
	Mel Johnson
	Howard Lee
	Lee W. Mason
	K.M. O'Donnell Jr.
	Gerrold Watkins
Manders, Harry 'Bunny'	**Philip José Farmer**
Mann, Abel	**John Creasey**
Manning, Adelaide F(rancis) O(ke)	*Manning Coles*
	Francis Gaite
Manning, David	**Frederick Schiller Faust**
Manton, Peter.	**John Creasey**
Maras, Karl.	**(Henry) Kenneth Bulmer** and **Peter Hawkins**
March, Maxwell	**Margery Louise Allingham**
Mariner, Scott.	**C(yril) M. Kornbluth** and **Frederik (George) Pohl**
Markham, Robert	**(Sir) Kingsley (William) Amis**
Marlowe, Stephen	**Milton Lesser**
Marner, Robert	**Algirdas Jonas Budrys**
Marquis, Don(ald Robert Perry)	*The Lantern*
	The Sundial
Marric, J.J.	**William Vivian Butler**
	John Creasey
Marsden, James	**John Creasey**
Marsh, Geoffrey L.	**Charles L(ewis) Grant**
Marsten, Richard.	**Salvatore A. Lombino**
Martin, Richard	**John Creasey**
Martin, Webber	**Robert Silverberg**
Martin-Georges, Georges.	**Georges Simenon**
Martinsen, Martin	**Ken(neth Martin) Follett**
Masefield, John, Junior	**Edward Alexander Crowley**
Marvel, Ik.	**Donald G(rant) Mitchell**

Mason, Ernest	**Frederik (George) Pohl (Jr.)**
Mason, Ernst	**Frederik (George) Pohl (Jr.)**
Mason, Frank	**Algirdas Jonas Budrys**
Mason, F(rank) van Wyck	*Geoffrey Coffin*
	Frank W. Mason
	Ward Weaver
Mason, Frank W.	**F(rank) van Wyck Mason**
Mason, Lee W.	**Barry N(orman) Malzberg**
Mason, Mason Jordon	**Judson Crews**
Mason, Michael	**Edgar Smith**
Mason, Tally	**August William Derleth**
Masterson, Whit.	**Bill Miller** and **Robert (Bob) Wade**
Master Therion	**Edward Alexander Crowley**
Matheson, Chris	**Richard Christian Matheson**
Matheson, Rodney	**John Creasey**
Maurois, André	**Emile Salomon Wilhelm Herzog**
Maynwaring, Archibald	**H(oward) P(hillips) Lovecraft**
Meade, Elizabeth Thomasina	**Elizabeth Thomasina Meade Smith**
Meade, L.T.	**Elizabeth Thomasina Meade Smith**
Meek, S.P.	**Sterner St. Paul Meek**
Meek, Sterner St. Paul	*S.P. Meek*
	Sterner St. Paul
Melmoth, Sebastian	**Oscar (Fingal O'Flahertie Wills) Wilde**
Mental Traveller, A	**Edward Alexander Crowley**
Merchant, Pau	*l*
	Harlan (Jay) Ellison
Merlyn, Arthur	**James (Benjamin) Blish**
Merrill, P.J.	**Holly Roth**
Merriman, Alex.	**Robert Silverberg**
Merritt, Aimee	**Forrest J(ames) Ackerman**
Metcalf, Suzanne	**L(yman) Frank Baum**
Meyer, Gustav	*Gustav Meyrink*
Meyrink, Gustav	**Gustav Meyer**
Michaelson, John Nairne	**Maxwell Anderson**
Miles	**Edward Alexander Crowley**
	Stephen Southwold
Militant	**Carl A. Sandburg**
Millar, Kenneth	*John Macdonald*
	John Ross Macdonald
	Ross Macdonald
Millay, Edna St. Vincent	*Edna St. Vincent Millay Boissevain*
	Nancy Boyd
Miller, Cincinnatus Heine	*Joaquin Miller*
Miller, Henry	*Phineas Flapdoodle*
Miller, Joaquin	**Cincinnatus Heine Miller**

Mills, S.J. . . . . **Edward Alexander Crowley**
Mitchell, Clyde . . . . **Harlan (Jay) Ellison** and **Robert Silverberg**
Mitchell, Clyde (T.) . . . . **(Gordon) Randall (Phillip David) Garrett**
Mitchell, Donald G(rant) . . . . *Ik Marvel*
Mohammed . . . . **Edward Alexander Crowley**
Mondelle, Wendayne . . . . **Forrest J(ames) Ackerman**
Moorcock, Michael (John) . . . . *Bill Barclay*
                                                    William Ewert Barclay
                                                    Michael Barrington
                                                   E(dward) P. Bradbury
                                                      James Colvin
                                                      Philip James
                                                      Hank Janson
                                                      Desmond Reid
Moore, C(atherine) L(ucille). . . . . *Keith Hammond*
                                                      Hudson Hastings
                                                      C.H. Liddell
                                               Mrs. Henry Kuttner
                                                      C.L. Moore
                                         Lawrence O'Donnell
                                                   Lewis Padgett
Morck, Paal . . . . **O(le) E(dvart) Rølvaag**
Morgan, Jane . . . . **James Fenimore Cooper**
Morgenstern, S. . . . . **William Goldman**
Morland, Peter Henry. . . . . **Frederick Schiller Faust**
Morley, Brian. . . . . **Marion Zimmer Bradley**
Morley, Wilfred Owen. . . . . **Robert (Augustine) W(ard) Lowndes**
Morpheus . . . . **Edward Alexander Crowley**
Morrison, Richard . . . . **Robert (Augustine) W(ard) Lowndes**
Morrison, Robert . . . . **Robert (Augustine) W(ard) Lowndes**
Morrison, Toni . . . . **Chloe Anthony Wofford**
Morton, Anthony . . . . **John Creasey**
Mourner Clad In Green, A . . . . **Edward Alexander Crowley**
Muddock, James Edward . . . . *Dick Donovan*
                           Joyce E(mmerson) Preston-Muddock
Mude, O.. . . . . **Edward (St. John) Gorey**
Multatuli . . . . **Eduard Douwes Dekker**
Mulvey, Thomas . . . . *Victor W. Appleton II*
Munchausen, Baron . . . . **Hugo Gernsback**
Mundy, Talbot . . . . **William L(ancaster) Gribbon**
Munro, H(ector) H(ugh) . . . . *Saki*
Munroe, Duncan H. . . . . **Eric F(rank) Russell**
Murgatroyd, Matthew. . . . . **James Athearn Jones**
Myles, Simon . . . . **Ken(neth Martin) Follett**
Nabokov, Vladimir Dmitrievich . . . . *V. Nabokov-Sirin*

Optic, Oliver	**William Taylor Adams**
Orczy, Baroness	**Mrs. Montague Barstow**
Orczy, Emma Magdalena Rosalia Maria Josefa Barbara	**Mrs. Montague Barstow**
O'Reilly, John	*Tex O'Reilly*
O'Reilly, Tex	**John O'Reilly**
Orson, Richard	*Frances & Richard Lockeridge*
Orwell, George	**Eric Arthur Blair**
Osborne, David	**Robert Silverberg**
Osborne, George	**Robert Silverberg**
Osceola	**Karen Christence Blixen-Finecke**
Otis, James	**James Otis Kaler**
Ouida	**(Marie) Louise de la Ramée**
Oursler, (Charles) Fulton	*Anthony Abbott*
	Arnold Fountain
	Samri Frikell
Ouspensky, P.D.	**Petr Uspenskii**
Oz, Amos	**Amos Klausner**
Padgett, Lewis	**Henry Kuttner** and **C(atherine) L(ucille) Moore**
Page,	**James Keena Page Jr.**
Page, James Keena, Jr.	*Jake Page*
Paget-Lowe, H(enry)	**H(oward) P(hillips) Lovecraft**
Paige, Richard	**Dean (Ray) Koontz**
Paley, Morton D.	**Sam(uel Kimball) Merwin Jr.**
Pansy	**Isabella MacDonald Alden**
Panurge	**Edward Alexander Crowley**
Park, Jordan	**C(yril) M. Kornbluth** and **Frederik (George) Pohl**
Park, Robert	**Erle Stanley Gardner**
Parker, Bert	**Harlan (Jay) Ellison**
Parker, Dorothy	**Dorothy Rothschild**
Parker, Leslie	**Angela (MacKail) Thirkell**
Parker, Lucas	**John Wyndham Parkes Lucas Beynon Harris**
Parkes, Lucas	**John Wyndham Parkes Lucas Beynon Harris**
Parkes, Wyndham	**John Wyndham Parkes Lucas Beynon Harris**
Parnell, Francis	**Festus Pragnell**
Parr, Robert	**Erle Stanley Gardner**
Parsons, Enid, aged twelve	**Edward Alexander Crowley**
Paul, Sterner St.	**S.P. Meek**
Pearson, Martin	**C(yril) M. Kornbluth** and **Donald A(llen) Wollheim**
Pellume, Noam D.	**Orson Scott Card**
Pendennis, Arthur	**William Makepeace Thackeray**
Pendleton,	**Chet Cunningham**
Pendleton, Don(ald Eugene)	*Dan Britain*
	Stephan Gregory
Pentecost, Hugh	**Judson (Pentecost) Phillips**

Percurabo .... **Edward Alexander Crowley**
Perdurabo .... **Edward Alexander Crowley**
Perdurabo, Frater .... **Edward Alexander Crowley**
Perdurabo, Prater. .... **Edward Alexander Crowley**
Perez, Juan .... **Manly Wade Wellman**
Perse, St. John .... **Aléxis St. Léger**
Person of Honour, ... **Jonathan Swift**
Person of Quality, A .... **Jonathan Swift**
Peshkov, Alexi Maximovitch .... *Maxim Gorki*
Petaja, Emil (Theodore) .... *Theodore Pine*
Peters, Curtis Arnoux .... *Peter Arno*
Pfaal, Hans .... **Edgar Allan Poe**
Philips, Hugh Pentecost .... **Judson Philips**
Philips, Judson .... *Hugh Pentecost Philips*
Phillips, James Atlee .... *Philip Atlee*
Phillips, Judson (Pentecost) .... *Phillips, Mark*
Phillips, Richard .... **Philip K(indred) Dick**
Phylos the Tibetan .... **Frederick S. Oliver**
Phypps, Hyacinthe .... **Edward (St. John) Gorey**
Pig, Edward .... **Edward (St. John) Gorey**
Pike, Robert L. .... **Robert L(loyd) Fish**
Pitcairn, J(ohn) J(ames) .... *Clifford Ashdown*
Plath, Sylvia .... *Sylvia Hughes*
Victoria Lucas
Platts, A. Monmouth. .... **A(nthony) B(erkeley) Cox**
Plick et Plock .... **Georges Simenon**
Plunkett, Edward John Moreton Drax .... *Lord Dunsany*
Poe, Edgar Allan .... *Hans Pfaal*
Quarles
Pohl, Frederik (George), (Jr.) .... *Elton V. Andrews*
Henry De Costa
Paul Flehr
S.D. Gottesman
Warren F. Howard
Walt Lasly
Paul Dennis Lavond
James MacCreigh
Scott Mariner
Ernest Mason
Ernst Mason
Edson McCann
Jordan Park
Charles Satterfield
Dirk Wylie
Allen Zweig

Porter, William Sydney .... *O. Henry*
Poum et Zette .... **Georges Simenon**
Pound, Ezra (Weston Loomis) .... *Alfred Venison*
Power, Cecil .... **Charles Grant Blairfindie Allen**
Pragnell, Festus .... *Francis Parnell*
Prather, Richard S(cott) .... *David Knight*
           Douglas Ring
Pratt, Dennis .... *Quentin Crisp*
Pratt, (Murray) Fletcher .... *George U. Fletcher*
           Irwin Lester
           B.F. Ruby
Prescot, Dray .... **(Henry) Kenneth Bulmer**
Prescot, J. .... **(Henry) Kenneth Bulmer**
Probationer. .... **Edward Alexander Crowley**
Prometheus .... **Edward Alexander Crowley**
Pronzini, Bill .... **William John Pronzini**
Pronzini, William John .... *Robert Hart Davis*
           Jack Foxx
           Brett Halliday
           William Jeffrey
           Bill Pronzini
           Alex Saxon
           Jack Saxon
Prospero and Caliban .... **Frederick William Rolfe**
Pryor, Vanessa .... **Chelsea Quinn Yarbro**
Pudor, Prob .... **Edward Alexander Crowley**
Putnam, Arthur Lee. .... **Horatio Alger**
Putnam, J. Wesley .... **Harry Sinclair Drago**
Puzo, Mario .... *Mario Cleri*
Pyeshkov, Aleksei Maksimovich .... *Maxim Gorki [Gorky]*
Q .... **Arthur T(homas) Quiller-Couch**
Quarles .... **Edgar Allan Poe**
Queen, Ellery .... **Frederic Dannay** and **Manfred Bennington Lepovsky**
Quiller, A., Jr. .... **Edward Alexander Crowley**
Quiller, Andrew .... **(Henry) Kenneth Bulmer**
Quiller-Couch, Arthur T(homas). .... *Q*
Quinn, Martin .... **Martin Cruz Smith**
Quinn, Simon .... **Martin Cruz Smith**
Quyth, Gabriel .... **Gary Jennings**
R., C.G. .... **Christina G(eorgina) Rossetti**
Rabelais, François .... *Alcofribas Nasier*
Rabinowitz, Sholem Yakov .... *Sholem Aleichem*
Rachen, Kurt Von .... **L(a Fayette) Ron(ald) Hubbard**
Raine, William MacLeod .... *Austin MacLeod*
Raleigh, Richard. .... **H(oward) P(hillips) Lovecraft**

Ramsay, Ethel . . . . **Edward Alexander Crowley**
Ramsay, Jay . . . . **(John) Ramsey Campbell**
Rand . . . . **Robert Silverberg**
Ranger, Ken . . . . **John Creasey**
Rawlins, Eustace . . . . **Eustace Robert Barton**
Rayner, Olive Pratt . . . . **Charles Grant Blairfindie Allen**
Reader, Constant . . . . **Dorothy Rothschild**
Reed, Eliot . . . . **Eric Ambler** and **Charles Rodda**
Reed, Ishmael . . . . *Emmett Coleman*
Reed, Peter . . . . **John D(ann) MacDonald**
Reilly, William K. . . . . **John Creasey**
Reizenstein, Elmer L(eopold) . . . . *Elmer (L.) Rice*
Remus, Uncle . . . . **Joel Chandler Harris**
Repp, Ed(ward) Earl . . . . *John Cody*
Peter Field
Reynolds, Ron . . . . **Ray(mond Douglas) Bradbury**
Rice, Elmer (L.) . . . . **Elmer L(eopold) Reizenstein**
Richards, Frank . . . . . **Robert (Ranke) Graves** and **Charles (Harold St. John)**
Hamilton
Ridgway, Jason . . . . **Milton Lesser**
Riley, James Whitcomb . . . . *Benj(amin) F. Johnson*
Riley, Tex . . . . **John Creasey**
Roberts, John . . . . **David Ernest Bingley**
Edward Alexander Crowley
Roberts, Kenneth . . . . **Lester Dent**
Roberts, Lawrence . . . . **Robert L(loyd) Fish**
Roberts, Terence . . . . **Ivan T. Sanderson**
Robertson, Constance (Pierrepont) Noyes . . . . *Dana Scott*
Robertson, Ellis . . . . **Harlan (Jay) Ellison** and **Robert Silverberg**
Rodman, Eric . . . . **Robert Silverberg**
Roeder, Pat . . . . **Harlan (Jay) Ellison**
Rogers, Doug . . . . **Ray(mond Douglas) Bradbury**
Rohmer, Sax . . . . **Arthur (Henry) Sarsfield Ward**
Rolfe, Frederick William . . . . *Baron (Frederick) Corvo*
Prospero and Caliban
Rølvaag, O(le) E(dvart) . . . . *Paal Morck*
Romaine, Jules . . . . **Louis Fairigoule**
Romanoff, Alexander Nicholayevitch . . . . *Achmed Abdullah*
Rome, Anthony (Tony) . . . . **Marvin H(ubert) Albert** and **J.D. Christilian**
Rosa Mundi, The Author of . . . . **Edward Alexander Crowley**
Ross, Leonard Q. . . . . **Leo Rosten**
Rossetti, Christina G(eorgina) . . . . *C.G.R.*
Rosten, Leo . . . . *Leonard Q. Ross*
Roth, Holly . . . . *K.G. Ballard*
P.J. Merrill

Rothschild, Dorothy .... *Dorothy Parker*
Constant Reader
Rotsler, William .... *Victor W. Appleton II*
Ruby, B.F. .... **(Murray) Fletcher Pratt**
Russell, George William .... *A.E.*
Ryan, Tim .... **Lester Dent**
Ryder, Jonathon .... **Robert Ludlum**
S., S.H. .... **Siegfried Sassoon**
S., S.O. .... **Edward Alexander Crowley**
Saki .... **H(ector) H(ugh) Munro**
Sand, George .... **Amandine-Aurore-Lucile Dupin**
Sand, Jules .... **Amandine-Aurore-Lucile Dupin**
Sandburg, Carl A. .... *Militant*
Sanders, Winston P. .... **Poul (William) Anderson**
Sanderson, Ivan T .... *Terence Roberts*
Sapiens, H. .... **Edward Alexander Crowley**
Sapper .... **H(erman) C(yril) McNeile**
Saroyan, William .... *Sirak Goryan*
Sassoon, Siegfried .... *Saul Kain*
Pynchbeck Lyre
S.H.S.
Sayers, Dorothy L(eigh) .... *Miss Di Chester*
Dorothy Leigh Sayers Fleming
Scarff, William .... **Algirdas Jonas Budrys**
Schoolcraft, John .... **Frederick Schiller Faust**
Scoppettone, Sandra .... *Jack Early*
Scot, ... **(Henry) Kenneth Bulmer**
Scotland, Jay. .... **John (William) Jakes**
Searls, Hank .... **Henry H(unt) Searls**
Searls, Henry H(unt) .... *Hank Searls*
Sebastian, Lee .... **Robert Silverberg**
Seton, Ernest Thompson .... *Wolf Thompson*
Seuss, Dr .... **Theodor Seuss Geisel**
Shackleton, C.C. .... **Brian W(ilson) Aldiss**
Shakespear, William, pp. Ouija Board .... **Edward Alexander Crowley**
Shannon, Dell .... **(Barbara) Elizabeth Linington**
Shaw, George Bernard .... *Corns Di Bassetto*
Shaw, Henry Wheeler .... *Josh Billings*
Shawn, Frank S. .... **Ron(ald Joseph) Goulart**
Sheldon, John .... **Robert (Albert) Bloch**
Shepherd, Michael .... **Robert Ludlum**
Sherwood, Nelson .... **(Henry) Kenneth Bulmer**
Shiel, M(atthew) P(hipps) .... *Gordon Holmes*
Shivaji, Mahatma Guru Sri Paramahansa .... **Edward Alexander Crowley**
S.H.S .... **Siegfried Sassoon**

Shute, Nevil . . . . **Nevil Shute Norway**
Shy, Timothy . . . . **D.B. Wyndham Lewis**
Siluriensis, Leolinus . . . . **Arthur Machen**
Silver, Nicholas . . . . **Frederick Schiller Faust**
Silver, Richard . . . . **(Henry) Kenneth Bulmer**
Silverberg, Robert . . . . *Gordon Aghill*
Robert Arnette
T.D. Bethlen
Alexander Blade
Ralph Burke
Robert Burke
Walter Chapman
Dirk Clinton
Walter Drummond
Don Elliot(t)
Richard Greer
E.K. Jarvis
Ivar Jorgenson
Warren Kastel
Calvin M. Knox
Dan Malcom
Webber Martin
Ray McKenzie
Alex Merriman
Clyde Mitchell
David Osborne
George Osborne
Robert Randall
Ellis Robertson
Eric Rodman
Lee Sebastian
Leonard G. Spencer
S.M. Tenneshaw
Hall Thornton
Gerald Vance
Richard F. Watson
L.T. Woodward MD
Simenon, Georges . . . . *Bobette*
Christian Brulls
J.K. Charles
Germain d'Antibes Georges d'Isly
Jacques Dersonne
Jean Dorsage
Luc Dorsan
Jean Dossage

Jean du Perry
Gom Gut, Kim
Georges Martin-Georges
Plick et Plock
Poum et Zette
Georges Sim
Georges Simm
Gaston Vialis
G. Vialo
G. Violis
X

Simm, Georges	**Georges Simenon**
Sinclair, Grant	**Harry Sinclair Drago**
Sinclair, Upton	*Frederick Garrison*
Sinistram, Super.	**Edward Alexander Crowley**
Sirin, V.	**Vladimir Dmitrievich Nabokov**
Six Six Six (666).	**Edward Alexander Crowley**
Six Six Six (666), The Prophet of the New Aeon	**Edward Alexander Crowley**
Sklar, Richard	*Victor W. Appleton II*
Slater, Ray	**Joe R. Lansdale**
Slaughter, Frank G(ill)	*G. Arnold Haygood*
	C.V. Terry
Sloluck, J. Milton	**Ambrose (Gwinnett) Bierce**
Smith, Charles H.	*Bill Arp*
Smith, Clark Ashton	*Timeus Gaylord*
	Chrisophe des Laurieres
Smith, Doc.	**E(dward) E(lmer) "Doc" Smith**
Smith, E(dward) E(lmer) "Doc"	*Doc Smith*
Smith, Elizabeth Thomasina Meade	*Elizabeth Thomasina Meade*
	L.T. Meade
Smith, Ernest Bramah	*Ernest Bramah*
Smith, Johnston	**Stephen Crane**
Smith, Joyce Carol Oates	**Joyce Carol Oates**
Smith, Kate Douglas	*Kate Douglas Wiggin*
Smith, Rosamond.	**Joyce Carol Oates**
Smith, T. Carlyle	**John Kendrick Bangs**
Smith, Woodrow Wilson.	**Henry Kuttner**
Snell, Roy. J.	*James Craig*
Softly, Edward	**H(oward) P(hillips) Lovecraft**
Solo, Jay	**Harlan (Jay) Ellison**
Somers, Jane	**Doris (May) Lessing**
Somers, Jonathan Swift, III	**Philip José Farmer**
Southern, Terry	*Maxwell Kenton*
Sparks, Timothy.	**Charles Dickens**
Spaulding, Douglas	**Ray(mond Douglas) Bradbury**

Spaulding, Leonard .... **Ray(mond Douglas) Bradbury**
Spencer, John .... **Roy (C.) Vickers**
Spencer, Leonard G. ... **(Gordon) Randall (Phillip David) Garrett** & **Robert Silverberg**
Stairs, Gordon .... **Mary H(unter) Austin**
Stanislavsky, Constantin. .... **Constantin Sergeyevich Alekseyev**
Stanton, Schuyler .... **L(yman) Frank Baum**
Stark, Richard .... **D(onald) E(dwin) Westlake**
Starr, Julian. .... **Horatio Alger**
Staunton, Schuyler .... **L(yman) Frank Baum**
Steele, Addison E. .... **Richard A(llen) Lupoff**
Stendahl. .... **Marie-Henri Beyle**
Stendahl, Baron de .... **Marie-Henri Beyle**
Steptoe, Lydia .... **Djuna Barnes**
Sterling, Brett .... **Ray(mond Douglas) Bradbury** and **Edmond (Moore) Hamilton**
Stewart, J(ohn) I(nnes) M(ackintosh) .... *Michael Innes*
St. John, David .... **E(verette) Howard Hunt Jr.**
St. John, Henry .... **John Creasey**
St. John, John .... **Edward Alexander Crowley**
Stoddard, Charles .... **Henry Kuttner**
Stone, I.F. .... **Isidor Feinstein**
Stone, Irving .... *Irving Tannenbaum*
Stowe, Harriet Beecher .... **Harriet (Elizabeth) Beecher**
Sturgeon, Theodore .... **Edward Hamilton Waldo**
Svaroff, Count Vladimir. .... **Edward Alexander Crowley**
Swift, Jonathan .... *Isaac Bickerstaff*
A Dissenter
M.B. Drapier
A Person of Honour
A Person of Quality
T.R.D.J.S.D.O.P.I.I.]
Swithen, John .... **Stephen (Edwin) King**
T., H.K. .... **Edward Alexander Crowley**
T., J. .... **Eric Temple Bell**
Tabasco, Alexander .... **Edward Alexander Crowley**
Taine, John .... **Eric Temple Bell**
Tait, Eric .... **Edward Alexander Crowley**
Tannenbaum, Irving .... **Irving Stone**
Tanner, William .... **(Sir) Kingsley (William) Amis**
Tarr, M.S. .... **Edward Alexander Crowley**
Tarrant, John .... **Clive Egleton**
Taylor, Phoebe Atwood .... *Alice Tilton*
T.B.A. .... **Thomas Bailey Aldrich**
Tenn, William .... **Philip (J.) Klass**

Book Collector's Price Guide

Terry, C.V. . . . . **Frank G(ill) Slaughter**
Thackeray, William Makepeace . . . . *Arthur Pendennis*
Michael Angelo Titmarsh
Theophile Wagstaff]
Thelema, Logos Aionos . . . . **Edward Alexander Crowley**
Theobold, Lewis, Jr. . . . . **H(oward) P(hillips) Lovecraft**
Therion . . . . **Edward Alexander Crowley**
Therion, Master . . . . **Edward Alexander Crowley**
Therion, To Mega DCLXVI . . . . **Edward Alexander Crowley**
Thibault, Jacques-Anatole- . . . . *Anatole France*
Gérôme
Thomas, David. . . . . **Edward Alexander Crowley**
Thornton, Hall. . . . . **Robert Silverberg**
Three, C. Three . . . . **Oscar Wilde**
Tiger, Derry . . . . **Harlan (Jay) Ellison**
Torquemada . . . . **John Dickson Carr**
Torr, Alice Wesley . . . . **Edward Alexander Crowley**
Tourgée, Albion W(inegar) . . . . *Henry Churton*
Edgar Henry
Traven, B. . . . . **Berick Traven Torsvan**
T.R.D.J.S.D.O.P.I.I. . . . . **Jonathan Swift**
Trevor, Glen . . . . **James Hilton**
Trueblood, Ernest V. . . . . **William (Cuthbert) Faulkner**
Tupper, M. . . . . **Edward Alexander Crowley**
Turner, J. . . . . **Edward Alexander Crowley**
Twain, Mark . . . . **Samuel Langhorne Clemens**
Undercliffe, Errol . . . . **(John) Ramsey Campbell**
Uriel, Henry . . . . **Frederick Schiller Faust**
Uspenskii, Petr . . . . *P.D. Ouspensky*
Vace, Geoffrey . . . . **Hugh B. Cave**
Vadé, Catherine . . . . **François Marie Arouet**
Vadé, Guillaume . . . . **François Marie Arouet**
Van Campen, Karl . . . . **John Wood Campbell Jr.**
Van Dine, S.S. . . . . **Willard Huntington Wright**
Van Dyne, Edith . . . . **L(yman) Frank Baum**
Vardeman, Robert (Bob) E(dward) . . . . *Victor W. Appleton II*
Paul Kenyon,
Daniel Moran
Vedder, John K. . . . . **Frank Gruber**
Verey, Rev C. . . . . **Edward Alexander Crowley**
Vernon, Olivia . . . . **Anne Brontë**
Vialis, Gaston. . . . . **Georges Simenon**
Vialo, G. . . . . **Georges Simenon**
Viaud, L.M. Julien . . . . *Pierre Loti*
Vicarion, Count Palmiro . . . . **Christopher Logue**

Victor	**Edward Alexander Crowley**
Vidal, Eugene Luther Gore, Jr.	*Edgar Box*
Viffa, Ananda	**Edward Alexander Crowley**
Vigil	**Arthur Koestler**
Vijja, Ananda	**Edward Alexander Crowley**
Vincey, Leo	**Edward Alexander Crowley**
Violis, G.	**Georges Simenon**
Viridis, Leo	**Edward Alexander Crowley**
Voltaire	**François Marie Arouet**
Von Drey, Howard	**Howard E(lmer) Wandrei**
von Rachen, Kurt	**L(a Fayette) Ron(ald) Hubbard Sr.**
Von Schartzkopf, Professor Theophilus, Ph.D, ...	**Edward Alexander Crowley**
Voyant, Claire.	**Forrest J(ames) Ackerman**
V Sign, The Author of the	**Edward Alexander Crowley**
W., M.	**Edward Alexander Crowley**
W., N.	**C(live) S(taples) Lewis**
Wagstaff, Theophile	**William Makepeace Thackeray**
Wallace, Irving	**Irving Wallechinsky**
Wallechinsky, Irving	*Irving Wallace*
Walley, Bryon.	**Orson Scott Card**
Walser, Sam	**Robert E(rvin) Howard**
Walter, Killiam Christian	**Hans Christian Andersen**
Wandrei, Howard E(lmer)	*Robert A. Garron*
	Howard W. Graham
	H.W. Guernsey
	Howard Von Drey
Warborough, Joseph	**Charles Grant Blairfindie Allen**
Warborough, Martin Leach	**Charles Grant Blairfindie Allen**
Ward, Artemus	**Charles Farrar Browne**
Ward, Arthur (Henry) Sarsfield	*Michael Furey*
	Sax Rohmer
Ward, ...	**Frederick Schiller Faust**
Ward, Robert	**Robert E(rvin) Howard**
Ward-Thomas (nee Stephens), Evelyn (Bridget Patricia)	*Evelyn Anthony*
	Eve Stephens
Warland, Allen.	**Donald A(llen) Wollheim**
Washington, Berwell	**James Branch Cabell**
Watkins, Gerrold	**Barry N(orman) Malzberg**
Watson, John H., MD.	**Philip José Farmer**
Watson, Richard F.	**Robert Silverberg**
Weary, Ogdred	**Edward (St. John) Gorey**
Webb, Christopher	**Leonard (Patrick O'Connor) Wibberley**
Weedy, Garrod	**Edward (St. John) Gorey**
Weinstein, Nathan Wellensten	*Nathaniel West*
Wellesley, Lord Charles	**Charlotte Brontë**

Wellman, Manly Wade .... *Levi Crow*
Manuel Ferney
Gans T. Field
Will Garth
Juan Perez
Hampton Wells
Wade Wells

Wells, Braxton. .... **Donald A(llen) Wollheim**
Wells, Hampton. .... **Manly Wade Wellman**
Wells, H(erbert) G(eorge) .... *Reginald Bliss*
Wells, Hubert George .... **Forrest J(ames) Ackerman**
Wells, John Jay. .... **Marion Zimmer Bradley** and **Juanita Coulson**
Wells, J. Wellington .... **L(yon) Sprague de Camp**
Wells, Mark .... **Edward Alexander Crowley**
Wells, Wade. .... **Manly Wade Wellman**
Wentworth, Robert .... **Edmond (Moore) Hamilton**
Wentworth, Thomas. .... **Edward Alexander Crowley**
Wentz, Elma .... **Robert Anson Heinlein**
West, C.P. .... **P(elham) G(renville) Wodehouse**
West, ... **August William Derleth**
West, Nathaniel .... **Nathan Wellensten Weinstein**
West, Owen .... **Dean (Ray) Koontz**
Westlake, D(onald) E(dwin) .... *John B. Allan*
Curt Clark
Tucker Coe
Timothy J. Culver
J. Morgan Cunningham
Samuel Holt
Sheldon Lord
Richard Stark

Westmacott, Mary .... **Agatha (Mary Clarissa Miller) Christie**
Wharton, Christabel .... **Edward Alexander Crowley**
White, E(lwyn) B(rooks) .... *E.B.W.*
White, Harlan .... **Harlan (Jay) Ellison**
White, Theodore Edward .... *Ron Archer*
Norman Edwards
Ted White

Whittlebot, Hernia. .... **(Sir) Noel (Pierce) Coward**
Wibberley, Leonard (Patrick O'Connor) .... *Leonard Holton*
Patrick O'Connor
Christopher Webb

Wick, Carter .... **Colin Wilcox**
Wiggin, Kate Douglas .... **Kate Douglas Smith**
Wilcox, Colin .... *Carter Wick*
Wilde, Jimmy .... **John Creasey**

Wilde, Oscar (Fingal O'Flahertie Wills). . . . . *C. Three Three (C.3.3)*
Sebastian Melmoth
Fingal O'Flahertie Wills

Wilder, Allen. . . . . **John (William) Jakes**

Wilkins, Mary. . . . . **Mary E(leanor) Wilkins Freeman**

Willer. . . . . **Edward A. Emshwiller**

Willey, Robert . . . . **Willy Ley**

Williams, J. Walker. . . . . **P(elham) G(renville) Wodehouse**

Williams, Tennessee . . . . **Thomas L(anier) Williams**

Williams, Thomas L(anier) . . . . *Tennessee Williams*

Willie, Albert Frederick . . . . **H(oward) P(hillips) Lovecraft**

Willington, James. . . . . **Oliver Goldsmith**

Willis, Charles . . . . **Arthur C(harles) Clarke**

Wills, Fingal O'Flahertie. . . . . **Oscar (Fingal O'Flahertie Wills) Wilde**

Wills, Thomas . . . . **William (Thomas) Ard**

Willy the Wisp. . . . . **Donald A(llen) Wollheim**

Wilmer, Old . . . . **Ring Lardner Jr.**

Wilson, John Anthony Burgess . . . . *Joseph Kell*

Windham, Basil . . . . **P(elham) G(renville) Wodehouse**

Windham, John . . . . **John Wyndham Parkes Lucas Beynon Harris**

Witherup, Anne Warrington. **John Kendrick Bangs**

Wodehouse, P(elham) G(renville) . . . . *Pelham Grenville*
P. WestC
J. Walker Williams
Basil Windham

Wolfe, Aaron . . . . **Dean (Ray) Koontz**

Wollheim, Donald A(llen) . . . . *Graham Conway*
Millard Verne Gordon
Verne Gordon
David Grinnell
Martin Pearson
Allen Warland
Braxton Wells
Braxton Wells
Willy the Wisp
Lawrence Woods
X

Woodard, Wayne . . . . *Hannes Bok*
Woolrich, Cornell . . . . **Cornell George Hopley-Woolrich**
Wrapper, Sumatra . . . . **Edward Alexander Crowley**
Wright, Robert . . . **Forrest J(ames) Ackerman & Robert (Augustine) W(ard)
Lowndes**
Wright, Weaver . . . . **Forrest J(ames) Ackerman**
Wright, Willard Huntington . . . . *S.S. Van Dine*
Wryde, Dogear . . . . **Edward (St. John) Gorey**
Wyndam, John . . . . **John Wyndham Parkes Lucas Benton Harris**
X . . . . **Georges Simenon**
Donald A(llen) Wollheim
Ya, Kwaw Li . . . . **Edward Alexander Crowley**
Yin, Leslie C(harles) B(owyer) . . . . *Leslie Charteris*
York, Jeremy . . . . **John Creasey**
York, Simon . . . . **Robert Anson Heinlein**
Young, Collier . . . . **Robert (Albert) Bloch**
Youngman-Carter, Margery Allingham . . . . **Margery Louise Allingham**
Yuen, Ko . . . . **Edward Alexander Crowley**
Zelazny, Roger (Joseph) . . . . *Harrison Denmark*
Zenobia, Alexandria . . . . **Anne Brontë**
Zetford, Tully . . . . **(Henry) Kenneth Bulmer**
Zoilus . . . . **H(oward) P(hillips) Lovecraft**
Zola, Emile . . . . **Eduoard Charles Antoine**
Zweig, Allen . . . . **Frederik (George) Pohl (Jr.)**
Zweig, Stefan . . . . *Stephen Branch*

Signature guide

Many years ago, I bought a collection of poetry books from a defunct bookstore. Once I had them all up on shelves, I noticed that there were quite a few copies of *Vagabond's House* by Don Blandings, 16 in all, as well as six copies of other books by Blandings *(Songs of the Seven Senses, Floridays, The Rest of the Road)*, all of them signed. A few days later, hanging around Fourth Avenue bookshops in New York, which was once very near my profession, I found exactly one copy of *Vagabond's House* that wasn't signed. I kidded the bookseller that he had an extremely rare copy. About the same period in my life, maybe a few years later, I used to go into a certain bookshop on Saturdays. About once a month, I'd run into a comic/columnist there named Joey Adams. He came in looking for old joke books for his column. Joey wrote a few books and, once, I caught him back in the stacks, surreptitiously signing the ones on the shelf. He'd take them up to the counter, and show the signatures to the daughter of the owner (who was off on Saturday). She'd mark them up and Joey would feel a whole lot better.

The point is that you can't really tell about signatures. Some cause a book's price to skyrocket; others are just there. If a book is a dog, then a signed copy of it is just a dog with a signature on it. In general, a signed copy by a living author is worth less than a dead author (who, presumably isn't going to make an appearance at a book signing). Also a living author might contract a disease I call the Blandings/Adams syndrome, signing any book within arm's reach. A limited and signed edition is usually better than a signed trade edition in that the publisher is, in a sense, guaranteeing the signature.

Below are sample signatures that I have verified one way or another. Some, I even watched being signed (which is no guarantee the signer was not an imposter). In short, be careful of paying a premium for signed books unless there is some verification of the signature. Even a grade school child can trace.

Allen Stang

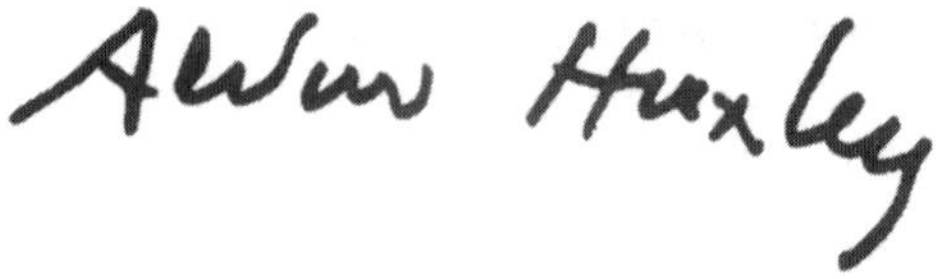

Aldous Huxley

Aliester Crowley

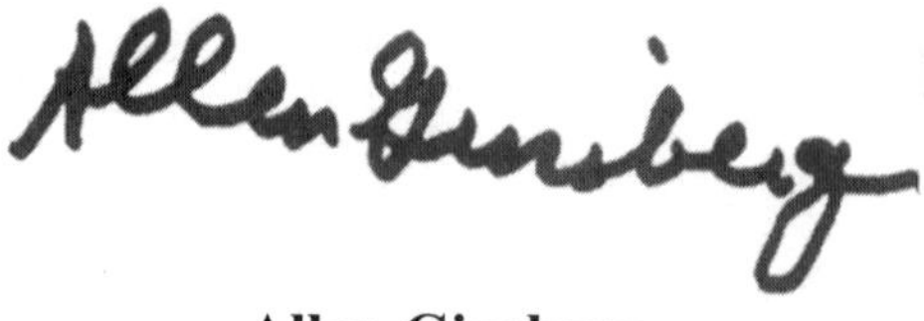

Allen Ginsberg

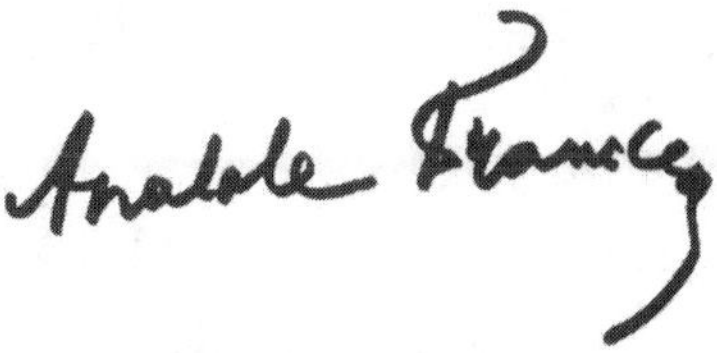

Antole France

Arthur Rackham

Andrew Lang

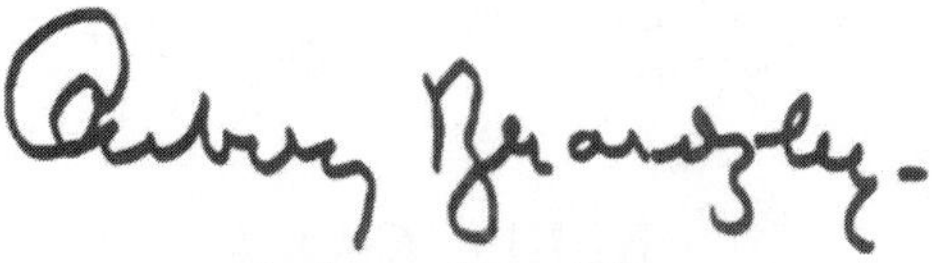

Aubrey Beadsley

Anne Rice

August Derleth

Archibald MacLeish

Bertrand Russell

Arthur Conan Doyle

Booth Tarkington

Arthur Machen

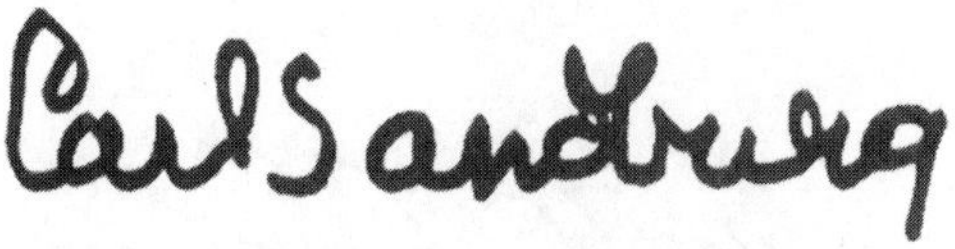

Carl Sandburg

Christina Rossetti

Eden Phillpots

Ciye Nino Cochise

Edgar Allen Poe

Dante Gabriel Rossetti

Edgar Lee Masters

D.H. Lawrence

Edna Ferber

Donald A. Wollheim

Edward Albee

Dorothy L. Sayer

Edwin Arlington Robinson

Edwin Markham

Eric Jong

e.e. cummings

Erma Bombeck

E.L. Doctorow

Eugene Fields

Elizebeth Barrett Browning

Eugene Lonesco

Ellery Queen Dannay

Evelyn Wagh

Ellery Queen Lee

Ezra Pound

George Santayana

Frank Ernest Hill

Gertrude Stein

Franz Kafka

Gore Vidal

Fredrick Remington

Gustave Dore

F. Scott Fitzgerald

Harlan Ellison

G. Bernard Shaw

Hart Crane

Henry D. Thoreau

Howard Pyle

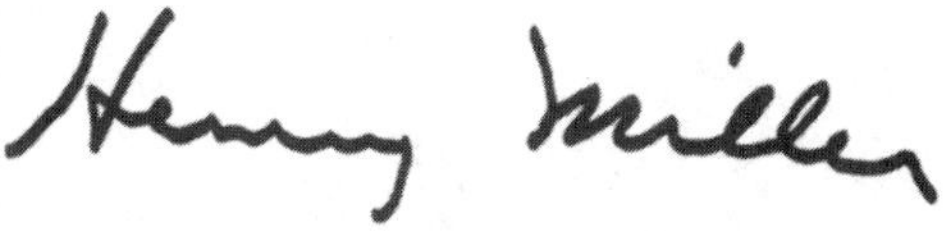

Henry James

H. Ryder Haggard

Henry Miller

Ian Fleming

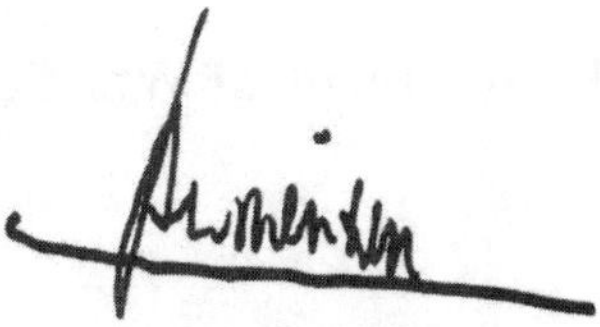

Herman Wouk

Immanuel Velikovsky

Hilda Doolittle

Jack Kerouac

H.L. Mencken

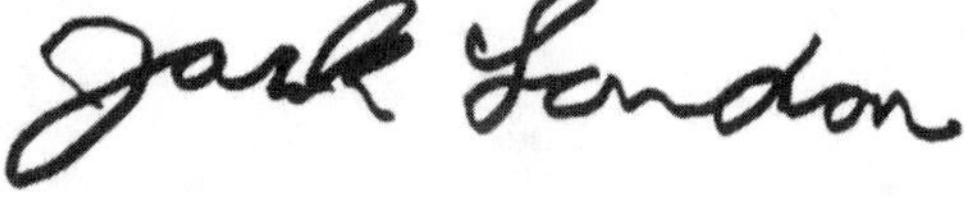

Jack London

Jack Page

James Whitcomb Riley

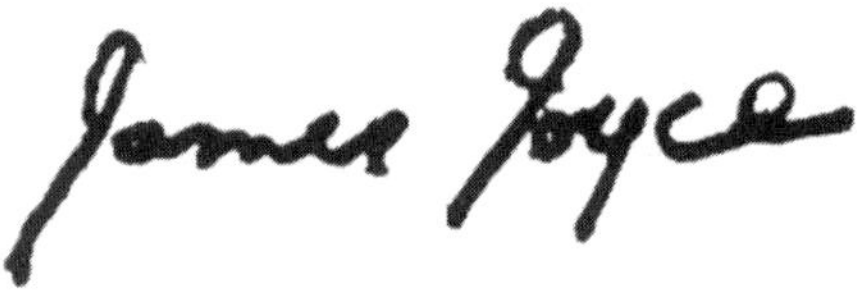

James Jones

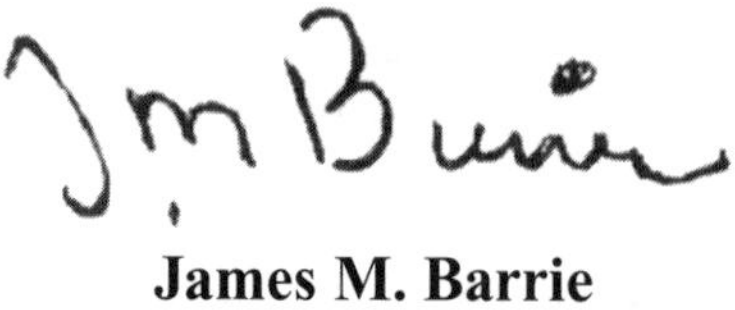

Jane Austen

James Joyce

J.D. Salinger

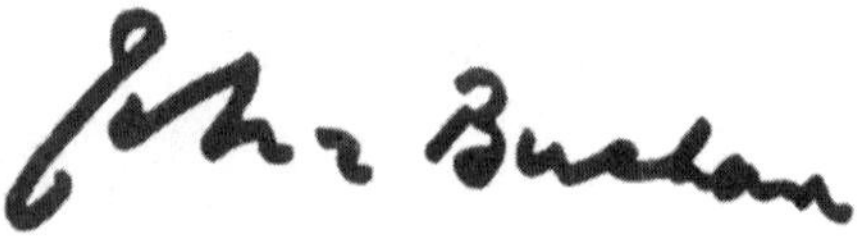

James M. Barrie

John Buchan

James Thurber

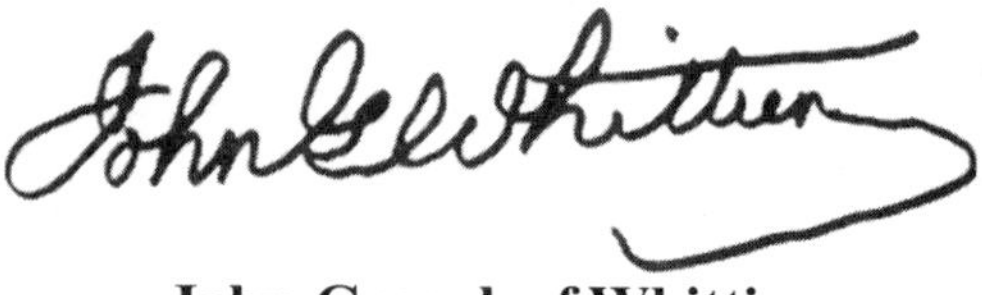

John Greenleaf Whittier

John Masefield

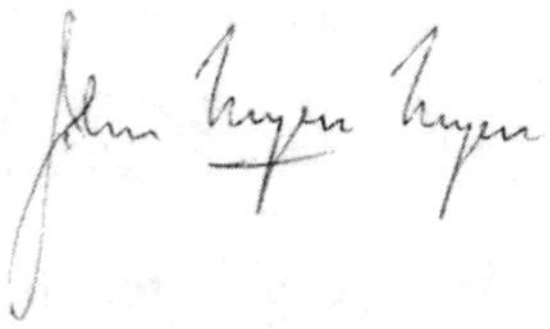

John Meyers Meyers

Joyce Kilmar

John P. Marquand

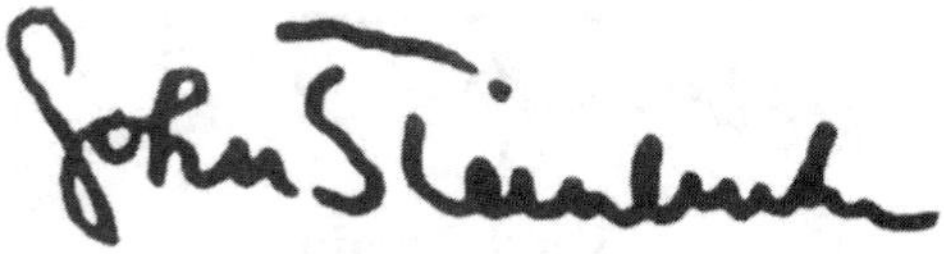

J.P. Donleavy

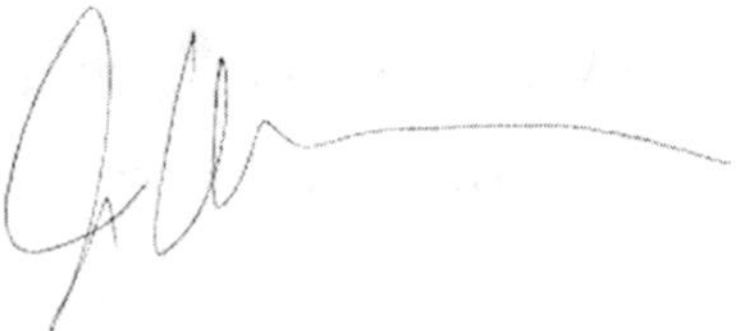

John Steinbeck

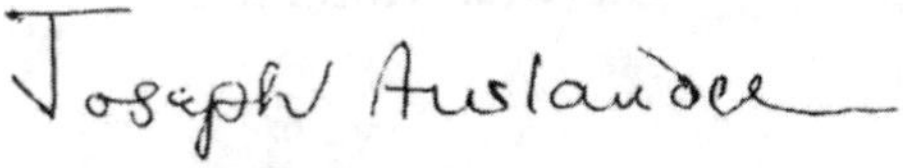

J.R.R. Tolkien

Johnathan Kellerman

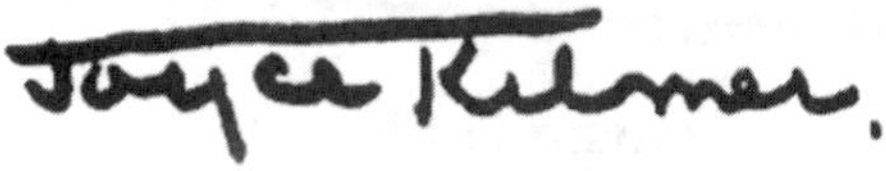

Lawrence Block

Joseph Auslander

Leon Uris

Joseph Conrad

L. Frank Baum

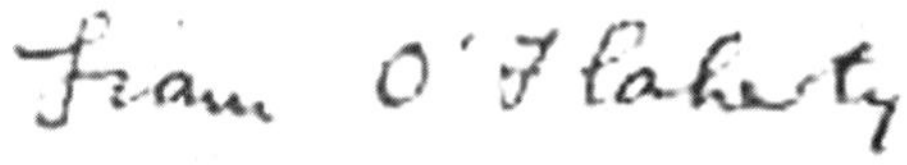

Liam O'Flaherty

Margaret Mitchell

Lord Dunsany

Marianne Moore

Louisa Mae Alcott

Mark Twain

Louis Anspacher

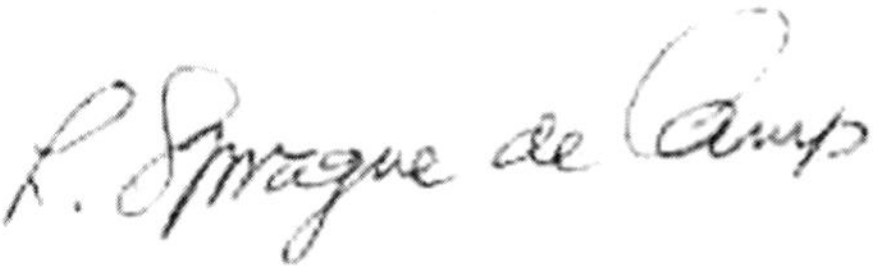

Max Beerbohm

L. Sprague de Camp

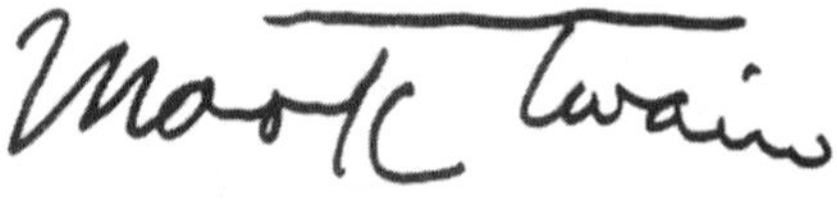

Maxwell Anderson

Madeleine L' Engle

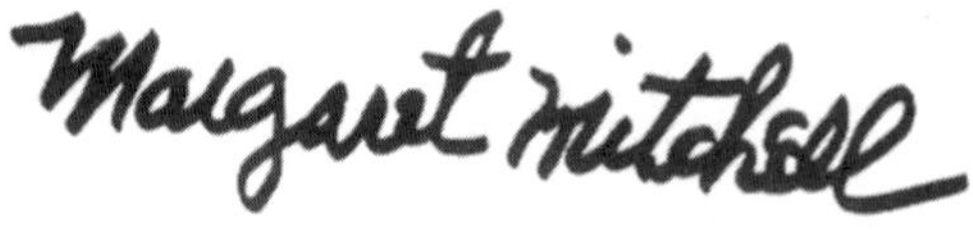

Meredith Wilson

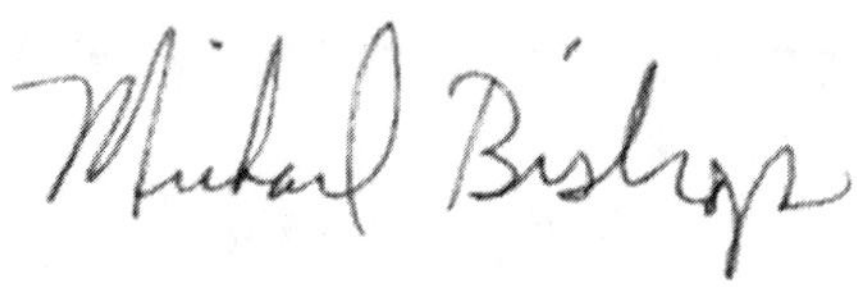

Michael Bishop

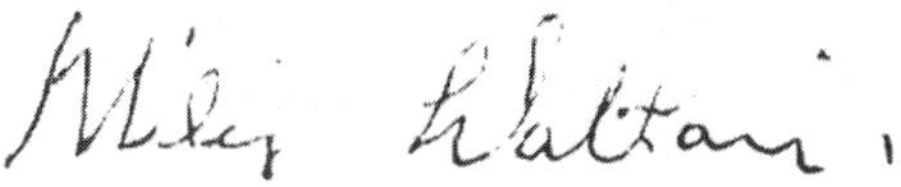

Paddy Chayefsky

Mika Waltari

Paul Goodman

M.P. Shiel

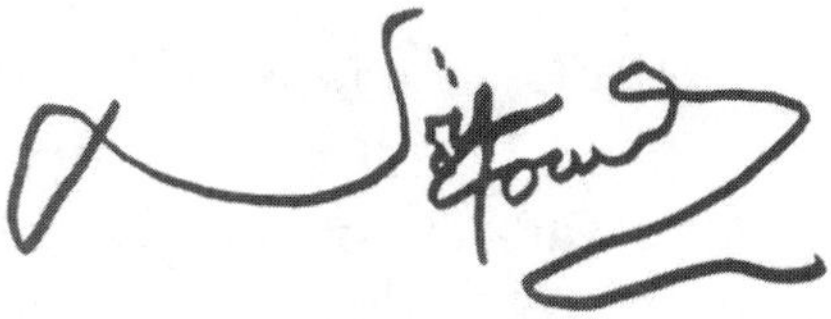

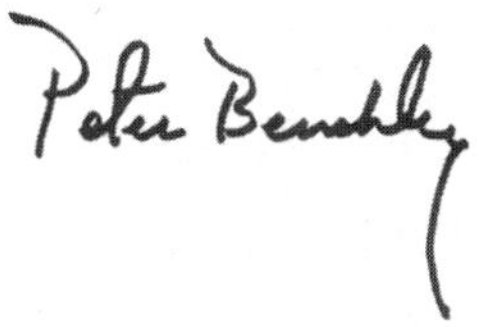

Peter Benchley

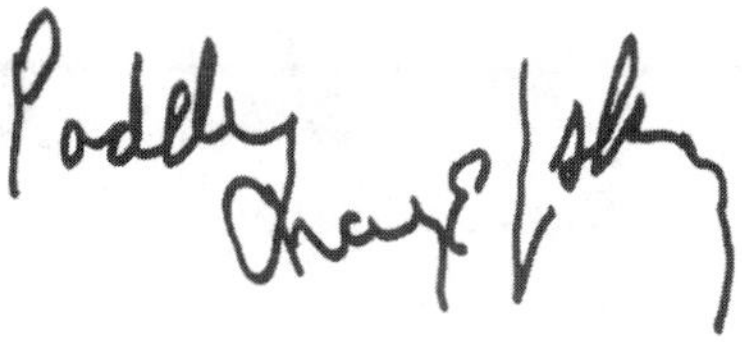

Noel Cowards

P.G. Wodehouse

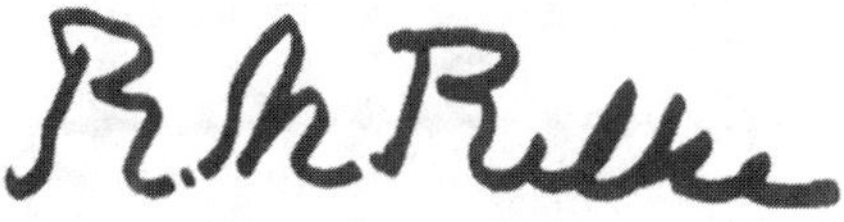

Norman Mailer

Rainer Marie Rilke

Orson Scott Card

Ralph Waldo Emerson

Randall Jarrell

Robert Browning

Ray Bradbury

Robert Creeley

Ray Russell

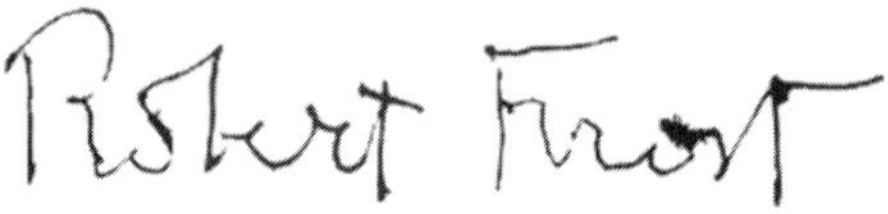

Robert Frost

Richard Le Gallienne

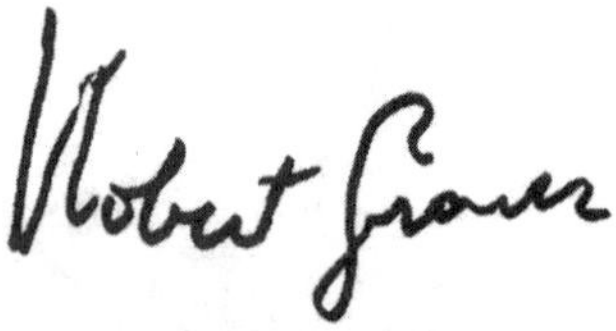

Robert Graves

Richard Wilbur

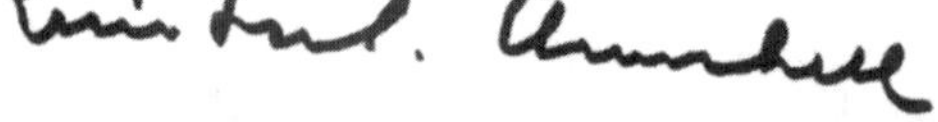

Robert W. Chambers

Robert Benchley

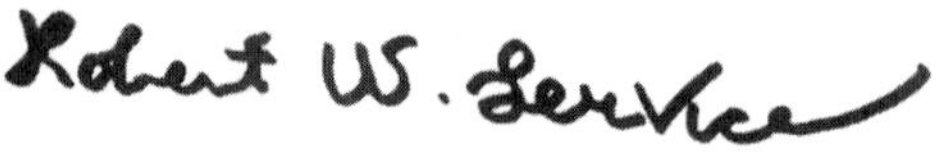

Robert W. Service

Robert B. Parker

Robinson Jeffers

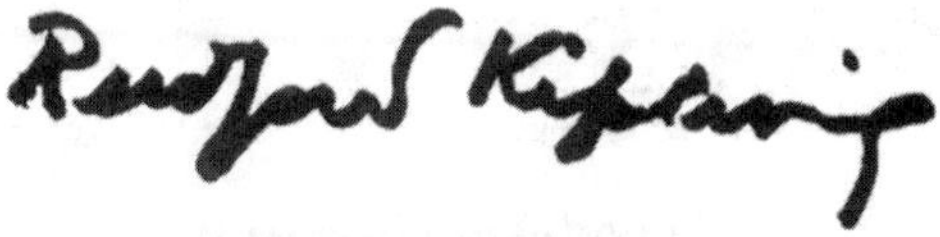

Rudyard Kipling

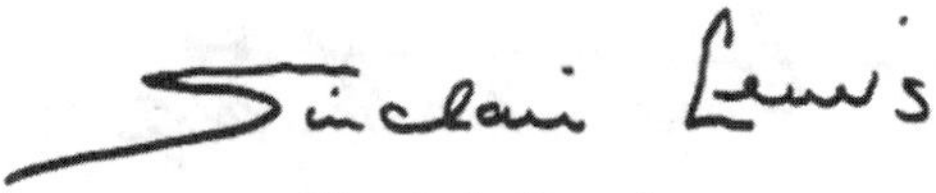

Sinclair Lewis

Samuel Langhorn Clemens

S.S. Van Dine

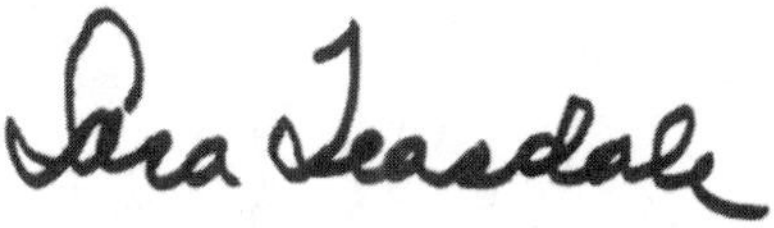

Sara Teasdale

Stephen Crane

Saul Bellow

Stephen Vincent Benet

Sheldon Siegel

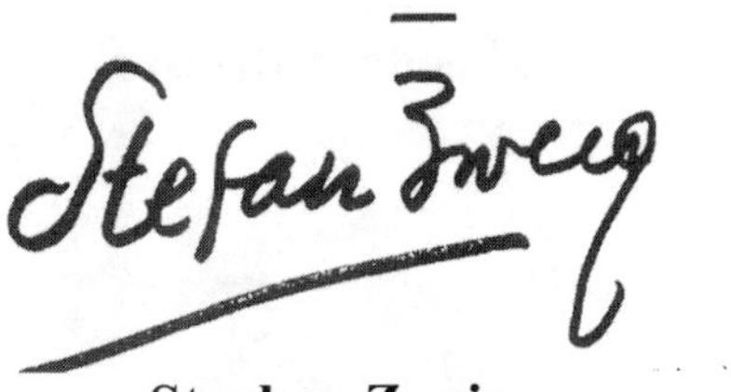

Stephen Zweig

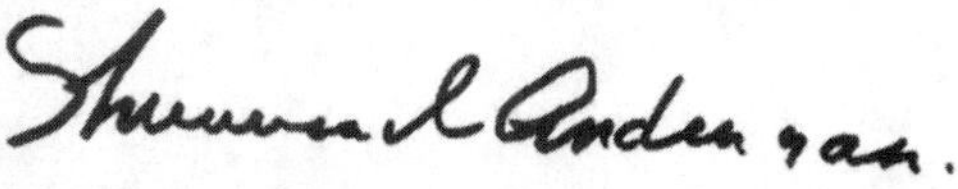

Sherwood Anderson

Steve Martini

Tangore

Theodosia Garrison

Tennessee Williams

Thornton Wilder

Terry Brooks

Tom Robbins

T.S. Eliot

Theodore Dreiser

Booksellers' Collecting Tips
ON COLLECTING

Book collecting normally begins with a passion for a particular subject or a favorite author. On the other hand, there are those who enjoy the search for potentially valuable books that have no strong area of focus. In either case, the problem of determining value is far more complex than in any other field of antique collecting. This is due to the sheer volume of books that have been kept for many generations that not only have not increased in value but border on being impossible to sell at any price. This is why the vast majority of books printed in the late 19th century can be found in serious stores at less than $25. The age of a book in itself does not guarantee you have a treasure.

The issue of value is based upon what is in demand. Once scarcity is determined in a general way, the book must be understood in terms of its edition and its condition. A later printing of most major authors has virtually no value in today's book market. A factor of supreme importance is a book's condition. As you become more familiar with books that are truly scarce or rare, you will realize how very small defects not only reduce the value but often make an actual first edition not collectible. Of course, it is obvious that most Bibles, encyclopedias, and sets of famous authors may inspire us by their content but seldom do they bring delight to the collector. It is the expert who distinguishes the vast majority of books from those few that have serious values.

Most of the books currently available are helpful to the beginner. Of course, visiting serious stores and noting the superb condition of the holdings will provide an instant education. While the Internet plays the predominant role in many of today's transactions, it is fueled by many who are uninformed and price books based upon the fantasies of individual sellers. Often these "would be" sellers ignore the intricacies of edition, condition, or the market itself. Besides the nightmare of the ex-library book, previous owner's inscriptions, underlinings, etc., may kill the book unless the perpetrator is of such international significance it provides an exception. In other words, the field of book collecting has many pitfalls but it can be a rewarding hobby or in rare cases a small business that is its own reward.

Richard Murian, Alcuin Books, Phoenix, Arizona

Beware the Book Club

Book club editions aren't always identifiable at first glance. They can say "First Edition," the Dust Jacket can have a price, the back board can be unmarked. Check all three before you buy a "First Edition." Make sure that the book is marked correctly as first edition of the particular publisher. In other words, if the dates for the title page and copyright don't match, it probably isn't a first and could be a book club. Except for small publishers (real small publishers) and vanity press books, the dust jacket should have a price. If it doesn't, there's a reason and chances are that the reason is that it's a book club edition. Check the back cover low and near the spine. Iis there a figure stamped or printed? If so, it's a book club. Other give-aways are the fact that the book is printed on thin paper, making it lighter and that it is smaller than the general run of books by the author. I can't remember how many times I've had to tell a customer that their prized first edition is a book club edition that is not worth anywhere near what they thought it was.

12th Street Books, New York, N.Y.

THE FIRST, THE SECOND AND THE THUS

When you read on the copyright page "First & Second printings Before Publication," note that this is not a book collector's First Edition.

"First Thus" frequently occurs in book descriptions. It usually means that this is a previously published work with new materials added.

Beware! Many book club editions will state "First Edition" on the copyright page.

Jerome Joseph, Brand Bookshop, Glendale, California

The 10,000 PERCENT Profit, A Fish Story (sort of)

No one's an expert in used books. If a genie made someone an expert in the field, it wouldn't last past the close of business tomorrow. I once bought a book for twenty-five cents, took it to the shop, and sold it for $25. There are not many businesses where you can make a 10,000 percent profit. I felt real good about it for about a week, until I learned the customer who bought it had sold it the next day for $300. That's expertise for you.

Basset Books, Monterey, California

Is "Flat Signed" Better?

This (or a variant of it) is probably the most often asked question I hear. What I'm talking about is, of course, whether it is better to buy a book (or get it autographed by the author) with just a signature alone or whether it is better to have it with a personalized inscription. With modern books by living authors, the popular wisdom states that it is better to have a "flat" (I hate that term) signed bookæthat is to say, a "stand-alone" signature, not a book with an inscription to an "unknown" person. For example, if I wrote a book, would you like me to sign it for you: "For (your first name here)- Hope you like it, Barry R. Levin," or just,

"Barry R. Levin." Many dealers will tell you that it is easier to resell your modern signed books if they are just "flat" signed. "No one named 'Bill,'" they will say, "wants a book signed 'For Bob.'"

Is this bit of popular wisdom true? Are flat signed books better? Well, yes and no.

The very best autograph dealers and authorities will tell you quite candidly that, in many cases, "a stand-alone" (or "flat"-if you must) signature in a modern book can be all but impossible to authenticate. Yes, he or she can rule out most fakes, but still can only tell you most of the time that a modern stand-alone signature "looks good," not that it is 100 percent authentic if the piece has no provenance.

A signature is almost (and in some languages in reality) a pictograph or symbol that represents a person's name, a stylized form of script often unlike the person's normal handwriting. It is possible with practice to copy that symbol. Yes, it helps if you know something about the mechanics of handwritingæalso of pens, inks, papers, etc., but a fair number of people can do a passable job of copying a given person's signature. It is extremely difficult, however, to copy a person's script, or handwriting in general. (I am not going to give you a primer here on the whys and wherefores of this for obvious reasons). Take my word for it, that is one of the reasons why the names of the handful of great forgers that have been caught are so well rememberedæit is a true (if despicable) art form.

For instance, I talked to an important collector of Stephen King the other day. He told me a very interesting story. He bought a copy of a proof for a new Stephen King novel over the Internet. The copy was described as being flat signed by the author. When the proof came, it was not signed. He e-mailed the seller, and the seller told him to send it back and he would send him a signed copy. Suspicious, the collector took a soft lead pencil and put a very small mark on a given page and sent the proof back. A week went by, and a signed copy of the proof was delivered to him. He looked at the signature (one that he is very familiar with) and it "looked good." He opened the proof to the page on which he had placed his mark on the copy that he had sent back, and lo and behold there is his mark. Now the collector knew that King was on vacation that week, and knew it was not possible for the seller to have gotten this particular copy signed in the time allotted-so even if the signature "looked good," it had to be a forgery.

Another collector sent me a scan of a very popular British author's stand-alone autograph. Once again, the "signed" book had been purchased on the Internet. She wanted to know if the signature was authentic. Now, it is almost impossible to truly authenticate an autograph from a scan and with no provenance, and it is not a free service we normally have time to render. Saying that, I did have time that day to look at the scan, so I did. This author's signature is one that is a little hard to get in this country, mostly because of the overwhelming demand at the moment. It is also, unfortunately, a particularly easy autograph to forge. I sent the collector an e-mailed note to that effect, along with an example I had of a signature known to be authentic. My advice was, and is, to only buy autograph material from an expert, one with proper credentials, especially flat or stand-alone examples of signatures.

In the last few years, I have seen a rise in the number of forged autographs of science fiction, fantasy, and horror authors-including Howard Phillips Lovecraft, Stephen King, Edgar Rice Burroughs, and even those of Ray Bradbury, whose signature is the most common authentic autograph in the field. My point in telling you all of this is simply to point out that the more words on your autographed items, the better! The number of people who can fool an autograph expert drops in direct proportion to the number of words on the page. If you are buying a stand-alone or flat signed book, the provenance for the piece can be as important as the honesty and knowledge of the seller.

It is also important to note that it is always a good idea, when having a book signed for you by an author, to have the author date the signature, especially if the book is being signed in the year, or, better yet, the month and year of publication. Books so signed are very desirable to collectors. Also, because the handwriting of authors often change over time, sometimes dramatically, the dating of the signature becomes doubly important. Ray Bradbury and Clark Ashton Smith are two notable examples of striking signature changes that come to mind.

None of us will live forever; no one is immortal. Collectors are one of the greatest conservators of our cultural heritage. The signed books we buy or have autographed for us today will one day bear the signature of a deceased author. How will people in the future know for sure that a particular signature is authentic? Some collectors put a note in their signed books (hopefully on acid-free paper) saying that they got the book signed at such and such a time and place. This is harmless and can be used as provenance to a point, but in the future it will be only as good as the reputation of the individual collector who wrote it. If he is not of note, it may prove to be almost as good in the future as a letter of authentication from a dishonest dealer or forger. No, the best measure of an item's authenticity is that which is integral and internal. Few if any collectors today care if Jules Verne or H. G. Wells inscribed a book to an unknown person. Just the opposite, a long inscription is preferred. Why is that true? Because, of course, these authors are now no longer signing anything, and it is easier to authenticate an inscribed and signed copy, so the more words from the master's hand, the better. Who knows, maybe in a hundred years, Ray Bradbury's signature may be worth something, and a book with a long inscription and maybe one of his drawings-priceless?

At this point, it would be wise to point out that even those collectors who do not like personalized inscriptions in their modern books will eagerly buy the following types of inscribed books:

* **ASSOCIATION COPY:** An inscribed or signed book that once belonged to someone the author knew or to someone very well known (i.e., another author, a movie star, a former president, etc.).

* **DEDICATION COPY** (sometimes called "THE COPY"): The copy inscribed by the author to the person or persons to whom the book is dedicated.

* **PRESENTATION COPY**: A copy of a book given by the author as a gift to the recipient, usually inscribed and often dated very near the time of publication. *(NOTE, not a copy signed by the author at the request of the autograph's recipient.)*

* **INSCRIBED SENTIMENT**: A copy

of a book that is inscribed without being personalized. An example would be a copy of my imaginary book, inscribed, "This is my favorite of all of my books. Barry R. Levin," or, "With my warmest regards, Barry R Levin." My favorite inscription of this type was on a book I once owned, signed by the author with the note, "This is the first copy of this book I ever signed." The "inscribed sentiment" may be the best of all worlds, for the collector of modern signed first editions by living authors.

So now you know why I have answered the question of "Is flat signed best?" with the answer, "Yes and no." For the purpose of resale in the lifetime of the author: "Yes," if there is no question of authenticity; and, "No," because an inscription makes it far easier to authenticate the handwriting of the author, and ipso facto, the signature, and thus the dictum applies, "The more words from the master's hand, the better."

So, how would you like me to sign my next imaginary book for you?

Barry R. Levin, Barry R. Levin Science Fiction & Fantasy Literature, Santa Monica, California

LONGSHOTS

When I was 18 years old and just finished my freshman year of college and first poetry workshop with Stephen Dunn (who later went on to win the Pulitzer Prize), my brother found a little typewritten, stapled poetry book in the trash and gave it to me. It was by a poet I never heard of, but I thought, hmm … he's not too bad. I wonder what ever became of him. The next time I was at a bookstore with a decent poetry selection I looked him up and there were two full

shelves of various titles. As it turns out this was Charles Bukowski's second chapbook, Longshot Pomes for Broke Players on 7 Poets Press. This was one of an edition of 200. I still have it. I have seen other copies listed for anywhere between $900 and $1,600.

I now own a used bookstore in Philadelphia with a pretty lively literary life. We have readings every week, publish a small poetry magazine (Joss) and are about to start more publishing projects. As part of our advocacy of self-publishing and small, friendly presses, we carry as many local publications as we can. I ask the writers to sign the books when they leave them here on consignment and display them prominently in the front of the store rather than filing them in the stacks where they would disappear, as most of them are saddle-stitched and virtually spineless. When I have the opportunity, I tell my Bukowski story. You really never know where a writer's career is going to lead, whether or not they are sanctioned by the universities and more established presses. If you buy one of these self-published books, the worst that can happen is you support a local artist and become familiar with some of his work. And there's always the chance that it will turn out to be a treasure.

Molly Russakoff, Molly's Cafe & Bookstore, Philadelphia, Pennsylvania (Note: Molly's chapbook: The Poverty Queen might be a good bet)

THE BOOKS YOU LOVE

Collect the books that you love, whether that means the book itself, the author's life, or even a film that was made from the book. Give an eye to condition always, and be sure to give in to the occasional impulse or temptation to take a risk with somethingæmore often than not, you'll be glad you did.

Kevin Johnson, Royal Books, Baltimore, Maryland

Print Making

Booksellers and many collectors soon learn that a book's illustrations can have as much or greater interest and value than its text. And they discover that it is important to know whether the illustrations are original works of art or reproductions. Print collectors, too, discover this need. At first, because the illustrations are produced in duplicate, one may conclude that they are reproductions. In a very real sense, however, they can be originals if they are made by certain methods, the three most common of which fall into these types: relief cuts, intaglio prints, and planographic prints.

Wood or linoleum block prints are examples of relief cuts created by cutting the surface of a block away, leaving the raised portion to be inked. Intaglio prints include engravings and etchings that are made by scratching or cutting a surface that is then inked and wiped, leaving ink in the cuts. The lithograph is a planographic print made by drawing on a surface with an oil-based instrument, wetting the surface, and then inking the surface with an oil-based ink. Since water will repel oil, only the drawn-on portions will print onto the paper. The products of these processes can be hand-colored afterwards. Or the lithograph can be made from more than one surface, each for a different color (chromolithography).

The prints made from these processes are limited in number because the surfaces will wear out, be damaged, or be ground down for a new use. They are considered the medium, and the images made from them are considered, therefore, all originals. They can be contrasted with today's photo-mechanical systems in which an original painting or drawing is photographed and prints are made from the negative. These are properly called reproductions and millions can be made from the negative. The original work continues to exist and can be photographed again and again.

Relief printing dates from ancient times and appears mostly in manuscripts and in books from the 15th through the 17th centuries. Engravings were most commonly used from the 17th through the 19th centuries. Lithography was used beginning around 1830 and chromolithography from around 1870. Artists, of course, continue to use these methods in their studios. Since around 1900, however, most book illustrations have been photo-mechanically produced.

Identifying the method by which an image was made can be difficult. A magnifying glass may be needed. A knowledge of the history of paper manufacture can be useful.

Here are a few indications to look for: regularly spaced dots that result from most photo-mechanical processes; an uneven mottled effect from the granular surface of the stone often used in lithography; a raised plate mark around the image from the pressure of the engraving press (sometimes trimmed off). The above is the briefest of introductions to this interesting subject. Consult the relevant articles in a good encyclopedia or the many books on the subject for more information.

Thomas P. Macaluso, Macaluso Rare and Fine Books, Kennett Square, Pennsylvania

Small Presses

Be aware that small presses, proportionately, are more likely to produce collectible books than the large trade publishers. If you know the author, but the publisher is obscure, it's a good bet that the book is desirable. There are probably a great many reasons this is true, but the most obvious is that a small press rarely has a run as large as a major trade house. Also, a writer, who is known, going to a small press is probably an indication that the book was one of his first, or that it is a radical departure from his trade publications.

George W. Skanse, Book Gallery, El Paso, Texas

The "Vanity" Press

Publishing is a for-profit venture. Larger publishing companies are conservative institutions and, for the most part, smaller publishers exist in profitable niches. This is not a new development, but rather a business necessity. It costs money to print and distribute a book. Because of this, publishing companies are selective, picking and choosing books they feel they can sell for a profit. If they didn't, of course, they would rather rapidly migrate to the bankruptcy courts of the world. Because the publishing companies are in the business of distribution, they control most of it. The effect is to freeze the state of literature and writing in general, keeping it within the bounds of the type of writing that has a winning "track record." This leads to an over saturation of narrowly defined books, reaching a point where nearly every commercially produced book is derivative in one way or another. When this reaches the saturation point, the collector shies away from the new book market. Derivative works, in the long run, do not become collectable. This is pretty much the condition of American publishing currently. In point of fact, with a very few exceptions, books published in the last decade in the United States will, over time, become worthless and fit only for dollar bins in the front of used bookstores. This is a cycle that gets repeated time and again in literature. Two factors change it and begin the cycle anew.

The small, niche publishers are always a factor. They are much more likely to venture into new areas in literature than larger trade publishers. However, they, too, quickly become specialized and even more closed to new innovations than the bigger trade houses. In short, they become a one-note samba, and only the first book or two they produce can be said to be important or collectable. A case in point might be California's Black Sparrow Press, launched in 1966 by John Martin to publish the work of the then little-known poet Charles Bukowski. It has prospered in its niche but has failed to seek out new "Bukowskis" and is mired in derivative works by a single small group of writers. So, while earlier books by Black Sparrow are collectable, later ones will find their way into the bargain bin eventually.

The so-called "vanity" press is a different matter. While disregarded by the publishing establishment as "amateur" and critics for much the same reason, the savvy collector knows they are both hidebound and dead wrong. Truly innovative literary artists and people with something unpopular to say are basically frozen out of publication through regular channels. Self-publication, or Vanity Press, companies are their only options. As the regular channels of publication become increasingly clogged with derivative and unimaginative books, the literary artist is forced into publication through his own efforts rather than rely on the conservative publishing establishment. What this means is that authors with innovative or informative, though unpopular, books will produce first editions, in very small printings, that will eventually become some of the most sought after and expensive books in the collectors market.

It is not a new situation. It has happened several times before. Percy Shelley published *Zastrozzi*. Edgar Allen Poe published *Tamerlaine*. Both were toward the beginning of the nineteenth century when publishing had become rigid, regionalized, and derivative. A first edition of either book might provide for an easy retirement. Edwin Arlington Robinson, D.H. Lawrence, James Joyce, all self-published or provided a subsidy to their publisher to publish what the establishment would not touch. One of the most expensive modern collectables: Grisham, John, *A Time To Kill*, New York: Wynwood Press, 1989, which has a value in the collector's market of about $4,000 in fine condition, was a subsidy publication.

Both the publishing and the literary (academic) establishments are very poor judges of literary art for the simple reason that it is against their interests to be good judges of it. A publisher will be very reluctant to bring out a truly innovative piece as it shows up the rest of the line as derivative and results in an overall decline in sales. In a similar manner, the reviewer or the teacher has invested a lot of time and effort in learning the conventions, patterns, etc., of the literature of the time. Since this "expert" knows the "right" way to construct a novel and has spent years learning this, a novel constructed differently will be disregarded almost as a matter of survival, in that a "new" novel makes their years of knowledge, study, and expertise obsolete. It is only the collector who seeks out the innovations, and tries to guess which will "catch on." In the end, only the collector stands to profit by doing so.

Throughout this book, in the publisher's slot, you will see the name of the author, or notations like "printed for the author." Some of these books will be worth several hundred, even several thousand, dollars. Some of the names will be well known, and some you'll never have heard of. These are really the prizes in the collecting game. These are the books that show the preeminence of the collector over every other form of literary expert. That little book that wasn't good enough for publishers' lists; wasn't worth a reviewer's time. Only a collector would know, could know, that it was destined to become a classic.

So when you pick up a book that was published by the author, or by a vanity press, read a few pages, skim a bit. If it's different, if it's good, pay the bookseller and take it home. It could replace your 401(k).

Americana

In the broadest sense, Americana is any book dealing with the United States or the area that is now the United States. It is also called Usiana, after the basic bibliography of the genre: Howes, Wright, *Usiana 1750-1950*, New York: R.R.Bowker, 1954, which, as a collectible itself, ranges from $70 to $100 depending on condition. Early Americana deals with the explorations of the English, French, and Spanish in the New World, and settles down to more specific works on geography, history, and culture by the eighteenth century.

The category allows for several sub-genres, some of which are very well collected. Beginning in the mid-1800s, the government began issuing books on exploration and the culture of various Indian groups. Three prime examples are: Marcy, Randolph B. and George B. McClellan, *Exploration of the Red River of Louisiana in the Year 1852*, Washington: Beverley Tucker, Senate Printer, 1854 ($75 to $200); *Fremont, Captain John C., Report of the Exploring Expedition to the Rocky Mountains in the Year 1842 and to Oregon and North California in the Years 1843-44*, House Document 166, Washington, D.C.: Gales and Seaton, 1845 ($1000 to $3000); and Featherstonhaugh, G. W., *Report of a Geological Reconnaissance Made in 1835 From the Seat of Government, By the Way of Green Bay and the Wisconsin Territory to the Coteau De Prairie*, Washington, D.C.: Gales and Seaton, 1836 ($400 to $850). In 1879, Congress commissioned

an annual report from the Bureau of American Ethnology (BAE), whose reports have become collectable.

Local history is another area. City, town, village, county, and state histories ranging from the early nineteenth century to the present day are the pride of many collectors of Americana. Atlases are also desirable. The American Guide Series, published under the depression's Works Progress Administration's Federal Writer's project, also fits in here.

The last half of the nineteenth century saw a fascination with the American West that hasn't really dwindled. Works on American Indians, Cowboys, and Western personalities such as Bill Cody, Bill Hickok, and the Earps, among others, remain solid sellers as new books and collectables as used ones. About the turn of the century, writers, photographers, and artists began producing art books based in western themes. Fredric Remington and Charles Russell are two of the best known and were followed by the quintessential cowboy, Will James. This lead to the twentieth century development of small presses specializing in Americana, such as Arthur H. Clarke, Grabhorn, and Caxton.

The Civil War has fostered an entire field of collectable and important books. In terms of sheer volume, it may be the single largest category within the area of Americana. From regimental histories to the photographs of early photographers such as Matthew Brady, the war between the states seems to hold an endless fascination for the book collector.

10 Classic Rarities

Dobie, J. Frank. *Mustangs*. Boston: Little, Brown, 1952. Bound in cowhide and issued in a slipcase.
Retail Value in:
  Near Fine to Fine Condition **$2000**
  Good to Very Good Condition. . . **$1500**

James, Will. *American Cowboy*. New York: Charles Scribner's Sons, 1942. Profit by fulfilling a childhood fancy.
Retail Value in:
  Near Fine to Fine Condition **$1250**
  Good to Very Good Condition. . . . **$800**

King, Jeff and Joseph Campbell and Maud Oakes. *Where the Two Came To Their Father; A Navajo War Ceremonial*. New York; Pantheon, 1943. A pamphlet in wraps.
Retail Value in:
  Near Fine to Fine Condition **$3000**
  Good to Very Good Condition. . . **$1100**

Lea, Tom. *The Hands of Cantu*. Boston: Little, Brown and Company; 1964. Limited edition.
Retail Value in:
  Near Fine to Fine Condition **$2000**
  Good to Very Good Condition. . . . **$900**

Remington, Frederic. *Done in the Open*. New York: R. H. Russell, Publisher, 1902. Signed, limited edition; with an introduction and verses by Owen Wister.
Retail Value in:
  Near Fine to Fine Condition **$3000**
  Good to Very Good Condition. . . **$1000**

Roosevelt, Theodore. *The Rough Riders*. New York: Charles Scribner's Sons, 1899.

The first edition is illustrated by Fredric Remington and Charles Dana Gibson.
Retail Value in:
  Near Fine to Fine Condition **$1200**
  Good to Very Good Condition. . . . **$800**

Russell, Charles M. *Good Medicine*. Garden City, NY: Doubleday, Doran & Co., 1929. Limited edition of 134 copies; introduction by Will Rogers.
Retail Value in:
  Near Fine to Fine Condition **$4000**
  Good to Very Good Condition. . . **$1500**

Schreyvogel, Charles. *My Bunkie and Others, Pictures of Western Frontier Life*. New York: Moffat, Yard & Co., 1909. Issued with a slipcase.
Retail Value in:
  Near Fine to Fine Condition **$1000**
  Good to Very Good Condition. . . . **$600**

Siringo, Charles. *A Texas Cow Boy or, Fifteen Years on the Hurricane Deck of a Spanish Pony*. Chicago: Rand McNally, 1886.
Retail Value in:
  Near Fine to Fine Condition $1500
  Good to Very Good Condition. . . . $850

Wheat, Carl I. *The Maps of the California Gold Region, 1848-1857. A Bibliocartography of an Important Decade*. San Francisco: Grabhorn Press, 1942.
Retail Value in:
  Near Fine to Fine Condition **$1800**
  Good to Very Good Condition. . . **$1000**

Price Guide

Abbott, Carl. *The Great Extravaganza;
Portland and the Lewis and Clark
Exposition.*
First Edition: Portland, OR: Oregon
Historical Society, 1981
Nr.Fine/Fine **$30**
Good/V.Good **$20**

Adams, Andy. *Texas Matchmaker.* First
Edition: Boston: Houghton, Mifflin, 1904.
Nr.Fine/Fine **$150**
Good/V.Good **$70**

Log of
a Cowboy
by Andy Adams

_____. *Log of a Cowboy.* First
Edition: Boston: Houghton, Mifflin, 1903.
Nr.Fine/Fine **$350**
Good/V.Good **$160**

_____. *The Outlet.* First Edition:
Boston: Houghton, Mifflin and Company,
1905.
Nr.Fine/Fine **$100**
Good/V.Good **$55**

Adams, Ramon F. *Come and Get It.*
First Edition: Norman, OK: University of
Oklahoma Press, 1952.
Nr.Fine/Fine **$45**
Good/V.Good **$20**

_____. *The Old Time Cowhand.*

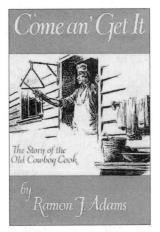

Come an' Get It
by Ramon J. Adams

First Edition: New York: Macmillan, 1961.
Nr.Fine/Fine **$25**
Good/V.Good **$15**

_____. *The Rampaging Herd.* First
Edition: Norman, OK: University of
Oklahoma Press, 1959.
Nr.Fine/Fine **$175**
Good/V.Good **$75**

_____. *Six-Guns & Saddle Leather.*
First Edition: Norman, OK: University of
Oklahoma Press, 1959.
Nr.Fine/Fine **$200**
Good/V.Good **$85**

Aken, David. *Pioneers of the Black Hills.*
First Edition: Milwaukee: Allied Printing,
1911.
Nr.Fine/Fine **$400**
Good/V.Good **$185**

Alexander, E. P. *Military Memoirs of a
Confederate.* First Edition: New York:
Charles Scribner's, 1907.
Nr.Fine/Fine **$250**
Good/V.Good **$145**

Alexander, Hartley Burr. *The World's
Rim: Great Mysteries of the North
American Indians.* First Edition: Lincoln,
NE: University of Nebraska Press, 1953.
Nr.Fine/Fine **$45**
Good/V.Good **$20**

_____. *The Mystery Of Life A Poetization of "The Hako" A Pawnee Ceremony*. First Edition: Chicago: Open Court Publishing, 1913.
Nr.Fine/Fine. **$80**
Good/V.Good. **$35**

Allen, William A. *Adventures with Indians and Game or Twenty Years in the Rocky Mountains*. First Edition: Chicago: A. W. Bowen & Co., 1903.
Nr.Fine/Fine. **$300**
Good/V.Good. **$175**

Alter, J. Cecil. *Jim Bridger*. First Edition: Salt Lake City: Shepard Book Co., 1925.
Nr.Fine/Fine. $350
Good/V.Good. $175

_____. *Through the Heart of the Scenic West*. First Edition: Salt Lake City: Shepard Book Co., 1927.
Nr.Fine/Fine. $150
Good/V.Good. $65

Alvord, Clarence Walworth and Lee Bidgood. *The First Explorations of the Trans-Allegheny Region by the Virginians, 1650-1674*. First Edition: Cleveland: Arthur H. Clark Company, 1912.
Nr.Fine/Fine. **$300**
Good/V.Good. **$175**

Alvord, Clarence Walworth. *Kaskaskia Records, 1778-1790*. First Edition: Springfield, IL: Illinois State Historical Library, 1909.
Nr.Fine/Fine. **$75**
Good/V.Good. **$25**

Amsden, Charles. *Navaho Weaving*. First Edition: Santa Ana, CA: Fine Arts Press, 1934.
Nr.Fine/Fine. **$400**
Good/V.Good. **$250**

Andrews, Mathew Page. *Social Planning By Frontier Thinkers*. First Edition: New York: Richard R. Smith, 1944.
Nr.Fine/Fine. **$25**
Good/V.Good. **$10**

Andrist, Ralph K. *The Long Death*. First Edition: New York: Macmillian, 1964.
Nr.Fine/Fine. **$35**
Good/V.Good. **$15**

_____. *The American Heritage History Of The Making Of The Nation, 1783-1860*. First Edition: New York: American Heritage Publishing Co., 1968.
Nr.Fine/Fine. **$65**
Good/V.Good. **$35**

Down to the Sea in Ships
by Ivin Anthony

Anthony, Irvin. *Down to the Sea in Ships*. First Edition: Philadelphia: The Penn Publishing Co., 1924.
Nr.Fine/Fine. **$80**
Good/V.Good. **$25**

_____. *Paddle Wheels and Pistols*. First Edition: Philadelphia: Macrae Smith Co., 1929.
Nr.Fine/Fine. **$85**
Good/V.Good. **$35**

Applegate, Frank G. *Indian Tales from the Pueblos*. First Edition: Philadelphia: J. B. Lippincott, 1929.
Nr.Fine/Fine. **$100**
Good/V.Good. **$45**

_____. *Native Tales from New Mexico*. First Edition: Philadelphia: J. B. Lippincott, 1932.
Nr.Fine/Fine. **$125**
Good/V.Good. **$55**

Arbor, Marilyn. *Tools & Trades of America's Past&the Mercer Collection.* First Edition: Doylestown, PA: Bucks County Historical Society, 1981.
Nr.Fine/Fine................... **$35**
Good/V.Good.................. **$15**

Arnold, R. Ross. *Indian Wars of Idaho.* First Edition: Caldwell, ID: Caxton Printers, Ltd., 1932.
Nr.Fine/Fine................... **$750**
Good/V.Good.................. **$400**

Arthur, John Preston. *Western North Carolina.* First Edition: Raleigh, NC: The Edward Buncombe Chapter of the Daughters of the American Revolution, of Asheville, N.C., 1914.
Nr.Fine/Fine................... **$175**
Good/V.Good.................. **$60**

Arthurs, Stanley. *The American Historical Scene.* First Edition: Philadelphia: University of Pennsylvania Press, 1935.
Nr.Fine/Fine................... **$85**
Good/V.Good.................. **$30**

Asbury, Herbert. *The Barbary Coast.* First Edition: New York: Alfred A Knopf, 1933.
Nr.Fine/Fine................... **$50**
Good/V.Good.................. **$20**

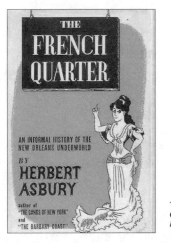

The French Quarter
by Herbert Asbury

_____. *The French Quarter.* First Edition: New York: Alfred A. Knopf, 1936.

Nr.Fine/Fine................... **$65**
Good/V.Good.................. **$30**

_____. *The Gangs of New York.* First Edition: New York: Alfred A. Knopf, 1928.
Nr.Fine/Fine................... **$165**
Good/V.Good.................. **$70**

_____. *The Great Illusion.* First Edition: Garden City, NY: Doubleday, 1950.
Nr.Fine/Fine................... **$45**
Good/V.Good.................. **$15**

_____. *Sucker's Progress: An Informal History Of Gambling In America From The Colonies To Canfield.* First Edition: New York: Dodd, Mead & Co., 1938.
Nr.Fine/Fine................... **$150**
Good/V.Good.................. **$75**

Ashley, Clifford, W. *The Yankee Whaler.* First Edition: Boston: Houghton Mifflin, 1926.
Nr.Fine/Fine................... **$200**
Good/V.Good.................. **$85**

Athearn, Robert G. *Forts of the Upper Missouri.* First Edition: Englewood Cliffs, NJ: Prentice Hall, 1967.
Nr.Fine/Fine................... **$65**
Good/V.Good.................. **$30**

_____. *Rebel of the Rockies.* First Edition: New Haven and London: Yale University Press, 1962.
Nr.Fine/Fine................... **$75**
Good/V.Good.................. **$35**

_____. *William Tecumseh Sherman and the Settlement of the West.* First Edition: Norman, OK: University of Oklahoma Press, 1956.
Nr.Fine/Fine................... **$75**
Good/V.Good.................. **$35**

Atherton, Gertrude. *California.* First Edition: New York: Harper & Brothers, 1914.

Nr.Fine/Fine. **$55**
Good/V.Good. **$20**

Ayers, James J. *Gold and Sunshine*. First
Edition: Boston: Richard G.
Badger/Gorham Press, 1922.
Nr.Fine/Fine. **$95**
Good/V.Good. **$55**

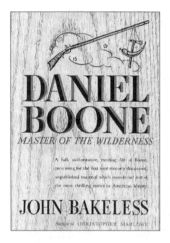

Daniel Boone:
Master of the
Wilderness
by John Bakeless

Bakeless, John. *Daniel Boone*. First
Edition: New York: William Morrow, 1939.
Nr.Fine/Fine. **$75**
Good/V.Good. **$30**

_____. *The Eyes of Discovery*.
First Edition: Philadelphia: J. B. Lippincott,
1950.
Nr.Fine/Fine. **$45**
Good/V.Good. **$20**

_____. *Lewis & Clark*.
First Edition: William Morrow & Company,
1947.
Nr.Fine/Fine. **$70**
Good/V.Good. **$30**

_____. *Spies of the Confederacy*.
First Edition: Philadelphia: J.B. Lippincott
Co., 1970.
Nr.Fine/Fine. **$50**
Good/V.Good. **$25**

Baker, Hozial. *Overland Journey to
Carson Valley, Utah*. First Edition: San

Francisco: The Book Club of California,
1973.
Nr.Fine/Fine. **$75**
Good/V.Good. **$35**

Ballantine, Betty. *The Art of Charles
Wysocki*. First Edition: New York:
Greenwick Press/Workman Publishing,
1985.
Nr.Fine/Fine. **$45**
Good/V.Good. **$20**

Bancroft, Hubert Howe. *The Native
Races Of The Pacific States*. (Five
Volumes).
First Edition: New York: D.Appleton And
Company, 1875-1886.
Nr.Fine/Fine. **$575**
Good/V.Good. **$300**

_____. *Popular
Tribunals. (Two Volumes)*. First Edition: San
Francisco: The History Company,
1887.Nr.Fine/Fine **$140**
Good/V.Good. **$60**

_____. *History of the
Northwest Coast. (Two Volumes)*. First
Edition: San Francisco: A.L. Bancroft &
Company, 1884.
Nr.Fine/Fine. **$250**
Good/V.Good. **$145**

Bandelier, Adolf F. *The Delight Makers*.
First Edition: New York: Dodd, Mead and
Co., 1890.
Nr.Fine/Fine. **$100**
Good/V.Good. **$65**

Bandini, Joseph and Giorda, *Joseph.
Smiimii Lu Tel Kaimintis Kolinzuten;
Narrative from the Holy Scripture in
Kalispell*. First Edition: Montana: St.
Ignatius Print, 1876.
Nr.Fine/Fine. **$450**
Good/V.Good. **$200**

Banta, R.E. *The Ohio.* First Edition: New
York: Rinehart and Company, 1949.
Nr.Fine/Fine. **$50**
Good/V.Good. **$25**

_____. *Indiana Authors and their Books 1816-1916*. First Edition: Crawfordsville, IN: Wabash College, 1949.
Nr.Fine/Fine. **$175**
Good/V.Good. **$65**

Barnard, Evan G. *A Rider on the Cherokee Strip*. First Edition: Boston: Houghton Mifflin, 1936.
Nr.Fine/Fine. **$125**
Good/V.Good. **$65**

Apaches &
Longhorns
by Will C. Barnes

Barnes, Will C. *Apaches and Longhorns*. First Edition: Los Angeles: Ward Ritchie Press, 1941.
Nr.Fine/Fine. **$225**
Good/V.Good. **$100**

_____ **and William MacLeod Raine**. *Cattle*. First Edition: New York: Doubleday Doran Co, 1930.
Nr.Fine/Fine. **$100**
Good/V.Good. **$45**

_____. *Tales from the Bar X Horse Camp*. First Edition: Chicago: Breeders' Gazette, 1920.
Nr.Fine/Fine. **$300**
Good/V.Good. **$145**

Barney, James. *Tales of Apache Warfare*. First Edition: Phoenix, AZ: James Barney, 1933. Points of Issue: printed wraps
Nr.Fine/Fine. $300
Good/V.Good $200

_____. *A Historical Sketch of the Volunteer Fire Department of Phoenix, Arizona*. First Edition: Phoenix, AZ: Phoenix Volunteer Fireman's Association, 1954.
Nr.Fine/Fine. **$30**
Good/V.Good. **$10**

Barry, Ada Loomis. *Yunini's Story of the Trail of Tears*. First Edition: London: Fudge & Co., 1932.
Nr.Fine/Fine. **$300**
Good/V.Good. **$125**

Bates, Finis L. *Escape and Suicide of John Wilkes Booth*. First Edition: Memphis, TN: Pilcher Printing Company, 1907.
Nr.Fine/Fine. **$125**
Good/V.Good. **$75**

Beard, Dan. *Hardly a Man is Now Alive*. First Edition: New York: Doubleday, Doran, 1939.
Nr.Fine/Fine. **$75**
Good/V.Good. **$45**

Bechdolt, Frederick. *Giants of the Old West*. First Edition: New York: The Century Co., 1930.
Nr.Fine/Fine. **$60**
Good/V.Good. **$25**

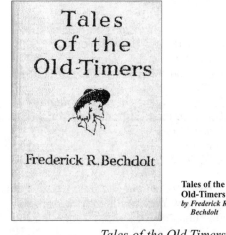

Tales of the
Old-Timers
by Frederick R. Bechdolt

_____. *Tales of the Old Timers*. First Edition: New York: The Century Co., 1924.
Nr.Fine/Fine. **$65**

Good/V.Good. **$30**

_____. *Horse Thief Trail*. First
Edition: Garden City, NY: Doubleday, 1932.
Nr.Fine/Fine. **$100**
Good/V.Good. **$45**

Beck, Henry Charlton. *The Roads of
Home-Lanes and Legends of New Jersey*.
First Edition: New Brunswick, NJ: Rutgers
Univ. Press, 1956.
Nr.Fine/Fine. **$35**
Good/V.Good. **$15**

_____. *Jersey Genesis:
The Story of the Mullica River*. First
Edition: New Brunswick, NJ: Rutgers Univ.
Press, 1945.
Nr.Fine/Fine. **$25**
Good/V.Good. **$10**

Beebe, Lucius. *The American West*. First
Edition: New York: E.P. Dutton & Co.,
1955.
Nr.Fine/Fine. **$55**
Good/V.Good. **$25**

_____. *Mr. Pullman's Palace Car*.
First Edition: Garden City: Doubleday &
Co., 1961.
Nr.Fine/Fine. **$125**
Good/V.Good. **$60**

_____. *Mansions on Wheels* First
Edition: Berkeley: Howell-North, 1959.
Nr.Fine/Fine. **$200**
Good/V.Good. **$85**

_____. *U. S. West: The Saga of
Wells Fargo*. First Edition: New York: E. P.
Dutton, 1949.
Nr.Fine/Fine. **$65**
Good/V.Good. **$30**

Bell, Horace. *On the Old West Coast*. First
Edition: New York: William Morrow, 1930.
Nr.Fine/Fine. **$200**
Good/V.Good. **$110**

_____. *Reminiscences of a Ranger*.
First Edition: Los Angeles: Yarness,

Caystile & Mathes, 1881.
Nr.Fine/Fine. **$750**
Good/V.Good. **$300**

Benedict, Carl P. A *Tenderfoot Kid on Gyp
Water*. First Edition: Austin, TX: Texas
Folklore Society, 1943.
Nr.Fine/Fine. **$250**
Good/V.Good. **$100**

Bennett, Estelline. *Old Deadwood Days*.
First Edition: New York: J.H. Sears & Co.,
1928.
Nr.Fine/Fine. **$125**
Good/V.Good. **$40**

Bennett, George. *Early Architecture of
Delaware*. First Edition: Wilmington, DE:
Historical Press, 1932.
Nr.Fine/Fine. **$175**
Good/V.Good. **$77**

Benton, Frank. *Cowboy Life on the Side
Track*. First Edition: Denver, CO: Western
Stories Syndicate, 1903.
Nr.Fine/Fine. **$125**
Good/V.Good. **$55**

Berry, Don. *Majority of Scoundrels*. First
Edition: New York: Harper & Brothers,
1961.
Nr.Fine/Fine. **$100**
Good/V.Good. **$65**

Bixby-Smith, Sarah. *Adobe Days*.
First Edition: Cedar Rapids, IA: The Torch
Press, 1925.
Nr.Fine/Fine. **$65**
Good/V.Good. **$30**

_____. *My Sagebrush
Garden*.
First Edition: Cedar Rapids, IA: The Torch
Press, 1924.
Nr.Fine/Fine. **$25**
Good/V.Good. **$10**

Black, Glenn. *Angel Site*. First Edition:
Indianapolis: Indiana Historical Society,
1967.
Nr.Fine/Fine. **$65**

Good/V.Good. **$35**

War Years With
Jeb Stuart
by W.W. Blackford

Blackford, W.W. *War Years with Jeb Stuart*. First Edition: New York: Charles Scribner's, 1945.
Nr.Fine/Fine. **$100**
Good/V.Good. **$45**

Boas, Franz. *Handbook of American Indian Languages (Two Volumes)*. First Edition: Washington, DC: Smithsonian, 1911 & 1922.
Nr.Fine/Fine. **$150**
Good/V.Good. **$85**

Boatright, Mody. *Backwoods to Border*. First Edition: Austin, TX: Texas Folklore Society, 1943.
Nr.Fine/Fine. **$50**
Good/V.Good. **$30**

_____. *From Hell to Breakfast*. First Edition: Austin, TX: Texas Folklore Society, 1944.
Nr.Fine/Fine. **$60**
Good/V.Good. **$25**

_____. *Tall Tales from Texas Cow Camps*. First Edition: Dallas, TX: The Southwest Press, 1934.
Nr.Fine/Fine. **$185**
Good/V.Good. **$95**

Bolton, Herbert Eugene. *Fray Juan CrespiæMissionary Explorer on the Pacific Coast 1769-1774*. First Edition: Berkeley, CA: University of California, 1927.
Nr.Fine/Fine. **$200**
Good/V.Good. **$125**

_____. *Rim of Christendom*. First Edition: New York: Macmillan, 1936.
Nr.Fine/Fine. **$150**
Good/V.Good. **$65**

Bolton, Reginald Pelham. *Indian Life of Long Ago in the City of New York*.First Edition: New York: Joseph Graham Boltons Books, 1934.
Nr.Fine/Fine. **$145**
Good/V.Good. **$65**

Bordeux, William. *Custer's Conqueror*. First Edition: np: Smith & Company, Publishers, 1952.
Nr.Fine/Fine. **$425**
Good/V.Good. **$325**

_____. *Conquering the Sioux*. First Edition: Sioux Falls, SD: William J. Bordeaux, 1929.
Nr.Fine/Fine. **$200**
Good/V.Good. **$125**

Bowman, Elizabeth Skaggs. *Land of High Horizons*. First Edition: Kingsport, TN: Southern Publishers, 1951.
Nr.Fine/Fine. **$75**
Good/V.Good. **$35**

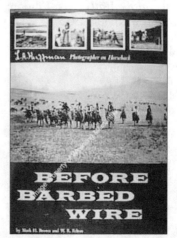

Before Barbed
Wire
by Mark Brown

Bowman, Isiah. *The Pioneer Fringe*. First Edition: New York: American Geographical Society, 1931.
Nr.Fine/Fin **$35**
Good/V.Good. **$15**

Brown, Dee. *Bury My Heart at Wounded Knee*. First Edition: New York: Holt, Rinehart & Winston, 1970.
Nr.Fine/Fin **$150**
Good/V.Good. **$65**

Brown, Mark. *Before Barbed Wire*. First Edition: New York Henry Holt & Co., 1956
Nr.Fine/Fin **$100**
Good/V.Good. **$55**

Bryant, Billy. *Children of Ol' Man River*. First Edition: New York: Lee Furman, Inc., 1936.
Nr.Fine/Fin **$85**
Good/V.Good. **$35**

Burman, Ben Lucian. *Children Of Noah*. First Edition: New York: Julian Messner, 1951.
Nr.Fine/Fin **$20**
Good/V.Good. **$8**

_____. *It's a Big Country: America Off the Highways*. First Edition: New York: Reynal and Co., 1956.
Nr.Fine/Fin **$15**
Good/V.Good. **$7**

Burnett, W. R. *Adobe Walls.* First Edition: New York: Alfred A. Knopf, 1953.
Nr.Fine/Fin **$100**
Good/V.Good. **$45**

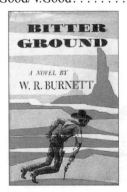

Bitter Ground
by W.R. Burnett

_____. *Bitter Ground*. First Edition: New York: Alfred A. Knopf, 1957.
Nr.Fine/Fin **$125**
Good/V.Good. **$50**

Burns, Walter Noble. *The Saga of Billy the Kid*. First Edition: Garden City, NY: Doubleday, Page & Co., 1926.
Nr.Fine/Fin **$45**
Good/V.Good. **$20**

_____. *Tombstone An Iliad of the Southwest*. First Edition: Garden City, NY: Doubleday, Page & Co., 1926.
Nr.Fine/Fin **$55**
Good/V.Good. **$25**

Carey, A. Merwyn. *American Firearms Makers*. First Edition: New York: Thomas Y. Crowell, 1953.
Nr.Fine/Fin **$65**
Good/V.Good. **$25**

Carr, John. *Pioneer Days in California. Historical and Personal Sketches*. First Edition: Eureka, CA: Times Publishing Company, 1891.
Nr.Fine/Fin **$525**
Good/V.Good. **$200**

Carroll, H. Bailey. *The Texas Santa Fe Trail*. First Edition: Canyon, TX: Panhandle-Plains Historical Society, 1951.
Nr.Fine/Fin **$125**
Good/V.Good. **$75**

Carson, James H. *Recollections Of The California Mines*. First Edition: Oakland, CA: Biobooks, 1950.
Nr.Fine/Fin **$85**
Good/V.Good. **$40**

Carter, Captain Robert G. T*he Old Sergeant's Story* First Edition: New York: Frederick H. Hitchcock, 1926.
Nr.Fine/Fin **$700**
Good/V.Good. **$425**

Cartland, Fernando G. *Southern Heroes or the Friends in War Time*. First Edition: Boston: Riverside Press, 1895.

Nr.Fine/Fin **$125**
Good/V.Good. **$60**

Casler, John O. *Four Years In The Stonewall Brigade*. First Edition: Girard, KS: Appeal Publishing Co., 1906.
Nr.Fine/Fin **$1800**
Good/V.Good. **$850**

The Teachings of Don Juan: A Yaqui Way of Knowledge
by Carlos Castaneda

Castaneda, Carlos. *The Teachings Of Don Juan: A Yaqui Way Of Knowledge*. First Edition: New York: Simon & Schuster, 1973. Nr.Fine/Fin. **$100**
Good/V.Good. **$50**

Castaneda, Carlos E. *Our Catholic Heritage in Texas*. First Edition: Austin, TX: The Knights of Columbus of Texas, 1936.
Nr.Fine/Fin **$1500**
Good/V.Good. **$650**

_____. *The Mexican Side of the Texas Revolution*. First Edition: Dallas: P.L. Turner, 1928.
Nr.Fine/Fin **$500**
Good/V.Good. **$350**

Catton, Bruce. *Army of the Potomac*. First Edition: Garden City, NY: Doubleday & Company, 1951.
N.Fine/Fin **$150**
Good/V.Good. **$60**

_____. *The Coming Fury*. First Edition: Garden City, NY: Doubleday & Company, 1961.
Nr.Fine/Fin **$60**
Good/V.Good. **$25**

_____. *Grant Moves South*. First Edition: Boston: Little, Brown & Co., 1960.
Nr.Fine/Fin **$35**
Good/V.Good. **$20**

Chabot, Frederick C. *The Alamo: Mission Fortress and Shrine*. First Edition: San Antonio, TX: The Leake Press, 1935.
Nr.Fine/Fin **$40**
Good/V.Good. **$25**

Chapman, Arthur. *The Pony Express*. First Edition: New York: G.P. Putnams, 1932.
Nr.Fine/Fin **$100**
Good/V.Good. **$45**

Claiborne, John Herbert. *Seventy Five Years in Old Virginia*. First Edition: New York and Washington: Neale Pub. Co., 1904.
Nr.Fine/Fin **$200**
Good/V.Good. **$85**

Clark, Thomas D. *The Kentucky*. First Edition: New York: Farrar & Rinehart Inc., 1942.
Nr.Fine/Fin **$75**
Good/V.Good. **$30**

_____. *Pills, Petticoats & Plows*. First Edition: Indianapolis: The Bobbs-Merrill Company, 1944.
Nr.Fine/Fin **$30**
Good/V.Good. **$15**

Clark, W. P. *The Indian Sign Language*. First Edition: Philadelphia: L. R. Hamersly, 1885.
Nr.Fine/Fin **$375**
Good/V.Good. **$150**

Clay, John. *My Life on the Range*. First Edition: Chicago: privately printed, 1924.
Nr.Fine/Fin **$600**
Good/V.Good. **$275**

Cleland, Robert Glass. *This Reckless Breed of Men.*First Edition: New York: Alfred A. Knopf, 1950.
Nr.Fine/Fin **$65**
Good/V.Good. **$25**

Clum, Woodworth. *Apache Agent*. First Edition: Boston: Houghton Mifflin, 1936.
Nr.Fine/Fin **$115**
Good/V.Good. **$60**

Coates, Harold Wilson. *Stories of Kentucky Feuds*. First Edition: Knoxville: Holmes-Darst Coal Corporation, 1942.
Nr.Fine/Fin **$55**
Good/V.Good. **$20**

Coates, Robert M. *The Outlaw Years*. First Edition: New York: The Macaulay Company, 1930.
Nr.Fine/Fin **$300**
Good/V.Good. **$145**

Cody, William F. *Story of the Wild West and Camp-fire Chats*. First Edition: Philadelphia: Historical Publishing Company, 1888.
Nr.Fine/Fin **$185**
Good/V.Good. **$90**

Cohn, David. *New Orleans and its Living Past*. First Edition (Limited to 1030 copies) Boston: Houghton Mifflin, 1941.
Nr.Fine/Fin **$1250**
Good/V.Good. **$675**

Cole, Faye Cooper. *Rediscovering Illinois*. First Edition: Chicago: University of Chicago Press, 1937.
Nr.Fine/Fin **$55**
Good/V.Good. **$25**

Collier, John. *Patterns and Ceremonials of the Indians of the Southwest*. First Edition: New York: E. P. Dutton, 1949.
Nr.Fine/Fin **$200**
Good/V.Good. **$85**

Connelley, William E. *Quantrill and the Border Wars*. First Edition: Cedar Rapids, IA: Torch Press, 1910.

Nr.Fine/Fin **$300**
Good/V.Good. **$175**

_____. *War with Mexico, 1846-1847*. First Edition: Kansas City: Bryant & Douglas, 1907.
Nr.Fine/Fin **$210**
Good/V.Good. **$95**

Conover, Charlotte Reeve. *Builders in New Fields*. First Edition: New York: G.P. Putnams, 1939.
Nr.Fine/Fin **$25**
Good/V.Good. **$12**

Cook, James H. *Fifty Years Out on the Old Frontier.* First Edition: New Haven: Yale University Press, 1923.
Nr.Fine/Fin **$200**
Good/V.Good. **$85**

_____. *Longhorn Cowboy* First Edition: New York: G.P. Putnam's, 1942.
Nr.Fine/Fin **$85**
Good/V.Good. **$35**

Coolidge, Dane and Mary. *The Navajo Indians.*First Edition: Boston: Houghton Mifflin, 1930.
Nr.Fine/Fin **$60**
Good/V.Good. **$30**

_____. *The Last of the Seris* .First Edition: New York: E. P. Dutton, 1939.
Nr.Fine/Fin **$60**
Good/V.Good. **$25**

Cooper, Courtney Ryley. *Annie Oakley-Woman At Arms*. First Edition: New York: Duffield and Co., 1927.
Nr.Fine/Fin **$165**
Good/V.Good. **$75**

Cornplanter, Jesse J. *Legends of the Longhouse*. First Edition: Philadelphia: J.B. Lippincott Co., 1938.
Nr.Fine/Fin **$135**
Good/V.Good. **$85**

Cossley-Batt, Jill L. *The Last of the*

California Rangers. First Edition: New York: Funk & Wagnalls, 1928.
Nr.Fine/Fin **$120**
Good/V.Good. **$45**

Croy, Homer. *Jesse James was My Neighbor*. First Edition: New York: Duell, Sloan & Pearce, 1949.
Nr.Fine/Fin **$110**
Good/V.Good. **$45**

Cruse, Thomas. *Apache Days and After*. First Edition: Caldwell, ID: The Caxton Printers, Ltd., 1941.
Nr.Fine/Fin **$350**
Good/V.Good. **$175**

Pistol Passport
by Eugene Cunningham

Cunningham, Eugene. *Pistol Passport*. First Edition: Boston: Houghton Mifflin Company, 1936.
Nr.Fine/Fin **$225**
Good/V.Good. **$135**

_____. *Triggernometry: A Gallery of Gunfights*. First Edition: New York: The Press of the Pioneers, 1934.
Nr.Fine/Fin **$400**
Good/V.Good. **$275**

Custer, Elizabeth. *Boots and Saddles*. First Edition: New York: Harper & Brothers, 1885.
Nr.Fine/Fin **$250**
Good/V.Good. **$95**

Custer, George. *My Life on the Plains, or Personal Experiences with Indians*. First Edition: New York: Sheldon and Company, 1874.
Nr.Fine/Fin **$2600**
Good/V.Good. **$1450**

Cutter, Donald. *Malaspina in California*. First Edition: San Francisco: John Howell, 1960.
Nr.Fine/Fin **$100**
Good/V.Good. **$45**

Dacus, J. A. *Life And Adventures Of Frank And Jesse James The Noted Western Outlaws*.
First Edition: St. Louis, MO.: W.S. Bryan, 1880.
Nr.Fine/Fin **$550**
Good/V.Good. **$250**

Cow Country
by Edward Everett Dale

Dale E. E. *Cow Country*. First Edition: Norman, OK: University of Oklahoma, 1942.
Nr.Fine/Fin **$115**
Good/V.Good. **$35**

_____. *Indians of the Southwest*. First Edition: Norman, OK: University of Oklahoma, 1949.
Nr.Fine/Fin **$75**
Good/V.Good. **$30**

Dalton, Emmett. *When the Daltons Rode*. First Edition: New York: Doubleday, Doran & Company, 1931.

Nr.Fine/Fin **$225**
Good/V.Good. **$100**

Dane, G. Ezra. *Ghost Town*. First Edition:
New York: Alfred A. Knopf, 1941.
Nr.Fine/Fin **$85**
Good/V.Good. **$30**

Davis, Mary Lee. *Uncle Sam's Attic
Alaska*.
First Edition: Boston: W.A. Wilde Co.,
1930.
Nr.Fine/Fin **$115**
Good/V.Good. **$50**

_____. *Sourdough Gold*. First
Edition: Boston: W.A. Wilde Co., 1931.
Nr.Fine/Fin **$50**
Good/V.Good. **$30**

DeVoto, Bernard. *Across the Wide
Missouri*. First Edition: Boston: Houghton
Mifflin, 1947.
Nr.Fine/Fin **$75**
Good/V.Good. **$25**

_____. *House of Sun-Goes-
Down*. First Edition: New York: Macmillan
Company, 1928.
Nr.Fine/Fin **$45**
Good/V.Good. **$25**

_____. *Year of Decision 1846*.
First Edition: Boston: Little, Brown & Co.,
1943.
Nr.Fine/Fin **$45**
Good/V.Good. **$15**

Dick, Everett. *The Sod-House Frontier
1854-1890*. First Edition: New York: D.
Appleton-Century, 1937.
Nr.Fine/Fin **$115**
Good/V.Good. **$45**

Dobie, J.Frank. *Coronado's Children*.
First Edition: Dallas, TX: The Southwest
Press, 1930. Points of Issue: First printing
dedication is from "a cowman of the Texas
soil."
Nr.Fine/Fin **$65**
Good/V.Good. **$25**

_____. *Apache Gold and Yaqui
Silver*. First Edition (Limited): Boston:
Little, Brown and Company, 1939.
Nr.Fine/Fin **$1200**
Good/V.Good. **$550**
First Edition (trade): Boston: Little, Brown
and Company, 1939.
Nr.Fine/Fin **$100**
Good/V.Good. **$45**

_____. *Mustangs*. First Edition
(trade): Boston: Little, Brown and Co.,
1952.
Nr.Fine/Fin **$100**
Good/V.Good. **$55**

Drago, Harry S. Great American Cattle
Trails.First Edition: New York: Dodd Mead,
1965.
Nr.Fine/Fin **$45**
Good/V.Good. **$20**

_____. *Great Range Wars*. First
Edition: New York: Dodd Mead, 1970.
Nr.Fine/Fin **$25**
Good/V.Good. **$10**

_____. *Outlaws on
Horseback*.First Edition: New York: Dodd,
Mead, 1964.
Nr.Fine/Fin **$95**
Good/V.Good. **$45**

_____. *Red River Valley*. First
Edition: New York: Clarkson N. Potter,
1962.
Nr.Fine/Fin **$65**
Good/V.Good. **$30**

Dunbar, Seymour. *A History of Travel in
America*. (Four Volumes). First Edition:
Indianapolis: Bobbs-Merrill Co., 1915.
Nr.Fine/Fin **$200**
Good/V.Good. **$110**

Earle, Alice Morse. *Colonial Days in Old
New York*. First Edition: New York: Charles

Scribners, 1896. Nr.Fine/Fin **$135**
Good/V.Good. **$70**

Elman, Robert. *Great American Shooting Prints*. First Edition: New York: Alfred A. Knopf, 1972
Nr.Fine/Fin **$150**
Good/V.Good. **$65**

Evans, Bessie. *American Indian Dance Steps*. First Edition: New York: A. S. Barnes & Co., 1931.
Nr.Fine/Fin **$200**
Good/V.Good. **$85**

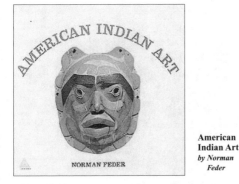

American Indian Art *by Norman Feder*

NORMAN FEDER

Feder, Norman. *American Indian Art*. First Edition: New York: Harry Abrams, 1965

Nr.Fine/Fin **$200**
Good/V.Good. **$95**

Fisher, Vardis. *Idaho Lore*. First Edition: Caldwell, ID: Caxton Printers, 1939
Nr.Fine/Fin **$450**
Good/V.Good. **$250**

Foreman, Grant. *Advancing the Frontier*. First Edition: Norman, OK: Univ. of Oklahoma Press, 1933
Nr.Fine/Fin **$200**
Good/V.Good. **$100**

Forrest, Earle R. *Missions and Pueblos of the Old Southwest*. First Edition: Cleveland: The Arthur H. Clark Company, 1929
Nr.Fine/Fin **$250**
Good/V.Good. **$125**

Freeman, Douglas Southall. *Lee's Lieutenants. (Three Volumes)*. First Edition: New York: Charles Scribners, 1942-1944
Nr.Fine/Fin **$1200**
Good/V.Good. **$500**

Fulmore, Z.T. *History and Geography of Texas*. First Editon: Austin: E. L. Steck, 1915
Nr.Fine/Fin **$125**
Good/V.Good. **$75**

Fundaburk, Emma Lila, and Mary Douglass Foreman. *Sun Circles and Human Hands: The Southeastern Indians–Art and Industry* First Edition: Luverne, AL: Emma Lila Fundaburk, 1957
Nr.Fine/Fin **$85**
Good/V.Good. **$30**

Garavaglia, Louis A. *Firearms of the American West 1803-1865*. First Edition: Albuquerque, NM: University Of New Mexico Press, 1984
Nr.Fine/Fin **$125**
Good/V.Good. **$85**

——————————. *Firearms of the American West 1866-1894*. First Edition: Albuquerque, NM: University Of New Mexico Press, 1984
Nr.Fine/Fin **$125**
Good/V.Good. **$85**

Gard, Wayne. *Sam Bass*. First Edition: Boston: Houghton Mifflin, 1936.
Nr.Fine/Fin **$75**
Good/V.Good. **$35**

——————————. *The Chisolm Trail*. First Edition: Norman, OK: University of Oklahoma Press, 1954
Nr.Fine/Fin **$75**
Good/V.Good. **$25**

——————————. *Frontier Justice*. First Edition: Norman, OK: University of Oklahoma Press, 1949
Nr.Fine/Fin **$75**
Good/V.Good. **$25**

Garland, Hamlin. *The Book of the American Indian*. First Edition: New York: Harper & Brothers, 1923
Nr.Fine/Fin **$400**
Good/V.Good................. **$175**

Gerhard, Peter. *Lower California Guidebook: A Descriptive Traveler's Guide* First Edition: Glendale, CA: Arthur H. Clarke Co., 1956
Nr.Fine/Fin **$65**
Good/V.Good.................. **$25**

_____. *Pirates on the West Coast of New Spain 1575-1742*.First Edition: Glendale, CA: Arthur H. Clarke Co., 1960
Nr.Fine/Fin **$125**
Good/V.Good.................. **$65**

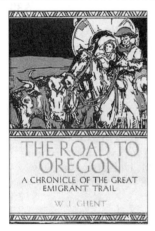

The Road to Oregon
by W.J. Ghent

Ghent, W.J. *The Early Far West* First Edition: New York: Longmans, Green, 1931
Nr.Fine/Fin **$40**
Good/V.Good.................. **$15**

_____. *The Road to Oregon*. First Edition: New York: Longmans, Green, 1929

Nr.Fine/Fin **$55**
Good/V.Good.................. **$25**

Gillett, James B. *Six Years with the Texas Rangers 1875-1881* First Edition: Austin, TX: VonBoeckmann-Jones Co., 1921
Nr.Fine/Fin **$550**
Good/V.Good................. **$250**

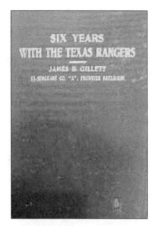

Six Years with the Texas Rangers
by James B. Gillett

Dona Lona: A Story of Taos and Santa Fe
by Blanche C. Grant

Grant, Blanche. *Dona Lona: A Story of Old Taos and Santa Fé*. First Edition: New York: Wilfred Funk, Inc., 1941
Nr.Fine/Fin **$85**
Good/V.Good.................. **$35**

_____. *When Old Trails Were New*. First Edition: New York: Press of the Pioneers, 1934
Nr.Fine/Fin **$95**
Good/V.Good.................. **$45**

Green, Ben K. *A Thousand Miles of Mustangin'* First Edition (Limited/Slipcased): Flagstaff, AZ: Northland Press, 1972.
Nr.Fine/Fin **$500**
Good/V.Good.................. **$300**
First Edition (trade): Flagstaff, AZ: Northland Press, 1972.

Nr.Fine/Fin **$165**
Good/V.Good. **$75**

_____. Village Horse Doctor West of the Pecos. First Edition: New York: Alfred A. Knopf, 1971
Nr.Fine/Fin **$75**
Good/V.Good. **$30**

_____. *Wild Cow Tales.* First Edition: New York: Alfred A. Knopf, 1969
Nr.Fine/Fin **$80**
Good/V.Good. **$35**

Gridley, Marion. *Indians of Yesterday.* First Edition: Chicago: M.A. Donohue & Co., 1940.
Nr.Fine/Fin **$75**
Good/V.Good. **$25**

Griffin, James B. *Archeology of the Eastern United States.*First Edition: Chicago: The University Of Chicago, 1952
Nr.Fine/Fin **$225**
Good/V.Good. **$85**

Grinnell, George Bird. *The Fighting Cheyennes.*
First Edition: New York: Scribners, 1915
Nr.Fine/Fin **$425**
Good/V.Good. **$200**

_____. *American Big Game in its Haunts.* First Edition: New York: Forest and Stream Publishing Company, 1904
Nr.Fine/Fin **$450**
Good/V.Good. **$150**

Hafen, Le Roy R. *The Overland Mail.* First Edition: Cleveland, OH: Arthur H. Clark Co., 1926
Nr.Fine/Fin **$250**
Good/V.Good. **$150**

Hafen, LeRoy R. & Ghent, W. J. *Broken Hand.* First Edition: Denver: The Old West Publishing Co., 1931.
Nr.Fine/Fin **$400**
Good/V.Good. **$175**

Halbert, Henry S. *A Dictionary of the Chocktaw Language.* First Edition: Washington, D.C.: U. S. Gov't. Printing Office, 1915
Nr.Fine/Fin **$75**
Good/V.Good. **$30**

Hale, Will T. *True Stories of Jamestown and Its Environs* First Edition: Nashville, TN: Smith & Lamar, 1907
Nr.Fine/Fin **$65**
Good/V.Good. **$25**

Hanley, J. Frank. *A Day in The Siskiyous an Oregon Extravaganza with fold out of Ashland Town.* First Edition: Indianapolis, IN: Art Press, 1916
Nr.Fine/Fin **$65**
Good/V.Good. **$35**

Haven, Charles T. *A History of the Colt Revolver.* First Edition (Limited/Slipcased): New York: William Morrow, 1940
Nr.Fine/Fin **$300**
Good/V.Good. **$150**
First Edition (trade): New York: William Morrow, 1940
Nr.Fine/Fin **$95**
Good/V.Good. **$40**

Havighurst, Walter. *Three Flags at the Straits The Forts of Mackinaw* First Edition: Englewood Cliffs, N.J.: Prentice-Hall, 1966
Nr.Fine/Fin **$35**
Good/V.Good. **$15**

Hebard, Grace R. *The Bozeman Trail. (Two Volumes).* First Edition: Cleveland, OH: Arthur H. Clark Co., 1922
Nr.Fine/Fin **$900**
Good/V.Good. **$600**

Henry, Alexander. *Travels and Adventures in Canada and the Indian Territories, Between the Years 1760 and 1776.*First Edition: New York: I. Riley, 1809
Nr.Fine/Fin **$1800**
Good/V.Good. **$1000**

Hinkle, James F. *Early Days Of A Cowboy On The Pecos* First Edition: Santa

Fe, NM: Stagecoach Press, 1965
Nr.Fine/Fin **$125**
Good/V.Good. **$50**

Mexico Bay
by Paul Horgan

Horgan, Paul. *Mexico Bay*. First Edition:
New York: Farrar, Straus Giroux, 1982
Nr.Fine/Fin **$70**
Good/V.Good. **$30**

Hough, Alfred Lacey. *Soldier in the West*.
First Edition: Philadelphia: Univ. of
Pennsylvania Press, 1957
Nr.Fine/Fin **$50**
Good/V.Good. **$20**

Howard, Helen Addison. *War Chief
Joseph*. First Edition: Caldwell, ID: The
Caxton Printers, Ltd: 1941.
Nr.Fine/Fin **$150**
Good/V.Good. **$50**

Hubbard, Harlan. *Shanty Boat*. First
Edition: New York: Dodd, Mead, 1954.
Nr.Fine/Fin **$65**
Good/V.Good. **$35**

Hughes, Langston. *A Pictorial History of
the Negro in America*. First Edition: New
York: Crown, 1956.
Nr.Fine/Fin **$150**
Good/V.Good. **$50**

Hungerford, Edward. *Locomotives on
Parade*. First Edition: New York: Thomas Y.
Crowell, 1940

Nr.Fine/Fin **$35**
Good/V.Good. **$20**

Hurston, Zora Neale. *Dust Tracks on the
Road*. First Edition: Philadelphia: J. B.
Lippincott, 1942
Nr.Fine/Fin **$425**
Good/V.Good. **$200**

Inverarity, Bruce. *Art of the Northwest
Coast Indians*. First Edition: Berkeley, CA:
University Of California, 1950
Nr.Fine/Fin **$75**
Good/V.Good. **$20**

James, Marquis. *Cherokee Strip*. First
Edition: New York: Viking, 1945
Nr.Fine/Fin **$65**
Good/V.Good. **$20**

**Uncle Bill: A Tale
of Two Kids and
a Cowboy**
by Will James

James, Will. *Uncle Bill. A Tale of Two Kids
and a Cowboy*. First Edition: New York:
Charles Scribners, 1932
Nr.Fine/Fin **$400**
Good/V.Good. **$175**

_____. *Smoky* Points of Issue: First
Issue has "Sand" as top title opposite title
page First Edition: New York: Charles
Scribners, 1929
Nr.Fine/Fin **$400**
Good/V.Good. **$175**

Johnson, Clifton. *Highways and Byways
of the Mississippi Valley*. First Edition: New

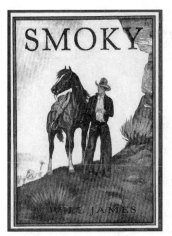

Smoky
by Will James

York: Macmillan, 1906
Nr.Fine/Fin **$100**
Good/V.Good................... **$55**

Johnson, Guion. *Ante-Bellum North Carolina*. First Edition: Chapel Hill, NC: Univ. of North Carolina Press, 1937
Nr.Fine/Fin **$150**
Good/V.Good................... **$65**

Kane, Harnett T. *Louisiana Hayride*. First Edition: New York: William Morrow, 1940
Nr.Fine/Fin **$65**
Good/V.Good................... **$30**

_____. *Gone Are the Days An Illustrated History of the Old South*. First Edition: New York: E. P. Dutton, 1960
Nr.Fine/Fin **$35**
Good/V.Good................... **$15**

Kelly, Charles. *The Outlaw Trail*. First Edition: Salt Lake City: published by the author, 1938
Nr.Fine/Fin **$1200**
Good/V.Good................... **$475**

King, Blanche Busey. *Under Your Feet*. First Edition: New York: Dodd Mead, 1939
Nr.Fine/Fin **$65**
Good/V.Good................... **$20**

Knox, Dudley W. *Naval Sketches of the War in California* Points of Issue: Printed by Grabhorn Press.

First Edition: New York: Random House, 1939
Nr.Fine/Fin **$345**
Good/V.Good................. **$185**

Mother Ditch
by Oliver La Farge

LaFarge, Oliver. *The Mother Ditch* First Edition: Boston: Houghton Mifflin, 1954
Nr.Fine/Fin **$30**
Good/V.Good................... **$12**

Lea, Tom. *George Catlin: Westward Bound a Hundred Years Ago*. First Edition: El Paso, TX: Pass of the North, 1939
Nr.Fine/Fin **$2500**
Good/V.Good................. **$1800**

_____. *The Wonderful Country*. First Edition: Boston: Little, Brown, & Co., 1952

A Bronco Pegasus
by Charles F. Lummis

Nr.Fine/Fin **$50**
Good/V.Good. **$20**

Lummis, Charles F. *A Bronco Pegasus*
First Edition: Boston: Houghton Mifflin, 1928
Nr.Fine/Fin **$125**
Good/V.Good. **$45**

_____. *Spanish Pioneers.* First
Edition: Chicago: A.C. McClurg and Co., 1893
Nr.Fine/Fin **$125**
Good/V.Good. **$60**

Mesa, Canon and Pueblo
by Charles E. Lummis

_____. *Mesa, Canon and Pueblo*.
First Edition: New York: The Century Co., 1925
Nr.Fine/Fin **$135**
Good/V.Good. **$65**

Mails, Thomas E. *Mystic Warriors of the Plains*. First Edition: Garden City, NY: Doubleday & Company, 1972
Nr.Fine/Fin **$200**
Good/V.Good. **$65**

_____. *Dog Soldiers, Bear Men and Buffalo Women*. First Edition: Englewood Cliffs, NJ: Prentice-Hall, 1973.
Nr.Fine/Fin **$200**
Good/V.Good. **$85**

McCracken, Harold. *The Frank Tenney Johnson Book*. First Edition: Garden City, NY: Doubleday & Company, 1974

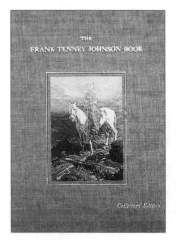

The Frank Tenney Johnson Book
by Harold McCracken

Nr.Fine/Fin **$350**
Good/V.Good. **$200**

_____. *The American Cowboy*. First Edition (Limited/Signed): Garden City, NY: Doubleday & Co, 1973
Nr.Fine/Fin **$125**
Good/V.Good. **$65**
First Edition (trade): Garden City, NY: Doubleday & Co, 1973
Nr.Fine/Fin **$45**
Good/V.Good. **$20**

_____. *Portrait of the Old West*.
First Edition: New York: McGraw-Hill Book Co., 1952.
Nr.Fine/Fin **$125**
Good/V.Good. **$50**

Miller, Joaquin. *Life Amongst the Modocs*. First Edition: London: Richard Bentley and Son, 1873
Nr.Fine/Fin **$350**
Good/V.Good. **$185**
First U.S. Edition: Hartford, CT: American Publishing Co., 1874
Nr.Fine/Fin **$150**
Good/V.Good. **$75**

Mitchell, John D. *Lost Mines of the Great Southwest* First Edition: Mesa, AZ: M.F. Rose, 1933
Nr.Fine/Fin **$250**
Good/V.Good. **$175**
First Hardcover Edition: Phoenix, AZ: The

Journal Co., Inc., 1933
Nr.Fine/Fin **$100**
Good/V.Good. **$65**

Moorehead, Warren K. *A Report on the Archaeology of Maine*. First Edition: Andover, MA: Andover Press, 1922
Nr.Fine/Fin **$225**
Good/V.Good. **$145**

Muir, John. *Picturesque California. (Two Volumes)*First Edition: New York and San Francisco: J. Dewing Publishing Company, 1888
Nr.Fine/Fin **$1500**
Good/V.Good. **$700**

The Yosemite
by John Muir

_____. *The Yosemite*. First Edition: New York: The Century Co., 1912
Nr.Fine/Fin **$300**
Good/V.Good. **$145**

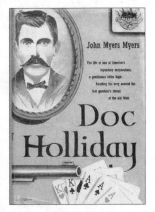

Doc Holliday
by john Myers Myers

Myers, John Myers. *Death of the Bravos*. First Edition: Boston: Little, Brown & Company, 1962
Nr.Fine/Fin **$100**
Good/V.Good. **$45**

_____. *Doc Holliday*. First Edition: Boston: Little, Brown & Company, 1955
Nr.Fine/Fin **$60**
Good/V.Good. **$25**

Neihardt, John G. *Black Elk Speaks: Being the Life Story of a Holy Man of the Oglala Sioux* First Edition: New York: William Morrow, 1932
Nr.Fine/Fin **$1200**
Good/V.Good. **$650**

The Real Billy The Kid
by Miguel Otero

Otero, Miguel. *The Real Billy the Kid*. First Edition: New York, Rufus Rockwell Wilson Inc., 1936
Nr.Fine/Fin **$400**
Good/V.Good. **$160**

_____. *My Nine Years as Governor of the Territory of New Mexico: 1897-1906*. First Edition: Albuquerque, NM: University of New Mexico Press, 1940
Nr.Fine/Fin **$250**
Good/V.Good. **$100**

Paine, Albert Bigelow. *Captain Bill McDonald, Texas Ranger. A Story of Frontier Reform*. First Edition: New York: J.

J. Little & Ives Co., 1909
Nr.Fine/Fin **$275**
Good/V.Good.................. **$175**

Pinkerton, Allan. *Strikers, Communists, Tramps and Detectives*. First Edition: New York: G.W. Carleton & Co., 1878.
Nr.Fine/Fin **$350**
Good/V.Good.................. **$150**

Quaife, M. M. *Chicago's Highways Old & New: from Indian Trail to Motor Road*. First Edition: Chicago: D.F. Keller & Company, 1923
Nr.Fine/Fin **$75**
Good/V.Good.................... **$25**

_____. *"Yellowstone Kelly": The Memoirs of Luther S. Kelly*. First Edition: New Haven, CT: Yale University Press, 1926
Nr.Fine/Fin **$150**
Good/V.Good.................. **$85**

Rascoe, Burton. *The Dalton Brothers*. First Edition: New York: Frederick Fell, 1954
Nr.Fine/Fin **$55**
Good/V.Good.................. **$25**

Reichard, Gladys. *Navajo Shepherd and Weaver* First Edition: New York: J.J. Augustin, 1936
Nr.Fine/Fin **$200**
Good/V.Good.................. **$75**

Richman, Irving B. *Ioway to Iowa*. First Edition: Iowa City, IA: State Hist. Soc. of Iowa, 1931
Nr.Fine/Fin **$75**
Good/V.Good.................. **$30**

Ridings, Sam P. *The Chisholm Trail*. First Edition: Guthrie, OK: Co-Operative Publ. Co., 1936 Nr.Fine/Fin **$350**
Good/V.Good.................. **$150**

Rister, Carl Coke. *The Southwestern Frontier, 1865-1881*. First Edition: Cleveland, OH: Arthur H. Clark Co., 1928
Nr.Fine/Fin **$275**

Good/V.Good.................. **$150**

_____. *Border Captives. The Traffic in Prisoners by Southern Plains Indians, 1835-1875*. First Edition: Norman, OK: University Of Oklahoma Press, 1940
Nr.Fine/Fin **$250**
Good/V.Good.................. **$110**

Roosevelt, Theodore. *Hunting Trips of a Ranchman*. First Edition: New York: G. P. Putnams, 1885
Nr.Fine/Fin **$1000**
Good/V.Good.................. **$600**

_____. *Naval War of 1812*. First Edition: New York: G. P. Putnams, 1882
Nr.Fine/Fin **$650**
Good/V.Good.................. **$300**

_____. *The Wilderness Hunter*. First Edition (Limited/Signed): New York: G. P. Putnams, 1893
Nr.Fine/Fin **$4200**
Good/V.Good.................. **$2600**
First Edition (trade): New York: G. P. Putnams, 1893
Nr.Fine/Fin **$600**
Good/V.Good.................. **$325**

Russell, Don. *The Lives And Legends Of Buffalo Bill* First Edition: Norman, OK: University of Oklahoma Press, 1960
Nr.Fine/Fin **$85**
Good/V.Good.................. **$40**

Rynning, Thomas. *Gun Notches*. First Edition: New York: Frederick A. Stokes Company, 1931
Nr.Fine/Fin **$100**
Good/V.Good.................. **$65**

Sabin, Edwin L. *Kit Carson Days*. First Edition: Chicago: A.C. McClurg, 1914
Nr.Fine/Fin **$300**
Good/V.Good.................. **$125**

_____. *Wild Men of the Wild West*.
First Edition: New York: Thomas Y. Crowell, 1929

Nr.Fine/Fin **$85**
Good/V.Good. **$35**

Sandoz, Mari. *Crazy Horse The Strange Man of the Oglalas* First Edition: New York: Alfred A. Knopf, 1942
Nr.Fine/Fin **$500**
Good/V.Good. **$275**

_____. *Old Jules.* First Edition: Boston: Little Brown and Company, 1935
Nr.Fine/Fin **$125**
Good/V.Good. **$65**

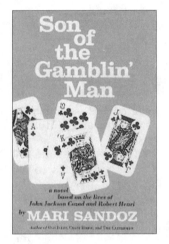

Son of the
Gamblin' Man
by Mari Sandoz

_____. *Son of the Gamblin' Man* First Edition: New York: Clarkson N. Potter, 1960.
Nr.Fine/Fin **$100**
Good/V.Good. **$45**

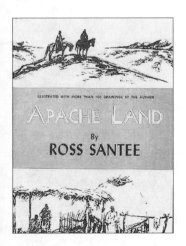

Apache Land
by Ross Santee

Santee, Ross. *Apache Land* First Edition: New York: Scribners, 1947
Nr.Fine/Fin **$150**
Good/V.Good. **$60**

_____. *Lost Pony Tracks.* First Edition: New York: Scribners, 1953.
Nr.Fine/Fin **$75**
Good/V.Good. **$35**

Seton, Ernest Thompson. *Lives of the Hunted.* First Edition: New York: Charles Scribners, 1901.
Nr.Fine/Fin **$450**
Good/V.Good. **$150**

Siringo, Charles A. *A Cowboy Detective.* First Edition: Chicago: W. B. Conkey Company, 1912
Nr.Fine/Fin **$450**
Good/V.Good. **$175**

_____. *A History of Billy the Kid.* First Edition: Santa Fe, NM: published for the author, 1920
Nr.Fine/Fin **$1800**
Good/V.Good. **$1000**

_____. *Lone Star Cowboy.* First Edition: Santa Fe, NM: published for the author, 1919
Nr.Fine/Fin **$350**
Good/V.Good. **$200**

_____. *Riata and Spurs.* First Edition: Boston: Houghton Mifflin Co., 1927
Nr.Fine/Fin **$135**
Good/V.Good. **$55**

Sprague, Marshall. *Money Mountain.* First Edition: Boston: Little, Brown and Company, 1953
Nr.Fine/Fin **$35**
Good/V.Good. **$15**

Spring, Agnes Wright. *The Cheyenne and Black Hills Stage and Express Routes.* First Edition: Glendale, CA: Arthur H. Clark Co., 1949
Nr.Fine/Fin **$225**

Good/V.Good **$115**

Standing Bear, Chief. *My People the Sioux*. First Edition: Boston: Houghton Mifflin Co., 1928
Nr.Fine/Fin **$150**
Good/V.Good **$95**

Stewart, Hilary. *Totem Poles*. First Edition: Seattle, WA: University Of Washington Press, 1990
Nr.Fine/Fin **$60**
Good/V.Good **$30**

Tarbell, Ida M. *The History of the Standard Oil Company*. First Edition: New York: McClure, Phillips & Co., 1904
Nr.Fine/Fin **$950**
Good/V.Good **$400**

Thompson, R.A. *Conquest of CaliforniaæCapture of Sonoma by the Bear Flag Men, Raising the American Flag in Monterey*. First Edition: Santa Rosa, CA: Sonoma Democrat Publishing, 1896
Nr.Fine/Fin **$200**
Good/V.Good **$95**

Tourgee, Albion W. *An Appeal to Caesar* First Edition: New York: Fords, Howard, & Hulbert, 1884
Nr.Fine/Fin **$145**
Good/V.Good **$45**

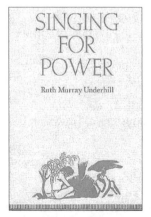
Singing for Power
by Ruth Underhill

Underhill, Ruth. S*inging for Power: The Song Magic of the Papago Indians of Southern Arizona* First Edition: Berkeley,

CA: University of California Press, 1938
Nr.Fine/Fin **$150**
Good/V.Good **$55**

Big Foot
Wallace
by Stanley Vestal

Vestal, Stanley. *Big Foot Wallace*. First Edition: Boston: Houghton and Mifflin, 1942
Nr.Fine/Fin **$150**
Good/V.Good **$100**

_____. *Happy Hunting Grounds*. First Edition: Chicago: Lyons and Carnahan, 1928
Nr.Fine/Fin **$200**
Good/V.Good **$65**

_____. *Warpath and Council Fire*. First Edition: New York: Random House, 1948
Nr.Fine/Fin **$115**
Good/V.Good **$40**

Walker, Tacetta. *Stories of Early Days in Wyoming*. First Edition: Casper, WY: Prairie Publishing Co., 1936.
Nr.Fine/Fin **$300**
Good/V.Good **$200**

Wall, Oscar Garrett. *Recollections Of The Sioux Massacre* First Edition: Lake City, MN: M. C. Russell, 1908.
Nr.Fine/Fin **$225**
Good/V.Good **$100**

Wallace, Ernest. *Commanches: Lords of*

the Plains. First Edition: Norman, OK:
University of Oklahoma Press, 1952
Nr.Fine/Fin **$45**
Good/V.Good. **$25**

Walsh, Richard J. *Making of Buffalo Bill:
A Study In Heroics*. First Edition:
Indianapolis, IN: Bobbs-Merrill, 1928
Nr.Fine/Fin **$175**
Good/V.Good. **$75**

Walters, Lorenzo D. *Tombstone's
Yesterday*. First Edition: Tucson: Acme
Printing Company, 1928
Nr.Fine/Fin **$450**
Good/V.Good. **$200**

Washington, Booker T. *The Man Farthest
Down* First Edition: Garden City, NY:
Doubleday Page, 1912
Nr.Fine/Fin **$1000**
Good/V.Good. **$650**

_____. *The Future of the
American Negro* First Edition: Boston:
Small, Maynard & Co., 1899
Nr.Fine/Fin **$400**
Good/V.Good. **$150**

Webb, Walter Prescott. *The Great Plains*.
First Edition: Boston: Ginn & Co. 1931.
Nr.Fine/Fin **$115**
Good/V.Good. **$45**

_____. *Texas Rangers*.
First Edition: Boston: Houghton Mifflin
Co., 1935
Nr.Fine/Fin **$275**
Good/V.Good. **$125**

White Horse Eagle, Big Chief. *We
Indians*.
First Edition: New York: E.P. Dutton, 1931
Nr.Fine/Fin **$200**
Good/V.Good. **$125**

Willcox, R. N. *Reminiscences of California
Life* First Edition: Avery, OH: Willcox
Printing, 1897
Nr.Fine/Fin **$900**
Good/V.Good. **$400**

Wilson, Mitchell. *American Science and
Invention*. First Edition: New York: Simon
and Schuster, 1954.
Nr.Fine/Fin **$25**
Good/V.Good. **$10**

Wilstach, Paul. *Hudson River Landings*.
First Edition: Indianapolis, IN: Bobbs
Merrill, 1933
Nr.Fine/Fin **$65**
Good/V.Good. **$25**

Wood, Frederic. T*he Turnpikes of New
England*. First Edition: Boston: Marshall
Jones Co, 1919
Nr.Fine/Fin **$125**
Good/V.Good. **$65**

Young, Harry. *Hard Knocks*. First Edition:
Portland, OR: Wells & Co., 1915.
Nr.Fine/Fin **$200**
Good/V.Good. **$100**

Art and Illustrated Books

Sometimes considered two separate and distinct categories, these two have a great deal in common and overlap in many places. The straight "art" book, such as: St Clair, Philip R., Frederic Remington, *The American West*, New York: Bonanza Books, 1981, which sells between $25 and $50 depending on condition, is overshadowed by Longfellow, Henry Wadsworth, *Song of Hiawatha* With Illustrations from Designs by Frederic Remington, Boston: Houghton, Mifflin and Company, 1891, which sells in the $2500 to $3500 range. That actually outdoes the first edition, Longfellow, Henry Wadsworth, *Song of Hiawatha*, Boston: Ticknor and Fields, 1855, which goes in the $800 to $1500 range. There are many books, both classic and popular, where the artist or illustrator is the important factor to the collector. Illustrators have established visual touchstones to classic characters that often overshadow the writer's descriptions, or depict them so closely that the artist's visualization finds its way into the public consciousness. Our mental portrait of a character is often that visualized by the artist or illustrator. A few examples are Sidney Paget's illustrations of Sherlock Holmes, Joseph Clement Coll's drawings of Fu Manchu, and renderings of Tarzan by both J. Allen St. John and John Coleman Burroughs. So the illustrated book becomes collectable based on the illustrator.

This can transcend the first edition, and creates another edition that the collector needs to be aware of, the first "thus." A "First Thus" is the first printing of any edition other than the first. In the example above, *The Song of Hiawatha* that is the most valuable is the first printing in 1891, which will be shown by a date on the title page matching the copyright date for Remington's illustrations on the verso.

Book illustration is hardly a new idea. The illuminated manuscripts of the Middle Ages were works of art as well as books. The more modern trend began with poet, designer William Morris and his famous Kelmscott Press. At Kelmscott, a book was produced as a piece of ensemble art, meshing together the artist, publisher, lithographer, typographer, printer, and binder. If the book was a new piece, the writer as well became a part of the team, working hand in glove to create the book. The books created by Kelmscott were wonders. Today, most are in museums and it takes a pretty hefty bankroll to own just one. Kelmscott had a major impact in France where the tradition created the "Livre d' Artiste," literally book of the Artist, which were books created in the close collaboration pioneered at Kelmscott.

Amboise Vollard created fine art books in a similar fashion, choosing the best artists of his generation, Picasso, Matisse, and Braque, among others. In the United States, an artist and writer named Howard Pyle changed book illustration on his own and then taught his technique to what has been called the Brandywine School, which included such artists as N.C. Wyeth, Frank Schoonover, Stanley Arthurs, Elizabeth Shippen Green, and Maxfield Parrish. Another group of American artists, the Ashcan School of Arthur B. Davies, Robert Henri, George Luks, William Glackens, John Sloan, Everett Shinn, Alfred Maurer, George Wesley Bellows, Edward Hopper, and Guy Pène Du Bois, also had a profound effect on book illustration.

10 Classic Rarities

Beardsley, Aubrey. *The Early Work; The Later Work; The Uncollected Work*. London: John Lane, Bodley Head, 1899-1925. Three limited edition volumes.
Retail Value in:
   Near Fine to Fine Condition **$3200**
   Good to Very Good Condition. . . **$2400**

Chagall, Marc. *The Jerusalem Windows*. New York/Monte Carlo: George Braziller & André Sauret, 1962 . Issued in a slipcase, text by Jean Leymarie.
Retail Value in:
   Near Fine to Fine Condition **$2600**
   Good to Very Good Condition. . . **$1500**

Duchamp, Marcel & Andre Breton. *Le Surréalisme en 1947*. Paris: "Pierre Feu," Maeght Editeur, 1947. THE surrealist source, art by Duchamp, Miro, Jean, Maria, Tanguy , Tanning, Bellmer, Brignoni, Calder, Capacci, Damme, de Diego, Donati, Hare, Lamba, Matta, Sage, Tanguy, and Toyen: texts by Breton, Bataille, Cesairek, Brun, Bellmer, Kiesler.
Retail Value in:
   Near Fine to Fine Condition **$8000**
   Good to Very Good Condition. . . **$5000**

Dulac, Edmund. *Lyrics Pathetic & Humorous from A to Z*. London: Frederick Warne & Co., 1908. Dulac's alphabet, the limited portfolio issued concurrently, brings auction prices in the stratosphere.
Retail Value in:
   Near Fine to Fine Condition **$1500**
   Good to Very Good Condition. . . **$1000**

Hassam, Childe. *The Etchings and Dry-Points of Childe Hassam*. New York: Charles Scribner's Sons, 1925. In the first edition, the initial etching "Cos Cob" is signed.
Retail Value in:
   Near Fine to Fine Condition **$2000**
   Good to Very Good Condition. . . **$1100**

Matisse, Henri. *Poèmes de Charles d'Orléans*. Manuscrits et illustrés par Henri Matisse. Paris: Tériade, 1950. Beautiful book, awesomely so.
Retail Value in:
   Near Fine to Fine Condition **$7000**
   Good to Very Good Condition. . . **$5000**

Miro, Joan. *Joan Miro. Lithographs. Volumes I, II, & III. Vol. I: Tudor*, 1972/ Vol. II: NY: Amiel, 1975/ Vol. III: Paris: Maeght, 1977.
Retail Value in:
   Near Fine to Fine Condition **$2000**
   Good to Very Good Condition. . . **$1200**

Picasso, Pablo. *Picasso, Le Gout Du Bonheur: a Suite of Happy, Playful, and Erotic Drawings*. New York: Abrams, 1970. Issued in slipcase in a limited edition of 666.
Retail Value in:
   Near Fine to Fine Condition **$2000**
   Good to Very Good Condition. . . **$1200**

Rackham, Arthur. *The Arthur Rackham Fairy Book*. Edinborough, Scotland: George G. Harrap & Co., Ltd., 1933. Limited edition of 460/signed.
Retail Value in:
   Near Fine to Fine Condition **$2900**
   Good to Very Good Condition. . . **$1800**

Warhol, Andy. *The Index Book*. New York: Random House, 1967. Issued with 1) colored pop-up castle 2) folding page with paper accordion 3) "The Chelsea Girls" paper disc; 4) colored pop-up airplane 4) mobile on a piece of black string 5) flexi-disc of the Velvet Underground illustrated with a portrait of Lou Reed 6) folding illustration of a nose 7) colored pop-up Hunt's Tomato Paste Cans 8) inflatable sponge 9) balloon 10) tear-out postcard.
Retail Value in:
   Near Fine to Fine Condition **$2800**
   Good to Very Good Condition. . . **$1700**

Price Guide

Aalto, Alvar. *Sketches*. First U.S. Edition: Cambridge, MA: The MIT Press, 1978.
Nr.Fine/Fine. **$95**
Good/V.Good. **$65**

Addams, Charles. *Night Crawlers*. First Edition: New York: Simon and Schuster, 1957.
Nr.Fine/Fine. **$45**
Good/V.Good. **$30**

_____. *Addams and Evil*. First Edition: New York: Random House, 1947.
Nr.Fine/Fine. **$100**
Good/V.Good. **$55**

Mac
by Cecil Aldin

Aldin, Cecil. *Mac*. First Edition: London: Henry Frowde and Hodder & Stoughton, 1912.
Nr.Fine/Fine $1200
Good/V.Good $500

_____. *White-ear & Peter-The Story of a Fox and a Fox Terrier*. (Neils Heiberg).
First Edition: London: Macmillan, 1912.
Nr.Fine/Fine. **$250**
Good/V.Good. **$150**

_____. *Old Inns*. First Edition: London: William Heinemann, 1921.
Nr.Fine/Fine. **$200**

Good/V.Good. **$95**

Anderson, Anne. *Briar Rose Book of Old Fairy Tales*. First Edition: London: T. C. & E. C. Jack, Ltd., 1930.
Nr.Fine/Fine. **$350**
Good/V.Good. **$200**

_____. *Sleeping Beauty*. First Edition Thus: London & New York: Thomas Nelson & Sons, 1928.
Nr.Fine/Fine. **$300**
Good/V.Good. **$95**

Anderson, C.W. *Horse Show*. First Edition: New York: Harper & Brothers, 1951.
Nr.Fine/Fine. **$150**
Good/V.Good. **$45**

_____. *Sketchbook: Horse Drawings* First Edition: New York: Macmillan, 1948.
Nr.Fine/Fine. **$200**
Good/V.Good. **$125**

Angelo, Valenti. *Valenti Angelo*. Author. Illustrator. Printer. First Edition: San Francisco: Book Club of California, 1976.
Nr.Fine/Fine. **$600**
Good/V.Good. **$400**

_____. *Salome*. (Oscar Wilde) First Edition Thus: San Francisco: Grabhorn Press, 1927.
Nr.Fine/Fine. **$300**
Good/V.Good. **$200**

_____. *The Long Christmas*. (Ruth Sawyer) First Edition: New York: Viking, 1941.
Nr.Fine/Fine. **$85**
Good/V.Good. **$35**

_____. *A Sentimental Journey Through France & Italy*. (Laurence Sterne) First Edition Thus: New York: Dodd Mead, 1929.
Nr.Fine/Fine. **$45**
Good/V.Good. **$20**

Arthurs, Stanley. *"Posson Jone" and Père Raphaël* .(George Washington Cable) First Edition: New York: Charles Scribner's Sons, 1909.
Nr.Fine/Fine **$175**
Good/V.Good **$85**.

_____. *Stanley Arthurs*. First Edition: Wilmington, DE: Delaware Art Museum, May 3-June 16, 1974.
Nr.Fine/Fine.................... **$35**
Good/V.Good.................. **$15**

Artzybasheff, Boris. *Poor Shaydullah*. First Edition: New York: Macmillan, 1931.
Nr.Fine/Fine................... $110
Good/V.Good................... $45

_____. *Orpheus; Myths of the World*.(Padraic Colum) First Edition (Limited/Signed): New York: Macmillan, 1930.
Nr.Fine/Fine.................. **$600**
Good/V.Good................. **$350**
First Edition (trade): New York: Macmillan, 1930.
Nr.Fine/Fine................... **$75**
Good/V.Good.................. **$30**

Austen, John. *Adventures of a Harlequin*.(Francis Bickley) First Edition: London: Selwyn and Blount Ltd, 1923.
Nr.Fine/Fine................... **$95**
Good/V.Good.................. **$35**

Avery, Milton. *Milton Avery-Prints & Drawings* First Edition: Brooklyn, NY: Brooklyn Museum, 1966.
Nr.Fine/Fine **$25**
Good/V.Good **$12**

Beardsley, Aubrey. *Le Morte D'Arthur*. (Sir Thomas Mallory) First Edition thus: London: J M Dent and Sons Ltd., 1893-94.
Nr.Fine/Fine................. **$2500**
Good/V.Good................ **$1500**

_____. *SalomÈ A Tragedy in One Act. Translated from the French of Oscar Wilde [by Lord Alfred Douglas]: Pictured by Aubrey Beardsley*. First Edition

Le Morte
D'Arthur
*by Aubrey
Beardsley*

in English: London: Elkin Matthews & John Lane, 1894.
Nr.Fine/Fine.................. **$3500**
Good/V.Good.................. **$2000**

_____. *The Early Work*. First Edition: London: John Lane/the Bodley Head, 1901.
Nr.Fine/Fine.................... **$300**
Good/V.Good..................... **$135**

Beerbohm, Max. *A Book of Caricatures*. First Edition: London: Methuen & Co., 1907.
Nr.Fine/Fine.................. **$550**
Good/V.Good.................. **$200**

_____. *Observations*. First Edition: London: William Heinemann, 1925.
Nr.Fine/Fine.................. **$450**
Good/V.Good.................. **$175**
Deluxe Edition: London: William Heinemann, 1926.
Nr.Fine/Fine.................. **$750**
Good/V.Good................. **$350**

Bellows, George W. *George W. Bellows: His Lithographs*. First Edition: New York and London: Alfred A. Knopf, 1927.
Nr.Fine/Fine.................... $220
Good/V.Good................... $100

Betts, Ethel Franklin. *While The Heart Beats Young (James Whitcomb Riley)* First Edition: Indianapolis: Bobbs Merrill, 1906.

While The Heart Beats Young *(James Whitcomb Riley)* *by Ethel Franklin Betts*

Nr.Fine/Fine. **$340**
Good/V.Good. **$225**

_____. *Humpty Dumpty.* *(Amma Alice Chapin)* First Edition: New York: Dodd, Mead, 1905.
Nr.Fine/Fine. **$155**
Good/V.Good. **$85**

Little Lord Fauntleroy *by Reginald B. Birch*

Birch, Reginald B. *Little Lord Fauntleroy*.(Francis Hodgeson Burnett) First Edition: New York: Scribners, 1886.
Nr.Fine/Fine. **$200**
Good/V.Good. **$85**
First U.K. Edition: London: Frederick Warne and Co., 1886.

Nr.Fine/Fine. **$100**
Good/V.Good. **$55**

_____. *The Vizier of the Two-Horned Alexander*. (Frank R. Stockton) First Edition: New York: The Century Company, 1899.
Nr.Fine/Fine. **$85**
Good/V.Good. **$25**

Blaine, Mahlon. *Hashish and Incense.* (Paul Verlaine) First Edition Thus: New York: Paul Verlaine Society, 1929.
Nr.Fine/Fine. **$175**
Good/V.Good. **$65**

_____. *Alraune*. (Hanns Heinz Ewers) First Edition Thus: New York: John Day, 1929.
Nr.Fine/Fine. **$85**
Good/V.Good. **$45**

_____. *The Monster Men*. (Edgar Rice Burroughs) First Edition Thus: New York Canaveral, 1962.
Nr.Fine/Fine. **$45**
Good/V.Good. **$25**

Boston, Peter. *Treasure of Green Knowe.* First Edition: New York: Harcourt Brace & World, 1958.
Nr.Fine/Fine. **$65**
Good/V.Good. **$35**

Boylan, Grace and Ike Morgan. Kids of Many Colors. First Edition: Chicago: Jamieson Higgins Co., 1901.
Nr.Fine/Fine. **$195**
Good/V.Good. **$75**

Bradley, Will. *Fringilla or Tales in Verse.* First Edition: Cleveland: Burrows Brothers, 1895.
Nr.Fine/Fine. **$1250**
Good/V.Good. **$850**

_____. *War is Kind*. (Stephen Crane) First Edition: New York: Frederick A. Stokes, 1899.
Nr.Fine/Fine. **$1000**
Good/V.Good. **$750**

Brangwyn, Frank and Walter Shaw Sparrow. *The Book of Bridges*. First Edition: London: John Lane/The Bodley Head, 1916
Nr.Fine/Fine. **$1000**
Good/V.Good. **$750**
First U.S. Edition: London and New York: John Lane The Bodley Head and John Lane Company, 1926.
Nr.Fine/Fine. **$850**
Good/V.Good. **$475**

Bransom, Paul. *The Wind in the Willows*. (Kenneth Graham) First Edition Thus: London: Methuen and Co., 1913.
Nr.Fine/Fine. **$450**
Good/V.Good. **$175**
First U.S. Edition Thus: New York: Charles Scribners, 1913.
Nr.Fine/Fine. **$275**
Good/V.Good. **$100**

_____. *The Argosy of Fables*. First Edition (Limited): New York: Frederick A. Stokes, 1921.
Nr.Fine/Fine. **$1750**
Good/V.Good. **$725**
First Edition (trade): New York: Frederick A. Stokes, 1921.
Nr.Fine/Fine. **$150**
Good/V.Good. **$45**

Braque, Georges. *Ten Works. With a Discussion by the Artist: Braque Speaks to Dora Vallier*. First Edition: New York: Harcourt, Brace & World, 1963.
Nr.Fine/Fine. **$4500**
Good/V.Good. **$1500**

_____. *Georges Braque*. First Edition: New York: Museum of Modern Art in collaboration with Cleveland Museum of Art, 1949.
Nr.Fine/Fine. **$45**
Good/V.Good. **$20**

Bratby, John. *Breakdown*. First Edition: London: Hutchinson, 1960.
Nr.Fine/Fine. **$50**
Good/V.Good. **$30**
First U.S. Edition: New York: The World

Publishing Co, 1960.
Nr.Fine/Fine. **$55**
Good/V.Good. **$20**

Brock, H.M. *The Scarlet Pimpernel*. (Baroness Orczy) First Edition Thus: London: Greening & Co., 1906
Nr.Fine/Fine. **$450**
Good/V.Good. **$175**

_____. *A Book of Old Ballads*.(Beverly Nichols) First Edition: London Hutchinson & Co., Ltd., 1934.
Nr.Fine/Fine. **$300**
Good/V.Good. **$75**

_____. *Songs and Ballads*. (William Makepeace Thackery) First Edition: London: Cassell and Co., 1896.
Nr.Fine/Fine. **$125**
Good/V.Good. **$35**

Brown, Ethel P. *Once Upon a Time in Delaware*. (Katherine Pyle) First Edition: Delaware: Society of the Colonial Dames of America, 1911.
Nr.Fine/Fine. **$25**
Good/V.Good. **$10**

Kidnapped
by Francis Brundage

Brundage, Francis. *Kidnapped*. (Robert Lewis Stevenson) First Edition Thus: Akron, OH: Saalfield Publishing Co., 1926.
Nr.Fine/Fine **$22**
Good/V.Good. **$10**

Buffet, Bernard. *Bernard Buffet Lithographs 1952-1966*. First Edition: New York: Tudor Publishing Company, 1968.
Nr.Fine/Fine. **$1000**
Good/V.Good. **$525**

A Child's
Garden of Verses
by Clara Burd

Burd, Clara. *A Child's Garden of Verses*. (Robert Lewis Stevenson) First Edition: Akron, OH: Saalfield Publishing Company, 1929.
Nr.Fine/Fine. **$85**
Good/V.Good. **$35**

Burroughs, John Coleman. *The Deputy Sheriff of Comanche County*. (Edgar Rice Burroughs) First Edition: Tarzana, CA: Burroughs, 1941.
Nr.Fine/Fine. **$2000**
Good/V.Good. **$800**

_____. *Llana of Gathol*. (Edgar Rice Burroughs) First Edition: Tarzana, CA: Burroughs, 1948.
Nr.Fine/Fine. **$450**
Good/V.Good. **$150**

_____. *Tarzan and the Foreign Legion*. (Edgar Rice Burroughs) First Edition: Tarzana, CA: Burroughs, 1947.
Nr.Fine/Fine. **$250**
Good/V.Good. **$90**

Caldecott, R. *A Sketch-Book of R. Caldecott's*. First Edition: London & New York: George Routledge, 1883.
Nr.Fine/Fine. **$200**

Good/V.Good. **$90**

Calder, Alexander. *Three Young Rats*. First Edition: New York: Curt Valentin, 1944.
Nr.Fine/Fine. **$1250**
Good/V.Good. **$550**

Campbell, Floyd V. *The Roosevelt Bears Their Travels and Adventures*. (Seymour Eaton) First Edition: Philadelphia: Edward Stern & Company, Inc., 1906.
Nr.Fine/Fine. **$650**
Good/V.Good. **$275**

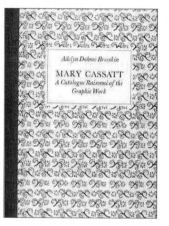

Mary Cassatt:
A Catalogue
Ratsonne of the
Graphic Work
by Mary Cassatt

Cassatt, Mary. *Mary Cassatt: A Catalogue Ratsonne of the Graphic Work*. First Edition: Washington, D.C.: Smithsonian Institution Press, 1970
Nr.Fine/Fine. **$1200**
Good/V.Good. **$750**

Cezanne, Paul. *Cezanne's Portrait Drawings*.First Edition: Cambridge, MA: MIT Press, 1970.
Nr.Fine/Fine. **$150**
Good/V.Good. **$60**

_____. *Cezanne's Composition*. First Edition: Berkeley, CA: University of California Press, 1950.
Nr.Fine/Fine. **$75**
Good/V.Good. **$25**

Chagall, Marc. *Chagall's Posters*. First Edition: New York: Crown, 1975.
Nr.Fine/Fine. **$175**

Good/V.Good. **$75**

_____. *Daphnis and Chloe*. First
Edition: New York: George Braziller, 1977.
Nr.Fine/Fine. **$145**
Good/V.Good. **$65**

_____. *The World of Marc Chagall*.
First Edition: Garden City: Doubleday,
1968. Nr.Fine/Fine **$125**
Good/V.Good. **$45**

Christo. Christo: *Running Fence: Sonoma
and Marin Counties, California, 1972-1976*.
First Edition (Limited/Signed/Hardcover):
New York: Harry Abrams, 1978.
Nr.Fine/Fine. **$500**
Good/V.Good. **$200**
First Edition (trade/Softcover): New York:
Harry Abrams, 1978.
Nr.Fine/Fine. **$55**
Good/V.Good. **$20**

Christy, Howard Chandler. *The
American Girl*. First Edition: New York:
Moffat, Yard, 1906.
Nr.Fine/Fine. **$200**
Good/V.Good. **$85**

_____. *The Christy
Girl*. First Edition: Indianapolis: Bobbs-
Merrill, 1906.
Nr.Fine/Fine. **$125**
Good/V.Good. **$55**

_____. *The Lion and
the Unicorn*. (Richard Harding Davis)
First Edition: New York: Scribners, 1899.
Nr.Fine/Fine. **$45**
Good/V.Good. **$20**

Coffin, Robert P. *Tristram. Mainstays Of
Maine*. First Edition: New York: Macmillan,
1944.
Nr.Fine/Fine. **$25**
Good/V.Good. **$12**

_____. *Lost Paradise:
a Boyhood on a Maine Coast Farm*. First
Edition: New York: Macmillan, 1934.
Nr.Fine/Fine. **$75**

Good/V.Good. **$30**

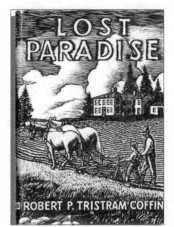

Lost Paradise:
A Boyhood On
A Maine Coast
Farm
by Robert P. Coffin

Coll, Joseph Clement. *Messiah of the
Cylinder*. (Victor Rousseau) First Edition:
Chicago: A. C. McClurg & Co., 1917.
Nr.Fine/Fine. **$125**
Good/V.Good. **$75**

_____. *King of the Khyber
Rifles*. (Talbot Mundy). First Edition:
Indianapolis, IN: Bobbs-Merrill, 1916.
Nr.Fine/Fine. **$145**
Good/V.Good. **$75**

_____. *Fire Tongue*. (Sax
Rohmer) First Edition: Garden City, NY:
Doubleday Page, 1922.
Nr.Fine/Fine. **$120**
Good/V.Good. **$45**

Constable, John. *Constable and his
Influence on Landscape Painting*. (C. J.
Holmes) First Edition: London; Archibald
Constable & Co., 1902.
Nr.Fine/Fine. **$450**
Good/V.Good. **$250**

Corbett, Bertha. *What We Saw at Madame
World's Fair*. (Elizabeth Gordon) First
Edition: San Francisco: Samuel Levinson,
1915.
Nr.Fine/Fine. **$65**
Good/V.Good. **$25**

Cox, Palmer. *The Brownie Yearbook*. First
Edition: New York: McLoughlin Brothers,

1895.
Nr.Fine/Fine $265
Good/V.Good $135

_____. *Brownies At Home* First
Edition: New York: The Century Co., 1893.
Nr.Fine/Fine. **$450**
Good/V.Good. **$200**

Crane, Walter. *The Flower Wedding*. First
Edition: London: Cassell, 1905.
Nr.Fine/Fine. **$375**
Good/V.Good. **$125**

_____. *Goody Two Shoes Picture
Book*. First Edition: London: George
Routledge, 1874.
Nr.Fine/Fine. **$1450**
Good/V.Good. **$800**

_____. *Claims of Decorative Art*.
First Edition: London: Lawrence and
Bullen, 1892.
Nr.Fine/Fine. **$165**
Good/V.Good. **$60**

Cruikshank, George. *Adventures of
Oliver Twist; Or, The Parish Boy's Progress.*
(Charles Dickens) First Edition Thus:
London: Bradbury and Evans, 1846.
Nr.Fine/Fine **$18,500**
Good/V.Good **$12,000**

Dali, Salvador. *Conquest of the Irrational*.
First Edition in English: New York: Julien
Levy, 1935.
Nr.Fine/Fine. **$1600**
Good/V.Good. **$850**

_____. *Hidden Faces*. First Edition
in English: New York: Dial Press, 1944.
Nr.Fine/Fine. $250
Good/V.Good $100

_____. *The Secret Life of Salvador
Dali*. First Edition: New York: Dial Press,
1942.
Nr.Fine/Fine. **$35**
Good/V.Good. **$125**

Davies, Arthur B. *The Etchings &*

Lithographs of Arthur B. Davies First
Edition: New York & London: Mitchell
Kennerley, 1929.
Nr.Fine/Fine. **$350**
Good/V.Good. **$200**

De Angeli, Marguerite. *The Door in the
Wall*. First Edition: Garden City, NY:
Doubleday & Company, 1949.
Nr.Fine/Fine. **$85**
Good/V.Good. **$30**

De Kooning, Willem. *De Kooning*. First
Edition: New York: Harold Rosenberg,
1974.
Nr.Fine/Fine. **$1500**
Good/V.Good. **$800**

_____. *Willem De Kooning
Drawings*.First Edition: Greenwich. CT:
Thomas R. Hess, 1972.
Nr.Fine/Fine. **$1250**
Good/V.Good. **$500**

Degas, Edgar. *Degas Dancers*. First
Edition: London: Faber and Faber, 1949.
Nr.Fine/Fine. **$200**
Good/V.Good. **$45**

_____. *Portraits by Degas*. First
Edition: Berkeley, CA: University of
California, 1962.
Nr.Fine/Fine. **$65**
Good/V.Good. **$25**

The
Wonderful
Wizard of Oz
*by W.W.
Denslow*

Denslow, W. W. *The Wonderful Wizard of*

OZ. (L. Frank Baum) First Edition: Chicago: George M. Hill, 1898.
Nr.Fine/Fine.............**$20000**
Good/V.Good.............**$12000**

_____. *An Arkansas Planter.(Opie Read)* First Edition: Chicago and New York: Rand, McNally & Company, 1896.
Nr.Fine/Fine..................**$75**
Good/V.Good.................**$35**

_____. *W. W. Denslow*. First Edition: np: Clarke Historical Library, Central Michigan University, 1976.
Nr.Fine/Fine..................**$50**
Good/V.Good.................**$30**

_____. *Denslow's Picture Book Treasury*. First Edition: New York: Arcade/Little, Brown, 1990.
Nr.Fine/Fine..................**$30**
Good/V.Good.................**$18**

Detmold, E. *Fabre's Book Of Insects. (Fabre; Alexander Teixeira De Mattos' translation, retold by Mrs. R. Stawell)*. First Edition: London: Hodder & Stoughton, 1920.
Nr.Fine/Fine.................**$350**
Good/V.Good................**$200**

_____. *Hours of Gladness. (Maurice Maeterlinck)* First Edition: London: George Allen & Unwin Ltd., 1912.
Nr.Fine/Fine.................**$225**
Good/V.Good................**$100**

_____. *The Book of Baby Birds. (Florence E. Dugdale)* First Edition: New York: Hodder & Stoughton, 1912.
Nr.Fine/Fine.................**$250**
Good/V.Good................**$100**

Dine, Jim. *The Poet Assassinated. (Guillaume Apollinaire translated by Ron Padgett)* First Edition Thus: New York: Henry Holt, 1968.
Nr.Fine/Fine.................**$275**
Good/V.Good................**$145**

_____. *Jim Dine: Painting What One Is*

(Contemporary Artists Series). (David Shapiro) First Edition: New York: Harry N. Abrams, 1981.
Nr.Fine/Fine..................**$175**
Good/V.Good.................**$85**

Duchamps, Marcel. *The Complete Works of Marcel Duchamps*. First Edition: New York: Harry N. Abrams, 1969.
Nr.Fine/Fine..................**$600**
Good/V.Good.................**$350**
First U.K. Edition: London:Thames and Hudson, 1969.
Nr.Fine/Fine..................**$600**
Good/V.Good.................**$350**

_____. *Marcel Duchamp: The Box in a Valise*. (Ecke Bonk) First Edition: New York: Rizzoli, 1989.
Nr.Fine/Fine..................**$200**
Good/V.Good.................**$85**

Durer, Albrecht. *Jerome.*(Randall Jarrell) First Edition: New York: Grossman, 1971.
Nr.Fine/Fine..................**$95**
Good/V.Good.................**$50**

Dufy, Raoul. *Dufy*. (Dora Perez-Tibi) First Edition: New York: Harry N. Abrams, Inc., 1989.
Nr.Fine/Fine..................**$100**
Good/V.Good.................**$35**

Dulac, Edmund. *Bells and Other Poems* . (Edgar Allen Poe) First Edition Thus: London Hodder and Stoughton, 1912.

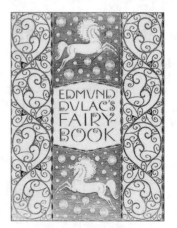

Edmund Dulac's Fairy-Book Fairy Tales of the Allied Nations *by Edmund Dulac*

Nr.Fine/Fine. **$1500**
Good/V.Good. **$600**

_____. *Edmund Dulac's Fairy-Book Fairy Tales of the Allied Nations.* First Edition: London: Hodder & Stoughton, 1916. Limited and Signed.
Nr.Fine/Fine. **$2850**
Good/V.Good. **$1500**
First Trade Edition: London: Hodder & Stoughton, 1916.
Nr.Fine/Fine. **$550**
Good/V.Good. **$250**

_____. *Sinbad the Sailor.* First Edition: London: Hodder and Stoughton, 1914.
Nr.Fine/Fine. **$4500**
Good/V.Good. **$2200**

_____. *The Sleeping Beauty and other Fairy Tales.* (Arthur Quiller-Couch) First Edition: London: Hodder and Stoughton, 1909.
Nr.Fine/Fine. **$3000**
Good/V.Good. **$1800**

Dwiggins, Clare Victor. *Only a Grain of Sand.* First Edition: Philadelphia: John C. Winston Company, 1905.
Nr.Fine/Fine. **$40**
Good/V.Good. **$25**

Edwards, George Wharton. *Thus Think and Smoke Tobacco: A Rhyme (XVII Century).* First Edition: New York: Frederick A. Stokes, 1891.
Nr.Fine/Fine. **$700**
Good/V.Good. **$325**

EMSH (Ed Emshsmiller). *Conan the Barbarian.* (Robert E. Howard) First Edition: New York: Gnome Press, 1954.
Nr.Fine/Fine. **$300**
Good/V.Good. **$175**

_____. *Highways In Hiding.* (George O. Smith) First Edition: New York: Gnome Press, 1955.
Nr.Fine/Fine. **$55**
Good/V.Good. **$25**

Ernst, Max. *Mr. Knife and Mrs. Fork.* (Rene Crevel) First Edition: Paris: The Black Sun Press, 1931.
Nr.Fine/Fine. **$5000**
Good/V.Good. **$2600**

Faberge, Karl. *The Art of Karl Faberge.* (Marvin C. Ross) First Edition: Norman: University of Oklahoma Press, 1965. Nr.Fine/Fine. **$175**
Good/V.Good. **$65**

Feiffer, Jules. *The Phantom Tollbooth.* (Norton Juster) First Edition: New York: Epstein & Carroll, 1961.
Nr.Fine/Fine. **$225**
Good/V.Good. **$100**

_____. *Sick Sick Sick.* First Edition: London: Collins, 1959.
Nr.Fine/Fine. **$15**
Good/V.Good. **$8**

Fisher, Harrison. *The American Girl.* First Edition: New York: Scribner's, 1909.
Nr.Fine/Fine. **$975**
Good/V.Good. **$450**

_____. *Bachelor Belles.* First Edition: New York: Dodd, Mead, 1908.
Nr.Fine/Fine. **$500**
Good/V.Good. **$300**

_____. *Cowardice Court.* (George Barr McCutcheon) First Edition: New York: Dodd, Mead & Company, 1906.
Nr.Fine/Fine. **$55**
Good/V.Good. **$18**

_____. *Maidens Fair.* First Edition: New York: Dodd, Mead, and Company, 1912.
Nr.Fine/Fine. **$1200**
Good/V.Good. **$800**

Frazetta, Frank. *Fantastic Art of Frank Frazetta Book 1.* First Edition: New York: Scribners, 1975.
Nr.Fine/Fine. **$250**
Good/V.Good. **$150**

_____. *Tarzan At the Earth's Core.*
(Edgar Rice Burroughs) First Edition: New
York: Canaveral Press, 1962.
Nr.Fine/Fine. **$65**
Good/V.Good. **$35**

Gag, Wanda. *The Funny Thing*. First
Edition: New York: Coward-McCann, 1929.
Nr.Fine/Fine. **$325**
Good/V.Good. **$175**

Garis, Howard R. *Uncle Wiggily's Travels.*
First Edition: New York: Platt & Munk,
1943.
Nr.Fine/Fine. **$100**
Good/V.Good. **$35**

Gauguin, Paul. *Gauguin: Watercolors and
Pastels.* (Jean Leymarie) First Edition: New
York: Abrams, 1962.
Nr.Fine/Fine. **$250**
Good/V.Good. **$175**

Gibson, Charles Dana. *Americans.* First
Edition: New York; R. H. Russell, 1900.
Nr.Fine/Fine. **$200**
Good/V.Good. **$65**

_____. *Drawings by
Charles Dana Gibson.* First Edition: New
York; R. H. Russell, 1894.
Nr.Fine/Fine. **$500**
Good/V.Good. **$200**

Glackens, William. *Santa Claus's Partner.*
(Thomas Nelson Page) First Edition: New
York: Charles Scribner's Sons, 1899.
Nr.Fine/Fine. $45
Good/V.Good. $25

_____. *A Traveler at Forty.*
(Theodore Dreiser) First Edition: New York:
The Century Co., 1914.
Nr.Fine/Fine. **$125**
Good/V.Good. **$65**

Goble, Warwick. *Green Willow and Other
Japanese Fairy Tales.* (Grace James) First
Edition: London: Macmillan and Co., 1910.
Nr.Fine/Fine. **$1000**
Good/V.Good. **$550**

Gorey, Edward. *Amphigorey Also.* First
Edition Limited: New York: Congdon &
Weed, 1983.
Nr.Fine/Fine. **$625**
Good/V.Good. **$400**
First Edition Trade: New York: Congdon &
Weed, 1983.
Nr.Fine/Fine. **$50**
Good/V.Good. **$35**

_____. *Dracula, A Toy Theater.*
First Edition: New York: Charles Scribner's
Sons, 1979.
Nr.Fine/Fine. **$500**
Good/V.Good. **$275**

**The Listing
Attic**
by Edward Gorey

_____. *The Listing Attic.* First
Edition: New York: Duell, Sloan and Pearce,
1954.
Nr.Fine/Fine. **$350**
Good/V.Good. **$150**

Goya. *Goya: Engravings and Lithographs.*
First Edition: London: Bruno Cassirer,
1964.
Nr.Fine/Fine. **$1150**
Good/V.Good. **$675**

Green, Elizabeth Shippen. *An Alliterative
Alphabet Aimed at Adult Abecedarians.*
(Huger Elliot) First Edition: Philadelphia:
David McKay Company, 1947.
Nr.Fine/Fine. **$250**

Good/V.Good. **$100**

_____. *The Book of the Little Past.* (Josephine Preston Peabody) First Edition: Boston; Houghton Mifflin Co. 1908
Nr.Fine/Fine. **$135**
Good/V.Good. **$75**

Greenaway, Kate. *Greenaway's Babies.* First Edition: Akron, OH: Saalfield, 1907.
Nr.Fine/Fine. **$150**
Good/V.Good. **$85**

_____. *The Language of Flowers.* First Edition: London: George Routledge, 1884.
Nr.Fine/Fine. **$1150**
Good/V.Good. **$500**

Mother Goose
by Kate Greenaway

_____. *Mother Goose.* First Edition: London: George Routledge, 1881.
Nr.Fine/Fine. **$2500**
Good/V.Good. **$750**

Gross, Milt. *Nize Baby.* First Edition: New York: George H. Doran Company, 1926.
Nr.Fine/Fine. **$85**
Good/V.Good. **$35**

_____. *Famous Fimmales Witt Odder Ewents From Heestory.* First Edition: Garden City, NY: Doubleday, Doran, 1928.
Nr.Fine/Fine. **$85**
Good/V.Good. **$40**

_____. *De Night in de Front From Chreesmas.* First Edition: New York: George H. Doran Company, 1927.
Nr.Fine/Fine. **$75**
Good/V.Good. **$30**

Grosz, George. *1001 Afternoons in New York.* (Ben Hecht) First Edition: New York: Viking Press, 1941.
Nr.Fine/Fine. **$150**
Good/V.Good. **$45**

_____. *Ecce Homo.* First U.S. Edition: New York: Jack Brussel, 1965.Nr.Fine/Fine **$95**
Good/V.Good. **$65**

Gruelle, Johnny. *Raggedy Ann's Magical Wishes.* First Edition: Chicago: Donohue, 1928.
Nr.Fine/Fine. **$300**
Good/V.Good. **$125**

Raggedy Ann And Betsy Bonnet String
by Johnny Gruelle

_____. *Raggedy Ann And Betsy Bonnet String.* First Edition: New York: Johnny Gruelle Company, 1943.
Nr.Fine/Fine. **$150**
Good/V.Good. **$65**

Hader, Berta & Elmer. *The Picture Book of Travel.* First Edition: New York: Macmillan, 1929.
Nr.Fine/Fine. **$45**
Good/V.Good. **$20**

_____. *Sonny Elephant.*
(Madge A. Bigham) First Edition: Boston:
Little, Brown and Company, 1930.
Nr.Fine/Fine. **$165**
Good/V.Good. **$55**

Henri, Robert. *Robert Henri, His Life and
Works*. First Edition: New York: Boni and
Liveright, 1921.
Nr.Fine/Fine. **$200**
Good/V.Good. **$85**

Hockney, David. *The Erotic Arts*. (Peter
Webb)First Edition: London: Secker &
Warburg, 1975.
Nr.Fine/Fine. **$5000**
Good/V.Good. **$2000**

_____. *Cameraworks*. First
Edition: London: Thames & Hudson, 1984.
Nr.Fine/Fine. **$250**
Good/V.Good. **$100**
First U.S. Edition: New York: Alfred A
Knopf, 1984.
Nr.Fine/Fine. **$350**
Good/V.Good. **$150**

The Road In
Storyland
*by Holling C.
Holling*

Holling, Holling C. *The Road In
Storyland. (Wally Piper)* First Edition: New
York: Platt & Munk, 1932.
Nr.Fine/Fine. **$125**
Good/V.Good. **$50**

_____. *Tree in the Trail*. First

Edition: Boston: Houghton Mifflin, 1942.
Nr.Fine/Fine. **$75**
Good/V.Good. **$25**

_____. *The Magic Story Tree.*
First Edition: New York: Platt & Munk,
1964.
Nr.Fine/Fine. **$85**
Good/V.Good. $20

Winslow
Homer
by Winslow Homer

Homer, Winslow. *Winslow Homer*. (John
Wilmerding) First Edition: New York:
Praeger, 1972.
Nr.Fine/Fine. **$75**
Good/V.Good. **$30**

Hopper, Edward. *Edward Hopper. The
Complete Prints*. (Gail Levin) First Edition:
New York: W.W. Norton, 1979.
Nr.Fine/Fine. **$45**
Good/V.Good. **$25**

Humphrey, Maud. *Children of the
Revolution*. First Edition: New York:
Frederick A. Stokes, 1900.
Nr.Fine/Fine. **$500**
Good/V.Good. **$225**

_____. *Little Heroes and
Heroines*. First Edition: New York:
Frederick A. Stokes, 1899.
Nr.Fine/Fine. **$450**
Good/V.Good. **$200**

_____. *Favorite Rhymes from*

Mother Goose. First Edition: New York: Frederick A. Stokes, 1891.
Nr.Fine/Fine. **$750**
Good/V.Good. **$450**

Icart, Louis. *The Etchings of Louis Icart*. First Edition: Exton, PA: Schiffer Publishing Ltd., 1982.
Nr.Fine/Fine. **$55**
Good/V.Good. **$30**

_____. *Icart*. First Edition: New York: Clarkson N. Potter, 1976.
Nr.Fine/Fine. **$65**
Good/V.Good. **$30**

Jasper Johns
by Jasper Johns

Johns, Jasper. *Jasper Johns: Paintings, Drawings and Sculpture 1954-1964*. (Alan R. Solomon, John Cage) First Edition: London: Whitechapel Gallery, 1964.
Nr.Fine/Fine. **$75**
Good/V.Good. **$45**

_____. *Jasper Johns* (Michael Crichton) First Edition: New York: Harry N. Abrams - Whitney Museum of American Art, 1977.
Nr.Fine/Fine. **$200**
Good/V.Good. **$85**

Kane, Paul. *Paul Kane's Frontier*. First Edition: Toronto: University of Toronto Press, 1971.
Nr.Fine/Fine. **$500**
Good/V.Good. **$300**

_____. *Wanderings of an Artist Among the Indians of North America*. First Edition: London: Longman, Brown, Green, Longmans, and Roberts, 1859.
Nr.Fine/Fine. **$7500**
Good/V.Good. **$3000**

Kay, Gertrude. *Tommy Tingle Tangle*. (Sarah Addington) First Edition: New York: P. F. Volland, 1927.
Nr.Fine/Fine. **$325**
Good/V.Good. **$165**

_____. *Through the Cloud Mountain*. (Florence Scott Bernard) First Edition: Philadelphia: J. B. Lippincott, 1922.
Nr.Fine/Fine. **$140**
Good/V.Good. **$65**

Kelly, Ellsworth. *Ellsworth Kelly: Drawings, Collages, Prints*. First Edition: Greenwich, CT: New York Graphic Society, 1971.
Nr.Fine/Fine. **$800**
Good/V.Good. **$425**

I Go Pogo
by Walt Kelly

Kelly, Walt. *I Go Pogo*. First Edition: New York: Simon & Schuster, 1952.
Nr.Fine/Fine. **$145**
Good/V.Good. **$50**

_____. *Uncle Pogo So-So Stories*. First Edition: New York: Simon & Schuster, 1953. Nr.Fine/Fine. **$125**

Good/V.Good **$45**

Uncle Pogo So-So
Stories
by Walt Kelly

Kent, Rockwell. *Moby Dick, or, The Whale*. (Three Volumes) (Herman Melville) First Edition Thus: Chicago: The Lakeside Press, 1930.
Nr.Fine/Fine **$6500**
Good/V.Good **$4500**

_____. *City Child*. (Selma Robinson) First Edition (Limited): New York: The Colophon Ltd., 1931.
Nr.Fine/Fine **$500**
Good/V.Good **$325**
First Edition (trade): New York: Farrar & Rinehart, 1931.
Nr.Fine/Fine **$75**
Good/V.Good **$30**

_____. *Salamina*. First Edition: New York: Harcourt, Brace, 1935.
Nr.Fine/Fine **$275**
Good/V.Good **$125**

Kirk, Maria. *Bimbi: Stories for Children*. (Louisa De La Rame) First Edition Thus: Philadelphia: J. B. Lippincott Company, 1910. **Points of Issue:** The first U.S. (Lippincott, 1900) was issued in green cloth. Illustrated by Edmund H. Garrett. This edition is in red cloth.
Nr.Fine/Fine **$40**
Good/V.Good **$15**

Klee, Paul. *The Thinking Eye*. First Edition: New York: George Wittenborn Inc., 1961.

Nr.Fine/Fine **$450**
Good/V.Good **$300**

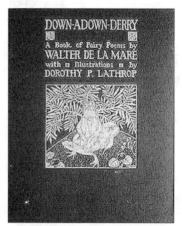

Down-Adown-Derry A Book of Fairy Poems
by Dorothy P. Lathrop

Lathrop, Dorothy P. *Down-Adown-Derry A Book of Fairy Poems*. (Walter De la Mare) First Edition: London: Constable and Co., 1922.
Nr.Fine/Fine **$150**
Good/V.Good **$85**

_____. *Fairy Circus*. First Edition: New York: The Macmillan Co., 1931.
Nr.Fine/Fine **$350**
Good/V.Good **$195**

Lawson, Robert. *Rabbit Hill*. First Edition: New York: Viking Press, 1944.
Nr.Fine/Fine **$100**
Good/V.Good **$60**

_____. *The Tough Winter*. First Edition: New York: Viking Press, 1954.
Nr.Fine/Fine **$95**
Good/V.Good **$45**

Le Mair, H. Willebeek. *Old Dutch Nursery Rhymes*. First Edition: Philadelphia: David McKay, 1917.
Nr.Fine/Fine **$425**
Good/V.Good **$175**
First U.K. Edition: London: Augener Ltd., 1917.
Nr.Fine/Fine **$350**
Good/V.Good **$150**

Lenski, Lois. *Prairie School*. First Edition: Philadelphia: J.B. Lippincott Co., 1951.
Nr.Fine/Fine.................**$150**
Good/V.Good.................**$45**

_____. *The Little Engine that Could*. (Watty Piper) First Edition: New York: Platt and Munk, 1930.
Nr.Fine/Fine.................**$40**
Good/V.Good.................**$22**

Lentz, Harold. *Jack The Giant Killer and Other Tales With "Pop-Up" Illustrations*. First Edition Thus: New York: Blue Ribbon Books, 1932.
Nr.Fine/Fine.................**$375**
Good/V.Good.................**$100**

Lichtenstein, Roy. *Roy Lichtenstein 1970-1980*. First Edition: New York: Hudson Hills Press, Inc., 1981.
Nr.Fine/Fine.................**$150**
Good/V.Good.................**$45**

Low, Loretta. *Timothy Toddlekin*. (Harriet Eunice) First Edition: New York: Cupples and Leon, 1914.
Nr.Fine/Fine.................**$55**
Good/V.Good.................**$20**

Luks, George. *George Luks: 1866-1933: An Exhibition of Paintings and Drawings Dating from 1889 to 1931*. First Edition: Utica, NY: Museum of Art, Munson-Williams-Proctor Institute, 1973.
Nr.Fine/Fine.................**$20**
Good/V.Good.................**$8**

Manet, Edouard. *Manet By Himself: Paintings, Pastels, Prints And Drawings*. First Edition: London: Macdonald, 1991.
Nr.Fine/Fine.................**$65**
Good/V.Good.................**$35**

_____. *Edouard Manet: Graphic Works; A Definitive Catalogue Raisonné*. First Edition: New York: Collectors Editions, 1970.
Nr.Fine/Fine.................**$375**
Good/V.Good.................**$155**

Marsh, Reginald. *Reginald Marsh*. First Edition: New York: Harry N. Abrams, Inc., 1972.
Nr.Fine/Fine.................**$225**
Good/V.Good.................**$100**

Matisse, Henri. *Etchings by Matisse*. First Edition: New York: The Museum of Modern Art, 1954.
Nr.Fine/Fine.................**$25**
Good/V.Good.................**$8**

_____. *Matisse: His Works and His Public*. First Edition: New York: The Museum of Modern Art, 1951.
Nr.Fine/Fine.................**$550**
Good/V.Good.................**$150**

The Goblin Scouts *(Harry Golding) by Thomas Maybank*

Maybank, Thomas. *The Goblin Scouts*. (Harry Golding)First Edition: London : Ward, Lock, no date.
Nr.Fine/Fine.................**$25**
Good/V.Good.................**$15**

Meteyard, Sidney N. *The Golden Legend*. (Henry Wadsworth Longfellow) First Edition Thus: London & New York: Hodder and Stoughton & George H. Doran, 1910.
Nr.Fine/Fine.................**$100**
Good/V.Good.................**$45**

Miro, Joan. *Miro Engravings 1928-1975*. (Four Volumes). First U.S. Edition Thus: New York: Rizzoli, 1989.
Nr.Fine/Fine.................**$1200**
Good/V.Good.................**$550**

_____. *Miro, Life and Work*. First
Edition: New York: Harry N. Abrams, 1962.
Nr.Fine/Fine................... **$350**
Good/V.Good................. **$155**

_____. *The Captured Imagination
Drawings by Joan Miro* First U.S. Edition:
New York: The American Federation of
Arts, 1987.
Nr.Fine/Fine................... **$60**
Good/V.Good.................. **$25**

Modigliani, Amedeo. *Forty-Five Drawings
By Modigliani*. First Edition: New York:
Grove Press, 1959.
Nr.Fine/Fine................... **$600**
Good/V.Good.................. **$400**

_____. *Modigliani*. First U.S.
Edition: New York: Harry N. Abrams, 1959.
Nr.Fine/Fine................... **$120**
Good/V.Good.................. **$45**

The Life and
Adventures of
Peter Croak
by Louis Moe

Moe, Louis. *The Life and Adventures of
Peter Croak*. First Editon Thus: London:
Thomas de la Rue, n.d.
Nr.Fine/Fine................... **$325**
Good/V.Good................. **$185**

Monet, Claude. *Monet: Catalogue
Raisonne*. First US Edition: New York:
Taschen America, LLC, 1996.
Nr.Fine/Fine................... **$250**
Good/V.Good................. **$100**

Moore, Henry. *As the Eye Moves...A
Sculpture*. First Edition: New York. Harry
N. Abrams, 1970.
Nr.Fine/Fine................... **$145**
Good/V.Good.................. **$75**

_____. *Mother And Child Etchings*.
First Edition: New York: Raymond Spencer

Company Limited, 1988.
Nr.Fine/Fine................... **$35**
Good/V.Good.................. **$18**

Moreau, Gustave. *Gustave Moreau with a
catalogue of the finished paintings,
watercolors and drawings*. First Edition:
Boston: New York Graphic Society, 1976.
Nr.Fine/Fine................... **$17**
Good/V.Good.................. **$80**

Young Folks'
Uncle Tom's
Cabin
by Ike Morgan

Morgan, Ike. *Young Folks' Uncle Tom's
Cabin*.(Harriet Beecher Stowe & Grace
Duffie Boylan) First Edition: Chicago:
Jamieson Higgins, 1901.
Nr.Fine/Fine................... **$65**
Good/V.Good.................. **$25**

Moses, Anna Mary Robertson. *Grandma
Moses: American Primitive*. First Edition:
Garden City, NY: Doubleday & Company,
1947.
Nr.Fine/Fine................... **$100**
Good/V.Good.................. **$45**

Motherwell, Robert. *The Dada Painters
and Poets*. First Edition: New York:
Wittenborn, Schultz, Inc. 1951.
Nr.Fine/Fine................... **$400**
Good/V.Good................. **$150**

Mucha, Alphonse. *Alphonse Maria
Mucha: His Life and Art*. First Edition: New
York: Rizzoli, 1989.
Nr.Fine/Fine................... **$85**

Good/V.Good **$45**
First U.K. Edition: London: Academy
Editions, 1989.
Nr.Fine/Fine **$70**
Good/V.Good **$30**

**The Marvelous
Land of OZ**
by John R. Neill

Neill, John R. *The Marvelous Land of OZ*.
(L. Frank Baum) First Edition: Chicago:
Reilly & Britton Co., 1904.
Nr.Fine/Fine **$1200**
Good/V.Good **$550**

_____. *The Curious Cruise of
Captain Santa*. (Ruth Plumly Thompson)
First Edition: Chicago: Reilly & Lee, 1926.
Nr.Fine/Fine **$550**
Good/V.Good **$250**

**The Wonder City
of OZ**
by John R. Neill

_____. *The Wonder City of
OZ*. First Edition: Chicago: Reilly & Lee,
1940.

Nr.Fine/Fine **$600**
Good/V.Good **$250**

Nelson, Emile A. *The Magic Airplane*.
First Edition: Chicago: Reilly & Lee, 1911.
Nr.Fine/Fine **$375**
Good/V.Good **$225**

Newell, Peter. *Ghosts I Have Met*. (John
Kendrick Bangs) First Edition: New York
Harper & Brothers, 1898.
Nr.Fine/Fine **$150**
Good/V.Good **$65**

Neilson, Kay. *East of the Sun and West of
the Moon*.First Edition: London: Hodder &
Stoughton, 1914.
Nr.Fine/Fine **$11,250**
Good/V.Good **$4500**

O'Keeffe, Georgia. *Georgia O'Keeffe*.
First Edition:New York: Viking Press, 1976.
Nr.Fine/Fine **$275**
Good/V.Good **$155**

**Georgia
O'Keeffe: the
New York Years**
*by Georgia
O'Keeffe*

Georgia O'Keeffe · The New York Years

_____. *Georgia O'Keeffe: the
New York Years*. First Edition: New York:
Alfred A. Knopf, 1991.
Nr.Fine/Fine **$80**
Good/V.Good **$45**

Olitski, Jules. *Jules Olitski*. First Edition:
Boston: New York Graphic Society, 1973.
Nr.Fine/Fine **$75**
Good/V.Good **$35**

Paget, Sidney. *The Hound of the*

Baskervilles. (Arthur Conan Doyle) First
Edition: London: George Newnes, 1902.
Nr.Fine/Fine. **$1600**
Good/V.Good. **$900**

Pape, Frank C. *The Revolt of the Angels*.
(Anatole France) First Edition: New York:
Dodd Mead, 1924.
Nr.Fine/Fine. **$60**
Good/V.Good. **$25**

_____. *The Silver Stallion*. (James
Branch Cabell) First Edition: New York:
Robert M. McBride, 1926.
Nr.Fine/Fine. **$65**
Good/V.Good. **$25**

Parker, Agnes Miller. *Down the River*.
First Edition: London: Victor Gollancz,
1937.
Nr.Fine/Fine. **$150**
Good/V.Good. **$45**

Parrish, Maxfield. *The Maxfield Parrish
Poster Book*. First Edition: New York:
Harmony. 1974.
Nr.Fine/Fine. **$500**
Good/V.Good. **$225**

_____. *The Knave of Hearts*.
(Louise Saunders) First Edition: New York:
Charles Scribners, 1925.
Nr.Fine/Fine. **$4000**
Good/V.Good. **$1550**

Mother Goose
in Prose
*by Maxfield
Parrish*

_____. *Mother Goose in Prose*.
(L. Frank Baum) First Edition: Chicago:

Way and Williams, 1897.
Nr.Fine/Fine. **$6000**
Good/V.Good. **$3500**

Round The
Mulberry Bush
by Fern Bisel Peat

Peat, Fern Bisel. *Round The Mulberry
Bush*. (Marion L. McNeil) First Edition:
Akron, OH: Saalfield Publishing, 1933.
Nr.Fine/Fine. **$125**
Good/V.Good. **$45**

Picasso, Pablo. *The Cubist Years 1907-
1916*. First Edition: London: Thames and
Hudson, 1979.
Nr.Fine/Fine. **$200**
Good/V.Good. **$85**

_____. *Lysistrata*. (Aristophanes)
First Edition: New York: Limited Editions
Club, 1934.
Nr.Fine/Fine. **$8500**
Good/V.Good. **$6500**

_____. *Picasso and the Human
Comedy*. First Edition: New York: Harcourt
Brace, 1954.
Nr.Fine/Fine. **$1100**
Good/V.Good. **$500**

_____. *Picasso's Posters*. First
Edition: New York: Random House,
1970/1971.
Nr.Fine/Fine. **$300**
Good/V.Good. **$120**

Pogany, Willy. *Rubáiyát of Omar
Khayyám*. First Edition Thus: London:

George G. Harrap, 1909.
Nr.Fine/Fine. **$800**
Good/V.Good. **$325**

Rubaiyat of Omar
Khayyam
by Willy Pogany

The King of
Ireland's Son
by Willy Pogany

Casanova Jones
by Willy Pogany

_____. *The King of Ireland's Son.*
(Padraic Colum) First Edition: New York:
Henry Holt, 1916.
Nr.Fine/Fine. **$350**
Good/V.Good. **$140**

_____. *Casanova Jones.* (Joseph
Anthony) First Edition: New York, The
Century Co., 1930.
Nr.Fine/Fine. **$100**
Good/V.Good. **$35**

Pollack, Jackson. *Jackson Pollack.* First
Edition: New York: Museum of Modern Art,
1967.
Nr.Fine/Fine. **$25**
Good/V.Good. **$10**

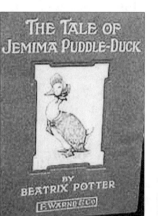

The Tale of
Jemima
Puddle-Duck
by Beatrix Potter

Potter, Beatrix. *Tale of Jemima Puddle-
Duck.* First Edition: London: Frederick
Warne and Co., 1908.
Nr.Fine/Fine. **$2500**
Good/V.Good. **$1000**

_____. *The Tale of Peter Rabbit.*
First Edition (Private Printing): London:
Privately printed, nd.
Nr.Fine/Fine **$35,000**
Good/V.Good **$25,000**
First Edition (Trade): London and New
York: Frederick Warne & Co., 1902.
Nr.Fine/Fine **$15,000**
Good/V.Good. **$8000**

Pyle, Howard. *The Ruby of Kishmoor.*
First Edition: New York: Harper and

Brothers, 1908.
Nr.Fine/Fine. **$225**
Good/V.Good. **$75**

The Ruby of Kishmoor
by Howard Pyle

_____. *Men of Iron.* First Edition: New York: Harper and Brothers, 1892.
Nr.Fine/Fine. **$200**
Good/V.Good. **$85**

_____. *Otto of the Silver Hand.* First Edition: New York: Scribners, 1888.
Nr.Fine/Fine. **$300**
Good/V.Good. **$175**

_____. *The First Christmas Tree.* (Henry Van Dyke) First Edition: New York: Scribners, 1897.
Nr.Fine/Fine. **$100**
Good/V.Good. **$35**

Grimm's Fairy Tales
by Arthur Rackham

Rackham, Arthur. *Grimm's Fairy Tales.* First Edition Thus: London: Constable, 1909.

Nr.Fine/Fine. **$2750**
Good/V.Good. **$1600**
First U.S. Edition Thus: Garden City, NY: Doubleday, Page, 1912.
Nr.Fine/Fine. **$200**
Good/V.Good. **$85**

_____. *The Book of Betty Barber.* (Maggie Brown) First Edition: London, Duckworth & Co., 1910.
Nr.Fine/Fine. **$1850**
Good/V.Good. **$700**

_____. *The Chimes.* (Charles Dickens)
First Edition Thus: London: Limited Editions Club, 1931.
Nr.Fine/Fine. **$800**
Good/V.Good. **$500**

_____. *A Christmas Carol.* (Charles Dickens) First Edition Thus: London: William Heinemann, 1915.
Nr.Fine/Fine. **$1200**
Good/V.Good. **$650**

Peter Pan in Kensington Gardens
by Arthur Rackham

_____. *Peter Pan in Kensington Gardens.* (James M. Barrie) First Edition: London: Hodder and Stoughton, 1906.
Nr.Fine/Fine. **$3000**
Good/V.Good. **$1600**

Rae, John. *Granny Goose.* First Edition: Joliet, IL: Volland, 1926.
Nr.Fine/Fine. **$100**
Good/V.Good. **$45**

_____. *American Indian Fairy Tales.*(W. T. L. Larned) First Edition: Chicago: PF Vollard, 1921.
Nr.Fine/Fine. **$30**
Good/V.Good. **$10**

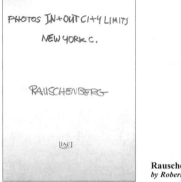

Rauschenberg
by Robert Rauschenberg

Rauschenberg, Robert. *Rauschenberg.* First Edition: West Islip, N.Y., ULAE Inc., 1982.
Nr.Fine/Fine. **$125**
Good/V.Good. **$45**

Remington, Frederic. *An Apache Princess.*
(Charles King) First Edition: New York: The Hobart Co., 1903.
Nr.Fine/Fine. **$40**
Good/V.Good. **$15**

_____. *Crooked Trails.* First Edition: New York: Harper & Brothers, 1898.
Nr.Fine/Fine. **$375**
Good/V.Good. **$125**

Remington's
Frontier Sketches
by Frederic Remington

_____. *Remington's Frontier Sketches.* First Edition: Chicago: The Werner Company, 1898.
Nr.Fine/Fine. **$2000**
Good/V.Good. **$850**

Sundown Leflare
by Frederic Remington

_____. *Sundown Leflare* First Edition: New York: Harpers & Brothers, 1899.
Nr.Fine/Fine. **$300**
Good/V.Good. **$140**

Rivera, Diego. *The Fresoes of Diego Rivera.* First Edition: New York: Harcourt, Brace, 1929.
Nr.Fine/Fine. **$1000**
Good/V.Good. **$625**

Robinson, Charles. *The Four Gardens.* (Handasyde) First Edition: London: William Heinemann, 1912.
Nr.Fine/Fine. **$125**
Good/V.Good. **$45**

The Farm Book
by Charles Robinson

_____. *The Farm Book.* (Walter Copeland) First Edition: London & New York: J. M. Dent, E. P. Dutton, 1901.

Nr.Fine/Fine. **$250**
Good/V.Good. **$150**

Robinson, W. Heath. *The Book of Goblins*. First Edition: London: Hutchinson, 1934.
Nr.Fine/Fine. **$400**
Good/V.Good. **$225**

Rockwell, Norman. *Norman Rockwell: Artist and Illustrator*. First Edition: New York: Harry N. Abrams, 1970.
Nr.Fine/Fine. **$100**
Good/V.Good. **$45**

_____. *The Secret Play*. (Ralph Henry Barbour) First Edition: New York: D. Appleton, 1915.
Nr.Fine/Fine. **$425**
Good/V.Good. **$200**

Rodin, Auguste. *Rodin: Drawings and Watercolors*. First Edition: London & New York: Thames and Hudson, 1983.
Nr.Fine/Fine. **$150**
Good/V.Good. **$85**

Rombola, John. *Rombola by Rombola*. First Edition: New York & London: A.S. Barnes And Co. & Thomas Yoseloff Ltd., 1965.
Nr.Fine/Fine. **$35**
Good/V.Good. **$15**

Ross, Penny. *Loraine and the Little People*. (Elizabeth Gordon) First Edition: Chicago: Rand McNally & Co., 1915.
Nr.Fine/Fine. **$65**
Good/V.Good. **$35**

Rouault, Georges. *Georges Rouault*. First Edition: New York: Harry N. Abrams, 1961.
Nr.Fine/Fine. **$165**
Good/V.Good. **$75**

Rountree, Harry. *The Poison Belt*. (Arthur Conan Doyle) First Edition: London: Hodder & Stoughton, 1913.
Nr.Fine/Fine. **$550**
Good/V.Good. **$200**

Rowlandson, Thomas. *The Watercolor Drawings of Thomas Rowlandson. From the Albert H. Wiggin Collection*. First Edition:

New York: Watson Guptil, 1947.
Nr.Fine/Fine. **$35**
Good/V.Good. **$12**

Ruscha, Edward. *Crackers*. First Edition: Hollywood, CA: Heavy Industry Publications, 1969.
Nr.Fine/Fine. **$450**
Good/V.Good. **$175**

Russell, Charles M. *The Charles M. Russell Book*. First Edition: Garden City, NY: Doubleday & Company, 1957.
Nr.Fine/Fine. **$85**
Good/V.Good. **$25**

_____. *Studies of Western Life*. First Edition: Cascade: The Albertype Co., 1890.
Nr.Fine/Fine. **$4500**
Good/V.Good. **$2500**

Samaras, Lucas. *Samaras Album*. First Edition: New York: Whitney Museum of American Art/Pace Editions, 1971.
Nr.Fine/Fine. **$450**
Good/V.Good. **$200**

Sargent, John Singer. *John Singer Sargent*. First Edition: New York: Harper & Row, 1970.
Nr.Fine/Fine. **$200**
Good/V.Good. **$125**

Schaeffer, Mead. *Wings of Morning*. (Louis Tracy) First Edition: New York: George H. Doran Co., 1924.
Nr.Fine/Fine. **$35**
Good/V.Good. **$15**

_____. *Wreck of the Grosvenor*. (W. Clark Russell) First Edition: New York: Dodd, Mead, nd.
Nr.Fine/Fine. **$55**
Good/V.Good. **$20**

Schoonover, Frank. *A Princess of Mars. (Edgar Rice Burroughs)* First Edition: Chicago: A.C. McClurg, 1917.
Nr.Fine/Fine. **$850**
Good/V.Good. **$350**

**Frank E. Schoonover.
Painter-Illustrator. A
Bibliography**
by Frank Schoonover

_____. *Frank E. Schoonover.
Painter-Illustrator. A Bibliography*. (John F.
Apgar) First Edition: np: John F. Apgar:
1969.
Nr.Fine/Fine. **$200**
Good/V.Good. **$85**

_____. *Yankee Ships in Pirate
Waters*. (Rupert Holland) First Edition:
Garden City, NY: Doubleday & Company,
1931.
Nr.Fine/Fine. **$35**
Good/V.Good. **$12**

Seuss, Dr. *The 500 Hats of Bartholomew
Cubbins*. First Edition: New York: The
Vanguard Press, 1938.
Nr.Fine/Fine. **$250**
Good/V.Good. **$100**

**You're Only Old
Once!**
by Dr. Seuss

_____. *You're Only Old Once*.
First Edition: New York: Random House,
1986. Nr.Fine/Fine. **$35**
Good/V.Good. **$15**

Shahn, Ben. *Ecclesiastes*. First U.S.
Edition (Limited/Signed): New York: Spiral
Press, 1965.
Nr.Fine/Fine. **$650**
Good/V.Good. **$300**
First Edition (trade): New York/Paris:

Grossman/Trianon, 1971.
Nr.Fine/Fine. **$55**
Good/V.Good. **$30**

Shepard, Ernest H. *When We Were Very
Young*. (A.A. Milne) First Edition: London:
Methuen & Co., 1924.
Nr.Fine/Fine. **$300**
Good/V.Good. **$100**
First U.S. Edition: New York: E. P. Dutton,
1924.
Nr.Fine/Fine. **$275**
Good/V.Good. **$85**

Shin, Everett. *A Christmas Carol*. (Charles
Dickens) First Edition: Philadelphia: John
C. Winston, 1938.
Nr.Fine/Fine. **$350**
Good/V.Good. **$150**

Sloan, John. *John Sloan's Prints*. First
Edition: New Haven, CT: Yale University
Press, 1969.
Nr.Fine/Fine. **$800**
Good/V.Good. **$225**

Smith, Jessie Willcox. *Boys and Girls of
Bookland*. (Nora Archibald Smith) First
Edition: New York: Cosmopolitan Book
Corporation, 1923
Nr.Fine/Fine. **$245**
Good/V.Good. **$125**

_____. *Dream Blocks*. (Aileen
Cleveland Higgins) First Edition: New York:
Duffield, 1908.
Nr.Fine/Fine. **$220**
Good/V.Good. **$135**

_____. *In the Closed Room*.
(Frances Hodgson Burnett) First Edition:
New York: McClure, Phillips & Co., 1904.
Nr.Fine/Fine. **$135**
Good/V.Good. **$45**

Soyer, Raphael. *Lost In America. (I. B.
Singer)* First Edition (Limited): Garden
City, NY: Doubleday & Company, 1981.
Nr.Fine/Fine. **$250**
Good/V.Good. **$100**
First Edition (trade): Garden City, NY:

Doubleday & Company, 1981.
Nr.Fine/Fine. **$25**
Good/V.Good. **$10**

Steele, Frederic Dorr. *The Scarlet Car*.
(Richard Harding Davis) First Edition: New
York Charles Scribner's Sons, 1907.
Nr.Fine/Fine. **$150**
Good/V.Good. **$65**

Strothman, F. *Over The Nonsense Road*.
(Lucile Gulliver) First Edition: New York:
D. Appleton, 1910.
Nr.Fine/Fine. **$65**
Good/V.Good. **$30**

Stuart, Gilbert. *Gilbert Stuart's Portraits
of George Washington*. First Edition:
Philadelphia: Privately printed, 1923.
Nr.Fine/Fine. **$250**
Good/V.Good. **$100**

Szyk, Arthur. *The New Order*. First
Edition: New York: G.P. Putnams, 1941.
Nr.Fine/Fine. **$250**
Good/V.Good. **$95**

Tenggren, Gustaf. *The Red Fairy Book*.
(Andrew Lang) First Edition Thus:
Philadelphia: David McKay, 1924.
Nr.Fine/Fine. **$145**
Good/V.Good. **$45**

_____. *Stories of the Magic
World*. (Elizabeth Woodruff) First Edition:
Springfield, MA: McLoughlin Bros., 1938.
Nr.Fine/Fine. **$325**
Good/V.Good. **$165**

Toulouse-Lautrec, Henri De. *The Circus*.
First Edition Thus: New York: Paris Book
Center, 1952.
Nr.Fine/Fine. **$500**
Good/V.Good. **$300**

_____. *Toulouse-
Lautrec*. First Edition: New York: Harry
Abrams, 1966.
Nr.Fine/Fine. **$65**
Good/V.Good. **$25**

Tudor, Tasha. *Alexander the Gander*. First
Edition: New York: Oxford University
Press, 1939.
Nr.Fine/Fine. **$450**
Good/V.Good. **$175**

Van Gogh, Vincent. *Van Gogh in Arles*.
First Edition: New York: Metropolitan
Museum Of Art, 1984.
Nr.Fine/Fine. **$50**
Good/V.Good. **$20**

_____. *The Works of Vincent Van
Gogh*. First Edition: New York: Reynal &
Co., 1970.Nr.Fine/Fine. **$85**
Good/V.Good. **$40**

Varga, Alberto. *Varga: The Esquire Years-
A Catalogue Raisonne*. First Edition: New
York: Alfred Van Der Marck, 1987.
Nr.Fine/Fine. **$150**
Good/V.Good. **$85**

Wagstaff, Dorothy. *Stories of Little Brown
Koko*. (Blanche Seale Hunt) First Edition:
Chicago and New York: American
Colortype Company, 1940.
Nr.Fine/Fine. **$125**
Good/V.Good. **$55**

Wain, Louis. *Cat's Cradle A Picture-Book
for Little Folk*. First Edition: London:
Blackie and Son, 1908.
Nr.Fine/Fine. **$1250**
Good/V.Good. **$750**

Ward, Lynd. *The Cat Who Went to Heaven*.
(Elizabeth Coatsworth) First Edition: New
York: Macmillan, 1931.
Nr.Fine/Fine. **$175**
Good/V.Good. **$55**

_____. *Impassioned Clay*.
(Llewellyn Powys) First Edition: New York
& London: Longmans, Green, 1931.
Nr.Fine/Fine. **$45**
Good/V.Good. **$20**

Warhol, Andy. *The Philosophy of Andy
Warhol (From A to B & Back Again)*. First
Edition: New York: Harcourt, Brace

Jovanovich, 1975.
Nr.Fine/Fine. **$175**
Good/V.Good. **$85**

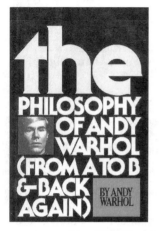

The Philosophy of
Andy Warhol
*(From A to B &
Back Again)*
by Andy Warhol

_____. *Wild Raspberries*. First
Edition: Boston: Bulfinch/Little, Brown,
1997.
Nr.Fine/Fine. **$30**
Good/V.Good. **$12**

Whistler, James McNeil. *Whistler
Lithographs*. First Edition: London: Jupiter
Books, 1975.
Nr.Fine/Fine. **$50**
Good/V.Good. **$20**

Williams, Garth. *Miss Bianca. (Margery
Sharp)* First Edition: Boston: Little Brown,
1962.
Nr.Fine/Fine. **$45**
Good/V.Good. **$20**

Wright, Alan. *Queen Victoria's Dolls*. First
Edition: London: George Newnes, 1894.
Nr.Fine/Fine. **$155**
Good/V.Good. **$70**

Wright, Frank Lloyd. *An American
Architecture*. First Edition: New York:
Horizon Press, 1955.
Nr.Fine/Fine. **$275**
Good/V.Good. **$120**

_____. **The Living City**.
First Edition: New York: Horizon Press,
1958.

Nr.Fine/Fine. **$125**
Good/V.Good. **$55**

Wulfing, Sulamith. *The Fantastic Art of
Sulamith Wulfing*. First Edition: New York:
Peacock Press/Bantam Books, 1978.
Nr.Fine/Fine. **$65**
Good/V.Good. **$40**

Wyeth, Andrew. *Christina's World*. First
Edition: Boston: Houghton Mifflin, 1982.
Nr.Fine/Fine. **$125**
Good/V.Good. **$55**

_____. *Wyeth at Kuerners*. First
Edition: Boston: Houghton Mifflin, 1976.
Nr.Fine/Fine. **$85**
Good/V.Good. **$35**

Wyeth, N.C. *Beth Norvell*. (Randall
Parrish) First Edition: Chicago: A. C.
McClurg, 1907.
Nr.Fine/Fine. **$65**
Good/V.Good. **$15**

_____. *Captain Blood*. (Rafael
Sabatini)
First Edition Thus: Boston: Houghton
Mifflin, 1922.
Nr.Fine/Fine. **$45**
Good/V.Good. **$20**

_____. *The Deerslayer*. (James
Fenimore Cooper) First Edition Thus: New
York: Charles Scribners, 1925.
Nr.Fine/Fine. **$200**
Good/V.Good. **$85**

_____. *The Mysterious Stranger*.
(Mark Twain) First Edition: New York:
Harper & Brothers, 1916.
Nr.Fine/Fine. **$350**
Good/V.Good. **$150**

_____. *The Yearling*. (Marjorie
Kinnan Rawlings) First Edition: New York:
Charles Scribner's Sons, 1939.
Nr.Fine/Fine. **$175**
Good/V.Good. **$65**

Banned Books

Ever since man invented written communication, there has been someone, somewhere who didn't want THAT communicated. The writer and the censor have walked hand in hand through human history. Babylonian kings kept a chisel for clay tablets they didn't care for, and every Pharaoh knew that papyrus burns very nicely. In a way, banned books provide pictures of society; it's mores and taboos, neuroses and psychoses.

In a very general way, banned books can be broken down into four major categories: Religious, Political, Societal, and Sexual, though it should be admitted that Sexual is a sub-category of Societal. There are fertile fields for collectors in very small and specialized areas of it. I have helped collectors build collections of early Christian heresies, as well as collections of sex manuals and horn books.

In any society, part of the artist's role is to challenge the givens. Literary art often takes the lead. And literary artists often pay the highest prices for their anti-social stands. The Emperor Augustus personally banished Ovid and his nasty little book, *Ars Amatoria*, from the Imperial city. The Pope himself decreed the execution of Giordano Bruno and burning of his heretical work *On the Infinite Universe and Worlds*.

For the collector, banned books can be an especially rewarding field. Because of bans and burnings, collectible, rare copies are a rule rather than an exception. And where else in the world do you have the opportunity to snub a Pope, flip the bird at an Emperor, or give the razzberry to your local Puritan?

The Twentieth Century ushered in four publishers who would challenge society on every level. The first was "Booklegger Jack" Kahane and his Obelisk Press. Between the First and the Second World Wars, the expatriate Englishman, crippled by German arms, started a bang that is still echoing. In the summer of 1932, Kahane picked up the first of many books that would challenge society, literature, and the entire publishing world. The book had been handed to him personally by an impoverished author, who, probably at the time, could not even afford the postage to mail it. The book was called *The Tropic of Cancer* and the would-be writer was Henry Miller. Kahane was looking for a direction for his new publishing house, which was centered in Paris but was to publish in English, Obelisk.

That was the start. Literary pornography, or straight pornography used to finance literature. Books that scandalized even the liberal Parisians. Books that scandalized a world, and changed forever what literature would be. "Booklegger Jack" he called himself, and he bragged that he published: "...what others feared to publish." And that he never published a book that someone, somewhere hadn't banned.

Kahane brought a lot of controversy into the literary world. In the eight years between his establishment of Obelisk and the disruption of the Second World War, he published Henry Miller, Anais Nin, Durrell's *The Black Book*, James Joyce, Radcliffe Hall, Frank Harris, and Cyril Connolly's *The Rock Pool*.

It took a war, and a visit from the grim reaper, to stop "Booklegger Jack." Hitler invaded and Jack died in 1939. Having shocked the world in every other possible way, he decided to leave before things got messy. Obelisk died with Jack, only to rise like a phoenix in 1953 under his son Maurice Girodias as the famous, and infamous, Olympia Press.

With the death of "Booklegger Jack" Kahane, control of Obelisk Press fell to his son, but the collapse of France and the German occupation firmly nailed the coffin shut. Maurice changed his name to Girodas to escape problems during the occupation and, in 1940, tried and failed to re-establish Obelisk's second imprint Editions du Chene. The real re-birth of Obelisk had to wait until 1953.

Girodas re-established his father's business as Olympia Press and set out to shock the world as his father had by publishing Samuel Beckett's *Watt* and Henry Miller's *Sexus* as well as reprinting DeSade and Apollonaire.

Shocking the world was profitable enough to further shock everyone with *The Story of O* in 1954. And 1955 brought *Lolita, Molloy*, and *The Ginger Man*, then the roof fell in. In 1956, the French government banned most of Olympia Press' list. In early 1957, J.P. Donleavy began his protracted legal battle with Olympia over the rights to *The Ginger Man*, a battle that raged until 1978. Then the Fourth Republic collapsed and Olympia was back.

Moving to rue Grand Severin, Girodas boldly introduced *Candy*. Then, in 1959, the *Beckett Trilogy (Molloy, Malone Dies, The Unnamable)*, Burroughs' *Naked Lunch,* and Roger Casement's *Black Diaries* were printed. Things were looking up (or down as the case may be with Olympia). Girodas opened a restaurant-nightclub complex on rue Grand Severin, a scandalous watering hole for the rich and decadent.

It all collapsed in 1964. Girodas was banned from publishing in France. He tried New York in 1965, with some help from protégé Barney Rosset, whose Grove Press reprinted Olympia titles in the American market. By 1967, Girodas was back, but the fire was out. In 1974, Olympia-New York collapsed under a pile of unpaid bills. Between 1974 and his death in 1990, Girodas wrote and looked for publishers, who were rarely as kind to him as he had been to the misfit geniuses he published in his heyday. His two-volume autobiography was finally published in Paris in 1990.

Olympia published Georges Bataille, Samuel Beckett, William Burroughs, Roger Casement, Jean Cocteau, J.P. Donleavy, Lawrence Durrell, Jean Genet, Henry Miller, Vladamir Nabokov, Terry Southern, and Pauline Reage, as well as preserved the works of DeSade, Apollonaire, and Cleland (among others). Literature owes a large debt to the little man who called himself "the Frog Prince." It's too bad it was paid with censorship.

For more than 50 years, since 1949, John Calder's literary enterprises have remained on the cutting edge, rising on a wave of change, or falling into a valley of persecution, censorship, and prejudice. While Maurice Giordias and Olympia were rising from the ashes of the Second World War and Obelisk, Calder was establishing a British counterpart. Unlike Olympia, however, Calder has weathered the storm.

Naked Lunch, Tropic of Cancer and *Last Exit to Brooklyn* all saw the light of day in Great Britain due to Calder. He published, and was banned, fought his way through, and published some more. Now, he is an "educational trust" and the leading exponent of "nouveau roman" through Calder Publications Ltd. in Britain, Riverrun Press Inc. in the U.S, and Calder Publications in France, publishing Claude Simon, Alain Robbe-Grillat, Marguerite Duras, and others. Unlike Olympia's Maurice Giordias, he has survived.

While Maurice Giordias was lifting French petticoats and John Calder was being shockingly un-Victorian, a young man from the Midwest moved to New York with the aim of un-Puritanizing America. Buying Grove Press, Barney Rosset set to work to challenge the concepts of obscenity we brought with us from the 19th century.

He built a publishing catalog that reads like a who's who of banned and challenged authors, including: Emmanuelle Arsan, Alan Ayckbourn, Imamu Amiri Baraka, Samuel Beckett, Eric Berne, Paul Bowles, James Broughton, William S. Burroughs, Marguerite Duras, Wallace Fowlie, Robert Frank, Jean Genet, Allen Ginsberg, Maurice Girodias, Witold Gombrowicz, Juan Goytisolo, Nat Hentoff, André Hodeir, Eugène Ionesco, Jack Kerouac, D.H. Lawrence, Henry Miller, Pablo Neruda, Frank O'Hara, Charles Olson, Joe Orton, Harold Pinter, George Reavey, John Rechy, Kenneth Rexroth, Alain Robbe-Grillet, Michael Rumaker, Hubert Selby, Gilbert Sorrentino, Amos Tutuola, Parker Tyler, Tomi Ungerer, and Alan Watts. He spearheaded legal battles to overturn censorship restrictions, and, in doing so, brought Henry Miller home, among other successes.

He sold Grove and moved on to Blue Moon Books, then to Arcade, but never stopped challenging our concepts of culture, obscenity, and censorship.

When the shouting dies down, when we can reflect on the direction of literary art in the 20th century, four figures will dominate what it was, and what it will become. Barney Rosset is the fourth, taking his place next to Jack Kahane, Maurice Girodias, and John Calderæthe men who saw the future and helped shape it.

A Note on Rebinding

From the 1920s through the 1960s, Parisian bookbinders carried on a special sideline, rebinding banned books to allow the purchaser to slip them through customs in the United States or United Kingdom. Rebinds of Henry Miller's Tropics are somewhat common and have served to preserve what would have become fragile paperbacks. Often the title was changed. I have seen several copies of the *Kama Sutra* in black buckram, titled *The Sacred Principles of the Brahmans*, apparently a specialty of a certain bookbinder. One of the more interesting specimens to pass through my hands was a rebind of Maurice Giorodias' first reprint of Frank Harris' *My Life and Loves*, four paperback volumes bound together in half leather in a custom made slipcase emblazoned with the title: Birds of the Mediterranean (obviously done in the late '50s or early '60s, given the double entendre). I know and have dealt with several collectors who specialize in collecting these rebindings.

10 Classic Rarities

Bannerman, Helen. *The Story of Little Black Sambo*. London: Grant Richards, 1899. Find this and forsake politically correct behavior forever.
Retail Value in:
Near Fine to Fine **$12,000**
Good to Very Good **$8500**

Burroughs, William S. *Naked Lunch*. Paris: Olympia Press, 1959. A green paperback, No. 79 in the Traveler's Companion Series. No dust jacket (added a month after publication). A green border on the title page.
Retail Value in:
Near Fine to Fine **$2500**
Good to Very Good **$1500**

Faulkner, William. *As I Lay Dying*. New York: Jonathan Cape/Harrison Smith, 1930. Initial "I" on page 11 misaligned hardcover in Dust Jacket.
Retail Value in:
Near Fine to Fine **$10000**
Good to Very Good **$6000**

Ginsberg, Allen. *Howl and Other Poems*. San Francisco: City Lights, 1956. Pocket Poets Series: Number Four. Stapled black wrappers with white wraparound pastedown.
Retail Value in:
Near Fine to Fine **$5000**
Good to Very Good **$3500**

Golding, William. *Lord of the Flies*. London: Faber & Faber, 1954. Red cloth, white titles to spine, hardcover in Dust Jacket.
Retail Value in:
Near Fine to Fine **$8000**
Good to Very Good **$4500**

Huxley, Aldous. *Brave New World*. London: Chatto & Windus, 1932. Blue cloth hardback in blue Dust Jacket. It will be a new world for you if you pick this up.
Retail Value in:
Near Fine to Fine **$4000**
Good to Very Good **$2200**

Kerouac, Jack. *Mexico City Blues*. New York: Grove Press, Inc., 1959. Gray cloth, white pictorial dust jacket, printed in black, design by Roy Kuhlman, author's photograph to rear panel, by William Eichel. Finding this a cure for the blues anywhere.
Retail Value in:
Near Fine to Fine **$3500**
Good to Very Good **$2000**

Miller, Henry. *Tropic of Capricorn*. Paris: Obelisk Press, 1939. Errata slip, and price (60 francs) stamped on back, in red wrappers lettered in black. Find this and study the Tropics from Club Med.
Retail Value in:
Near Fine to Fine **$2000**
Good to Very Good **$1000**

Nabokov, Vladimir. *Lolita*. Paris: Olympia Press, 1955. Two volumes, a green paperback issue #66 in Olympia's Traveller's Companion Series. Find it and you can join Chevalier in singing "Thank Heaven for Little Girls."
Retail Value in:
Near Fine to Fine **$7500**
Good to Very Good **$5000**

Price Guide

Ableman, Paul. *I Hear Voices*. First edition: Paris: Olympia Press, 1957.
Nr.Fine/Fine. **$35**
Good/V.Good. **$15**

Allard, Henry. *Bumps in the Night*. First Edition: New York: Doubleday, 1979.
Nr.Fine/Fine. **$30**
Good/V.Good. **$12**

Allende, Isabelle. *The House of Spirits*. First American Edition: New York: Alfred A. Knopf, 1985.
Nr.Fine/Fine. **$100**
Good/V.Good. **$50**
First U.K. Edition: London: Jonathan Cape, 1985.
Nr.Fine/Fine. **$65**
Good/V.Good. **$40**

Angelique, Pierre (Georges Bataille). *The Naked Beast at Heaven's Gate*. First Edition in English: Paris: Olympia Press, 1956.
Nr.Fine/Fine. **$500**
Good/V.Good. **$350**

_____. *A Tale of Satisfied Desire*. First Edition in English: Paris: Olympia Press, 1953.
Nr.Fine/Fine. **$500**
Good/V.Good. **$350**

Angelou, Maya. *I Know Why the Caged Bird Sings*. First Edition: New York: Random House, 1969.
Nr.Fine/Fine. **$300**
Good/V.Good. **$200**

Anonymous. *Go Ask Alice*. First Edition: Englewood Cliffs, NJ; Prentice-Hall, 1971.
Nr.Fine/Fine. **$175**
Good/V.Good. **$100**

_____. *I'm for Hire*. First Edition: Paris: Olympia Press, 1955.
Nr.Fine/Fine. **$150**
Good/V.Good. **$80**

First U.S. Edition: as by Marie Therese. North Hollywood: Brandon House, 1966.
Nr.Fine/Fine. **$50**
Good/V.Good. **$20**

_____ **(Diane Bataille)**. *The Whip Angels*. First Edition: Paris: Olympia, 1955.
Nr.Fine/Fine. **$100**
Good/V.Good. **$65**
First U.S. Edition: as by Selena Warfield. New York: Olympia Book Society, 1968.
Nr.Fine/Fine. **$45**
Good/V.Good. **$25**

Anaya, Rudolfo. *Bless Me, Ultima*. First Edition: Berkeley: Quinto Sol, 1972.
Nr.Fine/Fine. **$500**
Good/V.Good. **$350**

Apollinaire, Guillaume. *Amorous Exploits of a Young Rakehell*. First Edition in English: Paris: Olympia Press, 1953. Original French publication in 1907.
Nr.Fine/Fine. **$50**
Good/V.Good. **$35**

_____. *The Debauched Hospodar*. First Edition in English: Paris: Olympia Press, 1953. Original French publication in 1906.
Nr.Fine/Fine. **$50**
Good/V.Good. **$35**

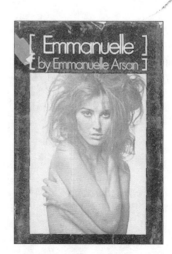

Emmanuelle
by Emmanuelle Arsan

Arsan, Emanuelle. *Emanuelle*. First
Edition: New York: Grove Press, 1971.
Nr.Fine/Fine. **$35**
Good/V.Good. **$15**

Emmanuelle II
*by Emmanuelle
Arsan*

_____. *Emanuelle II*. First
Edition: New York: Grove Press, 1974.
Nr.Fine/Fine. **$65**
Good/V.Good. **$35**

Ash, Sholem. *The God of Vengence*. First
Edition in English: Boston: The Stratford
Co., 1918.
Nr.Fine/Fine. **$225**
Good/V.Good. **$100**

Atwood, Margaret. *The Handmaid's Tale*.
First Edition: Toronto: McClelland &
Stewart, 1985.
Nr.Fine/Fine. **$100**
Good/V.Good. **$55**

Baldwin, James. *Another Country*. First
Edition: New York: The Dial Press, 1962.
Nr.Fine/Fine. **$250**
Good/V.Good. **$100**
First U.K. Edition: London: Michael
Joseph, 1963.
Nr.Fine/Fine. **$50**
Good/V.Good. **$30**

Baron, Willy (Baird Bryant). *Play My
Love*. First Edition: Paris: Olympia Press,
1960.
Nr.Fine/Fine. **$25**

Good/V.Good. **$10**

Baudelaire, Charles. *Les Fleurs du mal*.
First Edition: Paris: by the author, 1857.
Nr.Fine/Fine **$17,500**
Good/V.Good **$12,000**

Beardsley, Aubrey & John Glasco.
Under the Hill. First Edition: Paris:
Olympia Press, 1959.
Nr.Fine/Fine. **$100**
Good/V.Good. **$50**

Beckett, Samuel. *Molloy*. First Edition:
Paris: Olympia Press, 1955.
Nr.Fine/Fine. **$350**
Good/V.Good. **$200**

_____. *Molloy, Malone Dies,
The Unnamable*. First Edition: Paris:
Olympia Press, 1959.
Nr.Fine/Fine. **$200**
Good/V.Good. **$125**

**The Return
of Angela**
by Jean Blanche

Blanche, Jean. *The Return of Angela*. First
Edition: New York: Castle Books, 1956.
Nr.Fine/Fine. **$15**
Good/V.Good. **$8**

Blume, Judy. *Are You There, God? It's Me,
Margaret*. First Edition: Englewood Cliffs,
NJ: Bradbury, 1970.
Nr.Fine/Fine. **$20**
Good/V.Good. **$8**

_____. *Blubber*. First Edition:
Scarsdale, NY: Bradbury, 1974.
Nr.Fine/Fine **$25**
Good/V.Good **$10**

_____. *Tiger Eyes*. First Edition:
Scarsdale, NY: Bradbury Press, 1981.
Nr.Fine/Fine **$80**
Good/V.Good **$35**

Boff, Leonardo. *Church: Charism and Power: Liberation Theology and the Institutional Church*. First Edition in English: New York: Crossroads, 1985.
Nr.Fine/Fine **$25**
Good/V.Good **$15**

Blonde Flames
by Pamela Boyer

Boyer, Pamela. *Blonde Flames*. First Edition: New York: Key Publishing, 1957.
Nr.Fine/Fine **$15**
Good/V.Good **$8**

Bradbury, Ray. *Fahrenheit 451*. First Edition: New York: Ballantine, 1953. Points of Issue: Contains two short stories, The Playground & the Rock Cried.
Nr.Fine/Fine **$500**
Good/V.Good **$300**

Broughton, James. *Almanac for Amorists*. First Edition: Paris: Collections Merlin in collaboration with the Olympia Press, 1955.
Nr.Fine/Fine **$65**
Good/V.Good **$30**

Brown, Claude. *Manchild in the Promised Land*. First Edition: New York: Macmillan, 1965.
Nr.Fine/Fine **$75**
Good/V.Good **$35**

Burgess, Anthony. *A Clockwork Orange*. First Edition: London: Heinemann, 1962.
Nr.Fine/Fine **$5000**
Good/V.Good **$3500**
First U.S. Edition: New York: W.W.Norton, 1963.
Nr.Fine/Fine **$300**
Good/V.Good **$175**

Burns, R. Bernard. *The Ordeal of the Rod*. First Edition: Paris: Olympia Press, 1958.
Nr.Fine/Fine **$30**
Good/V.Good **$12**

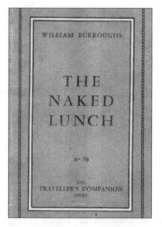

The Naked Lunch
by William S. Burroughs

Burroughs, William S. *Naked Lunch*. First U.S. Edition: New York: Grove Press, 1959.
Nr.Fine/Fine **$900**
Good/V.Good **$375**
First U.K. Edition: London: John Calder, 1959.
Nr.Fine/Fine **$650**
Good/V.Good **$250**

_____. *The Soft Machine.*
First Edition: Paris: Olympia Press, 1961.
Nr.Fine/Fine **$250**
Good/V.Good **$175**
First U.S. Edition: New York: Grove Press,
1966.
Nr.Fine/Fine **$95**
Good/V.Good **$65**
First U.K. Edition: London: Calder &
Boyars, 1968.
Nr.Fine/Fine **$100**
Good/V.Good **$65**

_____. *The Ticket that
Exploded.* First Edition: Paris: Olympia
Press, 1961.
Nr.Fine/Fine **$750**
Good/V.Good **$350**
1st U.S. Edition: New York: Grove Press,
1967
Nr.Fine/Fine $175
Good/V.Good . . . . $85.

Butz, A.R. *The Hoax of the Twentieth
Century.* First Edition: Richmond, Surrey:
Historical Review Press, 1976.
Nr.Fine/Fine **$35**
Good/V.Good **$15**

First U.S. Edition: Los Angeles: Noontide
Press, 1977.
Nr.Fine/Fine **$65**
Good/V.Good **$35**

Cabell, James Branch. *Jurgen.* First
Edition: New York: Robert M. McBride &
Co., 1919.
Nr.Fine/Fine **$1850**
Good/V.Good **$950**

Cadivec, Edith. *Eros: The Meaning of My
Life.* First Edition: New York: Grove Press,
1969.
Nr.Fine/Fine **$35**
Good/V.Good **$15**

Carroll, Jock. *Bottoms Up* First Edition:
Paris: Olympia Press, 1961.
Nr.Fine/Fine **$65**
Good/V.Good **$35**

Eros: The
Meaning
of My Life
by Edith Cadivec

Casement, Roger. *The Black Diaries.* First
Edition: Paris: Olympia Press, 1959.
Nr.Fine/Fine $300
Good/V.Good $145

**Caughey, John W., John Hope Franklin
and Ernest R. May**. *Land of the Free.*
First Edition: New York: Benziger Brothers,
Inc., 1965.
Nr.Fine/Fine **$30**
Good/V.Good **$12**

Childress, Alice. *A Hero Ain't Nothin' but
a Sandwich.* First Edition: New York:
Cowand-McCann, 1973.
Nr.Fine/Fine **$50**
Good/V.Good **$22**

Cleaver, Eldridge. *Soul on Ice.* First
Edition: New York: McGraw-Hill/Ramparts,
1968.
Nr.Fine/Fine **$175**
Good/V.Good **$85**

Cohen, Daniel. *Curses, Hexes and Spells.*
First Edition: London: J.M. Dent, 1977.
Nr.Fine/Fine **$55**
Good/V.Good **$30**

Cole, Babette. *Mommy Laid An Egg.* First
Edition: San Francisco, CA.: Chronicle
Books, 1993.
Nr.Fine/Fine **$20**
Good/V.Good **$8**

Cole, Joanna. *Asking About Sex and Growing Up*. First Edition: New York: Morrow Junior Books, 1988.
Nr.Fine/Fine. **$25**
Good/V.Good. **$12**

Conly, Jane Leslie. *Crazy Lady*. First Edition: New York: HarperCollins Children's Book Group, 1993.
Nr.Fine/Fine. **$25**
Good/V.Good. **$12**

Cooney, Caroline B. *The Face on the Milk Carton*. First Edition: New York: Bantam, 1990.
Nr.Fine/Fine. **$20**
Good/V.Good. **$8**

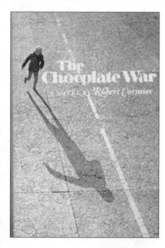

The Chocolate War
by Robert Cormier

Cormier, Robert. *The Chocolate War*. First Edition: New York: Pantheon, 1974.
Nr.Fine/Fine. **$100**
Good/V.Good. **$40**
First U. K. Edition: London: Victor Gollancz, 1974
Nr.Fine/Fine. **$35**
Good/V.Good. **$15**

_____. *Fade*. First Edition: New York: Delacorte Press, 1988.
Nr.Fine/Fine. **$55**
Good/V.Good. **$20**
First U.K. Edition: London: Victor Gollancz Ltd., 1988.
Nr.Fine/Fine. **$15**

Good/V.Good. **$6**

_____. *I Am the Cheese*. First Edition: New York: Pantheon, 1977.
Nr.Fine/Fine. **$18**
Good/V.Good. **$10**

Corso, Gregory. *The American Express*. First Edition: Paris: Olympia Press, 1961.
Nr.Fine/Fine. **$265**
Good/V.Good. **$130**

Cousins, Sheila (Graham Greene and Ronald Matthews). *To Beg I am Ashamed*. First Edition: London: Roultedge, 1938.
Nr.Fine/Fine. **$22000**
Good/V.Good. **$15000**
Paris Edition: Paris: Obelisk Press, 1938.
Nr.Fine/Fine. **$275**
Good/V.Good. **$125**
First American Edition: New York: The Vanguard Press, 1938.
Nr.Fine/Fine. **$255**
Good/V.Good. **$100**

Crannach, Henry (Marilyn Meeske). *Flesh and Bone*. First Edition: Paris: Olympia Press, 1957.
Nr.Fine/Fine. **$45**
Good/V.Good. **$20**

Crutcher, Chris. *Athletic Shorts*. First Edition: New York: Greenwillow Books, 1989.
Nr.Fine/Fine. **$25**
Good/V.Good. **$10**

Dahl, Roald. *James and the Giant Peach*. First Edition: New York: Alfred A. Knopf, 1961.
Nr.Fine/Fine. **$1200**
Good/V.Good. **$550**
First U.K. Edition: London: George Allen & Unwin, 1967.
Nr.Fine/Fine. **$450**
Good/V.Good. **$200**

Daimler, Harriet (Iris Owens). *Darling*. First Edition: Paris: Olympia Press, 1956.
Nr.Fine/Fine. **$75**
Good/V.Good. **$40**

_____. *Innocence*.
First Edition: Paris: Olympia Press, 1956.
Nr.Fine/Fine.................... **$45**
Good/V.Good................... **$20**

_____. *The
Organization*. First Edition: Paris: Olympia
Press, 1957.
Nr.Fine/Fine.................... **$65**
Good/V.Good................... **$35**

_____. *The Woman
Thing*. First Edition: Paris: Olympia Press,
1958.
Nr.Fine/Fine.................... **$45**
Good/V.Good................... **$20**

**Daimler, Harriet and Crannach, Henry
(Iris Owens and Marilyn Meeske)**. *The
Pleasure Thieves*. First Edition: Paris:
Olympia Press, 1958.
Nr.Fine/Fine.................... **$45**
Good/V.Good................... **$20**

Darwin, Charles. *On the Origin of
Species*. First Edition: London: John
Murray, 1859.
Nr.Fine/Fine **$50,000**
Good/V.Good **$30,000**

**de Farniente, Beauregard (J.C.
Gervaise de Latouche)**. *The Adventures of
Father Silas*. First Edition: Paris: Olympia
Press, 1958.
Nr.Fine/Fine.................... **$55**
Good/V.Good................... **$25**

De Leeuw, Hendrik. *Fallen Angels*. First
Edition: London: Arco Publishers, 1954.
Nr.Fine/Fine.................... **$50**
Good/V.Good................... **$17**

**Del Piombo, Akbar (Norman
Rubington)**. *The Boiler Maker*. First
Edition: Paris: Olympia Press, 1961.
Nr.Fine/Fine.................... **$65**
Good/V.Good................... **$30**

_____.
Cosimo's Wife. First Edition: Paris: Olympia
Press, 1957.

Nr.Fine/Fine.................... $50
Good/V.Good $25

Desmond, Robert. *An Adult's Story*. First
Edition: Paris: Olympia Press, 1954.
Nr.Fine/Fine.................... **$35**
Good/V.Good................... **$15**

_____. *Heaven, Hell and the
Whore*. First Edition: Paris: Olympia Press,
1956.
Nr.Fine/Fine.................... **$35**
Good/V.Good................... **$15**

_____. *Iniquity*. First edition:
Paris: Olympia Press, 1958.
Nr.Fine/Fine.................... **$35**
Good/V.Good................... **$15**

_____. *The Libertine*. First
Edition: Paris: Olympia Press, 1955.
Nr.Fine/Fine.................... **$35**
Good/V.Good................... **$15**

_____. *Professional Charmer*.
First Edition: Paris: Olympia Press, 1961.
Nr.Fine/Fine.................... **$15**
Good/V.Good................... **$12**

_____. *The Sweetest Fruit*. First
Edition: Paris: Olympia Press, 1951.
Nr.Fine/Fine.................... **$35**
Good/V.Good................... **$15**

Acapulco
Nocturne
by Barry Devlin

Devlin, Barry. *Acapulco Nocturne*. First

Edition: New York: Vixen Press, 1952.
Nr.Fine/Fine. **$30**
Good/V.Good. **$12**

Chains of Silk
by Barry Devlin

_____. *Chains of Silk*.First Edition:
New York: Vixen Press, 1954.
Nr.Fine/Fine. **$25**
Good/V.Good. **$10**

Moonkissed
by Barry Devlin

_____. *Moon-Kissed*. First Edition:
New York: Vixen Press, 1953.
Nr.Fine/Fine. **$25**
Good/V.Good. **$12**

_____. *No Holds Barred*. First
Edition: New York: Vixen Press, 1954.
Nr.Fine/Fine. **$15**
Good/V.Good. **$8**

Dickens, Charles. *Oliver Twist*. First
Edition: as by Boz: London: Richard

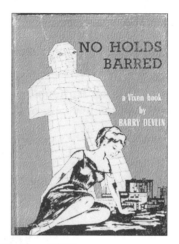

No Holds
Barred
by Barry Devlin

Bentley, 1838.
Nr.Fine/Fine **$12,500**
Good/V.Good. **$9500**

d'Musset, Alfred. *Passion's Evil*. First
Edition: Paris: Olympia Press, 1953.
Nr.Fine/Fine. **$35**
Good/V.Good. **$15**

The Ginger Man
by J.P. Donleavy

Donleavy, J.P. *The Ginger Man*. First
Edition: Paris: Olympia Press, 1955. Points
of Issue: #7 in Traveler's Companion Series,
Price on rear cover is "Francs 1,500."
Nr.Fine/Fine. **$800**
Good/V.Good. **$600**
First U.S. Edition: New York McDowell,
Obolensky 1958.
Nr.Fine/Fine. **$125**
Good/V.Good. **$50**

First U.K. Edition: London: Neville
Spearman, 1956.
Nr.Fine/Fine.................. **$135**
Good/V.Good.................. **$60**

Drake, Hamilton (Mason Hoffenberg).
Sin for Breakfast. First Edition: Paris:
Olympia Press, 1957.
Nr.Fine/Fine.................. **$65**
Good/V.Good.................. **$25**

Dreiser, Theodore. *An American Tragedy*.
First Edition: New York: Boni and
Liveright, 1925.
Nr.Fine/Fine.................. **$1500**
Good/V.Good.................. **$875**

_____. *The Genius*. First
Edition: New York: John Lane, 1915.
Nr.Fine/Fine.................. **$425**
Good/V.Good.................. **$175**

Duncan, Lois. *Killing Mr. Griffin*. First
Edition: Boston: Little, Brown and
Company, 1978.
Nr.Fine/Fine.................. **$15**
Good/V.Good.................. **$8**

Duras, Marguerie and Alain Resnais.
Hiroshima Mon Amour. First Edition: New
York: Grove Press, 1961.
Nr.Fine/Fine.................. **$25**
Good/V.Good.................. **$15**

Durrell, Lawrence. *The Black Book*. First
Edition: Paris: The Obelisk Press, 1938.
Nr.Fine/Fine.................. **$1500**
Good/V.Good.................. **$600**

First U.S. Edition: New York: E. P. Dutton,
1960.
Nr.Fine/Fine.................. **$125**
Good/V.Good.................. **$65**

Edward, Brett. *The Passion of Youth*. First
Edition: Paris: Olympia Press, 1960.
Nr.Fine/Fine.................. **$35**
Good/V.Good.................. **$15**

Ellis, Bret Easton. *American Psycho*. First
Edition: New York: Vintage, 1991.
Nr.Fine/Fine.................. **$50**
Good/V.Good.................. **$30**

El Saadawi, Nawal. *The Hidden Face of
Eve: Women in the Arab World*. First U.K.
Edition: London: Zed Press, 1980.
Nr.Fine/Fine.................. **$25**
Good/V.Good.................. **$10**

Faulkner, William. *Sanctuary*. First
Edition: New York: Jonathan Cape &
Harrison Smith, 1931.
Nr.Fine/Fine.................. **$12500**
Good/V.Good.................. **$5000**

Feral, Rex. *Hit Man: A Technical Manual
for Independent Contractors*. First Edition:
Denver: Paladin Press, 1983.

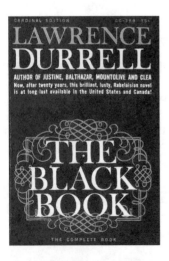

The Black Book
*by Lawrence
Durrell*

Lust
by Gerald Foster

Nr.Fine/Fine. **$125**
Good/V.Good. **$55**

Follett, Ken. *Pillars of the Earth.* First Edition: New York: Wm. Morrow & Co., 1989.
Nr.Fine/Fine. **$55**
Good/V.Good. **$35**

Foster, Gerald. *Lust.* First Edition: New York: Balzac Press, 1949.
Nr.Fine/Fine. **$35**
Good/V.Good. **$15**

Frank, Anne. *Anne Frank: The Diary of a Young Girl.* First Edition in English: New York: Doubleday, 1952.
Nr.Fine/Fine. **$250**
Good/V.Good. **$125**
First U.K. Edition: London: Constellation Books, 1952.
Nr.Fine/Fine. **$100**
Good/V.Good. **$65**

Freedman, Nancy. *The Prima Donna.* First Edition: New York: William Morrow, 1981.
Nr.Fine/Fine. **$18**
Good/V.Good. **$6**

Friday, Nancy. *Women on Top: How Real Life Has Changed Women's Sexual Fantasies.* First Edition: New York: Simon & Schuster, 1991.
Nr.Fine/Fine. **$20**
Good/V.Good. **$8**

Garden, Nancy. *Annie on My Mind.* First Edition: New York: Farrar, Straus, Giroux, 1982.
Nr.Fine/Fine. **$75**
Good/V.Good. **$30**

George, Jean Craighead. *Julie of the Wolves.* First Edition: New York: Harper and Row, 1972.
Nr.Fine/Fine. **$320**
Good/V.Good. **$180**

Ginzberg, Ralph (ed.). *Eros Magazine.* Quarterly Magazine issued in 1962 (4

Issues).
Nr.Fine/Fine. **$100**
Good/V.Good. **$60**

Gordimer, Nadine. *Burger's Daughter.* First Edition: London: Jonathon Cape, 1979.
Nr.Fine/Fine. **$85**
Good/V.Good. **$35**

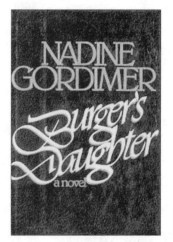

Burger's Daughter
by Nadine Gordimer

First U.S. Edition: New York: Viking Press, 1979.
Nr.Fine/Fine. **$75**
Good/V.Good. **$25**

Grass, Gunther. *The Tin Drum.* First Edition in English: London: Secker & Warburg, 1959.
Nr.Fine/Fine. **$65**
Good/V.Good. **$25**
First American Edition: New York: Pantheon, 1959.
Nr.Fine/Fine. **$75**
Good/V.Good. **$35**

Greene, Bette. *The Drowning of Stephan Jones.* First Edition: New York: Bantam, 1991.
Nr.Fine/Fine. **$35**
Good/V.Good. **$15**

_____. *The Summer of My German Soldier*. First Edition: New York: The Dial Press, 1973.
Nr.Fine/Fine. **$65**
Good/V.Good. **$25**

Griffin, John Howard. *Black Like Me*. First Edition: Boston: Houghton Mifflin, 1961.
Nr.Fine/Fine. **$400**
Good/V.Good. **$150**

Guest, Judith. *Ordinary People*. First Edition: New York: Viking Press, 1976.
Nr.Fine/Fine. **$125**
Good/V.Good. **$55**

Guterson, David. *Snow Falling on Cedars*. First Edition: New York: Harcourt Brace, 1994.
Nr.Fine/Fine. **$250**
Good/V.Good. **$150**

The Well of
Loneliness
by Radclyffe Hall

Hall, Radclyffe. *The Well of Loneliness*. First Edition: New York: Covici-Friede, 1928.
Nr.Fine/Fine. **$150**
Good/V.Good. **$65**

Hamilton, David. *The Age Of Innocence*. First Edition: London. Aurum Press, 1995.
Nr.Fine/Fine. **$100**
Good/V.Good. **$55**

Hammer, Stephen (John Coleman). *The Itch*. First Edition: Paris: Olympia Press, 1956.
Nr.Fine/Fine. **$30**
Good/V.Good. **$15**

Hardy, Thomas. *Jude the Obscure*. First Edition: New York: Harper and Brothers, 1895.
Nr.Fine/Fine. **$400**
Good/V.Good. **$200**
First U.K. Edition: London: Osgood, McIlvaine & Co, 1896.
Nr.Fine/Fine. **$3000**
Good/V.Good. **$500**

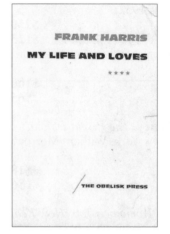

My Life
and Loves
by Frank Harris

Harris, Frank. *My Life and Loves*. First Edition: Paris and Nice: Privately printed for the Author, 1922-27. Note: Harris privately printed his memoirs in bits and pieces over a five-year period; a complete collection of these fragments is worth about $8000. The fragments run, according to size and condition, from $100 to $500.
First Trade Edition: Paris: Obelisk, 1933.
Nr.Fine/Fine. **$700**
Good/V.Good. **$450**

_____ **(Alexander Trocchi)**. *My Life and Loves Volume 5*. First Edition: Paris: Olympia Press, 1954.
Nr.Fine/Fine. **$40**
Good/V.Good. **$25**

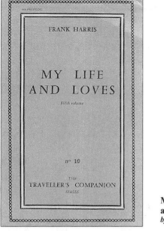

My Life
and Loves
by Frank Harris

Harris, Robie H. *It's Perfectly Normal*.
First Edition: Cambridge, MA: Candlewick
Press, 1994.
Nr.Fine/Fine. **$30**
Good/V.Good. **$12**

Hawthorne, Nathaniel. *The Scarlet
Letter*. First Edition: Boston: Ticknor, Reed
& Fields, 1850.
Nr.Fine/Fine. **$8500**
Good/V.Good. **$5500**

Heckstall-Smith, Anthony. *The Consort*.
First Edition: New York: Grove Press, 1965.
Nr.Fine/Fine. **$45**
Good/V.Good. **$25**

Heller, Joseph. *Catch 22*. First Edition:
New York: Simon & Schuster, 1961.
Nr.Fine/Fine. **$5000**
Good/V.Good. **$2500**

Helper, Hinton Rowan. *The Impending
Crisis in the South-How to Meet It*. First
Edition: New York: Burdick Brothers, 1857.
Nr.Fine/Fine. **$250**
Good/V.Good. **$150**

Himes, Chester. *Pinktoes*. First Edition:
Paris: Olympia Press, 1961.
Nr.Fine/Fine. **$180**
Good/V.Good. **$100**
First U.S. Edition: New York: Putnam/Stein
& Day, 1965.

Nr.Fine/Fine. **$175**
Good/V.Good. **$95**

Hinton, S.E. *The Outsiders*. First Edition:
New York: Viking Press, 1967.
Nr.Fine/Fine. $500
Good/V.Good . . . . $200.

_____. *That Was Then, This is Now*.
First Edition: New York: The Viking Press,
1971.
Nr.Fine/Fine. **$60**
Good/V.Good. **$25**

Hitler, Adolf. *Mein Kampf*. First Edition:
Munich: Eher Verlag, 1925.
Nr.Fine/Fine **$12,000**
Good/V.Good. **$5000**

Homer and Associates (Michel Gall). *A
Bedside Odyssey*. First Edition: Paris:
Olympia Press, 1962.
Nr.Fine/Fine. **$35**
Good/V.Good. **$20**

Hughes, Langston (ed.). *The Best Short
Stories by Negro Writers*. First Edition:
Boston: Little, Brown & Company, 1967.
Nr.Fine/Fine. **$50**
Good/V.Good. **$30**

Humphrey, Derek. *Final Exit*. First
Edition: Eugene, OR: The Hemlock Society,
1991.
Nr.Fine/Fine. **$15**
Good/V.Good. **$8**

Huxley, Aldous. *Brave New World*.
First U.S. Edition: Garden City, NY:
Doubleday, Doran, 1932 (LTD, Signed).
Nr.Fine/Fine. **$3000**
Good/V.Good. **$1800**
First U.S. Edition: Garden City, NY:
Doubleday, Doran, 1932 (trade).
Nr.Fine/Fine. **$200**
Good/V.Good. **$80**

Huysmans, J(oris). K(arl). *A Rebours*.

First U.S. Edition: New York: Lieber & Lewis, 1922.
Nr.Fine/Fine. **$50**
Good/V.Good. **$30**

_____. *La Bas*. First edition in English: New York: Albert & Charles Boni, 1924.
Nr.Fine/Fine. **$325**
Good/V.Good. **$200**

Jones, Henry (John Coleman). *The Enormous Bed*. First Edition: Paris: Olympia Press, 1955.
Nr.Fine/Fine. **$35**
Good/V.Good. **$20**

Joyce, James. *Ulysses*. First Edition: Paris: Shakespeare & Co., 1922.
Nr.Fine/Fine. **$60000**
Good/V.Good. **$45000**

Justice, Jean. *Murder vs. Murder*. First Edition: Paris: Olympia Press, 1964.
Nr.Fine/Fine. **$50**
Good/V.Good. **$30**

Kantor, MacKinlay. *Andersonville*. First Edition: Cleveland, OH: World Publishing Company, 1955.
Nr.Fine/Fine. **$125**
Good/V.Good. **$75**

Kazantzakis, Nikos. *The Last Temptation of Christ*. First Edition in English: New York: Simon & Schuster, 1960.
Nr.Fine/Fine. **$65**
Good/V.Good. **$25**

Kenton, Maxwell. (Terry Southern and Mason Hoffenberg). *Candy*. First Edition: Paris: Olympia Press, 1958.
Nr.Fine/Fine. **$250**
Good/V.Good. **$150**
First U.S. Edition: New York: G.P. Putnam's Sons, 1964.
Nr.Fine/Fine. **$175**
Good/V.Good. **$50**
First U.K. Edition: London: Bernard Geis, 1968.
Nr.Fine/Fine. **$100**

Good/V.Good. **$45**

Kesey, Ken. *One Flew Over the Cuckoo's Nest*. First Edition: New York: Viking Press, 1962.
Nr.Fine/Fine. **$10000**
Good/V.Good. **$7500**

Keyes, Daniel. *Flowers for Algernon*. First Edition: New York: Harcourt Brace & World, 1966.
Nr.Fine/Fine. **$650**
Good/V.Good. **$300**

King, Stephen. *Carrie*. First Edition: Garden City, N.Y.: Doubleday & Co., Inc., 1974.
Nr.Fine/Fine. **$2200**
Good/V.Good. **$1000**

_____. *Christine*. First Edition: New York: Viking Penguin, 1983.
Nr.Fine/Fine. **$10**
Good/V.Good. **$5**

_____. *Cujo*. First Edition: New York: Viking Press, 1981.
Nr.Fine/Fine. **$10**
Good/V.Good. **$5**

_____. *The Dead Zone*. First Edition: New York: The Viking Press, 1979.
Nr.Fine/Fine. **$100**
Good/V.Good. **$45**

Kung, Hans. *Infallible? An Inquiry*. First U. S. Edition: Garden City, NY: Doubleday And Company, 1971.
Nr.Fine/Fine. **$25**
Good/V.Good. **$10**

LaFarge, Oliver. *Laughing Boy*. First Edition: Boston: Houghton Mifflin Company, 1929.
Nr.Fine/Fine. **$100**
Good/V.Good. **$25**

Landshot, Gustav. *How To Do It*. First Edition: Paris: Olympia Press, 1956.
Nr.Fine/Fine. **$35**
Good/V.Good. **$15**

Lawrence, D.H. *Women in Love*. First Edition: New York: Privately printed, 1920.
Nr.Fine/Fine. **$2500**
Good/V.Good. **$950**

Lederer, William J. & Eugene Burdick. *The Ugly American*. First Edition: New York: W.W. Norton, 1958.
Nr.Fine/Fine. **$150**
Good/V.Good. **$25**

Lee, Harper. *To Kill a Mockingbird*. First Edition: Philadelphia and New York: J.B. Lippincott Company, 1960.
Nr.Fine/Fine. **$15000**
Good/V.Good. **$4000**

Lengel, Frances (Alexander Trocchi). *The Carnal Days of Helen Seferis*. First Edition: Paris: Olympia Press, 1954.
Nr.Fine/Fine. **$35**
Good/V.Good. **$15**

_____. *Helen and Desire*. First Edition: Paris: Olympia Press, 1954.
Nr.Fine/Fine. **$35**
Good/V.Good. **$15**

L'Engle, Madeleine. *A Wrinkle in Time*. First Edition: New York: Farrar, Straus & Giroux, 1962.
Nr.Fine/Fine. **$25**
Good/V.Good. **$10**

Lesse, Ruth. *Lash*. First Edition: Paris: Olympia Press: 1962.
Nr.Fine/Fine. **$35**
Good/V.Good. **$15**

Lincoln, James & Christopher Collier. *Jump Ship to Freedom*. First Edition: New York: Delacorte, 1981.
Nr.Fine/Fine. **$15**
Good/V.Good. **$5**

_____. *My Brother Sam is Dead*. First Edition: New York: Four Winds, 1974.
Nr.Fine/Fine. **$20**
Good/V.Good. **$12**

Lowry, Lois. *The Giver*. First Edition: Boston: Houghton Mifflin Company, 1993.
Nr.Fine/Fine. **$100**
Good/V.Good. **$65**

Madonna. *Sex*. First Edition: New York: Warner Books, 1992.
Nr.Fine/Fine. **$300**
Good/V.Good. **$200**

Malamud, Bernard. *The Fixer*. First Edition: New York: Farrar, Straus & Giroux, 1966. Nr.Fine/Fine. **$200**
Good/V.Good. **$100**

Mardaan, Attaullah. *Deva-Dasi*. First Edition: Paris: Olympia Press, 1957.
Nr.Fine/Fine. **$35**
Good/V.Good. **$15**
First U.S. Edition: New York: The Macaulay Company, 1959.
Nr.Fine/Fine. **$20**
Good/V.Good. **$12**

Mathabane, Mark. *Kaffir Boy*. First edition: New York: Macmillan Publishing Co., 1986.
Nr.Fine/Fine. **$50**
Good/V.Good. **$20**

Matthiesen, Peter. *In the Spirit of Crazy Horse*.First Edition: New York: Viking Press, 1983.
Nr.Fine/Fine. **$100**
Good/V.Good. **$65**

McCarthy, Mary. *The Group*. First Edition: New York: Harcourt Brace & World, 1963.
Nr.Fine/Fine. **$75**
Good/V.Good. **$45**

Meng, Wu Wu (Sinclair Beiles). *Houses of Joy*. First Edition: Paris: Olympia Press, 1958.
Nr.Fine/Fine. **$55**
Good/V.Good. **$25**

Merriam, Eve. *Halloween ABC*. First Edition: New York Macmillan Publishing Co., 1987.

Nr.Fine/Fine. **$20**
Good/V.Good. **$8**

Metalious, Grace. *Peyton Place*. First
Edition: New York: Julian Messner, 1956.
Nr.Fine/Fine. **$200**
Good/V.Good. **$95**

Miller, Henry. *Nexus*. First Edition: Paris:
Corrêa, 1960 (in French).
Nr.Fine/Fine. **$200**
Good/V.Good. **$145**
First Edition in English: Paris: Obelisk
Press, 1960.
Nr.Fine/Fine. **$125**
Good/V.Good. **$75**
First U.S. Edition: New York: Grove Press,
1965.
Nr.Fine/Fine. **$50**
Good/V.Good. **$20**
First U.K. Edition: London: Weidenfeld &
Nicolson, 1964.
Nr.Fine/Fine. **$100**
Good/V.Good. **$45**

_____. *Plexus*. First Edition: Paris:
Correa, 1952.
Nr.Fine/Fine. **$100**
Good/V.Good. **$45**
First Edition in English: Paris: Olympia
Press, 1953.
Nr.Fine/Fine. **$100**
Good/V.Good. **$45**

_____. *Quiet Days in Clichy*. First
Edition: Paris: Olympia Press, 1956.
Nr.Fine/Fine. **$2000**
Good/V.Good. **$1100**

_____. *Sexus*. First Edition: Paris:
Obelisk Press, 1949.
Nr.Fine/Fine. **$600**
Good/V.Good. **$300**

_____. *Tropic of Cancer*. First
Edition: Paris: The Obelisk Press, 1934.
Nr.Fine/Fine. **$4500**
Good/V.Good. **$1500**

_____. *Tropic of Capricorn*. First
Edition: Paris: The Obelisk Press, 1934.

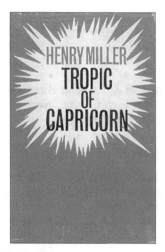

Tropic of
Capricorn
by Henry Miller

Nr.Fine/Fine. **$4500**
Good/V.Good. **$1500**

_____. *The World of Sex*. First
Edition: Printed by J.H.N. for Friends of
Henry Miller. [Chicago: Ben Abramson,
1941].
Nr.Fine/Fine. **$400**
Good/V.Good. **$250**

Moravia, Alberto. *The Wayward Wife*. First
U.S. Edition: New York: Farrar, Straus and
Cudahy, 1960.
Nr.Fine/Fine. **$45**
Good/V.Good. **$20**

_____. *Two-A Phallic Novel*.
First U.S. Edition: New York: Farrar Straus
Giroux, 1972.
Nr.Fine/Fine. **$25**
Good/V.Good. **$12**

Morris, Desmond. *The Naked Ape*. First
Edition: London: Jonathan Cape, 1967.
Nr.Fine/Fine. **$55**
Good/V.Good. **$25**

Morrison, Toni. *Beloved*. First Edition:
New York: Alfred A. Knopf, 1987.
Nr.Fine/Fine. **$400**
Good/V.Good. **$150**
First U.K. Edition: London: Chatto &
Windus, 1987.
Nr.Fine/Fine. **$55**

Good/V.Good. **$25**

_____. *The Bluest Eye*. First Edition: New York: Holt, Rinehart & Winston, 1970.
Nr.Fine/Fine. **$7500**
Good/V.Good. **$4500**
First U.K. Edition: London: Chatto and Windus, 1970.
Nr.Fine/Fine. **$450**
Good/V.Good. **$200**

_____. *The Song of Solomon*. First Edition: New York: Alfred A Knopf, 1977.
Nr.Fine/Fine. **$300**
Good/V.Good. **$125**

Nesbit, Malcom (Alfred Chester). *Chariot of Flesh*. First Edition: Paris: Olympia Press. 1955.
Nr.Fine/Fine. **$35**
Good/V.Good. **$15**

Newman, Leslea. *Heather Has Two Mommies*. First Edition: Los Angeles: Alyson Wonderland, 1989.
Nr.Fine/Fine. **$65**
Good/V.Good. **$25**

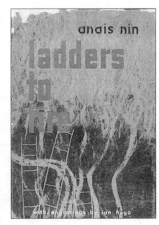

Ladders to Fire
by Anais Nin

Nin, Anais. *Ladders to Fire*. First Edition: New York: E.P. Dutton, 1946.
Nr.Fine/Fine. **$85**
Good/V.Good. **$40**

_____. *Nearer the Moon*. First Edition:

New York and San Diego: Harcourt Brace, 1996.
Nr.Fine/Fine. **$20**
Good/V.Good. **$12**

O'Hara, John. *Appointment in Samarra*. First Edition: New York: Harcourt, Brace and Co., 1934.
Nr.Fine/Fine. **$5000**
Good/V.Good. **$2500**

O'Neill, Peter. *The Corpse Wore Grey*. First Edition: Paris: Olympia Press, 1962.
Nr.Fine/Fine. **$35**
Good/V.Good. **$15**

_____. *Hell is Filling Up*. First Edition: Paris: Olympia Press, 1961.
Nr.Fine/Fine. **$35**
Good/V.Good. **$15**

Orwell, George. *Animal Farm*. First Edition: London: Martin Secker & Walburg Ltd., 1945.
Nr.Fine/Fine. **$3500**
Good/V.Good. **$2500**
First U.S. Edition: New York: Harcourt, Brace and Co., 1946.
Nr.Fine/Fine. **$400**
Good/V.Good. **$150**

_____. *1984*. First Edition: London: Secker & Warburg, 1949.
Nr.Fine/Fine. **$1750**
Good/V.Good. **$900**
First U.S. Edition: New York: Harcourt Brace & Co., 1949.
Nr.Fine/Fine. **$950**
Good/V.Good. **$400**

Parkinson, J. Hume. *Sextet*. First Edition: Paris: Olympia Press, 1965.
Nr.Fine/Fine. **$45**
Good/V.Good. **$25**

Pasternak, Boris. *Doctor Zhivago*. First U.S. Edition: New York: Pantheon Books, 1958.
Nr.Fine/Fine. **$85**
Good/V.Good. **$35**
First U.K. Edition: London: Collins &

Harvill, 1958.
Nr.Fine/Fine. **$300**
Good/V.Good. **$95**

Paterson, Katherine. *Bridge to Terabithia*.
First Edition: New York: Thomas Y.
Crowell, 1977.
Nr.Fine/Fine. **$75**
Good/V.Good. **$25**

_____. *The Great Gilly
Hopkins*. First Edition: New York: Thomas
Y. Crowell, 1978.
Nr.Fine/Fine. **$75**
Good/V.Good. **$25**

Peck, Robert Newton. *A Day No Pigs
Would Die*. First Edition: New York: Alfred
A Knopf, 1972.
Nr.Fine/Fine. **$50**
Good/V.Good. **$15**

Peters, Solimon. *Business as Usual*. First
Edition: Paris: Olympia Press, 1958.
Nr.Fine/Fine. **$35**
Good/V.Good. **$15**

Plath, Sylvia. *The Bell Jar*. First Edition:
As by Victoria Lucas. London: Heinemann,
1963.
Nr.Fine/Fine. **$2000**
Good/V.Good. **$950**
First U.S. Edition: New York: Harper &
Row, 1971.
Nr.Fine/Fine. **$100**
Good/V.Good. **$55**

Pomeroy, Wardell B. *Boys and Sex*. First
Edition: New York: Delacorte Press, 1968.
Nr.Fine/Fine. **$15**
Good/V.Good. **$8**

_____. *Girls and Sex*.
First Edition: New York: Delacorte Press,
1981.
Nr.Fine/Fine. **$15**
Good/V.Good. **$10**

Pond, Lily & Russo, Richard.*Yellow Silk*.
First Edition: New York: Harmony, 1990.
Nr.Fine/Fine. **$20**

Good/V.Good. **$12**

Powell, William. *The Anarchist Cookbook*.
First Edition: New York: Lyle Stuart, Inc.
1971.
Nr.Fine/Fine. **$100**
Good/V.Good. **$75**

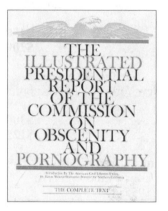

The Illustrated
Presidential
Report of the
Commission on
Obscenity and
Pornography
*by Presidential
Report*

Presidential Report. *The Illustrated
Presidential Report of the Commission on
Obscenity and Pornography*. First Edition:
San Diego: Greenleaf, 1970.
Nr.Fine/Fine. **$225**
Good/V.Good. **$125**

Queneau, Raymond. *Zazi Dans le Metro*.
First Edition: Paris: Olympia Press, 1959.
Nr.Fine/Fine. **$65**
Good/V.Good. **$35**

Reage, Pauline (Dominique Aury). *The
Story of O*. First Edition: Simultaneous in
French and in English: Paris: Olympia
Press, 1954.
Nr.Fine/Fine. **$600**
Good/V.Good. **$400**

Reich, Wilhelm. *The Discovery of the
Orgone / Volume Two/ The Cancer Biopathy*.
First Edition: New York: Orgone Institute
Press, 1948.
Nr.Fine/Fine. **$165**
Good/V.Good. **$85**

Remarque, Erich Maria. *All Quiet on the
Western Front*. First U.S. Edition: Boston:
Little, Brown and Co., 1929.

Nr.Fine/Fine. **$300**
Good/V.Good. **$100**

Commander
Amanda
Nightingale
by George Revelli

Revelli, George. *Commander Amanda Nightingale*. First U.S. Edition: New York: Grove Press, 1968.
Nr.Fine/Fine. **$25**
Good/V.Good. **$10**

Rodriguez, Luis J. *Always Running La Vida Loca: Gang Days in L.A.* First Edition: Willimantic, CT: Curbstone Press, 1993.
Nr.Fine/Fine. **$50**
Good/V.Good. **$20**

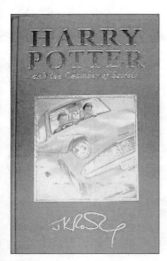

Harry Potter
and The
Chamber of
Secrets
by J.K. Rowling

Rowling, J.K. *Harry Potter Series*. First Editions: Harry Potter and the Philosopher's Stone. London: Bloomsbury, 1997.
Nr.Fine/Fine. **$30000**
Good/V.Good. **$20000**
Harry Potter and the Chamber of Secrets. London: Bloomsbury, 1998.
Nr.Fine/Fine. **$6000**
Good/V.Good. **$2250**
Harry Potter and the Prisoner of Azkaban. London: Bloomsbury, 1999.
Nr.Fine/Fine. $5200
Good/V.Good . . . . $2450.
Harry Potter and the Goblet of Fire. London: Bloomsbury, 2000.
Nr.Fine/Fine. **$1500**
Good/V.Good. **$500**

Rushdie, Salmon. *The Satanic Verses*. First Edition: London: Viking Press, 1988.
Nr.Fine/Fine. **$100**
Good/V.Good. **$45**

Sachar, Louis. *The Boy Who Lost His Face.* First Edition: New York: Alfred A. Knopf, 1989.
Nr.Fine/Fine. **$12**
Good/V.Good. **$8**

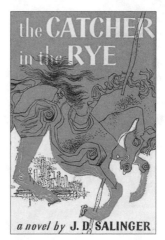

The Catcher in
the Rye
by J.D. Salinger

Salinger, J.D. *The Catcher in the Rye*. First Edition: Boston, Little, Brown & Co., 1951.
Nr.Fine/Fine. **$15000**
Good/V.Good. **$12000**
First U.K. Edition: London: Hamish

Hamilton, 1951.
Nr.Fine/Fine.................. **$1400**
Good/V.Good.................. **$600**
Points of Issue: First state dust jacket
carries a photo of Salinger.

Bent to Evil
by Kim Savage

Savage, Kim. *Bent to Evil*. First Edition:
New York: Vixen, 1952.
Nr.Fine/Fine.................... **$45**
Good/V.Good.................. **$25**

Hellion
by Kim Savage

_____. *Hellion*. First Edition: New
York: Vixen, 1951.
Nr.Fine/Fine.................... **$40**
Good/V.Good.................. **$25**

Schwartz, Alvin. *Cross Your Fingers, Spit
in Your Hat*. First Edition: New York &

Philadelphia: Lippencott, 1974.
Nr.Fine/Fine.................. **$125**
Good/V.Good.................. **$50**

Selby, Hubert, Jr. *Last Exit to Brooklyn*.
First Edition: New York: Grove Press, 1964.
Nr.Fine/Fine.................. **$300**
Good/V.Good.................. **$100**
First U. K. Edition: London: Calder and
Boyars, 1966
Nr.Fine/Fine.................. **$200**
Good/V.Good.................. **$75**

Sendak, Maurice. *In the Night Kitchen*.
First Edition: New York: Harper & Row,
1970.
Nr.Fine/Fine.................. **$650**
Good/V.Good.................. **$275**

Shaw, (George) Bernard. *Plays Pleasant
and Unpleasant: The First Volume,
Containing the Three Unpleasant Plays*.
First Edition: New York: Brentano's, 1905.
Nr.Fine/Fine.................. **$25**
Good/V.Good.................. **$12**

Silverstein, Charles and Felice Picano.
The New Joy of Gay Sex. First Edition: New
York: HarperCollins, 1992.
Nr.Fine/Fine.................. **$30**
Good/V.Good.................. **$15**

Silverstein, Shel. *A Light in the Attic*. First
Edition: New York: Harper & Row, 1981.
Nr.Fine/Fine.................. **$85**

**I Am Curious
(yellow)**
by Vilgot Sjoman

Good/V.Good. **$35**

Sjoman, Vilgot. *I Am Curious (Yellow)*.
First U.S. Edition: New York: Grove, 1960.
Nr.Fine/Fine. **$35**
Good/V.Good. **$20**

Snepp, Frank. *Decent Interval*. First
Edition: New York: Random House, 1977.
Nr.Fine/Fine. **$500**
Good/V.Good. **$300**

Solzhenitsyn, Aleksandr I. *The Gulag
Archipelago*. First English Language
Edition: New York, Evanston, San Francisco
and London: Harper & Row Publishers,
1973.
Nr.Fine/Fine. **$75**
Good/V.Good. **$40**

Steinbeck, John. *The Grapes of Wrath*.
First Edition: New York: Viking Press,
1939.
Nr.Fine/Fine. **$10000**
Good/V.Good. **$4750**

_____. *Of Mice and Men*. First
Edition: New York: The Viking Press, 1939.
Nr.Fine/Fine. **$8500**
Good/V.Good. **$2250**
Points of Issue: First Issue with bullet
between the 8's on page 88 and "and only
moved because the heavy hands were
pendula" on page 9, line 20 and 21 and "J.J.
Little and Ives Company " (versus Haddon
Craftsmen) on copyright page.

Stern, Howard. *Private Parts*. First
Edition: New York: Simon & Schuster,
1993.
Nr.Fine/Fine. **$30**
Good/V.Good. **$10**

Stone, Scott. *Blaze*. First Edition: New
York: Vixen Press, 1954.
Nr.Fine/Fine. **$25**
Good/V.Good. **$12**

Stowe, Harriet Beecher. *Uncle Tom's
Cabin*. First Edition: Boston and Cleveland:
Jewett, Proctor & Worthington, 1852.

Blaze
by Scott Stone

Nr.Fine/Fine. **$21000**
Good/V.Good. **$9500**

Sturges, Jock. *Radiant Identities*. New
York: Aperture, 1994.
Nr.Fine/Fine. **$150**
Good/V.Good. **$75**

Love
by Bernard Talmey

Talmey, Bernard. *Love*. First Edition: New
York: Practitioners' Publishing Co., 1916.
Nr.Fine/Fine. **$45**
Good/V.Good. **$20**

Tjele, Henrik. *Two and Two*. First Edition:
New York: Grove Press, 1970.
Nr.Fine/Fine. **$15**
Good/V.Good. **$9**

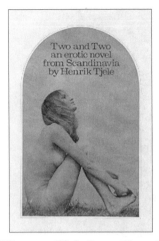

Two and Two
by Henrik Tjele

Oh! Calcutta!
by Kenneth Tynan

Thomas, Piri. *Down These Mean Streets.*
First Edition: New York: Alfred A. Knopf,
1967.
Nr.Fine/Fine. **$125**
Good/V.Good. **$45**

Trumbo, Dalton. *Johnny got His Gun.*
First Edition: Philadelphia: J. B. Lippincott,
1939.
Nr.Fine/Fine. **$1500**
Good/V.Good. **$450**

Twain. Mark (Samuel L. Clemens). *The
Adventures of Huckleberry Finn.* First
Edition: London: Chatto and Windus, 1884.
Nr.Fine/Fine. **$10000**
Good/V.Good. **$4500**
Frist U.S. Edition: New York: Charles L.
Webster and Co., 1885.
Nr.Fine/Fine. **$21000**
Good/V.Good. **$14000**

_____. *The Adventures of
Tom Sawyer.* First U.S. Edition: American
Publishing Co.: Hartford, Chicago,
Cincinnati, 1876.
Nr.Fine/Fine. **$35000**
Good/V.Good. **$15000**

Tynan, Kenneth. *Oh! Calcutta!* First
Edition: New York: Grove Press, 1969.
Nr.Fine/Fine. **$1200**
Good/V.Good. **$700**

*United States Vietnam Relations 1945-1967
(The Pentagon Papers).* First Edition:
Washington, D.C.: United States
Government printing Office, 1971.
Nr.Fine/Fine. **$750**
Good/V.Good. **$300**

Updike, John. *Rabbit Run.* First Edition:
New York: Alfred A. Knopf, 1960.
Nr.Fine/Fine. **$1200**
Good/V.Good. **$700**

Vonnegut, Kurt. *Slaughterhouse-Five; or
The Children's Crusade.* First Edition: New
York: Delecorte Press, 1969.
Nr.Fine/Fine. **$1000**
Good/V.Good. **$450**

Walker, Alice. *The Color Purple.* First
Edition: New York: Harcourt Brace
Jovanovich, 1982.
Nr.Fine/Fine. **$600**
Good/V.Good. **$300**

Willhoite, Michael. *Daddy's Roommate.*
First Edition: Boston: Alyson Wonderland,
1990.
Nr.Fine/Fine. **$35**
Good/V.Good. **$15**

Whitman, Walt. *Leaves of Grass.* First
Edition: Brooklyn, NY: Privately printed,
July 1855.
Nr.Fine/Fine **$125,000**
Good/V.Good **$65,000**
Whitman continued to add and revise the

book so there are several "firsts" of different revisions up to the "Deathbed" edition: David McKay, Philadelphia, 1891-92.
Nr.Fine/Fine. **$500**
Good/V.Good. **$225**

Memoirs of
Hecate County
by Edmund Wilson

Wilson, Edmund. *Memoirs of Hecate County*. First Edition: Garden City, NY: Doubleday & Co. Inc., 1946.
Nr.Fine/Fine. **$350**
Good/V.Good. **$160**

Winsor, Kathleen. *Forever Amber*. First Edition: New York: Macmillan Company, 1944.
Nr.Fine/Fine. **$650**
Good/V.Good. **$325**

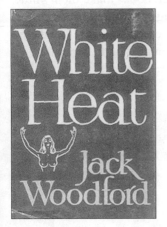

White Heat
by Jack Woodford

Woodford, Jack. *White Heat*. First U.S. Edition: New York: Woodford, 1947.
Nr.Fine/Fine. **$20**
Good/V.Good. **$10**

Spy Catcher
by Peter Wright

Wright, Peter. *Spycatcher*. First Edition: Melbourne: William Heinneman, 1987.
Nr.Fine/Fine. **$45**
Good/V.Good. **$20**
First U.S. Edition: New York: Viking Press, 1987.
Nr.Fine/Fine. **$35**
Good/V.Good. **$15**

Wright, Richard. *Black Boy*. First Edition: New York and London: Harper & Brothers, 1945.
Nr.Fine/Fine. **$400**
Good/V.Good. **$250**
Points of Issue: Stated First Edition with code M-T Dust Jacket-$2.50 price, "5760" on front flap, "5761" on back flap, and "No.2209" on back cover of jacket.

_____. *Native Son*. First Edition: New York: Harper & Brothers, 1940.
Nr.Fine/Fine. **$1000**
Good/V.Good. **$350**
Points of Issue: First state dust jacket is yellow and green.

Zindal, Paul. *The Pigman*. First Edition: New York: Harper & Row, 1968.
Nr.Fine/Fine. $18
Good/V.Good. $10

Biographies

Let's face it, there is a little of the voyeur in all of us. Peeks inside the private world of other people are a source of endless fascination. If the person is prominent, a celebrity, well so much the better. This fascination has carried us through history. We love the gossip, the facts, and the rumors about those we admire. We are also enamored of clay feet, deriving a simple, if satisfying, pleasure from reading about scandals or even small private vices, in those our society seeks to venerate. So, for the last few thousand years, we've been writing it all down.

Biographies also present a personalized view of history. In many cases, the individual view of world events is more accessible to the average reader than the academic exercises that we call history. The impact of history is seen much more clearly in biographies, memoirs, and autobiographies. Many collections of biography center on a particular era in history for this reason.

Other collections I have seen are built around a particular profession or pursuit. Politics, literature, and art are major focal points, but by no means the only focus of biographical collections. One client I have worked with for many years has a collection of movie star biographies, arranged with photoplay editions of their motion pictures. Over the years, I have seen collections of biographies centered on medicine, exploration, philosophy, counter-culture, even one based on eccentricity.

Biography also expands the collector's base for signatures. A biography can be signed by either or both the writer and the subject. The value of such signed editions tends to favor the subject, though, occasionally, the author might be favored based on his relative status with regard to the subject.

A modern trend in biography bases the form on that of a novel. Sometimes a stretch, it provides a readable and enjoyable story for those who aren't enamored of biography per se. Plot devices in such books make them border on fiction, might be called "faction," but they seem to sell well and the trend can probably be counted on to continue.

10 Classic Rarities

Blixen, Karen. *Out Of Africa*. London: Putnam, 1937. Maroon cloth boards stamped in gilt at spine, scarce first of a common book.
Retail value in:
    Near Fine to Fine **$3000**
    Good to Very Good. **$1250**

Churchill, Winston S. *Marlborough. His Life and Times*. London: George G. Harrap & Co. Ltd., 1934-38. 4 vols. Nice value without the blood, sweat or tears.
Retail value in:
    Near Fine to Fine **$4000**
    Good to Very Good **$2500**

(Clay, John) as by: His Eldest Son. *John Clay: A Scottish Farmer*. Chicago: Privately printed, 1906. The founder of a large ranch and cattle company profiles his pioneer father.
Retail value in:
    Near Fine to Fine **$3500**
    Good to Very Good. **$2000**

Darrow, Clarence. *The Story of My Life*. New York: Charles Scribner's Sons, 1932. A limited edition of 294 numbered and signed copies with some unnumbered and signed copies apparently slipping by.
Retail value in:
    Near Fine to Fine **$2500**
    Good to Very Good **$1500**

Graves, Robert. *Good-Bye To All That: An Autobiography*. London: Jonathan Cape. First Edition, 1929. The first state carries a poem by Sassoon Pp 341-343.
Retail value in:
    Near Fine to Fine **$1900**
    Good to Very Good **$1200**

Lewis, Wyndham. *Hitler*. London: Chatto & Windus, 1931. One of the first denunciations of the Nazis, Goebbels pulped or burned every copy he got a hold of.
Retail value in:
    Near Fine to Fine **$1500**
    Good to Very Good **$900**

Nesbit, Evelyn. *Prodigal Days the Untold Story*. New York: Julian Messner, Inc., 1934. Sheds some light on an old scandal.
Retail value in:
    Near Fine to Fine **$4500**
    Good to Very Good **$2500**

Vasari, Giorgio & Gaston du C. de Vere. *Lives of the Most Eminent Painters, Sculptors & Architects: in 10 volumes*. London: Macmillan and Co. & The Medici Society, 1912. THE source for this type of biography.
Retail value in:
    Near Fine to Fine **$2000**
    Good to Very Good **$1250**

Washington, Booker T. *Up From Slavery*. New York: Doubleday, Page & Company, 1901. A best seller in its day, this book should be findable.
Retail value in:
    Near Fine to Fine **$1500**
    Good to Very Good **$900**

Yeats, William Butler. *The Trembling of the Veil*. London: T. Werner Laurie, 1922. There are 1000 copies, signed and numbered, only about half of which can be found.
Retail value in:
    Near Fine to Fine **$1800**
    Good to Very Good **$1000**

Price Guide

Abbott, Jack Henry. *In the Belly of the Beast: Letters from Prison*. First Edition: New York: Random House, 1981.
Nr.Fine/Fine **$50**
Good/V.Good **$25**

Ackerley, J.R. *My Father and Myself*. First Edition: New York: Coward-McCann, 1969.
Nr.Fine/Fine **$55**
Good/V.Good **$30**

Adams, Henry. *The Education of Henry Adams*. First Edition: Boston: Houghton Mifflin, 1918.
Nr.Fine/Fine **$250**
Good/V.Good **$100**

Adams, Samuel Hopkins. *Alexander Woolcott: his Life and his World*. First Edition: New York: Reynal & Hitchcock, 1945.
Nr.Fine/Fine **$20**
Good/V.Good **$8**
First Edition: New York: Hamish Hamilton, 1946.
Nr.Fine/Fine **$16**
Good/V.Good **$7**

Letters of James Agee to Father Flye *by James Agee*

Agee, James. *Letters of James Agee to Father Flye*. First Edition: New York: George Braziller, 1962.
Nr.Fine/Fine **$50**
Good/V.Good **$30**

Amburn, Ellis. *Dark Star: The Roy Orbison Story*. First Edition: Secaucus, NJ: Carol Publishing Group, 1990.
Nr.Fine/Fine **$25**
Good/V.Good **$10**

_____. *Subterranean Kerouac: The Hidden Life of Jack Kerouac*. First Edition: New York: St. Martin's Press, 1998.
Nr.Fine/Fine **$20**
Good/V.Good **$8**

Pearl; the Obsessions and Passions of Janis Joplin *by Ellis Amburn*

_____. *Pearl; the Obsessions and Passions of Janis Joplin*. First Edition: New York: Warner Books, 1992.
Nr.Fine/Fine **$15**
Good/V.Good **$6**

My Life in High Heels *by Loni Anderson and Larkin Warren*

Anderson, Loni, with Warren, Larkin. *My Life in High Heels*. First Edition: New York: William Morrow & Company Inc., 1995.
Nr.Fine/Fine **$15**
Good/V.Good **$6**

Anderson, Sherwood. *Tar: A Midwest*

Childhood. First Edition: New York: Boni and Liveright, 1926.
Nr.Fine/Fine **$85**
Good/V.Good **$45**

Arsan, Emmanuelle. *Emmanuelle*. First Edition: New York: Boni and Liveright, 1926.
Nr.Fine/Fine **$55**
Good/V.Good **$30**

_____. *Emmanuelle II*.
First Edition: New York: Alfred A. Knopf, 1993.
Nr.Fine/Fine **$100**
Good/V.Good **$65**

Ashe, Arthur. *Days of Grace: A Memoir*.
First Edition: New York: Alfred A. Knopf, 1993.
Nr.Fine/Fine **$15**
Good/V.Good **$7**

Asimov, Isaac. *In Memory Yet Green the Autobiography of Isaac Asimov, 1920-1954*. First Edition: Garden City, NY: Doubleday, 1979.
Nr.Fine/Fine $20
Good/V.Good $12

_____. *In Joy Still Felt: The Autobiography of Isaac Asimov, 1964-1978*. First Edition: Garden City, NY: Doubleday & Company, 1980.
Nr.Fine/Fine **$25**
Good/V.Good **$15**

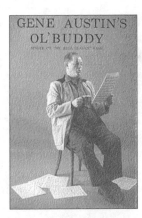

Gene Austin's
Ol' Buddy
by Gene Austin

Auster, Paul. *Hand To Mouth: A Chronicle Of Early Failure*. First Editon: New York: Henry Holt, 1997.
Nr.Fine/Fine **$35**
Good/V.Good **$15**

Austin, Gene. *Gene Austin's Ol' Buddy*.
First Edition: Phoenix, AZ: Augury Press, 1984.
Nr.Fine/Fine **$35**
Good/V.Good **$20**

Bacall, Lauren. *Lauren Bacall By Myself*. First Edition: New York: Alfred A Knopf, 1978.
Nr.Fine/Fine **$35**
Good/V.Good **$10**

Marlene Dietrich
by Stephen Bach

Bach, Stephen. *Marlene Dietrich*. First Edition: New York: William Morrow, 1992.
Nr.Fine/Fine **$20**
Good/V.Good **$12**
First U.K. Edition: London: Harper Collins, 1992 Nr.Fine/Fine **$15**
Good/V.Good **$8**

Baez, Joan. *Daybreak*. First Edition: New York: Dial Press, 1968.
Nr.Fine/Fine **$25**
Good/V.Good **$10**

Bailey, F. Lee. *The Defense Never Rests*. First Edition: New York: Stein and Day, 1971
Nr.Fine/Fine **$20**
Good/V.Good **$10**

Bair, Deirdre. *Simone De Beauvoir: A Biography*. First Edition: New York: Summit Books, 1990.
Nr.Fine/Fine **$20**
Good/V.Good **$8**

_____. *Anais Nin: A Biography*. First Edition: New York: Putnam, 1995.
Nr.Fine/Fine $25
Good/V.Good $10

_____. *Samuel Beckett. A Biography*.First Edition: New York: Harcourt Brace Jovanovich, 1978.
Nr.Fine/Fine . . . . **$**
Good/V.Good . . . . **$**

Baker, Russell. *Growing Up*. First Edition: New York: Congdon & Weed, Inc., 1982.
Nr.Fine/Fine **$25**
Good/V.Good **$10**

Love Lucy
by Lucille Ball

Ball, Lucille. *Love Lucy*. First Edition: New York: G. P. Putnam, 1996.
Nr.Fine/Fine **$20**
Good/V.Good **$8**

Barrows, Sydney Biddle, with Novak, William. *Mayflower Madam*. First Edition: New York: Arbor House, 1986.Nr.Fine/Fine **$15**
Good/V.Good **$6**

Bate, W. Jackson. *Samuel Johnson*. First Edition: New York: Harcourt Brace Jovanovich, 1977.

Nr.Fine/Fine **$20**
Good/V.Good **$9**

Behrman, S.N. *Portrait of Max: An Intimate Memoir of Sir Max Beerbohm*. First Edition: New York: Random House, 1960.
Nr.Fine/Fine **$30**
Good/V.Good **$12**

Benchley, Robert. *Chips Off the Old Benchley*. First Edition: New York: Harper & Brothers, 1949. Nr.Fine/Fine **$35**
Good/V.Good **$15**

Birmingham, Stephen. *The Late John Marquand: A Biography*. First Edition: Philadelphia: J.B. Lippencott Co., 1972
Nr.Fine/Fine **$30**
Good/V.Good **$12**

_____. *Duchess: The Story of Wallis Warfield Windsor*. First Edition: Boston: Little, Brown and Company, 1981.
Nr.Fine/Fine **$15**
Good/V.Good **$8**

Blair, Gwenda. *Almost Golden: Jessica Savitch and the Selling of Television News*. First Edition: New York: Simon & Schuster, 1988.
Nr.Fine/Fine **$12**
Good/V.Good **$5**

Leaving A
Doll's House
by Claire Bloom

Bloom, Claire. *Leaving A Doll's House*. First Edition: Boston: Little Brown, 1996.

Nr.Fine/Fine **$18**
Good/V.Good **$8**

Bok, Edward. *The Americanization of Edward Bok*. First Edition: New York: Charles Scribner's Sons, 1922.
Nr.Fine/Fine **$45**
Good/V.Good **$20**

Bowen, Catherine Drinker. *Yankee from Olympus: Justice Holmes and His Family*.First Edition: Boston: Little, Brown & Company, 1944.
Nr.Fine/Fine **$25**
Good/V.Good **$10**

Brando: Songs My
Mother Taught Me
*by Marlon Brando and
Roberts Lindsey*

Brando, Marlon, with Lindsey, Robert. *Brando: Songs My Mother Taught Me*. First Edition: New York: Random House, 1994.
Nr.Fine/Fine **$12**
Good/V.Good **$6**

Bresler, Fenton. *The Mystery of Georges Simenon: A Biography*. First Edition: London: William Heinemann/Quixote Press, 1983.
Nr.Fine/Fine **$35**
Good/V.Good **$15**
First U.S. Edition: New York, Beaufort, 1983.
Nr.Fine/Fine **$20**
Good/V.Good **$8**

Brightman, Carol. *Writing Dangerously: Mary McCarthy And Her World*. First Edition: New York: Clarkson Potter, 1992.
Nr.Fine/Fine **$25**

Good/V.Good **$12**

Brinnin, John Malcolm. *The Third Rose: Gertrude Stein and Her World*. First Edition: Boston: Little, Brown, 1959.
Nr.Fine/Fine **$35**
Good/V.Good **$20**

_____. *Dylan Thomas in America: An Intimate Journal*.First Edition: Boston: Little, Brown and Company, 1955.
Nr.Fine/Fine **$45**
Good/V.Good **$20**

Courtney Love:
The Real Story
by Poppy Z. Brite

Brite, Poppy Z. *Courtney Love: The Real Story*. First Edition: New York: Simon & Schuster, 1997.
Nr.Fine/Fine **$15**
Good/V.Good **$7**

Frank Harris:
The Life and Loves
of the Scoundrel
by Vincent Brome

Brome, Vincent. *Frank Harris: the Life and Loves of a Scoundrel*. First Edition:

New York: Thomas Yoseloff, 1959.
Nr.Fine/Fine **$25**
Good/V.Good **$15**

Brown, Larry. *On Fire*. First Edition:
Chapel Hill, NC: Algonquin Books, 1994.
Nr.Fine/Fine **$30**
Good/V.Good **$15**

Brownstein, Rachel M. *Tragic Muse:
Rachel of the Comedie-Francaise*. First
Edition: New York: Alfred A. Knopf,
1993.
Nr.Fine/Fine **$45**
Good/V.Good **$20**

Burgess, Anthony. *Flame into Being: the
Life and Work of D.H. Lawrence*. First
Edition: London: Heinemann, 1985.
Nr.Fine/Fine **$30**
Good/V.Good **$20**
First Edition: New York: Arbor House,
1985.
Nr.Fine/Fine **$20**
Good/V.Good **$10**

Burns, George. *Gracie: A Love Story*.
First Edition: New York: G.P. Putnam's,
1988.
Nr.Fine/Fine **$25**
Good/V.Good **$10**

Campbell, James. *Talking at the Gates:
A Life of James Baldwin*. First Edition:
New York: Viking, 1991.
Nr.Fine/Fine **$25**
Good/V.Good **$10**

Canby, Henry Seidel. *Walt Whitman, An
American*. First Edition: Boston:
Houghton, Mifflin, 1943.
Nr.Fine/Fine **$40**
Good/V.Good **$15**

Carr, John Dickson. *The Life Of Sir
Arthur Conan Doyle*. First Edition:
London: John Murray, 1949.
Nr.Fine/Fine **$80**
Good/V.Good **$45**
First Edition: New York: Harper and
Brothers, 1949.
Nr.Fine/Fine **$60**

Good/V.Good **$25**

Cate, Curtis. *George Sand*. First Edition:
Boston: Houghton Mifflin, 1975.
Nr.Fine/Fine **$30**
Good/V.Good **$12**

Cerf, Bennett. *At Random: The
Reminiscences of Bennett Cerf*. First
Edition: New York: Random House, 1977.
Nr.Fine/Fine **$20**
Good/V.Good **$8**

Charters, Ann. *Kerouac: A Biography*.
First Edition: San Francisco: Straight
Arrow Press, 1973.
Nr.Fine/Fine **$50**
Good/V.Good **$30**

Chaplin, Charles. *My Autobiography*.
First Edition: New York: Simon &
Schuster, 1964.
Nr.Fine/Fine $30
Good/V.Good $12

Cheever, John. *The Journals Of John
Cheever*. First Edition: New York: Alfred
A. Knopf, 1991.
Nr.Fine/Fine **$35**
Good/V.Good **$15**

Cheever, Susan. *Home Before Dark: a
Biographical Memoir of John Cheever By
His Daughter*. First Edition: Boston:
Houghton Mifflin, 1984.
Nr.Fine/Fine **$25**
Good/V.Good **$10**

Christie, Agatha. *An Autobiography*. First
Edition: London: Collins, 1977.
Nr.Fine/Fine **$35**
Good/V.Good **$20**
First U.S. Edition: New York: Dodd Mead,
1977.
Nr.Fine/Fine **$25**
Good/V.Good **$10**

Clark, Ronald W. Einstein. *The Life and
Times*. First Edition: New York, World
Publishing, 1971.
Nr.Fine/Fine **$35**
Good/V.Good **$15**

Clarke, Gerald. *Capote: A Biography*. First Edition: New York: Simon & Schuster, 1988.
Nr.Fine/Fine **$45**
Good/V.Good **$15**

Cobb, Irvin S. *Exit Laughing*. First Edition: Indianapolis: Bobbs-Merrill, 1941.
Nr.Fine/Fine **$45**
Good/V.Good **$20**

In My Own Words
by Mickey Cohen

Cohen, Mickey. *In My Own Words*. First Edition: Englewood Cliffs, NJ: Prentice-Hall, 1975.
Nr.Fine/Fine **$75**
Good/V.Good **$40**

Colson, Charles W. *Born Again: What Really Happened to the White House Hatchet Man*. First Edition: Old Tappan, NJ: Fleming H. Revell (Chosen Books), 1976.
Nr.Fine/Fine **$15**
Good/V.Good $6

Connell, Evan S. *Son of the Morning Star*. First Edition: San Francisco: North Point Press, 1984.
Nr.Fine/Fine **$175**
Good/V.Good **$85**

Coward, Noel. *Present Indicative*. First Edition: London: William Heinemann Ltd., 1937.
Nr.Fine/Fine **$75**
Good/V.Good **$45**

First Edition: New York: Doubleday, Doran & Co., Inc., 1937.
Nr.Fine/Fine **$35**
Good/V.Good **$15**

Cowley, Malcolm. *Exile's Return*. First Edition: New York: Norton, 1934.
Nr.Fine/Fine **$500**
Good/V.Good **$275**
First U.K. Edition: London: Jonathon Cape, 1935.
Nr.Fine/Fine **$400**
Good/V.Good **$250**
Limited/Signed: New York: Limited Editions Club, 1981.
Nr.Fine/Fine **$300**
Good/V.Good **$150**

Craven, Margaret. *Again Calls The Owl*. First Edition: New York: Putnam, 1980.
Nr.Fine/Fine **$25**
Good/V.Good **$10**

Cronkite, Walter. *A Reporter's Life*. First Edition: New York: Alfred A Knopf, 1996.
Nr.Fine/Fine **$15**
Good/V.Good **$8**

Day, Donald. *Will Rogers: A Biography*. First Edition: New York: David McKay, 1962.
Nr.Fine/Fine **$25**
Good/V.Good **$10**

Dean, John. *Blind Ambition: The White House Years*. First Edition: New York: Simon & Schuster, 1976.
Nr.Fine/Fine **$20**
Good/V.Good **$8**

Dillard, Annie. *An American Childhood*. First Edition: New York: Harper & Row, 1987.
Nr.Fine/Fine **$15**
Good/V.Good **$6**

_____. *The Writing Life*. First Edition: New York: Harper & Row, 1989.
Nr.Fine/Fine **$15**
Good/V.Good **$6**

Dillon, Millicent, ed. *Out in the World: Selected Letters of Jane Bowles 1935-1970*. First Edition (Signed & Limited): Santa Barbara: Black Sparrow, 1985.
Nr.Fine/Fine **$60**
Good/V.Good **$35**

_____. *A Little Original Sin: The Life and Work of Jane Bowles*. First Edition: New York: Holt, Rinehart and Winston, 1981.
Nr.Fine/Fine **$45**
Good/V.Good **$25**

Donald, David H. *Look Homeward: A Life of Thomas Wolfe*. First Edition: Boston: Little, Brown and Co., 1987.
Nr.Fine/Fine **$35**
Good/V.Good **$20**

Donaldson, Scott. *John Cheever: A Biography*. First Edition: New York: Random House, 1988.
Nr.Fine/Fine **$25**
Good/V.Good **$10**

_____. *Archibald MacLeish: An American Life*. First Edition: Boston: Houghton Mifflin Co., 1992.
Nr.Fine/Fine **$24**
Good/V.Good **$10**

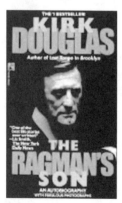
The Ragman's Son
by Kirk Douglas

Douglas, Kirk. *The Ragman's Son*. First Edition: New York: Simon & Schuster, 1988.
Nr.Fine/Fine **$25**
Good/V.Good **$12**

Drabble, Margaret. *Angus Wilson: A Biography*. First Edition: London: Secker & Warburg, 1995.
Nr.Fine/Fine **$20**
Good/V.Good **$12**

Dunaway, David King. *Huxley in Hollywood*. First Edition: New York: Harper & Row, 1989.
Nr.Fine/Fine **$25**
Good/V.Good **$10**

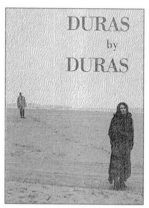
Duras by Duras
by Marguerite Duras

Duras, Marguerite. *Duras by Duras*. First Edition: San Francisco: City Lights Books, 1987.Nr.Fine/Fine **$12**
Good/V.Good **$6**

Edwards, Anne. *Sonya. The Life of Countess Tolstoy*. First Edition: New York: Simon and Schuster, 1981.
Nr.Fine/Fine **$20**
Good/V.Good **$8**

Elledge, Scott. *E. B. White: A Biography*. First Edition: New York: W. W. Norton & Company, 1984.
Nr.Fine/Fine **$25**
Good/V.Good **$15**

Ellmann, Richard. *Oscar Wilde*. First Edition: London: Hamish Hamilton, 1987.
Nr.Fine/Fine **$85**
Good/V.Good **$45**
First U.S. Edition: New York: Knopf : Distributed by Random House, 1988.
Nr.Fine/Fine **$35**

Good/V.Good $15

_____. *James Joyce*. First
Edition: New York: Oxford University
Press, 1959.
Nr.Fine/Fine $45
Good/V.Good $25

Epstein, Edward Jay. *Legend: The Secret
World of Lee Harvey Oswald*. First
Edition: New York: McGraw Hill, 1978.
Nr.Fine/Fine $20
Good/V.Good $12

Fast, Howard. *Being Red: A Memoir*.
First Edition: Boston: Houghton Mifflin
Co., 1990.
Nr.Fine/Fine $25
Good/V.Good $12

Field, Andrew. *Nabokov: His Life in Art*.
First Edition: Boston: Little, Brown,
1967.
Nr.Fine/Fine $45
Good/V.Good $25

Winchell, Gossip,
Power and the
Culture of Celebrity.
by Neal Gabler

Gabler, Neal. *Winchell, Gossip, Power
and the Culture of Celebrity*. First
Edition: New York: Alfred A. Knopf,
1994.
Nr.Fine/Fine $20
Good/V.Good $8

Galbraith, John Kenneth. *A Life in our
Times*. First Edition: Boston: Houghton
Mifflin Co., 1981.

Nr.Fine/Fine $35
Good/V.Good $15

_____. *Ambassador's
Journal: A Personal Account of the
Kennedy Years*. First Edition: Boston:
Houghton Mifflin, 1969.
Nr.Fine/Fine $20
Good/V.Good $8

Gide, Andre. *The Journals of Andre
Gide*. (Four Volumes)First Edition:
London: Secker & Warburg, 1947-1949.
Nr.Fine/Fine $100. Good/V.Good
$65.First Edition: New York. Alfred A.
Knopf, 1947-1951.
Nr.Fine/Fine $85
Good/V.Good $45

Gifford, Barry and Lawrence Lee.
*Jack's Book: An Oral Biography of Jack
Kerouac*. First Edition: New York: St
Martin's, 1978.
Nr.Fine/Fine $50
Good/V.Good $20

Gifford, Frank. *The Whole Ten Yards*.
First Edition: New York: Random House,
1993.
Nr.Fine/Fine $25
Good/V.Good $10

Gill, Brendan. *Here At The New Yorker*.
First Edition: New York: Random House,
1975.
Nr.Fine/Fine $25
Good/V.Good $12

The Frog Prince:
An Autobiography
by Maurice Girodias

Girodias, Maurice. *The Frog Prince: An Autobiography*. First Edition: New York: Crown, 1980.
Nr.Fine/Fine **$35**
Good/V.Good **$15**

Glendinning, Victoria. *Rebecca West: A Life*. First Edition: London: Weidenfeld & Nicolson, 1987.
Nr.Fine/Fine **$45**
Good/V.Good **$20**
First Edition: New York: Alfred A. Knopf, 1987.
Nr.Fine/Fine **$25**
Good/V.Good **$10**

_____. *Vita-A Biography of Vita Sackville-West*.First Edition: London: Weidenfeld & Nicolson, 1983.
Nr.Fine/Fine $45
Good/V.Good $20
First Edition: New York: Alfred A. Knopf, 1983.
Nr.Fine/Fine $35
Good/V.Good $15

_____. *Tollope*.First Edition: London: Hutchinson, 1992.
Nr.Fine/Fine **$30**
Good/V.Good **$10**
First Edition: New York: Alfred A. Knopf, 1992.
Nr.Fine/Fine **$25**
Good/V.Good **$8**

Goldman, Albert. *The Lives Of John Lennon*. First Edition: New York: William Morrow, 1988.
Nr.Fine/Fine **$30**
Good/V.Good **$15**

_____. *Ladies and Gentlemen: Lenny Bruce!!* First Edition: New York: Random House, 1974.
Nr.Fine/Fine **$35**
Good/V.Good **$18**

Gray, Francine du Plessix. *Rage and Fire a Life of Louise Colet Pioneer Feminist, Literary Star, Flaubert's Muse*. First Edition: New York: Simon &

Schuster, 1994.
Nr.Fine/Fine **$30**
Good/V.Good **$12**

Griffin, Peter. *Along With Youth: Hemingway, The Early Years*. First Edition: New York: Oxford University Press, 1985.
Nr.Fine/Fine **$45**
Good/V.Good **$25**

_____. *Less Than a Treason: Hemingway in Paris*.First Edition: New York: Oxford University Press, 1990.
Nr.Fine/Fine **$25**
Good/V.Good **$15**

Hale, Janet Campbell. *Bloodlines: Odyssey of A Native Daughter*. First Edition: New York: Random House, 1993.
Nr.Fine/Fine **$20**
Good/V.Good **$12**

Gentleman of Leisure A Year in the Life of a Pimp.
by Susan Hall

A Drinking Life.
by Pete Hamill

Hall, Susan. *Gentleman of Leisure A Year in the Life of A Pimp*. First Edition: New York: New American Library/Prairie Press, 1972
Nr.Fine/Fine **$65**
Good/V.Good **$35**

Hamill, Pete. *A Drinking Life*. First Edition: Boston: Little, Brown, 1994.
Nr.Fine/Fine **$35**
Good/V.Good **$15**

Hammarskjold, Dag. *Markings*. First Edition in English: New York: Alfred A Knopf, 1964. Nr.Fine/Fine. **$45**
Good/V.Good **$20**

Hamilton, Ian. *Robert Lowell*. First Edition: New York: Random House, 1982.
Nr.Fine/Fine **$35**
Good/V.Good **$20**

Harrer, Heinrich. *Seven Years in Tibet*. First Edition in English: London: Rupert Hart-Davis, 1953.
Nr.Fine/Fine $85
Good/V.Good $45
First U.S. Edition: New York: E.P. Dutton, 1954. Nr.Fine/Fine **$75**
Good/V.Good **$40**

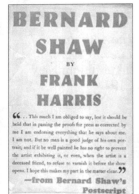

Bernard Shaw. An Unauthorized Biography Based on Firsthand Information. With a Postscript by Mr. Shaw
by Frank Harris

Harris, Frank. *Bernard Shaw. An Unauthorized Biography Based on Firsthand Information. With a Postscript by Mr. Shaw*. First Edition: London: Victor Gollancz Ltd., 1931
Nr.Fine/Fine **$125**

Good/V.Good **$60**
First U.S. Edition: New York: Simon and Schuster, 1931
Nr.Fine/Fine **$55**
Good/V.Good **$30**

_____. *Oscar Wilde His Life and Confessions*. First Edition: New York: Frank Harris, 1918.
Nr.Fine/Fine **$300**
Good/V.Good **$175**

_____. *New Preface To "The Life and Confessions of Oscar Wilde."* First Edition: London: The Fortune Press, 1925.
Nr.Fine/Fine **$65**
Good/V.Good **$35**
First U.S. Edition *(as-Oscar Wilde; including the hitherto unpublished Full and final confession by Lord Alfred Douglas and My memories of Oscar Wilde by George Bernard Shaw.)* New York: Covici. Friede, 1930.
Nr.Fine/Fine **$75**
Good/V.Good **$45**

Hart, Moss. *Act One: An Autobiography*. First Edition: New York: Random House, 1959.
Nr.Fine/Fine **$50**
Good/V.Good **$30**

Hathaway, Katharine Butler. *The Little Locksmith*. First Edition: New York: Coward-McCann, 1943.
Nr.Fine/Fine **$25**
Good/V.Good **$10**

Hellman, Lillian. *Scoundrel Time*. First Edition: Boston: Little, Brown, 1976.
Nr.Fine/Fine **$35**
Good/V.Good **$20**

_____. *An Unfinished Woman*. First Edition: Boston: Little Brown, 1969.
Nr.Fine/Fine **$45**
Good/V.Good **$25**

_____. *Pentimento: A Book of Portraits*. First Edition: Boston: Little, Brown, 1973.

Nr.Fine/Fine **$35**
Good/V.Good **$25**

Hemingway, Ernest. *A Moveable Feast: Sketches of the author's life in Paris in the Twenties*. First Edition: New York: Scribners, 1964.
Nr.Fine/Fine **$300**
Good/V.Good **$125**

_____. *The Dangerous Summer*. First Edition: New York: Scribners; 1985.
Nr.Fine/Fine **$150**
Good/V.Good **$50**

_____. *The Green Hills of Africa*. First Edition: New York: Scribner's, 1935
Nr.Fine/Fine **$3000**
Good/V.Good **$1800**

Hemingway, Gregory H. *Papa—A Personal Memoir*. First Edition: Boston: Houghton Mifflin, 1976. Nr.Fine/Fine**$30**
Good/V.Good **$12**

Hemingway, Jack. *Misadventures of a Fly Fisherman: My Life With & Without Papa*. First Edition: Lanham, MD: Taylor Publishing Company, 1986.
Nr.Fine/Fine **$50**
Good/V.Good **$20**

Hemingway, Mary Welsh. *How It Was*. First Edition: New York: Alfred A. Knopf, 1976.
Nr.Fine/Fine **$45**
Good/V.Good **$25**

Herrmann, Dorothy. *S.J. Perelman A Life*. First Edition: New York: G.P. Putnam's Sons, 1986.
Nr.Fine/Fine **$35**
Good/V.Good **$15**

Heymann, C. David. *Poor Little Rich Girl*. First Edition: New York: Random House, 1983. Nr.Fine/Fine. **$30**
Good/V.Good **$12**

_____. *A Woman Named Jackie*. First Edition: Secaucus, NJ: Carol

Publishing Group, 1989. Nr.Fine/Fine**$25**
Good/V.Good **$10**

_____. *Liz: An Intimate Biography of Elizabeth Taylor*. First Edition: New York: Birch Lane Press, 1995.
Nr.Fine/Fine **$15**
Good/V.Good **$8**

Errol Flynn:
The Untold Story
by Charles Higham

Higham, Charles. *Errol Flynn: The Untold Story*. First Edition: New York: Doubleday, 1980.
Nr.Fine/Fine **$45**
Good/V.Good **$25**

_____. *Lucy: The Real Life of Lucille Ball*. First Edition: New York: St. Martin's Press, 1986.
Nr.Fine/Fine **$35**
Good/V.Good **$15**

_____. *The Adventures of Conan Doyle: The Life of Creator of Sherlock Holmes*. First Edition: New York: W.W. Norton, 1976.
Nr.Fine/Fine **$25**
Good/V.Good **$10**

Hobson, Laura Z. *Laura Z. A Life*. First Edition: New York: Arbor House, 1983.
Nr.Fine/Fine **$20**
Good/V.Good **$8**

Holmes, Charles S. *The Clocks of Columbus. The Literary Career of James Thurber*. First Edition: New York: Atheneum, 1972.
Nr.Fine/Fine **$30**
Good/V.Good **$12**

Holmes Jr., Oliver Wendell. *Touched with Fire Civil War Letters and Diary*. First Edition: Cambridge, MA: Harvard University Press, 1946.
Nr.Fine/Fine **$25**
Good/V.Good **$15**

Holroyd, Michael. *Lytton Strachey: A Critical Biography*. First Edition: New York: Holt, Rinehart & Winston, 1967.
Nr.Fine/Fine $100
Good/V.Good $45

_____. *Augustus John-A Biography*. (Two Volumes) First Edition: Chatham, Kent: Printed by W. & J. Mackay for William Heinemann, 1974-1975. Nr.Fine/Fine **$400**
Good/V.Good **$175**

_____. *Bernard Shaw; A Biography*. (5 Volumes) First Edition: London: Chatto & Windus, 1988-1992.
Nr.Fine/Fine **$150**
Good/V.Good **$85**

Hotchner, A.E. *Papa Hemingway*. First Edition: New York: Random House, 1966.
Nr.Fine/Fine **$50**
Good/V.Good **$20**

Howard, John Tasker. *Stephen Foster: America's Troubadour*. First Edition: New York: Thomas Y. Crowell: 1934.
Nr.Fine/Fine **$50**
Good/V.Good **$30**

A Margin of Hope:
An Intellectual
Autobiography.
by Irving Howe

Howe, Irving. *A Margin of Hope: An*

Intellectual Autobiography. First Edition: New York: Harcourt Brace Jovanovich, 1982.
Nr.Fine/Fine **$25**
Good/V.Good **$10**

Huffington, Arianna Stassinopoulos. *Picasso: Creator and Destroyer*. First Edition: New York: Simon and Schuster, 1988.
Nr.Fine/Fine **$12**
Good/V.Good **$6**

Huntley, Chet. *The Generous Years Remembrances of a Frontier Boyhood*. First Edition: New York: Random House, 1968.
Nr.Fine/Fine **$12**
Good/V.Good **$5**

Huxley, Elspeth. *The Flame Trees of Thika: Memories of an African Childhood*. First Edition: London: Chatto & Windus, 1959.
Nr.Fine/Fine **$60**
Good/V.Good **$25**
First U.S. Edition: New York: William Morrow and Co., 1959.
Nr.Fine/Fine $30
Good/V.Good $15

Huxley, Laura Archera. *This Timeless Moment: A Personal View of Aldous Huxley.*First Edition: New York: Farrar, Straus & Giroux, 1968.
Nr.Fine/Fine **$60**
Good/V.Good **$25**
First U.K. Edition: London: Chatto &

Iacocca An
Autobiography
*by Lee Iacocca and
William Novak*

Windus, 1969.
Nr.Fine/Fine **$30**
Good/V.Good **$15**

Iacocca, Lee (w/William Novak).
Iacocca An Autobiography. First Edition:
New York: Bantam Books, 1984.
Nr.Fine/Fine **$12**
Good/V.Good **$6**

Jackson, Shirley. *Life Among the
Savages.* First Edition: New York: Farrar,
Straus, & Young, 1953.
Nr.Fine/Fine $150
Good/V.Good $65

Johnson, Diane. *Dashiell Hammett: A
Life.*First Edition: New York: Random
House, 1983. Nr.Fine/Fine. **$35**
Good/V.Good **$15**

Johnson, Edgar. *Charles Dickens: His
Tragedy and Triumph.* (Two Volumes)
First Edition: Boston: Little, Brown and
Co., 1952.
Nr.Fine/Fine **$75**
Good/V.Good **$40**

Johnson, Lyndon B. *The Vantage Point:
Perspectives of the Presidency, 1963-
1969.* First Edition: New York: Holt,
Rinehart and Winston, 1971.
Nr.Fine/Fine **$25**
Good/V.Good **$10**

Kalb, Marvin & Kalb, Bernard.
Kissinger. First Edition: Boston: Little,
Brown and Company, 1974.
Nr.Fine/Fine **$30**
Good/V.Good **$12**

Kanin, Garson. *Tracy and Hepburn an
Intimate Memoir.* First Edition: New
York: Viking Press, 1971.
Nr.Fine/Fine **$30**
Good/V.Good **$15**

Kaplan, Justin. *Mr. Clemens and Mark
Twain: A Biography.* First Edition: New
York: Simon and Schuster, 1966.
Nr.Fine/Fine **$75**
Good/V.Good **$35**

_____. *Walt Whitman: A Life.*
First Edition: New York: Simon and
Schuster, 1980.
Nr.Fine/Fine **$30**
Good/V.Good **$12**

Karr, Mary. *The Liar's Club.* First
Edition: New York: Viking, 1995.
Nr.Fine/Fine **$75**
Good/V.Good **$25**

Kazin, Alfred. *New York Jew.* First
Edition: New York: Alfred A. Knopf,
1978.
Nr.Fine/Fine **$45**
Good/V.Good **$20**

Keats, John. *You Might As Well Live The
Life and Times of Dorothy Parker.* First
Edition: New York: Simon and Schuster,
1970. Nr.Fine/Fine **$40**
Good/V.Good **$15**

Kelley, Kitty. *His Way: Unauthorized
Biography.* First Edition: New York:
Bantam Books, 1986.
Nr.Fine/Fine **$20**
Good/V.Good **$10**

_____. *Nancy Reagan: The
Unauthorized Biography.* First Edition:
New York: Simon & Schuster, 1991.
Nr.Fine/Fine **$15**
Good/V.Good **$6**

Kennedy, John F. *Profiles in Courage.*
First Edition: New York: Harper &
Brothers, 1956.
Nr.Fine/Fine **$300**
Good/V.Good **$100**

Kincaid, Jamaica. *My Brother.* First
Edition: New York: Farrar Straus Giroux,
1997. Nr.Fine/Fine **$55**
Good/V.Good **$20**

Kreyling, Michael. *Author and Agent
Eudora Welty and Diarmuid Russell.* First
Edition: New York: Farrar Straus Giroux,
1991. Nr.Fine/Fine **$25**
Good/V.Good **$15**

Krutch, Joseph Wood. *Samuel Johnson.*

First Edition: New York: Henry Holt and Company, 1944.
Nr.Fine/Fine **$40**
Good/V.Good **$25**

Kuralt, Charles. *A Life on the Road.* First Edition: New York: G.P. Putnam, 1990. Nr.Fine/Fine **$20**
Good/V.Good **$8**

L'Amour, Louis. *Education of a Wandering Man.* First Edition: New York: Bantam Books, 1989.
Nr.Fine/Fine **$30**
Good/V.Good **$12**

Lacey, Robert. *Sir Walter Raleigh.* First Edition: New York: Atheneum, 1974.
Nr.Fine/Fine **$15**
Good/V.Good **$8**

_____. *Ford: The Men and the Machine.* First Edition: Boston: Little, Brown and Company, 1986.
Nr.Fine/Fine **$25**
Good/V.Good **$10**

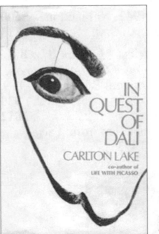

In Quest of Dali.
by Carlton Lake

Lake, Carlton. *In Quest Of Dali.* First Edition: New York: G.P. Putnam's, 1969.
Nr.Fine/Fine **$35**
Good/V.Good **$15**

_____ **& Gilot, Francoise**. *Life with Picasso.* First Edition: New York: McGraw-Hill Book Company, 1964.
Nr.Fine/Fine **$25**

Good/V.Good **$12**

Lash, Joseph P. *Eleanor: The Years Alone,* First Edition: New York: W. W. Norton, 1972. Nr.Fine/Fine **$55**
Good/V.Good **$30**

Leamer, Laurence. *King of The Night: Life of Johnny Carson.* First Edition: New York: Morrow & Co., 1989.Nr.Fine/Fine **$12**
Good/V.Good **$5**

Lee, Lawrence and Gifford, Barry. *Saroyan: A Biography.* First Edition: New York: Harper & Row, 1984. Nr.Fine/Fine **$20**
Good/V.Good **$8**

Leggett, John. *Ross & Tom Two American Tragedies.* First Edition: New York: Simon and Schuster, 1974.
Nr.Fine/Fine **$35**
Good/V.Good **$15**

Levin, Harry. *James Joyce. A Critical Introduction.* First Edition: Norfolk, CT.: New Directions Books, 1941.Nr.Fine/Fine **$40**
Good/V.Good **$25**

Lewis, C.S. *Surprised By Joy: The Shape of My Early Life.* First Edition: London: Geoffrey Bles, 1955. Nr.Fine/Fine . **$150**
Good/V.Good **$65**
First U.S. Edition: New York: Harcourt, Brace and Co., 1956. Nr.Fine/Fine . **$45**
Good/V.Good **$25**

The Joker is Wild
by Joe E. Lewis

Lewis, Joe E. *The Joker is Wild.* First

Edition: New York: Random House, 1955.
Nr.Fine/Fine **$65**
Good/V.Good **$25**

Emma Hamilton
by Nora Lofts

Lofts, Nora. *Emma Hamilton*. First
Edition: New York: Coward, McCann, &
Geoghegan, 1978.
Nr.Fine/Fine **$25**
Good/V.Good **$12**

Lovell, Mary S. *Straight On Till
Morning; The Biography of Beryl
Markham*. First Edition: New York: St.
Martins, 1987. Nr.Fine/Fine **$20**
Good/V.Good **$8**

_____. *The Sound of Wings: The
Life of Amelia Earhart*. First Edition: New
York: St. Martin's Press, 1989.
Nr.Fine/Fine **$25**
Good/V.Good **$10**

MacArthur, Douglas. *Reminiscences*.
First Edition: New York: McGraw-Hill,
1964. Nr.Fine/Fine **$45**

Good/V.Good **$25**

Malraux, Andre. *Anti-Memoirs*. First
Edition in English: New York: Holt,
Rinehart, Winston, 1968.
Nr.Fine/Fine **$30**
Good/V.Good **$15**

Manchester, William. *American Caesar-
Douglas MacArthur 1880-1964*. First
Edition: Boston: Little Brown, 1978.
Nr.Fine/Fine **$20**
Good/V.Good **$8**

Manso, Peter. *Mailer His Life and Times*
First Edition: New York: Simon &
Schuster, 1985.Nr.Fine/Fine **$20**
Good/V.Good **$10**

Maquet, Albert. *Albert Camus: The
Invincible Summer*. First Edition in
English: New York: George Braziller,
1958. Nr.Fine/Fine **$35**
Good/V.Good **$20**

Markham, Beryl. *West With the Night*.
First Edition: Boston: Houghton, Mifflin
and Company, 1942. Nr.Fine/Fine . **$600**
Good/V.Good **$325**

Marnham, Patrick. *The Man Who Wasn't
Maigret a Portrait of Georges Simenon*.
First Edition: London: Bloomsbury, 1992.
Nr.Fine/Fine **$30**
Good/V.Good **$12**
First U.S. Edition: New York: Farrar
Straus Giroux, 1993.

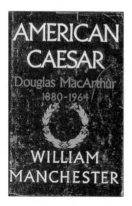

American Caesar
Douglas MacArthur
by William Manchester

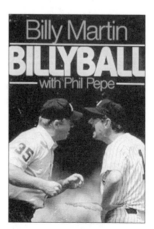

Billyball
by Billy Martin with
Phil Pepe

Nr.Fine/Fine **$25**
Good/V.Good **$10**

Martin, Billy. With Phil Pepe. *Billyball.*
First Edition: Garden City, NY:
Doubleday Inc., 1987.
Nr.Fine/Fine **$20**
Good/V.Good **$12**

Martin, Ralph G. *Jennie: The Life of
Lady Randolph Churchill 2 Volumes: Vol.1
The Romantic Years 1854-1895 & Vol.2
The Dramatic Years 1895-1921*. First
Edition: Englewood Cliffs, NJ: Prentice
Hall, 1969-1971. Nr.Fine/Fine **$45**
Good/V.Good **$20**

_____. *The Woman He Loved
the Story of the Duke & Duchess of
Windsor*. First Edition: New York: Simon
and Schuster, 1974. Nr.Fine/Fine. . . **$25**
Good/V.Good **$10**

Marx, Groucho. *Memoirs of a Mangy
Lover.* First Edition: New York: Bernard
Geis Associates, 1963.
Nr.Fine/Fine **$65**
Good/V.Good **$30**

Massie, Robert K. *Nicholas and
Alexandra*. First Edition: New York:
Atheneum, 1967.
Nr.Fine/Fine **$30**
Good/V.Good **$12**

Maugham, W. Somerset. *The Summing
Up.* (limited and signed): Garden City,
NY: Doubleday & Company, 1954.
Nr.Fine/Fine **$600**
Good/V.Good **$325**
First Edition: London: William
Heinemann, LTD., 1938.
Nr.Fine/Fine **$75**
Good/V.Good **$45**
First Edition: New York: Doubleday,
Doran, 1938.
Nr.Fine/Fine **$35**
Good/V.Good **$20**

Maurois, Andre. *Disraeli: A Picture of
the Victorian Age*. First Edition: New
York: D. Appleton & Company, 1928.

Nr.Fine/Fine **$50**
Good/V.Good **$30**

Mayfield, Sara. *The Constant Circle.
H.L. Mencken and His Friends*. First
Edition: New York: Delacorte Press, 1968.
Nr.Fine/Fine **$40**
Good/V.Good **$15**

Maynard, Joyce. *At Home in the World:
A Memoir*. First Edition: New York:
Picador, 1998.
Nr.Fine/Fine **$15**
Good/V.Good **$8**

Mayle, Peter. *A Year in Provience*. First
Edition: London: Hamish Hamilton,
1992.
Nr.Fine/Fine $25
Good/V.Good $12
First U.S. Edition: New York: Alfred A.
Knopf, 1990.
Nr.Fine/Fine $20
Good/V.Good $8

McCall, Nathan. *Makes Me Wanna
Holler: A Young Black Man in America*.
First Edition: New York: Random House,
1994.
Nr.Fine/Fine **$25**
Good/V.Good **$10**

Up 'til Now:
A Memoir
by Eugene McCarthy

McCarthy, Eugene. *Up 'til Now: A
Memoir*. First Edition: San Diego:
Harcourt Brace Jovanovich, 1987.
Nr.Fine/Fine **$15**

Good/V.Good **$7**

McCarthy, Mary. *How I Grew*. First Edition: New York: Harcourt Brace Jovanovich, 1987.
Nr.Fine/Fine **$25**
Good/V.Good **$12**

McCourt, Malachy. *A Monk Swimming*. First Edition: New York: Hyperion, 1998.
Nr.Fine/Fine **$25**
Good/V.Good **$10**

McGinniss, Joe. *The Last Brother*. First Edition: New York: Simon & Schuster, 1993.
Nr.Fine/Fine **$20**
Good/V.Good **$8**

Mead, Margaret. *Blackberry Winter: My Earlier Years*. First Edition: New York: William Morrow & Co., 1972.
Nr.Fine/Fine **$25**
Good/V.Good **$10**
First U.K. Edition: London: Angus & Robertson, 1973.
Nr.Fine/Fine **$20**
Good/V.Good **$8**

Mellow, James R. *Invented Lives: The Marriage of F. Scott & Zelda Fitzgerald*. First Edition: Boston & New York: Houghton Mifflin Company, 1984.
Nr.Fine/Fine **$45**
Good/V.Good **$25**

_____. *Charmed Circle: Gertrude Stein & Company.*First Edition: New York: Praeger Publishers, 1974.
Nr.Fine/Fine **$25**
Good/V.Good **$12**

_____. *Nathaniel Hawthorne and His Times*.
First Edition: Boston: Houghton Mifflin, 1980.
Nr.Fine/Fine **$20**
Good/V.Good **$8**

Middlebrook, Diane Wood. *Anne Sexton*. First Edition: Boston: Houghton Mifflin, 1991.

Nr.Fine/Fine **$20**
Good/V.Good **$8**

Miles, Barry. *Ginsberg*. First Edition: New York: Simon and Schuster, 1989.
Nr.Fine/Fine **$25**
Good/V.Good **$10**

Milford, Nancy. *Zelda*. First Edition: New York: Harper and Row, 1970.
Nr.Fine/Fine **$40**
Good/V.Good **$15**

Miller, Arthur. *Timebends, A Life*. First Edition: New York: Grove Press, 1987.
Nr.Fine/Fine **$35**
Good/V.Good **$15**

Miller, Donald L. *Lewis Mumford, A Life*. First Edition: New York: Weidenfeld & Nicolson, 1989.
Nr.Fine/Fine **$15**
Good/V.Good **$8**

Miller, Merle. *Plain Speaking: An Oral Biography of Harry S. Truman*. First Edition: New York: Berkley, 1974.
Nr.Fine/Fine **$30**
Good/V.Good` **$12**

W.C. Fields & Me
by Carlotta Monti with Cy Rice

Monti, Carlotta (w/Cy Rice). *W.C. Fields & Me.*First Edition: Englewood Cliffs, NJ: Prentice-Hall, Inc., 1971.
Nr.Fine/Fine **$20**
Good/V.Good **$9**

Mowat, Farley. *Woman in the Mist: The Story of Dianne Fossey and the Mountain*

Gorillas of Africa. First Edition: New York: Warner Books, 1987.
Nr.Fine/Fine **$12**
Good/V.Good **$6**

Nabokov, Vladimir. *Speak, Memory*.First Edition: London: Victor Gollancz Ltd., 1951.
Nr.Fine/Fine $350
Good/V.Good $175

Nin, Anais. *The Diary of Anais Nin Volumes 1 & 2*.First U.S. Editions: The Swallow Press, and Harcourt Brace & World, Inc. 1964-1966.
Nr.Fine/Fine **$35**
Good/V.Good **$15**

_____. *The Diary of Anais Nin. Volumes 3-7*. First U.S. Editions: San Diego & New York, Harcourt Brace et al, 1969-1980.
Nr.Fine/Fine **$20**
Good/V.Good **$10**

_____. *Incest*. First Edition: New York: Harcourt, Brace Jovanovich, 1992.
Nr.Fine/Fine **$30**
Good/V.Good **$15**

_____. *Henry and June*. First Edition: San Diego and New York: Harcourt Brace Jovanovich, 1986.
Nr.Fine/Fine **$35**
Good/V.Good **$20**

Niven, David. *The Moon's a Balloon*. First Edition: New York: G. P. Putnam, 1972
Nr.Fine/Fine **$10**
Good/V.Good **$5**

_____. *Bring on the Empty Horses*. First Edition: New York: G. P. Putnam, 1975.
Nr.Fine/Fine **$15**
Good/V.Good **$8**
First U.K. Edition: London: Hamish Hamilton, 1976. Nr.Fine/Fine **$15**
Good/V.Good **$8**

Nizer, Louis. *The Jury Returns*. First

Edition: Garden City, NY: Doubleday & Co., 1966.
Nr.Fine/Fine **$20**
Good/V.Good **$8**

Nolan, Christopher. *Under the Eye of the Clock: The Life Story of Christopher Nolan*. First Edition: London: Weidenfeld & Nicholson, 1987.
Nr.Fine/Fine **$45**
Good/V.Good **$20**
First U.S. Edition: New York: St. Martin's Press, 1987.
Nr.Fine/Fine **$25**
Good/V.Good **$10**

North, Sterling. *Rascal: A Memoir of a Better Era*. First Edition: New York: E. P. Dutton, 1963.
Nr.Fine/Fine **$30**
Good/V.Good **$15**

Nowell, Elizabeth. *Thomas Wolfe: A Biography*. First Edition: Garden City, N.Y.: Doubleday & Company, 1960.
Nr.Fine/Fine **$25**
Good/V.Good **$10**

I Remember: Sketch for an Autobiography
by Boris Pasternak

Pasternak, Boris. *I Remember: Sketch for an Autobiography*. First Edition: New York: Pantheon, 1959.
Nr.Fine/Fine **$30**
Good/V.Good **$15**

Paulsen, Gary. *Eastern Sun Winter Moon An Autobiographical Odyssey*. First Edition: New York: Harcourt Brace Jovanovich, 1993.

Nr.Fine/Fine **$15**
Good/V.Good **$8**

Payne, Robert. *The Life and Death of Adolf Hitler.* First Edition: New York: Praeger, 1972.
Nr.Fine/Fine **$35**
Good/V.Good **$18**

_____. *The Rise and Fall of Stalin.* First Edition: New York: Simon & Schuster, 1965.
Nr.Fine/Fine **$15**
Good/V.Good **$6**

Peacock, Molly. *Paradise, Piece By Piece.* First Edition: New York: Riverhead Books, Penguin Putnam Inc., 1998.
Nr.Fine/Fine **$12**
Good/V.Good **$6**

Phelan, James. *Howard Hughes: The Hidden Years.* First Edition: New York: Random House, 1976.
Nr.Fine/Fine **$25**
Good/V.Good **$15**

Phillips, Julia. *You'll Never Eat Lunch in This Town Again.* First Edition: New York; Random House, 1991.
Nr.Fine/Fine **$15**
Good/V.Good **$7**

Truman Capote: In Which Various Friends, Enemies, Acquaintances, and Detractors Recall His Turbulent Career
by George Plimpton

Plimpton, George. *Truman Capote: In Which Various Friends, Enemies, Acquaintances, and Detractors Recall His*

Turbulent Career. First Edition: New York: Doubleday, 1997.
Nr.Fine/Fine **$25**
Good/V.Good **$15**
First U.K. Edition: London: Picador, 1997.
Nr.Fine/Fine **$25**
Good/V.Good **$15**

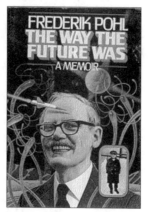

Fredrick Pohl: The Way the Future Was A Memoir
by Fredrick Pohl

Pohl, Frederik. *Frederik Pohl: The Way the Future Was-A Memoir.* First Edition: New York: Del Rey, 1978.
Nr.Fine/Fine **$15**
Good/V.Good **$7**

Presley, Priscilla Beaulieu. *Elvis and Me.* First Edition: New York: Putnam, 1985.
Nr.Fine/Fine **$12**
Good/V.Good **$6**

Price, Reynolds. *Clear Pictures: First Loves, First Guides.* First Edition: New York: Atheneum, 1989.
Nr.Fine/Fine **$35**
Good/V.Good **$20**

Pyle, Ernie. *Home Country.* First Edition: New York: William Sloane Associates, 1947.
Nr.Fine/Fine **$20**
Good/V.Good **$12**

Ramsland, Katherine. *Prism of the Night: A Biography of Anne Rice.* First Edition: New York: E. P. Dutton, 1991.
Nr.Fine/Fine **$20**

Good/V.Good $8

Rawlings, Marjorie Kinnan. *Cross Creek*.First Edition: New York: Charles Sribner's Sons, 1942.
Nr.Fine/Fine **$300**
Good/V.Good **$165**
First Edition: London: William Heinemann, 1942.
Nr.Fine/Fine **$200**
Good/V.Good **$100**

Ray, Gordon N. *H.G. Wells & Rebecca West*. First Edition: New Haven: Yale University Press, 1974.
Nr.Fine/Fine **$25**
Good/V.Good **$10**
First U.K. Edition: London: Macmillan, 1974
Nr.Fine/Fine **$20**
Good/V.Good $8

Roth, Philip. *The Facts: A Novelist's Autobiography*. First Edition: New York: Farrar, Straus & Giroux, 1988.
Nr.Fine/Fine **$35**
Good/V.Good **$15**

Russell, Bertrand. *The Autobiography of Bertrand Russell. (3 volumes)* First Edition: London: George Allen & Unwin, 1967.
Nr.Fine/Fine **$100**
Good/V.Good **$60**

Saint Exupery, Antoine De. *Wind, Sand and Stars*. First Edition in English: New York: Reynal & Hitchcock, 1939.
Nr.Fine/Fine **$100**
Good/V.Good **$35**

_____. *Night Flight*. First Edition in English: New York: Century Co., 1932.
Nr.Fine/Fine $150
Good/V.Good $50

_____. *Flight to Arras*.First Edition in English: New York: Reynal & Hitchcock, 1942.
Nr.Fine/Fine **$100**
Good/V.Good **$45**

Salter, James. *Burning The Days*. First Edition: New York: Random House, 1997.
Nr.Fine/Fine **$45**
Good/V.Good **$15**

Sartre, Jean-Paul. *The Words: The Autobiography of Jean-Paul Sartre*. First Edition: New York: George Braziller, 1964.
Nr.Fine/Fine **$50**
Good/V.Good **$25**

Saint Genet
by Jean-Paul Sartre

_____. *Saint Genet*. First Edition in English: New York: George Braziller, 1963.
Nr.Fine/Fine **$45**
Good/V.Good **$20**

Sassoon, Siegfried. *Memoirs of a Fox-Hunting Man*. First Edition: London: Faber & Gwyer Limited, 1928.
Nr.Fine/Fine **$750**
Good/V.Good **$300**

_____. *Memoirs of an Infantry Officer*. First Edition: London: Faber & Faber, 1930.
Nr.Fine/Fine **$250**
Good/V.Good **$135**

Sawyer-Laucanno, Christopher. *An Invisible Spectator: A Biography of Paul Bowles*. First Edition: New York: Weidenfeld and Nicolson, 1989.
Nr.Fine/Fine **$30**
Good/V.Good **$12**

Schorer, Mark. *Sinclair Lewis an American Life*. First Edition: New York: McGraw-Hill, 1961.
Nr.Fine/Fine **$30**
Good/V.Good **$12**

Seaman, Barbara. *Lovely Me: The Life of Jacqueline Susan*. First Edition: New York: William Morrow & Co., 1987.
Nr.Fine/Fine **$10**
Good/V.Good **$6**

See, Carolyn. *Dreaming: Hard Luck and Good Times in America*. First Edition: New York: Random House, 1995.
Nr.Fine/Fine **$15**
Good/V.Good **$8**

Shelden, Michael. *Friends of Promise: Cyril Connolly and the World of Horizon.* |First Edition: New York: Harper & Row, 1989.
Nr.Fine/Fine **$20**
Good/V.Good **$12**

Shiber, Etta. *Paris-Underground.* First Edition: New York: Charles Scribners Sons, 1946.
Nr.Fine/Fine **$15**
Good/V.Good **$8**

Silverman, Willa Z. *The Notorious Life of Gyp: Right-Wing Anarchist in Fin-de-Siecle France*. First Edition: New York: Oxford University Press, 1995.
Nr.Fine/Fine **$20**
Good/V.Good **$10**

Simon, Linda. *The Biography of Alice B. Toklas*.
First Edition: Garden City, NY: Doubleday & Co., 1977.
Nr.Fine/Fine **$20**
Good/V.Good **$8**

Sitwell, Edith. *Taken Care Of, An Autobiography*. First Edition: London: Hutchinson, 1965.
Nr.Fine/Fine **$55**
Good/V.Good **$25**

Sitwell, Osbert. *Autobiography: (I) Left Hand, Right Hand! An Autobiography. Vol. I: The Cruel Month. (II) The Scarlet Tree: Being the Second Volume of Left Hand, Right Hand! An Autobiography. (III) Great Morning: Being the Third Volume of Left Hand, Right Hand! An Autobiography. (IV) Laughter in the Next Room: Being the Fourth Volume of Left Hand, Right Hand! An Autobiography. (V) Noble Essences or Courteous Revelations: Being a Book of Characters and the Fifth and Last Volume of Left Hand, Right Hand! An Autobiography*. First Edition: London: Macmillan, 1945-1950.
Nr.Fine/Fine **$400**
Good/V.Good **$225**

Skinner, Cornelia Otis. *Madame Sarah*. First Edition: Boston: Houghton Mifflin, 1967.
Nr.Fine/Fine **$20**
Good/V.Good **$10**

Smith, Gene. *When The Cheering Stopped*. First Edition: New York: William Morrow, 1964.
Nr.Fine/Fine **$25**
Good/V.Good **$12**

Lo, the Former
Eygptian!
by H. Allen Smith

Smith, H. Allen. *Lo, the Former Egyptian!* First Edition: Garden City, NY: Doubleday, 1947.
Nr.Fine/Fine **$30**
Good/V.Good **$10**

Sonnenberg, Ben. *Lost Property:*

Memoirs & Confessions of a Bad Boy.
First Edition: New York: Summit Books,
1991.
Nr.Fine/Fine **$25**
Good/V.Good **$10**
First U.K. Edition: London: Faber &
Faber, 1991.
Nr.Fine/Fine **$25**
Good/V.Good **$12**

Souhami, Diana. *Gertrude & Alice*. First
Edition: London: Pandora Press, 1991.
Nr.Fine/Fine **$45**
Good/V.Good **$20**

Spender, Stephen. *World within World.*
The Autobiography of Stephen Spender.
First Edition: London: Hamish Hamilton,
1951.
Nr.Fine/Fine **$75**
Good/V.Good **$30**
First U.S. Edition: New York: Harcourt
Brace and Company, 1951.
Nr.Fine/Fine **$55**
Good/V.Good **$20**

Sperber, Ann M. *Murrow: His Life and*
Times. First Edition: New York:
Freundlich Books, 1986.
Nr.Fine/Fine **$20**
Good/V.Good **$8**

Starkie, Enid. *Arthur Rimbaud*. First
Edition: New York: New Directions, 1961.
Nr.Fine/Fine **$35**
Good/V.Good **$20**

Wars I Have Seen
by Gertrude Stein

Stein, Gertrude. *The Autobiography of*
Alice B. Toklas. First Edition: New York:
Harcourt, Brace and Company, 1933.
Nr.Fine/Fine **$725**
Good/V.Good **$350**
First U.K. Edition: London: John Lane
The Bodley Head, 1933.
Nr.Fine/Fine **$150**
Good/V.Good **$80**

_____. *Picasso*. First Edition in
English: London: B. T. Batsford, 1946.
Nr.Fine/Fine **$150**
Good/V.Good **$85**

_____. *Wars I Have Seen* First
Edition: London: Batsford, 1945.
Nr.Fine/Fine **$85**
Good/V.Good **$45**
First U.S. Edition: New York: Random
House, 1945.
Nr.Fine/Fine **$75**
Good/V.Good **$40**

Steinbeck, John. *Travels with Charley in*
Search of America. First Edition: New
York: The Viking Press, 1962.
Nr.Fine/Fine **$145**
Good/V.Good **$65**

Strouse, Jean. *Alice James-A Biography*.
First Edition: Boston: Houghton Mifflin,
1980.
Nr.Fine/Fine **$30**
Good/V.Good **$15**
First U.K. Edition: London: Johnathan
Cape, 1981.
Nr.Fine/Fine **$25**
Good/V.Good **$10**

Stuart, Jesse. *The Thread That Runs So*
True. First Edition: New York: Charles
Scribner's Sons, 1949.
Nr.Fine/Fine **$75**
Good/V.Good **$40**

Swanberg, W.A. *Luce and His Empire*.
First Edition: New York: Charles
Scribners, 1972.
Nr.Fine/Fine **$15**
Good/V.Good **$8**

Swanson, Gloria. *Swanson on Swanson*.
First Edition: New York: Random House,
1980.
Nr.Fine/Fine **$12**
Good/V.Good **$6**

Sykes, Christopher. *Evelyn Waugh: A
Biography*.
First Edition: London: Collins, 1975.
Nr.Fine/Fine **$25**
Good/V.Good **$10**
First U.S. Edition: Boston: Little, Brown
and Co., 1975.
Nr.Fine/Fine **$25**
Good/V.Good **$10**

Teichmann, Howard. *George S.
Kaufman*. First Edition: New York:
Atheneum, 1972.
Nr.Fine/Fine **$10**
Good/V.Good **$5**

Thomas, D.M. *Alexander Solzhenitsyn: A
Century in His Life*. First Edition: New
York: St. Martin's Press, 1998.
Nr.Fine/Fine **$20**
Good/V.Good **$8**

Thomas, Dylan. *A Child's Christmas in
Wales*. First Edition: Norfolk, CT: New
Directions, 1954.
Nr.Fine/Fine **$175**
Good/V.Good **$85**

Thurber, James. *My Life and Hard
Times*. First Edition: New York: Harper &
Brothers, 1933.
Nr.Fine/Fine **$100**
Good/V.Good **$35**

Thurman, Judith. *Isak Dinesen. The Life
of a Storyteller*. First Edition: New York:
St. Martin's Press, 1982.
Nr.Fine/Fine **$20**
Good/V.Good **$8**

Toklas, Alice B. *What Is Remembered*.
First Edition: London: Michael Joseph,
1963.
Nr.Fine/Fine **$100**
Good/V.Good **$55**
First U.S. Edition: New York: Holt,

Rinehart and Winston, 1963.
Nr.Fine/Fine **$75**
Good/V.Good **$35**

Tolson, Jay. *Pilgrim in the Ruins: A Life
of Walker Percy*. First Edition: New York:
Simon and Schuster, 1992.
Nr.Fine/Fine **$30**
Good/V.Good **$12**

Tomkins, Calvin. *Living Well is the Best
Revenge*. First Edition: New York: Viking
Press, 1971.
Nr.Fine/Fine **$35**
Good/V.Good **$15**

Treglown, Jeremy. *Roald Dahl: A
Biography*. First Edition: London: Faber
& Faber, 1994.
Nr.Fine/Fine **$25**
Good/V.Good **$10**

Turnbull, Andrew. *Scott Fitzgerald*. First
Edition: New York: Scribner's, 1962.
Nr.Fine/Fine **$30**
Good/V.Good **$20**
First UK Edition: London: Bodley Head,
1962.
Nr.Fine/Fine **$25**
Good/V.Good **$12**

Twain, Mark. *Life on the Mississippi*.
First Edition: London: Chatto & Windus,
1883.
Nr.Fine/Fine **$900**
Good/V.Good **$500**
First U.S. Edition: Boston: James R.
Osgood And Co., 1883. **Points of Issue:**
Page 411 tail-piece with urn, flames and
head of Twain; page 443 caption reads
"The St. Louis Hotel."
Nr.Fine/Fine **$2500**
Good/V.Good **$1500**

_____. *Roughing it*. First Edition:
Hartford: American Publishing Company,
1872.
Nr.Fine/Fine **$1500**
Good/V.Good **$850**

_____. *A Tramp Abroad*. First

Edition: Hartford: American Publishing
Company, 1880.
Nr.Fine/Fine **$3500**
Good/V.Good **$2000**
First U.K. Edition: London: Chatto &
Windus, 1880.
Nr.Fine/Fine **$3000**
Good/V.Good **$1800**

Tytell, John. *Ezra Pound. The Solitary
Volcano*. First Edition: New York: Anchor
Press/Doubleday, 1987. Nr.Fine/Fine **$25**
Good/V.Good **$10**

Ustinov, Peter. *Dear Me*. First Edition:
London: Heinemann, 1977.
Nr.Fine/Fine **$15**
Good/V.Good **$7**
First Edition: Boston: Little, Brown &
Company, 1977
Nr.Fine/Fine $12
Good/V.Good $5

Palm Sunday An
Autobiographical
Collage
by Kurt Vonnegut

Vonnegut, Kurt. *Palm Sunday An
Autobiographical Collage*. First Edition
(limited): New York: Delacorte Press,
1981.
Nr.Fine/Fine **$200**
Good/V.Good **$125**
First Edition *(trade)*: New York: Delacorte
Press, 1981.
Nr.Fine/Fine **$65**
Good/V.Good **$25**

Waugh, Evelyn. *A Little Learning*. First
Edition: London: Chapman & Hall, 1964.

Nr.Fine/Fine **$65**
Good/V.Good **$35**
First U.S. Edition: Boston: Little, Brown
and Company, 1964.
Nr.Fine/Fine **$40**
Good/V.Good **$20**

Welty, Eudora. *One Writer's Beginnings*.
First Edition: Cambridge and London:
Harvard University Press, 1984.
Nr.Fine/Fine **$100**
Good/V.Good **$65**

Beardsley
by Stanley Weintraub

Weintraub, Stanley. *Beardsley*. First
Edition: London: W.H. Allen, 1967.
Nr.Fine/Fine **$60**
Good/V.Good **$35**

First Edition: New York: George Braziller,
1967. Nr.Fine/Fine **$30**
Good/V.Good **$15**

White, Edmund. *Genet: A
Biography*.First Edition: London: Chatto
& Windus, 1993.
Nr.Fine/Fine **$35**
Good/v.Good. **$15**
First Edition: New York: Alfred A. Knopf,
1993.
Nr.Fine/Fine **$30**
Good/V.Good **$10**

White, William Allen. *The Autobiography
of William Allen White*. First Edition: New
York: Macmillan, 1946.
Nr.Fine/Fine **$40**
Good/V.Good **$25**

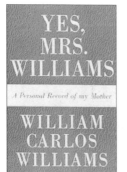

Yes, Mrs.
Williams: A
Personal Record
of My Mother
*by Willam Carlos
Williams*

Williams, William Carlos. *Yes, Mrs.
Williams: A Personal Record of My
Mother.* First Edition: New York:
McDowell, Oblensky Inc., 1959.
Nr.Fine/Fine **$55**
Good/V.Good **$30**

Wineapple, Brenda. *Sister Brother:
Gertrude and Leo Stein.* First Edition:
New York: G. P. Putnam's, 1996.
Nr.Fine/Fine **$25**

Good/V.Good **$10**

Wolff, Geoffrey. *The Duke of Deception:
Memories of My Father.* First Edition:
New York: Random House, 1979.
Nr.Fine/Fine **$25**
Good/V.Good **$15**

Wolff, Tobias. *This Boy's Life: A Memoir.*
First Edition: New York: Grove/Atlantic,
1989.
Nr.Fine/Fine **$85**
Good/V.Good **$50**

Zierold, Norman. *Garbo.* First Edition:
New York: Stein & Day, 1969.
Nr.Fine/Fine **$20**
Good/V.Good **$9**

Zweig, Stefan. *Balzac.* First Edition: New
York: The Viking Press, 1946.
Nr.Fine/Fine **$45**
Good/V.Good **$25**

Garbo
by Norman Zierold

Fantasy, Horror and Science Fiction

The capacity to create worlds beyond our own in our dreams and in our imagination forms what might be called the literature of the fantastic. The realm is a wide one, ranging from the pure invention of an entirely new universe, to a minor alteration in invention. As a literary form, it has been around as long as man has been able to dream and to write.

Man touched the moon with his feet for the first time in 1968, but in his mind he has been roaming its surface for centuries. The wind, rustling the branches of trees in the night, congers up phantoms of the supernatural. Beyond the hills we know, there may lie worlds of magic and mystery. The automobile changed forever the face of our civilization; what other invention might alter the world of tomorrow? All this is the stuff of the literature of the fantastic.

Roughly, it can be broken down into three broad areas. The first, Science Fiction, involves a forecasting of the future. Strictly, given the name, it should involve rather rigid guidelines, a possible future, one that conforms to scientific principles, but this is not necessarily the case. Works classed as science fiction can consist of an entirely new civilization on a far planet where science, as we know it, does not exist. It has been written by high school dropouts, and scientists with walls full of degrees. The second, Horror, is the addition of the supernatural to reality. Within it, the primal fears of things that go bump in the night are exploited to frighten us, thrill us, and entertain us. The last, Fantasy, is an exercise in being a God. It is the literary equivalent of saying "...let there be light." It is the creation of a new universe, with new rules and new laws. It's the realm of fairies, ogres, trolls, and sorcerers. All three are an exercise in dreaming and imagining.

Science fiction has been traced back to Ancient Greece, but its impact in the modern world probably began in the Renaissance. As early as 1516, Sir Thomas More would choose it as the medium for his satire on English society, *Utopia*. Johannes Kepler used it to popularize his scientific/mathematical model of the universe in *Somnium*. Francis Bacon assayed the form in *The New Atlantis*, which was among the first stories to forecast submarines and airplanes. Throughout the seventeenth century, authors such as Tommaso Campanella, Cyrano de Bergerac, Francis Godwin, and the ever popular Anonymous were finding earthly Utopias tucked in corners of the globe and flying to the moon and the planets. The trend continued into the eighteenth and nineteenth centuries, mixing with other genres in the romances of writers like H. Rider Haggard, and Jack London as well as holding on to a scientific base with scientist/writers such as H. G. Wells and Arthur Conan Doyle, M.D.

What is called science fiction probably began in the last half of the nineteenth century with Sir Edward

Bulwer-Lytton's *Vril*, which forecast atomic energy in 1871. What followed was an era of "scientific romance," extending to the depression era beginning in the late 1920s. Jules Verne, H. G. Wells, and Edgar Rice Burroughs joined an international parade of writers mixing science, romance, and political commentary with the future. H. Rider Haggard dotted the continent of Africa with lost civilizations and W. H. Hudson did the same for South America. Samuel Butler, Robert W. Chambers, James Ames Mitchell, among others, found future forecasting a way of explaining political ideas. Jacques Futrell gave us a synthetic diamond long before the Home Shopping Network and Karel Capek built robots long before any engineer could put one together.

The American dime novel and the British penny dreadful ushered in the next step in science fiction, the pulp era, in America often associated with the editor of Amazing Stories, Hugo Gernsback. It is an era where fantasy and science fiction cross-pollinate in formula stories and novels. Prehistory is recast along the lines of anthropology, archeology, and the theories of Darwin. The space opera has mankind flying between the stars while acting like the hero of a cowboy movie. The traces of the era remain today. We still read the prehistorical soap operas of Jane Auel, and watch what is perhaps the greatest of space operas, the movie *Star Wars*.

The end of the Second World War ushered in what we might, rather gratuitously, call modern science fiction. The explosion of an atomic weapon, the pre-eminence science displayed on the battlefield, ushered in a more rigid science fiction, some written by scientists and engineers such as Isaac Asimov, Robert Heinlein, L. Sprague DeCamp, and Fred Hoyle. Political polemics, lost races, alien contact, technological surmises, new philosophies, and theologies remained in the science fiction sphere while pure fantasy and gothic horror, detective stories, super spies, and divine intervention were booted out of the science fiction camp. Novels became increasingly formula productions, relying on characterization, or outre' concepts, to distinguish themselves. Solid sellers, but not topping the best seller lists as they had in previous eras, fantastic literature's blockbusters would come from the sub-genre of horror.

Horror has been a part of literature for as long as we can record its existence. Man has been pitting himself against the malevolent creatures of an unseen world for as long as there have been creative artists to imagine those horrors. There are witches in the Bible, and vampires in the Apocrypha. Historical figures have become mythical monsters. Even today, in parts of the Eastern world children are cautioned to stay in bed or Iksander (Alexander the Great) will get them. Today, horror authors such as Stephen King, Anne Rice, and Dean Koontz are fixtures of any best-seller list, often claiming the top spot. We love to be frightened, whether by a witch, a vampire, or the haunted precincts of a world that only touches us in the dark.

Modern horror began with the Napoleonic Wars. The Marquis De Sade noted that, at this time in history, the real terrors of war forced writers to delve into the supernatural to create things more horrible than reality. This was called the Gothic era and not only did it produce classic works of horror, it established a lot of the myths, plot devices, and themes of the modern horror genre. *The Castle of Otranto* by Horace Walpole is generally given credit as the first Gothic in 1764. Haunted castles, and ruins, fantastic landscapes and, above all, the supernatural became staples of a literary diet through such writers as Ann Radcliffe, M .G. Lewis, and C. R. Maturin. The early nineteenth century brought classics with Mary Shelley's *Frankenstein*, J. Sheridan LeFanu's *Carmilla*, and John Polidori's *The Vampyre*, originally attributed to Lord Byron. Penny dreadfuls drew their nickname from the Gothic stories they published, such as *A String of Pearls*, by Thomas Prest, the story that gave the world Sweeney Todd, the demon barber of Fleet Street. Before the end of the century, Bram Stoker had contributed Dracula to our nightmares. And, of course, one of the three great writers who would shape horror into its modern incarnation, Edgar Allen Poe, plied his trade in the nineteenth century.

The early twentieth century brought with it a second and a third master of the horror story. A Welch mystic, actor, and newspaperman named Arthur Machen, and a Rhode Island recluse named Howard Phillips Lovecraft would finish up what Poe began in creating what we now call modern horror fiction. The Gothics gave us the cast, the vampire, the monster, the ghost, the mummy, the changling as well as the settings. Starting with Poe, the emphasis began to shift

from the physical to the mental. Though supernatural at the base, Poe's stories centered on the horrors of the mind, the psychology of fright, and the depths to which a man's own thoughts could sink him. Machen found the avenue to conveying the subtle menace of the world, making a trip aboard on a London street at noon an occasion of foreboding, and, like Poe, he often trapped his readers in the mind of a man going mad. Machen found a shadowy underworld of malevolence, lurking just below the veneer we call reality. H. P. Lovecraft explored it. Rats in the walls to monsters in the sewers, Lovecraft found the hidden terrors in the commonest places.

Horror is tied to reality. The most horrible monster, in a fantasy land, has very little ability to frighten us. Fantasy is what results when all bonds to reality are dissolved. Possibly the oldest literary form, and always with us in fairy tales and myths, modern fantasy is, in fact, the latest developing of the three sub-genres of the literature of the fantastic. The conventions of it as a literary form finally solidified in the 1950s with the work of classics professor J.R.R. Tolkien. If we trace its origins, we need go back no further than the poet, printer, designer William Morris. Morris became fascinated with the saga. Scandinavian and Anglo Saxon tales of fantastic worlds overlayed on our own. Seeing these, he decided to create adult fairy tales. These have all of the fantastic elements of fairy tales and Scandinavian sagas in mature tales for the adult reader. Before he was through, he would take us to the *Well at the World's End, Across the Glittering Plain*; introduce us to *The Fair Jehane,* and offer us a goblet of *The Water of the Wondrous Isles*. Through the first half of the twentieth century, fantasy tried to find footing. Lord Dunsany followed in the footsteps of Morris, as did E. R. R. Eddison. Pulp writers, such as Robert E. Howard, combined elements of the science fiction of Edgar Rice Burroughs to create what is called sword and sorcery. Then, in the 1950s, it all came together with *The Hobbit* and *The Lord of the Rings*. There resides a fully formed universe with its own rules, its own natural law, Middle Earth. Fantasy has found its way onto the best-seller list with such writers as Terry Brooks and David Eddings. It should be remembered, however, that it is a young genre, with room to grow and develop.

Fantastic literature, for the collector, ranges wide. There are collections based solely on going to the Moon, or to Mars. Collections of a mythos developed by a single author and explored by others such as Lovecraft's *Cluthlu* or Andre Norton's *Witch World*. Collections based on publishers such as Fantasy Press, Shasta Publications, Gnome Press or Arkham House. Like the field of literature it is, the field of collecting it has spawned is nearly as limitless as time, and extends beyond the farthest star.

10 Classic Rarities

Asimov, Isaac. *Pebble In The Sky*. Garden City, NY: Doubleday & Co., 1950. Needle in a haystack, pebble in the sky, hard to find but the pebble is more rewarding.
Retail value in:
Near Fine to Fine **$1900**
Good to Very Good **$1000**

Bradbury, Ray. *Dark Carnival*. Sauk City, WI: Arkham House, 1947. Issued without a Dust Jacket. Finding one of the 80 copies of Dark Carnival can shed a lot of light on your finances.
Retail value in
Near Fine to Fine **$3000**
Good to Very Good **$2200**

Burroughs, Edgar Rice. *The Outlaw of Torn*. Chicago: A.C. McClurg & Company, 1927. Issued with Dust Jacket. Find this and make out like a bandit.
Retail value in:
Near Fine to Fine **$4500**
Good to Very Good **$2000**

Dick, Philip K. *A Handful of Darkness*. London: Rich & Cowen, 1955. No listing of "World of Chance" on rear panel. Covert this to a handful of money.
Retail value in:
Near Fine to Fine **$2500**
Good to Very Good **$1200**

Heinlein, Robert A. *Stranger in a Strange Land*. New York: G. P. Putnam's, 1961. The first printing has a code C22 on page 408. Find it and be as strange as you like.
Retail value in:
Near Fine to Fine **$2300**
Good to Very Good **$1200**

Herbert, Frank. *Dune*. Philadelphia:

Chilton Books, 1965. Blue binding, dust jacket price of $5.95. Great way to start a vacation would be to find this.
Retail value in:
Near Fine to Fine **$7500**
Good to Very Good. **$2500**

Lovecraft, H. P. *The Shadow Over Innsmouth*. Everett, PA: Visionary Publishing Co., 1936. Find it and cast some light in your own shadow.
Retail value in:
Near Fine to Fine **$5000**
Good to Very Good. **$3500**

Machen, Arthur. *The Cosy Room*. London: Rich & Cowan, 1936. Finding this could certainly make things "cosier" around your room.
Retail value in:
Near Fine to Fine **$2000**
Good to Very Good. **$1500**

Tolkien, J.R.R. *The Hobbit or There and Back Again*. London: George Allen & Unwin, 1937. "Dodgeson" (should be Dodgson) on rear Dust Jacket flap. Go there, back again or anywhere at all if you find this.
Retail value in:
Near Fine to Fine **$85000**
Good to Very Good. **$27000**

Wells, H.G. *The Time Machine*. London: William Heinemann, 1895. First Edition. Grey stamped in purple with 16 pages of ads. Time will be on your side with this.
Retail value in:
Near Fine to Fine **$3500**
Good to Very Good **$2000**

Price Guide

Inter Ice Age 4
by Kobe Abe

Abe, Kobo. *Inter Ice Age 4*. First U.S. Edition: New York: Alfred A. Knopf, 1970.
Nr.Fine/Fine **$25**
Good/V.Good **$15**

Barefoot in
the Head
by Brian W. Aldiss

Aldiss, Brian W. *Barefoot in the Head*. First Edition: London: Faber and Faber, 1969.
Nr.Fine/Fine **$65**
Good/V.Good **$25**
First U.S. Edition: New York: Doubleday, 1970.
Nr.Fine/Fine **$45**
Good/V.Good **$15**

_____. *Frankenstein Unbound*.

First Edition: London: Jonathan Cape, 1973.
Nr.Fine/Fine **$55**
Good/V.Good **$20**
First U.S. Edition: New York: Random House, 1973.
Nr.Fine/Fine **$45**
Good/V.Good **$15**

Aldrich, Thomas Bailey. *The Queen of Sheba*. First Edition: Boston, James R. Osgood, 1877.
Nr.Fine/Fine **$65**
Good/V.Good **$35**

Allingham, Garry. *Verwoerd: The End: A Look-back from the Future*. First Edition: Cape Town, S.A.: Purnell & Sons, 1961.
Nr.Fine/Fine **$15**
Good/V.Good **$8**
First U.K. Edition: London, Boardman, 1961.
Nr.Fine/Fine **$10**
Good/V.Good **$6**

Amosoff, N. *Notes from the Future*. First Edition: New York: Simon & Schuster, 1970.
Nr.Fine/Fine **$12**
Good/V.Good **$8**

Anderson, Olof W. *The Treasure Vault of Atlantis* First Edition: 511 Masonic Temple, MN: Midland Publishing Co., 1925.
Nr.Fine/Fine **$45**
Good/V.Good **$25**

Anderson, Poul. *The High Crusade*. First Edition: Garden City, NY: Doubleday, 1960.
Nr.Fine/Fine **$200**
Good/V.Good **$125**

_____. *Harvest the Fire*. First edition: New York: Tom Doherty Associates, 1995.
Nr.Fine/Fine **$10**
Good/V.Good **$6**

Anthony, Piers. *On a Pale Horse*. First Edition: New York: Ballantine Books,

1983.
Nr.Fine/Fine **$20**
Good/V.Good **$8**

Harvest the Fire
by Poal. Anderson

_____. *Harpy Thyme*. First
Edition: New York: Tor Books, 1994.
Nr.Fine/Fine **$10**
Good/V.Good **$6**

Asimov, Isaac. *I, Robot*. First Edition:
New York, Gnome Press, 1950.
Nr.Fine/Fine **$1000**
Good/V.Good **$695**

_____. *The Gods Themselves*.
First Edition: New York: Doubleday &
Company, 1972.
Nr.Fine/Fine **$95**
Good/V.Good **$25**

_____. *Foundation and Earth*.
First Edition: New York: Doubleday &
Company, 1986.
Nr.Fine/Fine **$25**
Good/V.Good **$12**

Bahnson Jr, Agnew H. *The Stars Are Too
High*. First Edition: New York: Random
House, 1959.
Nr.Fine/Fine **$35**
Good/V.Good **$12**

Ballard, J.G. *The Crystal World*. First
Edition: London: Jonathon Cape, 1966.
Nr.Fine/Fine **$225**

Good/V.Good **$135**
First U.S. Edition: New York: Farrar,
Straus & Giroux, 1966.
Nr.Fine/Fine **$125**
Good/V.Good **$65**

The Crystal World
by J.G. Ballard

_____. *The Day of Creation*. First
Edition: London: Victor Gollancz, 1987.
Nr.Fine/Fine **$35**
Good/V.Good **$12**
First U.S. Edition: New York: Farrar,
Straus & Giroux, 1967.
Nr.Fine/Fine **$25**
Good/V.Good **$10**

Balmer, Edwin and Philip Wylie. *When
Worlds Collide*. First Edition: New York:
Frederick A Stokes, 1933.
Nr.Fine/Fine **$150**
Good/V.Good **$85**

_____. *After
Worlds Collide*. First Edition: New York:
Frederick Stokes, 1934.
Nr.Fine/Fine **$150**
Good/V.Good **$85**

Barker, Clive. *Weaveworld*. First Edition
(LTD and Signed): London: Collins, 1987
Nr.Fine/Fine **$300**
Good/V.Good **$250**
First Edition (trade): London: Collins,
1987
Nr.Fine/Fine **$55**
Good/V.Good **$35**
First U.S. Edition (LTD and Signed): NY:

Poseidon Press, 1987.
Nr.Fine/Fine **$300**
Good/V.Good **$125**
First US Edition (trade): NY: Poseidon
Press, 1987.
Nr.Fine/Fine **$25**
Good/V.Good **$12**

Barjavel, Rene. *The Ice People*. First
U.K. Edition: London: Rupert Hart-Davis,
1970.
Nr.Fine/Fine **$25**
Good/V.Good **$10**
First U.S. Edition: New York: William
Morrow and Co., 1971.
Nr.Fine/Fine **$30**
Good/V.Good **$12**

Barnes, Arthur. *Interplanetary Hunter*.
First Edition: New York: Gnome Press,
1956.
Nr.Fine/Fine **$35**
Good/V.Good **$15**

Barth, John. *Giles Goat-Boy or, The
Revised New Syllabus*. First Edition:
Garden City, NY: Doubleday & Co.,
1966.
Nr.Fine/Fine $45
Good/V.Good $25
First U.K. Edition: London: Secker &
Warburg, 1967.
Nr.Fine/Fine **$40**
Good/V.Good **$15**

Beagle, Peter S. *The Last Unicorn*. First
Edition: New York: Viking Press, 1968.
Nr.Fine/Fine **$85**
Good/V.Good **$55**

_____. *The Innkeeper's Song*.
First Edition: New York: Roc Books,
1993.
Nr.Fine/Fine **$25**
Good/V.Good **$12**

Benford, Gregory. *Timescape*. First
Edition: New York: Simon and Schuster,
1980.
Nr.Fine/Fine **$55**
Good/V.Good **$25**

Timescape
by Gregory Benford

_____. *Against Infinity*. First
Edition: New York: Timescpe, 1983.
Nr.Fine/Fine **$15**
Good/V.Good **$8**

Bennett, Margot. *The Long Way Back*.
First Edition: London: The Bodley Head,
1954
Nr.Fine/Fine **$45**
Good/V.Good **$25**
First U.S. Edition: New York Coward-
McCann, 1955.
Nr.Fine/Fine **$20**
Good/V.Good **$12**

Best, Herbert. *The Twenty-fifth Hour*.
First Edition: New York: Random House,
1940.
Nr.Fine/Fine **$75**
Good/V.Good **$25**

Bester, Alfred. *The Demolished Man*.
First Edition: Chicago: Shasta Publishers,
1953.
Nr.Fine/Fine **$550**
Good/V.Good **$275**

_____ . *The Demolished Man*.
First Edition: New York: Berkley Putnam,
1976.
Nr.Fine/Fine **$35**
Good/V.Good **$20**

Blackwood, Algernon. *John Silence*. First
Edition: London, Eveleigh Nash, 1908.
Nr.Fine/Fine **$345**
Good/V.Good **$225**

First U.S. Edition: New York: Macmillan, 1912.
Nr.Fine/Fine **$55**
Good/V.Good **$35**

Psycho
by Robert Bloch

Bloch, Robert. *Psycho.* First Edition: New York: Simon and Schuster, 1959.
Nr.Fine/Fine **$1500**
Good/V.Good **$900**

_____. *King of Terrors.* First Edition: New York (LTD and Signed): Mysterious Press, 1977.
Nr.Fine/Fine **$125**
Good/V.Good **$85**
First Edition (trade): New York: Mysterious Press, 1977.
Nr.Fine/Fine **$35**
Good/V.Good **$15**

Binder, Eando. *Lords of Creation.* First Edition: Philadelphia Prime Press, 1949.
Nr.Fine/Fine **$55**
Good/V.Good **$25**

Blish, James. *Jack of Eagles.* First Edition: New York: Greenberg Publisher, 1952.
Nr.Fine/Fine **$75**
Good/V.Good **$40**

_____. *The Star Trek Reader.* First Edition: New York: E.P. Dutton, 1976.
Nr.Fine/Fine **$25**
Good/V.Good **$15**

Garden on the Moon
by Pierre Boulle

Boulle, Pierre. *Garden on the Moon.* First U.S. Edition: New York: Vanguard Press, 1965.
Nr.Fine/Fine **$25**
Good/V.Good **$12**

_____. *Planet of the Apes.* First U.S. Edition: New York: Vanguard Press, 1963.
Nr.Fine/Fine **$700**
Good/V.Good **$400**

Bouve, Edward T. *Centuries Apart.* First Edition: Boston: Little, Brown and Co., 1894.
Nr.Fine/Fine **$95**
Good/V.Good **$75**

Bowen, John. *After the Rain.* First Edition: London: Faber and Faber, 1958.
Nr.Fine/Fine **$35**
Good/V.Good **$15**
First U.S. Edition: New York: Random House, 1967.
Nr.Fine/Fine **$20**
Good/V.Good **$10**

Boyd, John. *The Last Starship From Earth.* First Edition: New York: Weybright and Talley, 1968.
Nr.Fine/Fine **$60**
Good/V.Good **$25**
First U.K. Edition: London: Gollancz, 1969.
Nr.Fine/Fine **$10**
Good/V.Good **$5**

Brackett, Leigh. *The Starmen.* First

Edition: New York: Gnome Press, 1952.
Nr.Fine/Fine **$95**
Good/V.Good **$55**

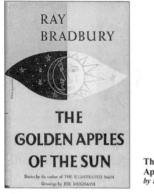

The Golden
Apples of the Sun
by Ray Bradbury

Bradbury, Ray. *The Golden Apples Of The Sun*. First Edition: Garden City, NY: Doubleday & Co., Inc., 1953.
Nr.Fine/Fine **$450**
Good/V.Good **$275**

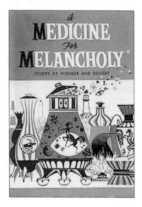

A Medicine
for Melancholy
by Ray Bradbury

_____. *A Medicine for Melancholy*. First Edition: Garden City, NY: Doubleday & Co., Inc., 1959.
Nr.Fine/Fine **$200**
Good/V.Good **$85**

_____. *Graveyard For Lunatics*. First Edition: New York: Alfred Knopf, 1990.
Nr.Fine/Fine **$20**
Good/V.Good **$12**

Bradshaw, William R. *The Goddess of Atvatabar*. First Edition: New York: J. F. Douthitt, 1892.
Nr.Fine/Fine **$300**
Good/V.Good **$200**

Bradley, Marion Zimmer. *The Mists of Avalon*. First Edition: New York: Alfred A. Knopf, 1982.
Nr.Fine/Fine **$150**
Good/V.Good **$85**

_____. *The Forest House*. First Edition: New York: Viking, 1993.
Nr.Fine/Fine **$15**
Good/V.Good **$8**

The Sword of
Shannara
by Terry Brooks

Brooks, Terry. *The Sword of Shannara*. First Edition: New York: Random House, 1977.
Nr.Fine/Fine **$450**
Good/V.Good **$275**

_____. *The Black Unicorn*. First Edition: New York: Ballantine Books/Del Rey, 1987.
Nr.Fine/Fine **$20**
Good/V.Good **$12**

_____. *Running With The Demon*. First Edition: New York: Ballantine Books/Del Rey, 1997.
Nr.Fine/Fine **$15**
Good/V.Good **$7**

The Black
Unicorn
by Terry Brooks

Angels and
Spaceships
by Fredric Brown

Brown, Fredric. *Angels and Spaceships*.
First Edition: New York: Dutton, 1954.
Nr.Fine/Fine **$300**
Good/V.Good **$125**

Brunner, John. *The Sheep Look Up*. First
Edition: New York: Harper & Row, 1972.
Nr.Fine/Fine **$80**
Good/V.Good **$50**
First U.K. Edition: London: J. M. Dent &
Sons Ltd., 1974.
Nr.Fine/Fine **$25**
Good/V.Good **$12**

_____. *Stand on Zanzibar*. First
Edition: Garden City, NY: Doubleday,
1968.
Nr.Fine/Fine **$175**

Good/V.Good **$125**
First UK Edition: London: Macdonald &
Co., 1969.
Nr.Fine/Fine **$125**
Good/V.Good **$95**

_____. *Quicksand*. First
Edition: Garden City, NY: Doubleday,
1967.
Nr.Fine/Fine **$25**
Good/V.Good **$12**
First U.K. Edition: London: Sidgwick &
Jackson, 1969.
Nr.Fine/Fine **$20**
Good/V.Good **$8**

Brunngraber, Rudolf. *Radium*. First
Edition: New York: Random House, 1937.
Nr.Fine/Fine **$35**
Good/V.Good **$25**

Burgess, Anthony. *A Clockwork Orange*.
First Edition: London: Heinemann, 1962.
Nr.Fine/Fine **$5000**
Good/V.Good **$2000**
First U.S. Edition: New York: W. W.
Norton & Company Inc., 1963.
Nr.Fine/Fine **$300**
Good/V.Good **$125**

Burgess, Gelett. *The White Cat*. First
Edition: Indianapolis: Bobbs, Merrill,
1907.
Nr.Fine/Fine **$75**
Good/V.Good **$45**

Burroughs, Edgar Rice. *The Chessmen
of Mars*. First Edition: Chicago: A. C.
McClurg & Co., 1922.
Nr.Fine/Fine **$2000**
Good/V.Good **$750**
Reprint Edition: Tarzana, CA: Burroughs,
1922.
Nr.Fine/Fine **$35**
Good/V.Good **$25**

_____. *John Carter of
Mars*. First Edition: New York: Canaveral
Press, 1964.
Nr.Fine/Fine **$75**
Good/V.Good **$50**

_____. *The Land That Time Forgot.* First Edition: Chicago: A. C. McClurg & Co., 1924. Nr.Fine/Fine$450.
Good/V.Good . . . . $250.
Reprint Edition: New York: Canaveral, 1962.
Nr.Fine/Fine **$45**
Good/V.Good **$25**

Pirates of Venus
by Edgar Rice Burroughs

_____. *Pirates of Venus.* First Edition: Tarzana. CA: Burroughs, 1934.
Nr.Fine/Fine **$550**
Good/V.Good **$400**
Reprint Edition: New York: Canaveral, 1962.
Nr.Fine/Fine **$45**
Good/V.Good **$25**

_____. *Tanar of Pellucidar.* First Edition: New York: Metropolitan Books, 1930.
Nr.Fine/Fine **$250**
Good/V.Good **$75**
Reprint Edition: New York Canaveral, 1962.
Nr.Fine/Fine **$50**
Good/V.Good **$25**

_____. *Tarzan of the Apes* First Edition: Chicago: A.C. McClurg, 1914.
Nr.Fine/Fine **$5000**
Good/V.Good **$3500**

_____. *Tarzan and the Foreign Legion.* First Edition: Tarzana, CA: Burroughs, 1947.
Nr.Fine/Fine **$100**
Good/V.Good **$55**

Tarzan and the Foreign Legion
by Edgar Rice Burroughs

Nova Express
by William S. Burroughs

Burroughs, William S. *Nova Express.* First Edition: New York: Grove Press, Inc., 1964.
Nr.Fine/Fine **$125**
Good/V.Good **$75**

_____. *The Wild Boys.* First Edition: New York: Grove Press, Inc., 1971.
Nr.Fine/Fine **$100**
Good/V.Good **$65**
First U.K. Edition: London: Calder &

Boyars, 1972.
Nr.Fine/Fine **$125**
Good/V.Good **$85**

Butler, Samuel. *Erewhon or Over the Range* First Edition: London: Trubner & Co., 1872.
Nr.Fine/Fine **$200**
Good/V.Good **$100**

_____. *Erewhon Revisited*. First Edition: London. Grant Richards, 1901.
Nr.Fine/Fine **$200**
Good/V.Good **$145**

Caidin, Martin. *Cyborg*. First Edition: New York: Arbor House, 1972.
Nr.Fine/Fine **$75**
Good/V.Good **$40**

_____. *The God Machine*. First Edition: New York: E.P. Dutton, 1968.
Nr.Fine/Fine **$35**
Good/V.Good **$15**

Calisher, Hortense. *Journal from Ellipsia*. First Edition: Boston: Little, Brown, 1965.
Nr.Fine/Fine **$45**
Good/V.Good **$25**

Calvino, Italo. *Cosmicomics*. First U.S. Edition: New York: Harcourt Brace & World, Inc., 1968.
Nr.Fine/Fine **$350**
Good/V.Good **$175**
First U.K. Edition: London: Jonathan Cape, 1969.
Nr.Fine/Fine **$450**
Good/V.Good **$285**

Cameron, John. *The Astrologer*. First Edition: New York: Random House, 1972.
Nr.Fine/Fine **$12**
Good/V.Good **$8**

Campbell, John W. Jr. *The Black Star Passes*. First Edition: Reading, PA: Fantasy Press, 1953.
Nr.Fine/Fine **$125**
Good/V.Good **$45**

_____. *Islands of Space*.

First Edition: Reading, PA: Fantasy Press, 1956.
Nr.Fine/Fine **$100**
Good/V.Good **$35**

_____. *Invaders From The Infinite*. First Edition: New York: Gnome Press, 1961.
Nr.Fine/Fine **$45**
Good/V.Good **$25**

_____. *The Mightiest Machine*. First Edition: Providence, RI: Hadley Publishing Company, 1947.
Nr.Fine/Fine **$100**
Good/V.Good **$55**

_____. *Who Goes There?* First Edition: Chicago: Shasta Publishers, 1948.
Nr.Fine/Fine **$500**
Good/V.Good **$350**

Campbell, Ramsey. *Hungry Moon*. First Edition: New York: Macmillan, 1986.
Nr.Fine/Fine **$15**
Good/V.Good **$8**
First U.K. Edition: London, Century/Hutchinson Ltd., 1987.
Nr.Fine/Fine **$10**
Good/V.Good **$6**

Demons by Daylight
by Ramsey Campbell

_____. *Demons by Daylight*. First Edition: Sauk City, WI: Arkham House, 1973.

Nr.Fine/Fine **$45**
Good/V.Good **$20**

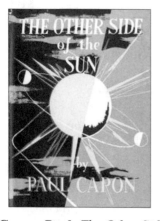

The Other Side
of the Sun
by Paul Capon

Capon, Paul. *The Other Side of the Sun.*
First Edition: London: Heinemann, 1950.
Nr.Fine/Fine **$35**
Good/V.Good **$12**

Capek, Karel. *The Absolute at Large.*
First Edition: New York: Macmillan,
1927.
Nr.Fine/Fine **$100**
Good/V.Good **$50**

War With
The Newts
by Karel Capek

_____. *War with the Newts.* First
Edition: London: Allen & Unwin, 1937.
Nr.Fine/Fine **$300**
Good/V.Good **$100**
First U.S. Edition: New York: G. P.
Putnam's Sons, 1937.
Nr.Fine/Fine **$275**

Good/V.Good **$100**

_____. *R. U. R.: Rossom's
Universal Robotsœa Fantastic
Melodrama.* First Edition: Garden City,
NY: Doubleday, Page & Co., 1923.
Nr.Fine/Fine **$85**
Good/V.Good **$45**

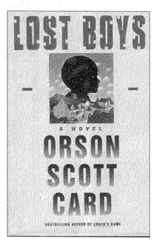

Lost Boys
by Orson Scott Card

Card, Orson Scott. *Lost Boys*. First
Edition: New York: Harper Collins, 1992.
Nr.Fine/Fine **$15**
Good/V.Good **$8**

Carr, Robert Spencer. *Beyond Infinity.*
First Edition (LTD and Signed): Reading,
PA: Fantasy Press, 1951.
Nr.Fine/Fine **$125**
Good/V.Good **$65**
First Edition (Trade): Reading, PA:
Fantasy Press, 1951.
Nr.Fine/Fine **$50**
Good/V.Good **$25**

Carter, Angela. *The Magic Toyshop.* First
Edition: New York: Simon and Schuster,
1967.
Nr.Fine/Fine **$100**
Good/V.Good **$25**

_____. *Nights at the Circus.* First
Edition: London: Chatto and Windus,
1984.
Nr.Fine/Fine **$50**
Good/V.Good **$25**

The Magic
Toyshop
by Angela Carter

First U.S. Edition: New York: Viking, 1985.
Nr.Fine/Fine $35
Good/V.Good . . . . $15.

Chambers, Robert W. *The King In Yellow*. First Edition: Chicago: F. Tennyson Neely, 1895. First state is green cloth with no frontespiece.
Nr.Fine/Fine **$1200**
Good/V.Good **$750**
Later states with 1895 on Title page.
Nr.Fine/Fine **$250**
Good/V.Good **$125**

_____. *The Green Mouse*. First Edition: New York: Appleton,1910.
Nr.Fine/Fine **$40**
Good/V.Good **$25**

Chandler, A. Bertram. *The Rim of Space*. First Edition: New York: Avalon Books, 1961.
Nr.Fine/Fine **$65**
Good/V.Good **$35**

Chester, George Randolph. *The Jingo*. First Edition: Indianapolis, IN: Bobbs-Merrill Co., 1912.
Nr.Fine/Fine **$35**
Good/V.Good **$20**

Clarke, Arthur C. *Childhood's End*. First Edition: New York: Ballantine, 1953.

Nr.Fine/Fine **$1200**
Good/V.Good **$800**
First U.K. Edition: London: Sidgwick and Jackson, 1954.
Nr.Fine/Fine **$800**
Good/V.Good **$450**

Childhood's
End
by Arthur C. Clarke

_____. *Rendezvous With Rama*. First Edition: London: Victor Gollancz, 1973.
Nr.Fine/Fine **$250**
Good/V.Good **$100**
First U.S. Edition: New York: Harcourt Brace Jovanovich, 1973.
Nr.Fine/Fine **$45**
Good/V.Good **$25**

_____. *2061: Odyssey Three*. First Edition: New York: Del Rey/Ballantine, 1988.
Nr.Fine/Fine **$15**
Good/V.Good **$10**
First U.K. Edition: London, Grafton Books, 1988.
Nr.Fine/Fine **$10**
Good/V.Good **$6**

Clarke, Arthur C. and Gentry Lee. *Cradle*. First Edition: New York: Warner Books, 1988.
Nr.Fine/Fine **$15**
Good/V.Good **$10**
First U.K. Edition: London: Victor Gollancz Ltd., 1988.
Nr.Fine/Fine **$10**

Good/V.Good **$6**

Clement, Hal. *Needle*. First Edition: Garden City, NY: Doubleday & Co., 1950.
Nr.Fine/Fine **$125**
Good/V.Good **$75**

_____. *Mission of Gravity*. First Edition: Garden City, NY: Doubleday & Co., 1952.
Nr.Fine/Fine **$750**
Good/V.Good **$500**
First U.K. Edition: London: Robert Hale Publishers, 1955.
Nr.Fine/Fine **$1200**
Good/V.Good **$900**

Clifton, Mark. *Eight Keys to Eden*. First Edition: Garden City, NY: Doubleday & Co., 1960.
Nr.Fine/Fine **$35**
Good/V.Good **$20**

Coblentz, Stanton A. *Hidden World*. First Edition: New York: Avalon, 1957.
Nr.Fine/Fine **$60**
Good/V.Good **$25**

_____. *The Sunken World*. First Edition: Los Angeles: Fantasy Publishing Co., 1948.
Nr.Fine/Fine **$65**
Good/V.Good **$25**

Cole, Everett B. *The Philosophical Corps*. First Edition: Hicksville, NY: Gnome Press, Inc., 1961.
Nr.Fine/Fine **$25**
Good/V.Good **$15**

Collier, John. *Tom's A-Cold. A Tale*. First Edition: London: Macmillan, 1933.
Nr.Fine/Fine **$85**
Good/V.Good **$30**
First U.S. Edition (as: Full Circle) New York: D. Appleton, 1933.
Nr.Fine/Fine **$300**
Good/V.Good **$125**

Copper, Basil. *The House of the Wolf*. First Edition: Sauk City, WI: Arkham

House, 1983.
Nr.Fine/Fine **$25**
Good/V.Good **$15**

Corelli, Marie. *The Mighty Atom*. First Edition: London: Hutchinson, 1896.
Nr.Fine/Fine **$65**
Good/V.Good **$30**
First U.S. Edition: Philadelphia: Lippincott, 1896.
Nr.Fine/Fine **$35**
Good/V.Good **$20**

The Andromeda Strain
by Michal Crichton

Crichton, Michael. *The Andromeda Strain*. First Edition: New York: Alfred A. Knopf, Inc, 1969.
Nr.Fine/Fine **$200**
Good/V.Good **$85**

_____. *Jurassic Park*. First Edition: New York: Alfred A. Knopf, Inc., 1969.
Nr.Fine/Fine **$20**
Good/V.Good **$8**

Cummings, Ray. *Brigands of the Moon*. First Edition: Chicago. A.C. McClurg, 1931.
Nr.Fine/Fine **$45**
Good/V.Good **$25**

_____. *The Girl in The Golden Atom*. New York: Harper & Brothers Publishers, 1923. First state is dark yellow stamped in black
Nr.Fine/Fine **$135**
Good/V.Good **$45**

Second state: Blue stamped in yellow.
Nr.Fine/Fine **$75**
Good/V.Good **$25**

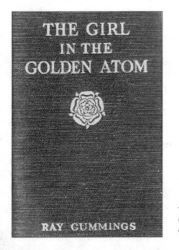

The Girl in the
Golden Atom
by Ray Cummings

Cummins, Harle Oren. *Welsh Rarebit
Tales*. First Edition: Boston: Mutual Book
Co., 1902.
Nr.Fine/Fine **$75**
Good/V.Good **$25**

DeCamp, L.Sprague. *The Rogue Queen*.
First Edition: New York: Doubleday and
Co., 1951.
Nr.Fine/Fine **$55**
Good/V.Good **$25**

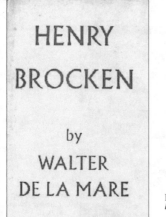

HENRY

BROCKEN

by

WALTER

DE LA MARE

Henry Brocken
*by Walter De
La Mare*

De La Mare, Walter. *Henry Brocken*
First Edition: London: Collins nd [1924].

Nr.Fine/Fine **$65**
Good/V.Good **$25**
First U.S. Edition: New York: Alfred A.
Knopf, 1924.
Nr.Fine/Fine **$45**
Good/V.Good **$25**

del Rey, Lester. *Marooned on Mars*. First
Edition: Philadelphia: The John C.
Winston Company, 1952.
Nr.Fine/Fine **$95**
Good/V.Good **$35**

DeMille, James. *A Strange Manuscript
Found in a Copper Cylinder*. First
Edition: New York: Harper & Brothers,
1888.
Nr.Fine/Fine **$95**
Good/V.Good **$45**

Delany, Samuel R. *Stars in my Pocket
Like Grains of Sand*. First Edition: New
York: Bantam, 1984.
Nr.Fine/Fine **$20**
Good/V.Good **$8**

Derleth, August. *Dwellers in Darkness*.
First Edition: Sauk City, WI: Arkham,
1976.
Nr.Fine/Fine **$50**
Good/V.Good **$30**

Derleth, August, and Lovecraft, H.P.
The Watchers Out of Time and Others.
First Edition: Sauk City, WI: Arkham,
1974.
Nr.Fine/Fine **$85**
Good/V.Good **$40**

Dick, Philip K. *Flow My Tears the
Policeman Said*. First Edition: New York:
Doubleday, 1974. Points of Issue: Code
O50 on page 231.
Nr.Fine/Fine **$650**
Good/V.Good **$250**

_____. *The Divine Invasion*. First
Edition: New York: Timescape Books,
1981.
Nr.Fine/Fine **$35**
Good/V.Good **$20**

Disch, Thomas. *On Wings of Song* First Edition: London, Victor Gollancz Ltd., 1979.
Nr.Fine/Fine **$35**
Good/V.Good **$20**
First US Edition: New York: St. Martin's, 1979
Nr.Fine/Fine **$25**
Good/V.Good **$10**

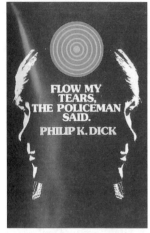

Flow My
Tears, The
Policeman Said
by Philip K. Dick

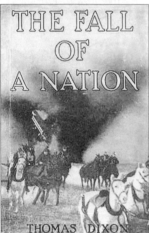

The Fall
of a Nation
by Thomas Dixon

Dixon, Thomas. *The Fall of a Nation—a Sequel to "The Birth of a Nation"* First Edition: New York: D. Appleton & Co., 1916.
Nr.Fine/Fine **$85**
Good/V.Good **$35**

Donnelly, Ignatius (as by Edmund Boisgilbert, M.D.). *Doctor Huguet. A Novel.* First Edition: Chicago: Schulte, 1891.
Nr.Fine/Fine **$100**
Good/V.Good **$75**

Donnelly, Ignatius. *The Golden Bottle* First Edition: New York and St. Paul, MN: D.D. Merrill Co., 1892.
Nr.Fine/Fine **$125**
Good/V.Good **$85**

Doyle, Arthur Conan. *The Land of Mist.* First Edition: London, Hutchinson, 1926.
Nr.Fine/Fine **$450**
Good/V.Good **$200**
First U.S. Edition: New York: George H. Doran, 1926.
Nr.Fine/Fine **$300**
Good/V.Good **$85**

_____. *The Lost World.* First Edition: London: Hodder & Stoughton, 1912.
Nr.Fine/Fine **$600**
Good/V.Good **$250**
First U.S. Edition: New York: Hodder & Stoughton and George H. Doran, 1912.
Nr.Fine/Fine **$350**
Good/V.Good **$175**

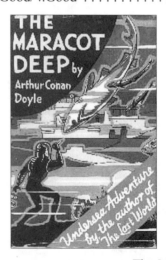

The
Maracot Deep
by Arthur Conan Doyle

_____ . *The Maracot Deep and Other Stories.* First Edition: London:

John Murray, 1929.
Nr.Fine/Fine **$1500**
Good/V.Good **$500**
First U.S. Edition: New York: Doubleday, Doran. 1929.
Nr.Fine/Fine **$550**
Good/V.Good **$250**

_____ . *The Poison Belt. Being an Account of Another Amazing Adventure of Professor Challenger*. First Edition: London: Hodder and Stoughton, 1913.
Nr.Fine/Fine **$650**
Good/V.Good **$300**
First US Edition: New York: Hodder and Stoughton/George H. Doran, 1913.
Nr.Fine/Fine **$450**
Good/V.Good **$150**

Dunsany, Lord. *The Charwoman's Shadow*. First Edition: London & New York: G.P. Putnam's Sons, 1926.
Nr.Fine/Fine **$450**
Good/V.Good **$250**
_____. *The King of Elfland's Daughter*. First Edition: London & New York: G.P. Putnam's Sons, 1924.
Nr.Fine/Fine **$150**
Good/V.Good **$85**

_____. *Dreamer's Tales*. First Edition: London: George Allen & Sons, 1910.
Nr.Fine/Fine **$350**
Good/V.Good **$185**
First U.S. Edition: Boston: John W. Luce, 1916
Nr.Fine/Fine **$250**
Good/V.Good **$100**

Eddings, David. *The King of Murgos*. First Edition: New York: A Del Rey Book/Ballantine Books, 1988.
Nr.Fine/Fine **$25**
Good/V.Good **$15**
_____. *The Ruby Knight*. First Edition: New York: A Del Rey Book/Ballantine Books, 1989.
Nr.Fine/Fine **$25**

Good/V.Good **$15**

Eddison, E.R. *Mistress of Mistresses*. First Edition: London: Faber & Faber, 1935.
Nr.Fine/Fine **$250**
Good/V.Good **$115**
First U.S. Edition: New York: E.P. Dutton & Co. Inc., 1935.
Nr.Fine/Fine **$200**
Good/V.Good **$75**

_____. *The Worm Ouroboros*. First Edition: London: Jonathan Cape, 1922.
Nr.Fine/Fine **$350**
Good/V.Good **$145**
First U.S. Edition: New York: Albert & Charles Boni, 1926.
Nr.Fine/Fine **$125**
Good/V.Good **$65**

_____. *Styrbiorn The Strong*. First Edition: London: Jonathan Cape, 1926.
Nr.Fine/Fine **$400**
Good/V.Good **$200**
First U.S. Edition: New York: Albert & Charles Boni, 1926
Nr.Fine/Fine **$400**
Good/V.Good **$200**

Ellison, Harlan. *Deathbird Stories*. First Edition: New York: Harper & Row, 1975.
Nr.Fine/Fine **$75**
Good/V.Good **$30**

England, George Allen. *The Flying Legion*. First Edition: Chicago: A. C. McClurg, 1920.
Nr.Fine/Fine **$45**
Good/V.Good **$20**

_____. *Darkness and Dawn*. First Edition: Boston: Small, Maynard & Company, 1914.
Nr.Fine/Fine **$100**
Good/V.Good **$45**

Ewers, Hans Heinz. *Alraune*. First Edition: München (Munich), Georg Müller Verlag, 1916.

Nr.Fine/Fine **$2500**
Good/V.Good **$1500**
First U.S. Edition: New York: John Day, 1929
Nr.Fine/Fine **$100**
Good/V.Good **$65**

Farley, Ralph Milne. *The Radio Man.* First Edition: Los Angeles: Fantasy Publishing Co., 1948.
Nr.Fine/Fine **$55**
Good/V.Good **$25**

Farmer, Philip Jose. *Lord Tyger.* First Edition: Garden City: Doubleday, 1970.
Nr.Fine/Fine **$150**
Good/V.Good **$85**

Red Orc's Rage
by Philip Jose Farmer

_____. *Red Orc's Rage.*
First Edition: New York: Tom Doherty Associates, 1991.
Nr.Fine/Fine **$12**
Good/V.Good **$8**

Farris, John. *The Fury.* First Edition: Chicago: Playboy Press, 1976.
Nr.Fine/Fine **$25**
Good/V.Good **$12**

_____. *All Heads Turn as the Hunt Goes By.* First Edition: Chicago: Playboy Press, 1977.
Nr.Fine/Fine **$20**
Good/V.Good **$10**

The Fury
by John Farris

Finney, Jack. *The Woodrow Wilson Dime.* First Edition: New York: Simon & Schuster, 1968.
Nr.Fine/Fine **$135**
Good/V.Good **$75**

Fuller, Alvarado M. *A.D. 2000.* First Edition: Chicago: Laird & Lee, 1925.
Nr.Fine/Fine **$350**
Good/V.Good **$150**

Futrelle, Jacques. *The Diamond Master.* First Edition: Indianapolis, IN: Bobbs Merrill, 1909.
Nr.Fine/Fine **$75**
Good/V.Good **$55**

Ganpat (Gompertz, M. L. A.). *Mirror Of Dreams.* First Edition: Garden City, NY: Doubleday, Doran & Company, 1928.
Nr.Fine/Fine **$75**
Good/V.Good **$45**

Gardner, John. *Grendel.* First Edition: New York: Alfred A. Knopf, 1971.
Nr.Fine/Fine **$300**
Good/V.Good **$125**

Gernsback, Hugo. *Ralph 124C 41+ A Romance of the Year 2660.* First Edition: Boston: The Stratford Company, 1925.
Nr.Fine/Fine **$750**
Good/V.Good **$500**

Gibbons, Floyd. *The Red Napoleon.* First Edition: New York: Jonathan Cape and

Harrison Smith, 1929.
Nr.Fine/Fine **$200**
Good/V.Good **$50**

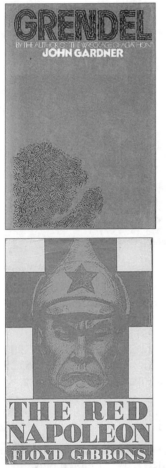

Grendel
by John Gardner

The Red
Napoleon
by Floyd Gibbons

Godfrey, Hollis. *The Man Who Ended War*. First Edition: Boston: Little, Brown & Company, 1908.
Nr.Fine/Fine **$100**
Good/V.Good **$75**

Gunn, James. *This Fortress World*. First Edition: Hicksville, NY: Gnome Press, 1955.
Nr.Fine/Fine **$75**
Good/V.Good **$25**

_____. *The End of the Dreams* First Edition: New York: Charles Scribner's Sons, 1975.

Nr.Fine/Fine **$25**
Good/V.Good **$12**

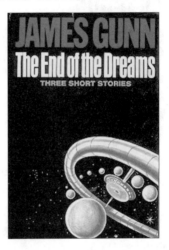

The End of
the Dream
by James Gunn

Haggard, H. Rider. *Allan Quatermain*. First Edition: London: Longmans,Green & Co, 1887.
Nr.Fine/Fine **$700**
Good/V.Good **$100**

_____. *King Solomon's Mines*. First Edition: London, Cassell & Co., 1886.
Nr.Fine/Fine **$8000**
Good/V.Good **$6000**
Second Issue: London, Cassell & Co., 1887.
Nr.Fine/Fine **$150**
Good/V.Good **$65**

_____. *She A History of Adventure*. First Edition: London: Longmans, Green, and Co., 1887.
Nr.Fine/Fine **$1000**
Good/V.Good **$750**

Hamilton, Edmond. *The Haunted Stars*. First Edition: New York: Dodd, Mead & Company, 1960.
Nr.Fine/Fine **$65**
Good/V.Good **$25**

_____. *The Star Kings*. First Edition: New York: Frederick Fell, 1949.
Nr.Fine/Fine **$100**
Good/V.Good **$45**

The Star Kings
by Edmond Hamilton

Harper, Vincent. *The Mortgage on the Brain*. First Edition: New York: Harper & Brothers Publishers, 1905.
Nr.Fine/Fine **$75**
Good/V.Good **$50**

Harrison, Harry. *The Stainless Steel Rat*. First Edition: New York: Bantam Books, 1987.
Nr.Fine/Fine **$15**
Good/V.Good **$6**

Hastings, Milo. *The City of Endless Night*. First Edition: New York: Dodd, Mead, 1920.
Nr.Fine/Fine **$300**
Good/V.Good **$200**

Hatfield, Richard. *Geyserland: Empiricisms in Social Reform*. First Edition: Washington D.C: Printed for Richard Hatfield, 1907.
Nr.Fine/Fine **$85**
Good/V.Good **$50**

Heinlein, Robert A. *The Puppet Masters*. First Edition: Garden City, NY: Doubleday, 1951.
Nr.Fine/Fine **$300**
Good/V.Good **$125**

_____. *The Green Hills of Earth*. First Edition: Chicago: Shasta, 1951.
Nr.Fine/Fine **$350**

Good/V.Good **$150**

_____. *Job: A Comedy of Justice*. First Edition: New York: Del Rey/Ballantine, 1984.
Nr.Fine/Fine **$35**
Good/V.Good **$15**

Dune Messiah
by Frank Herbert

Herbert, Frank. *Dune Messiah*. First Edition: New York: G. P. Putnams' Sons, 1969.
Nr.Fine/Fine **$500**
Good/V.Good **$225**
First U.K. Edition: London: Gollancz, 1971.
Nr.Fine/Fine **$100**
Good/V.Good **$45**

_____. *Dragon in the Sea*. First Edition: Garden City: Doubleday & Company, Inc., 1956.
Nr.Fine/Fine **$300**
Good/V.Good **$175**

Howard, Robert E. *The Coming of Conan*. First Edition: New York, Gnome Press, 1953.
Nr.Fine/Fine **$375**
Good/V.Good **$250**

_____. *Conan the Conqueror*. First Edition: New York, Gnome Press, 1950.
Nr.Fine/Fine **$400**
Good/V.Good **$275**

First U.K. Edition: London: T. V.
Boardman, 1954.
Nr.Fine/Fine **$350**
Good/V.Good **$185**

Howells, W.D. *Through the Eye of the
Needle.* First Edition: New York: Harper
& Brothers Publishers, 1907.
Nr.Fine/Fine **$25**
Good/V.Good **$15**

_____. *A Traveler from Altruria.*
First Edition: New York: Harper &
Brothers Publishers, 1894.
Nr.Fine/Fine **$85**
Good/V.Good **$35**

Hoyle, Fred. *The Black Cloud.* First
Edition: London: Heinemann, 1957.
Nr.Fine/Fine **$40**
Good/V.Good **$15**
First U.S. Edition: New York: Harper &
Brothers, 1957.
Nr.Fine/Fine **$35**
Good/V.Good **$15**

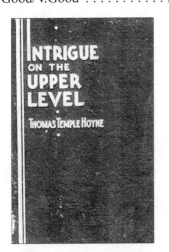

Intrigue on the
Upper Level
*by Thomas Temple
Hoyne*

Hoyne, Thomas Temple. *Intrigue on the
Upper Level.* First Edition: Chicago:
Reilly and Lee, 1934.
Nr.Fine/Fine **$95**
Good/V.Good **$45**

Hubbard, L. Ron. *Battlefield Earth.* First
Edition: New York: St. Martin's Press,
1982.

Nr.Fine/Fine **$100**
Good/V.Good **$45**

Battlefield
Earth
*by L. Ron.
Hubbard*

_____. *Typewriter in the Sky.*
First Edition: New York: Gnome Press,
1951.
Nr.Fine/Fine **$125**
Good/V.Good **$55**

Hudson, W. H. *A Crystal Age.* First
Edition: London: T. Fisher Unwin, 1887.
Nr.Fine/Fine **$400**
Good/V.Good **$150**
First U.S. Edition: New York: E. P. Dutton
and Company, 1906.
Nr.Fine/Fine **$50**
Good/V.Good **$35**

Huxley, Aldous. *Brave New World.* First
Edition: London: Chatto & Windus; 1932.
Nr.Fine/Fine **$4500**
Good/V.Good **$1500**
First US Edition: Garden City, NY:
Doubleday, 1932.
Nr.Fine/Fine **$85**
Good/V.Good **$35**

James, M. R. *Ghost Stories of an
Antiquary.* First Edition: London: Edward
Arnold, 1904.
Nr.Fine/Fine **$1250**
Good/V.Good **$850**

Johnson, Owen. *The Coming of the*

Amazons. First Edition: New York: Longmans, Green, & Co., 1931.
Nr.Fine/Fine **$85**
Good/V.Good **$40**

Jones, Raymond. *This Island Earth*. First Edition: Chicago: Shasta, 1952.
Nr.Fine/Fine **$450**
Good/V.Good **$175**
First U.K. Edition: London, T.V. Boardman & Co. Ltd., 1955
Nr.Fine/Fine **$125**
Good/V.Good **$55**

Men
Without Bones
by Gerald Kersh

Kersh, Gerald. *Men Without Bones*. First Edition: London, William Heinemann, 1955.
Nr.Fine/Fine **$150**
Good/V.Good **$65**

Flowers for
Algernon
by Daniel Keyes

Keyes, Daniel. *Flowers for Algernon*. First Edition: New York; Harcourt, Brace & World, 1966.
Nr.Fine/Fine **$450**
Good/V.Good **$245**

King, Stephen. *Carrie*. First Edition: New York: Doubleday & Co., 1974.
Nr.Fine/Fine **$1250**
Good/V.Good **$800**

_____. *Pet Sematary*. First Edition: New York: Doubleday & Co., 1983.
Nr.Fine/Fine **$65**
Good/V.Good **$45**

_____. *Insomnia*. First Edition: New York: Viking Publishers, 1994
Nr.Fine/Fine **$12**
Good/V.Good **$5**

Kline, Otis Adelbert. *Maza of the Moon* First Edition: Chicago: A.C. McClurg 1930.
Nr.Fine/Fine **$200**
Good/V.Good **$140**

_____. *The Planet of Peril*. First Edition: Chicago: A. C. McClurg & Co., 1930.
Nr.Fine/Fine **$175**
Good/V.Good **$120**

Koontz, Dean R. *Strangers*. First Edition: New York: G.P. Putnam's Sons, 1986.
Nr.Fine/Fine **$45**
Good/V.Good **$20**

_____. *Whispers*. First Edition: New York: G.P. Putnam's Sons, 1980.
Nr.Fine/Fine **$550**
Good/V.Good **$285**

_____. *Watchers*. First Edition: New York: G.P. Putnam's Sons, 1987.
Nr.Fine/Fine $65
Good/V.Good $40

_____. *Mr. Murder*. First Edition: New York: G.P. Putnam's Sons, 1993.
Nr.Fine/Fine **$25**

Good/V.Good **$10**

Kornbluth, C.M. *The Mindworm*. First Edition: London: Michael Joseph, 1955.
Nr.Fine/Fine $55
Good/V.Good **$20**

Kuttner, Henry. *Ahead of Time*. First Edition: New York, Ballantine Books, 1953.
Nr.Fine/Fine **$125**
Good/V.Good **$85**
First U.K. Edition: London: Weidenfeld & Nicolson, 1954.
Nr.Fine/Fine **$35**
Good/V.Good **$20**

Large, E.C. *Sugar in the Air*First Edition: New York: Charles Scribner's Sons, 1937.
Nr.Fine/Fine **$45**
Good/V.Good **$20**

LeGuin, Ursula. *The Lathe of Heaven.* First Edition: New York: Scribner's, 1971.
Nr.Fine/Fine **$350**
Good/V.Good **$185**
First U.K. Edition: London: Victor Gollancz, 1972.
Nr.Fine/Fine **$75**
Good/V.Good **$30**

Leiber, Fritz. *The Green Millennium.* First Edition: New York, Abelard Press, 1953.
Nr.Fine/Fine **$90**
Good/V.Good **$35**

Leinster, Murray. *The Last Space Ship*. First Edition: New York: Frederick Fell, Inc., 1949.
Nr.Fine/Fine **$85**
Good/V.Good **$45**

Lem, Stanislaw. *Memoirs Found in a Bathtub*. First U.K. Edition: London: Andre Deutsch, 1992.
Nr.Fine/Fine **$35**
Good/V.Good **$12**
First U.S. Edition: New York: Seabury Press, 1973.
Nr.Fine/Fine **$35**
Good/V.Good **$12**

Lewis, C. S. *Out of the Silent Planet.* First Edition: London: John Lane The Bodley Head, 1938.
Nr.Fine/Fine **$850**
Good/V.Good **$400**
First U.S. Edition: The Macmillan Company, 1943.
Nr.Fine/Fine **$375**
Good/V.Good **$185**

Lewis, Sinclair. *It Can't Happen Here.* First Edition: Garden City, NY: Doubleday, Doran & Co., 1935.
Nr.Fine/Fine **$95**
Good/V.Good **$40**

Lightner, A. M. *Star Dog*. First Edition: New York: McGraw Hill, 1973.
Nr.Fine/Fine **$75**
Good/V.Good **$45**

London, Jack. *Before Adam*. First Edition: New York. Macmillan, 1907.
Nr.Fine/Fine **$150**
Good/V.Good **$55**

_____. *The Iron Heel*. First Edition: New York: The Macmillan Company, 1908.
Nr.Fine/Fine **$125**
Good/V.Good **$45**

Lovecraft, H.P. *The Dunwich Horror And Others*. First Edition: Sauk City, WI; Arkham House, 1963.
Nr.Fine/Fine **$125**
Good/V.Good **$55**

_____. *At the Mountains of Madness*. First Edition: Sauk City, WI; Arkham House, 1964.
Nr.Fine/Fine **$125**
Good/V.Good **$45**

Machen, Arthur. *Three Imposters or The Transmutations* First Edition: London: John Lane. 1895.
Nr.Fine/Fine **$350**
Good/V.Good **$200**
First U.S. Edition: Boston: Roberts Brothers, 1895.
Nr.Fine/Fine **$350**

Good/V.Good **$200**
Reprint First Thus: New York: Alfred A.
Knopf, 1923.
Nr.Fine/Fine **$75**
Good/V.Good **$25**

_____. *The Shining
Pyramid*. First Edition: Chicago: Covici-
McGee, 1923.
Nr.Fine/Fine **$150**
Good/V.Good **$75**
First Edition U.K. (differs from original):
London: Martin Secker, 1925.
Nr.Fine/Fine **$100**
Good/V.Good **$50**
First U.S. Edition (differs from original,
reprints U.K. first): New York: Alfred A.
Knopf, 1925
Nr.Fine/Fine **$75**
Good/V.Good **$25**

Mathison, Richard. *Hell House*. First
Edition: New York: Viking, 1971.
Nr.Fine/Fine **$175**
Good/V.Good **$95**

McCaffrey, Anne. *Moreta: Dragonlady of
Pern*. First Edition: New York: Ballantine
Books/Del Rey, 1983.
Nr.Fine/Fine **$15**
Good/V.Good **$6**

McKenna, Richard. *Casey Agonistes and
Other Science Fiction and Fantasy
Stories*. First Edition: New York: Harper
and Row, 1973.
Nr.Fine/Fine **$45**
Good/V.Good **$20**

Merritt, A. *The Face in the Abyss*. First
Edition: New York: Horace Liveright,
1931.
Nr.Fine/Fine **$275**
Good/V.Good **$65**

_____. *The Ship of Ishtar* First
Edition: New York: G.P. Putnam's Sons,
1926.
Nr.Fine/Fine **$250**
Good/V.Good **$75**
Reprint Edition (illustrated by Virgil

Finlay): Los Angeles: Borden Publishing
Company, 1949.
Nr.Fine/Fine **$100**
Good/V.Good **$45**

Miller, Walter. *A Canticle For Leibowitz*.
First Edition: Philadelphia: Lippincott,
1960.
Nr.Fine/Fine **$750**
Good/V.Good **$265**

Moorcock, Michael. *Stormbringer*. First
Edition: London: Herbert Jenkins, 1965.
Nr.Fine/Fine **$425**
Good/V.Good **$250**

Moore, C. L. *Judgment Night*. First
Edition: New York: Gnome Press, 1952.
Nr.Fine/Fine **$75**
Good/V.Good **$45**

Mundy, Talbot. *Jimgrim*. First Edition:
New York & London: The Century Co.,
1931.
Nr.Fine/Fine **$150**
Good/V.Good **$65**

Niven, Larry. *Ringworld*. First Edition:
New York: Holt, Rinehart and Winston,
1977.
Nr.Fine/Fine **$175**
Good/V.Good **$95**

Norton, Andre. *Star Man's Son: 2250
A.D.* First Edition: New York: Harcourt
Brace & Company, 1952.
Nr.Fine/Fine **$550**
Good/V.Good **$300**

_____. *Mirror of Destiny*. First
Edition: New York: Morrow/Avon, 1995.
Nr.Fine/Fine **$20**
Good/V.Good **$10**

Orwell, George. *1984*. First Edition:
London: Secker & Warburg, 1949.
Nr.Fine/Fine **$1800**
Good/V.Good **$1200**
First U.S. Edition: New York: Harcourt
Brace, 1949.
Nr.Fine/Fine **$1000**
Good/V.Good **$650**

Paine, Albert Bigelow. *The Mystery of Evelin Delorme*. First Edition: Boston: Arena Publishing Co., 1894.
Nr.Fine/Fine **$175**
Good/V.Good **$100**

Pallen, Conde B. *Crucible Island: a Romance, an Adventure and an Experiment*. First Edition: New York: The Manhattanville Press, 1919.
Nr.Fine/Fine **$55**
Good/V.Good **$30**

Parry, David M. *The Scarlet Empire*. First Edition: Indianapolis, Bobbs-Merrill, 1906.
Nr.Fine/Fine **$65**
Good/V.Good **$35**

Percy, Walker. *Love in the Ruins*. First Edition: New York: Farrar Straus Giroux, 1971.
Nr.Fine/Fine **$165**
Good/V.Good **$75**

Powys, T.F. *Mr. Weston's Good Wine*. First Edition: London Chatto & Windus, 1927.
Nr.Fine/Fine **$125**
Good/V.Good **$65**
First U.S. Edition: New York: The Viking Press, 1928.
Nr.Fine/Fine **$85**
Good/V.Good **$45**

_____. *Unclay*. First Edition: London Chatto & Windus, 1931.
Nr.Fine/Fine **$100**
Good/V.Good **$85**
First U.S. Edition: New York: The Viking Press, 1932.
Nr.Fine/Fine **$100**
Good/V.Good **$75**

Pseudoman, Akkad. *Zero to Eighty*. First Edition: Princeton, NJ: Scientific Publishing Company, 1937.
Nr.Fine/Fine **$55**
Good/V.Good **$30**

Read, Herbert. *The Green Child*. First Edition: London: William Heinemann

Ltd., 1935. Nr.Fine/Fine **$95**
Good/V.Good **$50**

Reeve, Arthur B. *The Poisoned Pen* First Edition: New York: Harper & Bros, 1911.
Nr.Fine/Fine **$25**
Good/V.Good **$10**

Reynolds, Mack. *The Case of the Little Green Men*. First Edition: New York: Phoenix Press, 1951.
Nr.Fine/Fine **$155**
Good/V.Good **$85**

Rice, Anne. *Interview with a Vampire*. First Edition: New York: Alfred A. Knopf, 1976.
Nr.Fine/Fine **$950**
Good/V.Good **$500**

_____. *The Witching Hour*. First Edition: New York: Alfred A. Knopf, 1990.
Nr.Fine/Fine **$75**
Good/V.Good **$25**

_____. *The Vampire Armand*. First Edition: New York: Alfred A. Knopf, 1998.
Nr.Fine/Fine **$25**
Good/V.Good **$10**

Roberts, Keith. *The Chalk Giants*. First Edition: London: Hutchinson, London, 1974.
Nr.Fine/Fine **$150**
Good/V.Good **$85**
First US Edition: New York: G.P. Putnam's Sons, 1975
Nr.Fine/Fine **$85**
Good/V.Good **$35**

Robinson, C.H. *Longhead: the Story of the First Fire* First Edition: Boston: L.C. Page, 1913.
Nr.Fine/Fine **$95**
Good/V.Good **$45**

Rohmer, Sax. *Grey Face*. First Edition: Garden City: Doubleday, Page & Company, 1924.
Nr.Fine/Fine **$350**

Good/V.Good **$150**
First U.K. Edition: London: Cassell, 1924.
Nr.Fine/Fine **$350**
Good/V.Good **$150**

Rousseau, Victor. *The Messiah of the Cylinder*. First Edition: Chicago: A.C. McClurg & Co., 1917. Points of Issue: Illustrated by Joseph Clement Coll.
Nr.Fine/Fine **$125**
Good/V.Good **$75**

Saul, John. *Creature*. First Edition: New York: Bantam Books, 1989.
Nr.Fine/Fine **$15**
Good/V.Good **$5**

_____. *Black Lightning*. First Edition: New York: Fawcett Columbine, 1995.
Nr.Fine/Fine **$15**
Good/V.Good **$5**

Serviss, Garrett P. *The Columbus of Space*. First Edition: New York: D. Appleton & Co., 1911.
Nr.Fine/Fine **$325**
Good/V.Good **$125**

_____. *The Moon Metal*. First Edition: New York and London: Harper & Brothers, 1900.
Nr.Fine/Fine **$200**
Good/V.Good **$85**

Shiel, M.P. *Purple Cloud*. First Edition: London: Chatto & Windus, 1901.
Nr.Fine/Fine **$1500**
Good/V.Good **$1150**
First U.S. Edition: New York: Vanguard, 1930.
Nr.Fine/Fine **$100**
Good/V.Good **$55**

Silverberg, Robert. *The Book of Skulls*. First Edition: New York: Charles Scribner's Sons, 1972.
Nr.Fine/Fine **$25**
Good/V.Good **$12**

Simak, Clifford D. *Cosmic Engineers*. First Edition: New York. Gnome Press,

1950.
Nr.Fine/Fine **$125**
Good/V.Good **$75**

Siodmak, Curt. *Donovan's Brain*. First Edition: New York: Alfred A. Knopf, 1943.
Nr.Fine/Fine **$325**
Good/V.Good **$175**

Smith, Clark Ashton. *Genius Loci and Other Tales*. First Edition: Sauk City, WI: Arkham, 1948.
Nr.Fine/Fine **$175**
Good/V.Good **$100**

Smith, E.E. *Spacehounds of IPC*. First Edition Limited and Signed: Reading, PA: Fantasy Press, 1947.
Nr.Fine/Fine **$500**
Good/V.Good **$350**
First Edition Trade: Reading, PA: Fantasy Press, 1947.
Nr.Fine/Fine **$55**
Good/V.Good **$25**

_____. *Children of the Lens*. First Edition Limited and Signed: Reading, PA: Fantasy Press, 1954.
Nr.Fine/Fine **$450**
Good/V.Good **$275**
First Edition Trade: Reading, PA: Fantasy Press, 1947.
Nr.Fine/Fine **$200**
Good/V.Good **$125**

_____. *Skylark of Valeron*. First Edition: Reading, PA: Fantasy Press, 1949.
Nr.Fine/Fine **$90**
Good/V.Good **$60**

Snell, Edmund. *Kontrol*. First Edition: Philadelphia: J.B. Lippincott, 1928.
Nr.Fine/Fine **$50**
Good/V.Good **$25**

Spinrad, Norman. *Bug Jack Barron*. First Edition: New York: Walker and Company, 1969.
Nr.Fine/Fine **$85**
Good/V.Good **$35**

Stapledon, Olaf. *Star Maker*. First
Edition: London: Methuen, 1932.
Nr.Fine/Fine **$700**
Good/V.Good **$450**

_____. *Odd John*. First Edition:
London: Methuen, 1937.
Nr.Fine/Fine **$1000**
Good/V.Good **$650**

Stark, Harriett. *The Bacillus of Beauty*.
First Edition: New York: Frederick A.
Stokes & Co., 1900.
Nr.Fine/Fine **$125**
Good/V.Good **$75**

Stewart, George R. *The Earth Abides*.
First Edition: New York: Random House,
1949.
Nr.Fine/Fine **$350**
Good/V.Good **$185**

Stockton, Frank R. *Great Stone of
Sardi*s. First Edition: New York: Harper &
Brothers, 1899.
Nr.Fine/Fine . , ... **$45**
Good/V.Good **$25**

Sturgeon, Theodore. *More Than Human*.
First Edition: New York: Farrar, Straus
and Young, 1953.
Nr.Fine/Fine **$375**
Good/V.Good **$200**
First U.K. Edition: London: Victor
Gollancz, 1954.
Nr.Fine/Fine **$85**
Good/V.Good **$35**

Taine, John. *The Crystal Horde*. First
Edition: Reading, PA: Fantasy Press,
1952.
Nr.Fine/Fine **$85**
Good/V.Good **$35**

_____. *Forbidden Garden*. First
Edition: Reading, PA: Fantasy Press,
1947.
Nr.Fine/Fine **$85**
Good/V.Good **$45**

Thomas, Chauncey. *The Crystal Button*.
First Edition: Boston: Houghton Mifflin,

1891.
Nr.Fine/Fine **$75**
Good/V.Good **$50**

Thompson, Vance. *Green Ray*. First
Edition: Indianapolis, IN: Bobbs-Merrill
Co., 1924.
Nr.Fine/Fine **$25**
Good/V.Good **$10**

Tolkien, J.R.R. *The Fellowship of the
Ring*. First Edition: London: Allen &
Unwin, 1954.
Nr.Fine/Fine **$12,500**
Good/V.Good **$10,150**
First U.S. Edition: Boston: Houghton
Mifflin Company, 1954.
Nr.Fine/Fine **$2500**
Good/V.Good **$1650**

_____. *The Two Towers*. First
Edition: London: Allen & Unwin, 1954.
Nr.Fine/Fine **$12500**
Good/V.Good **$10150**
First U.S. Edition: Boston: Houghton
Mifflin Company, 1954.
Nr.Fine/Fine **$2500**
Good/V.Good **$1650**

_____. *The Return of the King*.
First Edition: London: Allen & Unwin,
1954.
Nr.Fine/Fine **$12500**
Good/V.Good **$10150**
First U.S. Edition: Boston: Houghton
Mifflin Company, 1954.
Nr.Fine/Fine **$2500**
Good/V.Good **$1650**

_____. *The Return of the
Shadow*. First Edition: London: Allen &
Unwin, 1988.
Nr.Fine/Fine **$150**
Good/V.Good **$85**
First U.S. Edition: Boston: Houghton
Mifflin Company, 1988.
Nr.Fine/Fine **$50**
Good/V.Good **$35**

**Train, Arthur, and Robert Williams
Wood.** *The Man Who Rocked the Earth.*

First Edition: New York: Doubleday, Page & Co., 1915. Points of Issue- "O" italicized on spine.
Nr.Fine/Fine **$175**
Good/V.Good **$65**

Van Vogt, A.E. *The Book of Ptath*. First Edition: Reading, PA: Fantasy Press, 1947.
Nr.Fine/Fine **$100**
Good/V.Good **$35**

Vonnegut, Kurt. *Slaughterhouse-Five or the Children's Crusade*. First Edition: New York: Delacorte 1976.
Nr.Fine/Fine **$40**
Good/V.Good **$20**
First U.K. Edition: London: Jonathan Cape, 1976
Nr.Fine/Fine **$35**
Good/V.Good **$15**

Waterloo, Stanley. *Armageddon*. First Edition: Chicago: Rand, McNally, 1898.
Nr.Fine/Fine **$150**
Good/V.Good **$55**

_____. *The Story of Ab. A Tale of The Time of the Cave Man*.
First Edition: Chicago: Way & William, 1897.
Nr.Fine/Fine **$200**
Good/V.Good **$125**

Weinbaum, Stanley G. *The Black Flame*. First Edition (LTD add . $20,): Reading, PA: Fantasy Press, 1948.
Nr.Fine/Fine **$95**
Good/V.Good **$45**

Wells, H.G. *The Island of Doctor Moreau*. First Edition: London, William Heinemann, 1896.
Nr.Fine/Fine **$1000**
Good/V.Good **$600**
First U.S. Edition: New York: Stone & Kimball, 1896.
Nr.Fine/Fine **$350**
Good/V.Good **$185**

_____. *The Invisible Man*. First Edition: London: C. Arthur Pearson, 1897.
Nr.Fine/Fine **$2500**
Good/V.Good **$1500**
First U.S. Edition: New York: Edward Arnold, 1897.
Nr.Fine/Fine **$600**
Good/V.Good **$275**

_____. *The War of the Worlds*. First Edition: London, William Heinemann, 1898. Points of Issue: 16 pp of advertisements at end.
Nr.Fine/Fine **$3000**
Good/V.Good **$1200**
First U.S. Edition: New York: Harper & Brothers, 1898.
Nr.Fine/Fine **$650**
Good/V.Good **$300**

_____. *The First Men in the Moon*. First Edition: London: George Newnes, 1901.
Nr.Fine/Fine **$450**
Good/V.Good **$225**
First US Edition: Indianapolis: Bowen-Merrill Company, 1901
Nr.Fine/Fine **$350**
Good/V.Good **$175**

White, Stewart Edward. *The Sign at Six*. First Edition: Indianapolis: The Bobbs-Merrill Company, 1912.
Nr.Fine/Fine **$45**
Good/V.Good **$25**

Wicks, Mark. *To Mars Via The Moon*. First Edition: London: Seeley & Co., 1911.
Nr.Fine/Fine **$100**
Good/V.Good **$75**
First U.S. Edition: Philadelphia: J.B. Lippincott Company. 1911.
Nr.Fine/Fine **$150**
Good/V.Good **$100**

Williams, Charles. *Descent into Hell*. First Edition: London: Faber and Faber, 1937.
Nr.Fine/Fine **$250**
Good/V.Good **$150**
First U.S. Edition: New York: Pelligrini &

Cudahy, 1949.
Nr.Fine/Fine **$65**
Good/V.Good **$35**

Williamson, Jack. *The Legion of Time*.
First Edition: Reading PA: Fantasy Press,
1952.
Nr.Fine/Fine **$50**
Good/V.Good **$25**

_____. *Darker Than You Think*.
First Edition (LTD and Signed): Reading
PA: Fantasy Press, 1948.
Nr.Fine/Fine **$250**
Good/V.Good **$155**
First Edition (Trade): Reading PA:
Fantasy Press, 1948.
Nr.Fine/Fine **$50**
Good/V.Good **$25**

Wilson, Colin. *The Philosopher's Stone*.
First Edition: London: Arthur Barker,
1969.
Nr.Fine/Fine **$125**
Good/V.Good **$65**
First U.S. Edition: New York: Crown,
1969.
Nr.Fine/Fine **$50**
Good/V.Good **$20**

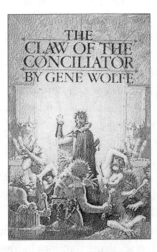

The Claw of the
Concilliator
by Gene Wolfe

Wolfe, Gene. *The Claw of the
Concilliator*. First Edition: New York:
Timescape Books/Simon and Schuster,
1981.

Nr.Fine/Fine **$45**
Good/V.Good **$25**

_____. *The Fifth Head of
Cerberus*. First Edition: New York:
Scribners, 1972.
Nr.Fine/Fine **$60**
Good/V.Good **$35**

Wright, S. Fowler. *Deluge*. First Edition:
New York: Cosmopolitan, 1928.
Nr.Fine/Fine **$100**
Good/V.Good **$45**

Wyndham, John. *The Day of the Triffids*.
First Edition: London: Michael Joseph,
1951.
Nr.Fine/Fine **$750**
Good/V.Good **$385**
First U.S. Edition: Garden City:
Doubleday & Company, 1951.
Nr.Fine/Fine **$450**
Good/V.Good **$225**

_____. *The Midwich Cuckoos*.
First Edition: London: Michael Joseph,
1957.
Nr.Fine/Fine **$160**
Good/V.Good **$95**
First U.S. Edition: New York: Ballantine,
1957.
Nr.Fine/Fine **$85**
Good/V.Good **$35**

Yarbo, Chelsea Quinn. *The Palace*. First
Edition: New York: St. Martins, 1978.
Nr.Fine/Fine **$25**
Good/V.Good **$12**

Zelazny, Roger. *Nine Princes in Amber*.
First Edition: Garden City: Doubleday,
1970.
Nr.Fine/Fine **$2500**
Good/V.Good **$1000**

_____. *The Courts of Chaos*.
First Edition: Garden City: Doubleday,
1976.
Nr.Fine/Fine **$45**
Good/V.Good **$18**

Literature in Translation

Much as the information may prove shocking, the greatest literary artists in the world have not all written in English. In point of fact, very few of them have. As a language, English is a relative newcomer and, due to its major fracture along the relative coasts of the Atlantic, fairly loose in its rules and constructions. An example I have always found amusing is "knocking up." On the eastern coast of the Atlantic it refers to a wake-up call. On the west coast, its meaning is somewhat different. Which is why I was so confused when I registered in a little inn in Wales and asked if I would like to be "knocked up."

Older languages have explored further than English, establishing new and rather unique areas of literature. One example is what the French call "nouveau roman" or, literally, "new novel." Essentially plotless and lacking an omniscient narrator, it reads like a slice of real life. Pioneered by such writers as Alain Robbe-Grillet, Michel Butor, Marguerite Duras, Robert Pinget, Nathalie Sarrault, Nobel Prize winner Claude Simon, and others, it is currently one of the hottest trends in American book collecting. During the nineties, nouveau roman crept out of the dollar bins and has begun a steady rise to the twenty to thirty dollar level in their first translated editions. Classics such as Simon, Claude, *Flanders Road*, New York: George Braziller, 1961, flirt with the $100 level in trade edition. And limiteds like Robbe-Grillet, Alain, *The Voyeur*, New York: Grove, 1958, break the $500 level. As modern American fiction has become more derivative and predictable, collectors, most of whom are essentially readers, are embracing more and more translated and unique works in literature.

Nor are the French the only innovators. Spanish, fractured like English by the Atlantic, has produced highly collectible works on both continents. Germans, Scandinavians, and Eastern Europeans produce as many Nobel Prize winners as those who write in English. An interesting development within the twentieth century is the appearance of Oriental authors in book collections. China, Japan, and Korea have what are perhaps the oldest continuing literary traditions in the World. Some of the work of Oriental literary artists combining this tradition with the Western forms has produced very interesting and enjoyable works, which are beginning to find room in American collections.

The largest single area of collecting translated works is collecting Nobel Prize winners. Such a collection is so full of translated works that books in English seem like interlopers on the shelves with them. I have used an asterisk to identify the Nobel Prize winners below.

10 Classic Rarities

Broch, Hermann. *The Death of Virgil.*
New York: Pantheon, 1945. Curious, as
this is also the true first, preceding the
German version.
Retail value in:
Near Fine to Fine **$1500**
Good to Very Good **$700**

Brunhoff, Jean de. *The Travels of Babar.*
New York: Harrison Smith & Robert
Haas, 1934.
Retail value in:
Near Fine to Fine **$2000**
Good to Very Good **$800**

Collodi, Carlo. *Story of a Puppet or The
Adventures of Pinocchio.* London: T.
Fisher Unwin, 1892. And you thought it
was Disney.
Retail value in:
Near Fine to Fine **$6500**
Good to Very Good **$3500**

Dumas, Alexandre. *Celebrated Crimes,*
Philadelphia: George Barrie & Son Pub.,
1895. Eight Volume set limited to 50
copies.
Retail value in:
Near Fine to Fine **$3000**
Good to Very Good **$1800**

Ernst, Max and Eluard, Paul.
Misfortunes of the Immortals. New York:
Black Sun Press, 1943. One of 110
copies.
Retail value in:
Near Fine to Fine **$3000**
Good to Very Good **$800**

*Mann, Thomas. *Buddenbrooks.* New
York: Knopf, 1924. Two volumes.
Retail value in:
Near Fine to Fine **$2000**
Good to Very Good. **$800**

*Marquez, Gabriel Garcia. *One
Hundred Years of Solitude.* New York:
Harper and Row, 1970. The first state of
the Dust Jacket has a "!" at the end of the
first paragraph on the front flap.
Retail value in:
Near Fine to Fine **$5500**
Good to Very Good **$4200**

Rimbaud, Arthur. *A Season in Hell.*
New York: Limited Editions Club, 1986.
A limited edition of 1000 illustrated by
Robert Mapplethorp.
Retail value in:
Near Fine to Fine **$2000**
Good to Very Good **$1200**

Saint-Exupery, Antoine De. *The Little
Prince.* New York: Reynal & Hitchcock,
1943. The first state Dust Jacket carries
the publisher's address on Fourth Avenue.
Retail value in:
Near Fine to Fine **$2600**
Good to Very Good **$1000**

Sand, George. *The Masterpieces of
George Sand.* Philadelphia: George Barrie
and Sons, 1900-1902. Printed in a limited
set of 20 Volumes for subscribers.
Retail value in:
Near Fine to Fine **$9000**
Good to Very Good **$6000**

Price Guide

Abell, Kjeld. *Three from Minikoi.*
First Edition in English: London: Seker
and Warburg, 1960.
Nr.Fine/Fine **$25**
Good/V.Good **$10**

*Agnon, Shmuel Yosef. *In the Heart of
the Seas.* First U.S. Edition: New York:
Schocken Books, 1947.
Nr.Fine/Fine **$65**
Good/V.Good **$20**

_____. *Days of Awe.* First
U.S. Edition: New York: Schocken Books,
1948.
Nr.Fine/Fine **$25**
Good/V.Good **$8**

_____. *A Book That Was
Lost: And Other Stories.* First U.S.
Edition: New York: Schocken Books,
1995.
Nr.Fine/Fine **$20**
Good/V.Good **$10**

Ahad, Ha-'Am. *Selected Essays.* First
Edition: Philadelphia: Jewish Publication
Society, 1912.
Nr.Fine/Fine **$18**
Good/V.Good **$6**

Ahlin, Lars. *Cinnamon Candy.* First U.S.
Edition: New York: Garland Publishing,
1990.
Nr.Fine/Fine **$45**
Good/V.Good **$20**

*Aleixandre, Vicente. *Destruction or
Love.* First Edition in English: Santa
Cruz, CA: Green Horse Three, 1976.
Nr.Fine/Fine **$65**
Good/V.Good **$25**

_____. *World Alone.* First
U.S. Edition: Great Barrington, MA:
Penmaen Press, 1982.
Nr.Fine/Fine **$45**
Good/V.Good **$20**

Allende, Isabel. *Of Love and Shadows.*
First U.S. Edition: New York: Alfred A.
Knopf, 1987.
Nr.Fine/Fine **$50**
Good/V.Good **$20**

_____. *The Stories of Eva Luna.*
First U.S. Edition: New York: Atheneum,
1991.
Nr.Fine/Fine **$25**
Good/V.Good $12

Alvaro, Corrado. *Man Is Strong.*
First U.S. Edition: New York: Alfred A.
Knopf, 1948.
Nr.Fine/Fine **$55**
Good/V.Good **$30**

_____. *Revolt in Aspromonte.* First
U.S. Edition: New Haven, CT: New
Directions, 1962.
Nr.Fine/Fine **$50**
Good/V.Good **$25**

Andersch, Alfred. *My Disappearance in
Providence & Other Stories.* First Edition
in English: Garden City, NY: Doubleday
and Co., 1978.
Nr.Fine/Fine **$65**
Good/V.Good **$25**

*Andric, Ivo. *The Bridge on the Drina.*
First Edition in English: London: Allen &
Unwin, 1959.
Nr.Fine/Fine **$325**
Good/V.Good **$155**

_____. *Bosnian Story.* First Edition
in English: London: Lincolns-Prager,
1960
Nr.Fine/Fine **$65**
Good/V.Good **$35**

Andrzejewski, Jerzy. *The Appeal.* First
Edition: London: Weidenfeld and
Nicolson, 1971.
Nr.Fine/Fine **$45**
Good/V.Good **$20**

Apollinaire, Guillaume. *Zone.* First
Edition of Translation by Samuel Beckett:
Dublin/London: The Dolmen Press/Calder

& Boyars, 1972.
Nr.Fine/Fine **$800**
Good/V.Good **$575**

*Asturias, Miguel Angel. *The Green Pope*. First Edition in English: New York: Delacorte, 1971.
Nr.Fine/Fine **$200**
Good/V.Good **$85**

_____. *Strong Wind*. First Edition in English: New York: Delacorte, 1968.
Nr.Fine/Fine **$145**
Good/V.Good **$65**

Ayme, Marcel. *The Proverb and Other Stories*. First U.S. Edition: New York: Antheneum, 1961.
Nr.Fine/Fine **$85**
Good/V.Good **$35**

_____. *Conscience of Love*. First Edition in English: London: The Bodley Head, 1962
Nr.Fine/Fine **$30**
Good/V.Good **$15**
First U.S. Edition: New York: Antheneum, 1961.
Nr.Fine/Fine **$35**
Good/V.Good **$20**

Barash, Asher. *Pictures from a Brewery*. First Edition: Indianapolis: Bobbs-Merrill, 1971.
Nr.Fine/Fine **$25**
Good/V.Good **$10**

Bataille, Georges. *L'Abbe C*. First U.K. Edition: London: Marion Boyars, 1983.
Nr.Fine/Fine **$45**
Good/V.Good **$25**

_____. *My Mother, Madame Edwarda, The Dead Man*. First U.K. Edition: London: Marion Boyars, 1989.
Nr.Fine/Fine **$35**
Good/V.Good **$20**

Benda, Julien. *The Great Betrayal*. First Edition in English: London: George Routledge, 1928.

Nr.Fine/Fine **$85**
Good/V.Good **$50**

The Arcades Project
by Walter Benjamin

Benjamin, Walter. *The Arcades Project*. First U.S. Edition: Cambridge, MA: Harvard University Press, 1999.
Nr.Fine/Fine **$45**
Good/V.Good **$25**

*Bergson, Henri. *Time & Free Will*. First Edition in English: London: Swan Sonnenschein, 1910.
Nr.Fine/Fine **$200**
Good/V.Good **$125**

_____. *Laughter: An Essay On the Meaning of the Comic*. First Edition in English: London & New York: Macmillan, 1911.
Nr.Fine/Fine **$75**
Good/V.Good **$30**

Bernanos, Georges. *Mouchette*. First Edition in English: New York: Holt, Rinehart and Winston, 1966.
Nr.Fine/Fine **$35**
Good/V.Good **$15**

Billetdoux, Francois. *A Man and His Master*. First U.K. Edition: London: Secker & Warburg, 1963.
Nr.Fine/Fine **$45**
Good/V.Good **$20**

Billetdoux, Raphaele. *Night Without Day*. First Edition: New York: Viking, 1987.
Nr.Fine/Fine **$25**

Good/V.Good **$10**

*Boll, Heinrich. *Billiards At Half-Past Nine*.First Edition of Paul Bowles Translation: London: Weidenfeld and Nicolson, 1961.
Nr.Fine/Fine **$200**
Good/V.Good **$125**

_____. *Acquainted With the Night*. First U.S. Edition: New York: Henry Holt & Co, 1954.
Nr.Fine/Fine **$100**
Good/V.Good **$45**

_____. *Group Portrait with Lady*. First Edition in English: London: Secker and Warburg, 1973
Nr.Fine/Fine **$55**
Good/V.Good **$25**
First U.S. Edition: New York: McGraw-Hill, 1973.
Nr.Fine/Fine **$45**
Good/V.Good **$15**

_____. *The Clown*. First U.S. Edition: New York: McGraw Hill Book Co., 1965.
Nr.Fine/Fine **$55**
Good/V.Good **$25**

The Bridge on the River Kwai
by Pierre Boulle

Boulle, Pierre. *The Bridge on the River Kwai*. First U.K. Edition: London: Secker & Warburg, 1954.
Nr.Fine/Fine **$600**

Good/V.Good **$250**

Sophia
by Pierre Boulle

_____. *Sophia*. First Edition: New York: Vanguard Press, Inc., 1959.
Nr.Fine/Fine **$45**
Good/V.Good **$20**

Breton, Andre. *Young Cherry Trees Secured against Hares*. First Edition in English: New York: View Editions, 1946.
Nr.Fine/Fine **$500**
Good/V.Good **$275**

*Bunin, Ivan. *Dark Avenues*.First Edition in English: London: John Lehmann, 1949.
Nr.Fine/Fine **$225**
Good/V.Good **$115**

_____. *Grammar of Love*.First U.S. Edition: New York: Harrison Smith and Robert Haas, 1934.
Nr.Fine/Fine **$85**
Good/V.Good **$35**

_____. *The Well of Days*.First U.S. Edition: New York: Alfred A. Knopf, 1934.
Nr.Fine/Fine **$125**
Good/V.Good **$65**

Butor, Michel. *Degrees*. First Edition in English: New York, Simon and Schuster, 1961.
Nr.Fine/Fine **$55**
Good/V.Good **$30**
First U.K. Edition: London: Methuen &

Co., 1962.
Nr.Fine/Fine **$35**
Good/V.Good **$15**

_____. *Second Thoughts*. First
Edition: London: Faber and Faber, 1958.
Nr.Fine/Fine **$75**
Good/V.Good **$45**

Buzzati, Dino. *The Bears' Famous
Invasion of Italy*. First Edition: New York:
Pantheon, 1947.
Nr.Fine/Fine **$275**
Good/V.Good **$145**

Calvino, Italo. *The Castle Of Crossed
Destinies*.First U.S. Edition: New York:
Harcourt Brace Jovanovich, 1977.
Nr.Fine/Fine **$125**
Good/V.Good **$35**

_____. *Path to the Nest of Spiders*.
First Edition in English: London: Collins,
1956.
Nr.Fine/Fine **$775**
Good/V.Good **$300**
First U.S. Edition: Boston: Beacon Press,
1957.
Nr.Fine/Fine **$300**
Good/V.Good **$125**

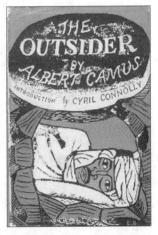

The Outsider
by Albert Camus

*Camus, Albert. *The Outsider*. First
Edition in English: London: Hamish
Hamilton, 1946.
Nr.Fine/Fine **$650**
Good/V.Good **$250**

_____. *The Fall*. First Edition in
English: London: Hamish Hamilton,
1957.
Nr.Fine/Fine **$125**
Good/V.Good **$55**
First U.S. Edition: New York: Alfred A.
Knopf, 1957.
Nr.Fine/Fine **$85**
Good/V.Good **$25**

**The Exile and
the Kingdom**
by Albert Camus

_____. *The Exile and the
Kingdom*. First Edition in English:
London: Hamish Hamilton, 1958.
Nr.Fine/Fine **$150**
Good/V.Good **$70**
First U.S. Edition: New York: Alfred A.
Knopf, 1958.
Nr.Fine/Fine **$100**
Good/V.Good **$40**

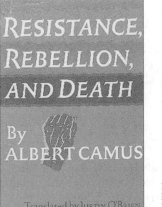

**Resistance,
Rebellion, and
Death**
by Albert Camus

_____. *Resistance, Rebellion, and Death*.First Edition in English: London: Hamish Hamilton, 1961.
Nr.Fine/Fine **$95**
Good/V.Good **$30**
First U.S. Edition: New York: Alfred A. Knopf, 1961.
Nr.Fine/Fine **$75**
Good/V.Good **$25**

Capek, Karl. *Krakatit*. First U.S. Edition: New York: Macmillan, 1925.
Nr.Fine/Fine **$75**
Good/V.Good **$30**

*Carducci, Giosue. *Odi Barbare* First Edition in English: New York: Vanni, 1950.
Nr.Fine/Fine **$45**
Good/V.Good **$20**

Castro, Ferreira de. *Jungle: a Tale of the Amazon Rubber-Tappers*. First U.S. Edition: New York: Viking Press, 1935.
Nr.Fine/Fine **$150**
Good/V.Good **$85**

Cayrol, Jean. *All in a Night*. First Edition in English: London: Faber & Faber, 1956.
Nr.Fine/Fine **$25**
Good/V.Good **$12**

The Family of
Pascual Duarte
by Camilo Jose Cela

*Cela, Camilo José. *Pascual Duarte's Family*. First Edition in English: London: Eyre & Spottiswoode, 1946.
Nr.Fine/Fine **$550**

Good/V.Good **$155**
First U.S. Edition as *The Family of Pascual Duarte*: Boston: Atlantic-Little Brown, 1964.
Nr.Fine/Fine **$125**
Good/V.Good **$55**

_____. *The Hive*. First U.S. Edition: New York: Farrar, Straus & Young, 1953.
Nr.Fine/Fine **$85**
Good/V.Good **$35**
First U.K. Edition: London: Gollancz, 1953.
Nr.Fine/Fine **$45**
Good/V.Good **$20**

Cernuda, Luis. *The Poetry of Luis Cernuda*. First Edition: New York: New York University Press, 1971.
Nr.Fine/Fine **$30**
Good/V.Good **$20**

Char, Rene'. *Hypnos Waking*. First U.S. Edition: New York: Random House, 1956
Nr.Fine/Fine **$65**
Good/V.Good **$30**

_____. *The Dog of Hearts*. First U.S. Edition: Santa Cruz, CA: Green Horse, 1973.
Nr.Fine/Fine **$30**
Good/V.Good **$15**

Cocteau, Jean. *Opium The Diary of an Addict*. First U.K. Edition: London: Longmans, Green, 1932.
Nr.Fine/Fine **$100**
Good/V.Good **$55**

_____. *The Imposter*. First Edition Thus: New York: The Noonsday Press, 1957.
Nr.Fine/Fine **$125**
Good/V.Good **$65**

_____. *The Eagle has Two Heads*. First U.S. Edition: New York: Funk & Wagnalls, 1948.
Nr.Fine/Fine **$85**
Good/V.Good **$30**

The Eagle has
Two Heads
by Jean Cocteau

The
Innocent Wife
*by Colette and
Willy*

Colette. *Mitsou*, or, *How Girls Grow Wise*. First U.S. Edition: New York: Albert & Charles Boni, 1930.
Nr.Fine/Fine **$325**
Good/V.Good **$125**

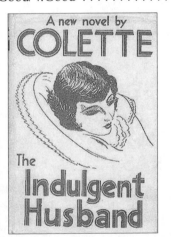

The Indulgent
Husband
*by Colette and
Willy*

Colette and Willy. *The Indulgent Husband*. First U.S. Edition: New York: Farrar & Rinehart, 1935.
Nr.Fine/Fine **$225**
Good/V.Good **$85**

_____. *The Innocent Wife*. First U.S. Edition: New York: Farrar & Rinehart, 1934.
Nr.Fine/Fine **$250**
Good/V.Good **$100**

Curtis, Jean-Louis. *Baccarat*. First Edition: London: Thames & Hudson,

1992.
Nr.Fine/Fine **$145**
Good/V.Good **$85**

D'Annunzio, Gabriele. *The Dead City*. First U.S. Edition: Chicago: Laird & Lee, 1902.
Nr.Fine/Fine **$500**
Good/V.Good **$275**

_____. *The Triumph of Death*. First U.S. Edition: New York: George H. Richmond, 1896.
Nr.Fine/Fine **$165**
Good/V.Good **$85**

Dery, Tibor. *Niki: The Story of a Dog*. First U.K. Edition: London: Secker & Warburg, 1958.
Nr.Fine/Fine **$25**
Good/V.Good **$10**

_____. *The Portuguese Princess*. First U.K. Edition: London: Calder & Boyars, 1966.
Nr.Fine/Fine **$30**
Good/V.Good **$12**

Dinesen, Isak. *Seven Gothic Tales*. First Edition: New York: Harrison Smith & Robert Haas, 1934.
Nr.Fine/Fine **$650**
Good/V.Good **$200**

_____. *Anecdotes of Destiny-Five Stories: The Diver, Babette's Feast,*

Tempests, The Immortal Story, The Ring.
First Edition: London: Michael Joseph,
1958.
Nr.Fine/Fine **$65**
Good/V.Good **$30**

Last Tales
by Isak Dinesen

_____. *Last Tales.*First U.S.
Edition: New York: Random House, 1957.
Nr.Fine/Fine **$125**
Good/V.Good **$50**
First U.K. Edition: London: Putnam,
1957.
Nr.Fine/Fine **$275**
Good/V.Good **$150**

Drieu La Rochelle, Pierre. *The Fire
Within*. First U.S. Edition: New York:
Alfred A. Knopf, 1965.
Nr.Fine/Fine **$35**
Good/V.Good **$20**

_____. *Will o' the Wisp.*
First U.K. Edition: London: Calder and
Boyars, 1963.
Nr.Fine/Fine **$35**
Good/V.Good **$15**

Druon, Maurice. *The Poisoned Crown*.
First U.S. Edition: New York: Scribners,
1957.
Nr.Fine/Fine **$120**
Good/V.Good **$45**

*Du Gard, Roger Martin. *The Thibaults*.
First U.S. Edition: New York: Boni and
Liveright, 1926.

Nr.Fine/Fine **$150**
Good/V.Good **$60**

_____. *The Postman.*
First Edition in English: London: Andre
Deutsch, 1954.
Nr.Fine/Fine **$100**
Good/V.Good **$45**
First U.S. Edition: New York: Viking,
1955.
Nr.Fine/Fine **$45**
Good/V.Good **$15**

_____. *Jean Barois.*
First U.S. Edition: New York: Viking,
1949.
Nr.Fine/Fine **$50**
Good/V.Good **$20**

Blue Eyes,
Black Hair
by Margerite Duras

Duras, Marguerite. *Blue Eyes, Black
Hair*. First Edition in English: New York:
Pantheon, 1987.
Nr.Fine/Fine **$35**
Good/V.Good **$20**
First U.K. Edition: London: Collins, 1988.
Nr.Fine/Fine **$25**
Good/V.Good **$12**

_____. *Summer Rain.*First U.S.
Edition: New York: Scribners, 1992.
Nr.Fine/Fine **$30**
Good/V.Good **$15**
First U.K. Edition: London:
HarperCollins, 1992.
Nr.Fine/Fine **$25**

Good/V.Good **$10**

Summer Rain
by Marguerite Duras

War: a Memoir
by Marguerite Duras

_____. *War: a Memoir*. First
U.S. Edition: New York: Pantheon, 1986.
Nr.Fine/Fine **$35**
Good/V.Good **$12**

*Echegaray, Jose. *The Son of Don Juan*.
First Edition Thus: Boston: Roberts
Brothers, 1895.
Nr.Fine/Fine **$55**
Good/V.Good **$30**

*Elytis, Odysseus. *Maria Nephele: A
Poem in Two Voices*. First U.S. Edition:
Boston: Houghton Mifflin, 1981.
Nr.Fine/Fine **$35**
Good/V.Good **$20**

_____. *The Sovereign Sun*.
First Edition: Philadelphia: Temple

University, 1974.
Nr.Fine/Fine **$25**
Good/V.Good **$15**

Estang, Luc. *The Better Song*. First U.S.
Edition: New York: Pantheon, 1963.
Nr.Fine/Fine **$25**
Good/V.Good **$10**
First U.K. Edition: London: Hodder &
Stoughton, 1964.
Nr.Fine/Fine **$20**
Good/V.Good **$10**

Faure, Elie. *The Dance Over Fire and
Water*. First Edition: New York: Harper &
Brothers, 1926.
Nr.Fine/Fine **$35**
Good/V.Good **$15**

Feuchtwanger, Lion. *Jew Suss A
Historical Romance*.First U.K. Edition
(Limited/Signed): London: Martin Secker,
1926.
Nr.Fine/Fine **$350**
Good/V.Good **$200**
First U.K. Edition (trade): London: Martin
Secker, 1926.
Nr.Fine/Fine **$125**
Good/V.Good **$60**

_____. *Success* First U.K.
Edition: London: Martin Secker, 1930.
Nr.Fine/Fine **$175**
Good/V.Good **$65**

*Fo, Dario. *Can't Pay? Won't Pay!* First
U.K. Edition: London: Pluto Press, 1982.
Nr.Fine/Fine **$35**
Good/V.Good **$20**

Fort, Paul. *Selected Poems and Ballads
of Paul Fort*. First U.S. Edition: New
York: Duffield and Company, 1921
Nr.Fine/Fine **$25**
Good/V.Good **$10**

*France, Anatole. *The Crime Of Sylvestre
Bonnard*.First Edition of Lafcadio Hearn
Translation: New York: Harper &
Brothers, 1890.
Nr.Fine/Fine **$275**
Good/V.Good **$135**

_____. *Bee the Princess of the Dwarfs*. First U.K. Edition: London: J. M. Dent, 1912.
Nr.Fine/Fine **$450**
Good/V.Good **$250**

_____. *The Aspirations of Jean Servien*. First U.K. Edition: London: John Lane The Bodley Head, 1912.
Nr.Fine/Fine **$55**
Good/V.Good **$20**

Frisch, Max. *I'm Not Stiller*. First U.K. Edition: London: Abelard-Schuman, 1958.
Nr.Fine/Fine **$150**
Good/V.Good **$75**

Fussenegger, Gertrud. *Noah's Ark*. First U.S. Edition: Philadelphia: J. B. Lippincott, 1982.
Nr.Fine/Fine **$25**
Good/V.Good **$10**

Fust, Milan. *The Story of My Wife*. First Edition in English: New York: Paj Publications, 1987.
Nr.Fine/Fine **$35**
Good/V.Good **$15**

acquainted with grief

Carlo Emilio Gadda

Acquainted
With Grief
*by Carlo Emilio
Gadda*

Gadda, Carlo Emilio. *Acquainted with Grief*. First U.S. Edition: New York: George Braziller, 1969.
Nr.Fine/Fine **$40**
Good/V.Good **$20**

The Roots
of Heaven
by Romain Gary

Gary, Romain. *The Roots of Heaven*. First U.S. Edition: New York: Simon & Schuster, 1958.
Nr.Fine/Fine **$45**
Good/V.Good **$20**

_____. *The Ski Bum*. First U.S. Edition: New York: Harper and Row, 1965.
Nr.Fine/Fine **$35**
Good/V.Good **$15**

Genet, Jean. *Our Lady of Flowers*. First Edition in English (Limited): Paris: Morihien, 1949.
Nr.Fine/Fine **$200**
Good/V.Good **$115**
First U.S. Edition: New York: Grove Press, 1963.
Nr.Fine/Fine **$55**
Good/V.Good **$25**
First U.K. Edition: London: Anthony Blond, 1964.
Nr.Fine/Fine **$45**
Good/V.Good **$20**

Gide, Andre. *Oscar Wilde. A Study*. First Edition in English: London: The Holywell Press, 1905.
Nr.Fine/Fine **$350**
Good/V.Good **$185**

_____. *Two Symphonies*. First U.S. Edition: New York: Alfred A. Knopf,

1931.
Nr.Fine/Fine $70
Good/V.Good $20
First U.K. Edition: London: Cassell, 1931.
Nr.Fine/Fine $85
Good/V.Good $45

_____. *Urien's Voyage*. First U.S.
Edition: New York: Philosophical Library,
1964.
Nr.Fine/Fine **$55**
Good/V.Good **$20**
First U.K. Edition: London: Peter Owen,
1964.
Nr.Fine/Fine **$35**
Good/V.Good **$15**

The Malediction
by Jean Giono

Giono, Jean. *The Malediction*. First U.S.
Edition: New York Criterion Books, 1955.
Nr.Fine/Fine **$175**
Good/V.Good **$100**

Girandoux, Jean. *Tiger at the Gates*.
First Edition: New York: Oxford, 1955.
Nr.Fine/Fine **$35**
Good/V.Good **$15**

Gombrowicz, Witold. *Ferdydurke*. First
U.K. Edition: London: Macgibbon and
Kee, 1961.
Nr.Fine/Fine **$225**
Good/V.Good **$125**

_____. *Pornografia*. First U.S.
Edition: New York: Grove Press, 1966.
Nr.Fine/Fine **$65**
Good/V.Good **$25**

Gomez de la Serna, Ramon. *Movie land*.
First Edition: New York: Macaulay, 1930.
Nr.Fine/Fine **$165**
Good/V.Good **$90**

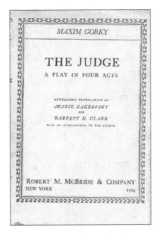

The Judge
by Maxim Gorky

Gorky, Maxim. *The Judge*. First Edition:
New York: McBride, 1924.
Nr.Fine/Fine **$75**
Good/V.Good **$30**

Gracq, Julien. *A Dark Stranger*. First
Edition: New York: New Directions, 1951.
Nr.Fine/Fine **$50**
Good/V.Good **$30**

*Grass, Gunther. *The Flounder*. First
U.S. Edition: New York: Harcourt Brace
Jovanovich, 1977.
Nr.Fine/Fine **$75**
Good/V.Good **$40**

_____. *Show Your Tongue*. First
U.K. Edition: London: Secker Warburg,
1989.
Nr.Fine/Fine **$25**
Good/V.Good **$12**

_____. *The Call of the Toad*. First
U.S. Edition: New York: Harcourt Brace
Jovanovich, 1992.
Nr.Fine/Fine **$25**
Good/V.Good **$10**

Green, Julien. *The Distant Lands* First
U.S. Edition: New York: M. Boyars,
Distributed By Rizzoli International.

Publications, 1991
Nr.Fine/Fine **$30**
Good/V.Good **$12**

Gyllensten, Lars. *The Testament of Cain*.
First Edition: London: Calder & Boyars,
1967.
Nr.Fine/Fine **$25**
Good/V.Good **$10**

*Hamsun, Knut. *Benoni*. First U.S.
Edition: New York: Alfred A, Knopf,
1925.
Nr.Fine/Fine **$375**
Good/V.Good **$165**

_____. *Hunger*. First U.S.
Edition: New York: Alfred A Knopf,
1920.
Nr.Fine/Fine **$300**
Good/V.Good **$125**

Dreamers
by Knut Hamsun

_____. *Dreamers*.First U.S.
Edition: New York: Alfred A Knopf,
1921.
Nr.Fine/Fine **$350**
Good/V.Good **$185**

*Hauptmann, Gerhart. *Phantom*. First
U.S. Edition: New York: B.W.Huebsch,
1922.
Nr.Fine/Fine **$150**
Good/V.Good **$75**
First U.K. Edition: London: Martin
Secker, 1923.

Nr.Fine/Fine **$145**
Good/V.Good **$55**

_____. *The Heretic of
Soana*. First Edition in English: New
York: B.W. Huebsch, 1923.
Nr.Fine/Fine **$75**
Good/V.Good **$25**

_____. *The Fool In
Christ*. First Edition: New York: B.W.
Huebsch, 1911.
Nr.Fine/Fine **$45**
Good/V.Good **$25**

*Hesse, Hermann. *Siddhartha*. First U.S.
Edition: New York: New Directions, 1951.
Nr.Fine/Fine **$1350**
Good/V.Good **$700**

_____. *Steppenwolf*. First U.S.
Edition: New York: Henry Holt, 1929.
Nr.Fine/Fine **$350**
Good/V.Good **$165**

_____. *Beneath the Wheel*. First
U.S. Edition: New York: Farrar, Strauss,
Giroux, 1968.
Nr.Fine/Fine **$85**
Good/V.Good **$35**

Huysmans, Joris-Karl. *Down Stream
and Other Works*. First U.S. Edition:
Chicago: Pascal Covici, 1927.
Nr.Fine/Fine **$100**
Good/V.Good **$45**

_____. *En Route*. First
U.S. Edition: New York: E. P. Dutton,
1920
Nr.Fine/Fine **$75**
Good/V.Good **$40**

Ishiguro, Kazuo. *A Pale View Of Hills*.
First U.K. Edition: London: Faber &
Faber, 1982.
Nr.Fine/Fine **$1250**
Good/V.Good **$655**

Jacob, Max. *The Story of King Kabul the
First and Gawain the Kitchen-Boy*. First
U.S. Edition: Lincoln, NE: University Of
Nebraska, 1994.

Big Foot Wallace
by Stanley Vestal 1942. $150 in Nr. Fine/Fine.

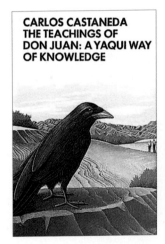

The Teachings of Don Juan: A Yaqui Way Of Knowledge
by Carlos Castaneda 1973. $100 in Nr. Fine/Fine.

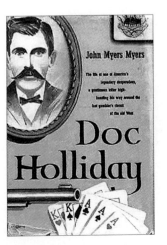

Doc Holliday
by John Myers Myers 1955. $60 in Nr. Fine/Fine.

Sucker's Progress: An Informal History Of Gambling In America From The Colonies To Canfield
by Herbert Asbury 1938. $150 in Nr. Fine/Fine.

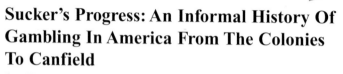

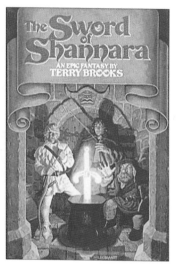

The Sword of Shannara
by Terry Brooks 1977. $450 in Nr. Fine/Fine.

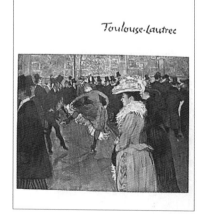

Toulouse-Lautrec
by Henri De Toulouse-Lautrec 1966. $265 in Nr. Fine/Fine.

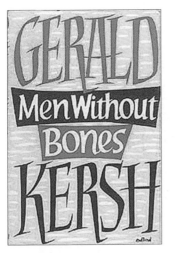

Georgia O'Keeffe: The New York Years
by Georgia O'Keeffe 1991. $80 in Nr. Fine/Fine.

Raggedy Ann's Magical Wishes
by Johnny Gruelle 1928. $300 in Nr. Fine/Fine.

Men Without Bones
by Gerald Kersh 1955. $150 in Nr. Fine/Fine.

Emmanuelle II
by Emmanuelle Arsan 1974. $65 in Nr. Fine/Fine.

The Ginger Man
by J.P. Donleavy 1955. $800 in Nr. Fine/Fine.

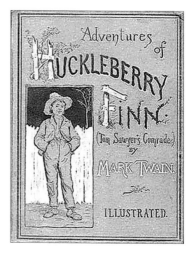

The Adventures of Huckleberry Finn
by Mark Twain 1884. $10,000 in Nr.
Fine/Fine.

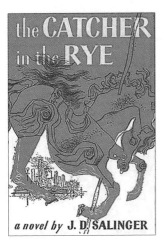

The Catcher in the Rye
by J.D. Salinger 1951. $15,000 in Nr. Fine/Fine.

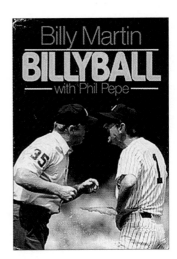

BillyBall
by Billy Martin with Phil Pepe 1987. $20 in Nr. Fine/Fine.

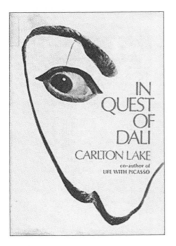

In Quest of Dali
by Carlton Lake 1969. $35 in Nr. Fine/Fine.

Lo, The Former Eygptian!
by H. Allen Smith 1947. $30 in Nr. Fine/Fine.

Love Lucy
by Lucille Ball 1996. $20 in Nr. Fine/Fine.

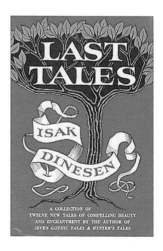

Last Tales
by Isak Dinesen 1957. $125 in Nr. Fine/Fine.

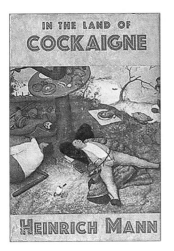

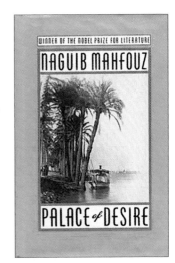

In the Land of Cockaigne
by Heinrich Mann 1929. $250 in Nr. Fine/Fine.

Palace of Desire
by Naguib Mahfouz 1991. $65 in Nr. Fine/Fine.

The Wonderful Clouds
by Francoise Sagan 1962. $70 in Nr. Fine/Fine.

Going Their Own Ways
by Alec Waugh 1938. $95 in Nr. Fine/Fine.

The Building of Jalna
by Mazo De La Roche 1944. $45 in Nr. Fine/Fine.

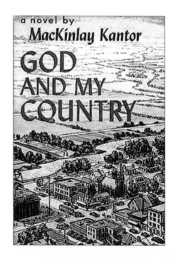

God and My Country
*by MacKinley Kantor 1954. $125 in
    Nr. Fine/Fine.*

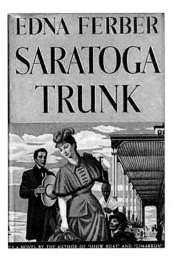

Saratoga Trunk
by Edna Ferber 1941. $135 in Nr. Fine/Fine.

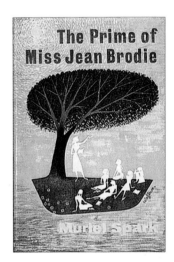

The Prime of Miss Jean Brodie
by Muriel Spark 1961. $275 in Nr. Fine/Fine.

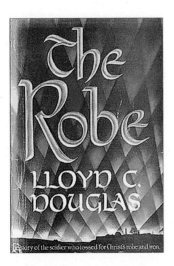

The Robe
*by Lloyd C. Douglas 1942. $550 in
Nr. Fine/Fine.*

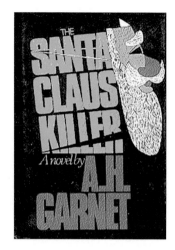

The Santa Claus Killer
by A.H. Garnet 1981. $20 in Nr. Fine/Fine.

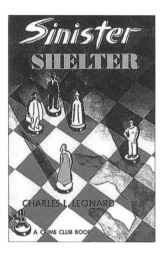

Sinister Shelter
by Charles L. Leonard 1949. $40 in
*   Nr. Fine/Fine.*

The Mystery of th Blue Train
by Agatha Christie 1928. $2,500 in
*   Nr. Fine/Fine.*

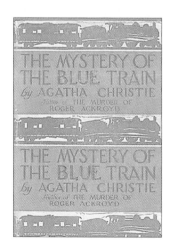

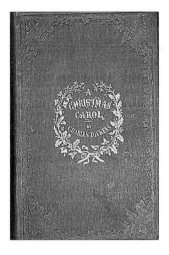

A Christmas Carol
by Charles Dickens 1941. $30,000 in Nr. Fine/Fine.

Death of a Dude
by Rex Stout 1969. $50 in Nr. Fine/Fine.

In My Own Way An Autobiography
by Alan W. Watts 1972. $120 in Nr. Fine/Fine.

Bigfoot and Other Legendary Creatures
by Paul Robert Walker 1992. $25 in
    Nr. Fine/Fine.

The Magical Records of the Beast 666
by Aleister Crowley 1972. $125 in Nr. Fine/Fine.

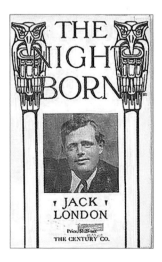

The Night Born
by Jack London 1959. $550 in Nr. Fine/Fine.

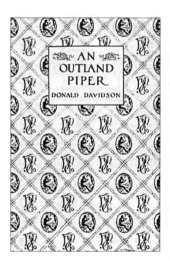

Angels: God's Secret Agents
by Billy Graham 1975. $20 in Nr. Fine/Fine.

An Outland Piper
by Donald Davidson 1924. $350 in Nr. Fine/Fine.

Creative Intuition In Art And Poetry
by Jacques Maritain 1953. $75 in Nr. Fine/Fine.

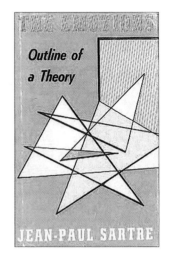

The Emotions, Outline of A Theory
by Jean-Paul Sartre 1948. $75 in Nr. Fine/Fine.

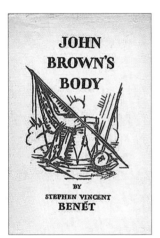

John Brown's Body
*by Stephen Vincent Benet 1928. $200 in
    Nr. Fine/Fine.*

Ham On Rye
*by Charles Bukowski 1982. $1,800 in
    Nr. Fine/Fine.*

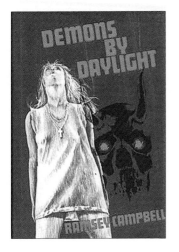

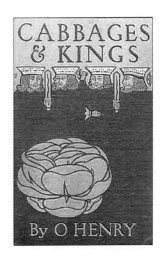

Demons By Daylight
by Ramsey Campbell 1973 $45 in Nr. Fine/Fine.

Cabbages & Kings
by O. Henry 1904. $550 in Nr. Fine/Fine.

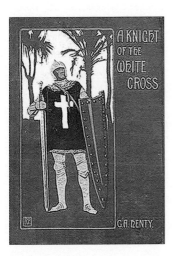

A Knight Of the White Cross
by G.G. Henty 1886 $165 in Nr. Fine/Fine.

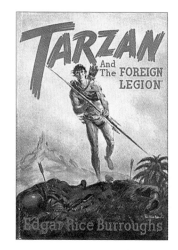

Tarzan and the Foreign Legion
by Edgar Rice Burroughs 1947. $100 in Nr. Fine/Fine.

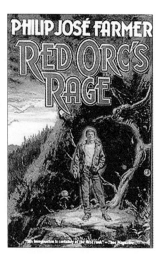

Red Orc's Rage
by Philip Jose Farmer 1991 $12 in Nr. Fine/Fine.

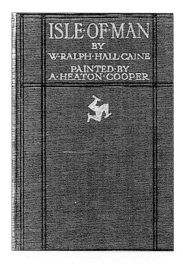

Isle of Man
by Hall Caine 1909. $150 in Nr. Fine/Fine.

Nr.Fine/Fine **$25**
Good/V.Good **$10**

Jens, Walter. *The Blind Man.* First U.K.
Edition: London: Andre Deutsch, 1954.
Nr.Fine/Fine **$30**
Good/V.Good **$12**

*Jensen, Johannes V. *The Long Journey.*
(Three Volumes) First U.K. Edition:
London: Gyldendal, 1922-1924.
Nr.Fine/Fine **$225**
Good/V.Good **$95**

*Jimenez, Juan Ramon. *Platero and I.*
First U.S. Edition: Austin, TX: University
of Texas, 1957.
Nr.Fine/Fine **$60**
Good/V.Good **$25**

_____. *Stories of Life and
Death.* First U.S. Edition: New York:
Paragon House, 1985.
Nr.Fine/Fine **$15**
Good/V.Good **$8**

*Johnson, Eyvind. *The Days of His
Grace.* First U.K. Edition: London: Chatto
and Windus, 1968.
Nr.Fine/Fine **$25**
Good/V.Good **$12**

Junger, Ernst. *Copse 125.* First U.K.
Edition: London: Chatto and Windus,
1930.
Nr.Fine/Fine **$200**
Good/V.Good **$110**

_____. *The Storm of Steel.* First
U.K. Edition: London: Chatto & Windus,
1929.
Nr.Fine/Fine **$225**
Good/V.Good **$125**

Kaleb, Vjekoslav. *Glorious Dust.* First
Edition: London: Lincolns-Prager, 1960.
Nr.Fine/Fine **$25**
Good/V.Good **$10**

*Kawabata, Yasunari. *House of the
Sleeping Beauties.* First Edition in
English: Palo Alto, CA: Kodansha, 1969.
Nr.Fine/Fine **$125**

Good/V.Good **$55**

1968 NOBEL Laureate
YASUNARI KAWABATA
HOUSE OF THE
SLEEPING BEAUTIES
AND OTHER STORIES
translated by
Edward G. Seidensticker

House of the
Sleeping
Beauties
*by Yasunari
Kawabata*

Kazantzakis, Nikos. *Zorba The Greek.*
First Edition: London: John Lehmann,
1952.
Nr.Fine/Fine **$200**
Good/V.Good **$85**
First U.S. Edition: New York: Simon and
Schuster, 1953
Nr.Fine/Fine **$250**
Good/V.Good **$100**

*Lagerkvist, Par. *The Sibyl.* First U.S.
Edition: New York: Random House, 1958.
Nr.Fine/Fine **$45**
Good/V.Good **$20**

_____. *The Dwarf.* First U.S.
Edition: New York: L. B. Fischer, 1954.
Nr.Fine/Fine **$65**
Good/V.Good **$30**

_____. *Pilgrim at Sea.* First
Edition in English: London: Chatto &
Windus, 1964.
Nr.Fine/Fine **$50**
Good/V.Good **$25**
First U.S. Edition: New York: Random
House, 1964.
Nr.Fine/Fine **$25**
Good/V.Good **$10**

*Lagerlof, Selma. *General's Ring.* First
U.S. Edition: Garden City, NY:
Doubleday, Doran, 1928.
Nr.Fine/Fine **$45**

Good/V.Good **$20**

_____. *Outcast*. First Edition
in English: London: Gyldendal, 1922.
Nr.Fine/Fine **$150**
Good/V.Good **$65**
First U.S. Edition: Garden City, NY:
Doubleday, Page, 1922.
Nr.Fine/Fine **$150**
Good/V.Good **$50**

_____. *The Wonderful Adventures
of Nils*. First U.K. Edition: London:
Arthur F. Bird, 1925.
Nr.Fine/Fine **$55**
Good/V.Good **$25**

*Laxness, Halldor. *Paradise Reclaimed*.
First U.S. Edition: New York: Thomas Y.
Crowell, 1962.
Nr.Fine/Fine **$150**
Good/V.Good **$65**

_____. *Fish Can Sing*. First
Edition: London: Methuen, 1966.
Nr.Fine/Fine **$250**
Good/V.Good **$95**

_____. *The Happy Warriors*
First U.K. Edition: London: Methuen,
1958.
Nr.Fine/Fine **$225**
Good/V.Good **$150**

Levi, Primo. *Other People's Trades*. First
U.S. Edition: New York: Summit, 1985.
Nr.Fine/Fine **$45**
Good/V.Good **$25**

_____. *If This Is a Man*. First U.S.
Edition: New York: Orion Press, 1959.
Nr.Fine/Fine **$225**
Good/V.Good **$100**

Lind, Jakov. *Travels to Enu: Story of a
Shipwreck*.First U.K. Edition: London:
Eyre Methuen, 1982.
Nr.Fine/Fine **$125**
Good/V.Good **$45**
First U.S. Edition: New York: St. Martin's,
1982.
Nr.Fine/Fine **$30**

Good/V.Good **$10**

Linna, Vaino. *The Unknown Soldier*. First
Edition: London: Collins, 1957.
Nr.Fine/Fine **$30**
Good/V.Good **$12**

Lorca, Federico Garcia. *The Poet in New
York and Other Poems of Federico* Garcia
Lorca. First Edition: New York: W.W.
Norton, 1940.
Nr.Fine/Fine **$2000**
Good/V.Good **$850**

*Maeterlinck, Maurice. *The Blue Bird*.
First U.S. Edition: New York: Dodd Mead
& Co., 1909.
Nr.Fine/Fine **$200**
Good/V.Good **$110**

_____. *The Life of the
Ant*. First U.S. Edition Thus: New York:
John Day, 1930.
Nr.Fine/Fine **$35**
Good/V.Good **$15**

_____. *The Life of The
Bee* First U.S. Edition: New York: Dodd,
Mead, 1901.
Nr.Fine/Fine **$155**
Good/V.Good **$65**

Palace of Desire
by Naguib Mahfouz

*Mahfouz, Naguib. *Palace of Desire*.
First U.S. Edition: Garden City, NY:
Doubleday, 1991.
Nr.Fine/Fine **$65**

Good/V.Good **$30**

_____. *Respected Sir*. First
U.K. Edition: London: Quartet, 1986.
Nr.Fine/Fine **$75**
Good/V.Good **$30**

_____. *Sugar Street*. First U.S.
Edition: Garden City, NY: Doubleday,
1992.
Nr.Fine/Fine **$50**
Good/V.Good **$20**

Malaparte, Curzio. *The Skin*. First U.S.
Edition: Boston: Houghton Mifflin, 1952.
Nr.Fine/Fine **$50**
Good/V.Good **$20**

Mallet-Joris, Francoise. *The Witches:
Three Tales of Sorcery*. First U.S. Edition:
New York: Farrar Strauss & Giroux, 1969.
Nr.Fine/Fine **$45**
Good/V.Good **$15**

Malroux, Andre. *Days of Wrath*. First
Edition: New York: Random House, 1936.

Nr.Fine/Fine **$25**
Good/V.Good **$12**

Mann, Heinrich. *In the Land of
Cockaigne*. First U.S. Edition: New York:
Macaulay, 1929.
Nr.Fine/Fine **$250**
Good/V.Good **$100**

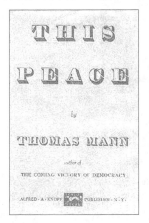

This Peace
by Thomas Mann

*****Mann, Thomas**. *This Peace*. First U.S.
Edition: New York: Alfred A. Knopf,

1938.
Nr.Fine/Fine **$225**
Good/V.Good **$95**

_____. *Joseph and His
Brothers*. First U.S. Edition: New York:
Alfred A. Knopf, 1934.
Nr.Fine/Fine **$750**
Good/V.Good **$275**

_____. *Death in Venice and
Other Stories*. First U.S. Edition: New
York: Alfred A. Knopf, 1925.
Nr.Fine/Fine **$550**
Good/V.Good **$200**

Marceau, Felicien. *The Flesh in the
Mirror*. First U.K. Edition: London:
Vision Press, 1957.
Nr.Fine/Fine **$75**
Good/V.Good **$45**

Marnau, Fred. *The Death of the
Cardinal*. First Edition: London: Grey
Walls, 1946.
Nr.Fine/Fine **$45**
Good/V.Good **$20**

No One Writes
to the Colonel
*by Gabriel Garcia
Marquez*

*****Marquez, Gabriel Garcia**. *No One
Writes to the Colonel and Other Stories*.
First U.S. Edition: New York: Harper &
Row, 1968.
Nr.Fine/Fine **$950**
Good/V.Good **$375**
First U.K. Edition: London: Cape, 1971.
Nr.Fine/Fine **$650**
Good/V.Good **$200**

_____. *In Evil Hour*.
First U.S. Edition: New York: Harper &
Row, 1979.
Nr.Fine/Fine **$175**
Good/V.Good **$75**

_____. *Love in the
Time of Cholera*. First Edition: New York:
Alfred A. Knopf, 1988.
Nr.Fine/Fine **$75**
Good/V.Good **$25**

*Martinson, Harry. *The Road*. First U.K.
Edition: London: Jonathan Cape, 1955.
Nr.Fine/Fine **$675**
Good/V.Good **$400**

_____. *Aniara: a Review
of Man in Time and Space*. First U.S.
Edition: New York: Alfred A Knopf,
1963.
Nr.Fine/Fine **$45**
Good/V.Good **$20**

_____. *Wild Bouquet*.
First U.S. Edition: Kansas City, Mo.:
BKMK Press, 1985.
Nr.Fine/Fine **$45**
Good/V.Good **$15**

Matute, Ana Maria. *The Lost Children*.
First U.S. Edition: New York: Macmillian,
1965.
Nr.Fine/Fine **$35**
Good/V.Good **$15**

The Frontenac
Mystery
by Francois Mauriac

Mauriac, Francois. *The Frontenac

Mystery. First Edition: London: Eyre &
Spottiswoode, 1951.
Nr.Fine/Fine **$65**
Good/V.Good **$25**

Mape: The
World of Illusion
by Andre Maurois

Maurois, Andre. *Mape: The World of
Illusion*. First U.S. Edition: New York: D.
Appleton & Company, 1926.
Nr.Fine/Fine **$85**
Good/V.Good **$35**

The Weigher
of Souls
by Andre Maurois

_____. *The Weigher of Souls*.
First U.S. Edition: New York: D. Appleton
& Company, 1931.
Nr.Fine/Fine **$95**
Good/V.Good **$40**

Meyrink, Gustav. *The Golem*. First U.S.
Edition: Boston: Houghton Mifflin, 1928.
Nr.Fine/Fine **$450**
Good/V.Good **$200**

Mikhalov, Sergei. *Jolly Hares*. First

Edition in English: Moscow: Progress
Publishers, 1969.
Nr.Fine/Fine **$20**
Good/V.Good **$12**

*Milosz, Czeslaw. *Bells In Winter.* First
U.S. Edition: New York: The Ecco Press,
1978.
Nr.Fine/Fine **$35**
Good/V.Good **$20**

_____. *Beginning With My*
Streets. First U.S. Edition: New York;
Farrar Straus & Giroux, 1991.
Nr.Fine/Fine **$45**
Good/V.Good **$25**

_____. *The Usurpers.* First
Edition in English: London: Faber &
Faber, 1955.
Nr.Fine/Fine **$125**
Good/V.Good **$40**

Mirbeau, Octave. *Torture Garden.*
First Edition: New York: Claude Kendall,
1931.
Nr.Fine/Fine **$75**
Good/V.Good **$35**

_____. *Celestine: Being the*
Diary of a Chambermaid. First Edition:
New York: William Faro, 1932.
Nr.Fine/Fine **$55**
Good/V.Good **$30**

*Mistral, Frederic. *Anglore: The Song of*
the Rhone. First U.S. Edition: Claremont,
CA: Saunders Studio Press, 1937.
Nr.Fine/Fine **$75**
Good/V.Good **$30**

*Mistral, Gabriela. *Crickets And Frogs.*
First U.S. Edition: New York: Atheneum,
1972.
Nr.Fine/Fine **$75**
Good/V.Good **$40**

Moravia, Alberto. *Wheel Of Fortune.*
First U.S. Edition: New York: Viking,
1937.
Nr.Fine/Fine **$125**
Good/V.Good **$45**

Satura: Poems
1962-1970
by Eugenio Montale

*Montale, Eugenio. *Satura: Poems 1962-*
1970. First U.S. Edition: New York: W.W.
Norton, 1998
Nr.Fine/Fine **$45**
Good/V.Good **$20**

_____. *The Butterfly of*
Dinard. First U.S. Edition: Lexington,
KY: University Press of Kentucky, 1971.
Nr.Fine/Fine **$50**
Good/V.Good **$30**

The Elephant
by Slawomir Mrozek

Mrozek, Slawomir. *The Elephant.* First
U.S. Edition: New York: Grove Press,
1962.
Nr.Fine/Fine **$40**
Good/V.Good **$15**

*Neruda, Pablo. *Splendor And Death Of*
Joaquin Murieta. First U.S. Edition: New
York: Farrar Straus & Giroux, 1972.
Nr.Fine/Fine **$125**
Good/V.Good **$45**

_____. *The Heights of Macchu Picchu*. First U.S. Edition: New York: Farrar Straus & Giroux, 1967.
Nr.Fine/Fine **$100**
Good/V.Good **$35**

_____. *Residence On Earth*. First U.S. Edition: Norfolk, CT: New Directions, 1946.
Nr.Fine/Fine **$145**
Good/V.Good **$65**

Days in the Sun
by Martin Andersen Nexo

Nexo, Martin Andersen. *Days in the Sun*. First U.S. Edition: New York: Coward-McCann, 1929.
Nr.Fine/Fine **$75**
Good/V.Good **$25**

Nossack, Hans Erich. *The Impossible Proof*. First Edition: New York: Farrar, Straus & Giroux, 1968.
Nr.Fine/Fine **$35**
Good/V.Good **$12**

Odojewski, Wlodzimierz. *The Dying Day*. First U.S. Edition: New York: Harcourt, Brace & World, 1959.
Nr.Fine/Fine **$25**
Good/V.Good **$10**

***Oe, Kenzaburo**. *A Personal Matter*. First U.S. Edition: New York: Grove Press, 1968.
Nr.Fine/Fine **$175**
Good/V.Good **$65**

_____. *Silent Cry*. First Edition

in English: Tokyo: Kodansha International, 1974.
Nr.Fine/Fine **$95**
Good/V.Good **$35**

A Personal Matter
by Kenzaburo Oe

The Silent Cry
by Kenzaburo Oe

_____. *Nip the Buds, Shoot the Kids*. First Edition in English: London & New York: Marion Boyars, 1995.
Nr.Fine/Fine **$50**
Good/V.Good **$20**

Ortega Y Gasset, Jose. *Man and Crisis*. First U.S. Edition: New York: W.W. Norton, 1958.
Nr.Fine/Fine **$65**
Good/V.Good **$25**

Otero, Blas De. *Twenty Poems*. First Edition: Madison, MN: Sixties Press, 1964.
Nr.Fine/Fine **$55**
Good/V.Good **$25**

Doctor Zhivago
by Boris Pasternak

*Pasternak, Boris. *Doctor Zhivago*. First U.K. Edition: London: Collins and Harvill Press, 1958.
Nr.Fine/Fine **$425**
Good/V.Good **$250**
First U.S. Edition: New York: Pantheon, 1958.
Nr.Fine/Fine **$175**
Good/V.Good **$65**

_____. *Sister My Life, Summer, 1917*. First U.S. Edition: New York: Washington Square Press, 1967.
Nr.Fine/Fine **$70**
Good/V.Good **$25**

_____. *Selected Poems*. First Edition: London: Lindsay Drummond, 1946.
Nr.Fine/Fine **$85**
Good/V.Good **$35**

*Paz, Octavio. *The Siren and the Seashell*. First U.S. Edition: Austin, TX: University of Texas Press, 1976.
Nr.Fine/Fine **$85**
Good/V.Good **$30**

_____. *The Labyrinth of Solitude*.First U.S. Edition: New York: Grove Press, 1961.
Nr.Fine/Fine **$165**
Good/V.Good **$85**
First U.K. Edition: London: Allen Lane/Penguin Press, 1967.
Nr.Fine/Fine **$125**
Good/V.Good **$55**

_____. *Alternating Current*.First U.S. Edition: New York: Viking Press, 1973.
Nr.Fine/Fine **$75**
Good/V.Good **$40**

*Perse, St. John. *Anabasis.* First U.K. Edition: London: Faber & Faber, 1930.
Nr.Fine/Fine **$200**
Good/V.Good **$75**

_____. *Birds*. First Edition Thus: New York: Bollingen Foundation, 1966.
Nr.Fine/Fine **$100**
Good/V.Good **$55**

_____. *Seamarks*. First Edition: New York: Pantheon Books, 1958.
Nr.Fine/Fine **$65**
Good/V.Good **$25**

Petersen, Nis. *Whistlers in the Night*. First U.S. Edition: Philadelphia: Nordic Books, 1983
Nr.Fine/Fine **$20**
Good/V.Good **$8**

Peyre, Joseph. *Glittering Death*. First Edition: New York: Random House, 1937.
Nr.Fine/Fine **$75**
Good/V.Good **$30**

_____. *Rehearsal in Oviedo*. First Edition: New York: Knight Publishers, 1937.
Nr.Fine/Fine **$65**
Good/V.Good **$25**

Pinget, Robert. *The Inquisitory*. First U.K. Edition: London: Calder and Boyars, 1966.
Nr.Fine/Fine **$55**
Good/V.Good **$35**
First U.S. Edition: New York: Grove Press, 1966.
Nr.Fine/Fine **$65**
Good/V.Good **$25**

_____. *Recurrent Memory (Passacaille)*. First U.K. Edition: London: Calder & Boyars, 1975.

Nr.Fine/Fine **$45**
Good/V.Good **$20**

*Luigi Pirandello. *Horse in the Moon: Twelve Short Stories*. First U.S. Edition: New York: E. P. Dutton, 1932.
Nr.Fine/Fine **$350**
Good/V.Good **$200**

_____. *One, None and a Hundred Thousand*. First U.S. Edition: New York: E. P. Dutton, 1933.
Nr.Fine/Fine **$100**
Good/V.Good **$45**

_____. *The Naked Truth*.First U.S. Edition: New York: E. P. Dutton, 1935.
Nr.Fine/Fine **$75**
Good/V.Good **$30**

Proust, Marcel. *Cities of the Plain*. (Two Volumes) First U.S. Edition: New York: Albert and Charles Boni, 1927.
Nr.Fine/Fine **$125**
Good/V.Good **$75**

_____. *Jean Santeuil*. First U.K. Edition: London: Weidenfeld and Nicholson, 1955.
Nr.Fine/Fine **$65**
Good/V.Good **$35**

*Quasimodo, Salvatore. *To Give and To Have and Other Poems*. First U.S. Edition: Chicago: Henry Regnery, 1969.
Nr.Fine/Fine **$75**
Good/V.Good **$30**

_____. *The Tall Schooner: A Poem*. First U.S. Edition: New York: Red Ozier Press, 1980.
Nr.Fine/Fine **$75**
Good/V.Good **$40**

_____. *The Poet and the Politician and other Essays*. First Edition: Carbondale, IL: Southern Illinois University Press, 1964.
Nr.Fine/Fine **$35**
Good/V.Good **$15**

Ramuz, Charles F. *Terror On the Mountain*. First U.S. Edition: New York: Harcourt, Brace & World, 1967.
Nr.Fine/Fine **$45**
Good/V.Good **$20**

Raynal, Paul. T*he Unknown Warrior*. First U.K. Edition: London: Methuen, 1928.
Nr.Fine/Fine **$70**
Good/V.Good **$35**

Remarque, Erich Maria. *The Road Back*. First U.K. Edition: London: Putnams, 1931.
Nr.Fine/Fine **$400**
Good/V.Good **$185**
First U.S. Edition: Boston: Little, Brown, 1931.
Nr.Fine/Fine **$300**
Good/V.Good **$125**

_____. *Three Comrades*. First U.S. Edition: Boston: Little, Brown & Co., 1937.
Nr.Fine/Fine **$125**
Good/V.Good **$60**

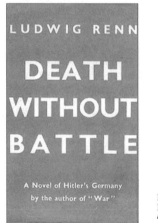

Death Without Battle
by Ludwig Renn

Renn, Ludwig. *Death Without Battle*.First U.K. Edition: London: Martin Secker, 1937.
Nr.Fine/Fine **$100**
Good/V.Good **$45**

Ribeiro, Aquilino. *When the Wolves Howl*. First U.S. Edition: New York: Macmillan, 1963.

Nr.Fine/Fine **$35**
Good/V.Good **$20**

Robbe-Grillet, Alain. *Jealousy*. First U.S. Edition: New York: Grove Press, 1959.
Nr.Fine/Fine **$22**
Good/V.Good **$12**

_____. *La Maison De Rendezvous*. First U.S. Edition: New York: Grove Press, 1966.
Nr.Fine/Fine **$55**
Good/V.Good **$25**

Annette and Sylvie
by Romain Rolland

Rolland, Romain. *Annette and Sylvie*. First U.S. Edition: New York: Henry Holt, 1925.
Nr.Fine/Fine **$85**
Good/V.Good **$40**

_____. *The Game of Love and Death*. First U.S. Edition: New York: Henry Holt, 1926.
Nr.Fine/Fine **$100**
Good/V.Good **$60**

Romains, Jules. *Verdun*. First Edition: New York: Alfred A. Knopf, 1939.
Nr.Fine/Fine **$95**
Good/V.Good **$55**

Roy, Jules. *The Navigator*. First Edition: New York: Alfred A. Knopf, 1955.
Nr.Fine/Fine **$55**
Good/V.Good **$20**

Sabato, Ernesto. *The Outsider*. First U.S. Edition: New York: Alfred A. Knopf, 1950.

Nr.Fine/Fine **$350**
Good/V.Good **$185**

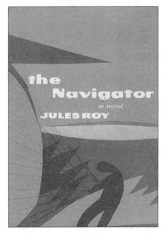

The Navigator
by Jules Roy

_____. *The Angel of Darkness*. First U.K. Edition: London: Jonathan Cape, 1991.
Nr.Fine/Fine **$45**
Good/V.Good **$20**
First U.S. Edition: New York: Ballantine Books, 1991
Nr.Fine/Fine **$35**
Good/V.Good **$15**

*Sachs, Nelly. *O The Chimneys*. First U.S. Edition: New York: Farrar, Straus and Giroux, 1967.
Nr.Fine/Fine **$75**
Good/V.Good **$30**

_____. *The Seeker and Other Poems*. First U.S. Edition: New York: Farrar Straus Giroux, 1970.

The Wonderful Clouds
by Francoise Sagan

Nr.Fine/Fine **$45**
Good/V.Good **$20**

Sagan, Francoise. *The Wonderful Clouds*. First U.S. Edition: New York: E.P. Dutton, 1962.
Nr.Fine/Fine **$70**
Good/V.Good **$30**

_____. *Bonjour Tristesse*.First U.S. Edition: New York: E.P. Dutton, 1955.
Nr.Fine/Fine **$125**
Good/V.Good **$55**

*Saramago, Jose. *The Gospel According to Jesus Christ*. First U.S. Edition: New York: Harcourt Brace, 1994.
Nr.Fine/Fine **$45**
Good/V.Good **$20**

Blindness
by Jose Saramago

_____. *Blindness*. First U.S. Edition: New York: Harcourt Brace Jovanovich, 1997.
Nr.Fine/Fine **$65**
Good/V.Good **$30**

_____. *The Stone Raft*. First U.S. Edition: New York: Harcourt Brace, 1995.
Nr.Fine/Fine **$35**
Good/V.Good **$15**

Sarraute, Nathalie. *Portrait of a Man Unknown*. First U.S. Edition: New York: George Braziller, 1958.
Nr.Fine/Fine **$65**
Good/V.Good **$25**

_____. *Do You Hear Them?*

First U.S. Edition: New York: George Braziller, 1973.
Nr.Fine/Fine **$45**
Good/V.Good **$15**

*Sartre, Jean-Paul. *In The Mesh*. First U.K. Edition: London: Andrew Dakers, 1954.
Nr.Fine/Fine **$185**
Good/V.Good **$100**

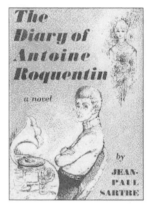
The Diary of
Antoine Roquentin
by Jean-Paul Sartre

_____. *The Diary Of Antoine Roquentin*. First U.K. Edition: London: John Lehmann, 1949.
Nr.Fine/Fine **$125**
Good/V.Good **$70**
First U.S. Edition as *Nausea*: Norfolk, CT: New Directions, 1949.
Nr.Fine/Fine **$100**
Good/V.Good **$35**

_____. *The Chips are Down*. First Edition in English: New York: Lear, 1948.
Nr.Fine/Fine **$225**
Good/V.Good **$110**
First Edition: London: Rider and Company, 1951.
Nr.Fine/Fine **$200**
Good/V.Good **$95**

*Seferis, George. *Three Secret Poems*. First Edition: Cambridge, MA: Harvard University Press, 1969.
Nr.Fine/Fine **$75**
Good/V.Good **$25**

_____. *The King of Asine*. First

Edition: London: John Lehmann, 1948.
Nr.Fine/Fine **$350**
Good/V.Good **$155**

*Seifert, Jaroslav. *Selected Poetry of Jaroslav Seifert.*First Edition: London: Andre Deutsch, 1986.
Nr.Fine/Fine **$35**
Good/V.Good **$15**
First U.S. Edition: New York: Macmillan, 1986.
Nr.Fine/Fine **$20**
Good/V.Good **$10**

The Long Voyage
by Jorge Semprun

Semprun, Jorge. *The Long Voyage.* First U.S. Edition: New York: Grove Press, 1964.
Nr.Fine/Fine **$45**
Good/V.Good **$15**

*Sholokhov, Mikhail. *And Quiet Flows The Don.* First U.S. Edition: New York: Alfred A. Knopf, 1934.
Nr.Fine/Fine **$75**
Good/V.Good **$30**

_____. *Seeds of Tomorrow.* First U.S. Edition: New York: Alfred A. Knopf, 1935.
Nr.Fine/Fine **$70**
Good/V.Good **$30**

_____. *Harvest on The Don.* First U.K. Edition: London: G.P. Putnams, 1960.
Nr.Fine/Fine **$35**
Good/V.Good **$20**
First U.S. Edition: New York: Alfred A.

Knopf, 1961.
Nr.Fine/Fine **$30**
Good/V.Good **$20**

Harvest on the Don
by Mikhail Sholokhov

*Sienkiewicz, Henryk. *Yanko the Musician and Other Stories.* First U.S. Edition: Boston: Little Brown, 1893.
Nr.Fine/Fine **$325**
Good/V.Good **$175**

_____. *Quo Vadis?* First U.S. Edition: Boston: Little Brown, 1896.
Nr.Fine/Fine **$225**
Good/V.Good **$95**

_____. *On The Bright Shore.* First U.S. Edition: Boston: Little Brown, 1898.
Nr.Fine/Fine **$50**
Good/V.Good **$30**

*Sillanpaa, Frans Eemil. *Mid Silja: The History of the Last Offshoot of an Old Family Tree.*
First U.S. Edition: New York: Macmillan, 1933.

Nr.Fine/Fine **$25**
Good/V.Good **$15**

_____. *People In the Summer Night. An Epic Suite.* First U.S. Edition: Madison, WI: The University of Wisconsin Press, 1966.
Nr.Fine/Fine **$25**
Good/V.Good **$12**

*Simon, Claude. *The Wind.* First U.S. Edition: New York: George Braziller,

1959.
Nr.Fine/Fine **$65**
Good/V.Good **$35**

_____. *The Palace*. First
Edition: First U.S. Edition: New York:
George Braziller, 1963.
Nr.Fine/Fine **$40**
Good/V.Good **$15**

_____. *Triptych*. First U.S.
Edition: New York: Viking, 1976
Nr.Fine/Fine **$50**
Good/V.Good **$30**

Sollers, Phillipe. *A Strange Solitude*.
First U.S. Edition: New York: Grove Press
Inc., 1959.
Nr.Fine/Fine **$40**
Good/V.Good **$25**

*Solzhenitsyn, Aleksandr I. *The Gulag
Archipelago*. First U.S. Edition: New
York: Harper & Row, 1974.
Nr.Fine/Fine **$75**
Good/V.Good **$30**

_____. *One Day In
The Life Of Ivan Denisovich*. First Edition
in English: London: Victor Gollancz,
1963.
Nr.Fine/Fine **$300**
Good/V.Good **$175**
First U.S. Edition: New York: Praeger,
1963.
Nr.Fine/Fine **$200**
Good/V.Good **$85**

_____. *Cancer Ward*.
(Two Volumes) First U.K. Edition:
London: Bodley Head, 1968-69.
Nr.Fine/Fine **$100**
Good/V.Good **$45**

*Spitteler, Carl. *Selected Poems*. First
Edition: New York: Macmillan, 1928.
Nr.Fine/Fine **$35**
Good/V.Good **$20**

*Szymborska, Wisława. *View with a
Grain of Sand*. First U.S. Edition: New
York: Harcourt Brace, 1995.

Nr.Fine/Fine **$45**
Good/V.Good **$20**

_____. *Poems New and
Collected, 1957-1997*. First Edition: New
York: Harcourt Brace & Company, 1998.
Nr.Fine/Fine **$35**
Good/V.Good **$12**

Leonardo's Bicycle
by Paco Taibo

Taibo, Paco. *Leonardo's Bicycle*. First
U.S. Edition: New York: Mysterious
Press, 1995.
Nr.Fine/Fine **$25**
Good/V.Good **$10**

_____. *An Easy Thing*. First Edition:
New York: Viking, 1990.
Nr.Fine/Fine **$40**
Good/V.Good **$15**

Teirlinck, Herman. *The Man in the
Mirror*. First Edition: London: Sythoff
Leyden/Heinemann, 1963.
Nr.Fine/Fine **$25**
Good/V.Good **$10**

Theotokas, George. *Leonis*. First Edition:
Minneapolis, MN: Nostos Books, 1985.
Nr.Fine/Fine **$20**
Good/V.Good **$12**

Toller, Ernst. *Letters from Prison*.
First Edition in English: London John
Lane/The Bodley Head, 1936.
Nr.Fine/Fine **$75**
Good/V.Good **$30**

_____. *Pastor Hall: A Play In Three
Acts*. First Edition of Stephen Spender

Translation: London: John Lane/The
Bodley Head, 1938.
Nr.Fine/Fine **$125**
Good/V.Good **$55**

Tolstoy, Count Alexei. *Tsar Fyodor
Ivanovitch.* First U.S. Edition: New York:
Brentano's, 1922.
Nr.Fine/Fine **$70**
Good/V.Good **$30**

Troyat, Henri. *The Mountain.* First U.S.
Edition: New York: Simon & Schuster,
1953
Nr.Fine/Fine **$20**
Good/V.Good **$8**

**Tucholsky, Kurt (as by John
Heartfield).** *Deutschland, Deutschland,
Ÿber alles.* First Edition in English:
Amherst, MA: University of
Massachusetts Press, 1972.
Nr.Fine/Fine **$100**
Good/V.Good **$65**

*Unset, Sigrid. *Happy Times in Norway.*
First U.S. Edition: New York: Alfred A.
Knopf, 1942.
Nr.Fine/Fine **$45**
Good/V.Good **$25**

_____. *The Faithful Wife.* First
U.S. Edition: New York: Alfred A. Knopf,
1937.
Nr.Fine/Fine **$55**
Good/V.Good **$30**

_____. *The Bridal Wreath.* First
U.S. Edition: New York: Alfred A. Knopf,
1929
Nr.Fine/Fine **$75**
Good/V.Good **$30**

Vailland, Roger. *The Law.* First U.K.
Edition: London: Jonathan Cape, 1958.
Nr.Fine/Fine **$50**
Good/V.Good **$20**

Valery, Paul. *The Graveyard by the Sea.*
First U.S. Edition: Philadelphia, PA: The
Centaur Press, 1932.
Nr.Fine/Fine **$275**

Good/V.Good **$150**

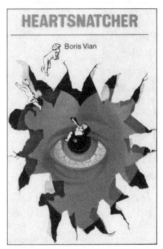

Heartsnatcher
by Boris Vian

Vian, Boris. *Heartsnatcher.* First U.K.
Edition: London: Rapp & Whiting, 1968.
Nr.Fine/Fine **$85**
Good/V.Good **$50**

Vidale, Albert. *Moonlight Jewelers.* First
U.S. Edition: New York: Farrar, Straus and
Cudahy, 1958.
Nr.Fine/Fine **$25**
Good/V.Good **$12**

*Von Heidenstam, Verner. *The Charles
Men.* First U.K. Edition: London:
Jonathan Cape, 1933.
Nr.Fine/Fine **$55**
Good/V.Good **$20**
First U.S. Edition: New York: The
American-Scandinavian Foundation,
1961.
Nr.Fine/Fine **$35**
Good/V.Good **$12**

_____. *The Tree of
the Folkungs.*First U.S. Edition: New
York: Alfred A. Knopf, 1925.
Nr.Fine/Fine **$50**
Good/V.Good **$30**

Waltari, Mika. *The Egyptian.* First U.S.
Edition: New York: G.P. Putnams, 1949.
Nr.Fine/Fine **$150**
Good/V.Good **$65**

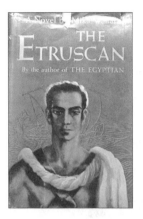

The Etruscan
by Mika Waltari

_____. *The Etruscan*. First U.S. Edition: New York: G.P. Putnams, 1956.
Nr.Fine/Fine **$75**
Good/V.Good **$25**

Wasserman, Jacob. *Kerkhoven's Third Existence*. First Edition: New York: Liveright Publishing Corp., 1934.
Nr.Fine/Fine **$55**
Good/V.Good **$20**

Bodies and Shadows
by Peter Weiss

Weiss, Peter. *Bodies and Shadows*. First U.S. Edition: New York: Delacorte Press A Seymour Lawrence Book, 1969.
Nr.Fine/Fine **$45**
Good/V.Good **$20**

Werfel, Franz. *The Song of Bernadette.* First Edition: New York: Viking, 1942.
Nr.Fine/Fine **$75**
Good/V.Good **$30**

*Xingjian, Gao. *Soul Mountain*. First Edition: New York: HarperCollins, 2000.
Nr.Fine/Fine **$35**
Good/V.Good **$12**

Yevtushenko, Yevgeny. *Stolen Apples.* First U.S. Edition: New York: Doubleday & Company, 1971.
Nr.Fine/Fine **$75**
Good/V.Good **$30**

_____. *Wild Berries. A Novel*. First U.S. Edition: New York: William Morrow, 1984.
Nr.Fine/Fine **$35**
Good/V.Good **$12**

Zweig, Arnold. T*he Case of Sergeant Grischa*. First U.S. Edition: New York: Viking Press, 1928.
Nr.Fine/Fine **$55**
Good/V.Good **$20**

Zweig, Stefan. *The Buried Candelabrum.* First U.S. Edition: New York: Viking Press, 1937.
Nr.Fine/Fine **$65**
Good/V.Good **$25**

Modern First Editions

Modern first editions are, perhaps, the largest category of book collecting. A general definition for the area is the first appearance of a work by a contemporary author. Several dealers currently divide the field by centuries, a modern first having been published in the twentieth century. Authors who began publishing in the nineteenth century may also be included if the bulk of their work was published in the twentieth. For example, James M. Barrie, H. G. Wells, and Arthur Conan Doyle all began their careers in the late nineteenth century, but continued well into the twentieth. The book might be a novel, a volume of poetry, a collection of essays, a short story omnibus, or even a play. The field is, basically, collected by author, though I have seen some collections that cross over into other genres of collecting. Newer genres, such as fantasy or mystery, might be confined to modern firsts, and older genres such as religion or philosophy might be confined to the current century, though this is not very common.

Condition is of great importance to the collector of modern first editions. Small faults that might be overlooked in other areas of collecting are not tolerated by collectors of modern firsts. Even faults that might serve to enhance the value of a book in other areas, such as notes in the text by a prominent owner, devalue modern firsts. Dust jackets are also very important, as the vast majority of books published in the twentieth century were originally issued with them. The state comes into play as well with a greater emphasis than in other areas of collecting. Later states are worth corresponding less as they become further and further removed from the original state.

There are specialized areas to be dealt with in collecting modern firsts. A great many modern firsts were preceded by an advance reading copy, either as a corrected or uncorrected proof. Some collectors prefer these as they are, in actuality, the first appearance of a work.

10 Classic Rarities

Anderson, Sherwood. *Winesburg, Ohio. A Group of Tales of Ohio Small Town Life.* New York: B.W. Heubsch, 1919. First edition, first issue, with line 5 of p.86 reading "lay" and with broken type in "the" in line 3 of p.251. Top edge stained yellow; map on front pastedown.
Retail value in
  Near Fine to Fine. **$12,000**
  Good to Very Good **$10,000**

Bowles, Paul. *The Sheltering Sky.* London: John Lehmann, 1949. Find this and more than sky will shelter you.
Retail value in:
  Near Fine to Fine **$7500**
  Good to Very Good **$3500**

Buck, Pearl S. *The Good Earth.* New York: John Day Company, 1931. With "flees" for "fleas" on page 100.
Retail value in:
  Near Fine to Fine **$9500**
  Good to Very Good **$2500**

Conrad, Joseph. *Lord Jim.* Edinburgh and London: Blackwood, 1900. Originally issued in green card covers with thistle gilt on spine.
Retail value in:
  Near Fine condition **$5500**
  Good to Very Good **$2500**

Durrell, Lawrence. *Pied Piper of Lovers.* London: Cassell, 1935. Spine of case misprints title as 'Pied Pipers of Lovers.'
Retail value in:
Near Fine to Fine **$2000**
Good to Very Good **$1000**

Faulkner, William. *The Sound and the Fury.* New York: Jonathan Cape & Harrison Smith, 1929. Humanity Uprooted is priced at $3.00 on first state Dust Jacket.
Retail value in:
  Near Fine to Fine. **$35,000**
  Good to Very Good **$20,000**

Fitzgerald, F. Scott. *Tales of the Jazz Age.* New York. Charles Scribner's Sons. 1922. "Published September, 1922 and Scribner's Seal" on the copyright page, with "and" for "an" on p. 232, line 6.
Retail value in:
  Near Fine to Fine. **$12,000**
  Good to Very Good **$8000**

Mitchell, Margaret. *Gone with the Wind.* New York: The Macmillan Company, 1936. Has "first published, May, 1936" on copyright page.
Retail value in:
  Near Fine to Fine. **$10,000**
  Good to Very Good **$7000**

Steinbeck, John. *The Grapes of Wrath.* New York: Viking, 1939. "First Edition" on lower corner of front Dust Jacket flap.
Retail value in:
  Near Fine condition **$10,000**
  Good to Very Good **$7500**

Wodehouse, P.G. *The Pothunters.* London: Adam and Charles Black, 1902. There are no advertisements in the first state.
Retail value in:
  Near Fine to Fine **$3500**
  Good to Very Good **$1800**

Price Guide

Abbey, Edward. *The Monkey Wrench Gang.* First Edition: Philadelphia, PA: J.B. Lippincott, 1975.
Nr.Fine/Fine **$650**
Good/V.Good **$250**

Abdullah, Achmed. *Steel and Jade.* First Edition: New York: George H. Doran, 1927.
Nr.Fine/Fine **$550**
Good/V.Good **$200**

Acton, Harold. *Humdrum.* First Edition: London: Chatto & Windus, 1928.
Nr.Fine/Fine **$600**
Good/V.Good **$400**

Ade, George. *The Old-Time Saloon.* First Edition: New York: Ray Long & Richard R. Smith, 1931.
Nr.Fine/Fine **$60**
Good/V.Good **$25**

AE. *Voices of the Stones.* First Edition: London: Macmillan, 1925.
Nr.Fine/Fine **$85**
Good/V.Good **$35**

Agee, James. *A Death in the Family.* First Edition: New York: McDowell, Obolensky, 1957.
Nr.Fine/Fine **$250**
Good/V.Good **$100**

Aiken, Conrad. *King Coffin.* First Edition: New York: Charles Scribner's Sons, 1935.
Nr.Fine/Fine **$125**
Good/V.Good **$50**

Albee, Edward. *All Over.* First Edition: New York: Atheneum, 1971.
Nr.Fine/Fine **$55**
Good/V.Good **$30**

Aldrich, Bess Streeter. *Spring Came On Forever.* First Edition: New York: D. Appleton, 1935.

Nr.Fine/Fine **$95**
Good/V.Good **$55**

The Man With
the Golden Arm
by Nelson Algren

Algren, Nelson. *The Man with the Golden Arm.* First Edition: Garden City, NY: Doubleday, 1949
Nr.Fine/Fine **$650**
Good/V.Good **$200**

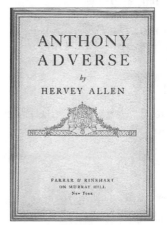

Anthony Adverse
by Hervey Allen

Allen, Hervey. *Anthony Adverse.* First Edition: New York: Farrar and Rinehart, 1933.
Nr.Fine/Fine **$250**
Good/V.Good **$100**

Amis, Kingsley. *Lucky Jim.* First Edition: London: Victor Gollancz, 1953.
Nr.Fine/Fine **$3750**
Good/V.Good **$1400**

Anderson, Maxwell. *Winterset.* First Edition: Washington: Anderson House, 1935.
Nr.Fine/Fine **$45**
Good/V.Good **$15**

Antin, Mary. *The Promised Land.* First Edition: Boston: Houghton Mifflin, 1912.
Nr.Fine/Fine **$45**
Good/V.Good **$20**

The
Power House
by Benjamin Appel

Appel, Benjamin. *The Power House.* First Edition: New York: E. P. Dutton, 1939.
Nr.Fine/Fine **$600**
Good/V.Good **$250**

Arlen, Michael J. *Men's Mortality.* First Edition: London: William Heinemann, 1933.
Nr.Fine/Fine **$250**
Good/V.Good **$140**

Atherton, Gertrude. *Dido Queen of Hearts.* First Edition: New York: Horace Liveright, 1929.
Nr.Fine/Fine **$100**
Good/V.Good **$60**

Auchincloss, Louis. *Portrait In Brownstone.* First Edition: Boston: Houghton Mifflin, 1962.
Nr.Fine/Fine **$100**
Good/V.Good **$35**

Auden, W.H. *Collected Shorter Poems*

1927-1957. First Edition: New York: Random House, 1966.
Nr.Fine/Fine **$125**
Good/V.Good **$50**

Hell in Harness
by Joseph Auslander

Auslander, Joseph. *Hell in Harness.* First Edition: Garden City, NY: Doubleday Doran, 1929
Nr.Fine/Fine **$125**
Good/V.Good **$50**

Austin, Mary. *The Land Of Journey's Ending.* First Edition: New York: The Century Co., 1924
Nr.Fine/Fine **$450**
Good/V.Good **$125**

Bacheller, Irving. *Uncle Peel.* First Edition: New York: Fredrick Stokes, 1933.
Nr.Fine/Fine **$45**
Good/V.Good **$20**

Bacon, Leonard. *Guinea-Fowl and Other Poultry.* First Edition: New York: Harper & Brothers, 1927
Nr.Fine/Fine **$75**
Good/V.Good **$35**

Baker, Dorothy. *Young Man With A Horn.* First Edition: Boston: Houghton Mifflin, 1938.
Nr.Fine/Fine **$350**
Good/V.Good **$110**

Baldwin, Faith. *Thresholds.* First Edition: Boston: Small, Maynard, 1923.

Nr.Fine/Fine. **$350**
Good/V.Good **$115**

Baldwin, James. *Just Above My Head.*
First Edition: New York: Dial Press, 1979.
Nr.Fine/Fine **$65**
Good/V.Good **$25**

Bangs, John Kendrick. *The Foothills of
Parnassus.* First Edition: New York:
Macmillan, 1914.
Nr.Fine/Fine **$150**
Good/V.Good **$60**

Barnes, Djuna. *Nightwood.* First Edition:
London: Faber and Faber, 1936.
Nr.Fine/Fine **$500**
Good/V.Good **$275**

Barth, John. *The Floating Opera.* First
Edition: New York: Appleton-Century
Crofts, 1956.
Nr.Fine/Fine **$400**
Good/V.Good **$135**

Beauregard:
The Great Creole
by Hamilton Basso

Basso, Hamilton. *Beauregard: The Great
Creole.* First Edition: New York:
Scribners, 1933.
Nr.Fine/Fine **$200**
Good/V.Good **$85**

Beach, Rex. *Flowing Gold.* First Edition:
New York & London: Harper & Brothers,
1922.
Nr.Fine/Fine **$85**
Good/V.Good **$50**

Behan, Brendan. *Borstal Boy.* First
Edition: London: Hutchinson, 1958.
Nr.Fine/Fine **$200**
Good/V.Good **$65**

Belasco, David. *The Theatre Through Its
Stage Door.* First Edition: New York:
Harper & Brothers, 1919.
Nr.Fine/Fine **$200**
Good/V.Good **$75**

Bellow, Saul. *Dangling Man.* First
Edition: New York: Vanguard, 1947.
Nr.Fine/Fine **$2100**
Good/V.Good **$750**

The Castle
Number Nine
*by Ludwig
Bemelmans*

Bemelmans, Ludwig. *The Castle Number
Nine.* First Edition: New York: Viking
Press, 1937.
Nr.Fine/Fine **$350**
Good/V.Good **$100**

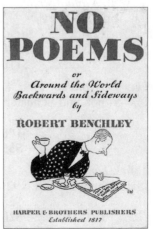

No Poems.
Or Around
the World
Backwards
and Sideways
by Robert Benchley

Benchley, Robert. *No Poems. Or Around the World Backwards and Sideways.* First Edition: New York: Harper & Brothers, 1932.
Nr.Fine/Fine $425
Good/V.Good $200

Benet, Stephen Vincent. *Young People's Pride.* First Edition: New York: Henry Holt, 1922.
Nr.Fine/Fine $100
Good/V.Good $45

Bennett, Arnold. *Elsie and the Child: A Tale of Riceyman Steps and Other Stories.* First Edition: London: Cassell and Company, 1924.
Nr.Fine/Fine $200
Good/V.Good $85

Ninth Avenue
by Maxwell Bodenheim

Bodenheim, Maxwell. *Ninth Avenue.* First Edition: New York: Horace Liveright, 1926.
Nr.Fine/Fine $300
Good/V.Good $110

Boyle, Kay. *Primer for Combat.* First Edition: New York: Simon and Schuster, 1942.
Nr.Fine/Fine $100
Good/V.Good $35

Bradford, Gamaliel. *Darwin.* First Edition: Boston: Houghton Mifflin, 1926
Nr.Fine/Fine $55
Good/V.Good $20

Bradford, Roark. *This Side of Jordan.* First Edition: New York: Harper and Brothers, 1929.
Nr.Fine/Fine $375
Good/V.Good $120

A Confederate General From Big Sur
by Richard Brautigan

Brautigan, Richard. *A Confederate General From Big Sur.* First Edition: New York: Grove Press, 1964.
Nr.Fine/Fine $450
Good/V.Good $150

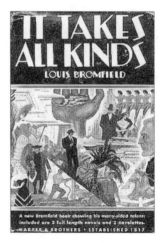

It Takes All Kinds
by Louis Bromfield

Bromfield, Louis. *It Takes All Kinds.* First Edition: New York; Harper & Brothers, 1939.
Nr.Fine/Fine $110
Good/V.Good $40

Broun, Heywood. *Gandle Follows His Nose.* First Edition: New York: Boni & Liveright, 1926.
Nr.Fine/Fine.................. **$75**
Good/V.Good **$25**

Buck, Pearl S. *The Promise.* First Edition: New York: John Day, 1943.
Nr.Fine/Fine **$45**
Good/V.Good **$15**

Burgess, Anthony. *A Clockwork Orange.* First Edition: London: Heinemann, 1962.
Nr.Fine/Fine **$6500**
Good/V.Good **$2000**

The Maxims
of Noah
by Gelett Burgess

Burgess, Gelett. *The Maxims of Noah. Derived from His Experience with Women Both Before and After the Flood as Given in Counsel to his Son Japhet.* First Edition: New York: Frederick A. Stokes, 1913.
Nr.Fine/Fine **$75**
Good/V.Good **$35**

Burgess, Thornton W. *Blacky the Crow.* First Edition: New York: Boston: Little Brown, 1922.
Nr.Fine/Fine **$350**
Good/V.Good **$125**

Byrne, Donn. *Destiny Bay.* First Edition: Boston: Little, Brown, 1928.
Nr.Fine/Fine **$45**
Good/V.Good **$15**

Destiny Bay
by Donn Byrne

Cabell, Branch. *Smirt: An Urban Nightmare.* First Edition: New York: Robert McBride, 1934.
Nr.Fine/Fine **$100**
Good/V.Good **$45**

Cable, George Washington. *Bylow Hill.* First Edition: New York: Scribners, 1902.
Nr.Fine/Fine **$25**
Good/V.Good **$10**

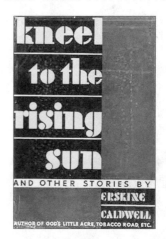

Kneel to the
Rising Sun
by Erskine Caldwell

Caldwell, Erskine. *Kneel to the Rising Sun.* First Edition: New York: Viking Press, 1935
Nr.Fine/Fine **$275**
Good/V.Good **$110**

Caldwell, Taylor. *The Final Hour.* First Edition: New York: Scribners, 1944.
Nr.Fine/Fine **$125**

Good/V.Good **$55**

The
Home-Maker
by Dorothy Canfield

Canfield, Dorothy. *The Home-Maker.*
First Edition: New York: Harcourt, Brace,
1924.
Nr.Fine/Fine **$85**
Good/V.Good **$25**

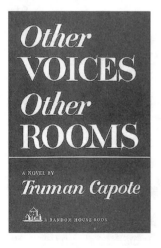

Other Voices
Other Rooms
by Truman Capote

Capote, Truman. *Other Voices, Other
Rooms.* First Edition: New York: Random
House, 1948.
Nr.Fine/Fine **$800**
Good/V.Good **$275**

Carver, Raymond. *Will You Please Be
Quiet, Please?* First Edition: New York:
McGraw-Hill Book Co., 1976.
Nr.Fine/Fine **$2200**

Good/V.Good **$850**

Cary, Joyce. *The Horse's Mouth.* First
Edition: London: Michael Joseph, 1944.
Nr.Fine/Fine **$300**
Good/V.Good **$100**

Cather, Willa. *Death Comes for the
Archbishop.* First Edition: New York:
Alfred A. Knopf, 1927.
Nr.Fine/Fine **$950**
Good/V.Good **$200**

Catton, Bruce. *Michigan: A Bicentennial
History.* First Edition: New York: W.W.
Norton & Company, 1976.
Nr.Fine/Fine **$40**
Good/V.Good **$15**

Chambers, Robert W. *The Laughing
Girl.* First Edition: New York: D.
Appleton, 1918.
Nr.Fine/Fine **$225**
Good/V.Good **$85**

Chayefsky, Paddy. *The Tenth Man.* First
Edition: New York: Random House, 1959.
Nr.Fine/Fine **$50**
Good/V.Good **$20**

Cheever, John. *The Way Some People
Live.* First Edition: New York: Random
House, 1943.
Nr.Fine/Fine **$1500**
Good/V.Good **$650**

Chesterton, G. K. *The Poet And The
Lunatics.* First Edition: London: Cassell,
1929.
Nr.Fine/Fine **$2200**
Good/V.Good **$800**

Ciardi, John. *Lives of X.* First Edition:
New Brunswick, NJ: Rutgers University
Press, 1971.
Nr.Fine/Fine **$40**
Good/V.Good **$15**

Clavell, James. *King Rat.* First Edition:
Boston: Little, Brown, 1962.
Nr.Fine/Fine **$425**
Good/V.Good **$175**

Lives of X
by John Ciardi

Cobb, Irvin S. *Faith, Hope, and Charity.*
First Edition: Indianapolis, IN: Bobbs
Merrill, 1934.
Nr.Fine/Fine **$300**
Good/V.Good **$175**

Connell, Evan S. *Mrs. Bridge.* First
Edition: New York: Viking Press, 1959.
Nr.Fine/Fine **$175**
Good/V.Good **$45**

Connelly, Marc. *The Green Pastures.*
First Edition: New York: Farrar &
Rinehart, 1929.
Nr.Fine/Fine **$200**
Good/V.Good **$55**

Conrad, Joseph. *The Rover.* First Edition:
Garden City, NY: Doubleday, Page, 1923.
Nr.Fine/Fine **$850**
Good/V.Good **$325**

Cowley, Malcolm. *Exile's Return.* First
Edition: New York: W. W. Norton, 1934.
Nr.Fine/Fine **$950**
Good/V.Good **$375**

Cozzens, James Gould. *Ask Me
Tomorrow.* First Edition: New York:
Harcourt, Brace and Company, 1940.
Nr.Fine/Fine **$150**
Good/V.Good **$45**

Crane, Nathalia. *Venus Invisible and
Other Poems.* First Edition: New York:
Coward-McCann, 1928.

Nr.Fine/Fine **$55**
Good/V.Good **$12**

The Gospel Singer
by Harry Crews

Crews, Harry. *The Gospel Singer.* First
Edition: New York: William Morrow &
Company, 1968.
Nr.Fine/Fine **$800**
Good/V.Good **$300**

The Flaming
Forest
*by James Oliver
Curwood*

Curwood, James Oliver. *The Flaming
Forest.* First Edition: New York:
Cosmopolitan, 1921.
Nr.Fine/Fine **$150**
Good/V.Good **$55**

Dahl, Roald. *My Uncle Oswald.* First
Edition: London: Michael Joseph, 1979.
Nr.Fine/Fine **$55**

Good/V.Good **$25**

Dahlberg, Edward. *Do These Bones Live.* First Edition: New York: Harcourt, Brace, 1941.
Nr.Fine/Fine **$200**
Good/V.Good **$80**

Davies, W.H. *The Autobiography of a Super-Tramp.* First Edition: London: A.C. Fifield, 1908.
Nr.Fine/Fine **$300**
Good/V.Good **$125**

Davis, Clyde Brion. *The Great American Novel.* First Edition: New York: Farrar & Rinehart, 1938.
Nr.Fine/Fine **$40**
Good/V.Good **$15**

Davis, H.L. *Honey in the Horn.* First Edition: New York: Harper and Brothers, 1935.
Nr.Fine/Fine **$300**
Good/V.Good **$125**

Davis, Richard Harding. *With the Allies.* First Edition: New York: Charles Scribner's Sons, 1914.
Nr.Fine/Fine **$45**
Good/V.Good **$20**

Day, Clarence. *This Simian World.* First Edition: New York: Alfred A. Knopf, 1920.
Nr.Fine/Fine **$85**
Good/V.Good **$30**

Day-Lewis, Cecil. *The Magnetic Mountain.* First Edition: London: Leonard and Virginia Woolf at the Hogarth Press, 1933.
Nr.Fine/Fine **$550**
Good/V.Good **$325**

De La Mare, Walter. *Memoirs of a Midget.* First Edition: London: Collins, 1921.
Nr.Fine/Fine **$275**
Good/V.Good **$120**

De La Roche, Mazo. *The Building of Jalna.* First Edition: Boston: Atlantic

Little Brown, 1944.
Nr.Fine/Fine **$45**
Good/V.Good **$20**

The Building of Jalna
by Mazo De La Roche

But Who Wakes The Bugler?
by Peter De Vries

De Vries, Peter. *But Who Wakes The Bugler?* First Edition: Boston: Houghton Mifflin, 1940.
Nr.Fine/Fine **$425**
Good/V.Good **$175**

Dell, Floyd. *King Arthur's Socks And Other Village Plays.* First Edition: New York: Alfred A. Knopf, 1922.
Nr.Fine/Fine **$75**
Good/V.Good **$40**

Derleth, August. *Sac Prairie People.* First Edition: Sauk City, WI: Stanton & Lee, 1948.
Nr.Fine/Fine **$125**

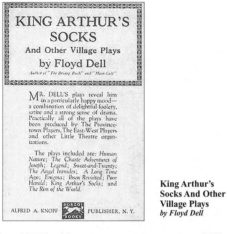

King Arthur's
Socks And Other
Village Plays
by Floyd Dell

Good/V.Good **$55**

Dickey, James. *Deliverance.* First
Edition: Boston: Houghton Mifflin. 1970.
Nr.Fine/Fine **$225**
Good/V.Good **$65**

Di Donato, Pietro. *Christ in Concrete.*
First Edition: Chicago: Esquire, 1937.
Nr.Fine/Fine **$85**
Good/V.Good **$35**

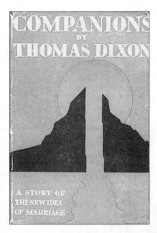

Companions
by Thomas Dixon

Dixon, Thomas. *Companions.* First
Edition: New York: Otis Publishing
Corporation, 1931.
Nr.Fine/Fine **$225**
Good/V.Good **$100**

Donleavy, J. P. *A Singular Man.* First
Edition: London: Bodley Head, 1964.

Nr.Fine/Fine **$120**
Good/V.Good **$50**

Doolittle, Hilda (as by H.D.). *Palimpsest.*
First Edition: Boston: Houghton Mifflin,
1926.
Nr.Fine/Fine **$400**
Good/V.Good **$125**

Dos Passos, John. *1919.* First Edition:
New York: Harcourt, Brace, 1932.
Nr.Fine/Fine **$550**
Good/V.Good **$200**

Douglas, Keith. *Alamein to Zem Zem-
with Poems and Drawings.* First Edition:
London: Editions Poetry, 1946.
Nr.Fine/Fine **$200**
Good/V.Good **$55**

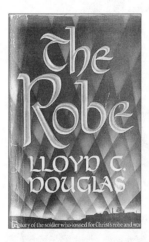

The Robe
by Lloyd C. Douglas

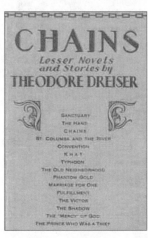

Chains Lesser
Novels and
Stories
by Theodore Dreiser

Douglas, Lloyd C. *The Robe.* First
Edition: Boston: Houghton Mifflin, 1942.
Nr.Fine/Fine **$550**
Good/V.Good **$200**

Doyle, Arthur Conan. *The Land of Mist.*
First Edition: London: Hutchinson, 1926.
Nr.Fine/Fine **$2200**
Good/V.Good **$950**

Dreiser, Theodore. *Chains Lesser Novels
and Stories.* First Edition: New York:
Boni & Liveright, 1927.
Nr.Fine/Fine **$350**
Good/V.Good **$125**

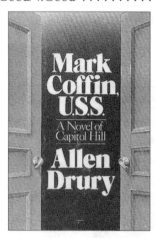

Mark Coffin
U.S.S., A Novel
Of Capitol Hill
by Allen Drury

Drury, Allen. *Mark Coffin U.S.S., A Novel
Of Capitol Hill.* First Edition: Garden
City, NY: Doubleday, 1979.
Nr.Fine/Fine **$45**
Good/V.Good **$15**

Du Maurier, Daphne. *Rebecca.* First
Edition: London: Victor Gollancz, 1938.
Nr.Fine/Fine **$2500**
Good/V.Good **$500**

Durrell, Lawrence. *A Private Country.*
First Edition: London: Faber & Faber,
1943.
Nr.Fine/Fine **$400**
Good/V.Good **$120**

Eastlake, William. *Go In Beauty.* First
Edition: New York: Harper & Brothers,
1956.

Nr.Fine/Fine **$500**
Good/V.Good **$175**

Chad Hanna
by Walter D. Edmonds

Edmonds, Walter D. *Chad Hanna.* First
Edition: Boston: Little Brown, 1940.
Nr.Fine/Fine **$65**
Good/V.Good **$25**

Eliot, T. S. *Old Possum's Book of
Practical Cats.* First Edition: London:
Faber and Faber, 1939.
Nr.Fine/Fine **$3250**
Good/V.Good **$1000**

Ellison, Ralph. *Shadow & Act.* First
Edition: New York: Random House, 1953.
Nr.Fine/Fine **$150**
Good/V.Good **$65**

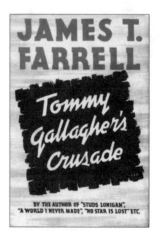

Tommy
Gallagher's
Crusade
by James T. Farrell

Farrell, James T. *Tommy Gallagher's Crusade.* First Edition: New York: Vanguard Press, 1939.
Nr.Fine/Fine **$150**
Good/V.Good **$45**

Fast, Howard. *Sparatcus.* First Edition: New York: Published by the Author, 1951.
Nr.Fine/Fine **$200**
Good/V.Good **$50**

Faulkner, William. *Go Down Moses.* First Edition: New York: Random House, 1942.
Nr.Fine/Fine **$4500**
Good/V.Good **$2000**

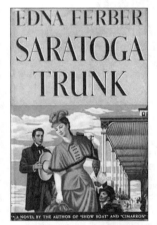

Saratoga Trunk
by Edna Ferber

Ferber, Edna. *The Saratoga Trunk.* First Edition: Garden City: Doubleday Doran, 1941.
Nr.Fine/Fine **$135**
Good/V.Good **$45**

Fergusson, Harvey. *The Conquest of Don Pedro.* First Edition: New York: William Morrow, 1954.
Nr.Fine/Fine **$100**
Good/V.Good **$45**

Ferlinghetti, Lawrence. *A Far Rockaway of the Heart.* First Edition: New York: New Directions, 1997.
Nr.Fine/Fine **$30**
Good/V.Good **$15**

Firbank, Ronald. *Valmouth.* First

Edition: London: Grant Richards, 1919.
Nr.Fine/Fine **$750**
Good/V.Good **$350**

Fisher, Vardis. *Sonnets to an Imaginary Madonna.* First Edition: New York: Harold Vinal, 1927.
Nr.Fine/Fine **$500**
Good/V.Good **$175**

Fitzgerald, F. Scott. *Taps At Reveille.* First Edition: New York: Scribners, 1935.
Nr.Fine/Fine **$5500**
Good/V.Good **$2250**

Forster, E. M. *A Room with a View.* First Edition: London: Edwin Arnold, 1908.
Nr.Fine/Fine **$250**
Good/V.Good **$100**

Fowles, John. *The Collector.* First Edition: London: Jonathan Cape, 1963.
Nr.Fine/Fine **$1000**
Good/V.Good **$550**

Frank, Waldo. *The Bridegroom Cometh.* First Edition: Garden City, NY: Doubleday, 1939.
Nr.Fine/Fine **$75**
Good/V.Good **$35**

Freeman, Mary E. Wilkins. *The Debtor.* First Edition: New York: Harper & Brothers, 1905.
Nr.Fine/Fine **$425**
Good/V.Good **$200**

Borgia
by Zona Gale

Gale, Zona. *Borgia.* First Edition: New York: Alfred A. Knopf, 1929.
Nr.Fine/Fine **$125**
Good/V.Good **$45**

Gardner, John. *The Resurrection.* First Edition: New York: New American Library, 1966.
Nr.Fine/Fine **$1150**
Good/V.Good **$500**

Glasgow, Ellen. *The Builders.* First Edition: Garden City, NY: Doubleday, Page, 1919.
Nr.Fine/Fine **$450**
Good/V.Good **$180**

Birth of a Hero
by Herbert Gold

Gold, Herbert. *Birth Of A Hero.* First Edition: New York: Viking, 1951.
Nr.Fine/Fine **$65**
Good/V.Good **$25**

Golding, William. *The Brass Butterfly.* First Edition: London: Faber & Faber, 1958.
Nr.Fine/Fine **$250**
Good/V.Good **$100**

Goldman, William. *Tinsel.* First Edition: New York: Delacorte, 1978.
Nr.Fine/Fine **$35**
Good/V.Good **$15**

Goodman, Paul. *The Empire City.* First Edition: Indianapolis: Bobbs-Merrill,

1959.
Nr.Fine/Fine **$95**
Good/V.Good **$25**

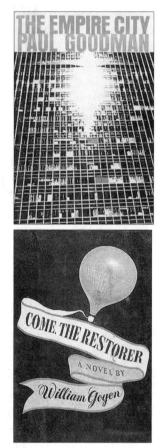

The Empire City
by Paul Goodman

Come, The Restorer
by William Goyen

Goyen, William. *Come, the Restorer.* First Edition: Garden City, NY: Doubleday, 1974.Nr.Fine/Fine **$55**
Good/V.Good **$20**

Grau, Shirley Ann. *The Keepers of the House.* First Edition: New York: Alfred A. Knopf, 1964.
Nr.Fine/Fine **$145**
Good/V.Good **$65**

Graves, Robert. *Goodbye To All That.* First Edition: London: Jonathan Cape, 1929.
Nr.Fine/Fine **$1850**
Good/V.Good **$1250**

Guthrie, A. B. *The Big Sky.* First Edition: Boston: Houghton Mifflin, 1947.
Nr.Fine/Fine **$350**
Good/V.Good **$125**

Haggard, H. Rider. *Belshazzar.* First Edition: London: Stanley Paul, 1930.
Nr.Fine/Fine **$1600**
Good/V.Good **$500**

Halper, Albert. *The Golden Watch.* First Edition: New York: Henry Holt, 1953.
Nr.Fine/Fine **$35**
Good/V.Good **$12**

Harris, Mark. *The Southpaw.* First Edition: Indianapolis: Bobbs Merrill, 1953.
Nr.Fine/Fine **$250**
Good/V.Good **$115**

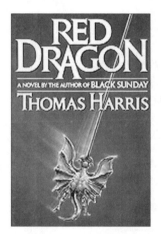

Red Dragon
by Thomas Harris

Harris, Thomas. *Red Dragon.* First Edition: New York: Putnam, 1981.
Nr.Fine/Fine **$160**
Good/V.Good **$55**

Heller, Joseph. *Catch 22.* First Edition: New York: Simon and Schuster, 1961.
Nr.Fine/Fine **$3350**
Good/V.Good **$1100**

Hellman, Lillian. *Watch On The Rhine.* First Edition: New York: Random House, 1941.
Nr.Fine/Fine **$225**
Good/V.Good **$85**

Hemingway, Ernest. *The Torrents of Spring.* First Edition: New York: Scribners, 1926.
Nr.Fine/Fine **$6000**
Good/V.Good **$1800**

Henry, O. *Postscripts.* First Edition: New York: Harper & Brothers, 1923.
Nr.Fine/Fine **$225**
Good/V.Good **$95**

The Limestone Tree
by Joseph Hergesheimer

Hergesheimer, Joseph. *The Limestone Tree.* First Edition: New York: Alfred A. Knopf, 1931.
Nr.Fine/Fine **$80**
Good/V.Good **$30**

Hersey, John. *Antonietta.* First Edition: New York: Alfred A, Knopf, 1991.
Nr.Fine/Fine **$35**
Good/V.Good **$12**

Mother of Gold
by Emerson Hough

Hilton, James. *Nothing So Strange.* First Edition: Boston: Little, Brown, 1947.
Nr.Fine/Fine **$75**
Good/V.Good **$20**

Hough, Emerson. *Mother of Gold.* First Edition: New York: D. Appleton, 1924.
Nr.Fine/Fine **$75**
Good/V.Good **$30**

Howells, W. D. *Between the Dark and the Daylight: Romances.* First Edition: New York: Harper & Brothers, 1907.
Nr.Fine/Fine **$120**
Good/V.Good **$45**

Hughes, Langston. *Fine Clothes To The Jew.* First Edition: New York: Alfred A. Knopf, 1927.
Nr.Fine/Fine **$2000**
Good/V.Good **$900**

Hughes, Rupert. *Within These Walls.* First Edition: New York: Harper & Brothers, 1923.
Nr.Fine/Fine **$150**
Good/V.Good **$55**

Huneker, James. *Ivory Apes And Peacocks.* First Edition: New York: Scribners, 1915.
Nr.Fine/Fine **$75**
Good/V.Good **$30**

Hunter, Evan. *The Blackboard Jungle.* First Edition: New York: Simon & Schuster, 1954.

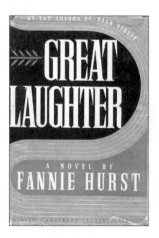

Great Laughter
by Fannie Hurst

Nr.Fine/Fine **$250**
Good/V.Good **$75**

Hurst, Fannie. *Great Laughter.* First Edition: New York: Harper & Brothers, 1936.
Nr.Fine/Fine **$325**
Good/V.Good **$80**

Hurston, Zora Neale. *Jonah's Gourd Vine.* First Edition: Philadelphia: J.B. Lippincott, 1934.
Nr.Fine/Fine **$2500**
Good/V.Good **$1000**

Huxley, Aldous. *Ape and Essence.* First Edition: London: Chatto & Windus, 1949.
Nr.Fine/Fine **$85**
Good/V.Good **$35**

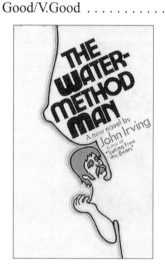

The Water Method Man
by John Irving

Irving, John. *The Water-Method Man.* First Edition: New York: Random House, 1972.
Nr.Fine/Fine **$675**
Good/V.Good **$225**

Isherwood, Christopher. *Sally Bowles.* First Edition: London: The Hogarth Press, 1937.
Nr.Fine/Fine **$1250**
Good/V.Good **$500**

Jackson, Charles. *The Lost Weekend.* First Edition: New York: Farrar & Rinehart, 1944.

Nr.Fine/Fine **$750**
Good/V.Good **$150**

Jackson, Shirley. *The Road through the Wall.* First Edition: New York: Farrar, Straus, 1948.
Nr.Fine/Fine **$1050**
Good/V.Good **$400**

Janvier, Thomas. *Santa Fe's Partner.* First Edition: New York: Harper & Brothers, 1907.
Nr.Fine/Fine **$25**
Good/V.Good **$10**

Blood for a
Stranger
by Randall Jarrell

Jarrell, Randall. *Blood for a Stranger.* First Edition: New York: Harcourt, Brace, 1942.
Nr.Fine/Fine **$1100**
Good/V.Good **$250**

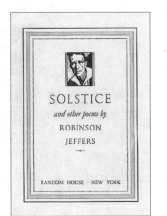

Solstice and
Other Poems
by Robinson Jeffers

Jeffers, Robinson. *Solstice and Other Poems.* First Edition: New York: Random House, 1935.
Nr.Fine/Fine **$510**
Good/V.Good **$225**

Georgina of
the Rainbows
*by Annie Fellows
Johnston*

Johnston, Annie Fellows. *Georgina of the Rainbows.* First Edition: New York: Britton Publishing, 1916.
Nr.Fine/Fine **$100**
Good/V.Good **$35**

Johnston, Mary. *The Exile.* First Edition: Boston: Little, Brown, 1927.
Nr.Fine/Fine **$125**
Good/V.Good **$45**

From Here To
Eternity
by James Jones

Jones, James. *From Here to Eternity.* First Edition: New York: Scribners, 1951.

Nr.Fine/Fine **$650**
Good/V.Good **$200**

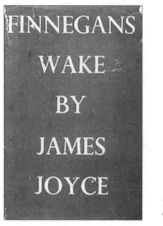

Finnegans Wake
by James Joyce

Joyce, James. *Finnegans Wake.* First
Edition: London/New York: Faber &
Faber/Viking Press, 1939.
Nr.Fine/Fine **$18,000**
Good/V.Good **$7500**

Do Re Mi
by Garson Kanin

Kanin, Garson. *Do Re Mi.* First Edition:
Boston: Little, Brown, 1955.
Nr.Fine/Fine **$95**
Good/V.Good **$35**

Kantor, MacKinlay. *God and My
Country.* First Edition: Cleveland, OH:
World Publishing, 1954.
Nr.Fine/Fine **$125**
Good/V.Good **$40**

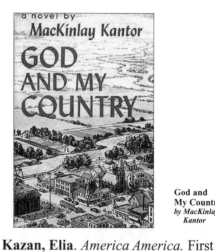

God and
My Country
*by MacKinlay
Kantor*

Kazan, Elia. *America America.* First
Edition: New York: Stein and Day, 1962.
Nr.Fine/Fine **$60**
Good/V.Good **$20**

Kelland, Clarence Buddington. *The
Sinister Strangers.* First Edition: New
York: Dodd, Mead, 1961.
Nr.Fine/Fine **$20**
Good/V.Good **$8**

Kennedy, William. *Billy Phelan's
Greatest Game.* First Edition: New York:
Viking, 1978.
Nr.Fine/Fine **$155**
Good/V.Good **$50**

Kerouac, Jack. *On the Road.* First
Edition: New York: Viking, 1957.
Nr.Fine/Fine **$11,000**
Good/V.Good **$4500**

Kesey, Ken. *One Flew Over the Cuckoo's
Nest.* First Edition: New York: Viking,
1962.
Nr.Fine/Fine **$6500**
Good/V.Good **$1500**

Kerr, Jean. *The Snake Has All The Lines.*
First Edition: Garden City, NY:
Doubleday, 1960.
Nr.Fine/Fine **$35**
Good/V.Good **$10**

Kipling, Rudyard. *Puck of Pook's Hill.*
First Edition: London: Macmillan & Co,
1906.

Nr.Fine/Fine **$1000**
Good/V.Good **$550**

Knowles, John. *A Separate Peace.* First Edition: London: Secker & Warburg, 1959.
Nr.Fine/Fine **$1150**
Good/V.Good **$650**

Kotzwinkle, William. *The Fan Man.* First Edition: New York: Harmony Books, 1974.
Nr.Fine/Fine **$75**
Good/V.Good **$25**

Kyne, Peter B. *Cappy Ricks Retires.* First Edition: New York: Cosmopolitan, 1922.
Nr.Fine/Fine **$125**
Good/V.Good **$35**

La Farge, Oliver. *The Enemy Gods.* First Edition: Boston: Houghton Mifflin Company, 1937.
Nr.Fine/Fine **$115**
Good/V.Good **$35**

Lardner, Ring. *Lose With A Smile.* First Edition: New York: Scribner's, 1933.
Nr.Fine/Fine **$400**
Good/V.Good **$175**

Lawrence, D. H. *Fantasia of the Unconscious.* First Edition: New York: Thomas Seltzer, 1922.
Nr.Fine/Fine **$950**
Good/V.Good **$350**

Winsome Winnie and Other New Nonsense Novels
by Stephen Leacock

Leacock, Stephen. *Winsome Winnie and Other New Nonsense Novels.* First Edition: New York: John Lane, 1920.
Nr.Fine/Fine **$225**
Good/V.Good **$75**

Le Gallienne, Richard. *There Was a Ship.* First Edition: Garden City, NY: Doubleday Doran, 1930. Points of Issue: Dust jacket and Frontispiece by Erte.
Nr.Fine/Fine **$75**
Good/V.Good **$30**

The Grass is Singing
by Doris Lessing

Lessing, Doris. *The Grass is Singing.* Points of Issue: First issue had a band over the Dust Jacket advertising that the book was a Daily Graphic pick of the month. First Edition: London, Michael Joseph, 1950.
Nr.Fine/Fine **$550**
Good/V.Good **$125**

The Double Image
by Denise Levertoff

Levertov, Denise as by Denise Levertoff.
The Double Image. First Edition: London:
The Cresset Press, 1946.
Nr.Fine/Fine **$425**
Good/V.Good **$200**

Levin, Meyer. *Citizens.* First Edition:
New York: Viking, 1940.
Nr.Fine/Fine **$150**
Good/V.Good **$35**

Lewis, Sinclair. *Elmer Gantry.* Points of
Issue: The spine of the first state
substitutes a "C" for the "G" in "Gantry."
First Edition: New York: Harcourt Brace,
1927.
Nr.Fine/Fine **$2500**
Good/V.Good **$600**

The Apes of God
by Wyndham Lewis

Lewis, Wyndham. *The Apes of God.* First
Edition: London: Arthur Press, 1930.
Nr.Fine/Fine **$850**
Good/V.Good **$200**

Lewisohn, Ludwig. *Israel.* First Edition:
New York: Boni & Liveright, 1925.
Nr.Fine/Fine **$100**
Good/V.Good **$35**

Liebling, A. J. *The Telephone Booth
Indian.* First Edition: Garden City, NY:
Doubleday Doran, 1942.
Nr.Fine/Fine **$350**
Good/V.Good **$100**

Lockridge, Ross. *Raintree County.* First
Edition: Boston: Houghton Mifflin, 1948.

Nr.Fine/Fine **$250**
Good/V.Good **$45**

Loos, Anita. *Gentlemen Prefer Blondes.*
First Edition: New York: Boni and
Liveright, 1925.
Nr.Fine/Fine **$1200**
Good/V.Good **$425**

Marvel, Ik. *Reveries of a Bachelor.* First
Edition: Indianapolis, IN: Bobbs Merrill,
1906.
Nr.Fine/Fine **$55**
Good/V.Good **$20**

McCarthy, Mary. *The Company She
Keeps.* First Edition: New York: Simon
and Schuster, 1942.
Nr.Fine/Fine **$425**
Good/V.Good **$70**

Machen, Arthur. *The Hill of Dreams.*
First Edition: London: Grant Richards,
1907.
Nr.Fine/Fine **$650**
Good/V.Good **$275**

The Heart is a
Lonely Hunter
by Carson McCullers

McCullers, Carson. *The Heart is a
Lonely Hunter.* First Edition: Boston:
Houghton Mifflin, 1940.

Nr.Fine/Fine **$2500**
Good/V.Good **$400**

McCutcheon, George Barr. *East of the
Setting Sun.* First Edition: New York:
Dodd, Mead, 1924.

Nr.Fine/Fine **$65**
Good/V.Good **$25**

McFee, William. *Command.* First
Edition: Garden City, NY: Doubleday
Page, 1922.
Nr.Fine/Fine **$85**
Good/V.Good **$25**

The Goose Girl
by Harold MacGrath

MacGrath, Harold. *The Goose Girl.*
First Edition: Indianapolis, IN: Bobbs-
Merrill, 1909.
Nr.Fine/Fine **$400**
Good/V.Good **$150**

McKenney, Ruth. *Mirage.* First Edition:
New York: Farrar, Strauss and Cudahy,
1956.
Nr.Fine/Fine **$35**
Good/V.Good **$10**

Mailer, Norman. *The Naked and the
Dead.* First Edition: New York: Rinehart,
1948.
Nr.Fine/Fine **$2500**
Good/V.Good **$750**

Malamud, Bernard. *The Natural.* First
Edition: New York: Harcourt, Brace,
1952.
Nr.Fine/Fine **$3500**
Good/V.Good **$1100**

Mansfield, Katherine. *Garden Party And
Other Stories.* First Edition: London:
Constable, 1922.

Nr.Fine/Fine **$200**
Good/V.Good **$75**

Repent In Haste
by John P. Marquand

Marquand, John P. *Repent in Haste.*
First Edition: Boston: Little Brown, 1945.
Nr.Fine/Fine **$65**
Good/V.Good **$20**

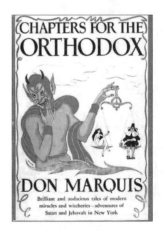

Chapters For
The Orthodox
by Don Marquis

Marquis, Don. *Chapters for the
Orthodox.* First Edition: Garden City, NY:
Doubleday Doran, 1934.
Nr.Fine/Fine **$125**
Good/V.Good **$45**

Matthiessen, Peter. *Race Rock.* First
Edition: New York: Harper & Brothers,
1954.
Nr.Fine/Fine **$600**
Good/V.Good **$225**

The Narrow Corner *by W. Somerset Maugham*

Maugham, W. Somerset. *The Narrow Corner.* First Edition: London: Heinemann, 1932.
Nr.Fine/Fine **$650**
Good/V.Good **$175**

Making a President/ A Footnote to the Saga of Democracy *by H.L. Mencken*

Mencken, H. L. *Making a President/A Footnote to the Saga of Democracy.* First Edition: New York: Alfred A. Knopf, 1932.
Nr.Fine/Fine **$525**
Good/V.Good **$175**

Michener, James. *The Fires of Spring.* First Edition: New York: Random House, 1949.
Nr.Fine/Fine **$2250**
Good/V.Good **$500**

Milne, A. A. *The Ivory Door.* First Edition: London: Chatto & Windus, 1929.
Nr.Fine/Fine **$175**
Good/V.Good **$65**

Montgomery, L. M. *Jane of Lantern Hill.* First Edition: Toronto: McClelland and Stewart, 1937.
Nr.Fine/Fine **$275**
Good/V.Good **$95**

Morley, Christopher. *Seacoast of Bohemia.* First Edition: Garden City, NY: Doubleday Doran, 1929.
Nr.Fine/Fine **$75**
Good/V.Good **$20**

Morrison, Toni. *Sula.* First Edition: New York: Alfred A. Knopf, 1974.
Nr.Fine/Fine **$450**
Good/V.Good **$100**

Morris, Wright. *My Uncle Dudley.* First Edition: New York: Harcourt Brace, 1942.
Nr.Fine/Fine **$1125**
Good/V.Good **$425**

Mowatt, Farley. *Sibir.* First Edition: Toronto: McClelland & Stewart, 1970.
Nr.Fine/Fine **$35**
Good/V.Good **$12**

Murdoch, Iris. *The Flight from the Enchanter.* First Edition: London: Chatto & Windus, 1956.
Nr.Fine/Fine **$1225**
Good/V.Good **$675**

Nabokov, Vladimir. *Bend Sinister.* First Edition: New York: Henry Holt, 1947.
Nr.Fine/Fine **$300**
Good/V.Good **$135**

Naipaul, Shiva. *Fireflies.* First Edition: London: Andre Deutsch, 1970.
Nr.Fine/Fine **$250**
Good/V.Good **$85**

Nathan, George Jean. *Monks Are Monks: A Diagnostic Scherzo.* First Edition: New York: Alfred A. Knopf, 1929.
Nr.Fine/Fine **$80**
Good/V.Good **$25**

Nathan, Robert. *Portrait of Jennie.* First Edition: New York: Alfred A. Knopf, 1940.
Nr.Fine/Fine **$75**
Good/V.Good **$30**

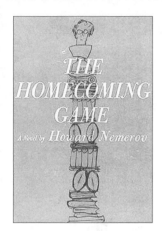

The Homecoming Game
by Harold Nemerov

Nemerov, Harold. *The Homecoming Game.* First Edition: New York: Simon and Schuster, 1957.
Nr.Fine/Fine **$60**
Good/V.Good **$25**

O'Casey, Sean. *The Green Crow.* First Edition: New York: George Braziller, 1956.
Nr.Fine/Fine **$30**
Good/V.Good **$12**

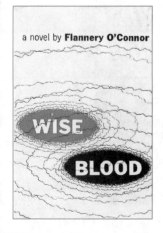

Wise Blood
by Flannery O'Connor

O'Connor, Flannery. *Wise Blood.* First Edition: New York: Harcourt, Brace,

1952.
Nr.Fine/Fine **$8000**
Good/V.Good **$3000**

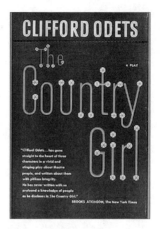

The Country Girl
by Clifford Odets

Odets, Clifford. *The Country Girl.* First Edition: New York: Viking, 1951.
Nr.Fine/Fine **$75**
Good/V.Good **$30**

O'Hara, John. *Butterfield 8.* First Edition: New York: Harcourt Brace, 1935.
Nr.Fine/Fine **$1225**
Good/V.Good **$275**

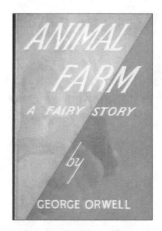

Animal Farm
by George Orwell

Orwell, George. *Animal Farm.* First Edition: London, Secker & Warburg, 1945.
Nr.Fine/Fine **$3000**
Good/V.Good **$975**

Enough Rope
by Dorothy Parker

Parker, Dorothy. *Enough Rope.* First Edition: New York: Boni & Liveright, 1926.
Nr.Fine/Fine **$675**
Good/V.Good **$350**

The Methodist Faun
by Anne Parrish

Parrish, Anne. *The Methodist Faun.* First Edition: New York: Harper & Brothers, 1929.
Nr.Fine/Fine **$75**
Good/V.Good **$30**

Patchen, Kenneth. *The Journal of Albion Moonlight.* First Edition: Mount Vernon, NY: By the Author, 1941.
Nr.Fine/Fine **$600**
Good/V.Good **$325**

Percy, Walker. *Early Architecture of*

Delaware. First Edition: New York: Farrar, Straus & Giroux, 1966.
Nr.Fine/Fine **$425**
Good/V.Good **$120**

Perelman, S. J. *The Road to Miltown or Under the Spreading Atrophy.* First Edition: New York: Simon & Schuster, 1957.
Nr.Fine/Fine **$95**
Good/V.Good **$30**

Black April
by Julia Peterkin

Peterkin, Julia. *Black April.* First Edition: Indianapolis: Bobbs Merrill, 1927.
Nr.Fine/Fine **$425**
Good/V.Good **$165**

Pale Horse, Pale Rider
by Katherine Anne Porter

Porter, Katherine Anne. *Pale Horse, Pale Rider.* First Edition: New York: Harcourt Brace, 1939.

Nr.Fine/Fine **$350**
Good/V.Good **$150**

Powys, John Cowper. *Visions and Revisions.* First Edition: London & New York: William Rider and G. Arnold Shaw, 1915.
Nr.Fine/Fine **$200**
Good/V.Good **$85**

Powys, Llewelyn. *Ebony and Ivory.* First Edition: London: Grant Richards, 1923.
Nr.Fine/Fine **$75**
Good/V.Good **$30**

Powys, T. F. *Unclay.* First Edition: London: Chatto & Windus, 1931.
Nr.Fine/Fine................. **$225**
Good/V.Good **$85**

Color of Darkness
by James Purdy

Purdy, James. *The Color of Darkness.* First Edition: Norfolk, CT: New Directions, 1957.
Nr.Fine/Fine **$125**
Good/V.Good **$45**

Pyle, Ernie. *Home Country.* First Edition: New York: William Sloane, 1947.
Nr.Fine/Fine **$25**
Good/V.Good **$8**

Rand, Ayn. *We the Living.* First Edition: London: Cassell, 1936.
Nr.Fine/Fine **$5500**
Good/V.Good **$2250**

Rawlings, Marjorie Kinnan. *Golden*

Apples. First Edition: New York: Scribner's, 1935.
Nr.Fine/Fine **$550**
Good/V.Good **$175**

Read, Opie. *The New Mr. Howerson.* First Edition: Chicago: Reilly & Britton, 1914.
Nr.Fine/Fine **$55**
Good/V.Good **$20**

Rhodes, Eugene Manlove. *Little World Waddies.* First Edition: Chico, CA: Carl Hertzog, Printer, 1946.
Nr.Fine/Fine **$375**
Good/V.Good **$175**

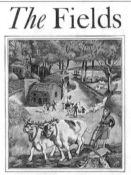

The Fields
by Conrad Richter

Richter, Conrad. *The Fields.* First Edition: New York: Alfred A. Knopf, 1946.
Nr.Fine/Fine **$75**
Good/V.Good **$30**

Rives, Amelie. *World's End.* First Edition: New York: Frederick A. Stokes, 1914.
Nr.Fine/Fine **$35**
Good/V.Good **$10**

Robbins, Harold. *A Stone for Danny Fisher.* First Edition: New York: Alfred A. Knopf, 1952.
Nr.Fine/Fine **$200**
Good/V.Good **$75**

Roberts, Kenneth. *Rabble In Arms.* First Edition: Garden City, NY: Doubleday

Doran, 1933.
Nr.Fine/Fine **$75**
Good/V.Good **$20**

Rosten, Leo, as by Leonard Q. Ross.
Education of Hyman Kaplan. First
Edition: New York: Harcourt Brace, 1937.
Nr.Fine/Fine **$85**
Good/V.Good **$20**

Roth, Philip. *Goodbye, Columbus And
Five Short Stories.* First Edition: Boston:
Houghton Mifflin, 1959.
Nr.Fine/Fine **$700**
Good/V.Good **$275**

Something of
Value
by Robert Ruark

Ruark, Robert. *Something of Value.* First
Edition: Garden City, NY: Doubleday,
1955
Nr.Fine/Fine **$125**
Good/V.Good **$35**

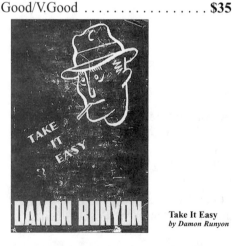

Take It Easy
by Damon Runyon

Runyon, Damon. *Take It Easy.* First
Edition: New York: Frederick Stokes,
1938.
Nr.Fine/Fine **$750**
Good/V.Good **$350**

Franny and
Zooey
by J.D. Salinger

Salinger, J. D. *Franny and Zooey.* First
Edition: Boston: Little Brown, 1961.
Nr.Fine/Fine **$750**
Good/V.Good **$225**

Purple and Fine
Women
by Edgar Saltus

Saltus, Edgar. *Purple and Fine Women.*
First Edition: Chicago: Pascal Covici,
1925.
Nr.Fine/Fine **$65**
Good/V.Good **$20**

Santayana, George. *The Last Puritan.*
First Edition: New York: Scribners, 1936,
Nr.Fine/Fine. **$350**

Good/V.Good **$85**

Saroyan, William. *Daring Young Man on the Flying Trapeze and Other Stories.* First Edition: New York: Random House, 1934.
Nr.Fine/Fine **$325**
Good/V.Good **$100**

Sarton, May. *The Single Hound.* First Edition: Boston: Houghton Mifflin, 1938.
Nr.Fine/Fine **$475**
Good/V.Good **$200**

The Harder
They Fall
by Budd Schulberg

Schulberg, Budd. *The Harder They Fall.* First Edition: New York: Random House, 1947.
Nr.Fine/Fine **$225**
Good/V.Good **$85**

Scott, Paul. *The Jewel in the Crown.* First Edition: London: Heinemann, 1966.
Nr.Fine/Fine **$175**
Good/V.Good **$75**

Seton, Anya. *The Winthrop Woman.* First Edition: Boston: Houghton Mifflin, 1958.
Nr.Fine/Fine **$85**
Good/V.Good **$35**

Sexton, Anne. *To Bedlam and Part Way Back.* First Edition: Cambridge, MA: Riverside Press, 1960.
Nr.Fine/Fine **$425**
Good/V.Good **$150**

Shaw, Irwin. *The Young Lions.* First Edition: New York: Random House, 1948.
Nr.Fine/Fine **$225**
Good/V.Good **$65**

Sillitoe, Alan. *Saturday Night and Sunday Morning.* First Edition: London: W. H. Allen, 1958.
Nr.Fine/Fine **$275**
Good/V.Good **$125**

Sinclair, Upton. *The Jungle.* First Edition: New York: The Jungle Publishing Company, 1906.
Nr.Fine/Fine **$1200**
Good/V.Good **$800**

Skinner, Cornelia Otis. *Excuse It, Please.* First Edition: New York: Dodd Mead, 1936.
Nr.Fine/Fine **$25**
Good/V.Good **$8**

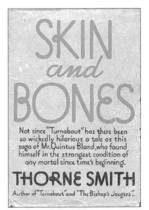

Skin and Bones
by Thorne Smith

Smith, Thorne. *Skin and Bones.* First Edition: Garden City, NY: Doubleday Doran, 1933.
Nr.Fine/Fine **$450**
Good/V.Good **$200**

Spark, Muriel. *The Prime of Miss Jean Brodie.* First Edition: London: Macmillan, 1961.
Nr.Fine/Fine **$275**
Good/V.Good **$125**

Stratton-Porter, Gene. *The White Flag.* First Edition: Garden City, NY:

Doubleday Page, 1923.
Nr.Fine/Fine **$300**
Good/V.Good **$95**

Stein, Gertrude. *Three Lives*. First
Edition: New York: Grafton Press, 1909.
Nr.Fine/Fine **$1400**
Good/V.Good **$500**

Steinbeck, John. *Cup of Gold*. First
Edition: New York: Robert M. McBride,
1929.
Nr.Fine/Fine **$25,000**
Good/V.Good **$15,000**

Stone, Irving. *Depths of Glory*. First
Edition: Franklin Centre, PA: The
Franklin Library, 1985
Nr.Fine/Fine.................. **$55**
Good/V.Good **$25**

These Bars of
Flesh
by T.S. Stribling

Stribling, T. S. *These Bars of Flesh*. First
Edition: Garden City, NY: Doubleday
Doran, 1938.
Nr.Fine/Fine **$100**
Good/V.Good **$50**

Styron, William. *Lie Down In Darkness*.
First Edition: Indianapolis, IN: Bobbs-
Merrill, 1951.
Nr.Fine/Fine **$500**
Good/V.Good **$150**

Tarkington, Booth. *The Magnificent
Ambersons*. First Edition: Garden City,
NY: Doubleday Page, 1918.
Nr.Fine/Fine **$850**

Good/V.Good **$375**

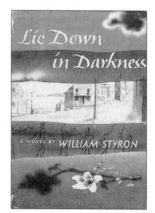

Lie Down in
Darkness
by William Styron

Terhune, Albert Payson. *A Dog Named
Chips*. First Edition: New York: Harper &
Brothers, 1931.
Nr.Fine/Fine **$85**
Good/V.Good **$40**

Thomas, D. M. *The White Hotel*. First
Edition: London: Victor Gollancz, 1981.
Nr.Fine/Fine **$95**
Good/V.Good **$35**

The Great Quillow
by James Thurber

Thurber, James. *The Great Quillow*. First
Edition: New York: Harcourt Brace, 1944.
Nr.Fine/Fine **$350**
Good/V.Good **$165**

Toole, John Kennedy. *A Confederacy of
Dunces*. First Edition: Baton Rouge:
Louisiana State University Press, 1980.
Nr.Fine/Fine **$4850**
Good/V.Good **$2200**

Totheroh, Dan. *Men Call Me Fool*. First

Edition: Garden City, N.Y: Doubleday, Doran, 1929
Nr.Fine/Fine **$85**
Good/V.Good **$35**

Traven, B. *The Treasure Of The Sierra Madre.* First Edition: London: Chatto & Windus, 1934.
Nr.Fine/Fine **$3750**
Good/V.Good **$1600**
First U.S. Edition (Revised): New York: Alfred A. Knopf, 1935.
Nr.Fine/Fine **$6250**
Good/V.Good **$2000**

Tyler, Anne. *If Morning Ever Comes.* First Edition: New York: Alfred A. Knopf, 1964.
Nr.Fine/Fine **$2000**
Good/V.Good **$750**

Rabbit, Run
by John Updike

Updike, John. *A Description of California in1828.* First Edition: New York: Alfred A. Knopf, 1960.
Nr.Fine/Fine **$1600**
Good/V.Good **$375**

Van Vechten, Carl. *Nigger Heaven.* First Edition: New York: Alfred A. Knopf, 1927.
Nr.Fine/Fine **$125**
Good/V.Good **$45**

Vidal, Gore. *In A Yellow Wood.* First Edition: New York: E. P. Dutton & Co. 1947.
Nr.Fine/Fine **$350**

Good/V.Good **$125**

America in the Coming Age of Electronics
PLAYER PIANO
A NOVEL BY
KURT VONNEGUT JR.
Player Piano
by Kurt Vonnegut Jr.

Vonnegut Jr., Kurt. *Player Piano.* First Edition: New York: Scribners, 1952.
Nr.Fine/Fine **$2200**
Good/V.Good **$550**

Walker, Alice. *The Color Purple.* First Edition: New York: Harcourt Brace Jovanovich, 1982.
Nr.Fine/Fine **$750**
Good/V.Good **$200**

Warren, Robert Penn. *Band Of Angels.* First Edition: New York Random House 1955.
Nr.Fine/Fine **$145**
Good/V.Good **$35**

Watts, Mary. *The Rise of Jennie Cushing.* First Edition: New York: The Macmillan Company, 1914.
Nr.Fine/Fine **$35**
Good/V.Good **$12**

Waugh, Alec. *Going Their Own Ways.* First Edition: London: Cassell, 1938.
Nr.Fine/Fine **$95**
Good/V.Good **$30**

Waugh, Evelyn. *Brideshead Revisited. The Sacred & Profane Memories of Captain Charles Ryder.* First Edition: London: Chapman & Hall Ltd., 1945.
Nr.Fine/Fine **$2750**
Good/V.Good **$1175**

Welty, Eudora. *A Curtain of Green.* First

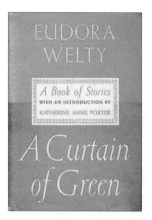

A Curtain
of Green
by Eudora Welty

Edition: Garden City, NY: Doubleday
Doran, 1941.
Nr.Fine/Fine **$800**
Good/V.Good **$335**

West, Jessamyn. *The Friendly
Persuasion.* First Edition: New York:
Harcourt, Brace, 1945.
Nr.Fine/Fine **$175**
Good/V.Good **$55**

West, Nathaniel. *The Day of the Locust.*
First Edition: New York: Random House,
1939.
Nr.Fine/Fine **$3200**
Good/V.Good **$1450**

Wharton, Edith. *Tales of the Old Timers.*
First Edition: New York, Scribners, 1923.
Nr.Fine/Fine **$350**
Good/V.Good **$85**

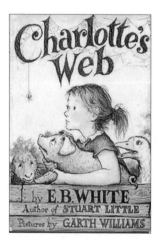

Charlotte's Web
by E.B. White

White, E. B. *Charlotte's Web.* First
Edition: New York, Harper & Brothers,
1952.
Nr.Fine/Fine **$2000**
Good/V.Good **$775**

White, Stewart Edward. *Gold.* First
Edition: Garden City, NY: Doubleday
Page, 1913.
Nr.Fine/Fine **$125**
Good/V.Good **$30**

White, T. H. *The Ill-Made Knight.* First
Edition: London: Collins, 1941.
Nr.Fine/Fine **$750**
Good/V.Good **$275**

Wilder, Thornton. *Bridge of San Luis
Rey.* First Edition: New York: Albert and
Charles Boni, 1927.
Nr.Fine/Fine **$850**
Good/V.Good **$345**

Williams, Ben Ames. *Splendor.* First
Edition: New York: E. P. Dutton, 1927.
Nr.Fine/Fine **$125**
Good/V.Good **$45**

Williams, Tennessee. *A Streetcar Named
Desire.* First Edition: New York: New
Directions, 1947.
Nr.Fine/Fine **$4500**
Good/V.Good **$1675**

Wilson, Harry Leon. *Merton of the
Movies.* First Edition: Garden City, NY:
Doubleday Page, 1922.
Nr.Fine/Fine **$125**
Good/V.Good **$35**

Wister, Owen. *When West Was West.* First
Edition: New York: Macmillan, 1928
Nr.Fine/Fine **$125**
Good/V.Good **$25**

Wodehouse, P. G. *Louder and Funnier.*
First Edition: London: Faber and Faber,
1932.
Nr.Fine/Fine **$850**
Good/V.Good **$375**

Wolfe, Thomas. *Look Homeward, Angel.*
First Edition: New York: Charles

Scribner's Sons, 1929.
Nr.Fine/Fine **$3000**
Good/V.Good **$1250**

Louder and Funnier
by P.G. Wodehouse

Woolf, Virginia. *Granite & Rainbow.*
First Edition: London: The Hogarth Press,
1958.
Nr.Fine/Fine **$450**
Good/V.Good **$125**

Wright, Harold Bell. *The Mine with the
Iron Door.* First Edition: New York: D.
Appleton, 1923.
Nr.Fine/Fine **$90**
Good/V.Good **$45**

Hemingway, Ernest. *The Sun Also Rises.*
First Edition: New York: Charles
Scribner's Sons, 1926.Points: First state
with "stoppped" on p. 181.
Nr.Fine/Fine **$25,000**
Good/V.Good **$9500**

Lofting, Hugh. *The Story of Doctor
Dolittle.*First Edition: New York:
Frederick A. Stokes, 1920.
Nr.Fine/Fine **$450**
Good/V.Good **$195**

Steinbeck, John. *Cannery Row* First
Edition: New York: Viking, 1945. Points:
First state issued in buff, not yellow,
cloth.
Nr.Fine/Fine **$2500**
Good/V.Good **$1200**

Mystery

The Mystery Genre is not new. The Chinese puzzle story borders on a millennium of existence and entertainment. In the modern, Western world, however, we can point to two definite events that ushered in the mystery genre as one of our most popular literary diversions. The first was April Fool's Day in 1841, when the fiction editor of *Graham's Magazine* published a little story called "The Murders in the Rue Morgue." That editor was Edgar Allen Poe, and the story created the genre we now know as mystery. C. Auguste Dupin, Poe's detective, would find a "Purloined Letter," solve the "Murder of Marie Roget," and confront a "Gold Bug." But the genre itself had to wait for a second event to find its way into the hearts of the public.

In the initial number of his new magazine, *The Strand*, George Newnes wrote of the street his offices were located on: "Of violent incident it has seen but little..." That statement remained true for six months, before becoming one of the greatest ironies ever printed. In July of 1891, *The Strand* published "A Scandal in Bohemia," the first adventure of Sherlock Holmes. While Holmes had seen print earlier, it was this story that broke open the floodgates and ushered in the mystery genre. *The Strand,* thus, became the origin, the starting point for rivers of fictional blood, murder, robbery, and mayhem.

There are older "crime" novels. Dickens' *Oliver Twist,* for example, was primarily a crime novel suggested to the author by the well-publicized trial of a fence, Ikey Solomon. One of the most chilling of these early crime novels was Edward Bulwer Lytton's *Lucretia: Or, The Children of Night,* suggested by the careers of two serial prisoners. These novels, however, bear little relation to the modern mystery genre of crime and detection.

Within a decade of the appearance of Sherlock Holmes, few popular magazines were complete without a mystery story. Amateur and professional, detectives caught bad guys monthly, and weekly. Soon the bad guys got their chance: genial con-man Colonel Clay fleeced London's upper crust in Grant Allen's stories, A. J. Raffles and Arsene Lupin burgled to their heart's content, while Fu Manchu schemed to take over the world and Madame Sarah, the Sorceress of the Strand, ruled London's underworld. Professional detectives came from the police and the private sector. Along with Holmes, private inquiry agents such as Martin Hewitt and Horace Dorrington roamed London's streets. Amateur detectives solved crimes from all manner of professions. Dr. Thorndyke listened to the tales told by murder victims. Father Brown knew the devil when he saw him. Even an advertising copywriter named Average Jones was able to apply his knowledge of humanity to solving crimes. American ex-patriot Dick Donovan ushered in the spy as detective in stories where he used his own name as his fictional agent of the Czar. Max Carrados, Ernest Brahmah's blind amateur detective, proved the handicapped made excellent detectives. After all a blind man can hardly be fooled by appearances.

As literary genres go, at least in the modern sense, mystery is still young. Outside of a couple volumes of Graham's, it can be contained in a collection beginning in 1891, just over a century. Doctors, lawyers, and Indians (if not a chief), have all had a hand at apprehending the bad guy. A good many collections, within the mystery genre, are built around a single classification or profession.

The nosy old lady does her bit in Agatha Christie's Miss Jane Marple stories, or as Hildegarde Withers, by Stuart Palmer. Lawyers like Arthur Train's Ephram Tutt or Erle Stanley Gardner's Perry Mason solved crimes detectives couldn't. Clergymen from G. K. Chesterton's Father Brown to Harry Kemelman's Rabbi David Small used everything from scholastic to talmudic logic to expose the criminal. The rich and the bored amused themselves ferreting out the miscreants in S. S. Van Dines' Philo Vance books or Dorothy Sayers' Lord Peter Wimsey stories. Criminals, active such as Lawrence Bloch's Bernie Rhodenburr and Richard Stark's Parker, are the heirs of A. J. Raffles, and reformed, like Leslie Charteris' Simon Templar, the Saint, or Michael Arlen's Falcon, skirt the law for the sake of justice, or profit. Historical figures such as Dr. Samuel Johnson, in Lillian De La Torre's books, solved the crimes of their era. Even a boat bum, John D. MacDonald's Travis McGee, gets in the act.

Public sector professionals run the gamut from the beat cop, such as Sax Rohmer's Red Kerry, to the top of the ranks in characters like John Creasey's Superintendent Roger West. In the private sector, down at the heels types like Dashiell Hammett's Sam Spade, tough guys like Mickey Spillane's Mike Hammer, the armchair crime solver Nero Wolfe by Rex Stout, and the hair trigger tempered Max Thursday by Wade Miller, are all private eyes. And lest we forget the ladies, G.G. Fickling's Honey West, Sue Grafton's Kinsey Millhone, Peter O'Donnell's Modesty Blaze, and Rex Stout's Theodolinda "Dol" Bonner, are better than the Mounties when it comes to getting their man, often in more ways than one.

Almost since its appearance as a genre, mystery has fascinated the collector, perhaps because of the hunt, the chase. Whether the clues are buried in the stacks of a bookstore, or out on the mean streets, one hunt is akin to the other. Whether it is the criminal that is exposed, or the first edition that is found, the detective and the book collector seem to have an affinity for each other. In mystery and in book collecting, the game is always afoot.

10 Classic Rarities

Cain, James M. *The Postman Always Rings Twice.* New York: Knopf, 1934. And you only have to find this once.
Retail value in:
    Near Fine to Fine **$2000**
    Good to Very Good **$1200**

Chandler, Raymond. *The Big Sleep.* New York: Alfred A, Knopf, 1939. Finding this is a ticket to sleeping well.
Retail value in:
    Near Fine to Fine. **$16,000**
    Good to Very Good **$10,000**

Christie, Agatha. *Ten Little Niggers.* London: Collins Crime Club, 1939. Issued in the U.S. as *And Then There Were None* then as *Ten Little Indians.*
Retail value in:
    Near Fine to Fine. **$10,000**
    Good to Very Good **$4000**

Fleming, Ian. *Casino Royale.* London: Jonathan Cape, 1953. Find this and avoid casinos, or buy one.
Retail value in:
    Near Fine condition **$21,000**
    Good to Very Good **$12,000**

Gardner, Erle Stanley. *The Case of the Stuttering Bishop.* New York: Morrow, 1936. Known to cause stuttering and other signs of surprise.
Retail value in:
    Near Fine to Fine **$1500**
    Good to Very Good **$1000**

Hammett, Dashiell. *The Maltese Falcon.* New York: Alfred Knopf, 1930. Probably better than finding the object of the book is finding a first edition in the unfindable Dust Jacket.
Retail value in:
    Near Fine to Fine **$8500**
    Good to Very Good **$1500**

Queen, Ellery. *The Siamese Twin Mystery.* New York: Fredrick A. Stokes, 1933. You only need one to make things a bit brighter.
Retail value in:
    Near Fine to Fine **$2500**
    Good to Very Good **$1250**

Sayers, Dorothy L. *Hangman's Holiday.* London: Victor Gollancz, 1933. Have your own holiday after finding this.
Retail value in:
    Near Fine to Fine **$5000**
    Good to Very Good **$3500**

Spillane, Mickey. *I, The Jury.* Dutton, 1947. And judge and just about whatever you want if you find this.
Retail value in:
    Near Fine to Fine **$3500**
    Good to Very Good **$2100**

Stout, Rex. *Too Many Cooks.* New York: Farrar & Rinehart, 1938. Includes recipe section so you can hire your own cook.
Retail value in:
    Near Fine to Fine **$4500**
    Good to Very Good **$2000**

Price Guide

Abbot, Anthony. *About The Murder of the Night Club Lady.* First Edition: New York: Covici-Friede, 1931.
Nr.Fine/Fine................. **$25**
Good/V.Good **$15**

Adams, Cleve F. *Sabotage.* First Edition: New York: E.P. Dutton & Co., 1940.
Nr.Fine/Fine **$35**
Good/V.Good **$15**

Adams, Samuel Hopkins. *Average Jones.* First Edition: Indianapolis: Bobbs-Merrill, 1911.
Nr.Fine/Fine **$325**
Good/V.Good **$150**

Aird, Catherine. *Henrietta Who?* First Edition: Garden City, NY: Doubleday/Crime Club, 1968.
Nr.Fine/Fine .... **$30.**
Good/V.Good **$12**

Alexander, David. *Terror on Broadway.* First Edition: New York: Random House, 1954.
Nr.Fine/Fine **$40**
Good/V.Good **$18**

Allen, Grant. *An African Millionaire. Episodes in the Life of the Illustrious Colonel Clay.* First Edition: London: Grant Richards Ltd., 1897.
Nr.Fine/Fine **$1250**
Good/V.Good **$600**

Allingham, Margery. *Death of a Ghost.* First Edition: London: Heinemann, 1934.
Nr.Fine/Fine **$250**
Good/V.Good **$100**
First U.S. Edition: Garden City, NY: Doubleday, Doran, 1934.
Nr.Fine/Fine **$175**
Good/V.Good **$85**

Ambler, Eric. *The Mask of Dimitrios.* First Edition: London: Hodder & Stoughton Ltd, 1939.
Nr.Fine/Fine **$12250**
Good/V.Good **$6200**
First U.S. Edition as *A Coffin for Dimitrios.* New York: Alfred A. Knopf, 1939.
Nr.Fine/Fine **$2000**
Good/V.Good **$850**

Ames, Delano. *The Body on Page One.* First Edition: New York; Rinehart & Co., 1951.
Nr.Fine/Fine **$150**
Good/V.Good **$85**

Anderson, Frederick Irving. *Adventures of the Infallible Godahl.* First Edition: New York: Thomas Y. Crowell, 1914.
Nr.Fine/Fine **$3000**
Good/V.Good **$1100**

Anderson, Poul. *Perish by the Sword.* First Edition: New York: Macmillan, 1959.
Nr.Fine/Fine **$100**
Good/V.Good **$45**

Anthony, Evelyn. *The Assassin.* First Edition: London: Hutchinson, 1970.
Nr.Fine/Fine **$25**
Good/V.Good **$12**
First U.S. Edition: New York: Coward-McCann, 1970.
Nr.Fine/Fine **$20**
Good/V.Good **$8**

Antony, Peter. *How Doth the Little Crocodile.* First Edition: London: Evans Brothers, 1952.
Nr.Fine/Fine **$525**
Good/V.Good **$200**
First U.S. Edition: New York: Macmillan, 1957.
Nr.Fine/Fine **$200**
Good/V.Good **$125**

Archer, Jeffrey. *A Quiver Full of Arrows.* First Edition: London: Hodder & Stoughton, 1980.
Nr.Fine/Fine **$40**
Good/V.Good **$15**
First U.S. Edition: New York: Linden

Press/Simon & Schuster, 1982.
Nr.Fine/Fine **$20**
Good/V.Good **$8**

Ard, William. *A Private Party.* First
Edition: New York: Rinehart & Co., 1953.
Nr.Fine/Fine **$45**
Good/V.Good **$20**

Arden, William. *A Dark Power.* First
Edition: New York: Dodd, Mead/Red
Badge, 1968.
Nr.Fine/Fine **$65**
Good/V.Good **$35**

Armstrong, Charlotte. *The Unsuspected.*
First Edition: New York: Coward-
McCann, 1946.
Nr.Fine/Fine **$165**
Good/V.Good **$60**

Arrighi, Mel. *Freak-Out.* First Edition:
New York: G. P. Putnam, 1968.
Nr.Fine/Fine **$45**
Good/V.Good **$25**

Ashdown, Clifford. *The Further
Adventures of Romney Pringle.* First
Edition: London: Cassell, 1903.
Nr.Fine/Fine **$300**
Good/V.Good **$175**

Ashford, Jeffrey. *The D. I.* First Edition:
New York: Harper & Brothers, 1961.
Nr.Fine/Fine **$15**
Good/V.Good **$8**

Atkey, Bertram. *Smiler Brun Gentleman
Crook.* First Edition: London: George
Newnes, Ltd., 1923.
Nr.Fine/Fine **$50**
Good/V.Good **$20**

Avallone, Michael. *The Case of the
Violent Virgin.* First Edition: London:
W.H. Allen, 1960.
Nr.Fine/Fine **$75**
Good/V.Good **$35**

Bagby, George. *Here Comes the Corpse.*
First Edition: Garden City, NY:
Doubleday, Doran/Crime Club, 1941.
Nr.Fine/Fine **$85**

Good/V.Good **$40**

Ball, John. *The Last Plane Out.* First
Edition: Boston: Little Brown, 1970.
Nr.Fine/Fine **$25**
Good/V.Good **$10**

_____. *In the Heat of the Night.* First
Edition: New York: Harper & Row, 1965.
|Nr.Fine/Fine **$650**
Good/V.Good **$300**

Bellairs, George. *The Tormentors.* First
Edition: London: John Gifford Ltd, 1962.
Nr.Fine/Fine **$20**
Good/V.Good **$6**

Benson, Ben. *The Ninth Hour.* First
Edition: New York: M. S. Mill Company
and William Morrow & Company, 1956.
Nr.Fine/Fine **$20**
Good/V.Good **$8**

Bentley, E. C. *Trent Intervenes.* First
Edition: London: Thomas Nelson, 1938.
Nr.Fine/Fine **$300**
Good/V.Good **$155**
First U.S. Edition: New York: Alfred A.
Knopf, 1938.
Nr.Fine/Fine **$250**
Good/V.Good **$125**

Berkeley, Anthony. *The Poisoned
Chocolates Case.* First Edition: Garden
City, NY: Doubleday, Doran & Co., 1929.
Nr.Fine/Fine **$600**
Good/V.Good **$275**

_____. *Trial and Error.* First
Edition: Garden City, NY: Doubleday
Doran, 1937.
Nr.Fine/Fine **$550**
Good/V.Good **$300**

Biggers, Earl Derr. *Charlie Chan
Carries On.* First Edition: Indianapolis:
Bobbs-Merrill, 1930.
Nr.Fine/Fine **$1600**
Good/V.Good **$750**

_____. *The House Without a
Key.* First Edition: New York: Bobbs-
Merrill, 1925.

Nr.Fine/Fine **$250**
Good/V.Good **$150**

The
Tormentors
*by George
Bellairs*

Blake, Nicholas. *The Beast Must Die.*
First Edition: London: Collins /Crime
Club, 1938.
Nr.Fine/Fine **$1900**
Good/V.Good **$1000**
First U.S. Edition: New York: Harpers,
1938.
Nr.Fine/Fine **$700**
Good/V.Good **$300**

Blochman, Lawrence G. *Diagnosis:
Homicide.* First Edition: Philadelphia:
Lippincott, 1950.
Nr.Fine/Fine **$100**
Good/V.Good **$45**

Block, Lawrence. *Burglar Who Liked to
Quote Kipling.* First Edition: New York:
Random House, 1979.
Nr.Fine/Fine **$15**
Good/V.Good **$7**

_____. *The Devil Knows
You're Dead.* First Edition: New York:
William Morrow, 1993.
Nr.Fine/Fine **$15**
Good/V.Good **$7**

Bodkin, McDonnell. *The Quests of Paul
Beck.* First Edition: Boston: Little Brown,
1910.

Nr.Fine/Fine **$500**
Good/V.Good **$200**

Boucher, Anthony. *The Case of the Seven
of Calvary.* First Edition: New York:
Simon & Schuster, 1937.
Nr.Fine/Fine **$600**
Good/V.Good **$275**

Box, Edgar. *Death in the Fifth Position.*
First Edition: New York: E.P. Dutton,
1952.
Nr.Fine/Fine **$150**
Good/V.Good **$80**

Bradbury, Ray. *Death is a Lonely
Business.* First Edition (Limited &

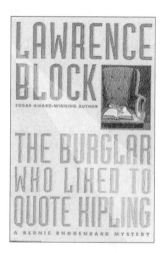

Burglar Who
Liked to Quote
Kipling
by Lawrence Block

Signed): Franklin Center, PA: Franklin
Library, 1985.
Nr.Fine/Fine **$100**
Good/V.Good **$45**
First Edition (trade): New York: Alfred A.
Knopf, 1985.
Nr.Fine/Fine **$45**
Good/V.Good **$20**

Bramah, Ernest. *The Eyes of Max
Carrados.* First Edition: London: Grant
Richards, 1923.
Nr.Fine/Fine **$3200**
Good/V.Good **$2100**
First U.S. Edition: New York: George H.
Doran, 1924.

The Devil
Knows You're
Dead
*by Lawrence
Block*

Nr.Fine/Fine **$1250**
Good/V.Good **$700**

Brand, Christianna. *Green for Danger.*
First Edition: London: John Lane The
Bodley Head, 1945.
Nr.Fine/Fine **$350**
Good/V.Good **$185**

Branson, H.C. *The Pricking Thumb.* First
Edition: New York: Simon & Schuster,
1942.
Nr.Fine/Fine **$65**
Good/V.Good **$25**

Braun, Lilian Jackson. *The Cat Who
Went into the Closet.* First Edition: New
York: G.P. Putnam, 1993.
Nr.Fine/Fine **$20**
Good/V.Good **$6**

Brean, Herbert. *Darker the Night.* First
Edition: New York: William Morrow &
Co., 1949.
Nr.Fine/Fine **$60**
Good/V.Good **$30**

Broun, Daniel. *The Subject of Harry
Egypt.* First Edition: New York: Holt,
Rhinehart and Winston, 1963.
Nr.Fine/Fine **$15**
Good/V.Good **$6**
First U.K. Edition: London: Victor
Gollancz, 1963.
Nr.Fine/Fine **$10**

Good/V.Good **$5**

Brown, Fredric. *The Dead Ringer.* First
Edition: New York: E.P. Dutton & Co.,
1948
Nr.Fine/Fine **$400**
Good/V.Good **$175**

Browne, Douglas G. *Too Many Cousins.*
First Edition: New York: Macmillan,
1953.
Nr.Fine/Fine **$25**
Good/V.Good **$10**

Bruce, Leo. *Cold Blood.* First Edition:
London: Victor Gollancz Ltd., 1952
Nr.Fine/Fine **$50**
Good/V.Good **$30**
First U.S. Edition: Chicago: Academy,
1980
Nr.Fine/Fine **$25**
Good/V.Good **$15**

Buchan, John. *The Thirty-Nine Steps.*
First Edition: London & Edinburgh:
William Blackwood and Sons, 1915.
Nr.Fine/Fine **$2100**
Good/V.Good **$1000**

Burke, James Lee. *In the Electric Mist
with Confederate Dead.* First Edition:
New York: Hyperion, 1993.
Nr.Fine/Fine **$20**
Good/V.Good **$12**

————————. *A Stained White
Radiance.* First Edition: New York:
Hyperion, 1992.
Nr.Fine/Fine **$25**
Good/V.Good **$15**

Burnett, W.R. *Little Caesar.* First
Edition: New York: Dial, 1929.
Nr.Fine/Fine **$500**
Good/V.Good **$200**

Burton, Miles. *Early Morning Murder.*
First Edition: London: Collins/Crime
Club, 1945.
Nr.Fine/Fine **$250**
Good/V.Good **$150**

First U.S. Edition as *Accidents Do Happen*. Garden City, NY: Doubleday/Crime Club, 1946.
Nr.Fine/Fine **$45**
Good/V.Good **$25**

Bush, Christopher. *The Perfect Murder Case*. First Edition: London: Heinemann, 1929.
Nr.Fine/Fine **$250**
Good/V.Good **$115**
First Edition: Garden City, NY: Doubleday/Crime Club, 1929.

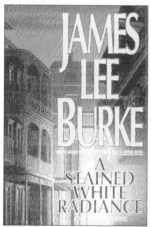

A Stained White
Radiance
by James Lee Burke

Nr.Fine/Fine **$400**
Good/V.Good **$175**

Butler, Ellis Parker. *Philo Gubb Correspondence School Detective*. First Edition: Boston: Houghton Mifflin, 1918.
Nr.Fine/Fine **$2000**
Good/V.Good **$1200**

Cain, James M. *The Magician's Wife*. First Edition: New York: Dial, 1965.
Nr.Fine/Fine **$65**
Good/V.Good **$25**

———————. *Past All Dishonor*. First Edition: New York: Alfred A. Knopf, 1946
Nr.Fine/Fine **$175**
Good/V.Good **$85**

Cannell, Stephen J. *King Con*. First Edition: New York: William Morrow, 1997.

Nr.Fine/Fine **$20**
Good/V.Good **$9**

Canning, Victor. *The Satan Sampler*. First Edition: New York: William Morrow, 1980.
Nr.Fine/Fine **$20**
Good/V.Good **$10**

Carnac, Carol. *Upstairs and Downstairs*. First Edition: Garden City, NY: Doubleday/Crime Club, 1950.
Nr.Fine/Fine **$75**
Good/V.Good **$25**

Carr, Caleb. *The Alienist*. First Edition (Limited & Signed): Franklin Center, PA: Franklin Library, 1985.
Nr.Fine/Fine **$200**
Good/V.Good **$95**
First Edition (trade): New York: Random House, 1994.
Nr.Fine/Fine **$65**
Good/V.Good **$30**

Carr, John Dickson. *The Arabian Nights Murder*. First Edition: New York: Harper & Brothers, 1936.
Nr.Fine/Fine **$1325**
Good/V.Good **$600**

———————. *The Dead Sleep Lightly*. First Edition: Garden City, NY: Doubleday, 1983.
Nr.Fine/Fine **$30**
Good/V.Good **$20**

Carvic, Heron. *Miss Seeton Sings*. First Edition: New York: Harper & Row, 1973.
Nr.Fine/Fine **$35**
Good/V.Good **$15**

Caunitz, William J. *One Police Plaza*. First Edition: New York: Crown Publishers, Inc., 1984.
Nr.Fine/Fine **$35**
Good/V.Good **$15**

Chandler, Raymond. *The Little Sister*. First Edition: London: Hamish Hamilton, 1949.
Nr.Fine/Fine **$1900**

Good/V.Good **$1100**
First U.S. Edition: Boston: Houghton
Mifflin, 1949.
Nr.Fine/Fine **$1850**
Good/V.Good **$1000**

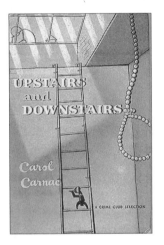

Upstairs and
Downstairs
by Carol Carnac

_____. *The Long Good-Bye.*
First Edition: London: Hamish Hamilton,
1953.
Nr.Fine/Fine **$1500**
Good/V.Good **$775**
First U.S. Edition: Boston: Houghton
Mifflin, 1954.
Nr.Fine/Fine. **$950**
Good/V.Good **$300**

_____. *Farewell, My Lovely.*
First Edition: New York: Alfred A. Knopf,
1940.
Nr.Fine/Fine **$2750**
Good/V.Good **$1000**

Charteris, Leslie. *The Ace Of Knaves.*
First Edition: London: Hodder &
Stoughton, 1937.
Nr.Fine/Fine **$1600**
Good/V.Good **$900**
First U.S. Edition: Garden City, NY:
Doubleday, Doran/Crime Club, 1937.
Nr.Fine/Fine **$550**
Good/V.Good **$200**

_____. *Thieves' Picnic.* First
Edition: London: Hodder & Stoughton,

1937.
Nr.Fine/Fine **$1375**
Good/V.Good $750
First U.S. Edition: Garden City, NY:
Doubleday/Crime Club, 1937.
Nr.Fine/Fine **$450**
Good/V.Good **$200**

Chesterton, G.K. *The Incredulity of
Father Brown.* First Edition: London:
Cassell, 1926.
Nr.Fine/Fine **$2650**
Good/V.Good **$800**
First U.S. Edition: New York: Dodd Mead,
1926.
Nr.Fine/Fine **$750**
Good/V.Good **$350**

Christie, Agatha. *Mrs. McGinty's Dead.*
First Edition: London: Collins/Crime
Club, 1952.
Nr.Fine/Fine **$145**
Good/V.Good **$65**
First Edition: New York: Dodd, Mead,
1952.
Nr.Fine/Fine **$75**
Good/V.Good **$35**

Thieves' Picnic
by Leslie Charteris

_____. *Death on the Nile.* First
Edition: London: Collins/Crime Club,
1937.
Nr.Fine/Fine **$4000**
Good/V.Good **$2400**

First Edition: New York: Dodd, Mead, 1938.
Nr.Fine/Fine **$500**
Good/V.Good **$275**

_____. *Lord Edgware Dies.*
First Edition: London: Collins/Crime Club, 1933.
Nr.Fine/Fine **$3200**
Good/V.Good **$2000**

_____. *The Mystery of the Blue Train.* First Edition: New York: Dodd, Mead, 1928.
Nr.Fine/Fine **$2500**
Good/V.Good **$850**

Clark, Douglas. *Premedicated Murder.*
First Edition: London: Victor Gollancz, 1975.
Nr.Fine/Fine **$150**
Good/V.Good **$80**
First Edition: New York: Scribners, 1975.
Nr.Fine/Fine **$20**
Good/V.Good **$10**

Death on
the Nile
by Agatha Christie

Clason, Clyde B. *Dragon's Cave.* First Edition: Garden City, NY: Doubleday/Crime Club, 1939.
Nr.Fine/Fine **$350**
Good/V.Good **$125**

Coe, Tucker. *Murder Among Children.*
First Edition: New York: Random House, 1967.

Nr.Fine/Fine **$75**
Good/V.Good **$30**

Lord Edgware
Dies
by Agatha Christie

Cohen, Octavus Roy. *Dangerous Lady.*
First Edition: New York: Macmillan, 1946.
Nr.Fine/Fine **$45**
Good/V.Good **$18**

The Mystery Of
The Blue Train
by Agatha Christie

Coles, Manning. *Now or Never.* First Edition: Garden City, NY: Doubleday/Crime Club, 1951.
Nr.Fine/Fine **$55**
Good/V.Good **$35**
First U.K. Edition: London: Hodder and Stoughton, 1951.
Nr.Fine/Fine **$35**

Good/V.Good **$20**

_____. *Drink to Yesterday.* First Edition: New York: Alfred A. Knopf, 1941.
Nr.Fine/Fine **$250**
Good/V.Good **$100**

Collins, Michael. *The Brass Rainbow.* First Edition: New York: Dodd, Mead, 1969.
Nr.Fine/Fine **$35**
Good/V.Good **$20**

Connington, J. J. *The Case With Nine Solutions.* First Edition: Boston: Little Brown, 1929.
Nr.Fine/Fine **$400**

Dangerous Lady
by Octavus Roy Cohen

Good/V.Good **$175**

Cornwell, Patricia. *Postmortem.* First Edition: New York: Scribner's, 1990.
Nr.Fine/Fine **$750**
Good/V.Good **$400**

Coxe, George Harmon. *Lady Killer.* First Edition: New York: Alfred A. Knopf, 1949.
Nr.Fine/Fine **$85**
Good/V.Good **$40**

Crane, Francis. *The Cinnamon Murder.* First Edition: New York: Random House, 1946.
Nr.Fine/Fine **$60**

Good/V.Good **$35**

Creasey, John. *The Toff and the Spider.* First Edition: London: Hodder & Stoughton, 1965.
Nr.Fine/Fine. **$35**
Good/V.Good **$15**
First U.S. Edition: New York: Walker & Company, 1965
Nr.Fine/Fine **$25**
Good/V.Good **$12**

_____. *The Depths.* First Edition: London: Hodder & Stoughton. 1963.
Nr.Fine/Fine **$45**
Good/V.Good **$25**
First Edition: New York: Walker, 1967.
Nr.Fine/Fine **$20**
Good/V.Good **$8**

Crispin, Edmund. *The Long Divorce.* First Edition: London: Victor Gollancz, 1951.
Nr.Fine/Fine **$100**
Good/V.Good **$50**
First U.S. Edition: New York: Dodd Mead, 1951.
Nr.Fine/Fine **$55**
Good/V.Good **$25**

Crofts, Freeman Wills. *Man Overboard.* First Edition: London: Collins/Crime Club, 1936.
Nr.Fine/Fine **$950**
Good/V.Good **$375**
First U.S. Edition: New York: Dodd, Mead, 1936.
Nr.Fine/Fine **$200**
Good/V.Good **$100**

Cumberland, Marten. *And Then Came Fear.* First Edition: Garden City, NY: Doubleday/Crime Club, 1948.
Nr.Fine/Fine **$85**
Good/V.Good **$60**

Cunningham, A.B. *Murder at Deer Lick.* First Edition: New York: Dutton, 1939.
Nr.Fine/Fine **$225**
Good/V.Good **$100**

Daly, Elizabeth. *Deadly Nightshade*. First Edition: New York: Farrar & Rinehart, 1940.
Nr.Fine/Fine **$300**
Good/V.Good **$135**

Dean, Spencer. *The Merchant of Murder*. First Edition: Garden City, NY: Doubleday, 1959.
Nr.Fine/Fine **$35**
Good/V.Good **$15**

Deighton, Len. *The Ipcress File*. First Edition: London: Hodder & Stoughton, 1962.
Nr.Fine/Fine **$1400**
Good/V.Good **$750**
First U.S. Edition: New York: Simon and Schuster, 1963.
Nr.Fine/Fine **$225**
Good/V.Good **$85**

De La Torre, Lillian. *Dr. Sam: Johnson, Detector*. First Edition: New York: Alfred A. Knopf, 1946.
Nr.Fine/Fine **$150**
Good/V.Good **$75**

Derleth, August. *Three Problems for Solar Pons*. First Edition: Sauk City, WI: Mycroft & Moran, 1952.
Nr.Fine/Fine **$325**
Good/V.Good **$200**

Dewey, Thomas B. *The Brave Bad Girls*. First Edition: New York: Simon & Schuster/Inner Sanctum, 1956.
Nr.Fine/Fine **$25**
Good/V.Good **$10**

Dickson, Carter. *Seeing is Believing*. First Edition: Cleveland and New York: The World Publishing Company, 1945.
Nr.Fine/Fine. **$45**
Good/V.Good **$20**

_____. *Lord of the Sorcerers*. First Edition: London: William Heinemann, 1946.
Nr.Fine/Fine **$275**
Good/V.Good **$85**

Diehl, William. *Sharky's Machine*. First Edition: New York: Delacorte, 1978.
Nr.Fine/Fine **$50**
Good/V.Good **$20**

Disney, Doris Miles. *Room For Murder*. First Edition: Garden City, NY: Doubleday, 1955.
Nr.Fine/Fine **$30**
Good/V.Good **$12**
First UK Edition: London: W.Foulsham & Co., 1959.
Nr.Fine/Fine **$25**
Good/V.Good **$10**

Doyle, Sir Arthur Conan. *His Last Bow*. First Edition: London: John Murray, 1917.
Nr.Fine/Fine **$2800**
Good/V.Good **$1600**
First U.S. Edition: New York: George H. Doran, 1917.
Nr.Fine/Fine **$2500**
Good/V.Good **$1000**

_____. *The Hound of the Baskervilles*. First Edition: London: Georges Newnes, 1902.
Nr.Fine/Fine **$2200**
Good/V.Good **$1200**

_____. *The Case-Book Of Sherlock Holmes*. First Edition: London: John Murray, 1927.
Nr.Fine/Fine **$7500**
Good/V.Good **$3100**
First Edition: New York: George H. Doran, 1927.
Nr.Fine/Fine **$1800**
Good/V.Good **$800**

DuBois, Theodora. *Death Is Late to Lunch*. First Edition: Boston: Houghton Mifflin, 1941.
Nr.Fine/Fine **$75**
Good/V.Good **$45**

Dunning, John. *Booked to Die*. First Edition: New York: Charles Scribners, 1992.
Nr.Fine/Fine **$500**

Good/V.Good **$275**

Booked to Die
by John Dunning

Eco, Umberto. *The Name Of The Rose.*
First Edition in English: London: Secker
& Warburg, 1983.
Nr.Fine/Fine **$250**
Good/V.Good **$140**
First U.S. Edition: New York: Harcourt
Brace, 1983.
Nr.Fine/Fine **$200**
Good/V.Good **$75**

Egan, Lesley. *My Name Is Death.* First
Edition: New York: Harper, 1964.
Nr.Fine/Fine **$25**
Good/V.Good **$10**

White Jazz
by James Ellroy

Ellroy, James. *White Jazz.* First Edition:
New York: Alfred A. Knopf, 1992.

Nr.Fine/Fine **$45**
Good/V.Good **$15**

Erskine, Margaret. *Case With Three
Husbands.* First Edition: Garden City,
NY: Doubleday/Crime Club, 1967
Nr.Fine/Fine **$55**
Good/V.Good **$25**
First U.K. Edition: London: Hodder and
Stoughton, 1967.
Nr.Fine/Fine **$30**
Good/V.Good **$15**

Fair, A.A. *Bachelors Get Lonely.* First
Edition: New York: William Morrow,
1961.
Nr.Fine/Fine **$95**
Good/V.Good **$40**

_____. *All Grass Isn't Green.* First
Edition: New York: William Morrow,
1970.
Nr.Fine/Fine **$65**
Good/V.Good **$30**
First U.K. Edition: London: Heinemann,
1970.
Nr.Fine/Fine **$25**
Good/V.Good **$15**

Faulkner, William. *Intruder in the Dust.*
First Edition: New York: Random House,
1948.
Nr.Fine/Fine **$1200**
Good/V.Good **$650**

Ferrigno, Robert. *Dead Man's Dance.*
First Edition: New York: G.P. Putnam,
1995.
Nr.Fine/Fine **$15**
Good/V.Good **$5**

Fickling, G. G. *Blood and Honey.* First
Edition: New York: Pyramid Books, 1961.
Points of Issue: Paperback Original
Pyramid #G-623
Nr.Fine/Fine **$25**
Good/V.Good **$12**

Fish, Robert L. *The Fugitive.* First
Edition: New York: Simon and Schuster,
1962.
Nr.Fine/Fine **$165**

Good/V.Good $75

_____. *The Murder League*. First Edition: New York: Simon & Schuster, 1968.
Nr.Fine/Fine $25
Good/V.Good $15

Hospitality For Murder
by Gerard Fisher

Fisher, Gerard. *Hospitality for Murder.* First Edition: New York: Washburn/Chantecler, 1959.
Nr.Fine/Fine $20
Good/V.Good $8

Fleming, Ian. *From Russia with Love.* First Edition: London: Jonathan Cape, 1957.
Nr.Fine/Fine $4000
Good/V.Good $1500
First U.S. Edition: New York: Macmillan, 1957.
Nr.Fine/Fine $175
Good/V.Good $85

_____. *The Spy Who Loved Me.* First Edition: London, Jonathan Cape, 1962.
Nr.Fine/Fine $700
Good/V.Good $300
First U.S. Edition: New York: Viking Press, 1962
Nr.Fine/Fine $150
Good/V.Good $65

Fletcher, Lucille. A novelization from the screenplay by Alan Ullmann. *Sorry, Wrong Number.* First Edition: New York: Random House, 1948.
Nr.Fine/Fine $45
Good/V.Good $25

Sorry Wrong Number
by Lucille Fletcher

Foley, Rae. *Wake the Sleeping Wolf.* First Edition: New York: Dodd, Mead, 1952.
Nr.Fine/Fine $180
Good/V.Good $75

Ford, Leslie. *The Woman in Black.* First Edition: New York: Charles Scribner's, 1947.
Nr.Fine/Fine $60
Good/V.Good $25

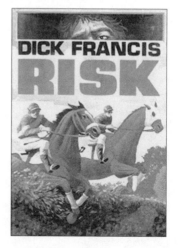

Risk
by Dick Francis

Francis, Dick. *Risk.* First Edition:

London: Michael Joseph, 1977.
Nr.Fine/Fine **$125**
Good/V.Good **$55**
First U.S. Edition: New York: Harper &
Row, 1977
Nr.Fine/Fine **$55**
Good/V.Good **$25**

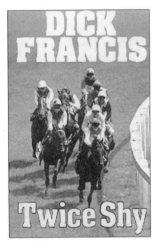

Twice Shy
by Dick Francis

_____. *Twice Shy.* First Edition:
London: Michael Joseph, 1981.
Nr.Fine/Fine **$80**
Good/V.Good **$45**
First U.S. Edition: New York: G.P.
Putnam's, 1982
Nr.Fine/Fine **$40**
Good/V.Good **$20**

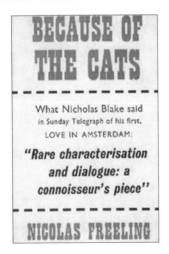

Because of the
Cats
*by Nicolas
Freeling*

Freeling, Nicolas. *Because of the Cats.*
First Edition: London: Victor Gollancz,
1963.
Nr.Fine/Fine **$85**
Good/V.Good **$40**
First Edition: New York: Harper & Row,
1964.
Nr.Fine/Fine **$25**
Good/V.Good **$10**

Freeman, R. Austin. *Pontifex, Son and
Thorndyke.* First Edition: London: Hodder
& Stoughton, 1931.
Nr.Fine/Fine **$650**
Good/V.Good **$275**
First Edition: New York: Dodd Mead,
1931.
Nr.Fine/Fine **$125**
Good/V.Good **$50**

Frome, David. *Mr. Pinkerton Has the
Clue.* First Edition: New York: Farrar &
Rinehart, 1936.
Nr.Fine/Fine **$145**
Good/V.Good **$65**

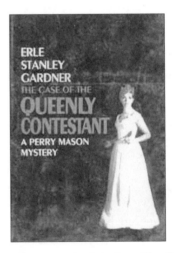

The Case of
the Queenly
Contestant
*by Erie Stanley
Gardner*

Gardner, Erle Stanley. *The Case of the
Queenly Contestant.* First Edition: New
York: William Morrow, 1967.

Nr.Fine/Fine **$65**
Good/V.Good **$30**

_____. *The Case of the
Troubled Trustee.* First Edition: New York:

William Morrow, 1965.
Nr.Fine/Fine **$55**
Good/V.Good **$25**

The Case of
the Troubled
Trustee
*by Erie Stanley
Gardner*

Garnet, A. H. *The Santa Claus Killer.*
First Edition: New Haven: Ticknor &
Fields, 1981.
Nr.Fine/Fine **$20**
Good/V.Good **$8**

Garve, Andrew. *The Narrow Search.* First
Edition: London: Collins/Crime Club,
1957.
Nr.Fine/Fine **$30**
Good/V.Good **$20**
First U.S. Edition: New York: Harper &
Brothers, 1957.
Nr.Fine/Fine **$25**

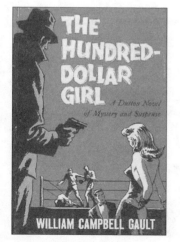

The Hundred
Dollar Girl
*by William
Campbell
Gault*

Good/V.Good **$10**

Gault, William Campbell. *The Hundred-
Dollar Girl.* First Edition: New York: E. P.
Dutton, 1961.
Nr.Fine/Fine **$175**
Good/V.Good **$65**

Murder by
Experts
by Anthony Gilbert

Gilbert, Anthony. *Murder by Experts.*
First Edition: New York: Dial Press, Inc.,
1937.
Nr.Fine/Fine **$125**
Good/V.Good **$70**

Gilbert, Michael. *Fear to Tread.* First
Edition: London: Hodder and Stoughton,
1953.
Nr.Fine/Fine **$150**
Good/V.Good **$50**
First U.S. Edition: New York: Harper &
Brothers, 1953.
Nr.Fine/Fine **$60**
Good/V.Good **$25**

Gilman, Dorothy. *A Palm for Mrs.
Pollifax.* First Edition: Garden City, NY:
Doubleday, 1973.
Nr.Fine/Fine **$35**
Good/V.Good **$10**

The Gordons. *Case File: FBI.* First
Edition: Garden City, NY:
Doubleday/Crime Club,
1953.Nr.Fine/Fine **$35**
Good/V.Good **$15**

First U.K. Edition: London: Macdonald, 1954.
Nr.Fine/Fine **$20**
Good/V.Good **$8**

Grafton, Sue. *E is for Evidence.* First Edition: New York: Henry Holt, 1988.
Nr.Fine/Fine **$145**
Good/V.Good **$65**

"F" is for Fugitive
by Sue Grafton

_____. *F Is For Fugitive.* First Edition: New York: Henry Holt, 1988.
Nr.Fine/Fine **$85**
Good/V.Good **$35**

Green, Anna-Katherine. *The Filigree Ball.* First Edition: Indianapolis: Bobbs-Merrill, 1903.
Nr.Fine/Fine **$75**
Good/V.Good **$30**

Greene, Graham. *The Captain and the Enemy.* First Edition: Toronto: Lester & Orpen Dennys, 1988.
Nr.Fine/Fine **$65**
Good/V.Good **$35**
First U.K. Edition: London: Reinhardt Books/Viking, 1988.
Nr.Fine/Fine **$55**
Good/V.Good **$30**
First U.S. Edition: New York: Viking, 1988.
Nr.Fine/Fine **$20**
Good/V.Good **$10**

Grisham, John. *The Firm.* First Edition:

New York: Doubleday, 1991.
Nr.Fine/Fine **$150**
Good/V.Good **$65**

The Firm
by John Grisham

Gruber, Frank. *The Silver Tombstone.* First Edition: New York: Farrar & Rinehart, 1945.
Nr.Fine/Fine **$75**
Good/V.Good **$30**

Haggard, William. *The Arena.* First Edition: London: Cassell & Co., 1961.
Nr.Fine/Fine **$35**
Good/V.Good **$15**
First U.S. Edition: New York: Ives Washburn , 1961.
Nr.Fine/Fine **$20**
Good/V.Good **$8**

Marked for Murder
by Brett Halliday

Halliday, Brett. *Marked for Murder.* First Edition: New York: Dodd Mead, 1945.
Nr.Fine/Fine **$100**
Good/V.Good **$40**

Framed in Blood
by Brett Halliday

_____. *Framed in Blood.* First Edition: New York: Dodd, Mead, 1951.
Nr.Fine/Fine **$30**
Good/V.Good **$20**

Hammett, Dashiell. *The Dain Curse.* First Edition: New York: Alfred A. Knopf, 1929.
Nr.Fine/Fine **$22,500**
Good/V.Good **$11,000**

_____. *The Thin Man.* First Edition: New York: Alfred A. Knopf, 1934.
Nr.Fine/Fine **$3950**
Good/V.Good **$1000**

Hare, Cyril. *That Yew Tree's Shade.* First Edition: London: Faber & Faber, 1954.
Nr.Fine/Fine **$60**
Good/V.Good **$30**
First U.S. Edition: as: *Death Walks The Woods.* Boston: Little, Brown, 1954.
Nr.Fine/Fine **$35**
Good/V.Good **$12**

Hart, Frances Noyes. *The Bellamy Trial.* First Edition: New York: Doubleday, Page, 1927.
Nr.Fine/Fine **$1250**
Good/V.Good **$750**

Harvester, Simon. *Red Road.* First Edition: London: Jarrolds, 1963
Nr.Fine/Fine **$30**
Good/V.Good **$15**

First U.S. Edition: New York: Walker, 1964
Nr.Fine/Fine **$20**
Good/V.Good **$8**

Hastings, Macdonald. *Cork in the Doghouse.* First Edition: London: Michael Joseph, 1957.
Nr.Fine/Fine **$50**
Good/V.Good **$20**
First U.S. Edition: New York: Alfred A. Knopf, 1958.
Nr.Fine/Fine **$40**
Good/V.Good **$15**

Head, Matthew. *The Devil in the Bush.* First Edition: New York: Simon and Schuster, 1945
Nr.Fine/Fine **$50**
Good/V.Good **$20**

Heard, H.F. *A Taste for Honey.* First Edition: New York: Vanguard, 1941.
Nr.Fine/Fine **$120**
Good/V.Good **$55**

Heberden, M.V. *The Case of the Eight Brothers.* First Edition: Garden City, NY: Doubleday/Crime Club, 1948.
Nr.Fine/Fine **$75**
Good/V.Good **$40**

Friends of
Eddie Coyle
*by George V.
Higgins*

Higgins, George V. *Friends of Eddie Coyle.* First Edition: New York: Alfred A. Knopf, 1972.
Nr.Fine/Fine **$100**
Good/V.Good **$45**

Hillerman, Tony. *Fly on the Wall.* First Edition: New York: Harper & Row, 1971.
Nr.Fine/Fine **$1200**
Good/V.Good **$500**

_____. *Skinwalkers.* First Edition: New York: Harper & Row, 1986
Nr.Fine/Fine **$80**
Good/V.Good **$45**

Hirschberg, Cornelius. *Florentine Finish.* First Edition: New York: Harper & Row, 1963.
Nr.Fine/Fine **$30**
Good/V.Good **$15**

Hoch, Edward D. *The Thefts of Nick Velvet.* First Edition (Limited): New York: Mysterious Press, 1978.
Nr.Fine/Fine **$100**
Good/V.Good **$65**
First Edition (Trade): New York: Mysterious Press, 1978.
Nr.Fine/Fine **$50**
Good/V.Good **$20**

Holmes, H.H. *Rocket To The Morgue.* First Edition: New York: Duell, Sloan & Pearce, 1942.
Nr.Fine/Fine **$650**
Good/V.Good **$250**

Holton, Leonard. *A Problem in Angels.* First Edition: New York: Dodd Mead, 1970.
Nr.Fine/Fine **$35**
Good/V.Good **$20**

Homes, Geoffrey. *The Doctor Died at Dusk.* First Edition: New York: William Morrow, 1936.
Nr.Fine/Fine **$200**
Good/V.Good **$75**

Hornung, E.W. *Mr. Justice Raffles.* First Edition: London: Smith, Elder & Co,

1909
Nr.Fine/Fine **$200**
Good/V.Good **$75**
First Edition: New York: Scribners, 1909.
Nr.Fine/Fine **$65**
Good/V.Good **$25**

Mr. Justice
Raffles
by E.W. Hornung

Hunter, Alan. *Gently With The Painters.* First Edition: London: Cassell, 1960.
Nr.Fine/Fine **$85**
Good/V.Good **$35**
First U.S. Edition: New York: Macmillan, 1976.
Nr.Fine/Fine **$25**
Good/V.Good **$10**

Iles, Francis. *Malice Aforethought. The Story of a Commonplace Crime.* First Edition: London: Mundanus [Victor Gollancz], 1931.
Nr.Fine/Fine **$750**
Good/V.Good **$300**

Innes, Michael. *Appleby's End.* First Edition: London: Victor Gollancz, 1945.
Nr.Fine/Fine **$125**
Good/V.Good **$55**
First Edition: New York: Dodd, Mead, 1945.
Nr.Fine/Fine **$50**
Good/V.Good **$35**

Irish, William. *Phantom Lady.* First Edition: Philadelphia: Lippincott, 1942.

Nr.Fine/Fine **$1350**
Good/V.Good **$350**

James, P. D. *Shroud for a Nightingale.*
First Edition: London: Faber and Faber,
1971.
Nr.Fine/Fine **$350**
Good/V.Good **$200**
First U.S. Edition: New York: Scribners
1971.
Nr.Fine/Fine **$175**
Good/V.Good **$90**

Kane, Henry. *Armchair in Hell.* First
Edition: New York: Simon & Schuster,
1948.
Nr.Fine/Fine **$35**
Good/V.Good **$15**

Keating, H.R.F. *The Sheriff of Bombay.*
First Edition: London: Collins, 1984
Nr.Fine/Fine **$35**
Good/V.Good **$15**

First U.S. Edition: Garden City, NY:
Doubleday/Crime Club, 1984

Nr.Fine/Fine **$15**
Good/V.Good **$8**

Keeler, Harry Stephen. *The Mysterious
Mr. I.* First Edition: New York: E. P.
Dutton, 1938
Nr.Fine/Fine **$300**
Good/V.Good **$100**

Keith, Carlton. *Crayfish Dinner.* First
Edition: Garden City, NY:
Doubleday/Crime Club, 1966
Nr.Fine/Fine **$35**
Good/V.Good **$10**

Kellerman, Faye. *Sacred and Profane.*
First Edition: New York: Arbor House,
1987
Nr.Fine/Fine **$25**
Good/V.Good **$10**

Kellerman, Jonathan. *The Clinic.* First
Edition: New York: Bantam Books, 1997
Nr.Fine/Fine **$10**
Good/V.Good **$5**

Kemelman, Harry. *Saturday the Rabbi
Went Hungry.* First Edition: New York:
Crown, 1966
Nr.Fine/Fine **$70**
Good/V.Good **$25**

Kendrick, Baynard. *Blind Man's Bluff.*
First Edition: Boston: Little, Brown, 1943
Nr.Fine/Fine **$75**
Good/V.Good **$25**

Kijewski, Karen. *Katwalk.* First Edition:
New York: St. Martin's Press, 1989
Nr.Fine/Fine **$100**
Good/V.Good **$35**

King, Rufus. *Museum Piece No. 13.* First
Edition: Garden City, NY:
Doubleday/Crime Club, 1946
Nr.Fine/Fine **$85**
Good/V.Good **$30**

Klinger, Henry. *Lust For Murder.* First
Edition: New York: Trident Press, 1966
Nr.Fine/Fine **$25**
Good/V.Good **$15**

Lacy, Ed. *Room to Swing.* First Edition:
New York: Harper & Brothers, 1957
Nr.Fine/Fine **$100**
Good/V.Good **$45**

Lathen, Emma. *Murder Without Icing.*
First Edition: New York: Simon and
Schuster, 1972
Nr.Fine/Fine **$60**

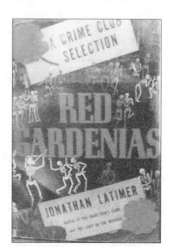

Red Gardenias
*by Jonathan
Latimer*

Good/V.Good **$20**

Latimer, Jonathan. *Red Gardenias.* First Edition: Garden City, NY: Doubleday Doran/Crime Club, 1939
Nr.Fine/Fine **$500**
Good/V.Good **$275**

Leblanc, Maurice. *The Woman of Mystery.* First Edition in English: New York: Macauley Company, 1916
Nr.Fine/Fine **$125**
Good/V.Good **$75**

LeCarre, John. *The Looking-Glass War.* First Edition: London: William Heinemann, 1965
Nr.Fine/Fine **$115**
Good/V.Good **$40**
First Edition: New York Coward-McCann, Inc., 1965
Nr.Fine/Fine **$30**
Good/V.Good **$10**

Sinister Shelter
by Charles L. Leonard

Leonard, Charles L. *Sinister Shelter.* First Edition: Garden City, NY: Doubleday/Crime Club, 1949
Nr.Fine/Fine **$40**
Good/V.Good **$15**

Leonard, Elmore. *Fifty-Two Pickup.* First Edition: New York: Delacorte Press, 1974
Nr.Fine/Fine **$450**
Good/V.Good **$175**

Linington, Elizabeth. *Date with Death.*

First Edition: New York: Harper & Row, 1966
Nr.Fine/Fine **$35**
Good/V.Good **$12**

Lockridge, Frances & Richard. *The Norths Meet Murder.* First Edition: Cleveland: World, 1946
Nr.Fine/Fine **$20**
Good/V.Good **$10**

Lorac, E.C.R. *Relative to Poison.* First Edition: London: Collins/Crime Club, 1947
Nr.Fine/Fine **$115**
Good/V.Good **$50**
First U.S. Edition: Garden City, NY: Doubleday/Crime Club, 1948
Nr.Fine/Fine **$100**
Good/V.Good **$40**

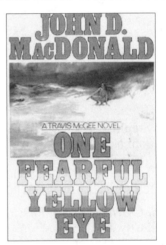

One Fearful
Yellow Eye
by John D. MacDonald

MacDonald, John D. *One Fearful Yellow Eye.* First Edition: Greenwich, CT: Fawcett Publications, Inc., 1966. Points of Issue: Paperback original Fawcett Gold Medal d1750
Nr.Fine/Fine **$40**
Good/V.Good **$18**
First Hardcover Edition: New York: Lippincott, 1977
Nr.Fine/Fine. **$425**
Good/V.Good **$300**

Free Fall in
Crimson
*by John D.
MacDonald*

_____. *Free Fall in Crimson*. First Edition: New York: Harper & Row, 1981
Nr.Fine/Fine **$35**
Good/V.Good **$15**

MacDonald, Philip. *Something To Hide*. First Edition: Garden City: Doubleday/Crime Club, 1952

Nr.Fine/Fine **$175**
Good/V.Good **$65**

MacDonald, Ross. *The Instant Enemy*. First Edition: New York: Alfred A. Knopf, 1968
Nr.Fine/Fine **$175**
Good/V.Good **$75**

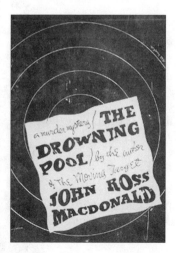

The Drowning
Pool
*by John Ross
MacDonald*

MacDonald, John Ross. *The Drowning Pool*. First Edition: New York: Alfred A. Knopf, 1950
Nr.Fine/Fine **$1250**
Good/V.Good **$575**

McBain, Ed. *So Long as You Both Shall Live*. First Edition: New York: Random House, 1976
 Nr.Fine/Fine **$45**
Good/V.Good **$15**

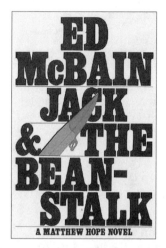

Jack & The
Beanstalk
by Ed McBain

_____. *Jack and the Beanstalk*. First Edition: New York: Holt Rinehart & Winston, 1984
Nr.Fine/Fine **$25**
Good/V.Good **$10**

McCloy, Helen. *The Imposter*. First Edition: New York: Dodd, Mead, 1977
Nr.Fine/Fine **$30**
Good/V.Good **$12**

McCutcheon, George Barr. *Anderson Crow Detective*. First Edition: New York: Dodd Mead, 1920
Nr.Fine/Fine **$75**
Good/V.Good **$25**

McDougald, Roman. *Purgatory Street*. First Edition: New York: Simon & Schuster, 1946
Nr.Fine/Fine **$30**
Good/V.Good **$15**

Purgatory
Street
*by Roman
McDougald*

False Scent
by Ngaio Marsh

Marric, J. J. *Gideon's Night.* First
Edition: London & Edinburgh: Hodder
and Stoughton, 1957
Nr.Fine/Fine **$25**
Good/V.Good **$12**
First US Edition: New York: Harper &
Brothers, 1957
Nr.Fine/Fine **$15**
Good/V.Good **$7**

Marquand, John P. *Mr. Moto is So
Sorry.* First Edition: Boston: Little Brown
Co, 1938
Nr.Fine/Fine **$135**
Good/V.Good **$55**

Marsh, Ngaio. *Died in the Wool.* First
Edition: London: Collins/Crime Club,
1945
Nr.Fine/Fine **$300**
Good/V.Good **$125**
First U.S. Edition: Boston: Little, Brown
and Company, 1945
Nr.Fine/Fine **$150**
Good/V.Good **$60**

_____. *False Scent.* First Edition:
London: Collins/Crime Club, 1960
Nr.Fine/Fine **$50**
Good/V.Good **$30**
First U.S. Edition: Boston: Little Brown,
1959
Nr.Fine/Fine **$30**
Good/V.Good **$15**

Martini, Steve. *Prime Witness.* First
Edition: New York: G. P. Putnam, 1993
Nr.Fine/Fine **$15**
Good/V.Good **$5**

Mason, A.E. W. *The House of the Arrow.*
First Edition: London & Edinburgh:
Hodder and Stoughton, 1924
Nr.Fine/Fine **$600**
Good/V.Good **$250**
First U.S. Edition: New York: George H.
Doran, 1924
Nr.Fine/Fine **$200**
Good/V.Good **$85**

Masterson, Whit. *The Gravy Train.* First
Edition: New York: Dodd, Mead, 1971
Nr.Fine/Fine **$30**
Good/V.Good **$15**

Maugham, W. Somerset. *Ashenden: or
The British Agent.* First Edition: London:
William Heinemann, 1928
Nr.Fine/Fine **$4200**
Good/V.Good **$500**
First U.S. Edition: Garden City, NY:
Doubleday Doran, 1928
Nr.Fine/Fine **$200**
Good/V.Good **$75**

Millar, Margaret. *The Devil Loves
Me.* First Edition: Garden City, NY:
Doubleday, Doran/Crime Club, 1942
Nr.Fine/Fine **$550**
Good/V.Good **$250**

Miller, Wade. *Shoot to Kill.* First Edition: New York: Farrar, Strauss & Young, 1948
Nr.Fine/Fine **$45**
Good/V.Good **$20**

Mitchell, Gladys. *Spotted Hemlock.* First Edition: London: Michael Joseph, 1958
Nr.Fine/Fine **$150**
Good/V.Good **$65**
First Edition: New York St. Martin's Press 1985
Nr.Fine/Fine **$15**
Good/V.Good **$8**

Morland, Nigel. *The Dear Dead Girls.* First Edition: London: Cassell, 1961
Nr.Fine/Fine **$70**
Good/V.Good **$30**

Morrison, Arthur. *The Hole in the Wall.* First Edition: London: Methuen, 1902
Nr.Fine/Fine **$300**
Good/V.Good **$125**

Morton, Anthony. *A Case for the Baron.* First Edition: London: Sampson Low, 1945
Nr.Fine/Fine **$100**
Good/V.Good **$65**
First U.S. Edition: New York: Duell, Sloan and Pearce, 1949
Nr.Fine/Fine **$65**
Good/V.Good **$25**

Mosley, Walter. *Devil in a Blue Dress.* First Edition: New York: Norton, 1990

Dead Men
Don't Ski
by Patricia Moyes

Nr.Fine/Fine **$100**
Good/V.Good **$55**

Moyes, Patricia. *Dead Men Don't Ski.* First Edition: London: Collins, 1959
Nr.Fine/Fine **$250**
Good/V.Good **$110**
First U.S. Edition: New York: Rinehart, 1959
Nr.Fine/Fine **$75**
Good/V.Good **$45**

Muller, Marcia. *Till The Butchers Cut Him Down.* First Edition: New York: Mysterious Press, 1994
Nr.Fine/Fine **$35**
Good/V.Good **$20**

Nolan, William F. *Death Is For Losers.* First Edition: Los Angeles: Sherbourne Press, 1968
Nr.Fine/Fine **$15**
Good/V.Good **$7**

Offord, Lenore Glen. *The Nine Dark Hours.* First Edition: New York: Duell, Sloan and Pearce, 1941
Nr.Fine/Fine **$55**
Good/V.Good **$20**

O'Hanlon, James. *As Good as Murdered.* First Edition: New York: Random House, 1940
Nr.Fine/Fine $45
Good/V.Good **$20**

Olsen, D.B. *Death Walks on Cat Feet.* First Edition: Garden City, NY: Doubleday/Crime Club, 1956
Nr.Fine/Fine **$35**
Good/V.Good **$15**

Orczy, Baroness. *The Old Man in the Corner.* First Edition: London: Greening & Co., 1909
Nr.Fine/Fine **$4000**
Good/V.Good **$2100**

Palmer, Stuart & Craig Rice. *People Vs. Withers & Malone.* First Edition: New York: Simon & Schuster, 1963
Nr.Fine/Fine **$75**

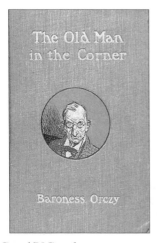

The Old Man
in the Corner
by Baroness Orczy

Good/V.Good **$30**

Paretsky, Sara. *Bitter Medicine*. First
Edition: New York: William Morrow,
1987
Nr.Fine/Fine **$65**
Good/V.Good **$35**

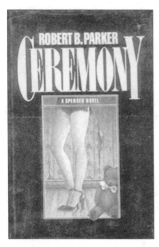

Ceremony
*by Robert B.
Parker*

Parker, Robert B. *Ceremony*. First
Edition: New York: Delacorte Press, 1982
Nr.Fine/Fine **$55**
Good/V.Good **$30**

_____. *Valediction*. First
Edition: New York: Delacorte, 1984
Nr.Fine/Fine **$45**
Good/V.Good **$25**

Patterson, James. *The Thomas Berryman*

Number. First Edition: Boston: Little
Brown, 1976
Nr.Fine/Fine **$400**
Good/V.Good **$225**

Patterson, Richard North. *The Lasko
Tangent*. First Edition: New York: W. W.
Norton, 1979
Nr.Fine/Fine **$400**
Good/V.Good **$225**

Paul, Elliot. *Hugger-Mugger in the
Louvre*. First Edition: New York: Random
House, 1940
Nr.Fine/Fine **$150**
Good/V.Good **$45**

Pentacost, Hugh. *The Champagne Killer*.
First Edition: New York: Dodd, Mead,
1972
Nr.Fine/Fine **$10**
Good/V.Good **$6**

Perowne, Barry. *The Return of Raffles:
Further Adventures of the Amateur
Cracksman*. First Edition: New York: John
Day Co., 1933
Nr.Fine/Fine **$75**
Good/V.Good **$30**

Peters, Ellis. *One Corpse Too Many*. First
Edition: London: Macmillan, 1979
Nr.Fine/Fine **$600**
Good/V.Good **$250**
First U.S. Edition: New York: Morrow,
1980
Nr.Fine/Fine **$150**
Good/V.Good **$65**

Peters, Elizabeth. *Lion in the Valley*. First
Edition: New York: Atheneum, 1986
Nr.Fine/Fine **$175**
Good/V.Good **$65**

Philips, Judson. *Murder as the Curtain
Rises*. First Edition: New York: Dodd
Mead, 1981
Nr.Fine/Fine **$30**
Good/V.Good **$15**

Porter, Joyce. *Dover One*. First Edition:
London: Jonathan Cape, 1964

Nr.Fine/Fine $125
Good/V.Good $65
First U.S. Edition: New York: Scribner's,
1964
Nr.Fine/Fine $55
Good/V.Good $25

Uncle Abner:
Master of
Mysteries
*by Melville Davisson
Post*

Post, Melville Davisson. *Uncle Abner:
Master of Mysteries.* First Edition: New
York & London: D. Appleton & Co, 1918
Nr.Fine/Fine $5000
Good/V.Good $2500

Postgate, Raymond, *Verdict of Twelve.*
First Edition: Garden City NY: Doubleday
Doran/Crime Club, 1940
Nr.Fine/Fine $500
Good/V.Good $275

Prather, Richard S. *Kill The Clown.* First
Edition: Greenwich, CT: Fawcett, 1962.
Points of Issue: Paperback original
Fawcett Gold Medal #s1208
Nr.Fine/Fine $10
Good/V.Good $5
First U.K. and Hardcover Edition:
London: Hammond & Hammond, 1967
Nr.Fine/Fine $35
Good/V.Good $15

Proctor, Maurice. *Devils Due.* First
Edition: New York: Harper Brothers, 1960
Nr.Fine/Fine $35
Good/V.Good $20

Propper, Milton M. *The Strange*

Disappearance of Mary Young. First
Edition: New York: Harper & Brothers,
1929
Nr.Fine/Fine $300
Good/V.Good $145

Punshon, E.R. *Night's Cloak.* First
Edition: New York: Macmillan, 1944
Nr.Fine/Fine $55
Good/V.Good $20

Puzo, Mario. *The Godfather.* First
Edition: New York: G.P. Putnams, 1969
Nr.Fine/Fine $1200
Good/V.Good $400

Queen, Ellery. *The Roman Hat Mystery.*
First Edition: New York: Fredrick Stokes,
1929
Nr.Fine/Fine $1950
Good/V.Good $850

There Was Wn
Old Woman
by Ellery Queen

_____. *There Was An Old Woman.*
First Edition: Boston: Little Brown, 1943
Nr.Fine/Fine $100
Good/V.Good $45

Quentin, Patrick. *My Son, the Murderer.*
First Edition: New York: Simon &
Schuster, 1954
Nr.Fine/Fine $45
Good/V.Good $15

Rawson, Clayton. *The Footprints on the
Ceiling.* First Edition: New York: Putnam,

1939
Nr.Fine/Fine **$800**
Good/V.Good **$350**

Pandora
by Arthur B. Reeve

Reeve, Arthur B. *Pandora.* First Edition: New York: Harper, 1926
Nr.Fine/Fine **$350**
Good/V.Good **$200**

Reichs, Kathy. *Deja Dead.* First Edition: New York: Scribners, 1997
Nr.Fine/Fine **$25**
Good/V.Good **$10**

Reilly, Helen. *Death Demands an Audience.* First Edition: Garden City, NY: Doubleday Doran/Crime Club, 1940
Nr.Fine/Fine **$125**
Good/V.Good **$45**

Rendell, Ruth. *The Secret House Of Death.* First Edition: London: John Long, 1968
Nr.Fine/Fine **$750**
Good/V.Good **$250**
First Edition: New York: Doubleday / Crime Club, 1968.
Nr.Fine/Fine **$140**
Good/V.Good **$80**

Rhode, John. *Hendon's First Case.* First Edition: New York: Dodd, Mead, 1935

Nr.Fine/Fine **$650**
Good/V.Good **$275**

Rice, Craig & Ed McBain. *The April*

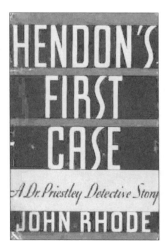

Hendon's First Case
by John Rhode

Robin Murders. First Edition: New York: Random House, 1958
Nr.Fine/Fine **$300**
Good/V.Good **$100**

Rinehart, Mary Roberts. *Tish.* First Edition: Boston: Houghton Mifflin, 1916
Nr.Fine/Fine **$250**
Good/V.Good **$90**

Roeburt, John. *The Hollow Man.* First Edition: New York: Simon & Schuster, 1954
Nr.Fine/Fine **$20**
Good/V.Good **$8**

Rohmer, Sax. *Bimbashi Baruk of Egypt.* First Edition: New York: Robert M. McBride Co., 1944
Nr.Fine/Fine **$250**
Good/V.Good **$110**

_____. *The Island Of Fu Manchu.* First Edition: London: Cassell, 1941
Nr.Fine/Fine **$1450**
Good/V.Good **$775**
First US Edition: Garden City, NY: Doubleday Doran/Crime Club, 1941
Nr.Fine/Fine **$850**
Good/V.Good **$400**

Roos, Kelley. *Grave Danger.* First Edition: New York: Dodd, Mead, 1965
Nr.Fine/Fine **$35**
Good/V.Good **$15**

Ross, Barnaby. *The Tragedy of X.* First
Edition: New York: Viking, 1932
Nr.Fine/Fine **$150**
Good/V.Good **$60**

Sanders, Lawrence. *The Anderson Tapes.*
First Edition: New York: G. P. Putnam's,
1970
Nr.Fine/Fine **$100**
Good/V.Good **$50**

Sandford, John. *Rules of Prey.* First
Edition: New York: G.P. Putnams, 1989
Nr.Fine/Fine **$65**
Good/V.Good **$30**

Tiny Carteret
by Sapper

Sapper. *Tiny Carteret.* First Edition:
London: Hodder & Stoughton, no date
[1930]
Nr.Fine/Fine **$225**
Good/V.Good **$100**

Sayers, Dorothy L. *Busman's
Honeymoon.* First Edition: New York:
Harcourt, Brace, 1937
Nr.Fine/Fine **$950**
Good/V.Good **$400**
First U.K. Edition: London: Victor
Gollancz Ltd., 1937
Nr.Fine/Fine **$1200**
Good/V.Good **$350**

Scherf, Margaret. *The Elk and the
Evidence.* First Edition: Garden City, NY:
Doubleday/Crime Club, 1952

Nr.Fine/Fine **$125**
Good/V.Good **$60**

Scoppettone, Sandra. *Playing Murder.*
First Edition: New York: Harper & Row,
1985
Nr.Fine/Fine **$35**
Good/V.Good **$20**

Shannon, Dell. *Coffin Corner: A Luis
Mendoza Mystery.* First Edition: New
York: William Morrow & Co., 1966.
Nr.Fine/Fine **$35**
Good/V.Good **$15**

The Shadow
Falls
*by Georges
Simenon*

Simenon, Georges. *Shadow Falls.* First
Edition in English: London: George
Routledge and Sons Ltd., 1945
Nr.Fine/Fine **$200**
Good/V.Good **$35**
First U.S. Edition: New York, Harcourt
Brace, 1945.
Nr.Fine/Fine **$300**
Good/V.Good **$50**

Smith, Martin Cruz. *Gorky Park.* First
Edition: New York: Random House, 1981

Nr.Fine/Fine **$50**
Good/V.Good **$20**
First U.K. Edition: London: Collins, 1981
Nr.Fine/Fine **$45**
Good/V.Good **$20**

Spillane, Mickey. *The Erection Set.* First
Edition: New York: E. P. Dutton, 1972

Nr.Fine/Fine **$100**
Good/V.Good **$55**

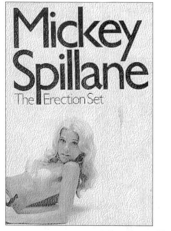

The Erection
Set
*by Mickey
Spillane*

_____. *The Last Cop Out.* First
Edition: New York: E.P. Dutton, 1973
Nr.Fine/Fine. **$75**
Good/V.Good **$25**

Death of a Dude
by Rex Stout

Stout, Rex. *Death of a Dude.* First
Edition: New York: Viking, 1969
Nr.Fine/Fine. **$50**
Good/V.Good **$30**

_____. *The Doorbell Rang.* First
Edition: New York: Viking, 1969
Nr.Fine/Fine **$75**
Good/V.Good **$35**

_____. *Fer-De-Lance* First Edition:
New York: Farrar & Rinehart, 1934.

Nr.Fine/Fine **$14000**
Good/V.Good **$6000**
First Edition: London: Cassell, 1935
Nr.Fine/Fine **$10,000**
Good/V.Good **$4000**

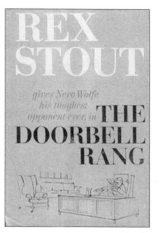

The Doorbell
Rang
by Rex Stout

Symonds, Julian. *The Killing of Francie
Lake.* First Edition: London: Collins,
1962
Nr.Fine/Fine **$15**
Good/V.Good **$7**

The Perennial
Boarder
*by Phoebe Atwood
Taylor*

Taylor, Phoebe Atwood. *The Perennial
Boarder.* First Edition: New York: W.W.
Norton & Co., 1941
Nr.Fine/Fine **$135**
Good/V.Good **$55**

Tey, Josephine. *Miss Pym Disposes.* First

Edition: New York: The Macmillan Co., 1947

Nr.Fine/Fine **$125**
Good/V.Good **$45**

Thayer, Lee. *Guilt Edged.* First Edition. New York: Dodd Mead, 1951

Nr.Fine/Fine **$45**
Good/V.Good **$25**

Thorp, Roderick. *Nothing Lasts Forever.* First Edition: New York: W.W. Norton, 1979

Nr.Fine/Fine **$65**
Good/V.Good **$35**

Tilton, Alice. *Dead Ernest.* First Edition: New York: W. W. Norton, 1944

Nr.Fine/Fine. **$100**
Good/V.Good **$35**

No Matter Where
by Arthur Train

Train, Arthur. *No Matter Where.* First Edition: New York: Scribners, 1933
Nr.Fine/Fine. **$70**
Good/V.Good **$40**

_____. *Page Mr. Tutt.* First Edition: New York: Charles Scribners, 1926
Nr.Fine/Fine. **$200**
Good/V.Good. **$85**

Traver, Robert. *Anatomy of a Murder.* First Edition: New York: St. Martins, 1958

Nr.Fine/Fine **$300**
Good/V.Good **$125**
First U.K. Edition: London: Faber & Faber, 1958
Nr.Fine/Fine **$75**
Good/V.Good **$30**

Tucker, Wilson. *Red Herring.* First Edition: New York: Rinehart, 1951
Nr.Fine/Fine **$35**
Good/V.Good **$20**
First Edition: London: Cassell & Co., 1953.
Nr.Fine/Fine **$30**
Good/V.Good **$15**

Uhnak, Dorothy. *The Investigation.* First Edition: New York: Simon and Schuster, 1977
Nr.Fine/Fine **$30**
Good/V.Good **$12**

Death of a
Swagman
by Arthur W. Upfield

Upfield, Arthur. *Death of a Swagman.* First Edition: Garden City, NY: Doubleday/Crime Club, 1945
Nr.Fine/Fine **$225**
Good/V.Good **$100**
First U.K. Edition: London: Francis Aldor, 1946
Nr.Fine/Fine **$100**
Good/V.Good **$45**
First Australian Edition: Sydney: Angus & Robertson, 1947
Nr.Fine/Fine. **$350**
Good/V.Good **$165**

**Encore The
Lone Wolf**
*by Louis Joseph
Vance*

Vance, Louis Joseph. *Encore the Lone Wolf.* First Edition: Philadelphia: J. B. Lippincott, 1933
Nr.Fine/Fine **$125**
Good/V.Good **$75**

Vandercook, John W. *Murder in Haiti.*
First Edition: New York: Macmillan, 1956
Nr.Fine/Fine **$35**
Good/V.Good **$18**

First Edition: London: Eyre & Spottiswoode, 1956
Nr.Fine/Fine **$25**
Good/V.Good **$10**

Van Dine, S.S. *The Dragon Murder Case.*
First Edition: New York: Scribners, 1933
Nr.Fine/Fine **$500**
Good/V.Good **$265**

_____. *The Gracie Allen Murder Case.* First Edition: New York: Charles Scribners, 1938.
Nr.Fine/Fine **$450**
Good/V.Good **$150**

Van Gulik, Robert. *The Chinese Maze Murders.* First Edition in English: The Hague and Bandung: W. Van Hoeve Ltd., 1956.
Nr.Fine/Fine **$1000**
Good/V.Good **$450**
First U.K. Edition: London: Michael Joseph, 1962
Nr.Fine/Fine **$225**

Good/V.Good **$85**

_____. *The Emperor's Pearl.* First Edition in English: London: Heinemann, 1963
Nr.Fine/Fine **$250**
Good/V.Good **$135**
First U.S. Edition: New York: Charles Scribner's Sons, 1963
Nr.Fine/Fine **$65**
Good/V.Good **$25**

Vickers, Roy. *The Department of Dead Ends* First Edition: London: Faber & Faber, 1949
Nr.Fine/Fine **$450**
Good/V.Good **$165**

Wade, Henry. *The Litmore Snatch.* First Edition: New York: Macmillan, 1957
Nr.Fine/Fine **$35**
Good/V.Good **$10**

Jack O' Judgment
by Edgar Wallace

Wallace, Edgar. *Jack O'Judgment.* First Edition: London: Ward, Lock, and Co., 1920
Nr.Fine/Fine **$550**
Good/V.Good **$250**

_____. *Murder Book of J. G. Reeder.* First Edition: Garden City, NY: Doubleday, Doran/Crime Club, 1929.
Nr.Fine/Fine **$365**
Good/V.Good **$155**

Walling, R.A.J. *Stroke of One.* First

The Murder Book of J.G. Reeder
by Edgar Wallace

Edition: New York: William Morrow, 1931
Nr.Fine/Fine **$175**
Good/V.Good **$100**
First U.K. Edition: London: Methuen & Co., 1931
Nr.Fine/Fine **$65**
Good/V.Good **$25**

Wambaugh, Joseph. *The Blue Knight.* First Edition: Boston: Atlantic/Little, Brown, 1972
Nr.Fine/Fine **$75**
Good/V.Good **$40**

The Girl Who Cried Wolf
by Hillary Waugh

Waugh, Hillary. *The Girl Who Cried Wolf.* First Edition: Garden City, NY: Doubleday/Crime Club, 1958

Nr.Fine/Fine **$65**
Good/V.Good **$35**

One For My Dame
by Jack Webb

Webb, Jack. *One For My Dame.* First Edition: New York: Holt, Rinehart, and Winston, 1961
Nr.Fine/Fine **$65**
Good/V.Good **$25**

Sleeping Dogs
by Carolyn Wells

Wells, Carolyn. *Sleeping Dogs.* First Edition: Garden City, N.Y.: Doubleday, Doran/Crime Club, 1929
Nr.Fine/Fine **$250**
Good/V.Good **$100**

Wentworth, Patricia. *Eternity Ring.* First Edition: Philadelphia & New York: Lippincott, 1948
Nr.Fine/Fine **$125**
Good/V.Good **$55**

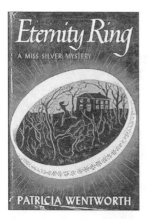

Eternity Ring
by Patricia Wentworth

Wilde, Percival. *P. Moran, Operative.*
First Edition: New York: Random House,
1947
Nr.Fine/Fine **$95**
Good/V.Good **$35**

The Curiosity of
Mr. Treadgold
by Valentine Williams

Williams, Valentine. *The Curiosity of Mr.
Treadgold.* First Edition: Boston:
Houghton Mifflin, 1937.
Nr.Fine/Fine **$85**
Good/V.Good **$35**

Woods, Sara. *Serpent's Tooth.* First
Edition: London: Collins/Crime Club,
1971
Nr.Fine/Fine **$60**
Good/V.Good **$30**
First U.S. Edition: New York: Holt
Rinehart Winston, 1971
Nr.Fine/Fine **$40**
Good/V.Good **$15**

Yaffe, James. *Mom Among The Liars.*
First Edition: New York: St. Martins
Press, 1992
Nr.Fine/Fine **$20**
Good/V.Good **$8**

Occult & Paranormal

A few years ago, on a bet, a mathematician analyzed the predictions of the psychics in a supermarket tabloid and statistically compared them to the weather reports on a major New York City television station. It was a direct confrontation of the scientific with the occult. The meteorologist, a scientist backed by years of study, using computers, radar, and all the other accoutrements of the modern age, versus the psychic who, somehow, sees, feels, or dreams what the future will be. Who came out on top? Who predicted the future with more accuracy? Actually it wasn't even close. The psychics outdid the scientists almost two to one. How? The entire fascination with the literature of the hidden and the unexplained is really a search for that answer.

The field is a broad one and a confusing one. Bookstores label it in different ways, and divide it into different categories. Astrology, numerology, divination, prophesy, magic, magick, occult, unexplained, witchcraft, UFO, metaphysics, secret societies, psychic, herbology, and New Age are all labels one can find on used bookstore shelves. A writer like Immanuel Velikovsky could end up in the Science section, while another, like Manly Palmer Hall, could be in Philosophy. That is a lot of the fun and the challenge in collecting it: it's hidden, like the name says—"Occult." Some categories are obvious. Astrology, for example, is always going to fit in and get grouped together. Other categories are not so out front, however. Herbs, naturopathic, homeopathic medicine and related areas can end up with Dr. Atkin's diet books in "Health and Nutrition."

Trying to classify it, there are only extremely broad, overlapping categories. There is a group of books one might call "magic" or, in some cases, "magick" to distinguish it from the illusions of the stage magician. Even at that, the category offers several subdivisions, such as theory; actual spell books, called grimoires; and biographies of magicians such as John Symonds' biography of Aleister Crowley, *The Great Beast*. And then, where does one stick Witchcraft, which runs the gamut between grimoires and religious documents based in nature worship? Shamanism might also overlap into this category; the knowledge of a Yaqui medicine man, in the work of Carlos Casteneda, or a Hawaiian Kahuna in Max Freedom Long's books. Various recastings of Eastern religion fit in partially through the work of the Theosophical Society and other smaller groups, as well as Western mysticism through the Freemasons and numerous other societies.

Divination could be another category. Basically, it's foretelling the future. It can be written in the stars, in astrology, or derived from numbers, in numerology. It can be the product of a psychic contact with the spirit world or the universe in general. It can be prophecy, handed from God to the prophet.

A relatively new field is UFOlogy, the studies, speculations and evidence that the Earth is being observed and/or visited by beings from another planet somewhere in the galaxy. This runs the gamut from scientific speculation to eyewitness accounts of abductions by a starship. A large area of it is given over to speculation on what the government does or does not hide about the subject.

Unexplained phenomena are also a modern development. Pioneered by Charles Fort in such works as *Book of the Damned, New Lands,* and *Lo!* it is a field that runs from a rainfall of frogs to the existence of dragons, abominable snowmen, and sea serpents. These are things that cannot happen, but apparently do. These are creatures we seem, somehow, not to have made acquaintance with yet on our little ball of clay and granite, or people who disappear without a trace, and those that show up from no place.

The study of cults plays a role in collecting in this area. Some cults pass through it into collections of Religion and Philosophy while others wither and remain part of an occult collection. A century ago, the books of Mary Baker Eddy and Joseph Smith were part of occult collections. Today, L. Ron Hubbard and the Wicca books of Gavin and Yvonne Frost are. A book like *Pistis Sophia, a Gnostic Gospel*, and G. R. S. Mead's *Fragments of a Faith Forgotten*, straddle the line, ending up in both the occult and religious areas.

Collecting occult books is a very old pursuit. Most of the classic works in the field are incunabula, with a scattering of other works through the eighteenth century. The work of Egyptologist A. E. Wallis Budge shows that collecting magical papyri was a pursuit of the Egyptian upper classes. Occult books of the nineteenth and twentieth century are, consequently, a good deal less expensive than books of more recent genres. Further, collections of classic occult works often consist, for the most part, of reprints and translations. There is very little reason for something like the Papyrus of Ani, also known as The Book of the Dead, to exist outside of a museum, as few people can read ancient Egyptian and 3000-year-old papyrus tends to be a bit fragile.

Many occultists have tried to explain or popularize their views in the form of novels. Viewed strictly as novels, they are rarely literary masterpieces, as they are meant to convey a philosophy rather than tell a story. In short, they are essays in novel form, or fables. Some of the better known are Edward Bulwer-Lytton's *Zanoni,* Aleister Crowley's *Moonchild,* and A. E. Waite's *The Quest of the Golden Stair.* In the sense that they are not strictly novels, many collectors find them an interesting addition to an occult collection.

Another factor to remember is that it is a small field, in many cases a playground for intellectuals. Therefore a lot of pivotal works have never been translated from Latin, Greek, or their native language. For example, less than half of the books in this area by Franz Hartmann, a medical doctor and leading German Theosophist and Rosicrucian, exist only in German. It is assumed, I guess, that collectors in this field are multi-lingual.

Books in this area are rarely on any best seller list, and those that do make it, such as Jay Anson's *Amityville Horror* or Van Daniken's *Chariots of the Gods*, tend to be a bit on the sensational and controversial side. Many books, however, tend to remain in print much longer than in other genres. Nineteenth and early twentieth century occult writers such as Aleister Crowley, Manly P. Hall, Dion Fortune, A. E. Waite, and Helena Blavatsky are all in print while their contemporaries in other genres are only available in the out of print market. All of this tends to compress the market a bit. While the more expensive end of the spectrum is considerably lower in price than other genres, the bottom tends toward higher prices. New books and more recent used books are a little more expensive than the normal run of trade publications. Perhaps it's because authors like H. P. Blavatsky and Aleister Crowley aren't really welcome at the book of the month club.

Like Illustration and the Philosophy/Religion genres, many, if not most, Occult books are collected as "First Thus" rather than true firsts. With a genre that is as old as this one, the true first may well be a stone tablet, which makes it a bit difficult to put it on a wooden bookcase, or display on a glass-topped table.

Ancient knowledge and modern speculation, things that really do go bump in the night and everything we can't explain. A collection of "curious and long forgotten lore" as Poe once termed it. It can be rewarding, very interesting and, who knows, it may allow you to turn that annoying neighbor into a frog.

10 Classic Rarities

Blavatsky, Helena Petrovna. *Isis Unveiled.* New York: Theosophical Society, 1877. One thousand copies of the first printing sold in a week. Three printings in 1877 are indistinguishable.
Retail Value in:
Near Fine to Fine. **$12,000**
Good to Very Good **$10,000**

Budge, E.A. Wallis. *The Book of the Dead: Facsimiles of the Papyri of Hunefer, Anhai, Karasher and Netchemet with Supplementary text from the papyrus of Nu, with transcripts, translations, etc.* London: British Museum, 1899. Find it and know what to do after your funeral.
Retail Value in:
Near Fine to Fine **$1350**
Good to Very Good **$900**

Crowley, Aleister. *777 Vel Prolegomena Symbolica Ad Systemam Sceptico-Mysticae Viae Explicandae, Fundamentum Hieroglyphicum Sanctissimorum Scientiae Summae (Liber DCCLXXVII).* London & Felling-on-Tyne: 1909. You won't need magick to profit from this one.
Retail Value in:
Near Fine to Fine **$3500**
Good to Very Good **$2500**

Frazer, Sir James George. *The Golden Bough. A Study in Magic & Religion.* London: 1911. Thirteen volumes bound in leather.
Retail Value in:
Near Fine to Fine **$2500**
Good to Very Good **$1500**

Hall, Manly P. *An Encyclopedic Outline of Masonic Hermetic Qabbalistic and Rosicrucian Symbolical Philosophy.* San Francisco: H. S. Crocker, 1928. The Fifth printing, a limited edition of 800 bound in vellum with a slipcase.:
Retail Value in:
Near Fine to Fine **$1100**

Good to Very Good **$800**

Kawaguchi, Ekai. *Three Years in Tibet—With the original Japanese illustrations.* Adyar, India: The Theosophical Office, 1909. One of the prettier publications of the Theosophical Press.
Retail Value in:
Near Fine to Fine **$1200**
Good to Very Good **$800**

Ouspensky, P.D. *The Symbolism of the Tarot (Philosophy of occultism in pictures and numbers. Pen-pictures of the twenty two tarot).* St. Petersburg (Russia): The Trood Printing and Publishing Co., 1913. Most of the English translation was shipped to the U.S.:
Retail Value in:
Near Fine to Fine **$1100**
Good to Very Good **$550**

Saint-Germain, Comte De. *La Tres Sainte Trinosophie: a parallel French and English text.* Los Angeles: The Phoenix Press, 1933.:
Retail Value in:
Near Fine to Fine **$2000**
Good to Very Good **$900**

Scott, Walter. *Letters on Demonology and Witchcraft, Addressed to J.G. Lockhart, Esq.* London: John Murray, 1830. The first edition is illustrated by George Cruikshank.
Retail Value in
Near Fine to Fine **$1500**
Good to Very Good **$1000**

Waite, A. E. *Saint-Martin the French Mystic and the Story of Modern Martinism.* London: William Rider and Son Ltd., 1922. A revised but definitve edition of the original 1901 publication.
Retail Value in:
Near Fine to Fine **$1000**
Good to Very Good **$450**

Price Guide

Achad, Frater. *Q.B.L. or, The Bride's Reception.* First Edition: Chicago, IL: Privately Printed for the Author Collegium Ad Spiritum Sanctum, 1922.
Nr.Fine/Fine **$350**
Good/V.Good **$100**

_____. *Thirty One Hymns to the Star Goddess.* First Edition: Chicago: Will Ransom, 1923.
Nr.Fine/Fine **$375**
Good/V.Good **$225**

Agrippa, Henry Cornelius. *Occult Philosophy or Magic Book One Natural Magic.* First Edition Thus: Chicago: Hahn & Whitehead, 1897.
Nr.Fine/Fine **$175**
Good/V.Good **$130**

_____. *On the Superiority of Woman over Man.* First Edition in English: New York: American News Company, 1873.
Nr.Fine/Fine **$200**
Good/V.Good **$85**

_____. *The Philosophy Of Natural Magic.* First Edition Thus: Chicago: de Laurence Scott, 1913
Nr.Fine/Fine **$60**
Good/V.Good **$35**

Albertus, Frater. *The Seven Rays of the Q.B.L.* First Edition: Salt Lake City, UT: Paracelsus Research Society, 1968
Nr.Fine/Fine **$150**
Good/V.Good **$65**

_____ *Gently I Answered And Said...* First Edition: Salt Lake City, UT: Paracelsus Research Society, 1978
Nr.Fine/Fine **$60**
Good/V.Good **$35**

Alder, Vera Stanley. *When Humanity Comes of Age.* First Edition: London:

Andrew Dakans, 1950
Nr.Fine/Fine **$35**
Good/V.Good **$20**

Andrews, George C. *Extra-Terrestrials Among Us.* First Edition: St. Paul, MN: Llewellyn Publications, 1986
Nr.Fine/Fine **$15**
Good/V.Good **$6**

Anson, Jay. *The Amityville Horror.* First Edition: Englewood Cliffs, N.J.: Prentice Hall, 1977
Nr.Fine/Fine **$25**
Good/V.Good **$10**

Arundale, George S. *Nirvana.* First Edition: Adyar: Theosophical Publishing House, 1926
Nr.Fine/Fine **$40**
Good/V.Good **$12**

Ashpole, Edward. *The Search for Extra-Terrestrial Intelligence.* First Edition: London: Blandford Press, 1989
Nr.Fine/Fine **$15**
Good/V.Good **$8**

Bailey, Alice A. *Letters on Occult Meditation.* First Edition: New York: Lucis Publishing Co, 1922
Nr.Fine/Fine **$40**
Good/V.Good **$15**

_____. *From Bethlehem to Calvery—The Initiations of Jesus.* First Edition: New York: Lucis Publishing

Nirvana
by George S. Arundale

Company, 1937
Nr.Fine/Fine **$35**
Good/V.Good **$15**

_____. *Education in the New Age.* First Edition: New York: Lucis Publishing Company, 1954
Nr.Fine/Fine **$20**
Good/V.Good **$12**

Baker, Alan. *The Encyclopaedia of Alien Encounters.* First Edition: London: Virgin, 1999
Nr.Fine/Fine **$12**
Good/V.Good **$6**

Barrett, Francis. *The Magus. A Complete System of Occult Philosophy.* Facsimile of 1801 Edition First Thus: New York: University Books, 1967
Nr.Fine/Fine **$125**
Good/V.Good **$55**

Baskin, Wade. *The Sorceror's Handbook.* First Edition: New York: Philosophical Library, 1974.
Nr.Fine/Fine. **$45**
Good/V.Good **$20**

_____. *A Dictionary of Satanism.* First Edition: New York: Philosophical Library, 1972
Nr.Fine/Fine **$30**
Good/V.Good **$15**

Bayless, Raymond. *Experiences Of A Psychical Researcher.* First Edition: New Hyde Park, NY: University Books, 1972
Nr.Fine/Fine **$30**
Good/V.Good **$12**

_____. *The Enigma of the Poltergeist.* First Edition: West Nyack, NY: Parker, 1967
Nr.Fine/Fine **$20**
Good/V.Good **$8**

Bergier, Jacques & Pauwels, Louis. *The Dawn of Magic.* First Edition in English: London: Anthony Goggs & Phillips, 1963.
Nr.Fine/Fine **$200**

Good/V.Good **$115**
First U.S. Edition as *Morning of the Magicians:* New York: Stein & Day, 1964.
Nr.Fine/Fine **$45**
Good/V.Good **$20**

_____.
Impossible Possibilities. First U.S. Edition: New York: Stein & Day, 1971.
Nr.Fine/Fine **$25**
Good/V.Good **$10**

Bergier, Jacques & the Editors of INFO. *Extraterrestrial Intervention.* First Edition Thus: Chicago: Henry Regnery, 1974
Nr.Fine/Fine. **$30**
Good/V.Good **$12**

Bergier, Jacques. *Secret Doors Of The Earth.* First U.S. Edition: Chicago: Henry Regnery, 1975
Nr.Fine/Fine **$40**
Good/V.Good $25

Berlitz, Charles & William L. Moore. *The Roswell Incident.* First Edition: New York Grosset & Dunlap, 1980
Nr.Fine/Fine **$35**
Good/V.Good **$12**

Berlitz, Charles. *The Mystery of Atlantis.* First Edition: New York: Grosset & Dunlap, 1971
Nr.Fine/Fine **$25**

Extraterrestrial Intervention
by Jacques Bergier & The Editors of INFO

Good/V.Good **$10**

_____. *The Bermuda Triangle.*
First Edition: Garden City, NY:
Doubleday, 1974
Nr.Fine/Fine **$20**
Good/V.Good **$8**

Bernstein, Morey. *The Search for Bridey
Murphy.* First Edition: Garden City, NY:
Doubleday, 1956
Nr.Fine/Fine **$50**
Good/V.Good **$20**

Besant, Annie. *The Building of the
Kosmos and Other Lectures.* First Edition:
London: Theosophical Publishing Society,
1894
Nr.Fine/Fine **$275**
Good/V.Good **$125**

_____. *The Ideals of Theosophy.*
First Edition: Madras, India: The
Theosophist Office, 1912.
Nr.Fine/Fine **$250**
Good/V.Good **$135**

_____. *Evolution and Occultism.*
First Edition: London: The Theosophical
Publishing Society, 1913
Nr.Fine/Fine **$200**
Good/V.Good **$85**

Besant, Annie & C. W. Leadbeater.
Occult Chemistry. First Edition: London:
Theosophical Publishing Society, 1908.
Nr.Fine/Fine **$350**
Good/V.Good **$200**

_____. *The
Lives of Alcyone.* (Two Volumes) First
Edition: Adyar, Madras: Theosophical
Publishing House, 1924.
Nr.Fine/Fine **$250**
Good/V.Good **$140**

Blavatsky, Helena Petrovna. *The Secret
Doctrine.* (Six Volumes) First Edition
Thus, Fourth Edition: Adyar:
Theosophical Publishing House, 1938
Nr.Fine/Fine **$125**
Good/V.Good **$80**

_____. *Nightmare Tales.*
First Edition: London: Theosophical
Publishing Society, 1892.
Nr.Fine/Fine **$500**
Good/V.Good **$200**

_____. *The Theosophical
Glossary.*
First Edition: London: Theosophical
Publishing Co., 1892
Nr.Fine/Fine **$325**
Good/V.Good **$200**

_____. *The Voice of the
Silence and Other Chosen Fragments.*
First Edition: New York: Elliott B. Page &
Co., 1899
Nr.Fine/Fine **$85**
Good/V.Good **$35**

_____. *A Modern
Panarion: A Collection Of Fugitive
Fragments.* First Edition: London: The
Theosophical Publishing Society, 1895
Nr.Fine/Fine **$70**
Good/V.Good **$30**

Blum, Howard. *Out There The
Government's Secret Quest for
Extraterrestrials.* First Edition: New York:
Simon and Schuster, 1990
Nr.Fine/Fine **$15**
Good/V.Good **$8**

Blum, Ralph H. *The Serenity
Runes—Five Keys to the Serenity Prayer.*
First Edition: New York: St. Martin Press,
1998
Nr.Fine/Fine **$15**
Good/V.Good **$6**

Boehme, Jacob. *Mysterium Magnum or
an Exposition of the First Book of Moses.*
First Edition Thus: London: John M.
Watkins, 1924
Nr.Fine/Fine **$750**
Good/V.Good **$425**

_____. *Concerning The Three
Principles of The Divine Essence.*
First Edition Thus: London: John M.
Watkins, 1910.

Nr.Fine/Fine **$325**
Good/V.Good **$135**

_____. *The Confessions of Jacob Boehme.*
First Edition: New York: Alfred A. Knopf, 1920
Nr.Fine/Fine **$225**
Good/V.Good **$110**

Bonewitz, Ra. *The Crystal Heart a Practical Guide to Healing the Heart Centre with Crystals.* First Edition: London: Aquarian Press, 1989
Nr.Fine/Fine **$20**
Good/V.Good **$9**

Occult Reich
by J.H. Brennan

Brennan, J.H. *Occult Reich* Points of Issue: Paperback Original First Edition: London: Futura Books, 1974
Nr.Fine/Fine **$25**

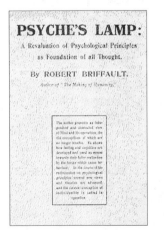

Psyche's Lamp:
A Revaluation of Psychological Principles as Foundation of All Thought
by Robert Briffault

Good/V.Good **$10**

Briffault, Robert. *Psyche's Lamp: a Revaluation of Psychological Principles as Foundation of All Thought* First Edition: London: Allen & Unwin, 1921.
Nr.Fine/Fine **$35**
Good/V.Good **$15**

Buckland, Raymond. *The Magick Of Chant-O-Matics* First Edition: Englewood Cliffs, NJ: Prentice Hall, 1977.
Nr.Fine/Fine **$45**
Good/V.Good **$15**

_____. *Buckland's Complete Book of Witchcraft* Points of Issue: Paperback Original First Edition: St. Paul MN: Llewellyn, 1995
Nr.Fine/Fine **$20**
Good/V.Good **$10**

Budge, E. A. Wallis. *The Gods of the Egyptians.* First Edition: London, Methuen & Co., 1904
Nr.Fine/Fine **$1500**
Good/V.Good **$900**

_____. *Egyptian Magic.* First Edition: London: Kegan Paul, Trench, Trübner/ New York: Henry Frowde, Oxford University Press, 1899
Nr.Fine/Fine **$125**
Good/V.Good **$70**

Bulwer-Lytton, Edward. *Zanoni.* (Two Volumes) First Edition Thus: Philadelphia: J. B. Lippincott Company, 1867.
Nr.Fine/Fine **$85**
Good/V.Good **$45**

Caddy, Eileen. *Spirit of Findhorn.* First Edition: New York: Harper & Row, 1976
Nr.Fine/Fine **$25**
Good/V.Good **$10**

Carrington, Hereward. *Modern Psychial Phenomena. Recent Researches and Speculations.* First Edition: New York: Dodd Mead, 1919

Nr.Fine/Fine **$90**
Good/V.Good **$35**

_____. *The Problems of
Psychical Research* First Edition: London:
William Rider, 1914.
Nr.Fine/Fine **$50**
Good/V.Good **$20**

Castaneda, Carlos. *Journey to Ixtlan: the
Lessons of Don Juan.* First Edition: New
York: Simon & Schuster, 1972.
Nr.Fine/Fine **$75**
Good/V.Good **$35**

The Teachings of
Don Jaun: A
Yaqui Way of
Knowledge
by Carlos Castaneda

_____. *The Teachings of Don
Juan. A Yaqui Way of Knowledge.* First
Edition: Berkeley: University of
California Press, 1968
Nr.Fine/Fine **$825**
Good/V.Good **$375**

Cayce, Edgar Evans. *Edgar Cayce on
Atlantis.* First Edition: New York:
Hawthorn Books, 1968
Nr.Fine/Fine **$25**
Good/V.Good **$12**

**Cayce, Edgar Evans and Hugh Lynn
Cayce.** *The Outer Limits of Edgar
Cayce's Power* First Edition: New York:
Harper & Row, Publishers, 1971
Nr.Fine/Fine **$25**
Good/V.Good **$10**

_____. *Faces of*

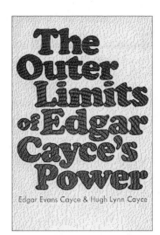

The Outer
Limits of Edgar
Cayce's Power
*by Edgar Evans
Cayce and Hugh
Lynn Cayce*

Fear. First Edition: San Francisco: Harper
& Row, 1980.
Nr.Fine/Fine **$25**
Good/V.Good **$12**

Cavendish, Richard. *The Black Arts.*
First Edition: London: Routledge &
Kegan Paul, 1967
Nr.Fine/Fine **$40**
Good/V.Good **$15**

Cerminara, Gina. *Many Mansions.* First
Edition: New York: William Sloane, 1950
Nr.Fine/Fine **$20**
Good/V.Good **$10**

Churchward, James. *Cosmic Forces: As
They Were Taught in Mu The Ancient Tale
that Religion and Science are Twin
Sisters.* First Edition: Mount Vernon, NY:
Published by the Author, 1934
Nr.Fine/Fine **$200**
Good/V.Good **$85**

_____. *Cosmic Forces: As
They Were Taught in Mu Relating to the
Earth.* First Edition: Mount Vernon, NY:
Published by the Author, 1935
Nr.Fine/Fine **$225**
Good/V.Good **$85**

_____. *The Lost Continent
of Mu The Motherland of Man.* First
Edition: New York: William Edwin
Rudge, 1926.
Nr.Fine/Fine **$300**

Good/V.Good **$135**

Clymer, R. Swinburne. *A Compendium of Occult Laws.* First Edition: Quakertown, PA: The Philosophical Publishing Company, 1938
Nr.Fine/Fine **$55**
Good/V.Good **$30**

_____. *Christisis. Higher Soul Culture.* First Edition: Allentown, PA: The Philosophical Publishing Company, 1911
Nr.Fine/Fine **$45**
Good/V.Good **$25**

Monsters, Giants
and Little Men
from Mars
by Daniel Cohen

Cohen, Daniel. *Monsters, Giants and Little Men from Mars.*First Edition: Garden City, NY: Doubleday, 1975
Nr.Fine/Fine **$35**
Good/V.Good **$15**

Conway, David. *Secret Wisdom: The Occult Universe Explored.* First Edition: London: Jonathan Cape, 1985.
Nr.Fine/Fine **$65**
Good/V.Good **$25**

Crowley, Aleister. *Magick.*First Edition thus: New York: Samuel Weiser, 1974
Nr.Fine/Fine **$65**
Good/V.Good **$30**

_____. *Magick in Theory and Practice.* First Edition: Paris: Lecram Press, 1929

Magik
by Aleister Crowley

Nr.Fine/Fine **$2200**
Good/V.Good **$1000**

Moonchild
by Aleister Crowley

_____. *Moonchild.*First Edition: London: The Mandrake Press, 1929
Nr.Fine/Fine **$1500**
Good/V.Good **$800**

_____. *The Magical Record of the Beast 666.* First Edition: London: Duckworth, 1972
Nr.Fine/Fine **$125**
Good/V.Good **$70**

_____. *The Vision and the Voice.* First Edition Thus: Dallas, TX: Sangreal, 1972.
Nr.Fine/Fine **$100**
Good/V.Good **$65**

The Magical Record of the Beast 666
by Aleister Crowley

The Vision & The Voice
by Aleister Crowley

Liber Aleph: The Book of Wisdom and Folly
by Aleister Crowley as by Master Therion

Doing Your Own Being
by Baba Ram Dass

Dass, Baba Ram. *Doing your own Being* First Edition: London: Neville Spearman , 1973.
Nr.Fine/Fine **$20**
Good/V.Good **$12**

Davies, Rodney. *Supernatural Disappearances.* First Edition: London: Robert Hale, 1995.
Nr.Fine/Fine **$20**
Good/V.Good **$12**

The Serpent & The Rainbow
by Wade Davis

Crowley, Aleister as by Master Therion.
Liber Aleph: The Book of Wisdom and Folly First Edition Thus: West Point, CA: Thelema Publishing Co., 1962.
Nr.Fine/Fine **$500**
Good/V.Good **$325**

Davis, Wade. *The Serpent & The Rainbow.* First Edition: New York: Simon & Schuster, 1985
Nr.Fine/Fine **$30**
Good/V.Good **$20**

Day, Harvey. *Occult Illustrated Dictionary.* First Edition: New York:

Oxford University Press, 1976
Nr.Fine/Fine **$20**
Good/V.Good **$10**

de Plancy, Colin. *Dictionary of Demonology.* First Edition of Wade Baskin Translation: London: Peter Owen, 1965.
Nr.Fine/Fine **$65**
Good/V.Good **$30**

Dixon, Jean. *My Life and Prophecies.* First Edition: New York: William Morrow, 1969
Nr.Fine/Fine **$20**
Good/V.Good **$8**

Doyle, Sir Arthur Conan. *The History of Spiritualism.* (Two Volumes) First Edition: London: Cassell, 1926
Nr.Fine/Fine **$1500**
Good/V.Good **$800**

_____. *The Coming of the Fairies.* First Edition: London: Hodder and Stoughton, 1922
Nr.Fine/Fine **$500**
Good/V.Good **$325**

First Edition: New York: George H. Doran Co., 1922
Nr.Fine/Fine **$800**
Good/V.Good **$550**

Ebon, Martin. *The Devil's Bride: Exorcism: Past and Present.* First Edition: New York: Harper & Row, 1974
Nr.Fine/Fine **$30**
Good/V.Good **$10**

_____. *Beyond Space and Time: An ESP Casebook.* First Edition: New York: The New American Library, 1967
Nr.Fine/Fine **$25**
Good/V.Good **$10**

Eliade, Mircea. *Myths, Dreams and Mysteries: The Encounter Between Contemporary Faiths and Archaic Realities.* First Edition in English: London: Harvill Press, 1960
Nr.Fine/Fine **$50**
Good/V.Good **$30**

First U.S. Edition: New York: Harper & Row, 1960
Nr.Fine/Fine **$45**
Good/V.Good **$20**

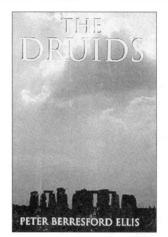

The Druids
by Peter Berresford Ellis

Ellis, Peter Berresford. *The Druids.* First Edition: Grand Rapids, MI: Eerdman, 1994
Nr.Fine/Fine **$25**
Good/V.Good **$12**

Evans, Christopher. *Cults of Unreason.* First Edition: London: Harrap, 1973.
Nr.Fine/Fine **$15**
Good/V.Good **$6**

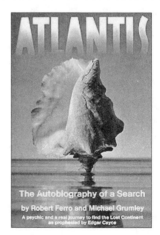

Atlantis— The Autobiography of a Search
by Robert Ferro and Michael Grumley

Ferro, Robert and Michael Grumley. *Atlantis—The Autobiography of a Search.* First Edition: Garden City, NY: Doubleday, 1970

Nr.Fine/Fine **$30**
Good/V.Good **$12**

Fort, Charles. *Book of the Damned* First Edition: New York: Boni & Liveright, 1919
Nr.Fine/Fine **$950**
Good/V.Good **$650**

_____. *New Lands.* First Edition: New York: Boni and Liveright, 1923.
Nr.Fine/Fine **$75**
Good/V.Good **$35**

_____. *Lo!* First Edition: New York: Claude Kendall, 1931
Nr.Fine/Fine **$150**
Good/V.Good **$85**

_____. *Wild Talents* First Edition: New York: Claude Kendall, 1931
Nr.Fine/Fine **$95**
Good/V.Good **$50**

Fortune, Dion *Goat—Foot God.* First Edition: London: Williams and Norgate, 1936
Nr.Fine/Fine **$750**
Good/V.Good **$425**

_____. *The Cosmic Doctrine.* First Edition: London: The Society of the Inner Light, 1949
Nr.Fine/Fine **$150**
Good/V.Good **$65**

_____. *Practical Occultism in Daily Life.* First Edition: London: Williams and Norgate, 1935
Nr.Fine/Fine **$100**
Good/V.Good **$40**

_____. *Moon Magic Being The Memoirs of a Mistress of that Art.* First Edition: London: The Aquarian Press, 1956
Nr.Fine/Fine **$90**
Good/V.Good **$40**

Fowler, Raymond. *The Andreasson Affair.* First Edition: Englewood Cliffs, NJ: Prentice-Hall, 1979
Nr.Fine/Fine **$30**

Good/V.Good **$12**

The Andreasson Affair
by Raymond Fowler

Frost, Gavin and Yvonne. *The Witch's Bible How to Practice the Oldest Religion.* First Edition: Los Angeles, CA: Nash, 1972.
Nr.Fine/Fine **$155**
Good/V.Good **$80**

_____. *Power Secrets from a Sorcerer's Private Magnum Arcanum.* First Edition: West Nyack, NJ: Parker Publishing, 1980.
Nr.Fine/Fine **$50**
Good/V.Good **$30**

Fox, Oliver. *Astral Projection. A Record of Out of the Body Experiences.* First Edition: New Hyde Park, NY: University Books, 1962
Nr.Fine/Fine **$25**
Good/V.Good **$10**

Friedman, Stanton T. *Top Secret/Majic.* First Edition: New York: Marlowe, 1996
Nr.Fine/Fine **$25**
Good/V.Good **$8**

Gardner, G. B. as by Scire. *High Magic's Aid.* First US Edition: Boston: Houghton Mifflin, 1949.
Nr.Fine/Fine **$275**
Good/V.Good **$150**

Gardner, G. B. *The Meaning of Witchcraft.* First Edition Thus: London &

New York: Aquarian Press/Samuel Weiser, 1971
Nr.Fine/Fine **$75**
Good/V.Good **$40**

George, Llewellyn. *A to Z Horoscope Maker and Delineator.* First Edition: Los Angeles: Llewellyn, 1928
Nr.Fine/Fine **$145**
Good/V.Good **$75**

_____. *Planetary Hour Book.* First Edition: Los Angeles, CA: Astrological Bulletina, 1929
Nr.Fine/Fine **$200**
Good/V.Good **$125**

Gibson, Walter B. and Litzka R. *The Complete Illustrated Book of the Psychic Sciences* First Edition: Garden City, NY: Doubleday, 1966.
Nr.Fine/Fine **$20**
Good/V.Good **$8**

_____. *Complete Illustrated Book of Divination and Prophecy.* First Edition: Garden City, NY: Doubleday, 1973.
Nr.Fine/Fine **$15**
Good/V.Good **$6**

Goodman, Linda. *Linda Goodman's Sun Signs.* First Edition: New York: Taplinger, 1968
Nr.Fine/Fine **$55**
Good/V.Good **$25**

_____. *Star Signs: Secret Codes Of The Universe.* First Edition: New York: St. Martin's Press, 1987
*Nr.*Fine/Fine **$30**
Good/V.Good **$12**

Grant, Kenneth. *Outside The Circles Of Time.* First Edition: London: Frederick Muller, 1980
Nr.Fine/Fine **$500**
Good/V.Good **$200**

_____. *The Magical Revival.* First Edition: London: Frederick Muller, 1972

Nr.Fine/Fine **$175**
Good/V.Good **$90**

First U.S. Edition: New York: Samuel Weiser, 1973
Nr.Fine/Fine **$125**
Good/V.Good **$55**

Gray, William G. *The Ladder Of Lights (or Qabalah Renovata).* First Edition: Toddington, UK: Helios Books, 1975.
Nr.Fine/Fine **$50**
Good/V.Good **$20**

_____. *The Talking Tree.* First U.S. Edition: New York Samuel Weiser, Inc., 1977.
Nr.Fine/Fine **$45**
Good/V.Good **$20**

Gurdjieff, G. *Meetings with Remarkable Men.* First Edition in English: London: Routledge & Kegan Paul, 1963.
Nr.Fine/Fine **$150**
Good/V.Good **$85**
First U.S. Edition: New York: E. P. Dutton, 1963
Nr.Fine/Fine **$75**
Good/V.Good **$35**

_____. *All and Everything. An Objective Impartial Criticism of the Life of Man, or Beelzebub's Tales to his Grandson.*
First US Edition: New York: Harcourt Brace, 1950.
Nr.Fine/Fine **$275**
Good/V.Good **$150**

_____. *Life is Real Only Then, When "I am."* First U.S. Edition: New York: E.P Dutton, 1981.
Nr.Fine/Fine **$55**
Good/V.Good **$30**

Hall, Manly P. *Shadow Forms.* First Edition: Los Angeles: Hall Publishing Co., 1925
Nr.Fine/Fine **$155**
Good/V.Good **$80**

_____. *The Lost Keys of Masonry:*

The Legend of Hiram Abiff. First Edition:
Los Angeles: Privately published by the
Author, 1923.
Nr.Fine/Fine **$125**
Good/V.Good **$75**

_____. *Lectures on Ancient
Philosophy.* First Edition: Los Angeles,
CA: The Hall Publishing Company, 1929
Nr.Fine/Fine **$95**
Good/V.Good **$55**

_____. *Codex Rosae Crucis.* First
Edition: Los Angeles: The Philosophers
Press, 1938.
Nr.Fine/Fine **$145**
Good/V.Good **$85**

_____. *Initiates of the Flame.*
First Edition: Los Angeles: The Phoenix
Press, 1922
Nr.Fine/Fine **$100**
Good/V.Good **$55**

Hartmann, Franz. *Among The Gnomes.
An Occult Tale of Adventure in the
Untersberg.* First Edition in English:
London: T. Fisher Unwin, 1895
Nr.Fine/Fine **$350**
Good/V.Good **$195**
First U.S. Edition: Boston: Occult
Publishing Company, 1896
Nr.Fine/Fine **$200**
Good/V.Good **$115**

_____. *Magic, White and Black,
or the Science of Finite and Infinite Life,
Containing Practical Hints for Students of
Occultism.*
Third Edition: London: George Redway,
1888
Nr.Fine/Fine **$175**
Good/V.Good **$55**

_____. *With the Adepts: An
Adventure Among The Rosicrucians.* First
U.S. Edition: Boston: Occult Publishing
Company, 1893
Nr.Fine/Fine **$185**
Good/V.Good **$100**

_____. *Cosmology, Or Cabala.*

*Universal Science. Alchemy. Containing
The Mysteries Of The Universe Regarding
God Nature Man. The Macrocosm and
Microcosm, Eternity and Time Explained
According To The Religion Of Christ, By
Means Of The Secret Symbols Of The
Rosicrucians Of The Sixteenth And
Seventeenth Centuries. Copied And
Translated From An Old German
Manuscript, And Provided With A
Dictionary Of Occult Terms.* First U.S.
Edition: Boston: Occult Publishing Co.,
1888
Nr.Fine/Fine **$1800**
Good/V.Good **$1100**

Hatch, D. P. *Some More Philosophy of
the Hermetics.* First US Edition: Los
Angeles: R. R. Baumgardt, 1898
Nr.Fine/Fine **$75**
Good/V.Good **$40**

_____. *Some Philosophy Of The
Hermetics.* First U.K. Edition: London:
Kegan, Paul, Trench, 1898
Nr.Fine/Fine **$120**
Good/V.Good **$45**

Heindel, Max. *Rosicrucian Cosmo-
Conception.* First Edition: Seattle, WA:
Rosicrucian Fellowship, 1909
Nr.Fine/Fine **$100**
Good/V.Good **$45**

_____. *Ancient and Modern
Initiation.* First Edition: Oceanside, CA:
Rosicrucian Fellowship, 1931.
Nr.Fine/Fine **$45**
Good/V.Good **$20**

_____. *Occult Principles of
Health and Healing.* First Edition:
Oceanside, CA: Rosicrucian Fellowship,
1938.
Nr.Fine/Fine **$35**
Good/V.Good **$15**

_____. *Teachings of an Initiate*
First Edition: Oceanside, CA: Rosicrucian
Fellowship, 1927.
Nr.Fine/Fine **$35**

Good/V.Good $20

Earth Magic
by Francis Hitching

Hitching, Francis. *Earth Magic.* First
Edition: New York: William Morrow,
1977
Nr.Fine/Fine $35
Good/V.Good $15

Holmes, Ronald. *Witchcraft in British
History* First Edition: London: Frederick
Muller, 1974.
Nr.Fine/Fine $140
Good/V.Good $80

Minds Without
Boundaries
by Stuart Holroyd

Holroyd, Stuart. *Minds without
Boundaries.* First Edition: n.p.: Danbury
Press, 1975.
Nr.Fine/Fine $15
Good/V.Good $8

Holzer, Hans. *Psychic Photography.
Threshold of a New Science?* First
Edition: New York: McGraw-Hill, 1969
Nr.Fine/Fine $85
Good/V.Good $35

_____. *The Aquarian Age Is There
Intelligent Life on Earth?* First Edition:
Indianapolis, IN: Bobbs Merrill, 1971
Nr.Fine/Fine $35
Good/V.Good $10

_____. *The Truth about Witchcraft.*
First Edition: Garden City, NY:
Doubleday, 1969
Nr.Fine/Fine $40
Good/V.Good $12

Howe, Ellic. *The Magicians Of The
Golden Dawn: A Documentary History Of
A Magical Order 1887-1923.*
First Edition: London: Routledge &
Kegan Paul, 1972
Nr.Fine/Fine $95
Good/V.Good $60

_____. *Urania's Children. The
Strange World of the Astrologers.*
First Edition: London: William Kimber,
1967
Nr.Fine/Fine $65
Good/V.Good $45

Hubbard, L. Ron. *Dianetics: The
Modern Science of Mental Health.* First
Edition: New York: Hermitage House,
1950.
Nr.Fine/Fine $425
Good/V.Good $175

Huson, Paul. *Mastering Witchcraft. A
Practical Guide for Witches, Warlocks,
and Covens.* First Edition: New York:
Putnams, 1970.
Nr.Fine/Fine $35
Good/V.Good $15

_____. *Mastering Herbalism.* First
Edition: New York: Stein & Day, 1974
*Nr.*Fine/Fine $40
Good/V.Good $15

Jones, Marc Edmund. *How to Learn Astrology.* First Edition: Philadelphia, PA:

Dianetics: the Modern Science of Mental Health *by L. Ron Hubbard*

David McKay, 1941
Nr.Fine/Fine **$50**
Good/V.Good **$20**

_____. *Key Truths of Occult Philosophy. An Introduction to the Codex Occultus* First Edition: Los Angeles, CA: J.F. Rowny Press, 1925
Nr.Fine/Fine **$55**
Good/V.Good **$30**

Judge, William Q. *The Ocean of Theosophy.* First Edition: New York and London: The Path & The Theosophical Publishing Society, 1893.
Nr.Fine/Fine **$125**
Good/V.Good **$45**

_____. *Practical Occultism.* First Edition: Pasadena, CA: Theosophical University Press, 1951.
Nr.Fine/Fine **$30**
Good/V.Good **$10**

Kardec, Allan. *Spiritualist's Philosophy. The Spirit's Book.* First Edition in English: London: Trubner & Co., 1875
Nr.Fine/Fine **$325**
Good/V.Good **$145**

_____. *Experimental Spiritism: Book On Mediums; Guide For Mediums And Invocators* First Edition Thus: New York: Samuel Weiser, 1970

Nr.Fine/Fine **$25**
Good/V.Good **$10**

Kautz, William H. and Melanie Branon; with foreword and forecast by Kevin Ryerson. *Channeling: The Intuitive Connection.* First Edition: San Francisco: Harper & Row, 1987
Nr.Fine/Fine **$15**
Good/V.Good **$6**

Khei, F. R.:C.: 0-X. *Rosicrucian Symbology : a treatise wherein the Discerning Ones will find the Elements of Constructive Symbology and Certain Other Things.* First Illustrated Edition: New York: Macoy Publishing & Masonic Supply Company, 1916
Nr.Fine/Fine **$75**
Good/V.Good **$50**

Khei, X. *Rosicrucian Fundamentals. A Synthesis of Religion, Science and Philosophy.* First Edition: New York:

Channeling: The Intuitive Connection *by William H. Kautz and Melanie Branon*

Societas Rosicruciana In America, 1920
Nr.Fine/Fine **$200**
Good/V.Good **$85**

King, Basil. *The Abolishing Of Death.* First Edition: New York: Cosmopolitan Book Corp., 1919.
Nr.Fine/Fine **$30**
Good/V.Good **$15**

King, Francis. *Sexuality, Magic and*

Perversion. First Edition: Secausus, NJ: The Citadel Press, 1972
Nr.Fine/Fine **$125**
Good/V.Good **$65**

_____. *The Magical World Of Aleister Crowley.* First U.S. Edition: New York: Coward, McCann & Geoghegan, 1978
Nr.Fine/Fine **$75**
Good/V.Good **$30**

_____. *The Secret Rituals of the O.T.O.* First Edition: London: C.W. Daniel, 1973.
Nr.Fine/Fine **$350**
Good/V.Good **$200**

King, Godfre Ray. *The "I AM" Discourses.* First Edition: Schaumburg, IL: Saint Germain Press, 1935
Nr.Fine/Fine **$50**
Good/V.Good **$25**

Kingsford, Anna & Edward Maitland. *The Virgin Of The World.* First Edition: Madras: P.Kailasam Bros., 1885
Nr.Fine/Fine **$300**
Good/V.Good **$165**

Knight, Gareth. *Practical Guide to Qabalistic Symbolism.* (Two Volumes) First Edition: Cheltenham: Helios, 1976.
Nr.Fine/Fine **$75**
Good/V.Good **$45**

_____. *The Practice of Ritual Magic.* First Edition: Cheltenham: Helios, 1969.
Nr.Fine/Fine **$60**
Good/V.Good **$25**

Lamb, Geoffrey. *Magic, Witchcraft and the Occult* First Edition: London: David & Charles, 1997
Nr.Fine/Fine **$40**
Good/V.Good **$15**

LaVey, Anton Szandor. *The Satanic Rituals.* First Edition: Seacaucus, NJ: University Books, Inc., 1972
Nr.Fine/Fine **$225**

Good/V.Good **$125**

_____. *The Compleat Witch or What to do When the Virtue Fails.* First Edition: New York: Dodd, Mead, 1971
Nr.Fine/Fine **$200**
Good/V.Good **$85**

Leadbeater, C. W. *The Perfume of Egypt and Other Weird Stories.* First Edition: Adyar, Madras, India: The Theosophist Office, 1911
Nr.Fine/Fine **$125**
Good/V.Good **$75**

_____. *The Other Side of Death.* First U.K. Edition: London: Theosophical Publishing Society, 1904
Nr.Fine/Fine **$45**
Good/V.Good **$25**

_____. *Some Glimpses Of Occultism. Ancient And Modern.* First U.S. Edition: Chicago: Theosophical Book Concern, 1903
Nr.Fine/Fine **$65**
Good/V.Good **$30**

Leek, Sybil. *ESP: The Magic Within You.* First Edition: London: Abelard-Schuman, 1971
Nr.Fine/Fine **$100**
Good/V.Good **$35**

_____. *Diary of a Witch.* First Edition: Englewood Cliffs, NJ: Prentice-Hall, 1968
Nr.Fine/Fine **$75**
Good/V.Good **$30**

Levi, Eliphas. *Transcendental Magic.* First Edition of translation by Arthur Edward Waite: London: George Redway, 1896
Nr.Fine/Fine **$350**
Good/V.Good **$200**

_____. *The Magical Ritual of the Sanctum Regnum.* First Edition of translation by W. Wynn Westcott: London: George Redway, 1896

Nr.Fine/Fine **$275**
Good/V.Good **$175**

Lewi, Grant. *Astrology for the Millions*
First Edition: New York: Doubleday,
Doran & Co., 1940
Nr.Fine/Fine **$25**
Good/V.Good **$10**

Lewis, H. Spencer. *Essays of a Modern*
Mystic. First Edition: San Jose: Supreme
Grand Lodge of AMORC, 1962
Nr.Fine/Fine **$30**
Good/V.Good **$12**

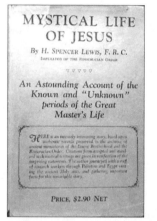

**Mystical Life
of Jesus**
by H. Spencer Lewis

_____. *The Mystical Life of*
*Jesus.*First Edition: San Jose, CA: The
Rosicrucian Press, 1929
Nr.Fine/Fine **$50**
Good/V.Good **$20**

_____. *Mansions of the Soul:*
The Cosmic Conception. First Edition:
San Jose, CA: The Rosicrucian Press,
1930
Nr.Fine/Fine **$35**
Good/V.Good **$15**

Lodge, Oliver J. *Christopher: A Study in*
Human Personality First Edition: London:
Cassell, 1918
Nr.Fine/Fine **$25**
Good/V.Good **$12**
First U.S. Edition: New York: George H.
Doran, 1919
Nr.Fine/Fine **$25**
Good/V.Good **$10**

_____. *Why I Believe in*
*Personal Immortality.*First Edition:
London: Cassell, 1928
Nr.Fine/Fine **$150**
Good/V.Good **$85**

_____. *The Immortality of the*
*Soul.*First Edition: Boston: The Ball
Publishing Co., 1908.
Nr.Fine/Fine **$165**
Good/V.Good **$75**

Long, Max Freedom. *Recovering the*
Ancient Magic. First Edition: London:
Rider & Co., 1936
Nr.Fine/Fine **$525**
Good/V.Good **$300**

_____. *The Secret Science*
Behind Miracles First Edition: Los
Angeles, CA: Kosmon Press, 1948
Nr.Fine/Fine **$75**
Good/V.Good **$35**

_____*Growing into Light.*
First Edition: Vista, CA: Huna Research,
1955
Nr.Fine/Fine **$20**
Good/V.Good **$10**

The Grail from
Celtic Myth to
Christian
Symbol
*by Roger Sherman
Loomis*

Loomis, Roger Sherman. *The Grail from*
Celtic Myth to Christian Symbol. First
Edition: Cardiff: University of Wales
Press, 1963
Nr.Fine/Fine **$55**
Good/V.Good **$25**

First U.S. Edition: New York: Columbia
University Press, 1963
Nr.Fine/Fine **$40**
Good/V.Good **$20**

Maple, Eric. *The Dark World of Witches.*
First Edition: London: Robert Hale, 1962.
Nr.Fine/Fine **$85**
Good/V.Good **$30**

_____. *The Domain of Devils.* First
Edition: London: Robert Hale, 1966
Nr.Fine/Fine **$45**
Good/V.Good **$20**

_____. *Witchcraft The story of
man's search for supernatural power.* First
Edition: London: Octopus Books, 1973
Nr.Fine/Fine **$25**
Good/V.Good **$12**

MacGregor-Mathers, S. L. (trans.) *The
Book of The Sacred Magic of Abra-Melin,
The Mage.* Second U.S. Edition: Chicago:
De Laurence Co., 1932
Nr.Fine/Fine **$275**
Good/V.Good **$200**

_____. *The
Grimoire of Armadel.* First Edition Thus:
New York: Samuel Weiser, 1980.
Nr.Fine/Fine **$65**
Good/V.Good **$30**

Astrology
by Louis MacNeice

MacNeice, Louis. *Astrology.* First U.S.
Edition: Garden City, NY: Doubleday,
1964

Nr.Fine/Fine **$25**
Good/V.Good **$10**

Mead, G.R.S. *Thrice-Greatest Hermes.*
(Three Volumes) First Edition: London
and Benares: The Theosophical
Publishing Society, 1906.
Nr.Fine/Fine **$350**
Good/V.Good **$150**

_____. *Fragments of a Faith
Forgotten.* First Edition: London: The
Theosophical Publishing Society, 1900.
Nr.Fine/Fine **$250**
Good/V.Good **$100**

_____. *Quests Old And New.* First
Edition: London: G. Bell & Sons, 1913.
Nr.Fine/Fine **$165**
Good/V.Good **$55**

Michell, John. *The View Over Atlantis.*
First Edition: London: Garnstone Press,
1969
Nr.Fine/Fine **$35**
Good/V.Good **$20**

Muldoon, Sylvan. *The Case for Astral
Projection.* First Edition: Chicago: The
Aries Press, 1936.
Nr.Fine/Fine **$55**
Good/V.Good **$30**

_____. *Psychic Experiences of
Famous People.* First Edition: Chicago:
The Aries Press, 1947.
Nr.Fine/Fine **$45**
Good/V.Good **$20**

Murray, Margaret Alice. *The Witch-Cult
in Western Europe.* First Edition: Oxford:
Clarendon Press, 1921
Nr.Fine/Fine **$125**
Good/V.Good **$75**

Nauman, St. Elmo. *Exorcism Through
the Ages.* First Edition: New York:
Philosophical Library, 1974
Nr.Fine/Fine **$25**
Good/V.Good **$10**

Norvell, Anthony. *How To Develop Your
Psychic Powers For Health, Wealth, and*

*Security.*First Edition: West Nyack, NY: Parker Publishing Company, 1969.
Nr.Fine/Fine **$20**
Good/V.Good **$8**

Exorcism
Through
the Ages
by St. Elmo Nauman

_____. *Mind Cosmology: How to Translate Your Inner Dreams Into The Outer Reality You Desire!* First Edition: West Nyack, N.Y.: Parker Publishing Company, 1971.
Nr.Fine/Fine **$15**
Good/V.Good **$6**

Olcott, Henry Steel. *Old Diary Leaves: The True Story of The Theosophical Society.* First Trade Edition: New York: Putnams, 1895
Nr.Fine/Fine **$175**
Good/V.Good **$95**

Ophiel. *The Oracle of Fortuna* First Edition: St. Paul, MN: Peach Publishing, 1969.
Nr.Fine/Fine **$55**
Good/V.Good **$20**

_____. *The Art and Practice of the Occult.* First Edition: St. Paul, MN: Peach Publishing, 1968.
Nr.Fine/Fine **$50**
Good/V.Good **$20**

_____. *The Art and Practice of Clairvoyance.*First Edition: St. Paul, MN: Peach Publishing, 1969.
Nr.Fine/Fine **$45**
Good/V.Good **$15**

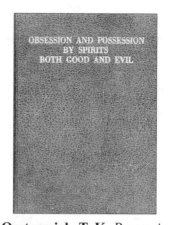

Possession,
Demoniacal and
Other, Among
Races, in
Antiquity, The
Middle Ages, and
Modern Times
by T.K. Oesterreich

Oesterreich, T. K. *Possession, Demoniacal and Other, among Primitive Races, in Antiquity, The Middle Ages, and Modern Times.*First Edition in English: London: Kegan, Paul & Trench, 1930
Nr.Fine/Fine **$85**
Good/V.Good **$50**
First U.S. Edition as: *Obsession and Possession by Spirits both Good and Evil*: Chicago: The de Laurence Company, 1935
Nr.Fine/Fine **$45**
Good/V.Good **$25**

Ostrander, Sheila & Lynn Schroeder. *Psychic Discoveries Behind the Iron Curtain* First Edition: Englewood Cliffs, NJ: Prentice-Hall, 1970.
Nr.Fine/Fine **$30**
Good/V.Good **$12**

Ouspensky, P.D. *Strange Life of Ivan Osokin.*First Edition in English: London: Stourton Press, 1947
Nr.Fine/Fine **$300**
Good/V.Good **$125**

_____. *In Search of the Miraculous.* First Edition: New York: Harcourt, Brace, 1949
Nr.Fine/Fine **$85**
Good/V.Good **$35**

_____. *The Fourth Way. A Record of Talks and Answers to Questions based in the teachings of G.I Gurdjieff.* First Edition: New York: Alfred A. Knopf,

1957
Nr.Fine/Fine **$65**
Good/V.Good **$35**

_____. *Talks With A Devil.*First
Edition: New York: Alfred A. Knopf,
1973
Nr.Fine/Fine **$50**
Good/V.Good **$20**

Panchadasi, Swami. *The Astral World: Its
Scenes, Dwellers, and Phenomena.* First
Edition: Chicago: Advanced Thought
Publishing Co., 1915
Nr.Fine/Fine **$25**
Good/V.Good **$15**

_____. *Clairvoyance and
Occult Powers.*First Edition: Chicago:
Advanced Thought Publishing Co., 1916
Nr.Fine/Fine **$40**
Good/V.Good **$25**

Papus. *The Tarot Of The Bohemians.* First
U.K. Edition: London: Chapman & Hall,
1892
Nr.Fine/Fine **$225**
Good/V.Good **$155**

_____. *The Qabalah—Secret Tradition of
the West.* First Edition Thus: New York:
Samuel Weiser, 1977
Nr.Fine/Fine **$55**
Good/V.Good **$35**

The Compleat
Astrologer
*by Derek and Julia
Parker*

Parker, Derek and Julia. *The Compleat
Astrologer.* First Edition: New York:
McGraw-Hill, 1971

Nr.Fine/Fine **$45**
Good/V.Good **$20**

Perriman, A.E. *Broadcasting from
Beyond* First Edition: London: Spiritualist
Press, 1952
Nr.Fine/Fine **$45**
Good/V.Good **$25**

Phylos the Thibetan. *A Dweller on Two
Planets or The Dividing of the Way.*First
Edition Thus: Los Angeles: Borden
Publishing, 1952
Nr.Fine/Fine **$125**
Good/V.Good **$45**

_____. *An Earth Dweller's
Return.* First Edition: Milwaukee, WI:
Lemurian Press, 1940
Nr.Fine/Fine **$65**
Good/V.Good **$20**

Price, Harry. *Rudi Schneider. A Scientific
Examination of His Mediumship.*First
Edition: London: Methuen & Co., 1930
Nr.Fine/Fine **$145**
Good/V.Good **$55**

_____. *Confessions of a Ghost
Hunter.* First Edition: London: Putnams,
1936
Nr.Fine/Fine **$65**
Good/V.Good **$25**

_____. *Leaves from a Psychist's
Case-Book.* First Edition: London:
Gollancz, 1933
Nr.Fine/Fine **$45**
Good/V.Good **$20**

Rampa, T. Lobsang. *The Third Eye: The
Autobiography of a Tibetan Lama.*First
US Edition: Garden City, NY: Doubleday,
1957
Nr.Fine/Fine **$55**
Good/V.Good **$20**

_____. *Doctor from Lhasa.*
First Edition: London: Souvenir Press,
1959
Nr.Fine/Fine **$35**
Good/V.Good **$15**

Doctor from Lhasa
by T. Lobsang Rampa

_____. *The Saffron Robe.*First Edition: New York: Pageant Press, 1966
Nr.Fine/Fine **$125**
Good/V.Good **$55**

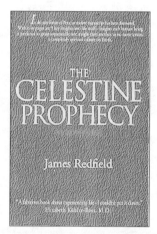

The Celestine Prophecy
by James Redfield

Redfield, James. *The Celestine Prophecy.* First Edition: New York: Warner Books, 1993
Nr.Fine/Fine **$85**
Good/V.Good **$30**

Redpath, Ian. *Messages from the Stars: Communication and Contact with Extraterrestrial Life.* First Edition: New York: Harper & Row, 1978
Nr.Fine/Fine **$30**
Good/V.Good **$15**

Regardie, Israel *Golden Dawn, Vols. 1-4, An Account of the Teachings, Rites and*

Messages from the Stars
by Ian Redpath

*Ceremonies of the Order of the Golden Dawn.*First Edition: Chicago: The Aries Press, 1937-1940
Nr.Fine/Fine **$600**
Good/V.Good **$350**

_____. *The Tree of Life: A Study in Magic.* First Edition: London: Rider & Co., 1932
Nr.Fine/Fine **$165**
Good/V.Good **$95**

_____. *The Middle Pillar: A Co-Relation of the Principles of Analytical Psychology and the Elementary Techniques of Magic* First Edition: Chicago: Aries Press, 1938.
Nr.Fine/Fine **$175**
Good/V.Good **$100**

Robbins, Rossell Hope. *The Encyclopedia of Witchcraft and Demonology.* First Edition: New York: Crown, 1959
Nr.Fine/Fine **$45**
Good/V.Good **$25**

Roberts, Jane. *Seth Speaks The Eternal Validity of the Soul.* First Edition: Englewood Cliffs, NJ: Prentice-Hall, 1972
Nr.Fine/Fine **$75**
Good/V.Good **$30**

_____. *A Seth Book: Dreams, "Evolution," And Value Fulfillment Volume II* First Edition: Englewood Cliffs, NJ: Prentice-Hall, 1986

Nr.Fine/Fine **$25**
Good/V.Good **$12**

Roberts, Susan. *The Magician of the Golden Dawn The Story of Aleister Crowley.* First Edition: Chicago: Contemporary Books, 1978
Nr.Fine/Fine **$65**
Good/V.Good **$20**

Rohmer, Sax. *The Romance of Sorcery.* First U.S. Edition: New York: E. P. Dutton, 1915
Nr.Fine/Fine **$225**
Good/V.Good **$100**

Saint-Germain, Comte C. De. *Practical Astrology: Scholarly, Simple, Complete Simple Method of Casting Horoscopes.* First U.S. Edition: Chicago: Laird & Lee, 1901
Nr.Fine/Fine **$135**
Good/V.Good **$60**

_____. *Study Of Palmistry For Professional Purposes And Advanced Students* First U.S. Edition: Chicago: Laird & Lee, 1900
Nr.Fine/Fine **$125**
Good/V.Good **$45**

Sepharial. *The Numbers Book* First Edition: Slough Bucks, England: W. Foulsham, 1957
Nr.Fine/Fine **$40**
Good/V.Good **$15**

_____. *The World Horoscope Hebrew Astrology.*First Edition: London: W. Foulsham, 1965
Nr.Fine/Fine **$25**
Good/V.Good **$15**

_____. *New Dictionary of Astrology.* First Edition: New York: Galahad, 1963.
Nr.Fine/Fine **$20**
Good/V.Good **$12**

Seth, Ronald. *In The Name of the Devil.* First Edition: New York: Walker, 1969
Nr.Fine/Fine **$25**
Good/V.Good **$10**

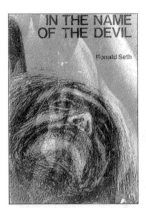

In The Name of
The Devil
by Ronald Seth

Sinnett, A. P. *Incidents in the Life of Madame Blavatsky.* First Edition: London: George Redway, 1886.
Nr.Fine/Fine **$65**
Good/V.Good **$30**

_____ *Growth of the Soul.* First U.K. Edition: London: Theosophical Publishing Society, 1896
Nr.Fine/Fine **$125**
Good/V.Good **$55**

Sladek, John. *The New Apocrypha: A Guide to Strange Science and Occult Beliefs.* First Edition: London: Hart-Davis, MacGibbon, 1973
Nr.Fine/Fine **$155**
Good/V.Good **$45**

Spence, Lewis. *The Mysteries of Britain, or the Secret Rites and Traditions of Ancient Britain Restored.*First Edition: London: Rider & Co, nd.
Nr.Fine/Fine **$185**
Good/V.Good **$100**

_____. *The Fairy Tradition In Britain.* First Edition: London: Rider & Co., 1948
Nr.Fine/Fine **$125**
Good/V.Good **$85**

_____. *The Magic Arts in Celtic Britain.*First Edition: London: Rider & Co, nd.
Nr.Fine/Fine **$100**
Good/V.Good **$45**

Watseka: America's
Most Extraordinary
Case of Possession
and Exorcism
by David St.Clair

St. Clair, David. *Watseka: America's Most Extraordinary Case of Possession and Exorcism.*First Edition: Chicago: Playboy Press, 1977
Nr.Fine/Fine **$200**
Good/V.Good **$85**

Stearn, Jess. *Edgar Cayce: The Sleeping Prophet.* First Edition: Garden City, NY: Doubleday, 1967
Nr.Fine/Fine **$45**
Good/V.Good **$15**

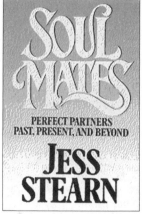

Soul Mates
by Jess Stearn

_____. *Soul Mates.* First Edition: New York: Bantam Books, 1984
Nr.Fine/Fine **$30**
Good/V.Good **$12**

_____. *The Search for the Girl With the Blue Eyes.*First Edition: Garden City, NY: Doubleday, 1968
Nr.Fine/Fine **$25**

Good/V.Good **$8**

Steiner, Rudolf. *Christianity as Mystical Fact.* Third Edition in English: London: Rudolf Steiner Publishing Company, 1938.
Nr.Fine/Fine **$55**
Good/V.Good **$20**

First Edition Thus: West Nyack, NY: Rudolph Steiner Publications, Inc., 1961.
Nr.Fine/Fine **$35**
Good/V.Good **$15**

_____. *The Gates of Knowledge.* First Edition in English: New York: Putnams, 1912
Nr.Fine/Fine **$200**
Good/V.Good **$90**

_____. *Anthroposophy: An Introduction.* First U.K. Edition: London: H. Collison, 1931
Nr.Fine/Fine **$65**
Good/V.Good **$45**

Cosmic Workings
in Earth and Man
by Rudolf Steiner

_____. *Cosmic Workings in Earth and Man.* First Edition in English: London: Rudolf Steiner Publishing Company, 1952
Nr.Fine/Fine **$75**
Good/V.Good **$30**

St George, E.A. *The Casebook of a Working Occultist.* First Edition: London: Rigel Press, 1972
Nr.Fine/Fine **$55**
Good/V.Good **$20**

Summers, Montague. *The Vampire: His Kith and Kin.* First Edition: London: Kegan, Paul, Trench, Trubner, 1928
Nr.Fine/Fine **$275**
Good/V.Good **$165**

_____. *The Vampire In Europe.* First Edition: London: Kegan, Paul, Trench, Trubner, 1929.
Nr.Fine/Fine **$450**
Good/V.Good **$250**

_____. *The Werewolf.* First Edition: London: Kegan, Paul, Trench, Trubner, 1933.
Nr.Fine/Fine **$375**
Good/V.Good **$200**

_____. *A Popular History of Witchcraft.* First Edition: London: Kegan, Paul, Trench, Trubner, 1937.
Nr.Fine/Fine **$175**
Good/V.Good **$100**

Swedenborg, Emmanuel. *A Treatise Concerning Heaven And Hell, And Of The Wonderful Things Therein.* First US Edition: Baltimore, MD: Anthony Miltenberger, 1812.
Nr.Fine/Fine **$500**
Good/V.Good **$265**

_____. *Arcana Coelestia.* (Thirteen Volumes) First Edition Thus: New York: Swedenborg Foundation, 1965
Nr.Fine/Fine **$150**
Good/V.Good **$100**

_____. *The Doctrine of Life for the New Jerusalem.* First Edition Thus: London, the Swedenborg Society, 1913.
Nr.Fine/Fine **$65**
Good/V.Good **$30**

_____. *Divine Love and Wisdom.* First Edition Thus: London: Swedenborg Society, 1890.
Nr.Fine/Fine **$75**
Good/V.Good **$30**

Symonds, John. *The Great Beast.* First

Edition: London, New York, Melbourne, Sydney, Cape Town: Rider and Company, 1951
Nr.Fine/Fine **$400**
Good/V.Good **$225**

_____. *The Magic Of Aleister Crowley.* First Edition: London: Frederick Muller Ltd, 1958
Nr.Fine/Fine **$125**
Good/V.Good **$55**

Companions of
the Unseen
by Paul Tabori

Tabori, Paul. *Companions of the Unseen.* First Edition: New Hyde Park, NY: University Books, 1968.
Nr.Fine/Fine **$15**
Good/V.Good **$8**

Tart, Charles. *Altered States of Consciousness.* First Edition: New York: John Wiley, 1969
Nr.Fine/Fine **$40**
Good/V.Good **$15**

_____. *Waking Up: Overcoming the Obstacles to Human Potential.* First Edition: Boston: Shambhala, 1986
Nr.Fine/Fine **$25**
Good/V.Good **$10**

Thomas, Eugene E. *Brotherhood of Mt. Shasta.* First Edition: Los Angeles, CA: DeVorss, 1946
Nr.Fine/Fine **$65**
Good/V.Good **$35**

Torrens, RG *Golden Dawn: Its Inner*

Teachings. First Edition: London: Neville Spearman Ltd., 1969
Nr.Fine/Fine **$100**
Good/V.Good **$40**

_____. *The Secret Rituals of the Golden Dawn.* First U.S. Edition: New York: Samuel Weiser, 1973
Nr.Fine/Fine **$165**
Good/V.Good **$95**

THE STORY OF ANTONIO C. AGPAOA, SPIRITUALIST HEALER OF THE PHILIPPINES, AND THE ASTOUNDING FACTS ABOUT SUCCESSFUL SURGERY WITHOUT INSTRUMENTS, ANESTHESIA, OR PAIN

By TOM VALENTINE

with a Foreword by Harold Sherman, author of *Wonder Healers of the Philippines*

Psychic Surgery
by Tom Valentine

Valentine, Tom. *Psychic Surgery.* First Edition: Chicago, IL: Regnery, 1973
Nr.Fine/Fine **$25**
Good/V.Good **$10**

Von Daniken, Erich. *Chariots of the Gods?* First U.S. Edition: New York: Putnams, 1968
Nr.Fine/Fine **$20**
Good/V.Good **$12**

_____. *The Gold of the Gods.* First Edition in English: London: Souvenir Press, 1972
Nr.Fine/Fine **$30**
Good/V.Good **$15**

_____. *Signs of the Gods* First Edition in English: London: Souvenir Press, 1980
Nr.Fine/Fine **$20**
Good/V.Good **$8**

Velikovsky, Immanuel. *Worlds in Collision.* First Edition: New York: The Macmillan Co., 1950.

Nr.Fine/Fine **$225**
Good/V.Good **$75**

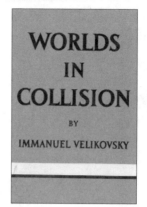

Worlds in Collision
by Immanuel Velikovsky

_____. *Ages In Chaos.* First Edition: Garden City, NY: Doubleday, 1952
Nr.Fine/Fine **$75**
Good/V.Good **$40**

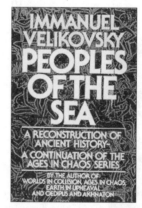

Peoples of the Sea
by Immanuel Velikovsky

_____. *Peoples of the Sea.* First Edition: Garden City, NY: Doubleday, 1977
Nr.Fine/Fine **$50**
Good/V.Good **$25**

Walker, Benjamin. *Encyclopedia of Metaphysical Medicine.* First Edition: London: Routledge & Kegan Paul, 1978
Nr.Fine/Fine **$35**
Good/V.Good **$15**

_____. *Tantrism: Its Secret Principles and Practices.* First Edition: Wellingborough, UK: Aquarian Press,

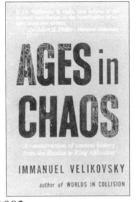

Ages in Chaos
by Immanuel Velikovsky

1982
Nr.Fine/Fine **$50**
Good/V.Good **$20**

_____. *Beyond the Body: The Human Double and the Astral Plane.*First Edition: London: Routledge & Kegan Paul, 1974.
Nr.Fine/Fine **$30**
Good/V.Good **$15**

The Brotherhood of the Rosy Cross
by Arthur Edward Waite

Waite, Arthur Edward. *The Brotherhood of the Rosy Cross* First Edition: London: William Rider & Son, 1924
Nr.Fine/Fine **$475**
Good/V.Good **$225**

_____. *The Book of Black Magic and Pacts.*First Edition: London: George Redway, 1898
Nr.Fine/Fine **$1500**
Good/V.Good **$1100**

_____. *The Holy Kabbalah A Study of the Secret Tradition in Israel.* First Edition: London: Williams and Norgate, 1929
Nr.Fine/Fine **$850**
Good/V.Good **$500**

_____. *The Secret Tradition in Goetia. The Book of Ceremonial Magic. Including the Rites and Mysteries of Goetic Theurgy, Sorcery And Infernal Necromancy.*First Edition: London: William Rider & Son, 1911.
Nr.Fine/Fine **$600**
Good/V.Good **$400**

_____. *The Quest of the Golden Stairs.*First Edition: London: Theosophical Publishing House, 1927.
Nr.Fine/Fine **$175**
Good/V.Good **$95**

Bigfoot and Other Legendary Creatures
by Paul Robert Walker

Walker, Paul Robert. *Bigfoot and Other Legendary Creatures.*First Edition: New York: Harcourt Brace, 1992
Nr.Fine/Fine **$25**
Good/V.Good **$15**

Watson, Lyall Gifts of Unknown Things.* First U.S. Edition: New York: Simon and Schuster, 1976
Nr.Fine/Fine **$35**
Good/V.Good **$20**

Watts, Alan W. *The Way of Zen.* First Edition: New York: Pantheon, 1957.
Nr.Fine/Fine **$250**

Good/V.Good **$100**

Gifts of
Unknown Things
by Lyall Watson

_____. *Nature, Man and Woman.*
First Edition: New York: Pantheon, 1958
Nr.Fine/Fine **$225**
Good/V.Good **$110**

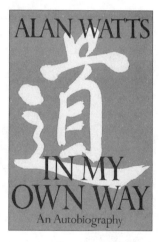

In My Own Way
by Alan Watts

_____. *In My Own Way An
Autobiography.* First Edition: New York:
Pantheon Books, 1972
Nr.Fine/Fine **$120**
Good/V.Good **$45**

Wellesley, Gordon. *Sex And The Occult.*
First Edition: London: Souvenir Press
Ltd., 1973.
Nr.Fine/Fine **$25**
Good/V.Good **$12**

W.Wynn Westcott (trans). *Isiac Tablet or*

the Bembine Table of Isis. Facsimile of
1887 First Edition: Los Angeles:
Philosophical Research Society, nd
Nr.Fine/Fine **$55**
Good/V.Good **$25**

Webb, James. *The Occult Establishment.*
First Edition: Glasgow, Scotland: Richard
Drew Publishing, 1981
Nr.Fine/Fine **$105**
Good/V.Good **$55**

_____. *The Occult Underground.*
First Edition: La Salle, IL: Open Court
Publishing Company, 1974
Nr.Fine/Fine **$85**
Good/V.Good **$50**

White, Stewart Edward. *The
Unobstructed Universe.* First Edition:
New York: Dutton, 1940
Nr.Fine/Fine **$45**
Good/V.Good **$25**

Wilcox, John. *An Occult Guide to South
America.* First Edition: New York: Laurel
Tape and Film, Inc., 1976
Nr.Fine/Fine **$20**
Good/V.Good **$6**

Wilson, Colin. *The Occult.* First Edition:
London: Hodder and Stoughton, 1971
Nr.Fine/Fine **$70**
Good/V.Good **$30**

_____. *Beyond the Occult: Twenty
Years' Research Into the Paranormal.*
First Edition: London: Bantam Press,
1988
Nr.Fine/Fine **$55**
Good/V.Good **$30**

_____. *Men of Mystery: A
Celebration Of the Occult.* First Edition:
London: W.H. Allen, 1977
Nr.Fine/Fine **$60**
Good/V.Good **$35**

Yates, Frances A. *The Occult Philosophy
in the Elizabethan Age.* First Edition:
London: Routledge & Kegan Paul, 1979
Nr.Fine/Fine **$110**

Good/V.Good **$65**

_____. *The Rosicrucian Enlightenment.* First Edition: London & Boston: Routledge & Kegan Paul, 1972
Nr.Fine/Fine **$100**
Good/V.Good **$60**

Zolar. *The History of Astrology.* First Edition: New York: Arco, 1972.
Nr.Fine/Fine **$15**
Good/V.Good **$6**

Poetry & Belles Lettres

Belles Lettres: to write for the sake of beauty alone. Literature is, after all is said and done, an art form. The well turned phrase, the beautiful description, the poem that makes your heart a dancer, these are Belles Lettres. It is writing simply for the sake of art, exploring the limits of what the soul can draw from rearrangements of the dictionary. The format can be almost anything. It can be a book of poetry, a collection of essays or stories, or even a novel. The telling factor is the beauty, the novelty, the art of it. Perhaps it can be called painting with words. Arthur Machen found it to be the perfect, sublime combination of terror and beauty. The dividing line for me has always been whether it appeals to my mind or to my emotions. If it makes me feel, it's Belles Lettres.

It is a field that holds a lot more small press and vanity publications than other genres. While novelists might get a healthy advance for their first book, poets, for the last two centuries or more, seem to be expected to prove themselves through small or vanity presses. Auden, Poe, Wordsworth, Coleridge, Machen, Dylan Thomas, and Paul Lawrence Dunbar all self or subsidy published their introductions to the world of publication. Small presses are a major factor in the genre. Black Sun, Sylvia Beach's Shakespeare and Co., Harriet Weaver's Egoist Press, Lawrence Ferlinghetti's City Lights, California's Black Sparrow Press have all brought out classics of Belles Lettres. The field is a specialized one, as the most sought after books are extremely rare and hence rather expensive. This is the champagne area in the collector's market, the high end.

It often crosses over into the art/illustration area, books that are a collaborative effort aimed at producing a multimedia experience. The artistic "marriage" of William Morris and Edward Bourne-Jones at Kelmscott Press is a prime example. More modern examples might be the LEC publication of Arthur Rimbaud's *A Season in Hell*, illustrated by Robert Mapplethorp, and the University of California's publication of Alain Robbe-Grillet's *La Belle Captive*, illustrated by Rene Magritte. Sometimes the collaboration of a literary and a graphic artist produces something so wondrous that it is pleasure just to hold in your hands.

This is an area that can be extremely personal. If it touches you, if you find, while reading, that you reach up to wipe a tear from your cheek, or if you are laughing so hard that you have to put the book down; well, then you've found a book that belongs in your collection of Belles Lettres. These are the books that never grow old. These books open new worlds, new thoughts, new interpretations every time they are opened; every time they are read from the first reading to readings extending to June 1st of never. They are as wondrous and beautiful as any work of art can be, for that is what they are, works of art. There are no other areas of art so accessible, so easily attainable by the average man as Belles Lettres. To hold the first edition, the very first appearance in the world of a book that touches you, that reaches you, is equivalent to owning the Mona Lisa, and no man in world today is rich enough to afford that.

10 Classic Rarities

Auden, W.H. *Poems.* (privately printed) S[tephen]. H[arold]. S[pender]. n.p. [Frognal, Hampstead], 1928.
Retail value . . . . **$50,000** in almost any condition

Bridges, Robert. *The Testament of Beauty.* (privately printed for the author) n.p. [Oxford] n.d. [1927-9]. Five volumes in unprinted wrappers.
Retail value in:
  Near Fine to Fine **$4000**
  Good to Very Good **$2200**

cummings, e.e. *The Enormous Room.* New York: Boni and Liveright, 1922. First issue, the word "shit" intact in the last line of page 219. In later issues the word was blocked out.
Retail value in:
  Near Fine to Fine **$3800**
  Good to Very Good. **$2500**

Dunbar, Paul Lawrence. *Majors and Minors.* Toledo, OH: Hadley & Hadley, Printers and Binders, 1895. Dunbar's second book, published at his own expense
Retail value in:
Near Fine to Fine **$2000**
Good to Very Good **$1100**

Eliot, T.S. *The Wasteland.* New York: Boni and Liveright, 1922 . "Mountain" correctly spelled on page 41
Retail value in:
  Near Fine to Fine. **$12,000**
  Good to Very Good **$8000**

Hughes, Langston. *Weary Blues.* New York: Alfred A. Knopf, 1926. Finding it cures the blues.
Retail value in:
  Near Fine to Fine. **$15,000**
  Good to Very Good **$10,000**

Pound, Ezra. *Imaginary Letters.* Paris: Black Sun Press, 1930. Printed on Japan Vellum. Finding this pays in real banknotes
Retail value in:
  Near Fine to Fine **$3500**
  Good to Very Good **$3000**

Stein, Gertrude. *Dix Portraits.* Paris: Editions de la Montagne, 1930. Trade Edition, one of 400 copies on Alpha Paper, numbered from 101 to 500
Retail value in:
  Near Fine to Fine **$2200**
  Good to Very Good **$1500**

Thomas, Dylan: *18 Poems.* London, The Sunday Referee and The Parton Bookshop, 1934. Price per poem is hefty
Retail value in:
  Near Fine condition **$4000**
  Good to Very Good **$1800**

Yeats, W.B. *The Wanderings of Oisin.* London: Kegan Paul, Trench, 1889. Dark blue cloth with black endpapers
Retail value in:
  Near Fine to Fine **$3000**
  Good to Very Good **$1600**

Price Guide

Adams, Leonie. *Those Not Elect.* First Edition: New York: Robert M. McBride, 1925.
Nr.Fine/Fine **$150**
Good/V.Good **$65**

Agee, James. *Permit Me Voyage.* First Edition: New Haven: Yale University Press, 1934
Nr.Fine/Fine **$850**
Good/V.Good **$425**

The Charnel Rose
by Conrad Aiken

Aiken, Conrad. *The Charnel Rose.* First Edition: Boston: The Four Seas Company, 1918
Nr.Fine/Fine **$725**
Good/V.Good **$400**

_____. *Priapus and The Pool.* First Edition: Cambridge: Dunster House, 1922
Nr.Fine/Fine **$450**
Good/V.Good **$250**

_____. *The Pilgrimage of Festus.* First Edition: New York: Alfred A. Knopf, 1923
Nr.Fine/Fine **$100**
Good/V.Good **$65**

Akers, Elizabeth. *The Silver Bridge.* First Edition: Boston: Houghton Mifflin, 1886.

Nr.Fine/Fine **$95**
Good/V.Good **$45**

Antoninus, Brother (William Everson). *San Joaquin.* First Edition: Los Angeles: Ritchie, 1939
Nr.Fine/Fine **$2500**
Good/V.Good **$1400**

The Last Crusade. First Edition: Berkeley: Oyez, 1969
Nr.Fine/Fine **$300**
Good/V.Good **$165**

The Crooked Lines of God: Poems 1949-1954. First Edition: Detroit: University of Detroit Press, 1959
Nr.Fine/Fine **$250**
Good/V.Good **$145**

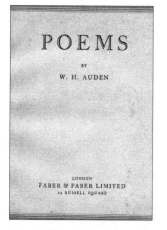

Poems
by W.H. Auden

Auden, W. H. *Poems.* First Edition: London: Faber & Faber, 1930
Nr.Fine/Fine **$1600**
Good/V.Good **$750**

_____. *The Dance of Death.* First Edition: London: Faber & Faber, 1933
Nr.Fine/Fine **$1000**
Good/V.Good **$600**

_____. *Collected Shorter Poems 1927-1957.* First U.S. Edition: New York: Random House, 1966.

Nr.Fine/Fine **$150**
Good/V.Good **$65**
First U.K. Edition: London: Faber &
Faber, 1966
Nr.Fine/Fine **$95**
Good/V.Good **$50**

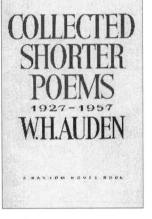

Collected Shorter
Poems 1927-1957
by W.H. Auden

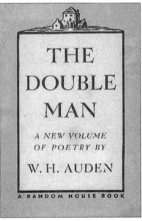

The Double Man
by W.H. Auden

_____. *The Double Man.* First
Edition: New York: Random House, 1941
Nr.Fine/Fine **$150**
Good/V.Good **$70**

Auslander, Joseph. *Riders at the Gate.*
First Edition: New York: The Macmillan
Company, 1938.
Nr.Fine/Fine **$85**
Good/V.Good **$35**

Bacon, Leonard. *The Legend of
Quincibald.* First Edition (limited in

slipcase): New York: Harper & Brothers,
1928
Nr.Fine/Fine **$200**
Good/V.Good **$125**
First Edition (trade): New York: Harper &
Brothers, 1928
Nr.Fine/Fine **$35**
Good/V.Good **$20**

The Legend of
Quincibald
by Leonard Bacon

_____. *Lost Buffalo and other
poems.* First Edition (limited): New York:
Harper and Bros., 1930
Nr.Fine/Fine **$80**
Good/V.Good **$35**
First Edition (trade): New York: Harper
and Bros., 1930
Nr.Fine/Fine **$45**
Good/V.Good **$25**

Barnes, Djuna. *Ryder.* First Edition: New
York: Horace Liveright, 1928
Nr.Fine/Fine **$500**
Good/V.Good **$300**

_____. *The Book of Repulsive
Women.* Points of Issue: A stapled
chapbook
First Edition: New York: Guido Bruno,
1915
Nr.Fine/Fine **$750**
Good/V.Good **$475**

_____. *A Book.* First Edition:
New York: Boni and Liveright, 1923
Nr.Fine/Fine **$1500**

Good/V.Good **$650**

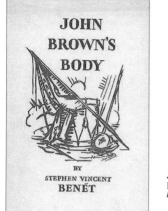

John Brown's
Body
*by Stephen Vincent
Benet*

Benet, Stephen Vincent. *John Brown's Body.* First Edition: Garden City, NY: Doubleday, Doran, 1928
Nr.Fine/Fine **$200**
Good/V.Good **$85**

_____. *Five Men and Pompey.* First Edition: Boston: Four Seas Company, 1915
Nr.Fine/Fine **$400**
Good/V.Good **$150**

_____. *Heavens and Earth.* First Edition: New York: Henry Holt and Company, 1920
Nr.Fine/Fine **$300**
Good/V.Good **$125**

Starry Harness
*by William Rose
Benet*

Benet, William Rose. *Starry Harness.* First Edition: New Haven, CT: Duffield and Green, 1933
Nr.Fine/Fine **$95**
Good/V.Good **$35**

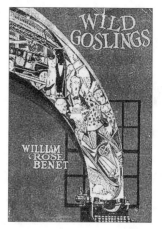

Wild Goslings: A
Selection of
Fugitive Pieces
*by William Rose
Benet*

_____. *Wild Goslings: A Selection of Fugitive Pieces.* First Edition: New York: George H. Doran Company, 1927
Nr.Fine/Fine **$85**
Good/V.Good **$30**

_____. *The Falconer of God.* First Edition: New Haven, CT: Yale University Press, 1914
Nr.Fine/Fine **$100**
Good/V.Good **$65**

Berryman, John. *77 Dream Songs.* First Edition: New York: Farrar, Straus, 1964.
Nr.Fine/Fine **$250**
Good/V.Good **$90**

Betjeman, John. *Continual Dew: A Little Book of Bourgeois Verse.* First Edition: London: John Murray, 1937.
Nr.Fine/Fine **$425**
Good/V.Good **$175**

_____. *First and Last Loves.* First Edition: London: John Murray, 1952.
Nr.Fine/Fine **$250**
Good/V.Good **$135**

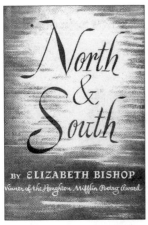

North and South
by Elizabeth Bishop

Bishop, Elizabeth. *North & South.* First Edition: Boston: Houghton Mifflin Company, 1946
Nr.Fine/Fine **$1500**
Good/V.Good **$725**

Blanding, Don. *The Virgin of Waikiki.* First Edition: New York: Henry M. Snyder, 1933
Nr.Fine/Fine **$45**
Good/V.Good **$20**

_____. *Floridays.* First Edition: New York: Dodd, Mead, 1941.
Nr.Fine/Fine **$55**
Good/V.Good **$25**

_____. *The Rest of the Road.* First Edition: New York: Dodd, Mead, 1937.
Nr.Fine/Fine **$45**
Good/V.Good **$15**

Bogan, Louise. *Dark Summer.* First Edition: New York: Charles Scribner's Sons, 1929
Nr.Fine/Fine **$550**
Good/V.Good **$200**

_____. *Body of This Death.* First Edition: New York: Robert M. McBride & Company, 1923
Nr.Fine/Fine **$525**
Good/V.Good **$200**

Branch, Anna Hempstead. *Sonnets from*

a Lock Box. First Edition: Boston; Houghton Mifflin, 1929
Nr.Fine/Fine **$40**
Good/V.Good **$15**

Bukowski, Charles. *Days Run Away Like Wild Horses over the Hills.* First Edition (Limited/Signed): Los Angeles: Black Sparrow, 1969
Nr.Fine/Fine **$1200**
Good/V.Good **$800**
First Edition (Trade Softcover): Los Angeles: Black Sparrow, 1969
Nr.Fine/Fine **$60**
Good/V.Good **$25**

_____. *Horsemeat.* First Edition: Santa Barbara: Black Sparrow, 1982
Nr.Fine/Fine **$2500**
Good/V.Good **$1800**

Ham on Rye
by Charles Bukowski

_____. *Ham on Rye.* First Edition (Limited/Signed): Santa Barbara: Black Sparrow Press, 1982
Nr.Fine/Fine **$1800**
Good/V.Good **$600**

Brinnin, John Malcolm. *The Garden is Political.* First Edition: New York; Macmillan, 1942

Nr.Fine/Fine **$65**
Good/V.Good **$25**

Annie Allen
by Gwendolyn Brooks

Brooks, Gwendolyn. *Annie Allen.* First Edition: New York: Harper & Brothers, 1949.
Nr.Fine/Fine **$750**
Good/V.Good **$450**

_____. *A Street in Bronzeville.* First Edition: New York: Harper & Brothers, 1945
Nr.Fine/Fine **$1050**
Good/V.Good **$400**

Bynner, Witter. *Indian Earth.* First Edition: New York: Alfred A. Knopf, 1929
Nr.Fine/Fine **$75**
Good/V.Good **$35**

Carlton, Will. *Farm Festivals.* First Edition: New York: Harper & Brothers, 1881
Nr.Fine/Fine **$55**
Good/V.Good **$25**

_____. *City Ballads.* First Edition: New York: Harper & Brothers, 1886
Nr.Fine/Fine **$45**
Good/V.Good **$20**

Carmen, Bliss. *By the Aurelian Wall and Other Elegies.* First U.S. Edition: Boston: Lamson, Wolffe and Company, 1898.
Nr.Fine/Fine **$110**
Good/V.Good **$60**

_____. *The Friendship Of Art.* First Edition: Boston: L. C. Page, 1904
Nr.Fine/Fine **$75**
Good/V.Good **$35**

As If
by John Ciardi

Ciardi, John. *As If.* First Edition: New Brunswick: Rutgers University Press, 1955
Nr.Fine/Fine **$75**
Good/V.Good **$30**

_____. *Homeward to America.* First Edition: New York: Henry Holt, 1939
Nr.Fine/Fine **$165**
Good/V.Good **$75**

Clark, Badger. *Sun and Saddle Leather.* First Edition: Boston: Richard G. Badger, 1917.
Nr.Fine/Fine **$80**
Good/V.Good **$45**

Coatsworth, Elizabeth. *Mouse Musings.* First Edition: Hingham, MA: Peuterschein, 1954
Nr.Fine/Fine **$225**
Good/V.Good **$125**

_____. *The Cat Who Went to Heaven.* First Edition: New York: Macmillan, 1930.
Nr.Fine/Fine **$125**
Good/V.Good **$70**

Coffin, Robert P. Tristram. *Strange Holiness.* First Edition: New York:

Macmillan 1935
Nr.Fine/Fine **$85**
Good/V.Good **$35**

SHIP'S
LOG
AND OTHER POEMS
by
Grace Hazard Conkling

G RACE HAZARD CONKLING, poet, lecturer, poetry teacher at Smith College, and mother of the well-known child poet, Hilda Conkling, stands among the finest women poets in America. Her latest book of verse elicits from Mark Van Doren the following comment: "This seems to be her best book. . . excellent in its kind, and I think sure to add to its author's already considerable reputation. . . I recognize in it extraordinary vigor and competence, and believe it will be effective with an important audience."

Alfred A. Knopf   Publisher, N. Y.

Ship's Log and
Other Poems
*by Grace Hazard
Conkling*

Conkling, Grace Hazard. *Ship's Log and Other Poems.* First Edition: New York: Alfred A. Knopf, 1924
Nr.Fine/Fine **$55**
Good/V.Good **$20**

_____. *Witch and Other Poems.* First Edition: New York: Alfred Knopf, 1929.
Nr.Fine/Fine **$45**
Good/V.Good **$20**

Cooke, Rose Terry. *Huckleberries Gathered from New England Hills.* First Edition: Boston: Houghton, Mifflin, 1892.
Nr.Fine/Fine **$75**
Good/V.Good **$35**

Corso, Gregory. *The Mutation of the Spirit: A Shuffle Poem.* Points of Issue: printed as separate sheets to be reordered to form new poems. First Edition: New York: Death Press, 1964
Nr.Fine/Fine **$450**
Good/V.Good **$300**

_____. *Vestal Lady On Brattle A Collection of Poems Written In Cambridge Massachusetts. 1954-1955.* Point of Issue: Paperback Original. First Edition: Cambridge, MA: Richard Brukenfeld, 1955

Nr.Fine/Fine **$375**
Good/V.Good **$225**

_____. *Gasoline.* Points of Issue: Paperback Original Pocket Poets Series #8. First Edition: San Francisco: City Lights Books, 1958
Nr.Fine/Fine **$200**
Good/V.Good **$125**

Corwin, Norman. *On a Note of Triumph.* First Edition: New York: Simon and Schuster, 1945
Nr.Fine/Fine **$85**
Good/V.Good **$30**

Crane, Hart. *The Bridge. A Poem.* First Edition: Paris: The Black Sun Press, 1930
Nr.Fine/Fine **$3500**
Good/V.Good **$1800**

_____. *White Buildings.* Points of Issue: Allen Tate's name incorrectly on title page First Edition: New York: Boni & Liveright, 1926
Nr.Fine/Fine **$2800**
Good/V.Good **$1600**

_____. *Collected Poems of Hart Crane.* First Edition: New York: Liveright, 1933
Nr.Fine/Fine **$500**
Good/V.Good **$275**

Crane, Nathalia. *The Janitor's Boy and Other Poems.* First Edition: New York: Thomas Seltzer, 1924.
Nr.Fine/Fine **$85**
Good/V.Good **$35**

_____. *Lava Lane and Other Poems.* First Edition: New York: Thomas Seltzer, 1925
Nr.Fine/Fine **$100**
Good/V.Good **$45**

cummings, e. e. *The Enormous Room.* Points of Issue: The word "shit" on Page 219 is inked out in later states. First Edition later states: New York: Boni & Liveright, 1922
Nr.Fine/Fine **$850**

Good/V.Good **$400**

Eimi
by e.e. cummings

_____. *Eimi*. First Edition:
New York: Covici-Friede, 1933
Nr.Fine/Fine **$1500**
Good/V.Good **$400**

_____. *Tulips And Chimneys*.
First Edition: New York: Thomas Seltzer,
1922
Nr.Fine/Fine **$1000**
Good/V.Good **$650**

_____. *Santa Claus: A Morality*.
First Edition: New York: Henry Holt,
1946
Nr.Fine/Fine **$200**
Good/V.Good **$115**

Day-Lewis, Cecil. *Noah and the Waters*.
First Edition: London: Leonard and
Virginia Woolf at the Hogarth Press, 1936
Nr.Fine/Fine **$225**
Good/V.Good **$100**

_____. *The Magnetic
Mountain*. First Edition: London: Leonard
and Virginia Woolf at the Hogarth Press,
1933
Nr.Fine/Fine **$450**
Good/V.Good **$250**

_____. *Country Comets*. First
Edition: London: Martin Hopkinson &

Company Ltd., 1928
Nr.Fine/Fine **$175**
Good/V.Good **$95**

Dickey, James. *Drowning With Others*.
First Edition: Middletown, CT: Wesleyan
University Press, 1962
Nr.Fine/Fine **$300**
Good/V.Good **$165**

_____. *Buckdancer's Choice*.
First Edition: Middletown, CT: Wesleyan
University Press, 1965
Nr.Fine/Fine **$225**
Good/V.Good **$85**

_____. *Helmets*. First Edition:
Middletown, CT: Wesleyan University
Press, 1964
Nr.Fine/Fine **$200**
Good/V.Good **$75**

Dickinson, Emily. *Further Poems of
Emily Dickinson: Withheld from
Publication by her Sister Lavinia*. First
Edition: Boston: Little Brown, 1929
Nr.Fine/Fine **$200**
Good/V.Good **$125**

_____. *Bolts of Melody*. First
Edition: New York: Harper & Brothers,
1945
Nr.Fine/Fine................ **$145**
Good/V.Good **$65**

Dillon, George. *The Flowering Stone*.
First Edition: New York: The Viking
Press, 1931
Nr.Fine/Fine **$125**
Good/V.Good **$55**

_____. *Boy in the Wind*. First
Edition: New York: The Viking Press,
1927
Nr.Fine/Fine **$100**
Good/V.Good **$45**

Doolittle, Hilda (as by H. D.). *By Avon
River*. First Edition: New York:
Macmillan, 1949
Nr.Fine/Fine **$200**
Good/V.Good **$85**

_____. *Red Roses for Bronze.* First Edition: London: Chatto & Windus, 1931.
Nr.Fine/Fine **$275**
Good/V.Good **$150**

_____. *Hedylus.* First Edition: London and Boston: Basil Blackwell and Houghton, Mifflin, 1928
Nr.Fine/Fine **$275**
Good/V.Good **$155**

Dugan, Alan. *Poems.* First Edition: New Haven, CT: Yale University Press, 1961
Nr.Fine/Fine **$200**
Good/V.Good **$85**

_____. *Poems 2.* First Edition: New Haven, CT: Yale University Press, 1963
Nr.Fine/Fine **$50**
Good/V.Good **$20**

Dunbar, Paul Lawrence. *The Heart of Happy Hollow.* First Edition: New York: Dodd, Mead, 1904
Nr.Fine/Fine **$600**
Good/V.Good **$275**

_____. *Poems of the Cabin and Field.* First Edition: New York: Dodd, Mead, 1899
Nr.Fine/Fine **$275**
Good/V.Good **$100**

_____. *When Malindy Sings.* First Edition: New York: Dodd, Mead, 1903
Nr.Fine/Fine **$275**
Good/V.Good **$165**

Eberhart, Richard. *A Bravery of Earth.* Points of Issue: First State contains an errata slip First Edition: London: Cape, 1930.
Nr.Fine/Fine **$300**
Good/V.Good **$185**

_____. *An Herb Basket.* First Edition: Cummington, MA: Cummington Press, 1950
Nr.Fine/Fine **$350**

Good/V.Good **$250**

Eliot, T. S. *The Cocktail Party.* Point of Issue: Misprint "here" for "her" on Page 29. First Edition: London: Faber and Faber, 1950
Nr.Fine/Fine **$1600**
Good/V.Good **$1000**

_____. *Prufrock And Other Observations.* First Edition: London: The Egoist Press: 1917.
Nr.Fine/Fine **$30000**
Good/V.Good **$25000**

_____. *Poems.* First Edition: New York: Alfred A. Knopf, 1920
Nr.Fine/Fine **$4000**
Good/V.Good **$1850**

_____. *Old Possum's Book Of Practical Cats.* First Edition: London: Faber and Faber, 1939.
Nr.Fine/Fine **$3500**
Good/V.Good **$2000**

_____. *The Sacred Wood.* First Edition: London: Methuen, 1920
Nr.Fine/Fine **$1800**
Good/V.Good **$775**

Engle, Paul. *Worn Earth.* First Edition: New Haven: Yale University Press, 1932
Nr.Fine/Fine **$125**
Good/V.Good **$55**

_____. *Always The Land.* First Edition: New York: Random House, 1941
Nr.Fine/Fine **$75**
Good/V.Good **$30**

Fearing, Kenneth. *Poems.* First Edition: New York: Dynamo, 1935
Nr.Fine/Fine **$145**
Good/V.Good **$75**

_____. *Stranger at Coney Island and Other Poems.* First Edition: New York: Harcourt, Brace, 1948
Nr.Fine/Fine **$100**
Good/V.Good **$45**

Ferlinghetti, Lawrence. *Pictures of the*

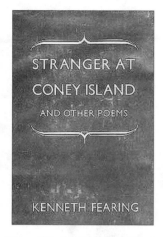

Stranger at Coney Island and Other Poems
by Kenneth Fearing

Gone World. Points of Issue: Stapled chapbook, Pocket Poets Series: Number One First Edition: San Francisco: City Lights Books, 1955
Nr.Fine/Fine **$450**
Good/V.Good **$200**

A Coney Island Of The Mind
by Lawrence Ferlinghetti

_____. *A Coney Island Of The Mind.* First Edition: Norfolk, CT: New Directions, 1958
Nr.Fine/Fine **$175**
Good/V.Good **$75**

_____. *The Old Italians Dying.* First Edition: San Francisco: City Lights Books, 1976
Nr.Fine/Fine **$300**
Good/V.Good **$200**

Field, Eugene. *Poems of Childhood.*

Points of Issue: Illustrated with color plates by Maxfield Parrish. First Edition: New York: Charles Scribners, 1904
Nr.Fine/Fine **$1000**
Good/V.Good **$625**

_____. *The Symbol and the Saint.* First Edition: Mt. Vernon, NY: William Edwin Rudge, 1924
Nr.Fine/Fine **$110**
Good/V.Good **$60**

_____. *The Love Affairs of A Bibliomaniac.* First Edition: New York: Scribners, 1896
Nr.Fine/Fine **$175**
Good/V.Good **$85**

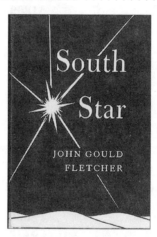

South Star
by John Gould Fletcher

Fletcher, John Gould. *South Star.* First Edition: New York: Macmillan, 1941
Nr.Fine/Fine **$95**
Good/V.Good **$40**

_____. *Fire and Wine.* First Edition: London: Grant Richards, 1913
Nr.Fine/Fine **$250**
Good/V.Good **$165**

_____. *Selected Poems.* First Edition: New York: Farrar & Rinehart, 1938
Nr.Fine/Fine **$55**
Good/V.Good **$20**

Ford, Charles Henri. *The Overturned Lake.* First Edition: Cincinnati, OH: Little

Man Press, 1941
Nr.Fine/Fine **$225**
Good/V.Good **$85**

_____. *Sleep In A Nest Of Flames.* First Edition: Norfolk, CT: New Directions, 1949
Nr.Fine/Fine **$75**
Good/V.Good **$45**

Frost, Robert. *A Boy's Will.* First Edition: London: David Nutt, 1913
Nr.Fine/Fine **$4500**
Good/V.Good **$2800**
First U.S. Edition: New York: Henry Holt, 1915
Nr.Fine/Fine **$3500**
Good/V.Good **$1800**

_____. *Mountain Interval.* First Edition: New York: Henry Holt, 1916
Nr.Fine/Fine **$3300**
Good/V.Good **$1000**

_____. *New Hampshire.* First Edition: New York: Henry Holt, 1923
Nr.Fine/Fine **$1200**
Good/V.Good **$375**

_____. *A Further Range.* First Edition (Limited): New York: Henry Holt, 1936
Nr.Fine/Fine **$600**
Good/V.Good **$275**
First Edition (Trade): New York: Henry

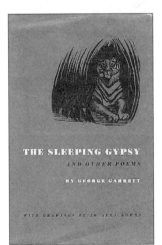

The Sleeping Gypsy
by George Garrett

Holt, 1936
Nr.Fine/Fine **$90**
Good/V.Good **$35**

Garrett, George. *The Sleeping Gypsy and Other Poems.* First Edition: Austin, TX: University of Texas Press, 1958
Nr.Fine/Fine **$75**
Good/V.Good **$30**

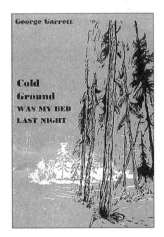

Cold Ground
Was My Bed
Last Night
by George Garrett

_____. *Cold Ground Was My Bed Last Night.* First Edition: Columbia, MO: University of Missouri Press, 1964
Nr.Fine/Fine **$45**
Good/V.Good **$20**

Garrique, Jean. *Selected Poems.* First Edition: Urbana, IL: University of Illinois Press, 1992
Nr.Fine/Fine **$25**
Good/V.Good **$10**

Ginsberg, Allen. *Reality Sandwiches.* First Edition: San Francisco: City Lights Books, 1963
Nr.Fine/Fine **$75**
Good/V.Good **$30**

_____. *T.V. Baby Poems.* First Edition (Hardcover Limited): London: Cape Goliard Press, 1967
Nr.Fine/Fine **$350**
Good/V.Good **$185**
First Edition (Softcover Trade):
Nr.Fine/Fine **$45**
Good/V.Good **$20**

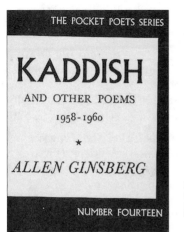

Kaddish and
Other Poems
1958-1960
*by Allen
Ginsberg*

_____. *Kaddish and Other Poems 1958-1960.* Points of Issue: Softcover, Number 14 in the Pocket Poets. First Edition: San Francisco: City Lights Books, 1961
Nr.Fine/Fine **$225**
Good/V.Good **$85**

The Dead of
Spring
by Paul Goodman

Goodman, Paul. *The Dead of Spring.* Point of Issue: Spiral bound. First Edition: Glen Gardner, NJ: Libertarian Press, 1950.
Nr.Fine/Fine **$200**
Good/V.Good **$60**

_____. *Parents Day.* First Edition: Saugatuck CT: The 5x8 Press, 1951
Nr.Fine/Fine **$125**

Good/V.Good **$75**

Parent's Day
by Paul Goodman

North Percy
by Paul Goodman

_____. *North Percy.* First Edition (Hardcover-Limited): Los Angeles: Black Sparrow Press, 1968
Nr.Fine/Fine **$100**
Good/V.Good **$45**
First Edition (Softcover-Trade): Los Angeles: Black Sparrow Press, 1968
Nr.Fine/Fine **$30**
Good/V.Good **$15**

Guest, Edgar A. *Passing Throng.* First Edition: Chicago: Reilly & Lee, 1923
Nr.Fine/Fine **$35**
Good/V.Good **$15**

_____. *Over Here.* First Edition: Chicago: Reilly and Britton, 1918

Passing Throng
by Edgar A. Guest

Nr.Fine/Fine **$55**
Good/V.Good **$30**

_____. *A Heap O' Livin.'* First
Edition: Chicago: Reilly & Lee, 1916
Nr.Fine/Fine **$40**
Good/V.Good **$20**

Guiney, Louise Imogen. *Happy Ending,
The Collected Lyrics of Louise Imogen
Guiney.* First Edition: Boston & NY:
Houghton Mifflin, 1909
Nr.Fine/Fine **$450**
Good/V.Good **$200**

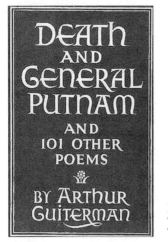

**Death and
General Putnam**
by Arthur Guiterman

Guiterman, Arthur. *Death and General
Putnam.* First Edition: New York: Dutton,
1935

Nr.Fine/Fine **$35**
Good/V.Good **$15**

_____. *Ballads of Old New
York.* First Edition: New York: Harper &
Brothers, 1920
Nr.Fine/Fine **$45**
Good/V.Good **$20**

Harris, Thomas Lake. *Star-Flowers, a
Poem of the Woman's Mystery.* (First
Canto) First Edition: Fountaingrove, CA:
Privately printed, 1886
Nr.Fine/Fine **$350**
Good/V.Good **$200**

Heyward, Dubose. *Skylines and
Horizons.* First Edition: New York:
Macmillan, 1924.
Nr.Fine/Fine **$155**
Good/V.Good **$65**

Hecht, Anthony. *A Summoning Of
Stones.* First Edition: New York:
Macmillan, 1954
Nr.Fine/Fine **$175**
Good/V.Good **$85**

_____. *The Venetian Vespers.*
First Edition (Limited-Signed): Boston:
David R. Godine, 1979
Nr.Fine/Fine **$450**
Good/V.Good **$275**
First Edition (Trade): New York:
Atheneum, 1979
Nr.Fine/Fine **$75**
Good/V.Good **$40**

Hillyer, Robert. *The Death Of Captain
Nemo.* First Edition: New York: Alfred A.
Knopf, 1949
Nr.Fine/Fine **$95**
Good/V.Good **$35**

_____. *The Relic and Other
Poems.* First Edition: New York: Alfred A.
Knopf, 1957
Nr.Fine/Fine **$45**
Good/V.Good **$15**

Holmes, John Clellon. *The Bowling
Green Poems.* First Edition: California,

PA: Arthur & Kit Knight, 1977
Nr.Fine/Fine **$125**
Good/V.Good **$65**

Howe, M. A. De Wolfe. *Shadows.* First
Edition: Boston: Copeland and Day, 1897
Nr.Fine/Fine **$85**
Good/V.Good **$55**

Hubbard, Elbert. *One Day; a Tale of the Prairies.* First Edition: Boston: Arena, 1893.
Nr.Fine/Fine **$850**
Good/V.Good **$400**

_____. *This Then is a William Morris Book: Being A Little Journey By Elbert Hubbard, & Some Letters, Heretofore Unpublished, Written To His Friend & Fellow Worker, Robert Thomson, All Throwing A Side-Light, More or Less, On The Man and His Times.* First Edition: East Aurora, NY, The Roycrofters, 1907
Nr.Fine/Fine **$155**
Good/V.Good **$65**

Hughes, Langston. *The Ways of White Folks.* First Edition: New York: Alfred A. Knopf, 1934
Nr.Fine/Fine **$275**
Good/V.Good **$135**

_____. *Tambourines to Glory.* First Edition: New York: John Day, 1958
Nr.Fine/Fine **$300**
Good/V.Good **$125**

_____. *Simple Speaks His Mind.* First Edition: New York: Simon & Schuster, 1950.
Nr.Fine/Fine **$300**
Good/V.Good **$200**

Hughes, Langston and Roy De Carava. *The Sweet Flypaper of Life.* First Edition: New York: Simon & Schuster, 1955
Nr.Fine/Fine **$850**
Good/V.Good **$350**

Hughes, Ted. *Crow.* First Edition: London: Faber and Faber, 1970
Nr.Fine/Fine **$300**

Good/V.Good **$140**

Crow
by Ted Hughes

_____. *The Hawk in the Rain.* First Edition: London, Faber and Faber, 1957.
Nr.Fine/Fine **$500**
Good/V.Good **$300**
First U.S. Edition: New York: Harper & Brothers, 1957
Nr.Fine/Fine **$200**
Good/V.Good **$85**

Gaudette
by Ted Hughes

_____. *Gaudette.* First Edition: London: Faber & Faber, 1977
Nr.Fine/Fine **$75**
Good/V.Good **$35**
First U.S. Edition: New York: Harper & Row, 1977

Nr.Fine/Fine **$55**
Good/V.Good **$25**

Jarrell, Randall. *The Lost World.* First
Edition: New York: Macmillan, 1965
Nr.Fine/Fine **$100**
Good/V.Good **$40**

_____. *A Sad Heart at the
Supermarket. Essays & Fables.* First
Edition: New York: Atheneum, 1962
Nr.Fine/Fine **$45**
Good/V.Good **$20**

_____. *The Seven League
Crutches.* First Edition: New York:
Harcourt Brace, 1951
Nr.Fine/Fine **$200**
Good/V.Good **$75**

Dear Judas
by Robinson Jeffers

Jeffers, Robinson. *Dear Judas.* First
Edition: New York: Horace Liveright,
1929
Nr.Fine/Fine **$225**
Good/V.Good **$100**

_____. *Thurso's Landing and
Other Poems.* First Edition: New York:
Horace Liveright, 1932
Nr.Fine/Fine **$250**
Good/V.Good **$125**

_____. *The Women at Point
Sur.* First Edition: New York: Boni &
Liveright, Inc., 1927
Nr.Fine/Fine **$165**
Good/V.Good **$75**

Kemp, Harry. *The Passing God.* First
Edition: New York: Brentano's, 1919
Nr.Fine/Fine **$45**
Good/V.Good **$20**

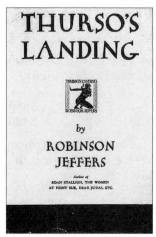

Thurso's
Landing and
Other Poems
by Robinson Jeffers

Kerouac, Jack. *Scattered Poems.* First
Edition: San Francisco: City Lights
Books, 1971
Nr.Fine/Fine **$75**
Good/V.Good **$45**

_____. *Book of Dreams.* Points of
Issue: The First State has dark blue wraps
First Edition: San Francisco: City Lights
Books, 1961
Nr.Fine/Fine **$200**
Good/V.Good **$85**

Kilmer, Joyce. *Trees and Other Poems.*
First Edition: New York: George H.
Doran, 1914
Nr.Fine/Fine **$450**
Good/V.Good **$250**

_____. *Main Street and Other
Poems.* First Edition: New York: George
H. Doran, 1917
Nr.Fine/Fine **$135**
Good/V.Good **$65**

Kipling, Rudyard. *Departmental Ditties,
Barrack-Room Ballads and Other Verses.*
First U.S. Edition: New York: United
States Book Company, successors to John
W. Lovell Company, 1890.

Nr.Fine/Fine **$300**
Good/V.Good **$135**

Kreymborg, Alfred. *Scarlet and Mellow.*
First Edition: New York: Boni &
Liveright, 1926
Nr.Fine/Fine **$85**
Good/V.Good **$35**

_____. *Manhattan Men.*
First Edition: New York: Coward-
McCann, 1929
Nr.Fine/Fine **$60**
Good/V.Good **$25**

Kunitz, Stanley. *The Wellfleet Whale.*
First Edition: New York: Sheep Meadow
Press, 1983
Nr.Fine/Fine **$135**
Good/V.Good **$55**

Lanier, Sidney. *Poems.* First Edition:
Philadelphia: J. B. Lippincott, 1877
Nr.Fine/Fine **$200**
Good/V.Good **$95**

Lazarus, Emma. *Admetus and Other
Poems.* First Edition: New York: Hurd
And Houghton, 1871
Nr.Fine/Fine **$325**
Good/V.Good **$150**

Le Gallienne, Richard. *The Religion of a
Literary Man.* First Edition: London:
Elkin Matthews & John Lane, 1893
Nr.Fine/Fine **$275**
Good/V.Good **$125**

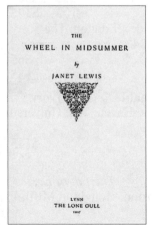

The Wheel in
Midsummer
by Janet Lewis

_____. *Painted Shadows.*
First U.S. Edition: Boston: Little, Brown,
1904
Nr.Fine/Fine **$250**
Good/V.Good **$110**

Lewis, Janet. *The Wheel in Midsummer.*
Points of Issue: Paperback Original. First
Edition: Lynn: The Lone Gull, 1927
Nr.Fine/Fine **$350**
Good/V.Good **$200**

_____. *The Wife of Martin Guerre.*
First Edition: San Francisco: Colt Press,
1941
Nr.Fine/Fine **$275**
Good/V.Good **$150**

The Tree of
Laughing Bells
by Vachel Lindsay

Lindsay, Vachel. *The Tree of Laughing
Bells.* First Edition: n.p.: by the Author,
1905
Nr.Fine/Fine **$2000**
Good/V.Good **$1200**

_____. *Rhymes To Be Traded
For Bread.* Points of Issue: Staple bound
on newsprint stock. First Edition:
Springfield, IL: by the Author, 1912
Nr.Fine/Fine **$850**
Good/V.Good **$500**

_____. *Every Soul is a Circus.*
First Edition: New York: Macmillan, 1929
Nr.Fine/Fine **$150**
Good/V.Good **$50**

_____. *The Golden Whales of
California and Other Rhymes in the*

American Language. First Edition: New York: Macmillan, 1920
Nr.Fine/Fine **$200**
Good/V.Good **$65**

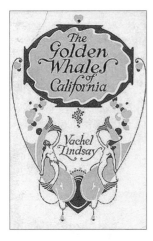

The Golden Whales of Califonia
by Vachel Lindsay

Lowell, Amy. *Men, Women And Ghosts.* First Edition: New York: Macmillan, 1916
Nr.Fine/Fine **$125**
Good/V.Good **$55**

_____. *Pictures of the Floating World.* First Edition: New York: Macmillan, 1919
Nr.Fine/Fine **$200**
Good/V.Good **$125**

_____. *Can Grande's Castle.* First Edition: New York: Macmillan, 1918
Nr.Fine/Fine **$85**
Good/V.Good **$35**

Lowell, Robert. *Land of Unlikeness.* First Edition: Cummington, MA: Cummington Press, 1944
Nr.Fine/Fine **$2750**
Good/V.Good **$1275**

_____. *Lord Weary's Castle.* First Edition: New York: Harcourt, Brace, 1946.
Nr.Fine/Fine **$325**
Good/V.Good **$145**

_____. *Near the Ocean.* First Edition: New York, Farrar, Straus and

Giroux, 1967
Nr.Fine/Fine **$125**
Good/V.Good **$55**

McCrae, John. *In Flanders Fields.* First U.K. Edition: London: Hodder & Stoughton, 1919
Nr.Fine/Fine **$75**
Good/V.Good **$30**
First U.S. Edition: New York: Putnams, 1919
Nr.Fine/Fine **$75**
Good/V.Good **$35**

McGinley, Phyllis. *A Short Walk from the Station.* First Edition: New York: Viking, 1951
Nr.Fine/Fine **$35**
Good/V.Good **$15**

_____. *The Plain Princess.* First Edition: Philadelphia: JB Lippincott, 1945
Nr.Fine/Fine **$45**
Good/V.Good **$20**

Machen, Arthur. *Ornaments in Jade.* First Edition: New York: Alfred A. Knopf, 1924
Nr.Fine/Fine **$225**
Good/V.Good **$125**

_____. *Strange Roads With the Gods in Spring.* First Edition (Limited-Signed): London: The Classic Press, 1924.
Nr.Fine/Fine **$300**
Good/V.Good **$175**
First Edition (Trade): London: The Classic Press, 1924.
Nr.Fine/Fine **$65**
Good/V.Good **$35**

Macleish, Archibald. *Tower of Ivory.* First Edition: New Haven: Yale University Press, 1917
Nr.Fine/Fine **$145**
Good/V.Good **$65**

_____. *The Pot of Earth.* First Edition: Boston: Houghton Mifflin, 1925

Nr.Fine/Fine **$85**
Good/V.Good **$40**

_____. *The Happy Marriage and Other Poems.* First Edition: Boston: Houghton Mifflin, 1924
Nr.Fine/Fine **$75**
Good/V.Good **$25**

March, Joseph Moncure. *The Wild Party.* First Edition: Chicago: Pascal Covici, 1928
Nr.Fine/Fine **$175**
Good/V.Good **$80**

_____. *The Set-Up.* First Edition: New York: Covici-Friede, 1928
Nr.Fine/Fine **$125**
Good/V.Good **$85**

Markham,Edwin. *The Man With The Hoe.* First Edition: San Francisco, CA: A. M. Robertson, 1899
Nr.Fine/Fine **$225**
Good/V.Good **$135**

_____. *Gates of Paradise and other Poems.* First Edition: Garden City, NY: Doubleday Page, 1920
Nr.Fine/Fine **$45**
Good/V.Good **$20**

Masefield, John. *Salt-Water Ballads.* First Edition: London: Grant Richards, 1902.
Nr.Fine/Fine **$1200**
Good/V.Good **$725**
First U.S. Edition: New York: Macmillan, 1913
Nr.Fine/Fine **$250**
Good/V.Good **$145**

_____. *The Midnight Folk.* First Edition: London: Heinemann, 1927.
Nr.Fine/Fine **$200**
Good/V.Good **$95**

_____. *Right Royal.* First Edition: London: Heinemann, 1920
Nr.Fine/Fine **$75**
Good/V.Good **$25**

Spoon River Anthology
by Edgar Lee Masters

Masters, Edgar Lee. *Spoon River Anthology.* First Edition: New York: Macmillan, 1915
Nr.Fine/Fine **$3000**
Good/V.Good **$1650**

_____. *Starved Rock.* First Edition: New York Macmillan, 1919.
Nr.Fine/Fine **$55**
Good/V.Good **$20**

Merwin, W. S. *A Mask For Janus.* First Edition: New Haven: Yale University Press, 1952
Nr.Fine/Fine **$1100**
Good/V.Good **$375**

Miles, Josephine. *Lines At Intersection.* First Edition: New York: Macmillan, 1939
Nr.Fine/Fine **$65**
Good/V.Good **$30**

Millay, Edna St. Vincent. *Renascence and Other Poems.* Points of Issue: Watermarked Paper First Edition: New York: Mitchell Kennerley, 1917
Nr.Fine/Fine **$2100**
Good/V.Good **$850**

_____. *Buck in the Snow and Other Poems.* First Edition: New York: Harper and Brothers, 1928
Nr.Fine/Fine **$145**
Good/V.Good **$55**

_____. *Wine from These*

Grapes. First Edition: New York: Harper & Brothers, 1934
Nr.Fine/Fine **$75**
Good/V.Good **$35**

The Buck in the Snow and Other Poems
by Edna St. Vincent Millay

_____. *Make Bright the Arrows.* First Edition: New York: Harper & Brothers, 1940
Nr.Fine/Fine **$55**
Good/V.Good **$25**

Miller, Joaquin. *In Classic Shades and Other Poems.* First Edition: Chicago: Belford-Clarke, 1890
Nr.Fine/Fine **$400**
Good/V.Good **$225**

Moore, Marianne. *Observations.* First Edition: New York: Dial Press, 1924
Nr.Fine/Fine **$2550**
Good/V.Good **$1400**

_____. *O To Be A Dragon.* First Edition: New York: Viking, 1959
Nr.Fine/Fine **$155**
Good/V.Good **$45**

Moore, Merrill M. *One Thousand Autobiographical Sonnets.* First Edition: New York: Harcourt, Brace, 1938
Nr.Fine/Fine **$150**
Good/V.Good **$95**

Nash, Ogden. *Hard Lines.* First Edition: New York: Simon and Schuster, 1931
Nr.Fine/Fine **$200**

Good/V.Good **$110**

_____. *The Face is Familiar.* First Edition: Boston: Little, Brown, 1940
Nr.Fine/Fine **$55**
Good/V.Good **$25**

_____. *Free Wheeling.* First Edition: New York: Simon & Schuster, 1931
Nr.Fine/Fine **$110**
Good/V.Good **$45**

Nathan, Robert. *Youth Grows Old.* First Edition: New York: Robert M. McBride, 1922
Nr.Fine/Fine **$115**
Good/V.Good **$65**

_____. *Morning in Iowa.* First Edition: New York: Alfred A. Knopf, 1944
Nr.Fine/Fine **$55**
Good/V.Good **$25**

_____. *A Cedar Box.* First Edition: Indianapolis Bobbs-Merrill, 1929
Nr.Fine/Fine **$85**
Good/V.Good **$35**

Noguchi, Yone. *Seen and Unseen.* First Edition: New York: Orientalia, 1920
Nr.Fine/Fine **$450**
Good/V.Good **$275**

O'Sheel, Shaemas. *The Blossomy Bough: Poems.* First Edition: New York: published by the author through The Franklin Press, 1911
Nr.Fine/Fine **$100**
Good/V.Good **$40**

Parker, Dorothy. *Sunset Gun.* First Edition (Limited): New York: Boni & Liveright, 1928
Nr.Fine/Fine **$650**
Good/V.Good **$400**
First Edition (Trade): New York: Boni & Liveright, 1928
Nr.Fine/Fine **$125**
Good/V.Good **$50**

_____. *Enough Rope.* First

Edition: New York: Boni & Liveright, 1926

Nr.Fine/Fine **$750**
Good/V.Good **350**

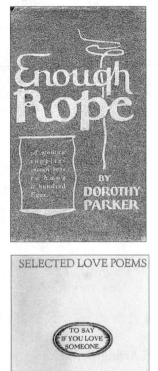

Enough Rope
by Dorothy Parker

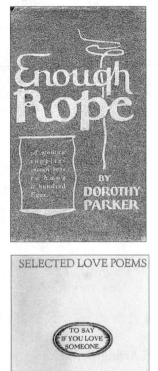

To Say If You Love Someone
by Kenneth Patchen

Patchen, Kenneth. *To Say If You Love Someone.* First Edition: Prairie City, IL: The Decker Press, 1948

Nr.Fine/Fine **$2750**
Good/V.Good **$1250**

_____. *First Will & Testament.*
First Edition: Norfolk, CT: New Directions, 1939

Nr.Fine/Fine **$650**
Good/V.Good **$225**

_____. *The Famous Boating Party*. First Edition: New York: New Directions, 1954

Nr.Fine/Fine **$135**
Good/V.Good **$55**

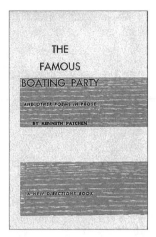

The Famous
Boating Party
by Kenneth Patchen

Plath, Sylvia. *The Colossus.* First Edition: London: Heinemann, 1960

Nr.Fine/Fine **$1600**
Good/V.Good **$575**

Pound, Ezra. *Lustra.* First Edition (Limited): London: Elkin Mathews, 1916.

Nr.Fine/Fine **$2,500**
Good/V.Good **$875**

First Edition (Trade-Abridged): London: Elkin Mathews, 1916.

Nr.Fine/Fine **$350**
Good/V.Good **$185**

_____. *Pavannes and Divisions.*
First Edition: New York: Alfred A. Knopf, 1918

Nr.Fine/Fine **$550**
Good/V.Good **$150**

_____. *Indiscretions.* First Edition: Paris: Three Mountains Press, 1923.

Nr.Fine/Fine **$1500**
Good/V.Good **$725**

Ransom, John Crowe. *Two Gentlemen In Bonds.* First Edition: New York: Alfred A.

Knopf, 1927
Nr.Fine/Fine **$550**
Good/V.Good **$200**

Reese, Lizette Woodworth. *A Branch of May.* First Edition: Baltimore: Cushings & Bailey, 1887
Nr.Fine/Fine **$400**
Good/V.Good **$180**

Rexroth, Kenneth. *The Art of Worldly Wisdom.* First Edition: Prairie City, IL: Decker Press, 1949
Nr.Fine/Fine **$450**
Good/V.Good **$250**

_____. *In What Hour.* Point of Issue: Contains errata slip. First Edition: New York: Macmillan, 1940
Nr.Fine/Fine **$350**
Good/V.Good **$165**

_____. *The Signature of All Things.* First Edition: New York: New Directions, 1949
Nr.Fine/Fine **$125**
Good/V.Good **$50**

Rich, Adrienne Cecile. *A Change of World.* First Edition: New Haven, CT: Yale University Press, 1951
Nr.Fine/Fine **$1000**
Good/V.Good **$600**

_____. *The Diamond Cutters And Other Poems.* First Edition: New York: Harper & Brothers, 1955
Nr.Fine/Fine **$300**
Good/V.Good **$125**

Riding, Laura. *The Life Of The Dead.* First Edition: London: Arthur Barker, 1933
Nr.Fine/Fine **$750**
Good/V.Good **$425**

Riley, James Whitcomb. *Child-World.* First Edition: Indianapolis, Bowen-Merrill, 1897
Nr.Fine/Fine **$550**
Good/V.Good **$200**

_____. *An Old Sweetheart of Mine.* First Illustrated Edition (Howard Chandler Christy): Indianapolis, IN: Bobbs-Merrill, 1902
Nr.Fine/Fine **$450**
Good/V.Good **$225**

An Old Sweetheart Of Mine *by James Whitcomb Riley*

_____. *Rubaiyat of Doc Sifers.* First Edition: New York: Century, 1897
Nr.Fine/Fine **$325**
Good/V.Good **$145**

Robinson, Edwin Arlington. *The Torrent and the Night Before.* First Edition: Gardiner, ME: Printed For The Author (Riverside Press), 1896
Nr.Fine/Fine **$2000**
Good/V.Good **$1200**

_____. *The Children of the Night.* First Edition: Boston: Richard G. Badger, 1897
Nr.Fine/Fine **$500**
Good/V.Good **$275**

_____. *Tristram.* First Edition: New York: Macmillan, 1927.
Nr.Fine/Fine **$75**
Good/V.Good **$35**

_____. *Cavender's House.* First Edition: New York: Macmillan, 1929
Nr.Fine/Fine **$95**
Good/V.Good **$50**

Roethke, Theodore. *Open House*. First Edition: New York: Alfred A. Knopf, 1941.
Nr.Fine/Fine **$950**
Good/V.Good **$350**

Rukeyser, Muriel. *Orpheus*. First Edition: San Francisco: Centaur Press, 1949.
Nr.Fine/Fine **$75**
Good/V.Good **$45**

Sandburg, Carl. *Cornhuskers*. First Edition: New York: Henry Holt and Co., 1918.
Nr.Fine/Fine **$950**
Good/V.Good **$355**

_____. *Chicago Poems*. First Edition: New York: Henry Holt, 1916
Nr.Fine/Fine **$1450**
Good/V.Good **$825**

_____. *Potato Face*. First Edition: New York: Harcourt Brace, 1930
Nr.Fine/Fine **$500**
Good/V.Good **$175**

Sarton, May. *Encounter in April*. First Edition: Boston: Houghton Mifflin. 1937
Nr.Fine/Fine **$500**
Good/V.Good **$250**

_____. *Inner Landscape*. First Edition: Boston: Houghton Mifflin, 1939
Nr.Fine/Fine **$225**
Good/V.Good **$100**

Schwartz, Delmore. *In Dreams Begin Responsibilities*. First Edition: Norfolk, CT: New Directions, 1938
Nr.Fine/Fine **$550**
Good/V.Good **$200**

_____. *Vaudeville For a Princess and Other Poems*. First Edition: Norfolk, CT: New Directions, 1950
Nr.Fine/Fine **$150**
Good/V.Good **$65**

Sexton, Anne. *The Book of Folly*. First Edition (Limited-Signed): Boston: Houghton Mifflin, 1972

Nr.Fine/Fine **$475**
Good/V.Good **$275**
First Edition (Trade): Boston: Houghton Mifflin, 1972
Nr.Fine/Fine **$85**
Good/V.Good **$35**

_____. *Transformations*. First Edition (Limited-Signed): Boston: Houghton Mifflin, 1971
Nr.Fine/Fine **$225**
Good/V.Good **$100**
First Edition (Trade): Boston: Houghton Mifflin, 1971
Nr.Fine/Fine **$100**
Good/V.Good **$45**

Shapiro, Karl. *Trial of a Poet*. First Edition (Limited-Signed): New York: Reynal & Hitchcock, 1947
Nr.Fine/Fine **$240**
Good/V.Good **$125**
First Edition (Trade): New York: Reynal & Hitchcock, 1947
Nr.Fine/Fine **$85**
Good/V.Good **$40**

_____. *In Defense of Ignorance*. First Edition: New York: Random House, 1960.
Nr.Fine/Fine **$45**
Good/V.Good **$20**

Simpson, Louis. *Caviare at the Funeral*. First Edition: New York: Franklin Watts, 1980
Nr.Fine/Fine **$25**
Good/V.Good **$12**

Snodgrass, W.D. *Heart's Needle*. First Edition: New York: Alfred A. Knopf, 1959
Nr.Fine/Fine **$275**
Good/V.Good **$125**

Snow, Wilbert. *Down East*. First Edition: New York: Gotham House, 1932
Nr.Fine/Fine **$50**
Good/V.Good **$15**

Snyder, Gary. *Riprap*. First Edition: Ashland, MA: Origin Press, 1959

Nr.Fine/Fine **$1000**
Good/V.Good **$650**

Riprap
by Gary Snyder

_____. *Six Sections From Mountains And Rivers Without End.* First Edition: San Francisco: Four Seasons Foundation, 1965
Nr.Fine/Fine **$85**
Good/V.Good **$35**

Earth House Hold
by Gary Snyder

_____. *Earth House Hold.* First Edition: New York: New Directions, 1969
Nr.Fine/Fine **$225**
Good/V.Good **$75**

Speyer, Leonora. *Slow Wall: Poems New and Selected.* First Edition: New York: Alfred A. Knopf, 1939

Nr.Fine/Fine **$45**
Good/V.Good **$20**

Slow Wall: Poems New and Selected
by Leonora Speyer

_____. *Fiddler's Farewell.* First Edition: New York: Alfred A. Knopf, 1926
Nr.Fine/Fine **$75**
Good/V.Good **$30**

Stein, Gertrude. *Two Poems.* First Edition: Paulet, VT: The Banyan Press, 1948
Nr.Fine/Fine **$250**
Good/V.Good **$110**

_____. *Rose Is A Rose Is A Rose Is A Rose.* First Edition: New York: William R. Scott, 1939
Nr.Fine/Fine **$275**
Good/V.Good **$150**

Stevens, Wallace. *Harmonium.* First Edition: New York: Alfred A. Knopf, 1923.
Nr.Fine/Fine **$3500**
Good/V.Good **$1800**

_____. *The Man With The Blue Guitar & Other Poems.* First Edition: New York: Alfred A. Knopf, 1937.
Nr.Fine/Fine **$1600**
Good/V.Good **$925**

_____. *The Auroras of Autumn.* First Edition: New York: Alfred A. Knopf, 1950.

Nr.Fine/Fine **$500**
Good/V.Good **$275**

_____. *Parts Of A World.* First Edition: New York: Alfred A. Knopf, 1942
Nr.Fine/Fine **$800**
Good/V.Good **$375**

Stoddard, Charles Warren. *South Sea Idyls.* First Edition: Boston: James R. Osgood, 1873
Nr.Fine/Fine **$325**
Good/V.Good **$165**

_____. *A Troubled Heart and How it was Comforted at Last.* First Edition: Notre Dame, IN: Joseph A. Lyons, 1885
Nr.Fine/Fine **$185**
Good/V.Good **$100**

Taylor, Bayard. *The Masque of the Gods.* First Edition: Boston: James R. Osgood and Company, 1872
Nr.Fine/Fine **$75**
Good/V.Good **$40**

Teasdale, Sara. *Rivers to the Sea.* First Edition: New York: Macmillan, 1915
Nr.Fine/Fine **$65**
Good/V.Good **$25**

_____. *Flame and Shadow.* First Edition: New York: Macmillan, 1920
Nr.Fine/Fine **$50**
Good/V.Good **$20**

_____. *Sonnets to Duse and other Poems.* First Edition: Boston: The Poet Lore Company Publishers, 1907
Nr.Fine/Fine **$2600**
Good/V.Good **$1450**

Thomas, Dylan. *Deaths and Entrances.* First Edition: London: J.M. Dent, 1946
Nr.Fine/Fine **$700**
Good/V.Good **$425**

_____. *Under The Milkwood.* First Edition: London: J.M. Dent, 1954
Nr.Fine/Fine **$175**
Good/V.Good **$60**
First U.S. Edition: New York: New Directions, 1954.
Nr.Fine/Fine **$100**
Good/V.Good **$35**

_____. *In Country Sleep.* First Edition (Limited): New York: New Directions, 1952.
Nr.Fine/Fine **$4600**
Good/V.Good **$2200**
First Edition (Trade): New York: New Directions, 1952.
Nr.Fine/Fine **$300**
Good/V.Good **$100**

Untermeyer, Louis. *Challenge.* First Edition: New York: The Century Co., 1914
Nr.Fine/Fine. **$90**
Good/V.Good **$35**

_____. *First Love: A Lyric Sequence.* First Edition: Boston: Sherman French, 1911
Nr.Fine/Fine **$100**
Good/V.Good **$40**

THE COUNTRY YEAR

Poems by Mark Van Doren

The Country Year
by Mark Van Doren

Van Doren, Mark. *The Country Year.*
First Edition: New York: William Sloane
Associates, 1946
Nr.Fine/Fine **$45**
Good/V.Good **$20**

_____. *Now the Sky & Other
Poems.* First Edition: New York: Albert &
Charles Boni, 1928
Nr.Fine/Fine **$175**
Good/V.Good **$75**

Van Dyke, Henry. *The Golden Key.* First
Edition: New York: Scribners, 1926
Nr.Fine/Fine **$175**
Good/V.Good **$95**

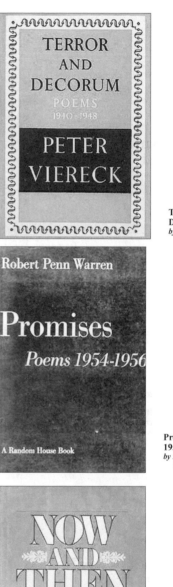

Terror and
Decorum
by Peter Viereck

The Blue Flower
by Henry Van Dyke

_____. *The Blue Flower.* First
Edition: New York: Scribners, 1902
Nr.Fine/Fine **$65**
Good/V.Good **$35**

Viereck, Peter. *Terror and Decorum-
Poems 1940-1948.* First Edition:
Nr.Fine/Fine **$30**
Good/V.Good **$12**

_____. *The Tree Witch.* First
Edition: New York: Scribners, 1961
Nr.Fine/Fine **$35**
Good/V.Good **$15**

Warren, Robert Penn. *Promises: Poems
1954-1956.* First Edition: New York:
Random House, 1957

Promises: Poems
1954-1956
*by Robert Penn
Warren*

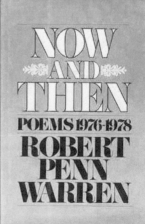

Now and Then:
Poems 1976-1978
*by Robert Penn
Warren*

Nr.Fine/Fine **$150**
Good/V.Good **$50**

_____. *Now And Then: Poems 1976-1978*. First Edition: New York: Random House, 1978.
Nr.Fine/Fine **$45**
Good/V.Good **$20**

_____. *Or Else: Poems, 1968-1973*. First Edition (Limited-Signed): New York: Random House, 1974.
Nr.Fine/Fine **$165**
Good/V.Good **$75**
First Edition (Trade): New York: Random House, 1974.
Nr.Fine/Fine **$30**
Good/V.Good **$12**

Widdemer, Margaret. *The Singing Wood*. First Edition: New York: Adelphi Company, 1926
Nr.Fine/Fine.................. **$35**
Good/V.Good **$15**

_____. *The Road to Downderry and Other Poems*. First Edition: New York: Farrar & Rinehart, 1932
Nr.Fine/Fine **$25**
Good/V.Good **$10**

Wilbur, Richard. *The Beautiful Changes and other Poems*. First Edition: New York: Renal & Hitchcock, 1947
Nr.Fine/Fine **$140**
Good/V.Good **$80**

_____. *Things of This World*. First Edition: New York: Harcourt Brace, 1956.
Nr.Fine/Fine **$145**
Good/V.Good **$65**

Wilcox, Ella Wheeler (As by Ella Wheeler). *Maurine*. First Edition: Milwaukee: Cramer, Aikens & Cramer, 1876.
Nr.Fine/Fine **$325**
Good/V.Good **$185**

_____. *Poems of Experience.* First Edition: London: Gay and Handcock, 1910

Nr.Fine/Fine **$95**
Good/V.Good **$50**

_____. *Poems of Passion*. First Edition: Chicago: Belford, Clarke & Co, 1883.
Nr.Fine/Fine **$75**
Good/V.Good **$30**

_____. *An Erring Woman's Love*. First Edition: Chicago, W.B. Conkey, 1892.
Nr.Fine/Fine **$55**
Good/V.Good **$25**

Williams, William Carlos. *An Early Martyr*. First Edition: New York: The Alcestis Press, 1935.
Nr.Fine/Fine **$1500**
Good/V.Good **$850**

_____. *Kora in Hell: Improvisations*. First Edition: Boston: The Four Seas Company, 1920
Nr.Fine/Fine **$850**
Good/V.Good **$350**

_____. *The Desert Music*. First Edition (Limited-Signed): New York: Random House, 1954
Nr.Fine/Fine **$1250**
Good/V.Good **$875**
First Edition (Trade New York: Random House, 1954
Nr.Fine/Fine **$150**
Good/V.Good **$40**

Winters, Yvor. *The Bare Hills: A Book of Poems*. First Edition: Boston: Four Seas Company, 1927
Nr.Fine/Fine **$275**
Good/V.Good **$135**

_____. *The Proof*. First Edition: New York: Coward-McCann, 1930.
Nr.Fine/Fine **$125**
Good/V.Good **$55**

Wurdemann, Audrey. *House of Silk*. First Edition: New York: Harold Vinal, 1927
Nr.Fine/Fine **$180**
Good/V.Good **$75**

_____. *The Seven Sins.*
First Edition: New York: Harper and
Brothers, 1935.
Nr.Fine/Fine **$45**
Good/V.Good **$15**

Wylie, Elinor. *Nets to Catch the Wind.*
First Edition: New York: Harcourt Brace,
1921
Nr.Fine/Fine **$125**
Good/V.Good **$55**

Black Armour
by Elinor Wylie

_____. *Black Armour.* First
Edition: New York: George H. Doran,
1923.
Nr.Fine/Fine **$75**
Good/V.Good **$30**

Zaturenska, Marya. *Threshold and
Hearth.* First Edition: New York:
Macmillan, 1934.
Nr.Fine/Fine **$50**
Good/V.Good **$20**

Riley, James Whitcomb. *The Old
Swimmin-Hole and 'leven More Poems, By
Benj. F. Johnson, of Boone.* First Edition:
Indianapolis, Indiana: George C. Hitt & Co.,
1883.
Nr.Fine/Fine **$750**
Good/V.Good **$325**

Philosophy & Religion

Like the Occult, this is a very old area featuring books that were originally handwritten, or even chiseled in stone. It is, perhaps, a little more volatile for the collector. Advances in philosophy or religion usually take time to become noticed or recognized. Who was the leading living theologian, or leading philosopher at the turn of the twenty-first century? The fact is that we don't know yet. That is a lot of the enjoyment in collecting it. The hunt for the future is in either field.

Who were the leading figures of the twentieth century? In philosophy, we might say Jean Paul Sartre with his popularization of Existentialism, but will the future recognize Martin Heidigger, Karl Jaspers, or possibly Sidney Hook? Or, we might go from the academic to the popular and name Ayn Rand and her brand of radical individualism as the leading philosopher of the century just passed. In theology, will the future go for the founders of new denominations such as Charles Taze Russell and Mary Baker Eddy; or those who expanded older theologies, like Thomas Merton or Sri Aurobindo?

Napoleon once remarked that, had he been truly great, he would have lived in a garret and written two books. The reference is to Spinoza, a lens grinder who lived in an attic, where he wrote and self-published two of the most influential books the world has ever seen. It is a modern conceit that we would recognize Spinoza if he lived today. If we are honest with ourselves, we should recognize that the odds against someone like Spinoza being published today are somewhat greater than at any time in history. Since his time we have added qualification after degree, after connections to the bare recognition that anyone is even called a philosopher. A degreeless lens grinder would have his work,

despite the fact that it was a significant advance in the history of thought, returned with a form letter should he even try publication. It is the age of science, or we might even say, the dark age of science, and thought that is not derived scientifically has a hard road indeed. For the collector, this means that philosophy is a target of opportunity. If you owned one of the first printed copies of Spinoza's *Ethics*, you could contact an auction house and, without a doubt, forget that work, as a term, has any practical meaning in your life.

Except for the older veins of theology and religion, which have established clear paths of publication for adherents, new ideas and concepts in the field, as in philosophy, stand very little chance of trade publication. Martin Luther once nailed an invitation to debate 95 theological points to the door of a church. Within a year, what were, basically, pirated books containing that invitation rocked the world. This could not happen today. If the most advanced theological thought in the world were nailed to the doors of every church in America tomorrow, the most advanced theological thought in the world would be part of a landfill by Thursday. Of course, if any collector rescued just one copy, his heirs would probably become unspeakably wealthy.

Much of this genre is collected as First Thus. It crosses culture barriers, withstands the passage of time, and transcends language. Few people today could read Plato in his original form, most people in the Western world would be lost in the ideograms of Confucius' first editions, and don't even think about Zoroaster.

I have always enjoyed reading in this area. Speculations, reasonings, conclusions about Man, God and the universe are things that I find to be utterly fascinating. The more I read, the more I notice how right Socrates was all those centuries ago. Told he was the wisest man in Athens, he replied that he knew nothing, but that he was the only man in Athens who knew that he knew nothing. Collecting and reading all these nothings have given me hour upon hour of pleasure. Selling and dealing in them has been both profitable and rewarding. It is a field full of small and obscure publishers, writers and thinkers, full of both tomorrow and the stuff of landfills. The successful collector will have both, and not only profit materially, but mentally and spiritually as well. Perhaps, that is one of the best deals going.

Note on Bibles

The Bible is, at least in the Western World, the commonest book. I have seen numerous copies of it from the 1700s in yard sales in older communities. In Europe, it is not uncommon to find earlier copies. I have also seen and helped collectors build collections of the Bible in all its variations. Despite being old, however, few copies of the Bible are worth much. Rare and important Bibles are extremely rare and most are the property of libraries and museums. *The Gutenberg Bible* was also the first printed book and very valuable. The first Bible in any language, such as *The Mentelin Bible* in German printed in 1460, is usually valuable. Oddities and misprints, such as the Devil's Bible that left a "not" or two out of the 10 commandments, are also desirable. Some Bibles, such as that illustrated by Gustave Dore, are valuable for the illustrations. The average Bible, however, even those two hundred or more years old, are not worth much in the used book market.

One other facet of Bible collecting has to do with the practice of keeping family history on the blank pages. A bible owned by a prominent family, or showing the birth of a prominent person, might bring a good deal due to its historical value.

10 Classic Rarities

Emerson, Ralph Waldo. *Nature*. Boston: James Munroe and Company, 1836. First edition, first state, has P. 94 misnumbered 92.
Retail value in:
    Near Fine to Fine $3500
    Good to Very Good $2100

Glover, Mary Baker. *Science and Health*. Boston: Christian Scientist Publishing Company, 1875. Note the name of the author; reprints are as by Mary Baker Eddy.
Retail value in:
    Near Fine to Fine **$4500**
    Good to Very Good **$2000**

Holmes, Oliver Wendell. *The Common Law*. Boston: Little, Brown, and Company, 1881. Original is bound in russet cloth.
Retail value in:
    Near Fine to Fine **$3500**
    Good to Very Good **$1750**

Hurston, Zora Neale. *Moses Man of the Mountain*. Philadelphia: J.B. Lippincott Co., 1939. A study of Moses from an African-American folklore standpoint —as the great "Voodoo Man" of the Bible.
Retail value in:
    Near Fine to Fine **$3000**
    Good to Very Good **$1750**

Kyoka, Izumi. *The Tale Of The Wandering Monk*. New York: The Limited Editions Club, 1995. First U.S. Edition bound in white silk.
Retail value in:
    Near Fine to Fine **$2000**
    Good to Very Good **$1500**

Lewis, C.S. *The Screwtape Letters*. London: Geoffrey Bles, 1942. Instructions from the Devil, find this and buy him out.
Retail value in:
    Near Fine to Fine **$1500**
    Good to Very Good **$1000**

Merton, Thomas. *The Tower of Babel*. Hamburg, Germany: Printed for James Laughlin, 1957. A limited edition of 250 copies signed by Merton and the artist G. Marcks.
Retail value in:
    Near Fine to Fine **$2500**
    Good to Very Good **$1800**

Rand, Ayn. *Capitalism: The Unknown Ideal*. New York: The New American Library, 1966. Limited to 700 copies signed by Rand.
Retail value in:
    Near Fine to Fine **$3000**
    Good to Very Good **$2500**

Russell, Bertrand. *German Social Democracy: Six Lectures*. London: Longmans Green & Co., 1896. There are four variant bindings, 1000 copies total in first edition.
Retail value in:
    Near Fine condition **$2500**
    Good to Very Good **$1200**

Thoreau, Henry David. *Walden: or, Life in the Woods*. Boston: Ticknor and Fields, 1854. Simplify your life by finding this.
Retail value in:
    Near Fine to Fine **$15,000**
    Good to Very Good **$9000**

Price Guide

Abbott, Lyman. *My Four Anchors.* First Edition: Boston: The Pilgrim Press, 1911
Nr.Fine/Fine **$20**
Good/V.Good **$8**

_____. *The Christian Ministry.* First Edition: Boston: Houghton Mifflin, 1905
Nr.Fine/Fine **$175**
Good/V.Good **$65**

Adams, Hannah. *The History of the Jews from The Destruction of Jerusalem to the Present Time.* First Edition: London: A. Macintosh, 1818
Nr.Fine/Fine **$365**
Good/V.Good **$175**

_____. *Truth and Excellence of the Christian Religion Exhibited.* First Edition: Boston: John West, 1804
Nr.Fine/Fine **$250**
Good/V.Good **$100**

_____. *A Narrative Of The Controversy Between The Rev. Jedidiah Morse, Dd, And The Author.* First Edition: Boston: Cummings & Hilliard, 1814
Nr.Fine/Fine **$225**
Good/V.Good **$95**

Addams, Jane. *Newer Ideals of Peace.* First Edition: New York: Macmillan, 1907
Nr.Fine/Fine **$300**
Good/V.Good **$100**

Adler, Mortimer J. *What Man has Made of Man. A Study of the Consequences of Platonism and Positivism in Psychology.* First Edition: New York: Longmans, Green and Co., 1937
Nr.Fine/Fine **$65**
Good/V.Good **$35**

_____. *Time of Our Lives, The: The Ethics of Common Sense.* First Edition: New York: Holt, Rinehart & Winston, 1970
Nr.Fine/Fine **$50**
Good/V.Good **$20**

_____. *Philosopher at Large.* First Edition: New York: Macmillan, 1977
Nr.Fine/Fine **$35**
Good/V.Good **$15**

_____. *The Conditions of Philosophy: Its Checkered Past, Its Present Disorder, and Its Future Promise.* First Edition: New York: Atheneum, 1965
Nr.Fine/Fine **$35**
Good/V.Good **$15**

Alcott, Amos Bronson. *Tablets.* First Edition: Boston: Roberts Brothers, 1868
Nr.Fine/Fine **$350**
Good/V.Good **$145**

Andrews, Stephen Pearl. *Discoveries in Chinese or the Symbolism of the Primitive Characters of the Chinese System of Writing.* First Edition: New York: Charles B. Norton, 1854
Nr.Fine/Fine **$400**
Good/V.Good **$225**

Appleyard, Brian. *Understanding The Present: Science and The Soul of Modern Man.* First Edition: London: Picador, 1992.
Nr.Fine/Fine **$25**
Good/V.Good **$10**

Arendt, Hannah. *The Origins of Totalitarianism.* First Edition: New York: Harcourt Brace, 1951
Nr.Fine/Fine **$750**
Good/V.Good **$450**

_____. *The Human Condition.* First Edition: Chicago: University of Chicago Press, 1958
Nr.Fine/Fine **$95**
Good/V.Good **$25**

_____. *Eichmann in Jerusalem. A Report on the Banality of Evil.* First Edition: London: Faber and Faber, 1963
Nr.Fine/Fine **$65**
Good/V.Good **$20**
First U.S. Edition: New York: Viking, 1963.
Nr.Fine/Fine **$35**
Good/V.Good **$15**

_____. *The Burden of Our Time.*
First Edition: London: Secker & Warburg,
1951
Nr.Fine/Fine **$50**
Good/V.Good **$30**

Arnold, Matthew *God & The Bible.* First
Edition: London: Smith, Elder, 1875
Nr.Fine/Fine **$210**
Good/V.Good **$100**

_____. *Literature and Dogma: An
Essay Towards a Better Apprehension of the
Bible.* First Edition: London: Smith, Elder,
1873
Nr.Fine/Fine **$200**
Good/V.Good **$95**

_____. *Culture and Anarchy. An
Essay in Political and Social Criticism.* First
Edition: London: Smith, Elder, 1869
Nr.Fine/Fine **$500**
Good/V.Good **$225**

Arthur, Timothy Shay. *Ten Nights In A
Barroom and What I Saw There.* First Edition:
Philadelphia: Lippincott, Grambo & Co., 1855
Nr.Fine/Fine **$125**
Good/V.Good **$65**

Aurobindo, Sri. *Lights on Yoga.* First Edition:
Howrah, Calcutta: N Goswami, 1935
Nr.Fine/Fine **$155**
Good/V.Good **$85**

_____. *The Human Cycle.* First

Edition: Pondicherry: Sri Aurobindo Ashram,
1949
Nr.Fine/Fine **$55**
Good/V.Good **$30**

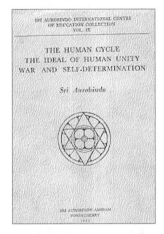

**The Human
Cycle**
by Sri Aurobindo

_____. *The Human
Cycle—The Ideal of Human Unity—War and
Self-Determination.* First Edition:
Pondicherry: Sri Aurobindo Ashram, 1962
Nr.Fine/Fine **$45**
Good/V.Good **$25**

_____. *Ilion. An Epic in Quanitative
Hexameters.* First Edition: Pondicherry: Sri
Aurobindo Ashram, 1957
Nr.Fine/Fine **$45**
Good/V.Good **$20**

Ayer, A. J. *Language Truth And Logic.* First
Edition: London: Gollancz, 1936
Nr.Fine/Fine **$1500**
Good/V.Good . . . . $**950**

_____. *Philosophical Essays.* First Edition:
London: Macmillan, 1954
Nr.Fine/Fine **$225**
Good/V.Good **$85**

_____. *The Problem of Knowledge.* First
Edition: London: Macmillan, 1956.
Nr.Fine/Fine **$115**
Good/V.Good **$45**

_____. *The Origins of Pragmatism.*
First Edition: London: Macmillan, 1968
Nr.Fine/Fine **$85**

Lights on Yoga
by Sri Aurobindo

Good/V.Good **$35**

Bain, Alexander. *Senses and the Intellect.*
First Edition: London: John W. Parker And
Son, 1855
Nr.Fine/Fine **$350**
Good/V.Good **$200**

_____. *The Emotions and the Will.*
First Edition: London: John W. Parker and
Son, 1859
Nr.Fine/Fine **$225**
Good/V.Good **$145**

_____. *Mental & Moral Science. a
compendium of psychology & ethics.*First
Edition: London: Longmans, 1868.
Nr.Fine/Fine **$225**
Good/V.Good **$110**

Ballou, Adin. *Practical Christian Socialism.*
First Edition: Hopewell & New York: The
author & Fowlers and Wells, 1854
Nr.Fine/Fine **$1250**
Good/V.Good **$500**

Baker, Herschel. *The Dignity of Man Studies
in the Persistence of an Idea.* First Edition:
Cambridge, MA: Harvard University Press,
1947
Nr.Fine/Fine **$45**
Good/V.Good **$20**

_____. *The Wars Of Truth.* First
Edition: Cambridge, MA: Harvard University
Press, 1952
Nr.Fine/Fine **$30**
Good/V.Good **$12**

Barzun, Jacques. *The Culture We Deserve.*
First Edition: Middletown, CT: Wesleyan
University Press, 1989.
Nr.Fine/Fine **$65**
Good/V.Good **$25**

Bebek, Borna. *The Third City: Philosophy At
War With Positivism.* First Edition: London.
Routledge & Kegan Paul, 1982
Nr.Fine/Fine **$35**
Good/V.Good **$20**

_____. *Santhana: One Man's Road to
the East.* First Edition: London: Bodley Head,

1980
Nr.Fine/Fine **$25**
Good/V.Good **$12**

Beecher, Henry Ward. *Royal Truths.* First
Edition: Boston: Tichnor and Fields, 1866
Nr.Fine/Fine **$155**
Good/V.Good **$70**

_____. *Lectures to Young Men
on Various Important Subjects.* First Edition:
New York: Derby and Jackson, 1859
Nr.Fine/Fine **$65**
Good/V.Good **$25**

_____. *Freedom and War.*
First Edition: Boston: Ticknor & Fields, 1863
Nr.Fine/Fine **$75**
Good/V.Good **$30**

Belloc, Hilaire. *On Nothing & Kindred
Subjects.* First Edition: London: Methuen,
1908.
Nr.Fine/Fine **$50**
Good/V.Good **$30**

_____. *On Something.* First Edition:
London: Methuen & Co., 1910
Nr.Fine/Fine **$45**
Good/V.Good **$25**

_____. *On Everything* First Edition:
London: Methuen & Co., 1909
Nr.Fine/Fine **$50**
Good/V.Good **$30**

Bergson, Henri. *Creative Evolution.*First U.K.
Edition: London: St. Martin's, 1911
Nr.Fine/Fine **$240**
Good/V.Good **$110**

First U.S. Edition: New York: Henry Holt,
1911
Nr.Fine/Fine **$125**
Good/V.Good **$70**

_____. *Time and Free Will. An Essay
on the Immediate Data of Consciousness.*
First U.K. Edition: London: Swan
Sonnenschein, 1910
Nr.Fine/Fine **$150**
Good/V.Good **$85**
First U.S. Edition: New York: Macmillan,

1910
Nr.Fine/Fine **$120**
Good/V.Good **$65**

_____. *Two Sources of Morality and Religion* First Edition in English: New York: Henry Holt, 1935
Nr.Fine/Fine **$145**
Good/V.Good **$80**

_____. *Creative Mind.* First Edition thus: New York: Philosophical Library, 1946
Nr.Fine/Fine **$50**
Good/V.Good **$20**

Berkeley, George. *The Works. To which is added, An Account of his Life, and Several of his Letters to Thomas Prior, Dean Gervais, and Mr. Pope.* (Two Volumes) First Edition: London: Printed for G. Robinson, 1784
Nr.Fine/Fine **$6500**
Good/V.Good **$3700**

_____. *Alciphron, or the Minute Philosopher. In Seven Dialogues. Containing an Apology for the Christian Religion, against those who are called Freethinkers* First Edition: London: J. Tonson, 1732
Nr.Fine/Fine **$2600**
Good/V.Good **$1250**

Berrigan, Daniel. *The Bow in the Clouds. Man's Covenant with God.* First Edition: New York: Coward-McCann, 1961
Nr.Fine/Fine **$55**
Good/V.Good **$25**

_____. *The Bride. Essays in the Church.* First Edition: New York: Macmillan, 1959
Nr.Fine/Fine **$65**
Good/V.Good **$30**

_____. *America Is Hard To Find.* First Edition: Garden City, NY: Doubleday, 1972
Nr.Fine/Fine **$65**
Good/V.Good **$25**

Berrigan, Philip. *Widen the Prison Gates Writing from Jails April 1970-December 1972.* First Edition: New York: Simon and

Schuster, 1973
Nr.Fine/Fine **$35**
Good/V.Good **$20**

_____. *A Punishment for Peace* First Edition: New York: Macmillan, 1969
Nr.Fine/Fine **$30**
Good/V.Good **$12**

Blood, Benjamin. *Optimism, The Lesson of Ages. A Compendium of Democratic Theology, Designed to Illustrate Necessities Whereby All Things are as They are, and to Reconcile Discontents of Men with the Perfect Love and Power of Ever-Present God.* First Edition: Boston: Bela Marsh, 1860
Nr.Fine/Fine **$725**
Good/V.Good **$400**

Bonhoeffer, Dietrich. *Act and Being.* First U.S. Edition: New York: Harper & Brothers, 1961
Nr.Fine/Fine $35
Good/V.Good$15 First U.K. Edition: London: Collins, 1962
Nr.Fine/Fine **$20**
Good/V.Good **$12**

_____. *Sanctorum Communio.* First Edition: London: Collins, 1963
Nr.Fine/Fine **$35**
Good/V.Good **$20**

Bosanquet, Bernard. *A History of Aesthetic.* First Edition: London: Swan Sonnenschein, 1892
Nr.Fine/Fine **$325**
Good/V.Good **$150**

_____. *The Meeting of Extremes in Contemporary Philosophy.* First Edition: London, Macmillan, 1921
Nr.Fine/Fine **$215**
Good/V.Good **$95**

_____. *Implication and Linear Inference.* First Edition: London: Macmillan, 1920
Nr.Fine/Fine **$45**
Good/V.Good **$20**

Boteach, Shmuel. *Wrestling With The Devine:*

A Jewish Response to Suffering. First Edition: Northvale, NJ: Jason Aronson Inc., 1995
Nr.Fine/Fine **$25**
Good/V.Good **$10**

Blondel, Maurice. *The Letter On Apologetics and History and Dogma.* First U.S. Edition: New York: Holt, Rinehart and Winston, 1964
Nr.Fine/Fine **$30**
Good/V.Good **$15**

Bradley, Francis Herbert. *Appearance and Reality.* First Edition: London: Swan Sonnenschein, 1893
Nr.Fine/Fine **$155**
Good/V.Good **$85**

Brandeis, Louis D. *Other People's Money.* First Edition: New York: Frederick A. Stokes, 1914
Nr.Fine/Fine **$650**
Good/V.Good **$275**

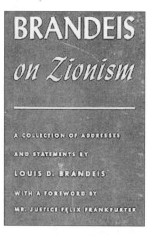

Brandeis on
Zionism
by Louis D. Brandeis

_____. *Brandeis on Zionism. A Collection of Addresses and Statements by Louis D. Brandeis* First Edition: Washington, D.C.: Zionist Organization of America, 1942
Nr.Fine/Fine **$25**
Good/V.Good **$10**

Brisbane, Albert. *Social Destiny of Man: or, Association and Reorganization of Industry.* First Edition: Philadelphia: C. F. Stollmeyer, 1840
Nr.Fine/Fine **$200**
Good/V.Good **$125**

Brownson, Orestes A. *An Oration on the Scholar's Mission* Points of Issue: Paperback Original. First Edition: Boston: Benjamin H Green, 1843
Nr.Fine/Fine **$165**
Good/V.Good **$85**

Burke, Kenneth. *Permanence and Change: An Anatomy of Purpose.* First Edition: New York: New Republic, Inc., 1935
Nr.Fine/Fine **$150**
Good/V.Good **$90**

_____. *The Rhetoric Of Religion Studies In Logology.* First Edition: Boston: Beacon Press, 1961
Nr.Fine/Fine **$35**
Good/V.Good **$18**

_____. *The Philosophy of Literary Form: Studies in Symbolic Action.* First Edition: Baton Rouge, LA: Louisiana State University, 1941
Nr.Fine/Fine **$75**
Good/V.Good **$30**

Bushnell, Horace. *Nature and the Supernatural.* First Edition: New York: Scribner, 1858
Nr.Fine/Fine **$165**
Good/V.Good **$80**

_____. *Views Of Christian Nurture, And Of Subjects Adjacent Thereto.* First Edition: Hartford, CT: Edwin Hunt, 1847
Nr.Fine/Fine **$110**
Good/V.Good **$65**

_____. *Moral Uses of Dark Things.* First Edition: New York: Scribners, 1868
Nr.Fine/Fine **$85**
Good/V.Good **$45**

Butler, Nicholas Murray. *The Meaning of Education and Other Essays and Addresses.* First Edition: New York: Macmillan, 1898
Nr.Fine/Fine **$45**
Good/V.Good **$20**

_____. *The International Mind.* First Edition: New York: Scribers, 1912
Nr.Fine/Fine **$55**

Good/V.Good **$25**

Carnap, Rudolf. *Unity of Science.* First
Edition in English: London: Kegan, Paul
Trench, Trubner, 1934
Nr.Fine/Fine **$400**
Good/V.Good **$150**

_____. *The Logical Syntax of
Language.* First Edition in English: London:
Kegan Paul, Trench, Trubner, 1937
Nr.Fine/Fine **$300**
Good/V.Good **$175**

Cassirer, Ernest. *The Myth of the State.* First
Edition: New Haven, CT: Yale University
Press, 1946
Nr.Fine/Fine **$150**
Good/V.Good **$80**

Channing, William Ellery. *Duties Of
Children. A Sermon, Delivered On The Lord's
Day, April 12, 1807, To The Religious Society
In Federal-Street.* Points of Issue: Paperback
original in Marbled Wraps First Edition:
Boston: Manning & Loring, 1807
Nr.Fine/Fine **$450**
Good/V.Good **$250**

_____. *Slavery.* First
Edition: Boston: James Munroe, 1835
Nr.Fine/Fine **$350**
Good/V.Good **$200**

_____. *Conversations in
Rome: Between an Artist, A Catholic, and a
Critic.* First Edition: Boston: W. Crosby and
H. P. Nichols, 1847
Nr.Fine/Fine **$225**
Good/V.Good **$100**

Chardin, Pierre Teilhard de. *The Future of
Man.* First U.S. Edition: New York: Harper &
Row, 1964
Nr.Fine/Fine **$65**
Good/V.Good **$30**
First U.K. Edition: London: Collins, 1964
Nr.Fine/Fine **$35**
Good/V.Good **$15**

_____. *Science and
Christ.* First U.S. Edition: New York: Harper

& Row, 1965.
Nr.Fine/Fine **$25**
Good/V.Good **$10**

The Future
of Man
*by Pierre Teilhard de
Chardin*

Chatterji, Mohini M. *The Bhagavad Gita or
The Lord's Lay.* First U.S. Edition: Boston:
Ticknor, 1887
Nr.Fine/Fine **$50**
Good/V.Good **$20**

Chesterton, G. K. *What's Wrong with the
World.* First Edition: London: Cassell, 1910.
Nr.Fine/Fine **$125**
Good/V.Good **$70**
First U.S. Edition: New York: Dodd, Mead,
1910
Nr.Fine/Fine **$75**
Good/V.Good **$35**

_____. *The Resurrection of Rome.*
First Edition: London: Hodder and Stoughton,
1930
Nr.Fine/Fine **$200**
Good/V.Good **$65**
First U.S. Edition: New York: Dodd, Mead,
1930
Nr.Fine/Fine **$75**
Good/V.Good **$40**

_____. *The Catholic Church and
Conversion.* First Edition: London: Burnes,
Oates & Washbourne Ltd., 1927
Nr.Fine/Fine **$45**
Good/V.Good **$20**

_____. *The Thing: Why I am a*

Catholic.First U.S. Edition: New York: Dodd, Mead, 1930
Nr.Fine/Fine **$65**
Good/V.Good **$30**

Chetwood, Thomas B *God and Creation.*First Edition: New York, Benziger Brothers, 1928
Nr.Fine/Fine **$30**
Good/V.Good **$12**

_____. *A Handbook of Newman*. First Edition: New York: Schwartz, Kirwin and Fauss, 1927
Nr.Fine/Fine **$25**
Good/V.Good **$10**

Clarke, James Freeman. *Ten Great Religions*. First Edition: Boston: James R. Osgood and Company, 1871
Nr.Fine/Fine **$100**
Good/V.Good **$45**

_____. *Modern Unitarianism*. First Edition: Philadelphia: Lippincott, 1886
Nr.Fine/Fine **$75**
Good/V.Good **$35**

_____. *Nineteenth Century Questions*. First Edition: Boston: Houghton Mifflin, 1897
Nr.Fine/Fine **$65**
Good/V.Good **$35**

Clifford, William Kingdon. *The Common Sense of the Exact Sciences* First U.S. Edition: New York: D. Appleton, 1885
Nr.Fine/Fine **$200**
Good/V.Good **$125**

_____. *Mathematical Papers*. First Edition: London: Macmillan, 1882
Nr.Fine/Fine **$675**
Good/V.Good **$325**

_____. *Lectures and Essays*. First Edition: London: Macmillan, 1879.
Nr.Fine/Fine **$350**
Good/V.Good **$185**

Cobbe, Frances Power. *Religious Duty*. First Edition: Boston: William V. Spencer, 1865
Nr.Fine/Fine **$110**
Good/V.Good **$65**

Cohen, Morris. *The Faith of a Liberal*. First Edition: New York: Henry Holt, 1946
Nr.Fine/Fine **$75**
Good/V.Good **$30**

_____. *The Meaning of Human History* First Edition: LaSalle, IL: Open Court, 1947
Nr.Fine/Fine **$65**
Good/V.Good **$25**

Collingwood, Robin George. *Speculum Mentis or the Map of Knowledge.*First Edition: Oxford: At the Clarendon Press, 1924
Nr.Fine/Fine **$125**
Good/V.Good **$85**

_____. *Essay on Metaphysics*. First Edition: Oxford: At the Clarendon Press, 1940
Nr.Fine/Fine **$140**
Good/V.Good **$75**

_____. *The Principles of Art*. First Edition: Oxford: At the Clarendon Press, 1940
Nr.Fine/Fine **$75**
Good/V.Good **$35**

Conant, James Bryant *General Education in a Free Society*. First Edition: Cambridge, MA: Harvard University Press, 1945
Nr.Fine/Fine **$80**
Good/V.Good **$30**

_____. *Our Fighting Faith*. First Edition: Cambridge, MA: Harvard University Press, 1942
Nr.Fine/Fine **$50**
Good/V.Good **$20**

Constant, Benjamin. *Adolphe and The Red NoteBook*. First Edition: London: Hamish Hamilton, 1948
Nr.Fine/Fine **$35**
Good/V.Good **$15**
First U.S. Edition: Indianapolis, IN: Bobbs Merrill, 1959
Nr.Fine/Fine **$25**
Good/V.Good **$10**

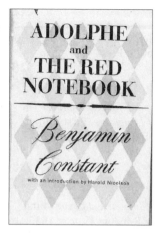

Adolphe and The
Red NoteBook
*by Benjamin
Constant*

Dalberg-Acton, John Emerich Edward. *The History of Freedom and other Essays.* First Edition: London: Macmillan, 1907
Nr.Fine/Fine **$95**
Good/V.Good **$40**

_____ .

Lectures On Modern History First Edition: London: Macmillan, 1906
Nr.Fine/Fine **$110**
Good/V.Good **$60**

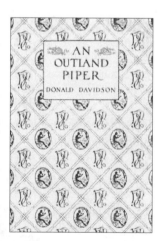

An Outland Piper
by Donald Davidson

Davidson, Donald. *An Outland Piper.* First Edition: Boston: Houghton Mifflin, 1924
Nr.Fine/Fine **$350**
Good/V.Good **$125**

_____ . *The Attack on Leviathan.*

First Edition: Chapel Hill, NC: University of North Carolina, 1938
Nr.Fine/Fine **$275**
Good/V.Good **$150**

Davidson, Thomas. *Rousseau and Education According to Nature.* First Edition: New York: Scribners, 1898.
Nr.Fine/Fine **$125**
Good/V.Good **$60**

Debs, Eugene V. *Labor and Freedom.* First Edition: St. Louis, MO: Phil Wagner, 1916
Nr.Fine/Fine **$135**
Good/V.Good **$55**

_____ . *Walls and Bars.* First Edition: Chicago: Socialist Party, 1927
Nr.Fine/Fine **$100**
Good/V.Good **$45**

Deleuze, Gilles & Felix Guattari. *Anti-Oedipus: Capitalism and Schizophrenia.* First Edition: New York: Viking: 1977
Nr.Fine/Fine **$85**
Good/V.Good **$40**

Dewey, John. *Studies in Logical Theory.* First Edition: Chicago: University of Chicago Press, 1903
Nr.Fine/Fine **$350**
Good/V.Good **$185**

_____ . *The Quest for Certainty: A Study of the Relation of Knowledge and Action.* First Edition: New York: Minton Balch, 1929
Nr.Fine/Fine **$75**
Good/V.Good **$30**

_____ . *The Study of Ethics: A Syllabus.* First Edition: Ann Arbor: The Inland Press 1897
Nr.Fine/Fine **$170**
Good/V.Good **$120**

Dresser, Horatio W. *Health and the Inner Life.*
First Edition: New York: G.P. Putnams, 1906
Nr.Fine/Fine **$65**
Good/V.Good **$30**

Dummett, Michael. *Origins of Analytic*

Philosophy. First Edition: London: Duckworth, 1993
Nr.Fine/Fine **$75**
Good/V.Good **$40**

_____. *The Interpretation of Frege's Philosophy.* First Edition: London: Duckworth, 1981
Nr.Fine/Fine **$60**
Good/V.Good **$25**

Durant, Will. *Philosophy and the Social Problem.* First Edition: New York: Macmillan, 1917
Nr.Fine/Fine **$55**
Good/V.Good **$25**

_____. *The Mansions of Philosophy; A Survey of Human Life and Destiny.* First Edition: New York: Simon & Schuster, 1929
Nr.Fine/Fine **$30**
Good/V.Good **$15**

Eddy, Mary Baker. *Pulpit and Press.* First Edition: Concord, NH: Republican Press Association, 1895.
Nr.Fine/Fine **$650**
Good/V.Good **$375**

_____. *Unity of Good.* First Edition: Boston, by the Author 1888
Nr.Fine/Fine **$85**
Good/V.Good **$50**

_____. *Christian Healing and The People's Idea of God: Sermons Delivered at Boston* First Edition: Boston: Allison Stewart. 1909
Nr.Fine/Fine **$110**
Good/V.Good **$55**

Eddy, Sherwood. *A Pilgrimage of Ideas: The Re-Education of Sherwood Eddy.* First Edition: New York: Farrar & Rinehart, 1934
Nr.Fine/Fine **$55**
Good/V.Good **$25**

_____. *The Kingdom of God and the American Dream. The Religious and Secular Ideals of American History.* First Edition: New York: Harper & Brothers, 1941

Nr.Fine/Fine **$75**
Good/V.Good **$35**

_____ *God In History.* First Edition: New York: Association Press, 1947.
Nr.Fine/Fine **$25**
Good/V.Good **$15**

Edie, James M. *Speaking & Meaning: The Phenomenology of Language.* First Edition: Bloomington, IN: Indiana University Press, 1976.
Nr.Fine/Fine **$30**
Good/V.Good **$12**

Eisley, Loren. *The Immense Journey.* First Edition: New York: Random House, 1957
Nr.Fine/Fine **$100**
Good/V.Good **$45**

_____. *The Mind as Nature.* First Edition: New York: Harper & Row, 1962
Nr.Fine/Fine **$60**
Good/V.Good **$35**

_____. *Darwin and the Mysterious Mr. X: New Light on the Evolutionists.* First Edition: New York: E. P. Dutton, 1979
Nr.Fine/Fine **$30**
Good/V.Good **$12**

Emerson, Ralph Waldo. *The Method of Nature. An Oration delivered before the Society of the Adelphi, in Waterville.* First Edition: Boston: Samuel Simkins, 1841
Nr.Fine/Fine **$650**
Good/V.Good **$350**

_____. *English Traits.* First Edition: Boston: Phillips, Sampson, and Company, 1856
Nr.Fine/Fine **$650**
Good/V.Good **$200**

_____. *Society and Solitude.* First Edition: Boston: Fields, Osgood & Co., 1870
Nr.Fine/Fine **$525**
Good/V.Good **$300**

Farber, Marvin. *The Foundation of Phenomenology Edmund Husserl and the Quest for a Rigorous Science of Philosophy.* First Edition: Cambridge, MA: Harvard

University Press, 1943
Nr.Fine/Fine **$65**
Good/V.Good **$30**

_____. *Naturalism and Subjectivism.* First Edition: Albany, NY: Charles C. Thomas, 1959
Nr.Fine/Fine **$25**
Good/V.Good **$12**

Fiske, John. *Tobacco and Alcohol.* First Edition: New York: Leypoldt and Holt, 1869
Nr.Fine/Fine **$250**
Good/V.Good **$110**

_____. *A Century of Science And Other Essays.* First Edition: Boston: Houghton Mifflin, 1899
Nr.Fine/Fine **$85**
Good/V.Good **$50**

_____. *Myths and Myth-Makers: Old Tales and Superstitions interpreted by Comparative Mythology.* First Edition: Boston: James R. Osgood and Company, 1874.
Nr.Fine/Fine **$155**
Good/V.Good **$75**

Frege, Gottlob. *The Foundations of Arithmetic. A logico-mathematic enquiry into the concept of number.* First U.K. Edition: Oxford: Basil Blackwell, 1950
Nr.Fine/Fine **$200**
Good/V.Good **$120**

Frothingham, Octavius Brooks. *Transcendentalism in New England.* First Edition: New York: G.P. Putnams, 1876
Nr.Fine/Fine **$175**
Good/V.Good **$95**

_____. *The Cradle of the Christ. A Study in Primitive Christianity.* First Edition: New York: G.P. Putnams, 1877
Nr.Fine/Fine **$155**
Good/V.Good **$80**

_____. *Recollections and Impressions, 1822-1890* First Edition: New York: G.P. Putnams, 1891
Nr.Fine/Fine **$85**

Good/V.Good **$55**

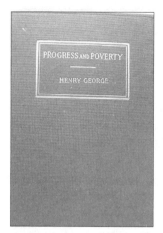

Progress and
Poverty
by Henry George

George, Henry. *Progress and Poverty.* First Edition: San Francisco: by the Author, 1879
Nr.Fine/Fine **$3500**
Good/V.Good **$2100**
First Trade Edition: New York: D. Appleton, 1880
Nr.Fine/Fine **$325**
Good/V.Good **$185**

Angels: God's
Secret Agents
by Billy Graham

Graham, Billy. *Peace with God.* First Edition: Garden City, NY: Doubleday, 1953.
Nr.Fine/Fine **$25**
Good/V.Good **$10**

_____. *Angels: God's Secret Agents.* First Edition: Garden City, NY: Doubleday, 1975
Nr.Fine/Fine **$20**

Good/V.Good **$8**

Hall, G. Stanley. *Senescence. The Last Half of Life.* First Edition: New York: D. Appleton, 1922
Nr.Fine/Fine **$75**
Good/V.Good **$40**

_____. *Life and Confessions of a Psychologist.* First Edition: New York & London: D. Appleton, 1923
Nr.Fine/Fine **$75**
Good/V.Good **$30**

_____. *Founders of Modern Psychology.* First Edition: New York: D. Appleton, 1912
Nr.Fine/Fine **$65**
Good/V.Good **$25**

Harris, Thomas Lake. *The New Republic A Discourse of the Prospects, Dangers, Duties and Safeties of the Times.* First Edition: Santa Rosa, CA: Fountaingrove Press, 1891.
Nr.Fine/Fine **$600**
Good/V.Good **$375**

_____. *The Breath of God with Man. An Essay On The Grounds And Evidences Of Universal Religion.* First Edition: New York: Brotherhood Of New Life, 1867
Nr.Fine/Fine **$275**
Good/V.Good **$150**

Hedge, Frederic Henry. *The Sick Woman. A Sermon for the Time.* First Edition: Boston: Prentiss and Deland, 1863
Nr.Fine/Fine **$75**
Good/V.Good **$45**

_____. *The Primeval World Of Hebrew Tradition.* First Edition: Boston: Roberts Brothers, 1870
Nr.Fine/Fine **$120**
Good/V.Good **$50**

Hegel, Georg Wilhelm Friedrich. *Hegel's Science of Logic.* First U.K. Edition: London: George Allen & Unwin, 1929
Nr.Fine/Fine **$375**
Good/V.Good **$200**

_____. *Lectures on the Philosophy of Religion.* First U.K. Edition: London: Kegan Paul, 1895.
Nr.Fine/Fine **$350**
Good/V.Good **$275**

_____. *The Phenomenology of Mind.* First U.K. Edition: London: Swan Sonnenschein, 1910
Nr.Fine/Fine **$200**
Good/V.Good **$125**

Heidegger, Martin. *Existence and Being.* First Edition in English: London: Vision Press, 1949
Nr.Fine/Fine **$225**
Good/V.Good **$100**

_____. *Being and Time.* First Edition in English: London: SCM Press, 1962
Nr.Fine/Fine **$400**
Good/V.Good **$250**

_____. *Introduction to Metaphysics.* First U.S. Edition: New Haven: Yale University Press, 1959.
Nr.Fine/Fine **$150**
Good/V.Good **$85**

Hicks, Granville. *Eight Ways of Looking at Christianity.* First Edition: New York: The Macmillan Company, 1926
Nr.Fine/Fine **$200**
Good/V.Good **$85**

Hocking, William Ernest. *The Lasting Elements of Individualism.* First Edition: New Haven: Yale University Press, 1937
Nr.Fine/Fine **$45**
Good/V.Good **$20**

_____. *Man and the State* First Edition: New Haven: Yale University Press, 1926
Nr.Fine/Fine **$85**
Good/V.Good **$50**

_____. *Thoughts on Death and Life.* First Edition: New York: Harper and Brothers, 1937
Nr.Fine/Fine **$30**
Good/V.Good **$15**

Hook, Sydney. *The Metaphysics of Pragmatism.* First Edition: Chicago & London: The Open Court Publishing Company, 1927
Nr.Fine/Fine **$300**
Good/V.Good **$185**

_____. *Pragmatism and the Tragic Sense of Life.* First Edition: New York: Basic Books, 1974.
Nr.Fine/Fine **$35**
Good/V.Good **$20**

_____. *The Hero In History: A Study in Limitation and Possibility.* First Edition: New York: John Day, 1943
Nr.Fine/Fine **$65**
Good/V.Good **$30**

Hopkins, Mark. *Lectures on Moral Science.* First Edition: New York: Sheldon, 1862.
Nr.Fine/Fine **$120**
Good/V.Good **$70**

_____. *Miscellaneous Essays and Discourses.* First Edition: Boston: T. R. Marvin, 1847
Nr.Fine/Fine **$75**
Good/V.Good **$40**

_____. *The Scriptural Idea of Man.* First Edition: New York: Scribners, 1883
Nr.Fine/Fine **$25**
Good/V.Good **$12**

Howe, Julia Ward. *From the Oak to The Olive.* First Edition: Boston: Lee and Shepard, 1868
Nr.Fine/Fine **$275**
Good/V.Good **$125**

_____. *Is Polite Society Polite? And Other Essays.* First Edition: Boston & New York: Lamson, Wolfe, & Company, 1895
Nr.Fine/Fine **$300**
Good/V.Good **$185**

Hume, David. *An Enquiry Concerning The Principles Of Morals.* First Edition: London: Printed for A. Millar, 1751.

Nr.Fine/Fine **$6000**

Good/V.Good **$4200**

James, Henry, Sr. *The Nature of Evil.* First Edition: New York: D. Appleton, 1855
Nr.Fine/Fine **$275**
Good/V.Good **$150**

James, William. *The Will to Believe and Other Essays in Popular Philosophy.* First Edition: New York: Longmans Green, 1897
Nr.Fine/Fine **$400**
Good/V.Good **$225**

_____. *A Pluralistic Universe.* First Edition: New York: Longmans Green, 1909
Nr.Fine/Fine **$200**
Good/V.Good **$120**

_____. *Pragmatism, A New Name for Some Old Ways of Thinking.* First Edition: New York: Longmans Green, 1907
Nr.Fine/Fine **$625**
Good/V.Good **$185**

Jaspers, Karl. *Philosophy.* (Three Volumes) First U.S. Edition: Chicago: University of Chicago Press, 1969-71
Nr.Fine/Fine **$125**
Good/V.Good **$75**

_____. *Truth and Symbol.* First Edition in English: London: Vision Press, 1959
Nr.Fine/Fine **$75**
Good/V.Good **$40**

_____. *Man in the Modern Age.* First Edition: New York: Henry Holt, 1933
Nr.Fine/Fine **$160**
Good/V.Good **$100**

Jeans, Sir James Hopwood. *Astronomy and Cosmogony.* First Edition: Cambridge: University Press, 1928.
Nr.Fine/Fine **$85**
Good/V.Good **$40**

Jung, C G. *Memories, Dreams, Reflections.* First Edition: London: Collins, 1963
Nr.Fine/Fine **$110**
Good/V.Good **$60**

Kojeve, Alexandre. *Introduction to the*

Reading of Hegel. First US Edition: New York: Basic Books, 1969
Nr.Fine/Fine **$45**
Good/V.Good **$15**

Lang, Graham A. *Towards Technocracy.* First Edition: Los Angeles: The Angelus Press, 1933.
Nr.Fine/Fine **$45**
Good/V.Good **$20**

Lerner, Max. *Actions and Passions Notes on the Multiple Revolution of Our Time.* First Edition: New York: Simon and Schuster, 1949
Nr.Fine/Fine **$25**
Good/V.Good **$10**

_____. *America as a Civilization Life and Thought in the United States Today.* First Edition: New York: Simon and Schuster, 1957
Nr.Fine/Fine **$20**
Good/V.Good **$8**

_____. *The Age of Overkill.* First Edition: New York: Simon & Schuster, 1962
Nr.Fine/Fine **$25**
Good/V.Good **$15**

Lewis, Clarence Irving. *The Ground & Nature Of The Right.* First Edition: New York: Columbia University Press, 1955
Nr.Fine/Fine **$45**
Good/V.Good **$20**

_____. *Mind and the World Order.* First Edition: New York: Scribners, 1929
Nr.Fine/Fine **$65**
Good/V.Good **$45**

_____. *Values and Imperatives: Studies in Ethics.* First Edition: Palo Alto, CA: Stanford University Press, 1969
Nr.Fine/Fine **$35**
Good/V.Good **$15**

Lewis, C.S. *The Screwtape Letters.* First U.S. Edition: New York: Macmillan, 1943
Nr.Fine/Fine **$900**
Good/V.Good **$500**

_____. *Reflections on the Psalms* First Edition: London: Geoffrey Bles, 1958.
Nr.Fine/Fine **$200**
Good/V.Good **$85**

_____*Great Divorce: A Dream.* First Edition: London: Geoffrey Bles/The Centenary Press, 1945
Nr.Fine/Fine **$200**
Good/V.Good **$125**
First U.S. Edition: New York: Macmillan, 1946
Nr.Fine/Fine **$190**
Good/V.Good **$100**

Lieber, Francis. *Letters to a Gentleman in Germany.* First Edition: Philadelphia: Carey, Lea and Blanchard, 1834
Nr.Fine/Fine **$275**
Good/V.Good **$130**

_____. *Stranger in America.* First Edition: Philadelphia: Carey, Lea and Blanchard, 1835
Nr.Fine/Fine **$225**
Good/V.Good **$100**

Lynd, Robert S. and Helen Merrell. *Middletown, A Study in American Culture* First Edition: New York, Harcourt, Brace and Company, 1929
Nr.Fine/Fine **$150**
Good/V.Good **$65**

_____.
Middletown In Transition: A Study of Cultural Conflicts First Edition: New York, Harcourt, Brace and Company, 1937
Nr.Fine/Fine **$50**
Good/V.Good **$20**

Lyotard, Jean-Francois. *Political Writings.* First Edition: Minneapolis, MN: University of Minnesota Press, 1993
Nr.Fine/Fine **$65**
Good/V.Good **$35**

_____. *The Differend.* First Edition: Minneapolis, MN: University of Minnesota Press, 1988
Nr.Fine/Fine **$75**
Good/V.Good **$45**

Marcuse, Herbert. *Eros and Civilization.*
First Edition in English: Boston: Beacon,
1955
Nr.Fine/Fine **$250**
Good/V.Good **$145**

_____. *Studies in Critical
Philosophy.* First U.S. Edition: Boston:
Beacon Press, 1972
Nr.Fine/Fine **$100**
Good/V.Good **$55**

_____. *Counter-Revolution and
Revolt.* First U.S. Edition: Boston: Beacon
Press, 1972
Nr.Fine/Fine **$75**
Good/V.Good **$35**

Creative
Intuition In Art
and Poetry
*by Jacques
Maritain*

Maritain, Jacques. *Creative Intuition In Art
And Poetry* First Edition: New York: Pantheon
Books, 1953
Nr.Fine/Fine **$75**
Good/V.Good **$45**

_____. *France My Country.
Through the Disaster.* First Edition: New York:
Longmans, Green, 1941
Nr.Fine/Fine **$40**
Good/V.Good **$15**

_____. *Man's Approach to God*
First U.S. Edition: Latrobe, PA: Archabbey
Press, 1960.
Nr.Fine/Fine **$125**
Good/V.Good **$70**

May, Rollo. *The Art of Counseling.*
First Edition: Nashville, TN: Abingdon Press,
1939
Nr.Fine/Fine **$300**
Good/V.Good **$125**

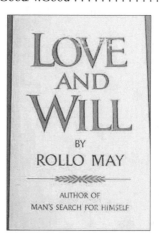

Love and Will
by Rollo May

_____. *Love & Will.* First Edition: New
York: W.W. Norton, 1969
Nr.Fine/Fine **$40**
Good/V.Good **$15**

_____. *Power and Innocence.* First
Edition: New York: W.W. Norton, 1972
Nr.Fine/Fine **$30**
Good/V.Good **$12**

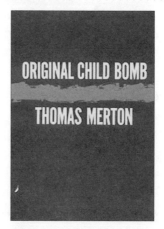

Original Child
Bomb
by Thomas Merton

Mead, George Herbert. *Philosophy of the Present.* First Edition: Chicago: Open Court, 1932
Nr.Fine/Fine **$200**
Good/V.Good **$110**

Merton, Thomas. *Original Child Bomb* First Edition (Limited/Signed): Norfolk, CT: New Directions, 1962
Nr.Fine/Fine **$825**
Good/V.Good **$500**
First Edition (Trade): Norfolk, CT: New Directions, 1962
Nr.Fine/Fine **$55**
Good/V.Good **$30**

The Ascent to Truth
by Thomas Merton

_____. *The Ascent of Truth.* First Edition: New York: Harcourt, Brace, 1951
Nr.Fine/Fine **$95**
Good/V.Good **$55**

Seeds of Contemplation
by Thomas Merton

_____. *The Seven Storey Mountain.* First Edition: New York: Harcourt, Brace, 1948.
Nr.Fine/Fine **$1200**
Good/V.Good **$550**

_____. *Seeds of Contemplation.* First Edition: Norfolk, CT: New Directions, 1949
Nr.Fine/Fine **$500**
Good/V.Good **$150**

Merleau-Ponty, Maurice. *Sense and Non-Sense.* First U.S. Edition: Evanston, IL: Northwestern University, 1964
Nr.Fine/Fine **$75**
Good/V.Good **$40**

_____. *The Structure of Behavior.* First U.S. Edition: Boston: Beacon Press, 1963
Nr.Fine/Fine **$65**
Good/V.Good **$35**

_____. *Humanism and Terror.* First U.S. Edition: Boston: Beacon Press, 1969
Nr.Fine/Fine **$25**
Good/V.Good **$15**

Meyerson, Emile. *Identity and Reality.* First U.K. Edition: London: George Allen & Unwin, 1930
Nr.Fine/Fine **$85**
Good/V.Good **$50**

Newman, John Henry. *Apologia Pro Vita Sua.* First Edition: London: Longman, Roberts and Green, 1864
Nr.Fine/Fine **$475**
Good/V.Good **$225**

_____. *Lyra Apostolica.* First Edition: Derby: Henry Mozley and Sons, 1836.
Nr.Fine/Fine **$450**
Good/V.Good **$195**

_____. *An Essay on the Development of Christian Doctrine.* First Edition: London: James Toovey, 1845
Nr.Fine/Fine **$275**

Good/V.Good **$145**

Neibuhr, Reinhold. *The Structure Of Nations And Empires.* First Edition: New York: Scribners, 1959
Nr.Fine/Fine **$30**
Good/V.Good **$12**

_____. *Pious and Secular America.* First Edition: New York: Scribners, 1958
Nr.Fine/Fine **$30**
Good/V.Good **$15**

Nietzsche, Friedrich. *Thus Spake Zarathustra.* First Edition in English: New York: Macmillan, 1896
Nr.Fine/Fine **$5200**
Good/V.Good **$2500**

_____. *Dawn of Day* First U.K. Edition: London: T. Fischer Unwin, 1903
Nr.Fine/Fine **$1250**
Good/V.Good **$750**

_____. *Beyond Good and Evil.* First U.S. Edition: New York: Macmillan, 1907
Nr.Fine/Fine **$775**
Good/V.Good **$425**

Palmer, Ray. *Hymns and Sacred Pieces.* First Edition: New York: Anson D. F. Randolph, 1865
Nr.Fine/Fine **$225**
Good/V.Good **$110**

Peirce, Charles Sanders. *Collected Papers.* (Six Volumes) First Edition: Cambridge, MA: Harvard University Press, 1931-1935
Nr.Fine/Fine **$1450**
Good/V.Good **$825**

Porter, Noah. *Elements of Intellectual Science.* First Edition: New York: Scribners, 1887
Nr.Fine/Fine **$65**
Good/V.Good **$25**

Rand, Ayn. *Capitalism: The Unknown Ideal* First Edition (Trade): New York: The New American Library, 1966
Nr.Fine/Fine **$100**
Good/V.Good **$45**

Capitalism: The Unknown Ideal by Ayn Rand

_____. *For the New Intellectual.* First Edition: New York: Random House, 1961
Nr.Fine/Fine **$225**
Good/V.Good **$95**

_____. *The Virtue of Selfishness a New Concept of Egoism.* First Edition: New York: New American Library, 1964
Nr.Fine/Fine **$100**
Good/V.Good **$45**

Rauschenbusch, Walter. *For God and the People: Prayers of the Social Awakening.* First Edition: Boston: Pilgrim Press, 1910
Nr.Fine/Fine **$45**
Good/V.Good **$25**

_____. *The Social Principles of Jesus.* First Edition: New York: Methodist Book Concern, 1916
Nr.Fine/Fine **$35**
Good/V.Good **$15**

_____. *Christianity and the Social Crisis.* First Edition: Boston: Pilgrim Press, 1915
Nr.Fine/Fine **$25**
Good/V.Good **$10**

Reed, Sampson. *Observations on the Growth of the Mind.* First Edition: Boston: Cummings, Hilliard, 1826
Nr.Fine/Fine **$275**
Good/V.Good **$185**

_____. *A Biographical Sketch Of Thomas Worcester, DD, For Nearly Fifty Years*

The Pastor of the Boston Society of the New Jerusalem, with Some Account of the Origin and Rise of That Society. First Edition: Boston: New Church Union, 1880
Nr.Fine/Fine **$65**
Good/V.Good **$30**

Reichenbach, Hans. *Atom And Cosmos.* First U.S. Edition: New York: Macmillan, 1933
Nr.Fine/Fine **$125**
Good/V.Good **$40**

_____. *The Rise of Scientific Philosophy.* First U.S. Edition: Berkeley and Los Angeles: University Of California Press, 1951
Nr.Fine/Fine **$65**
Good/V.Good **$30**

_____. *Experience and Prediction. An Analysis of the Foundations and the Structure of Knowledge* First Edition: Chicago: University Of Chicago Press, 1938.
Nr.Fine/Fine **$70**
Good/V.Good **$40**

Riley, Woodbridge. *Men and Morals: The Story of Ethics.* First Edition: Garden City, NY: Doubleday, 1929
Nr.Fine/Fine $25
Good/V.Good **$10**

_____. *The Founder of Mormonism.* First Edition: New York: Dodd, Mead, 1902
Nr.Fine/Fine **$150**
Good/V.Good **$85**

Ripley, George. *The Latest Form of Infidelity Examined. A Letter to Mr. Andrews Norton, Occasioned by His "Discourse Before the Association of the Alumni of the Cambridge Theological School," On the 19th of July, 1839. By an Alumnus of that School.* Points of Issue: Paperback Original. First Edition: Boston: James Munroe, 1839
Nr.Fine/Fine **$625**
Good/V.Good **$300**

Rorty, Richard. *Philosophy and the Mirror of Nature.* First Edition: Princeton, NJ: Princeton University Press, 1979.

Nr.Fine/Fine **$110**
Good/V.Good **$65**

_____. *Consequences of Pragmatism, (Essays: 1972-1980).* First Edition: Minneapolis, MN: University of Minnesota Press, 1982.
Nr.Fine/Fine **$100**
Good/V.Good **$45**

Achieving Our Country
by Richard Rorty

_____. *Achieving Our Country, Leftist Thought in Twentieth-Century America.* First Edition: Cambridge, MA: Harvard University Press, 1998
Nr.Fine/Fine **$25**
Good/V.Good **$12**

Runes, Dagobert D. *On the Nature of Man: An Essay in Primitive Philosophy.* First Edition: New York: Philosophical Library, 1956
Nr.Fine/Fine **$35**
Good/V.Good **$20**

_____. *A Book of Contemplation.* First Edition: New York: Philosophical Library, 1957
Nr.Fine/Fine **$30**
Good/V.Good **$15**

_____. *Classics In Logic: Readings in Epistemology Theory of Knowledge and Dialectics* First Edition: New York: Philosophical Library, 1962.
Nr.Fine/Fine **$35**

Good/V.Good **$25**

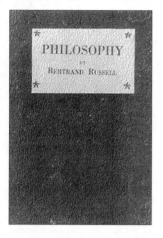

Philosophy
by Bertrand Russell

Russell, Bertrand. *Philosophy.* First Edition:
New York: W.W. Norton, 1927
Nr.Fine/Fine **$85**
Good/V.Good **$45**

**Mysticism and
Logic**
by Bertrand Russell

_____. *Mysticism and Logic* First
Edition: London: Longmans, Green, 1918
Nr.Fine/Fine **$200**
Good/V.Good **$110**
First U.S. Edition: New York: W.W. Norton,
1929
Nr.Fine/Fine **$100**
Good/V.Good **$65**

_____. *Introduction To Mathematical
Philosophy* First Edition: London; Allen &
Unwin, 1919.
Nr.Fine/Fine **$850**

Good/V.Good **$500**

Russell, Charles Taze. *Millennial Dawn.* First
Edition: Allegheny, PA: Watch Tower Bible
And Tract Society, 1906
Nr.Fine/Fine **$325**
Good/V.Good **$175**

_____. *Pastor Russell's
Sermons.* First Edition: Brooklyn, NY:
Peoples Pulpit Association, 1917
Nr.Fine/Fine **$250**
Good/V.Good **$145**

_____. *The Divine Plan of the
Ages.* First Edition: Brooklyn, NY: Watch
Tower Bible And Tract Society, 1915
Nr.Fine/Fine **$300**
Good/V.Good **$175**

Russell, George William. (as by A. E.) *The
Candle of Vision* First Edition: London:
Macmillan, 1919
Nr.Fine/Fine **$125**
Good/V.Good **$75**

_____.

Imagination and Reveries. First Edition:
Dublin and London: Maunsel, 1915
Nr.Fine/Fine **$75**
Good/V.Good **$40**

_____. *The
Living Torch.* First Edition: London:
Macmillan, 1937
Nr.Fine/Fine **$40**
Good/V.Good **$25**

Ryle, Gilbert. *Concept of Mind.* First Edition:
London: Hutchinson House, 1949
Nr.Fine/Fine **$500**
Good/V.Good **$275**
First U.S. Edition: New York: Barnes &
Noble, 1949.
Nr.Fine/Fine **$300**
Good/V.Good **$125**

_____. *Dilemmas.* First Edition:
Cambridge: Cambridge University Press,
1954
Nr.Fine/Fine **$85**
Good/V.Good **$55**

_____. *On Thinking.* First Edition:
London: Basil Blackwell, 1979
Nr.Fine/Fine **$65**
Good/V.Good **$30**

Santayana, George. *The Sense of Beauty Being the Outlines of Aesthetic Theory* First U.K. Edition: London: Adam and Charles Black, 1896
Nr.Fine/Fine **$125**
Good/V.Good **$70**
First U.S. Edition: New York: Scribners, 1896
Nr.Fine/Fine **$90**
Good/V.Good **$40**

_____. *Interpretations of Poetry and Religion.* First Edition: New York: Scribners, 1900
Nr.Fine/Fine **$110**
Good/V.Good **$50**

_____. *The Realm of Essence.* First Edition: New York: Charles Scribner's Sons, 1927
Nr.Fine/Fine **$115**
Good/V.Good **$60**

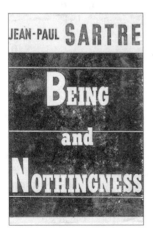

Being and Nothingness
by Jean-Paul Sartre

Sartre, Jean-Paul. *Being and Nothingness.* First Edition In English: New York: Philosophical Library, 1956.
Nr.Fine/Fine **$200**
Good/V.Good **$75**

_____. *Existentialism.* First U.S. Edition: New York: Philosophical Library, 1947.

Nr.Fine/Fine **$125**
Good/V.Good **$75**

Existentialism
by Jean-Paul Sartre

The Emotions, Outline Of A Theory
by Jean-Paul Sartre

_____. *The Emotions, Outline Of A Theory.* First U.S. Edition: New York: Philosophical Library, 1948.
Nr.Fine/Fine **$75**
Good/V.Good **$40**

Schuller, Robert H. *Reach Out for New Life.* First Edition: New York: Hawthorn Books, 1977
Nr.Fine/Fine **$15**
Good/V.Good **$6**

_____. *The Peak to Peek Principle.* First Edition: Garden City, NY: Doubleday, 1980
Nr.Fine/Fine **$20**

Good/V.Good **$10**

Reach Out for New Life
by Robert H. Schuller

Sheen, Fulton J. *The Moral Universe.* First
Edition: Milwaukee: Bruce Publishing, 1936
Nr.Fine/Fine **$170**
Good/V.Good **$75**

_____. *The Seven Last Words.* First
Edition: New York & London: Century Co.,
1933
Nr.Fine/Fine **$75**
Good/V.Good **$35**

_____. *The Mystical Body Of
Christ.* First Edition: New York: Sheed &
Ward, 1935
Nr.Fine/Fine **$45**
Good/V.Good **$25**

Smart, Ninian. *The Religious Experience of
Mankind.* First Edition: New York: Scribners,
1969
Nr.Fine/Fine **$35**
Good/V.Good **$15**

_____. *Worldviews: Crosscultural
Explorations of Human Beliefs.* First Edition:
New York: Scribners, 1983
Nr.Fine/Fine **$25**
Good/V.Good **$12**

_____. *Religion and the Western
Mind.* First Edition: Albany, NY: State
University of New York, 1987
Nr.Fine/Fine **$45**

Good/V.Good **$20**

Smith, Joseph W *Gleanings from the Sea:
Showing the Pleasures, Pains and Penalties of
Life Afloat, with Contingencies Ashore.* First
Edition: Andover, MA: Joseph W. Smith, 1887
Nr.Fine/Fine **$300**
Good/V.Good **$200**

Spencer, Herbert. *A System of Synthetic
Philosophy.* (Six Volumes) First Edition:
London: Williams and Norgate, 1898
Nr.Fine/Fine **$650**
Good/V.Good **$375**

_____. *Education Intellectual
Moral And Physical.* First Edition: London: G.
Mainwaring, 1861
Nr.Fine/Fine **$385**
Good/V.Good **$195**

Thompson, Francis. *Health & Holiness.* First
Edition: London: J. Masters, 1905.
Nr.Fine/Fine **$35**
Good/V.Good **$20**

Thoreau, Henry David. *Excursions.* First
Edition: Boston: Ticknor and Fields, 1863
Nr.Fine/Fine **$1650**
Good/V.Good **$750**

_____. *Maine Woods.* First
Edition: Boston: Ticknor & Fields, 1864
Nr.Fine/Fine **$1450**
Good/V.Good **$650**

_____. *A Week On The
Concord And Merrimac Rivers.* First Edition:
Boston and Cambridge: James Munroe, 1849
Nr.Fine/Fine **$15000**
Good/V.Good **$6500**

Trench, Richard Chenevix. *The Fitness of
Holy Scripture for Unfolding the Spiritual Life
of Men.* First Edition: London: Macmillan,
Barclay and Macmillan, John W. Parker, 1845
Nr.Fine/Fine **$95**
Good/V.Good **$45**

Trine, Ralph Waldo. *The Man Who Knew.*
First Edition: London: G. Bell, 1936
Nr.Fine/Fine **$115**
Good/V.Good **$65**

_____. *In The Fire Of The Heart.*
First Edition: New York: McClure, Phillips,
1906
Nr.Fine/Fine **$55**
Good/V.Good **$30**

_____. *In Tune with the Infinite.*
First Edition: New York: Thomas Y. Crowell &
Co. 1897
Nr.Fine/Fine **$45**
Good/V.Good **$20**

Veblen, Thorstein. *The Theory of the Leisure
Class.* First Edition: New York, Macmillan,
1899.
Nr.Fine/Fine **$6500**
Good/V.Good **$4250**

_____. *Absentee Ownership And
Business Enterprise In Recent Times.* First
Edition: New York: Huebsch, 1923.
Nr.Fine/Fine **$375**
Good/V.Good **$195**

_____. *The Place of Science in
Modern Civilization.* First Edition: New York:
Huebsch, 1919.
Nr.Fine/Fine **$350**
Good/V.Good **$175**

Von Hugel, Baron Frederich. *Essays and
Addresses on the Philosophy of Religion.* First
Edition: London: Dent, 1928
Nr.Fine/Fine **$30**
Good/V.Good **$12**

Wallace, Alfred Russel. *Studies Scientific and
Social.* (Two Volumes) First Edition: London:
Macmillan, 1900.
Nr.Fine/Fine **$750**
Good/V.Good **$400**

_____. *Bad Times.* First
Edition: London: Macmillan, 1885
Nr.Fine/Fine **$625**
Good/V.Good **$400**

Ward, William George. *Essays on the
Philosophy of Theism.* (Two Volumes) First
Edition: London: Kegan Paul, Trench, 1884
Nr.Fine/Fine **$145**
Good/V.Good **$65**

_____. *Essays on the
Church's Doctrinal Authority.* First Edition:
London: Burnes, Oates & Washbourne, 1889
Nr.Fine/Fine **$55**
Good/V.Good **$25**

Whitefield, George. *The Christian's
Companion.* First Edition: London: by the
booksellers, 1738
Nr.Fine/Fine **$650**
Good/V.Good **$400**

_____. *Fifteen Sermons
Preached on Various Important Subjects,
Carefully Corrected and Revised According to
the Best London Edition.* First U.S. Edition:
Philadelphia: Mathew Carey, 1794
Nr.Fine/Fine **$375**
Good/V.Good **$190**

Whitehead, Alfred North. *Process and
Reality.* First Edition: New York & London:
Macmillan, 1929
Nr.Fine/Fine **$450**
Good/V.Good **$275**

_____. *The Concept of
Nature.* First Edition: Cambridge: at the
University Press, 1920
Nr.Fine/Fine **$200**
Good/V.Good **$95**

_____. *Symbolism Its Meaning and
Effect.* First Edition: Cambridge: Cambridge
University Press, 1928
Nr.Fine/Fine **$150**
Good/V.Good **$85**

Wittgenstein, Ludwig. *Tractatus Logico-
Philosophicus.* First U.S. Edition: New York:
Harcourt, Brace, 1922
Nr.Fine/Fine **$1500**
Good/V.Good **$750**

Vintage Fiction

A box of old books has a certain smell. I've never been able to describe it. It's not quite musty, though I suppose that's as good a word for it as any. There are elements of tobacco and leather, and fine wine; elements of sunshine, and dark closed places. I first encountered it in my grandmother's attic on Long Island and I guess you could say it clung to me. If we view the craft of fiction, which is really being a very good, professional liar, by the conventions of the craft rather than a calendar, modern fiction began to develop in the nineteen twenties. Several eras preceded it. The odor I remember so well is how they smell in my mind when I find some of them.

A little more than a century ago, fiction writing was almost a language unto itself. Called "purple prose," the fiction of the nineteenth century featured overblown, poetic descriptions, and sentences that filled a page or two without stopping for a breath. It was fascinating, wonderful stuff to read. Its masters were Edward Bulwer-Lytton, Prime Minister Benjamin Disraeli, and the man from the Isle of Man, Hall Caine. For many years, the literary controversy over the finest novel centered on two books, *Pelham* by Bulwer-Lytton and *Vivian Grey* by Disraeli. The curious fact is that this era of overblown description, twisty allegory, and symbolic prose produced what is still considered the best, or certainly one of the best, novels ever written, Herman Melville's *Moby Dick, or the Whale*.

The eighteenth century produced many wonderful books as well. Some of these have become enduring classics, and were abridged for children and young readers. *Robinson Crusoe* and *Gulliver's Travels* top the list of great eighteenth century fiction commonly abridged to introduce children to literature. It was a lusty era, and many of the best eighteenth century novels are found in banned book collections. *Moll Flanders*, by Daniel Defoe, *The History of Tom Jones* by Henry Fielding, *Fanny Hill* by John Cleland, and Samuel Richardson's wonderful puzzle, *Pamela, or Virtue Rewarded* have all felt the bite of censorship. Nor were the English the only people lifting petticoats. The Marquis De Sade's best work stands up well against the dirty old men from across the channel. According to a French professor of my acquaintance, pornography is the last reason to read De Sade.

As the nineteenth century wound down, young writers began writing in a "conversational" style. Their books came out like a story told before a roaring fire on a winter's night. Arthur Conan Doyle, James M. Barrie, Henry Rider Haggard, and others began telling stories as if some old man were sitting with his grandchildren to remember the past. Some figures crossed over the lines between the "purple prose" era and the conversational style. Arthur Machen's unique prose, for example, would be exploited by horror and other writers right on to the best seller list today, a prime example being Stephen King.

For the collector, these old books can be a wonderful area to play about in. A lot of the books were best sellers in their day, and are still relatively common as well as relatively inexpensive. Vintage fiction is wonderful to read and fascinating to collect. The smell lingers in your mind and the thoughts stay on the tip of your brain.

10 Classic Rarities

Bierce, Ambrose. *Can Such Things Be?*
New York: Cassell, 1893. In this case,
obviously.
Retail value in:
   Near Fine to Fine **$5000**
   Good to Very Good **$3500**

Collins, Wilkie. *The Woman In White.*
(Three Volumes) London: Sampson Low,
Son & Co., 1860. No mystery to making
out on this.
Retail value in:
   Near Fine to Fine **$15,000**
   Good to Very Good **$3500**

Crane, Stephen (as by Johnston Smith).
Maggie a Girl of the Streets. New York:
Self-published, 1893. Should keep you off
the streets.
Retail value in:
   Near Fine to Fine **$35,000**
   Good to Very Good **$26,000**

Eliot, George. *The Mill on the Floss (3
Vol. set).* Edinburgh and London: William
Blackwood, 1860. Two Bindings: A)
original orange-brown cloth, with 16
pages of ads in volume three. No ad leaf
in the front of volume one. B) light brown
cloth with blindstamped covers and gilt
titles to the spine.
Retail value in:
   Near Fine to Fine **$5000**
   Good to Very Good **$2000**

Hawthorne, Nathaniel. *The Scarlet
Letter.* Boston: Ticknor, Reed & Fields,
1850. First State has a misprint
"reduplicate" for "repudiate" at line 20
page 21.
Retail value in:
   Near Fine to Fine **$8750**
   Good to Very Good **$5000**

James, Henry. *Daisy Miller: A Comedy
In Three Acts.* Boston: James R Osgood &
Co., 1883. First hardcover issue binding
with James R. Osgood colophon on spine.
Retail value in:
   Near Fine to Fine **$1000**
   Good to Very Good **$700**

Melville, Herman. *Moby Dick; or, The
Whale.* New York: Harper & Brothers,
1851. First American edition, first
unexpurgated edition. Most were
destroyed in a fire; those left are red hot
collectibles.
Retail value in:
   Near Fine to Fine **$85,000**
   Good to Very Good **$55,000**

Morris, William. *The Life and Death of
Jason.* Hammersmith: Kelmscott Press,
1895. Printed in red and black, with two
full-page illustrations by Edward Burne-
Jones and initials and decorations by
Morris. Bound in limp vellum with ribbon
ties.
Retail value in:
   Near Fine to Fine **$10,000**
   Good to Very Good **$4000**

Trollope, Anthony. *Prime Minister.*
London: Chapman & Hall, 1876. First
edition in the eight monthly parts: brown
cloth-cased with original printed wrappers
bound in.
Retail value in:
   Near Fine to Fine **$8500**
   Good to Very Good **$6500**

Twain, Mark. *The Adventures of Tom
Sawyer.* London: Chatto and Windus,
[June] 1876. The true first edition of the
American classic.
Retail value in:
   Near Fine to Fine **$17,500**
   Good to Very Good **$10,000**

Price Guide

Adams, Henry. *Democracy: An American Novel.* First Edition: New York: Henry Holt and Company, 1880
Nr.Fine/Fine **$400**
Good/V.Good **$225**

Adams, John Turvill. *Knight of the Golden Malice.* First Edition: New York: Derby & Jackson, 1857
Nr.Fine/Fine **$100**
Good/V.Good **$45**

_____. *The Lost Hunter: A Tale of Early Times.* First Edition: New York: Derby & Jackson, 1856
Nr.Fine/Fine **$165**
Good/V.Good **$75**

_____. *The White Chief Among Red Men.* First Edition: New York: Derby & Jackson, 1856
Nr.Fine/Fine **$120**
Good/V.Good **$65**

Aimard, Gustave. *The Last of the Incas, A Romance of the Pampas.* First Edition: London: Ward Lock, 1862
Nr.Fine/Fine **$300**
Good/V.Good **$165**

_____. *The Gold Seekers.* First Edition: London: Ward & Lock, 1862
Nr.Fine/Fine **$165**
Good/V.Good **$75**

_____. The *Indian Scout.* First Edition: London: Ward & Lock, 1861
Nr.Fine/Fine **$600**
Good/V.Good **$255**

Ainsworth, William Harrison. *Leaguer of Lathom.* First Edition: London: Tinsley Brothers, 1876
Nr.Fine/Fine **$600**
Good/V.Good **$245**

_____. *Rookwood.* First Edition: London, Richard Bentley, 1834

Nr.Fine/Fine **$500**
Good/V.Good **$210**

_____. *The Tower of London: A Historical Romance.* First Edition: London: Richard Bentley, 1840
Nr.Fine/Fine **$650**
Good/V.Good **$275**

Aldrich, Thomas Bailey. *Story Of A Bad Boy.* Points of Issue: First state with p. 14, line 20, reading "scattered" for " scatters," and p. 197, line 10, "abroad" for "aboard. First Edition: Boston: Fields, Osgood, & Co., 1870
Nr.Fine/Fine **$300**
Good/V.Good **$175**

_____. *The Course of True Love Never Did Run Smooth.* First Edition: New York: Rudd and Carleton, 1858
Nr.Fine/Fine **$160**
Good/V.Good **$55**

Alger, Jr., Horatio. *Luck and Pluck; or John Oakley's Inheritance.* First Edition: Boston: Loring, 1869
Nr.Fine/Fine **$2100**
Good/V.Good **$1200**

_____. *Ragged Dick; or, Street Life in New York with the Boot-Blacks.* First Edition: Boston: Loring, 1868
Nr.Fine/Fine **$2700**
Good/V.Good **$1400**

_____. *Boy's Fortune, or, The Strange Adventures of Ben Baker.* First Edition: Philadelphia: Henry T. Coates & Co., 1882
Nr.Fine/Fine **$400**
Good/V.Good **$100**

Anstey, F. *Vice Versa; Or A Lesson To Fathers.* First Edition: London: Smith, Elder and Co, 1882.
Nr.Fine/Fine **$75**
Good/V.Good **$40**

_____. *The Brass Bottle.* First Edition:

London: Smith, Elder & Co., 1900
Nr.Fine/Fine **$90**
Good/V.Good **$55**
First U.S. Edition: New York: D.
Appleton, 1900
Nr.Fine/Fine **$55**
Good/V.Good **$30**

_____. *Mr. Punch's Pocket Ibsen: A
Collection of Some of the Master's Best-
Known Dramas Condensed, Revised, and
Slightly Rearranged.* First Edition:
London: William Heinemann, 1893
Nr.Fine/Fine $125
Good/V.Good **$45**

Bangs, John Kendrick. *A House-Boat on
the Styx.* First Edition: New York: Harper
and Brothers, 1896
Nr.Fine/Fine **$150**
Good/V.Good **$65**

_____. *The Pursuit of the
House-Boat.* First Edition: New York:
Harper & Brothers Pubs., 1897
Nr.Fine/Fine **$125**
Good/V.Good **$65**

_____. *Toppleton's Client
Or, A Spirit in Exile.* First Edition: New
York: Charles L. Webster & Company,
1893
Nr.Fine/Fine **$225**
Good/V.Good **$100**

Baring-Gould, Sabine. *Domitia.* First
Edition: London: Methuen, 1898
Nr.Fine/Fine. **$75**
Good/V.Good **$35**

_____. *Richard Cable. The
Lightshipman.* (Three Volumes) First
Edition: London: Smith Elder, 1888
Nr.Fine/Fine. **$125**
Good/V.Good **$60**

_____. *Cheap Jack Zita.*
(Three Volumes) First Edition: London:
Methuen, 1893
Nr.Fine/Fine **$300**
Good/V.Good **$125**

Barrie, James M. *Sentimental Tommy.*
First Edition: London: Cassell, 1896
Nr.Fine/Fine **$150**
Good/V.Good **$50**

_____. *When a Man's Single.
A Tale of Literary Life.* First Edition:
London: Hodder & Stoughton, 1888
Nr.Fine/Fine **$255**
Good/V.Good **$100**

_____. *The Little Minister.*
(Three Volumes) First Edition: London:
Hodder & Stoughton, 1891
Nr.Fine/Fine **$525**
Good/V.Good **$195**

_____. *A Tillyloss Scandal.*
Points of Issue: This is an American
Pirate, cobbled together from magazine
pieces. The first edition carries the
address: "43, 45 and 47 East Tenth Street"
and was issued in buff colored wraps.
First Edition: New York: Lovell Coryell,
1893
Nr.Fine/Fine. **$245**
Good/V.Good **$95**

Beads of
Tasmer
by Amelia Barr

Barr, Amelia E. *Beads of Tasmer.* First
Edition: New York: James Clarke, 1893.
Nr.Fine/Fine **$250**
Good/V.Good **$95**

_____. *Jan Vedder's Wife.* First
Edition: New York: Dodd Mead, 1885

Nr.Fine/Fine $65
Good/V.Good **$25**

_____. *The Bow of Orange Ribbons.* First Edition: New York: Dodd, Mead, & Co., 1886.
Nr.Fine/Fine **$45**
Good/V.Good **$20**

_____. *Remember the Alamo.* First Edition: New York: Dodd Mead, 1888
Nr.Fine/Fine. **$35**
Good/V.Good **$15**

Bates, Arlo. *The Diary of a Saint.* First Edition: Boston: Houghton Mifflin, 1902
Nr.Fine/Fine **$45**
Good/V.Good **$25**

_____. *The Puritans.* First Edition: Boston: Houghton Mifflin, 1899
Nr.Fine/Fine. **$35**
Good/V.Good **$20**

Bellamy, Edward. *Looking Backward 2000-1887.* First Edition: Boston: Ticknor and Company, 1888
Nr.Fine/Fine **$625**
Good/V.Good **$200**

_____. *Equality.* First Edition: New York: D. Appleton & Co., 1897.
Nr.Fine/Fine **$700**
Good/V.Good **$300**

_____. *The Blindman's World.* First Edition: Boston: Houghton Mifflin, 1898
Nr.Fine/Fine **$85**
Good/V.Good **$35**

Bennett, Emerson. *Clara Moreland; or, Adventures in the Far South-West.* First Edition: Philadelphia: T. B. Peterson, 1853
Nr.Fine/Fine **$165**
Good/V.Good **$70**

Besant, Walter. *Beyond the Dreams of Avarice.* First Edition: London: Chatto & Windus, 1895

Nr.Fine/Fine **$145**
Good/V.Good **$65**

_____. *The World Went Very Well Then.* (Three Volumes) First Edition: London: Chatto & Windus, 1887
Nr.Fine/Fine **$175**
Good/V.Good **$70**

_____. *St. Katherine's by the Tower.* (Three Volumes) First Edition: London: Chatto & Windus, 1891
Nr.Fine/Fine **$525**
Good/V.Good **$200**

Bierce, Ambrose. *Black Beetles in Amber.* First Edition: San Francisco and New York: Western Authors Publishing Co., 1892
Nr.Fine/Fine **$625**
Good/V.Good **$275**

Shapes of Clay
by Ambrose Bierce

_____. *Shapes of Clay.* First Edition: San Francisco: W.E. Wood, 1903
Nr.Fine/Fine **$775**
Good/V.Good **$400**

_____. *Tales of Soldiers and Civilians.* First Edition: San Francisco: E.L.G. Steele, 1891
Nr.Fine/Fine **$600**
Good/V.Good **$275**

Blackmore, Richard Doddridge. *Cripps,*

the Carrier. A Woodland Tale. (Three
Volumes) First Edition: London: Sampson
Low, 1876
Nr.Fine/Fine **$165**
Good/V.Good **$90**

Borrow, George. *Lavengro: The Scholar -
The Gypsy -The Priest.* (Three Volumes)
First Edition: London: John
Murray, 1851
Nr.Fine/Fine **$500**
Good/V.Good **$250**

_____. *The Romany Rye; a
Sequel to "Lavengro."* First Edition:
London: John Murray, 1857
Nr.Fine/Fine **$275**
Good/V.Good **$140**

Bronte, Charlotte. (as by Currer Bell).
Jane Eyre. An Autobiography. First
Edition: London: Smith, Elder & Co.,
1847. (Three Volumes)
Nr.Fine/Fine **$38,000**
Good/V.Good **$22,500**
First U.S. Edition: New York: Harper &
Brothers, 1848.
Nr.Fine/Fine **$1450**
Good/V.Good **$775**

_____.
Shirley, A Tale. First Edition: London:
Smith, Elder & Co., 1849
Nr.Fine/Fine **$3750**
Good/V.Good **$1600**

_____.
Villette. First Edition: London: Smith,
Elder & Co, 1853
Nr.Fine/Fine **$2500**
Good/V.Good **$1350**
First U.S. Edition: New York: Harper And
Brothers, 1853
Nr.Fine/Fine **$750**
Good/V.Good **$400**

Bronte, Emily (as by Ellis Bell).
Wuthering Heights. First U.S. Edition:
New York: Harper & Brothers Publishers,
1848
Nr.Fine/Fine **$14500**

Good/V.Good **$7500**

Bunner, H. C. *"Short Sixes" Stories to be
Read while the Candle Burns.* First
Edition: New York: Puck, Keppler &
Schwarzmann, 1891
Nr.Fine/Fine **$165**
Good/V.Good **$75**

_____. *More "Short Sixes."* First
Edition: New York: Puck, Keppler &
Schwarzmann, 1894
Nr.Fine/Fine **$75**
Good/V.Good **$30**

_____. *A Woman of Honor.* First
Edition: Boston: James R. Osgood, 1883
Nr.Fine/Fine **$200**
Good/V.Good **$75**

Burnett, Francis Hodgson. *Little Lord
Fauntleroy.* Points of Issue: First State has
Devinne Press seal on Page 201. First
Edition: New York: Scribners, 1886
Nr.Fine/Fine **$1475**
Good/V.Good **$800**
First U.K. Edition: London, Frederick,
Warne and Co., 1886
Nr.Fine/Fine **$375**
Good/V.Good **$165**

_____. *A Lady of
Quality.* First Edition: New York:
Scribners, 1896.
Nr.Fine/Fine **$110**
Good/V.Good **$50**

_____. *Louisiana.*
First Edition: New York: Scribners, 1880.
Nr.Fine/Fine **$75**
Good/V.Good **$40**

Butler, Samuel. *The Way of All Flesh.*
First Edition: London: Grant Richards,
1903
Nr.Fine/Fine **$650**
Good/V.Good **$300**
First U.S. Edition: New York: E. P.
Dutton, 1910.
Nr.Fine/Fine **$275**
Good/V.Good **$165**

Bynner, Edwin Lassetter. *Damen's Ghost.* First Edition: Boston: Houghton Mifflin/James R. Osgood, 1881
Nr.Fine/Fine **$65**
Good/V.Good **$30**

_____. *Agnes Surriage.*
First Edition: Boston: Ticknor And Company, 1887
Nr.Fine/Fine **$85**
Good/V.Good **$40**

Cable, George Washington. *The Grandissimes: A Story of Creole Life.*
First Edition: New York: Scribners, 1880
Nr.Fine/Fine **$120**
Good/V.Good **$45**

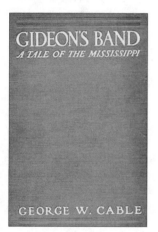

Gideon's Band: A
Tale of the
Mississippi
by George W. Cable

_____. *Gideon's Band: A Tale of the Mississippi.* First Edition: New York: Scribner's, 1914
Nr.Fine/Fine **$100**
Good/V.Good **$45**

_____. *The Cavalier.*
First Edition: New York: Charles Scribner's, 1901
Nr.Fine/Fine **$65**
Good/V.Good **$30**

Caine, Hall. *A Son of Hagar: A Romance of Our Time.* First Edition: London: Chatto and Windus, 1887.

Nr.Fine/Fine **$500**
Good/V.Good **$275**

_____. *The Scapegoat: A Romance.*
First Edition: London: William Heinemann, 1891
Nr.Fine/Fine **$375**
Good/V.Good **$190**

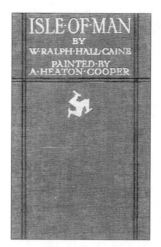

Isle of Man
by Hall Caine

Caine, Hall (as by W. Ralph Hall Caine). *Isle of Man.* First Edition: London: Adam and Charles Black, 1909
Nr.Fine/Fine **$150**
Good/V.Good **$65**

Carroll, Lewis. *Alice's Adventures in Wonderland.* First Edition: London: Macmillan, 1866
Nr.Fine/Fine **$24,000**
Good/V.Good **$18,000**
First U.S. Edition: New York: D. Appleton, 1866
Nr.Fine/Fine **$20,000**
Good/V.Good **$12,000**

_____. *The Hunting of the Snark.*
First Edition: London: Macmillan, 1876
Nr.Fine/Fine **$2000**
Good/V.Good **$600**

_____. *Though the Looking Glass.*
First Edition: London, Macmillan, 1872
Nr.Fine/Fine **$8500**
Good/V.Good **$4000**

Caruthers, William Alexander. *The Cavaliers of Virginia, or The Recluse of Jamestown. An Historical Romance of the*

Old Dominion. (Two Volumes) First Edition: New York: Harper & Brothers, 1834-1835
Nr.Fine/Fine **$300**
Good/V.Good **$165**

Catherwood, Mary. *The Queen of the Swamp, and Other Plain Americans.* First Edition: Boston: Houghton, Mifflin, 1899
Nr.Fine/Fine **$85**
Good/V.Good **$30**

_____. *The White Islander.* First Edition: New York: The Century Co., 1893.
Nr.Fine/Fine **$50**
Good/V.Good **$30**

Chopin, Kate. *A Night in Acadie.* First Edition: Chicago: Way & Williams, 1897.
Nr.Fine/Fine **$2000**
Good/V.Good **$875**

_____. *Bayou Folk.* First Edition: Boston: Houghton Mifflin, 1894
Nr.Fine/Fine **$700**
Good/V.Good **$275**

_____. *The Awakening.* First Edition: Chicago: Herbert S. Stone, 1899
Nr.Fine/Fine **$8200**
Good/V.Good **$3750**

The Gunmaker
of Moscow
by Sylvanus Cobb

Cobb, Sylvanus. *The Gunmaker of Moscow or Vladimir the Monk.* First

Edition: New York: Robert Bonner's Sons, 1888
Nr.Fine/Fine **$125**
Good/V.Good **$45**

_____. *Karmel the Scout or The Rebel of the Jerseys.* First Edition: Philadelphia: Henry T. Coates, 1896
Nr.Fine/Fine **$55**
Good/V.Good **$30**

Collins, Wilkie. *The Queen of Hearts.* (Three Volumes) First Edition: London: Hurst and Blackett, 1859
Nr.Fine/Fine **$2300**
Good/V.Good **$1000**

_____. *After Dark.* (Two Volumes) First Edition: London: Smith, Elder, 1856.
Nr.Fine/Fine **$12,500**
Good/V.Good **$4600**

_____. *The Moonstone.* (Three Volumes) First Edition: London: Tinsley Brothers, 1868
Nr.Fine/Fine **$7500**
Good/V.Good **$4500**

Conrad, Joseph. *Almayer's Folly: The Story of an Eastern River.* First Edition: London: T. Fisher Unwin, 1895
Nr.Fine/Fine **$3650**
Good/V.Good **$1500**

_____. *Lord Jim.* First Edition: Edinburgh and London, Blackwood, 1900
Nr.Fine/Fine **$3500**
Good/V.Good **$1200**

Cooper, James Fenimore. *Last of the Mohicans A Narrative of 1757.* First Edition: Philadelphia: H.C. Carey & I. Lea, 1826.
Nr.Fine/Fine **$20,000**
Good/V.Good **$12,000**

_____. *Pioneers, or the Sources of the Susquehanna; A Descriptive Tale.* First Edition: New York: Charles Wiley, 1823
Nr.Fine/Fine **$2000**

Good/V.Good **$850**

_____. *The Deerslayer: or, The First War-Path. A Tale.* First Edition: Philadelphia: Lea & Blanchard, 1841
Nr.Fine/Fine **$2500**
Good/V.Good **$1250**

_____. *Pathfinder; or, The Inland Sea.* First Edition: Philadelphia: Lea & Blanchard, 1840
Nr.Fine/Fine **$2850**
Good/V.Good **$1100**

Crane, Stephen (as by Johnston Smith). *Maggie a Girl of the Streets.* First Edition (Trade): New York: D. Appleton, 1896
Nr.Fine/Fine **$2400**
Good/V.Good **$1000**

_____. *Red Badge of Courage.* First Edition: New York D. Appleton and Company 1895
Nr.Fine/Fine **$3500**
Good/V.Good **$1850**

_____. *The Open Boat and Other Tales of Adventure.* First Edition: New York: Doubleday McClure, 1898
Nr.Fine/Fine **$125**
Good/V.Good **$45**

Via Crucis: A Romance of the Second Crusade *by Francis Marion Crawford*

Crawford, Francis Marion. *Via Crucis; a Romance of the Second Crusade.* First Edition: New York: Macmillan, 1899

Nr.Fine/Fine **$170**
Good/V.Good **$65**

_____. *The Ralstons.* (Two Volumes) First Edition: New York: Macmillan, 1895
Nr.Fine/Fine **$115**
Good/V.Good **$45**

Davis, Rebecca Harding. *Kent Hampden.* First Edition: New York: Scribners, 1892
Nr.Fine/Fine **$165**
Good/V.Good **$75**

Davis, Richard Harding. *Van Bibber and Others.* First Edition: New York: Harper & Brothers, 1892
Nr.Fine/Fine **$85**
Good/V.Good **$40**

_____. *In the Fog.* First Edition: New York: R. H. Russell, 1901
Nr.Fine/Fine **$120**
Good/V.Good **$50**

_____. *Gallegher and Other Stories.* First Edition: New York: Scribners, 1891
Nr.Fine/Fine **$85**
Good/V.Good **$40**

De Forest, John William. *Overland: A Novel.* First Edition: New York: Sheldon and Co., 1871
Nr.Fine/Fine **$100**
Good/V.Good **$45**

A Christmas Carol *by Charles Dickens*

Dickens, Charles. *Great Expectations.* (Three Volumes) First Edition: London: Chapman and Hall, 1861
Nr.Fine/Fine **$28,000**
Good/V.Good **$15,000**

_____. *A Christmas Carol.* First Edition: London: Chapman and Hall, 1843
Nr.Fine/Fine **$30,000**
Good/V.Good **$18,000**

Dickens, Charles (as by Boz). *Oliver Twist.* (Three Volumes) First Edition: London: Richard Bentley, 1838
Nr.Fine/Fine **$12,500**
Good/V.Good **$6500**

Disraeli, Benjamin. *Vivian Grey.* (Five Volumes) First Edition: London: Henry Colburn, 1826-27
Nr.Fine/Fine **$1850**
Good/V.Good **$1000**

_____. *Henrietta Temple, A Love Story.* (Three Volumes) First Edition: London: Henry Colburn, 1837
Nr.Fine/Fine **$550**
Good/V.Good **$300**
First U.S. Edition: Philadelphia: Carey and Hart, 1837
Nr.Fine/Fine **$250**
Good/V.Good **$125**

_____. *Endymion.* (Three Volumes) First Edition: London: Longmans, Green, 1880
Nr.Fine/Fine **$275**
Good/V.Good **$155**

Dodge, Mary Mapes. *Hans Brinker or the Silver Skates.* First Edition: New York: James O'Kane, 1866
Nr.Fine/Fine **$1500**
Good/V.Good **$800**

_____. *When Life Is Young.* First Edition: New York: Century, 1894.
Nr.Fine/Fine **$65**
Good/V.Good **$40**

Dostoievsky, Fedor. *Poor Folk.* First

Edition of Lena Milman Translation: London: Elkin Mathews, 1894.
Nr.Fine/Fine **$425**
Good/V.Good **$175**

Doyle, Arthur Conan. *The White Company.* (Three Volumes) First Edition: London; Smith, Elder, 1891
Nr.Fine/Fine **$10,000**
Good/V.Good **$4850**

_____. *The Refugees.* (Three Volumes) First Edition: London: Longmans Green, 1893
Nr.Fine/Fine **$2050**
Good/V.Good **$975**
First U.S. Edition: New York: Harper & Brothers, 1893
Nr.Fine/Fine **$375**
Good/V.Good **$225**

_____. *A Duet With An Occasional Chorus.* First Edition: London: Grant Richards, 1899.
Nr.Fine/Fine **$225**
Good/V.Good **$130**
First U.S. Edition: New York: D. Appleton, 1899
Nr.Fine/Fine **$75**
Good/V.Good **$25**

DuMaurier, George. *The Martian.* First Edition (Limited): London and New York: Harper & Brothers, 1897
Nr.Fine/Fine **$150**
Good/V.Good **$85**
First Edition: London and New York: Harper & Brothers, 1897
Nr.Fine/Fine **$65**
Good/V.Good **$30**
_____. *Trilby, A Novel.* First Edition: London: Osgood, McIlvaine, 1895
Nr.Fine/Fine **$100**
Good/V.Good **$45**
First U.S. Edition: New York: Harper & Brothers, 1894
Nr.Fine/Fine **$65**
Good/V.Good **$25**

_____. *Peter Ibbetson.* First

Edition: New York: Harper & Brothers,
1891
Nr.Fine/Fine **$55**
Good/V.Good **$20**
First U.K. Edition: London: Osgood,
McIlvaine, 1892. (Two Volumes)
Nr.Fine/Fine **$85**
Good/V.Good **$35**

Eliot, George. *Romola.* (Three Volumes)
First Edition (Trade): London: Smith,
Elder, 1863
Nr.Fine/Fine **$850**
Good/V.Good **$400**

_____. *Silas Marner The Weaver
of Raveloe.* First Edition: Edinburgh and
London: William Blackwood and Sons,
1861.
Nr.Fine/Fine **$5000**
Good/V.Good **$2800**

Daniel Deronda
by George Eliot

_____. *Daniel Deronda.* (Four
Volumes) First Edition: Edinburgh and
London: William Blackwood, 1876
Nr.Fine/Fine **$2575**
Good/V.Good **$1000**

Evans, Augusta Jane. *Beulah.* First
Edition: New York: Derby & Jackson,
1859
Nr.Fine/Fine **$150**
Good/V.Good **$80**

_____. *Inez: A Tale of the
Alamo.* First Edition: New York: Carleton,

1872
Nr.Fine/Fine **$65**
Good/V.Good **$30**

Flaubert, Gustave. *Madame Bovary.*
First Edition of Eleanor Marx-Aveling
translation: London: Vizetelly & Co.,
1886.
Nr.Fine/Fine **$7500**
Good/V.Good **$3000**

Foote, Mary Hallock. *The Desert and the
Sown.* First Edition: Boston: Houghton
Mifflin, 1902
Nr.Fine/Fine **$75**
Good/V.Good **$35**

_____. *A Touch of Sun
and Other Stories.* First Edition: Boston:
Houghton Mifflin, 1903
Nr.Fine/Fine **$85**
Good/V.Good **$45**

Ford, Paul Leicester. *A Warning To
Lovers.* First Edition: New York: Dodd,
Mead, 1906
Nr.Fine/Fine **$175**
Good/V.Good **$65**

_____. *Love Finds the Way.*
First Edition: New York: Dodd Mead,
1904
Nr.Fine/Fine **$200**
Good/V.Good **$85**

_____. *Wanted-A Matchmaker.*
First Edition: New York: Dodd Mead,
1900
Nr.Fine/Fine **$145**
Good/V.Good **$65**

Fox, John. *The Little Shepherd of
Kingdom Come.* First Edition: New York:
Scribners, 1903
Nr.Fine/Fine **$155**
Good/V.Good **$70**

_____. *The Trail of the Lonesome
Pine.* First Edition: New York: Charles
Scribner's Sons, 1908
Nr.Fine/Fine **$120**
Good/V.Good **$45**

_____. *"Hell fer Sartain": And Other Stories.* First Edition: New York: Harper & Brothers, 1897
Nr.Fine/Fine **$95**
Good/V.Good **$50**

Fuller, Henry B. *The Puppet-Booth.* First Edition: New York: Century Co., 1896
Nr.Fine/Fine **$255**
Good/V.Good **$95**

_____. *The Cliff-Dwellers.* First Edition: New York: Harper & Brothers, 1893
Nr.Fine/Fine **$165**
Good/V.Good **$95**

_____. *The Chatelaine of La Trinite.* First Edition: New York: The Century Co., 1892
Nr.Fine/Fine **$75**
Good/V.Good **$45**

Gaskell, Elizabeth. (as by Mrs. Gaskell) *Wives and Daughters.* (Two Volumes) First Edition: London: Smith, Elder, 1866
Nr.Fine/Fine **$665**
Good/V.Good **$325**
First U.S. Edition: New York: Harper & Brothers, 1866
Nr.Fine/Fine. **$500**
Good/V.Good **$225**

Gautier, Theophile. *One of Cleopatra's Nights.* First Edition of Lafcadio Hearn Translation: New York: R. Worthington, 1882
Nr.Fine/Fine **$575**
Good/V.Good **$200**

_____. *Clarimonde.* First Edition of Lafcadio Hearn Translation: New York: Brentano's, 1899
Nr.Fine/Fine. **$525**
Good/V.Good **$250**

Gissing, George. (as by Anonymous) *Demos.* First Edition: London: Smith, Elder, 1886.
Nr.Fine/Fine **$2000**
Good/V.Good **$875**

Gissing, George. *Denzil Quarrier. A Novel.* First Edition: London: Lawrence & Bullen, 1892
Nr.Fine/Fine **$525**
Good/V.Good **$300**

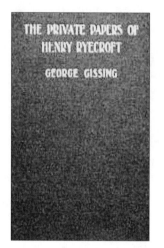

The Private Papers of Henry Ryecroft *by George Gissing*

_____. *The Private Papers of Henry Ryecroft.* First Edition: Westminster: Archibald Constable & Co., 1903.
Nr.Fine/Fine **$275**
Good/V.Good **$95**

Gogol, Nikolai. *Dead Souls.* First Edition in English: London: T. Fisher Unwin, 1893
Nr.Fine/Fine **$475**
Good/V.Good **$215**

_____. *The Inspector-General.* First Edition of Arthur Sykes translation: London: Walter Scott, 1892
Nr.Fine/Fine **$145**
Good/V.Good **$85**

Gould, Nat. *Who Did It?* First Edition: Manchester: George Routledge and Sons, 1896
Nr.Fine/Fine **$35**
Good/V.Good **$20**

_____. *The Old Mare's Foal.* First Edition: London: George Routledge and Sons, 1899
Nr.Fine/Fine **$95**

Good/V.Good **$45**

Habberton, John. *The Worst Boy in Town.* First Edition: New York: Putnam, 1880.
Nr.Fine/Fine **$135**
Good/V.Good **$75**

_____. *Helen's Babies.* First Edition: Boston: Loring, 1876
Nr.Fine/Fine **$200**
Good/V.Good **$85**

_____. *Other People's Children.* First Edition: New York: Putnam, 1877.
Nr.Fine/Fine **$100**
Good/V.Good **$45**

Haggard, H. Rider. *Dawn.* (Three Volumes) First Edition: London: Hurst and Blackett, 1884
Nr.Fine/Fine **$8250**
Good/V.Good **$5000**

The Wizard
by H. Rider Haggard

_____. *The Wizard.*
First Edition: Bristol & London: J. W. Arrowsmith & Simpkin, Marshall, Hamilton, Kent, n.d.
Nr.Fine/Fine **$625**
Good/V.Good **$300**
First U.S. Edition: New York Longmans, Green, and Co., 1896
Nr.Fine/Fine **$200**
Good/V.Good **$85**
_____. *Mr. Meeson's Will.*

First Edition: London: Spencer Blackett, 1888
Nr.Fine/Fine **$500**
Good/V.Good **$200**

Hale, Edward Everett. *Man Without a Country.* Points of Issue: Softcover in mauvre wraps. First Edition: Boston: Ticknor & Fields, 1865
Nr.Fine/Fine **$1200**
Good/V.Good **$725**

_____. *The Fortunes of Rachel.* First Edition: New York: Funk & Wagnalls, 1884
Nr.Fine/Fine **$165**
Good/V.Good **$55**

_____. *Philip Nolan's Friends, A Story Of The Change Of Western Empire.* First Edition: New York: Scribner, Armstrong, & Co., 1877
Nr.Fine/Fine **$110**
Good/V.Good **$45**

Hardy, Thomas. *Tess of the d'Urbervilles: A Pure Woman Faithfully Presented.* (Three Volumes) Points of Issue: Chapter XXV for 'Chapter XXXV on page 199 of volume 2. First Edition: London: James R. Osgood, McIlvaine, 1891
Nr.Fine/Fine **$12,225**
Good/V.Good **$6500**

_____. *Return of the Native.* First Edition: London: Smith, Elder, 1878
Nr.Fine/Fine **$5000**
Good/V.Good **$2250**

_____. *Two On A Tower.* (Three Volumes) First Edition: London: Sampson Low, Marston, Searle and Rivington, 1882
Nr.Fine/Fine **$2500**
Good/V.Good **$1400**

Harris, Joel Chandler. *Uncle Remus His Songs & His Sayings.* First Edition: New York: D. Appleton, 1881
Nr.Fine/Fine **$5800**
Good/V.Good **$2750**

_____. *Sister Jane.* First Edition: Boston: Houghton Mifflin, 1896
Nr.Fine/Fine. **$250**
Good/V.Good **$110**

_____. *The Story of Aaron (so named) the Son of Ben Ali.* First Edition: Boston & New York: Houghton Mifflin, 1896
Nr.Fine/Fine **$265**
Good/V.Good **$115**

Harrison, Constance Cary. (as by Mrs. Burton) *The Merry Maid of Arcady, His Lordship and Other Stories.* First Edition: Boston, London, New York: Lamson Wolffe, 1897
Nr.Fine/Fine **$85**
Good/V.Good **$40**

Harte, Bret. *The Lost Galleon and Other Tales.* First Edition: San Francisco: Towne and Bacon, 1867
Nr.Fine/Fine **$600**
Good/V.Good **$250**

_____. *Barker's Luck and Other Stories.* First Edition: Boston: Houghton, Mifflin and Company, 1896
Nr.Fine/Fine **$110**
Good/V.Good **$45**

_____. *A Sappho of Green Springs and Other Tales.* First Edition: London. Chatto & Windus, 1891
Nr.Fine/Fine **$125**
Good/V.Good **$75**
First U.S. Edition: Boston & New York: Houghton Mifflin, 1891
Nr.Fine/Fine **$50**
Good/V.Good **$25**

Hawthorne, Nathaniel. *Mosses from an Old Manse.* First Edition: New York: Wiley & Putnam, 1846.
Nr.Fine/Fine **$5750**
Good/V.Good **$2500**

_____. *Twice-Told Tales.* First Edition: Boston: American Stationers Co. John B. Russell, 1837
Nr.Fine/Fine. **$5250**

Good/V.Good **$2700**

_____. *The House of the Seven Gables.* First Edition: Boston: Ticknor, Reed & Fields, 1851
Nr.Fine/Fine **$4500**
Good/V.Good **$2450**

Hearn, Lafcadio. *Shadowings.* First Edition: Boston: Little, Brown and Company, 1900
Nr.Fine/Fine **$750**
Good/V.Good **$225**

_____. *Stray Leaves from Strange Literature.* First Edition: Boston: James R. Osgood, 1884
Nr.Fine/Fine. **$825**
Good/V.Good **$400**

_____. *Youma. The Story of a West-Indian Slave.* First Edition: New York: Harper & Brothers, 1890
Nr.Fine/Fine **$325**
Good/V.Good. **$125**

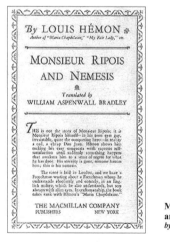

Monsieur Ripois and Nemesis
by Louis Hemon

Hemon, Louis. *Monsieur Ripois and Nemesis.* First Edition of William Aspenwall Bradley translation: New York: Macmillan, 1925.
Nr.Fine/Fine **$75**
Good/V.Good **$30**

Henry, O. *Strictly Business.* First Edition: New York: Doubleday Page, 1910

Nr.Fine/Fine **$2000**
Good/V.Good **$850**

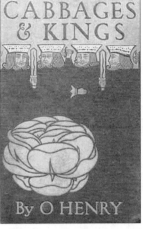

Cabbages & Kings
by O Henry

_____. *Cabbages & Kings.* First
Edition: New York: McClure Phillips,
1904
Nr.Fine/Fine **$600**
Good/V.Good **$250**

_____. *Heart of the West.* First
Edition: New York: The McClure
Company, 1907
Nr.Fine/Fine **$365**
Good/V.Good **$185**

Henty, G.A. *Under Drake's Flag: Tale of
the Spanish Main.* First Edition: London:
Blackie & Son, 1883
Nr.Fine/Fine **$175**
Good/V.Good **$50**

_____. *A Knight of the White Cross.*
First Edition: London: Blackie & Son,
1886
Nr.Fine/Fine **$165**
Good/V.Good **$70**

_____. *A March on London, Being
the Story of Wat Tyler's Insurrection.* First
Edition: New York: Scribners, 1897.
Nr.Fine/Fine. **$165**
Good/V.Good **$75**
First U.K. Edition: London: Blackie &
Son, 1898

Nr.Fine/Fine **$150**
Good/V.Good **$70**

Holland, J.G. *Nicholas Minturn.* First
Edition: New York: Scribner Armstrong ,
1877
Nr.Fine/Fine **$60**
Good/V.Good **$25**

**Holley, Marietta. (as by Josiah Allen's
Wife)** *Samantha on the Race Problem.*
First Edition: Boston: Union
Publishing/Dodd Mead, 1892
Nr.Fine/Fine **$110**
Good/V.Good **$50**

__. *Samantha Among the Brethren.* First
Edition: New York & London: Funk &
Wagnalls, 1890
Nr.Fine/Fine **$65**
Good/V.Good **$25**

__. *Samantha at Saratoga: Or, "Flirtin'
With Fashion."* First Edition: Philadelphia:
Hubbard Brothers, 1887
Nr.Fine/Fine **$75**
Good/V.Good **$30**

Howard, Blanche Willis. *The Garden of
Eden.* First Edition: New York: Scribners,
1900
Nr.Fine/Fine **$75**
Good/V.Good **$35**

_____. *Aunt Serena.*
First Edition: Boston: James R. Osgood,
1881
Nr.Fine/Fine **$65**
Good/V.Good **$35**

Howells, W. D. *The Rise of Silas Lapham.*
First Edition: Boston: Ticknor & Co.,
1885
Nr.Fine/Fine **$325**
Good/V.Good **$140**

_____. *The Lady of the
Aroostook.* First Edition: Cambridge, MA:
Houghton, Osgood and Co., 1879
Nr.Fine/Fine **$85**

Good/V.Good **$35**

_____. *Mouse-Trap and Other Farces.* First Edition: New York: Harper & Brothers, 1889
Nr.Fine/Fine **$65**
Good/V.Good **$30**

Ingraham, Col. Prentiss. *Buffalo Bill and the White Queen or, The Shadow of the Aztecs.* Points of Issue: Paperback Original. First Edition: New York; Street & Smith, 1911
Nr.Fine/Fine **$45**
Good/V.Good **$20**

_____. *The Corsair Queen; or, the Gipsies of the Sea.* Points of Issue: Paperback Original first is Beadle's Dime Library, vol. XII, no. 155. First Edition: New York: Beadle & Adams, 1881
Nr.Fine/Fine. **$50**
Good/V.Good **$35**

_____. *Buffalo Bill in the Land of Dread or, The Quest of the Unknown.* Points of Issue: Paperback Original. First Edition: New York; Street & Smith Corp, 1915
Nr.Fine/Fine **$35**
Good/V.Good **$20**

James, Henry. *Passionate Pilgrim and other Tales.* First Edition: Boston: James R. Osgood, 1875
Nr.Fine/Fine. **$3000**
Good/V.Good **$1200**

_____. *Watch and Ward.* First Edition: Boston Houghton, Osgood and Company, 1878.
Nr.Fine/Fine **$1250**
Good/V.Good **$525**

_____. *Better Sort.* First U.S. Edition: New York: Scribners, 1903
Nr.Fine/Fine. **$225**
Good/V.Good. **$95**
First U.K. Edition: London: Methuen, 1903
Nr.Fine/Fine **$200**

Good/V.Good **$90**

The Aztec Treasure-House
by Thomas A. Janvier

Janvier, Thomas A. *The Aztec Treasure-House.* First Edition: New York: Harper & Brothers, 1890
Nr.Fine/Fine **$100**
Good/V.Good **$45**

_____. *The Uncle of an Angel and Other Stories.* First Edition: New York: Harper and Brothers, 1891
Nr.Fine/Fine **$65**
Good/V.Good **$25**

Jewett, Sarah Orne. *A Native of Winby and Other Tales.* First Edition: Boston: Houghton Mifflin, 1893
Nr.Fine/Fine **$250**
Good/V.Good **$100**

_____. *The Country of the Pointed Firs.* First Edition: Boston: Houghton Mifflin, 1896
Nr.Fine/Fine **$400**
Good/V.Good **$175**

_____. *Country Doctor.* First Edition: Boston: Houghton Mifflin, 1884
Nr.Fine/Fine **$275**
Good/V.Good **$100**

Jones, John Beauchamp. *Rival Belles. Or, life in Washington.* First Edition: Philadelphia: T.B. Peterson & Bros., 1864
Nr.Fine/Fine **$50**

Good/V.Good **$30**

_____. *The Winkles. Or, the Merry Monomaniacs.* First Edition: New York: D. Appleton, 1855
Nr.Fine/Fine **$75**
Good/V.Good **$40**

Judson, Edward Zane Carroll. (as by Ned Buntline) *Matanzas; or A Brother's Revenge. A Tale of Florida.* Points of Issue: Paperback Original. First Edition: Boston: George H. Williams, 1848
Nr.Fine/Fine **$850**
Good/V.Good **$400**

_____. *The White Wizard or, The Great Prophet of the Seminoles. A Tale of Mystery in the South and North.* Points of Issue: Paperback Original. First Edition: New York: Frederic A. Brady, n.d
Nr.Fine/Fine................ **$750**
Good/V.Good **$350**

Kaler, James Otis. *Jenny Wren's Boarding House-A Story of Newsboy Life in New York.* First Edition: Boston: Estes & Lauriat, 1893.
Nr.Fine/Fine................ **$150**
Good/V.Good **$80**

Kaler, James Otis. (as by James Otis) *Toby Tyler, or Ten Weeks With a Circus.* First Edition: New York: Harper & Brothers, 1881
Nr.Fine/Fine **$325**
Good/V.Good **$100**

_____. *The Boy Captain.* First Edition: Boston: Estes and Lauriat, 1896
Nr.Fine/Fine **$125**
Good/V.Good **$55**

Lawrence, George Alfred. *Silverland.* First Edition: London: Chapman And Hall, 1873
Nr.Fine/Fine **$365**
Good/V.Good **$185**

_____. *Barren*

Honour. First Edition: London: Parker, Son, and Bourn, 1862
Nr.Fine/Fine **$325**
Good/V.Good **$145**

Lippard, George. *New York: Its Upper Ten And Lower Million.* First Edition: Cincinnati, OH: H. M. Rulison, 1853
Nr.Fine/Fine **$100**
Good/V.Good **$60**

The Night Born
by Jack London

London, Jack. *The Night Born.* First Edition: New York The Century Co., 1913
Nr.Fine/Fine **$550**
Good/V.Good **$200**

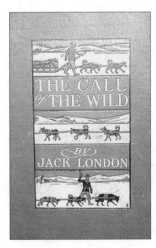

The Call of the Wild
by Jack London

_____. *The Call of the Wild.* First Edition: New York: Macmillan, 1903.

Nr.Fine/Fine **$8000**
Good/V.Good **$3750**

_____. *Burning Daylight.* First
Edition: New York: Macmillan, 1910
Nr.Fine/Fine **$3000**
Good/V.Good **$1200**

Loti, Pierre. *The Book of Pity and of
Death.* First Edition in English: London,
Paris and Melbourne: Cassell, 1892
Nr.Fine/Fine **$150**
Good/V.Good **$45**

_____. *Madame Chrysantheme.*
First Edition in English: London: George
Routledge and Sons, 1897
Nr.Fine/Fine **$75**
Good/V.Good **$30**

_____. *Ramuntcho.* First U.S.
Edition: New York: R. F. Fenno, 1897
Nr.Fine/Fine **$85**
Good/V.Good $30

Lytton, Edward Bulwer. *Pelham; or, The
Adventures of a Gentleman.* (Three
Volumes) First Edition: London: Henry
Colburn, 1828
Nr.Fine/Fine **$675**
Good/V.Good **$450**

_____. *The Last Days
of Pompeii.* (Three Volumes) First
Edition: London: Richard Bentley, 1834
Nr.Fine/Fine **$1200**
Good/V.Good **$475**
First U.S. Edition: New York: Harper &
Brothers, 1834. (Two Volumes)
Nr.Fine/Fine **$350**
Good/V.Good **$150**

_____. *Lucretia or the
Children of the Night.* (Three Volumes)
First Edition: London, Saunders and
Otley, 1846
Nr.Fine/Fine **$550**
Good/V.Good **$200**

Major, Charles. *Dorothy Vernon of
Haddon Hall.* First Edition: New York:
Macmillan, 1902

Nr.Fine/Fine **$65**
Good/V.Good **$30**

Marvel, Ik. *Reveries of a Bachelor: Or a
Book of the Heart.* First Edition: New
York: Baker & Scribner, 1850
Nr.Fine/Fine **$100**
Good/V.Good **$45**

_____. *Dream Life: A Fable of the
Seasons.* First Edition: New York: Charles
Scribner, 1851
Nr.Fine/Fine **$110**
Good/V.Good **$60**

_____. *Seven Stories, with Basement
and Attic.* First Edition: New York:
Charles Scribner, 1865
Nr.Fine/Fine **$65**
Good/V.Good **$25**

Melville, Herman. *The Piazza Tales.*
First Edition: New York and London: Dix
& Edwards and Sampson Low, 1856
Nr.Fine/Fine **$5250**
Good/V.Good **$1700**

_____. *Pierre; or The
Ambiguities.* First Edition: New York:
Harper & Brothers, 1852
Nr.Fine/Fine **$2500**
Good/V.Good **$1500**

_____. *Mardi: and a Voyage
Thither.* (Three Volumes) First Edition:
London: Richard Bentley, 1849
Nr.Fine/Fine **$3500**
Good/V.Good **$2100**
First U.S. Edition: New York: Harper &
Brothers, 1849
Nr.Fine/Fine **$4500**
Good/V.Good **$1500**

Mitchell, S. Weir. *Hugh Wynne Free
Quaker.* First Edition: New York: Century
Co., 1897
Nr.Fine/Fine **$250**
Good/V.Good **$110**

_____. *Constance Trescot. A
Novel.* First Edition: New York: Century
Co., 1905

Nr.Fine/Fine **$55**
Good/V.Good **$20**

Nesbit, Edith. *The Story of the Amulet.*
First Edition: London, T. Fisher Unwin.
1906
Nr.Fine/Fine **$400**
Good/V.Good **$185**

Yvernelle: A
Legend of
Feudal France
by Frank Norris

Norris, Frank. *Yvernelle: A Legend of
Feudal France.* First Edition:
Philadelphia: J. B. Lippincott, 1892
Nr.Fine/Fine **$2750**
Good/V.Good **$1500**

_____. *McTeague, A Story of San
Francisco.* Points of Issue: first state has
"moment" as last word on page 106. First
Edition: Garden City, NY: Doubleday &
McClure, 1899
Nr.Fine/Fine **$1100**
Good/V.Good **$375**

_____. *The Octopus: A Story of
California. The Epic of Wheat.* First
Edition: Garden City, NY: Doubleday,
Page, 1901
Nr.Fine/Fine **$300**
Good/V.Good **$125**

Optic, Oliver. *A Victorious Union: The
Blue and the Gray Afloat.* First Edition:
Boston: Lothrop, Lee & Shepard, 1893
Nr.Fine/Fine $500

Good/V.Good **$225**

_____. *The Boat Club.* First
Edition: Boston: Brown, Bazin, 1855
Nr.Fine/Fine **$125**
Good/V.Good **$45**

_____. *Marrying a Beggar or the
Angel in Disguise and Other Tales.* First
Edition: Boston: Wentworth, Hewes,
1859.
Nr.Fine/Fine **$175**
Good/V.Good **$85**

Ouida. *La Strega and Other Stories.* First
Edition: London, Sampson Low, Marston,
1899.
Nr.Fine/Fine **$75**
Good/V.Good **$40**

_____. *Ariadnê, The story of a dream.*
(Three Volumes) First Edition: London:
Chatto & Windus, 1877
Nr.Fine/Fine **$300**
Good/V.Good **$125**
First U.S. Edition: Philadelphia: J.B.
Lippincott, 1877
Nr.Fine/Fine **$120**
Good/V.Good **$55**

_____. *The Waters of Edera.* First Edition:
London, T. Fisher Unwin, 1900
Nr.Fine/Fine **$125**
Good/V.Good **$55**

Page, Thomas Nelson. *In Ole Virginia.*
First Edition: New York: Scribners, 1887.
Nr.Fine/Fine **$300**
Good/V.Good **$100**

_____. *Two Prisoners.*
First Edition: New York: R. H. Russell,
1898
Nr.Fine/Fine **$75**
Good/V.Good **$30**

_____. *Red Rock. A
Chronicle of Reconstruction.* First
Edition: New York: Scribners, 1898
Nr.Fine/Fine **$100**
Good/V.Good **$40**

Pansy. *Making Fate.* First Edition: Boston: Lothrop Publishing Company, 1895
Nr.Fine/Fine **$75**
Good/V.Good **$30**

_____. *A New Graft on the Family Tree.* First Edition: Boston: Lothrop Publishing Company, 1880
Nr.Fine/Fine **$55**
Good/V.Good **$20**

Pater, Walter. *Imaginary Portraits.* First Edition: London: Macmillan and Co. 1887.
Nr.Fine/Fine **$375**
Good/V.Good **$200**

_____. *Marius the Epicurean.* (Two Volumes) First Edition: London: Macmillan, 1885
Nr.Fine/Fine **$275**
Good/V.Good **$150**

Peck, George W. *Peck's Bad Boy and His Pa.* First Edition: Chicago: Bedford, Clarke, 1883
Nr.Fine/Fine **$225**
Good/V.Good **$75**

_____. *The Grocery Man and Peck's Bad Boy.* First Edition: Chicago: Bedford, Clarke & Co. 1883
Nr.Fine/Fine **$135**
Good/V.Good **$65**

Peterson, Charles Jacobs. (as by J. Thornton Randolph). *The Cabin and Parlor; Or, Slaves and Masters.* First Edition: Philadelphia: T. B. Peterson, 1852
Nr.Fine/Fine **$655**
Good/V.Good **$300**

Poe, Edgar Allen. *Manuscript Found in a Bottle in The Gift: A Christmas and New Year's Present for 1836.* First Edition: Philadelphia: E.L. Carey & A. Hart, 1835.
Nr.Fine/Fine **$1150**
Good/V.Good **$500**

Porter, Jane. *The Scottish Chiefs.* (Five Volumes) First Edition: London: Printed for Longman, Hurst, Rees, and Orme, 1810
Nr.Fine/Fine **$3000**
Good/V.Good **$1300**

Pyle, Howard. *Yankee Doodle, an Old Friend in a New Dress.* First Edition: New York: Dodd, Mead, 1881
Nr.Fine/Fine **$2000**
Good/V.Good **$875**

_____. *The Merry Adventures of Robin Hood of Great Renown, in Nottinghamshire.* First Edition: New York: Scribners, 1883.
Nr.Fine/Fine **$1000**
Good/V.Good **$650**

_____. *Otto of the Silver Hand.* First Edition: New York: Scribners, 1888.
Nr.Fine/Fine **$500**
Good/V.Good **$200**

Quiller-Couch, Arthur. *Dead Man's Rock.* First Edition: London: Cassell, 1887
Nr.Fine/Fine **$425**
Good/V.Good **$200**

Quiller-Couch, Arthur. (as by Q) *Noughts and Crosses Stories, Studies and Sketches.* First Edition: London: Cassell, 1891
Nr.Fine/Fine **$65**
Good/V.Good **$30**
First U.S. Edition: New York: Scribners, 1898
Nr.Fine/Fine **$75**
Good/V.Good **$35**

_____. *The Blue Pavilions.* First Edition: London: Cassell, 1891
Nr.Fine/Fine **$55**
Good/V.Good **$25**

Radcliffe, Ann. *The Mysteries of Udolpho, a Romance; Interspersed with Some Pieces of Poetry.* First Edition: London: G.G. & J. Robinson, 1794
Nr.Fine/Fine **$4000**

Good/V.Good **$2500**

_____. *Italian: Or the Confessional of the Black Penitents: A Romance.* (Three Volumes) First Edition: London: T. Cadell Jun And W. Davies, 1797
Nr.Fine/Fine **$2750**
Good/V.Good **$1200**

Read, Opie. *Judge Elbridge.* First Edition: New York: Rand, McNally & Co., 1899
Nr.Fine/Fine **$65**
Good/V.Good **$25**

_____. *A Kentucky Colonel.* First Edition: Chicago: F.J. Sculte, 1890
Nr.Fine/Fine **$75**
Good/V.Good **$30**

Bolanyo
by Opie Read

_____. *Bolanyo.* First Edition: Chicago: Way & Williams, 1897
Nr.Fine/Fine **$350**
Good/V.Good **$165**

Reade, Charles. *The Cloister and the Hearth. A Tale of the Middle Ages.* First Edition: London: W. Clowes for Trubner & Co, 1861
Nr.Fine/Fine **$7500**
Good/V.Good **$4000**

_____. *White Lies: A Story.* (Three Volumes) First Edition: London:

Trubner & Co., 1857
Nr.Fine/Fine................ **$425**
Good/V.Good **$150**

Reid, Captain Mayne. *The White Chief: A Legend of North Mexico.* (Three Volumes) First Edition: London: David Bogue, 1855
Nr.Fine/Fine **$1500**
Good/V.Good **$650**
First U.S. Edition: New York: Carleton, 1870.
Nr.Fine/Fine **$110**
Good/V.Good **$45**

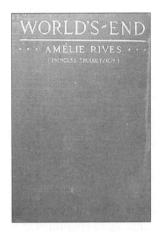

World's End
by Amelie Rives

Rives, Amelie. *World's-End.* First Edition: New York: Frederick A. Stokes, 1914
Nr.Fine/Fine $55
Good/V.Good **$25**

Opening a Chestnut Burr
by E.P. Roe

Roe, E. P. *Opening a Chestnut Burr.* First Edition: New York: Dodd Mead, 1874.
Nr.Fine/Fine. **$25**
Good/V.Good **$10**

Rolfe, Frederick William. (as by Baron Corvo). *Hadrian The Seventh.* First Edition: London: Chatto & Windus, 1904
Nr.Fine/Fine **$5000**
Good/V.Good **$3250**

_____. *Don Tarquinio. A Kataleptic Phantasmatic Romance.* First Edition: London: Chatto & Windus, 1905
Nr.Fine/Fine **$3200**
Good/V.Good **$1825**

_____. *Stories Toto Told Me.* Points of Issue: Paperback Original, green/grey wraps printed by John Wilson & Son at the University Press, Cambridge, Mass. First Edition: London: John Lane, The Bodley Head, 1898
Nr.Fine/Fine **$600**
Good/V.Good **$350**

Russell, William Clark. *A Strange Voyage.* First Edition: London: Sampson Low, Marston, Searle & Rivington, 1885
Nr.Fine/Fine **$200**
Good/V.Good **$110**

_____. *List Ye Landsmen! A Romance of Incident.* First Edition: London & New York: Cassell, 1892.
Nr.Fine/Fine **$55**
Good/V.Good **$20**

Saltus, Edgar. *Mr. Incoul's Misadventure.* First Edition: New York: Benjamin & Bell, 1887
Nr.Fine/Fine **$60**
Good/V.Good **$25**

_____. *Imperial Purple.* First Edition: Chicago: Morrill, Higgins, 1892
Nr.Fine/Fine **$65**
Good/V.Good **$25**

Shaw, Henry Wheeler. (as by Josh Billings) *Josh Billings on Ice.* First Edition: New York: G.W. Carleton, 1868
Nr.Fine/Fine **$95**
Good/V.Good **$40**

__. *Old Probability: Perhaps Rain-Perhaps Not.* First Edition: New York: G.W. Carleton, 1879
Nr.Fine/Fine **$100**
Good/V.Good **$50**

__. *Everybody's Friend.* First Edition: Hartford, CT: American Publishing, 1874.
Nr.Fine/Fine **$85**
Good/V.Good **$35**

Smith, Elizabeth Oakes. *Bertha and the Lily.* First Edition: Boston: Cinn Derby, 1854.
Nr.Fine/Fine **$300**
Good/V.Good **$110**

Southworth, Emma D.E.N. *The Bridal Eve.* Points of Issue: Paperback Original. First Edition: New York: Street & Smith, 1901
Nr.Fine/Fine **$35**
Good/V.Good **$12**

_____. *The Gipsy's Prophecy. A Tale of Real Life.* First Edition: Philadelphia: T.B. Peterson & Brothers, 1861
Nr.Fine/Fine **$165**
Good/V.Good **$70**

Spofford, Harriet Prescott. *The Thief in the Night.* First Edition: Boston: Roberts Brothers, 1872
Nr.Fine/Fine **$235**
Good/V.Good **$110**

_____. *The Maid He Married.* First Edition: Chicago: Herbert S. Stone, 1899
Nr.Fine/Fine. **$125**
Good/V.Good **$45**

Stephens, Ann Sophia. *Fashion and Famine: A Tale.* First Edition: London: W. Kent/Ward & Lock, 1854
Nr.Fine/Fine **$75**
Good/V.Good **$40**

David Balfour
*by Robert Lewis
Stevenson*

Stevenson, Robert Lewis. *David Balfour: Being Memoirs of his Adventure at Home and Abroad.* First Edition: London: Cassell, 1893.
Nr.Fine/Fine **$110**
Good/V.Good **$50**
First U.S. Edition: New York: Scribners, 1893
Nr.Fine/Fine **$85**
Good/V.Good **$45**

_____. *The Wrecker.* First Edition: London: Cassell, 1892
Nr.Fine/Fine **$245**
Good/V.Good **$125**

_____. *The Master of Ballantrae.* First Edition: London: Cassell & Co., 1889.
Nr.Fine/Fine **$185**
Good/V.Good **$80**
First U.S. Edition: New York: Scribners, 1889
Nr.Fine/Fine **$150**
Good/V.Good **$65**

Stockton, Frank R. *The Casting Away of Mrs. Lecks and Mrs. Aleshine.* Points of

Issue: Paperback Original.
First Edition: New York: Century Co., 1886
Nr.Fine/Fine **$95**
Good/V.Good **$35**

_____. *Ting-A-Ling.* First Edition: New York: Hurd and Houghton, 1870
Nr.Fine/Fine **$400**
Good/V.Good **$165**

_____. *The Lady, or the Tiger? and Other Stories.* First Edition: New York: Scribners, 1884
Nr.Fine/Fine **$750**
Good/V.Good **$400**

Stowe, Harriet Beecher. *Uncle Tom's Cabin.* (Two Volumes) First Edition: Boston & Cleveland, OH: John P. Jewett & Co. & Jewett, Proctor and Worthington, 1852
Nr.Fine/Fine **$21,000**
Good/V.Good **$9500**

_____. *Dred: A Tale of the Great Dismal Swamp.* (Two Volumes) First Edition: Boston: Phillips, Sampson, 1856
Nr.Fine/Fine **$850**
Good/V.Good **$350**

_____. *Oldtown Folks.* (Three Volumes) First Edition: London: Sampson Low, Son, and Marston, 1869
Nr.Fine/Fine **$750**
Good/V.Good **$300**
First U.S. Edition: Boston: Fields, Osgood, 1869
Nr.Fine/Fine **$250**
Good/V.Good **$110**

Stuart, Ruth McEnery. *In Simpkinsville.* First Edition: New York: Harper & Brothers, 1897
Nr.Fine/Fine. **$95**
Good/V.Good **$45**

_____. *The River's Children.* First Edition: New York: Phelps Publishing Company, 1904

Nr.Fine/Fine **$600**
Good/V.Good **$325**

Terhune, Mary Virginia (as by Marion Harland) *The Royal Road or Taking Him at His Word.* First Edition: New York: Anson D. F. Randolph and Company, 1894.
Nr.Fine/Fine **$75**
Good/V.Good **$30**

Thomas, Frederick William. *East and West. A Novel.* First Edition: Philadelphia: Carey, Lea & Blanchard, 1836
Nr.Fine/Fine. **$375**
Good/V.Good **$165**

Tolstoy, Leo N. (Tolstoi, Lyof N.) *Anna Karenina.* First Edition in English: New York: Thomas Y. Crowell and Co., 1886
Nr.Fine/Fine **$2500**
Good/V.Good **$1400**

_____. *War and Peace.* First U.S. Edition: New York, William S. Gottsberger, 1886
Nr.Fine/Fine **$17,500**
Good/V.Good **$12,225**

Tourgee, Albion Winegar. *A Fool's Errand.* First Edition: New York: Fords, Howard & Hulbert, 1879
Nr.Fine/Fine **$155**
Good/V.Good **$45**

Townsend, Mary Ashley. *Distaff and Spindle.* First Edition: Philadelphia: J. B. Lippincott, 1895
Nr.Fine/Fine **$100**
Good/V.Good. **$45**

Trollope, Anthony. *Lady Anna.* First Edition: London: Chapman and Hall, 1874
Nr.Fine/Fine **$2750**
Good/V.Good **$1400**

_____. *Barchester Towers.* (Three Volumes) First Edition: London Longman, Brown, Green, Longmans, & Roberts, 1857
Nr.Fine/Fine **$7500**

Good/V.Good **$4100**

Turgeniev, Ivan Sergheievitch. *Fathers and Sons.* First Edition in English: New York: Leypoldt & Holt, 1867
Nr.Fine/Fine **$6000**
Good/V.Good **$2850**

Twain, Mark. *The Celebrated Jumping Frog of Calaveras County.* First Edition: New York: C. H. Webb, 1867
Nr.Fine/Fine **$15,000**
Good/V.Good **$7000**

The Prince and
The Pauper
by Mark Twain

_____. *The Prince and the Pauper.* First Edition: Boston: James R. Osgood, 1882
Nr.Fine/Fine **$2750**
Good/V.Good **$1250**

_____. *Punch, Brothers, Punch! and Other Sketches.* First Edition: New York: Slote, Woodman, 1878
Nr.Fine/Fine **$950**
Good/V.Good **$350**

Wallace, Lew. *Ben-Hur. A Tale of the Christ.* First Edition: New York: Harper & Brothers, 1880
Nr.Fine/Fine **$1200**
Good/V.Good **$550**

_____. *The Prince of India.* (Two Volumes) First Edition: New York: Harper & Brothers Publishers, 1893

Nr.Fine/Fine **$125**
Good/V.Good **$45**

Wiggin, Kate Douglas. *Rebecca of Sunnybrook Farm.* First Edition: Boston and New York: Houghton Mifflin, 1903
Nr.Fine/Fine **$800**
Good/V.Good **$350**

_____. *Timothy's Quest.* First Edition: Boston and New York: Houghton, Mifflin, 1891
Nr.Fine/Fine **$85**
Good/V.Good **$20**

_____. *A Cathedral Courtship and Penelope's English Experiences.* First Edition: Boston and New York: Houghton, Mifflin, 1893
Nr.Fine/Fine **$30**
Good/V.Good **$12**

Woolson, Constance Fenimore. *For the Major.* First Edition: New York: Harper & Brothers, 1883
Nr.Fine/Fine **$70**
Good/V.Good **$45**

Alcott, Louisa May. *Little Men: Life at Plumfield with Jo's Boys.*First US Edition: Boston: Roberts Brothers, 1871.Points: First issue, with ads at front listing Pink and White Tyranny as "Nearly Ready."
Nr.Fine/Fine **$750**
Good/V.Good **$275**

Directory of Bookstores

Limitations of space and time, of knowledge first and second hand, necessarily limits this directory to booksellers I know or have had recommended by someone I trust. Please do not consider that I am in any way disparaging your local bookseller, or any bookshop that is not included here.

Section One

These booksellers are personal contacts: people I know and have learned to trust. As the area I travel is, by necessity, limited, this list is also limited. They do represent, however, the best booksellers I have come into contact with in a band stretching from Albuquerque to San Francisco and another from Baltimore to New York City.

Arizona

Alcuin Books
115 W. Camelback Rd.
Phoenix, AZ 85013

Anasazi Bookstore
10540 W. Indian School Rd #
3
Phoenix, AZ 85037

Arizona Book Gallery
121 W. Camelback Rd.
Phoenix, AZ 85013

Bent Cover
12428 N. 28th Dr.
Phoenix, AZ 85029

Book Gallery
169 W. Camelback Rd.
Phoenix, AZ 85013

Book Gallery
3643 E. Indian School Rd.
Phoenix, AZ 85018

Changing Hands Bookstore
6428 S. McClintock Dr #
C101
Tempe, AZ 85283

Dragon's Plunder
217 S. San Francisco St.
Flagstaff, AZ 86001

Guidon Books
7117 E. Main St.
Scottsdale, AZ 85251

Mesa Bookshop
50 W. Main St.
Mesa, AZ 85201

Old Town Books
518 S. Mill Ave.
Tempe, AZ 85281

California

Antiquarian Archive
379 State St.
Los Altos, CA 94022

Basset Books
800 Lighthouse Ave. # C

Monterey, CA 93940

Book Castle's-Movie World
212 N. San Fernando Blvd.
Burbank, CA 91502

Book Alley
611 E. Colorado Blvd.
Pasadena, CA 91101

Bookfellows
238 N. Brand Blvd.
Glendale, CA 91203

Book-Go-Round
14410 Oak St.
Saratoga, CA 95070

Brand Book Shop
231 N. Brand Blvd.
Glendale, CA 91203

Chelsea Book Shop
637 Irving St.
San Francisco, CA 94122

Dark Delicacies
4213 W. Burbank Blvd.
Burbank, CA 91505

Dutton's Books
5146 Laurel Canyon Blvd.
North Hollywood, CA 91607

Bart's Books
302 W. Matilija St.
Ojai, CA 93023

Lost Horizon Bookstore
703 Anacapa St.
Santa Barbara, CA 93101

Feldman's Books
1170 El Camino Real
Menlo Park, CA 94025

Green Apple Books & Music
506 Clement St.
San Francisco, CA 94118

Handee Books
5277 Prospect Rd.
San Jose, CA 95129

Iliad Book Shop
4820 Vineland Ave.
North Hollywood, CA 91601

Kayo Books
814 Post St.
San Francisco, CA 94109

Know Knew Books
415 S California Ave.
Palo Alto, CA 94306

Lighthouse Books
801 Lighthouse Ave.
Monterey, CA 93940

Lincoln Avenue Books
2194 Lincoln Ave.
San Jose, CA 95125

Old Capitol Books
639 Lighthouse Ave. # A
Monterey, CA 93940

Phoenix Books
990 Monterey St.
San Luis Obispo, CA 93401

Recycle Book Store
1066 The Alameda
San Jose, CA 95126

Sam Johnson's Bookshop
12310 Venice Blvd.
Los Angeles, CA 90066

Todd's Books
17391 Holiday Dr.
Morgan Hill, CA 95037

Wessex-Used Books &
Records
558 Santa Cruz Ave.
Menlo Park, CA 94025

Yesterday's Books
7902 Sandholt Rd. # E
Moss Landing, CA 95039

Maryland

Kelmscott Book Shop
32 W 25th St.
Baltimore, MD 21218

Royal Books
32 W 25th St.

Baltimore, MD 21218

Nevada

Albion Book Co
2466 E. Desert Inn Rd. # G
Las Vegas, NV 89121

Dead Poet Bookstore
3874 W. Sahara Ave.
Las Vegas, NV 89102

New Mexico

Book Stop
3410 Central Ave. SE
Albuquerque, NM 87106

Books & More Books
1341 Cerrillos Rd.
Santa Fe, NM 87505

Books Unlimited
1724 Paseo De Peralta
Santa Fe, NM 87501

Downtown Books & Beans
521 Central Ave. NE
Albuquerque, NM 87102

Nicholas Potter Book Seller
211 E. Palace Ave.
Santa Fe, NM 87501

Oasis Books
625 Amherst Dr. NE
Albuquerque, NM 87106

Page One Too Antiquarian
Books
11200 Montgomery Blvd. NE
Albuquerque, NM 87111

Reed Books
924 Paseo De Peralta # 4
Santa Fe, NM 87501

Simmons & Simmons Fine
Books
4616 Central Ave. SE
Albuquerque, NM 87108

Title Wave Books
7915 Menaul Blvd. NE
Albuquerque, NM 87110

New York

(My apologies here. New York City is one of the greatest book towns on the planet, still. There are many wonderful used/antiquarian bookstores throughout the five boroughs. I started there however; and the demise of Fourth Avenue as the book capital of the world fills me with an incredible sadness. To me, New York City is filled with the ghosts of stores and their proprietors. The spectres of those who are now, I'm sure, selling the latest offerings from the pens of the greatest authors who ever lived to the angels. I never linger for very long there, so my contacts are limited.)

12th St. Books & Records
11 E. 12th St. Front
New York, NY 10003

Strand Book Store Inc.
828 Broadway
New York, NY 10003

Pennsylvania

Baldwin's Book Barn
865 Lenape Rd.
West Chester, PA 19382

Bauman Rare Books
1215 Locust St.
Philadelphia, PA 19107

Hibberd's Books
1306 Walnut St.
Philadelphia, PA 19107

Molly's Cafe & Bookstore
1010 S. 9th St.
Philadelphia, PA 19147

Mostly Books
526 Bainbridge St.
Philadelphia, PA 19147

Russakoff's Books & Records
259 S 10th St.
Philadelphia, PA 19107

Thomas Macaluso Used &
Rare Books
130 S. Union St.
Kennett Square, PA 19348

Texas

Book Gallery
2706 E. Yandell
El Paso, TX 79903

Section Two

These are bookstores I have never set foot in. They are compiled from three sources. Some I have done business with for years, by mail, phone, and, lately, the Internet. Others are recommendations from the list above. Finally, there are recommendations from book scouts of my acquaintance. The final category requires some slight explanation. Book scouts differ in philosophy in how they approach bookstores. Personally, I am one of the loquacious group, making no secret of being a scout and often engaging the bookseller in conversation. It is, in fact, something I consider one of the true joys of my profession. It does, however, have an effect on the used book market. If scouts suddenly start buying a particular author or book, the price tends to increase. Other scouts, noting this, forego discounts and pay sales tax to avoid this effect. They never admit to being scouts, or even being in the book business, so their recommendations might carry different impressions, and certainly the weight of a "mystery shopper."

Alabama
The Alabama Booksmith
2626 19th Pl S.
Homewood, AL 35209

Arkansas
Arkansas Bookworm
120 E. Haywood St.
England, AR 72046

Just Books
120 King Arthur Ct.
Hot Springs, AR 71913

California
Acres Of Books
240 Long Beach Blvd.
Long Beach, CA 90802

Black Oak Books
1491 Shattuck Ave.
Berkeley, CA 94709

Book Baron
1236 S. Magnolia
Anaheim, CA 92804

The Bookman
840 N. Tustin Ave.
Orange, CA 92867

Serendipity Books
1201 University Ave.
Berkeley, CA 9470

Colorado
A Abracadabra Antiquarian
Bookshop
32 South Broadway
Denver, CO 80209

Aberdeen Bookstore
1360 West Littleton Blvd.
Littleton, CO 80120

AION Bookshop
1235 Pennsylvania Ave.
Boulder, CO 80302

Beat Book Shop
1713 Pearl St.
Boulder, CO 80302

Book Mountain
8851 Comanche Rd.
Longmont, CO 80503

Denver Book Mall
32 Broadway
Denver, CO 80203

Fahrenheits Books
38 Broadway
Denver, CO 80203

Mad Dog and the Pilgrim
Booksellers
6630 E. Colfax Ave.
Denver, CO 80220

Murder by the Book
1574 S. Pearl St.
Denver, CO 80210

Willow Creek Books
8100 S. Akron St.
Englewood, CO 80112

Connecticut
Barely Used Books
5 Roosevelt Ave.
Stonington, CT 06378

Book Barn
41 W. Main
East Lyme, CT 06333

Books & Company
1235 Whitney Ave.
Hamden, CT 06517

Brick Walk Bookshop
966 Farmington Ave.
West Hartford, CT 06107

Centerbridge Books
33 Deep River Rd.
Essex, CT 06426

Jumping Frog
585 Prospect Ave.
Hartford, CT 06105

McBlain Books
2348 Whitney Ave.
Hamden, CT 06518

Novel Trader
69 State St.
North Haven, CT 06473

On the Road Bookshop
163 Albany Turnpike
Canton, CT 06019

Rons Reading Room
11 Pine St.
Oxford, CT 06478

Whitlock Farm Booksellers
Sperry Road
Bethany, CT 06524

Delaware
Second Hand Prose
28 S. Walnut St.
Milford, DE 19963

Florida
Archives Book Cafe
1948 E. Sunrise Blvd.
Fort Lauderdale, FL 33304

Attic Bookshop
5201 Seminole Blvd. Ste. 8
Saint Petersburg, FL 33708

Backwater Book Store
328 Stiles Ave.
Orange Park, FL 32073

Beach Books
241 13th Ave. North
Jacksonville Beach, FL 32250

Book Bank USA
10500 Ulmerton Road
Largo, FL 33771

Book Bazaar
1488 Main St.
Sarasota, FL 34236

Book Emporium
4415 Bonita Beach Road
Bonita Springs, FL 34134

Books & Books Inc.
265 Aragon Ave.
Miami, FL 33134

Brandywine Books
114 South Park Ave.
Winter Park, FL 32789

Chamblin Book Mine
4551 Roosevelt Blvd.
Jacksonville, FL 32210

Gibsons Book Store
3728 Southwest 64th Ave.
Fort Lauderdale, FL 33314

Jerrys Bookshop
917 University Blvd. North
Jacksonville, FL 32211

Macintosh Book Shop
2365 Periwinkle Way
Sanibel, FL 33957

Old Tampa Book Company
Inc.
507 N. Tampa St.
Tampa, FL 33602

Paper Pad Book Store
2811 Tamiami Trail
Port Charlotte, FL 33952

Tappin Book Mine
705 Atlantic Blvd.
Atlantic Beach, FL 32233

Tees Books
5734 Old Cheney Highway
Orlando, FL 32807

Volume One Books
8910 Taft St.
Hollywood, FL 33024

Georgia
Atlanta Book Exchange
1000 N. Highland Ave.
Northeast
Atlanta, GA 30306

Barter Books
3120 Peach Orchard Rd.
Augusta, GA 30906

Book Source
2880 Holcomb Bridge Rd.
Alpharetta, GA 30022

C Dickens Books
56 E. Andrews Drive
Northwest
Atlanta, GA 30305

Golden Bough Vintage Books
371 Cotton Ave.
Macon, GA 31201

Memorable Books
5380 Manor Drive
Stone Mountain, GA 30083

Roswell Bookstore Inc.
11055 Alpharetta Highway
Roswell, GA 30076

Star Sapphire
3600 Cherokee St. Northwest
Kennesaw, GA 30144

Idaho
Browsers Book Store
2415 N. Government Way Ste.
2
Coeur D Alene, ID 83814

George Nolan Books
200 N. 4th St.
Coeur D Alene, ID 83814

Illinois
Abraham Lincoln Book Shop
357 W. Chicago Ave.
Chicago, IL 60610

Amaranth Books
828 Davis St.
Evanston, IL 60201

Babbitt's Books
104 North St.
Normal, IL 61761

Beasley Books
1533 W. Oakdale Ave.
Chicago, IL 60657

Book Den
1043 Chicago Ave.
Evanston, IL 60202

Book Ends
2375 South Lost Bridge Rd.
Decatur, IL 62521

Bookleggers Used Books
2907 N. Broadway
Chicago, IL 60607

Booknook Parnassus
2000 Maple Ave.
Evanston, IL 60201

Booksmith
108 S. Marion St.
Oak Park, IL 60302

Bookzeller
202 S. Main St.
Naperville, IL 60540

Chicago Rare Book Center
56 W. Maple St.
Chicago, IL 60610

Fagin N Books
459 N. Milwaukee Ave.
Chicago, IL 60610

Fortsas Books Limited
5458 N. Milwaukee Ave.
Chicago, IL 60630

Novel Idea Book Exchange
6310 Woodward Ave.
Downers Grove, IL 60516

Pages
300 S. Main St.
Wheaton, IL 60187

Prairie Avenue Bookshop
418 S. Wabash Ave.
Chicago, IL 60605

Rain Dog Books & Cafe
408 S. Michigan Ave.
Chicago, IL 60605

Sandpiper Book Exchange
160 S. Bloomingdale Rd.
Bloomingdale, IL 60108

Selected Works Bookstore
3510 N. Broadway
Chicago, IL 60607

Shake Rattle & Read Book
Box
4812 N. Broadway St.
Chicago, IL 60640

Stars Our Destination
705 Main St.
Evanston, IL 60202

Thomas J Joyce & Company
400 N. Racine Ave.
Chicago, IL 60622

Toad Hall Books
2106 Broadway
Rockford, IL 61104

Victorias Books Limited
13 W. Campbell St.
Arlington Heights, IL 60005

Indiana
Book World Inc.
7775 E. Washington St.
Indianapolis, IN 46219

Circle City Antiquarian Books
45 S. Franklin Rd.
Indianapolis, IN 46219

Idlewood Rare Books
6420 W.50 South
Lebanon, IN 46052

Miles Books
2816 Highway Ave.
Highland, IN 46322

Remarkable Book Shop
7227 Taft St.
Merrillville, IN 46410

Iowa
Big Table Books
330 Main St.
Ames, IA 50010

Haunted Bookshop
520 E. Washington St.
Iowa City, IA 52240

Read Books
215 2nd St. Southeast
Cedar Rapids, IA 52401

Upstart Crow Books
2810 Cottage Grove Ave.
Des Moines, IA 50311

Kansas
Blue Parrot Books
816 W. 13th St. North
Wichita, KS 67203

Book A Holic Inc.
924 S. Oliver St.
Wichita, KS 67218

Book Worm Book Store
112 S. Main St.
El Dorado, KS 67042

Dusty Bookshelf
922 E. Douglas Ave.
Wichita, KS 67202

Green Dragon Books
790 N. West St.
Wichita, KS 67203

Maple Drive Books
5840 Maple St.
Shawnee Mission, KS 66202

Rainy Day Books
2706 W. 53rd St.
Shawnee Mission, KS 66205

Watermark West-Rare Books
149 N. Broadway St.
Wichita, KS 67202

Kentucky
Black Swan Books
505 E. Maxwell St.
Lexington, KY 40502

Buy the Book
6103 Crestwood Station
Louisville, KY 40202

Gate 6 Bookstore
15226 Fort Campbell Blvd.
Oak Grove, KY 42262

Karens Book Barn
2295 Wolfpen Rd.
Sulphur, KY 40070

Outhouse Book Shop
4435 Taylorsville Rd.
Louisville, KY 40220

Readers Corner
115 Wiltshire Ave.
Louisville, KY 40207

Louisiana
Bayou Books
1005 Monroe St.
Gretna, LA 70053

Beckhams Book Shop
228 Decatur St.
New Orleans, LA 70130

Book Merchant
512 Front St.
Natchitoches, LA 71457

Book Worm of N O E
7011 Read Blvd.
New Orleans, LA 70127

Books Plus
5523 Main St.
Zachary, LA 70791

Cottonwood Books
3054 Perkins Rd.
Baton Rouge, LA 70808

Dauphine Street Books
410 Dauphine St.
New Orleans, LA 70112

Faulkner House Books
624 Pirates Alley
New Orleans, LA 70116

Great Acquisitions Books
8200 Hampson St.
New Orleans, LA 70118

Kitchen Witch
1214 N. Rampart St.
New Orleans, LA 70116

Librairie Book Shop
823 Chartres St.
New Orleans, LA 70116

Maine
ABCD Books
23 Bay View
Camden, ME 04843

Betts Bookstore
584 Hammond St.
Bangor, ME 04401

Maryland
19th Century Shop
1047 Hollins St.
Baltimore, MD 21223

Allens Book Shop
416 E. 31st St.
Baltimore, MD 21218

Baltimore Book Company Inc.
2114 N. Charles St.
Baltimore, MD 21218

Book Alcove Inc.
5976 Shady Grove Rd.
Gaithersburg, MD 20877

Books With A Past
2465 Md. Route 97
Glenwood, MD 21738

Briarwood Bookshop
66 Maryland Ave.
Annapolis, MD 21401

Georgetown Book Shop
7770 Woodmont Ave.
Bethesda, MD 20814

Second Edition
6490 Dobbin Rd.
Columbia, MD 21045

Washington Used Book Center
11910 Parklawn Drive
Rockville, MD 20852

Massachusetts
Another Story Used & Rare
Books
1145 Main St.
Worcester, MA 01603

Avenue Victor Hugo Book
Shop
339 Newbury St.
Boston, MA 02115

Barrow Book Store
79 Main St.
Concord, MA 01742

Bearly Read Books
320 Boston Post Rd.
Sudbury, MA 01776

Bookends
80 Maple St.
Florence, MA 01062

Books With A Past
17 Walden St.
Concord, MA 01742

Boston Book Company &
Boston Book Annex
906 Beacon St.
Boston, MA 02215

Brattle Book Shop
9 West St.
Boston, MA 02111

Commonwealth Books
134 Boylston St.
Boston, MA 02116

Cranberry Book Barn
164 Plymouth
North Carver, MA 02355

Half Moon Books
7 Pearl St.
Northampton, MA 01060

Isaiah Thomas Books & Prints
Inc.
4632 Falmouth Rd.
Cotuit, MA 02635

Ken Lopez Bookseller
51 Huntington Rd.
Hadley, MA 01035

McIntyre & Moore
Booksellers
255 Elm St.
Somerville, MA 02144

Meetinghouse Books
70 N. Main St.
South Deerfield, MA 01373

Odyssey Book Shop
9 College St.
South Hadley, MA 01075

Old Book Store
32 Masonic St.
Northampton, MA 01060

Page and Parchment
375 Elliot St.
Newton Upper Falls, MA
02464

Raven Used Book Shop
71 N. Pleasant St.
Amherst, MA 01002

Ten Pound Island Book Co.
76 Langsford St.
Gloucester, MA 01930

Troubadour Books
336 West St.
North Hatfield, MA 01066

Upper Story Books
1730 Massachusetts Ave.
Lexington, MA 02420

Valley Books
199 N. Pleasant St.
Amherst, MA 01002

Michigan
A & J RAU Booksellers
171 W. Main
Mecosta, MI 49332

Andrews & Rose Booksellers
105 E. Main St.
Niles, MI 49120

Another Look Books
22263 Goddard Rd.
Taylor, MI 48180

Archives Book Shop
517 W. Grand River Ave.
East Lansing, MI 48823

Athena Book Shop
154 S. Burdick St.
Kalamazoo, MI 49007

Avalon Bookshop
8314 Portage Rd.
Portage, MI 49002

Big Book Store
5911 Cass Ave.
Detroit, MI 48202

Book Barn
1673 Haslett Rd.
Haslett, MI 48840

Book Beat Limited
26010 Greenfield Rd.
Oak Park, MI 48237

Book-About
100 W. Main St.
Lowell, MI 49331

C MacNeill Book Dealer
3165 12 Mile Rd.
Berkley, MI 48072

Curious Book Shop
307 E. Grand River Ave.
East Lansing, MI 48823

Dove Booksellers
13904 Michigan Ave.
Dearborn, MI 48126

Golden Bough Books
2413 Parkview Ave.
Kalamazoo, MI 49008

John K King Books
901 West Lafayette Blvd.
Detroit, MI 48226

Kazoo Books
407 N. Clarendon St.
Kalamazoo, MI 49006

Links To the Past
52631 U. S. Route 131 North
Three Rivers, MI 49093

Lowrys Books
22 N. Main St.
Three Rivers, MI 49093

Mecosta Book Gallery
171 W. Main
Mecosta, MI 49332

Reading Books
7 Squires Street Square
Rockford, MI 49341

Rodeghers Used Books
23924 Michigan Ave.
Dearborn, MI 48124

Yesterdays Books
229 South Riverview Drive
Kalamazoo, MI 49004

Minnesota
Book House
429 14th Ave. Southeast
Minneapolis, MN 55414

Booksmart
2914 Hennepin Ave.
Minneapolis, MN 55408

Cummings Books
318 14th Ave. Southeast
Minneapolis, MN 55414

Dinkytown Antiquarian Book
Store
1316 4th St. Southeast
Minneapolis, MN 55414

Harpers Books
1053 Grand Ave.
Saint Paul, MN 55105

Magers & Quinn Booksellers
3038 Hennepin Ave.
Minneapolis, MN 55408

Midway Books
1579 University Ave. West
Saint Paul, MN 55104

Once Upon A Crime
604 W. 26th St.
Minneapolis, MN 55405

Rag & Bone Books
2812 W. 43rd St.
Minneapolis, MN 55410

Rulon-Miller Books
400 Summit Ave.
Saint Paul, MN 55102

Sixth Chamber Used Books
1332 Grand Ave.
Saint Paul, MN 55105

St Croix Antiquarian
Booksellers
232 Main St. South
Stillwater, MN 55082

Uncle Edgars Mystery
Bookstore
2864 Chicago Ave.
Minneapolis, MN 55407

Uncle Hugos Science Fiction
Bookstore
2864 Chicago Ave.
Minneapolis, MN 55407

Mississippi
Choctaw Books
926 North St.
Jackson, MS 39202

Lemuria
4465 I 55 North
Jackson, MS 39206

Spanish Trail Books
781 Howard Ave.
Biloxi, MS 39530

Missouri
Annies Book Stop
744 Florissant Meadows South
Florissant, MO 63033

Bloomsday Books
301 E. 55th St.
Kansas City, MO 64113

Blue & Grey Book Shoppe
107 W. Lexington Ave.
Independence, MO 64050

Bookworm Book Store
8109 Wornall Rd.
Kansas City, MO 64114

By the Book
9040 Manchester Rd.
Saint Louis, MO 63144

Green Trails Bookshop
14270 Ladue Rd.
Chesterfield, MO 63017

Left Bank Books
399 N. Euclid Ave.
Saint Louis, MO 63108

Old Book Shop
122 S. Main St.
Independence, MO 64050

Readers Heaven
105 W. Lexington Ave.
Independence, MO 64050

Montana
Birds Nest
219 N. Higgins Ave.
Missoula, MT 59802

Nevada
Not New Books
435 Spokane St. Ste. 2
Reno, NV 89512

New Hampshire
Antiquarian Bookstore
1070 Lafayette Rd.
Portsmouth, NH 03801

Bert Babcock-Bookseller, LLC
9 East Derry Rd.
Derry, NH 03038

New Jersey
Between the Covers
35 W. Maple Ave.
Merchantville, NJ 08109

Book Bin
725 Arnold Ave.
Point Pleasant Beach, NJ
08742

Book Garden
868 Monmouth Rd.
Cream Ridge, NJ 08514

Book Shop
430 Hillsdale Ave.
Hillsdale, NJ 07642

Book Stop
52 S. Washington Ave.
Bergenfield, NJ 07621

Book Store at Depot SQ
8 Depot Square
Englewood, NJ 07631

Booktrader of Hamilton
2402 Nottingham Way
Trenton, NJ 08619

Brier Rose Books
450 Cedar Lane
Teaneck, NJ 07666

Broadway Books Exclusive
914 Broadway
Bayonne, NJ 07002

Chatham Bookseller Inc.
8 Green Village Road
Madison, NJ 07940

Cindi's Book Barn
20 Alden St.
Cranford, NJ 07016

Curious Old Book Shop
5216 Atlantic Ave.
Ventnor City, NJ 08406

Gibson Galleries
14 Kramer Ave.
Caldwell, NJ 07006

Left Bank Books
28 N. Union St.
Lambertville, NJ 08530

Phoenix Books Lambertville
49 N. Union St.
Lambertville, NJ 08530

The Booklovers Outlet
31 Woodmere Drive
Summit, NJ 07901

New Mexico
Bookstore
121 S. Main St.
Belen, NM 87002

Craigs Book Exchange
1124 S. Solano Drive
Las Cruces, NM 88001

EVCO Books
1625 S. Main St.
Las Cruces, NM 88005

New York
A Bookmarx
28 Lincoln Ave.
Roslyn Heights, NY 11577

Alabaster Bookshop
122 4th Ave.
New York, NY 10003

Andersons Book Shop
96 Chatsworth Ave.
Larchmont, NY 10538

Aurora Fine Books
548 W. 28th St.
New York, NY 10001

Austin Book Shop
10429 Jamaica Ave.
Richmond Hill, NY 11418

Bay Ridge Bookstore
8508 4th Ave.
Brooklyn, NY 11209

Bee Cee Books Inc.
222 Smith St.
Freeport, NY 11520

Bensonhurst Discount Book
Store
1908 86th St.
Brooklyn, NY 11214

Book Ark
173 W. 81st St.
New York, NY 10024

Book Bin
234 Merrick Rd.
Oceanside, NY 11572

Book Corner
1801 Main St.
Niagara Falls, NY 14305

Book Emporium
235 Glen Cove Ave.
Sea Cliff, NY 11579

The Bookery
215 N. Cayuga St.
Ithaca, NY 14850

Book It
1430 N. Salina St.
Syracuse, NY 13208

Book Outlet
71 4th St.
Troy, NY 12180

Book-In-Hand
103 Condon Rd.
Stillwater, NY 12170

Booklovers Paradise
2972 Merrick Rd. # A
Bellmore, NY 11710

Books of Wonder
16 W. 18th St.
New York, NY 10011

Booktrader
252 Main St.
Saugerties, NY 12477

Dove & Hudson
296 Hudson Ave.
Albany, NY 12210

Fagan Books
6883 State Route 5 and 20
Bloomfield, NY 14469

Good Times Book Shop
150 E. Main St.
Port Jefferson, NY 11777

Gotham Book Mart
41 W. 47th St.
New York, NY 10036

Graham Holroyd
31 Lancer Place
Wbster, NY 14580

Gryphon Bookshop
2246 Broadway
New York, NY 10024

Heights Books
109 Montague St.
Brooklyn, NY 11201

High Ridge Books Inc.
Sunny Ridge Road
Harrison, NY 10528

Little Bookshop
230 E. 80th St.
New York, NY 10021

Mary Jane Books
215 Western Ave.
Albany, NY 12203

Murphys Downtown Books
212 E. Jefferson St.
Syracuse, NY 13202

Mysterious Book Shop
129 W. 56th St.
New York, NY 10019

Oracle Junction
2964 Delaware Ave.
Buffalo, NY 14217

Pomander Books
321 W. 94th St.
New York, NY 10025

Riverrun Books
7 Washington Ave.
Hastings On Hudson, NY
10706

Scarsdale Book Shop LLC
68 Garth Rd.
Scarsdale, NY 10583

Used Book Cafe
126 Crosby St.
New York, NY 10012

North Carolina
B J Exchange Used Books
4905 Murchison Rd.
Fayetteville, NC 28311

Book Trader
312 S. Elm St.
Greensboro, NC 27401

Bookshop
400 W. Franklin St.
Chapel Hill, NC 27516

Chapel Hill Rare Books &
Prints
310 W. University Drive
Chapel Hill, NC 27516

Dilworth Books
6720 Providence Lane West
Charlotte, NC 28226

Garden Gate
145 Wait Ave.
Wake Forest, NC 27587

Macneils
2 Bank Of America Plaza
Charlotte, NC 28202

Pages Past-Used & Rare
Books
1837 Spring Garden St.
Greensboro, NC 27403

Wentworth & Leggett Rare
Books
905 W. Main St.
Durham, NC 27701

Ohio
Acorn Bookshop Inc.
1464 W. 5th Ave.
Columbus, OH 43212

Book Harbor
32 W. College Ave.
Westerville, OH 43081

Book Shoppe
1844 S. Smithville Rd.
Dayton, OH 45420

Bookhaven of Springfield
1549 Commerce Rd.
Springfield, OH 45504

Cleveland Antiquarian Books
1239 W. 6th St.
Cleveland, OH 44113

Collector Book & Print
Gallery
1801 Chase Ave.
Cincinnati, OH 45223

Copperfield & Twist
Bookstore
7050 Market St.
Youngstown, OH 44512

Dickens Book Shop
26 S. Broadway St.
Lebanon, OH 45036

Dorian Books
802 Elm St.
Youngstown, OH 44505

Dust Jacket
3200 Linwood Ave.
Cincinnati, OH 45226

Duttenhofers Books
214 W. McMillan St.
Cincinnati, OH 45219

Frogtown Books
2131 N. Reynolds Rd.
Toledo, OH 43615

Grounds for Thought
174 S. Main St.
Bowling Green, OH 43402

Hoffmans Book Shop
211 E. Arcadia Ave.
Columbus, OH 43202

Karen Wickliff-Books
2579 N. High St.
Columbus, OH 43202

Keisogloff Rare Books Inc.
815 Superior Ave. East
Cleveland, OH 44114

Leyshons Books
320 Northridge Rd.
Columbus, OH 43214

Little Bookshop
58 E. Main St.
Westerville, OH 43081

Munchkin Book Shop
10435 Airport Highway
Swanton, OH 43558

Now and Again Books Inc.
126 S. Prospect Ave.
Hartville, OH 44632

Old Erie Street Bookstore
2128 E. 9th St.
Cleveland, OH 44115

Paupers Books
206 N. Main St.
Bowling Green, OH 43402

Royalty Books and Records
508 Canton Rd.
Akron, OH 44312

Significant Books
3053 Madison Rd.
Cincinnati, OH 45209

Twice-Loved Books
19 E. Midlothian Blvd.
Youngstown, OH 44507

Village Bookshop
2424 W. Dublin Granville Rd.
Columbus, OH 43235

Zubal Books
2969 W. 25th St.
Cleveland, OH 44113

Oklahoma
Aladdin Book Shoppe
5040 North May Ave.
Oklahoma City, OK 73112

Archives Books Inc.
1914 E. 2nd St.
Edmond, OK 73034

Book Place
24 E. Dewey Ave.
Sapulpa, OK 74066

Books Inc.
2442 E. 15C
Tulsa, OK 74104

First Edition Book Store
1502 E. 15th St.
Tulsa, OK 74120

Gardners Used Books Music
& Comics Inc.
4421 S. Mingo Rd.
Tulsa, OK 74146

Oak Tree Books
2812 E. 15th St.
Tulsa, OK 74104

Oregon
Authors Ink Books
5605 Southwest Rockwood
Court
Beaverton, OR 97007

Belmont Booksellers
4707 Southeast Belmont St.
Portland, OR 97215

Book Habit
390 Liberty St. Southeast
Salem, OR 97301

Booksmart
4908 River Road North
Salem, OR 97303

Booktique
3975 Mercantile Drive
Lake Oswego, OR 97035

Future Dreams
2205 E. Burnside St.
Portland, OR 97214

Hawthorne Boulevard Books
3129 Southeast Hawthorne
Blvd.
Portland, OR 97214

Holland Book Store
527 Southwest 12th Ave.
Portland, OR 97205

Longfellows Books
1401 Southeast Division St.
Portland, OR 97202

Murder by the Book
3210 Southeast Hawthorne
Blvd.
Portland, OR 97214

No Garbage Books
240 2nd Ave. Southwest
Albany, OR 97321

Powells City of Books
8725 Southwest Cascade Ave.
Beaverton, OR 97008

Readers Guide To Recycled
Literature
1105 Edgewater St. Northwest
Salem, OR 97304

South Salem Escape Fiction
3240 Triangle Drive Southeast
Salem, OR 97302

Title Wave Used Books
216 Northeast Knott St.
Portland, OR 97212

Treasure Island Books
2785 Commercial St.
Southeast
Salem, OR 97302

Wrigley-Cross Books
1809 Northeast 39th Ave.
Portland, OR 97212

Pennsylvania
Agvent Rare Books
291 Linden Rd.
Mertztown, PA 19539

Another Story
100 N. 9th St.
Allentown, PA 18102

The Archive
1800 Markley St.
Norristown, PA 19401

Blue Ridge Books
Northridge Antiques Mall
Carlisle, PA 17013

Book Bin Bookstore
Unlimited
36 E. Vine St.
Lancaster, PA 17602

Book Connection
20555 Route 19
Cranberry Twp, PA 16066

Book Haven
2022 Marietta Ave.
Lancaster, PA 17603

Book House
11N U.S. Route 15
Dillsburg, PA 17019

Book Tree
1008 3rd Ave.
New Brighton, PA 15066

Bookhaven
2202 Fairmount Ave.
Philadelphia, PA 19130

Bridge Street Old Books
1 Smoke Rise
New Hope, PA 18938

Chestnut Street Books
11 W. Chestnut St.
Lancaster, PA 17603

Cover To Cover Books
138 N. Hanover St.
Carlisle, PA 17013

DOE Run Valley Books
RR 1
Chadds Ford, PA 19317

Hermits Book House
34 Mount Zion Rd.
Wyoming, PA 18644

Mikes Library
92 South Main St.
Wilkes Barre, PA 18701

Mystery Books
916 W. Lancaster Ave.
Bryn Mawr, PA 19010

New Street Book Shop
513 N. New St.
Bethlehem, PA 18018

The Title Page
1 Franklin Ave.
Bryn Mawr, PA 19010

Twice Sold Tales
5911 Smithfield
Buena Vista, PA 15018

Yesterdays Books
3967 William Penn Highway
Murrysville, PA 15668

York Emporium
343 W. Market St.
York, PA 17401

Rhode Island
Cellar Stories Book Store
111 Mathewson St.
Providence, RI 02903

Myopic Books
5 S. Angell St.
Providence, RI 02906

Other Worlds
1281 N. Main St.
Providence, RI 02904

Reds Book Shop
131 Arnold St.
Woonsocket, RI 02895

Second Thoughts Book Store
1281 N. Main St.
Providence, RI 02904

Tysons Book Shop
334 Westminster St.
Providence, RI 02903

South Carolina
Bentleys Bookshop Inc.
123 N. Main St.
Greenville, SC 29601

Book Dispensary
1600 Broad River Rd.
Columbia, SC 29210

Book Gallery
622 Northeast Main St.
Simpsonville, SC 29681

Charleston Rare Book Co.
66 Church St.
Charleston, SC 29401

Eccentricities
701 Gervais St.
Columbia, SC 29201

Tennessee
Andover Square Books
805 Noragate Rd.
Knoxville, TN 37919

BLK Books
6503 Slater Rd.
Chattanooga, TN 37412

Bodacious Books
5133 Harding Pike
Nashville, TN 37205

Book Adventure
3546 Walker Ave.
Memphis, TN 38111

Book Bank
3161 Poplar Ave.
Memphis, TN 38111

Book Company
1920 S. Kelley St.
Chattanooga, TN 37404

Book Discoveries
2013 Belmont Blvd.
Nashville, TN 37212

Book Eddy
2537 Chapman Highway
Knoxville, TN 37920

Book Place
691 S. Mendenhall Rd.
Memphis, TN 38117

Bookman Rare and Used
Books
1713 21st Ave. South
Nashville, TN 37212

Burkes
1719 Poplar Ave.
Memphis, TN 38104

Cover To Cover
104 S. Magnolia St.
Maryville, TN 37803

Dads Old Book Store
4004 Hillsboro Pike
Nashville, TN 37215

Moody Books Inc.
128 Princeton Rd.
Johnson City, TN 37601

Sandmans Books N Things
110 Keith St. Southwest
Cleveland, TN 37311

Texas
Abracadabra Bookshop
601 E. Market St.
Rockport, TX 78382

Aldredge Book Store
2909 Maple Ave.
Dallas, TX 75201

All Books Used & Rare
2126 Richmond Ave.
Houston, TX 77098

Attal Galleries
3310 Red River St.
Austin, TX 78705

Bargain Books
22776 Cypresswood Drive
Houston, TX 77093

Beckers Books
7405 Westview Drive
Houston, TX 77055

Beckers Books
7405 Westview Drive
Houston, TX 77055

Book Cellar
600 Soledad St.
San Antonio, TX 78205

Book Collector
2347 University Blvd.
Houston, TX 77005

Book Den
449 McCarty Rd.
San Antonio, TX 78216

Book Gallery
2706 E. Yandell Drive
El Paso, TX 79903

Book Nook Trades
217 Fm 1960 Road West
Houston, TX 77090

Book Shoppe
1822 W. Berry St.
Fort Worth, TX 76110

Book Wizard
726 E. Pipeline Road
Hurst, TX 76053

Bookmark
7500 N. Mesa St.
El Paso, TX 79912

Books-N-Things
523 N. 1st St.
Harlingen, TX 78550

Cheever Books
140 Carnahan St.
San Antonio, TX 78209

Crime & Space Books
609 W. 6th St. # A
Austin, TX 78701

Detering Book Gallery
2311 Bissonnet St.
Houston, TX 77005

Front Street Books
121 E. Holland Ave.
Alpine, TX 79830

Galveston Bookshop
317 23rd St.
Galveston, TX 77550

Hart of Austin Antiquarian
Books
1009 W. 6th St.
Austin, TX 78703

Katy Budget Books
2450 Fry Rd.
Houston, TX 77084

Murder by the Book
2342 Bissonnet St.
Houston, TX 77005

Old Possums Books
3126 Handley Drive
Fort Worth, TX 76112

Park Springs Books
3901 W. Arkansas Lane
Arlington, TX 76016

Quarter Price Books
3820 S. Shepherd Drive
Houston, TX 77098

Read Em Again
2337 Nederland Ave.
Port Neches, TX 77651

Rerun Books
115 W. Southmore Ave.
Pasadena, TX 77502

River Oaks Book Store
3270 Westheimer Rd.
Houston, TX 77098

Twig Book Shop
5005 Broadway St.
San Antonio, TX 78209

Utah
B & W Collector Books
3466 S. 700 East
Salt Lake City, UT 84106

Book Attic
817 W. Center St.
Midvale, UT 84047

Bookshelf
2432 Washington Blvd.
Ogden, UT 84401

Exchange
149 E. 200 South
Clearfield, UT 84015

Ken Sanders Rare Books
268 S. 200 East
Salt Lake City, UT 84111

The Book Shelf
2432 Washington Blvd.
Ogden, UT 84401

Vermont
Tuttle Antiquarian Books Inc.
28 S. Main St.
Rutland, VT 05701

Virginia
Bargain Books
7524 Granby St.
Norfolk, VA 23505

Book People
536 Granite Ave.
Richmond, VA 23226

Chapter 2 Books
6945 Lakeside Ave.
Richmond, VA 23228

First Landing Books & Fine
Art
2708 Pacific Ave.
Virginia Beach, VA 23451

Jo Ann Reisler Limited
360 Glyndon St. Northeast
Vienna, VA 22180

John Lynch Bookstore
116 East Little Creek Rd. # A
Norfolk, VA 23505

Riverby Books
805 Caroline St.
Fredericksburg, VA 22401

Smithfield Rare Books
15064 Carrollton Blvd.
Carrollton, VA 23314

The Way We Were
32 E. Mellen St.
Hampton, VA 23663

Washington
Aunties Bookstore
402 W. Main Ave.
Spokane, WA 99201

B Brown & Associates
3534 Stone Way North
Seattle, WA 98103

B L M F Literary Saloon
1501 Pike Place
Seattle, WA 98101

Ballard Books
2232 Northwest Market St.
Seattle, WA 98107

Bibelots & Books
222 Westlake Ave. North
Seattle, WA 98109

Comstocks Bindery &
Bookshop
257 E. Main St.
Auburn, WA 98002

Gregor Books
3407 California Ave.
Southwest
Seattle, WA 98116

Gusdorfs Books
10525 E. Sprague Ave.
Spokane, WA 99206

Henderson Books
116 Grand Ave.
Bellingham, WA 98225

Inland Book Store
123 S. Wall St.
Spokane, WA 99201

Island Books Etc.
3014 78th Ave. Southeast
Mercer Island, WA 98040

Left Bank Books
92 Pike St.
Seattle, WA 98101

Magus Bookstore
1408 Northeast 42nd St.
Seattle, WA 98105

Morningstar Books
112 Grand Ave.
Bellingham, WA 98225

Open Books A Poem
Emporium
2414 N. 45th St.
Seattle, WA 98103

Ravenna Rare Books
5639 University Way
Northeast
Seattle, WA 98105

Renaissance Books
5554 27th Ave. Northeast
Seattle, WA 98105

Seattle Book Center
3530 Stone Way North
Seattle, WA 98103

Spencers Book Store
10411 Northeast Fourth Plain
Rd.
Vancouver, WA 98662

Spokane Book Center
626 N. Monroe St.
Spokane, WA 99201

Tacoma Book Center
324 E. 26th St.
Tacoma, WA 98421

Third Place Books
17171 Bothell Way Northeast
Seattle, WA 98155

Vandewater Books
1716 N. 45th St.
Seattle, WA 98103

Village Books
1210 11th St.
Bellingham, WA 98225

Vintage Books
6613 E. Mill Plain Blvd.
Vancouver, WA 98661

West Virginia
Trans Alleghney Books Inc.
725 Green St.
Parkersburg, WV 26101

Wisconsin
Aardvarks Bookstore
2750 E. Johnson St.
Madison, WI 53704

Alternate Realities
310 State St.
Madison, WI 53703

Booked for Murder Limited
2701 University Ave.
Madison, WI 53705

Bookworks
109 State St.
Madison, WI 53703

Constant Reader Bookshop
Limited
1627 E. Irving Place
Milwaukee, WI 53202

Foundry Book
105 Commerce St.
Mineral Point, WI 53565

McDermott Books
449 State St. Ste. D
Madison, WI 53703

Panther Books
3132 North Downer Ave.
Milwaukee, WI 53211

Pauls Book Store
670 State St.
Madison, WI 53703

Red Wheelbarrow Bookshop
2210 N. 2nd St.
Milwaukee, WI 53212

Renaissance Book Shop
834 N. Plankinton Ave.
Milwaukee, WI 53203

Yesterdays Memories Old
Book Shop
5631 W. Center St.
Milwaukee, WI 53210